TEACHING STUDENTS
WITH MILD
AND MODERATE
LEARNING PROBLEMS

TEACHING STUDENTS WITH MILD AND MODERATE LEARNING PROBLEMS

JOHN LANGONE
University of Georgia

ALLYN AND BACON
Boston   London   Sydney   Toronto

Series Editorial Assistant: Carol Craig
Production Administrator: Annette Joseph
Production Coordinator: Holly Crawford
Editorial-Production Service: Linda Zuk, WordCrafters Editorial Services, Inc.
Cover Administrator: Linda K. Dickinson
Cover Designer: Susan Slovinsky

Library of Congress Cataloging-in-Publication Data

Langone, John
  Teaching students with mild and moderate learning problems / John
Langone.
     p.   cm.
  "Portions of this text appeared in Teaching retarded learners"—
T.p. verso.
  Includes bibliographical references (p.).
  ISBN 0-205-12362-7
  1. Handicapped children—Education—United States.   2. Handicapped
children—Education—United States—Curricula.   3. Special
education—United States.   I. Langone, John, 1950–   Teaching
retarded learners.   II. Title.
LC4031.L348   1990
371.9'0973—dc20   89-48196
                                                                  CIP

Printed in the United States of America

10 9 8 7 6 5 4 3 2 1   95 94 93 92 91 90

Photo Credits

pp. 1, 57, 163, 252: Ken Karp
pp. 26, 126, 197, 288: DLM Teaching Resources, Allen, Texas
p. 92: Kay Shaw
p. 216: Carmine L. Galasso
p. 327: Shirley Zeiberg
p. 352: Laima Druskis
p. 373: Marc P. Anderson
p. 406: Neil Goldstein

BRIEF CONTENTS

CONTENTS

Chapter Four
DESIGNING CURRICULUM 92

Chapter Five
DEVELOPING INSTRUCTIONAL INTERVENTIONS, PART I: MEASUREMENT SYSTEMS 126

Chapter Six
DEVELOPING INSTRUCTIONAL INTERVENTIONS, PART II:
  TECHNIQUES FOR CHANGING LEARNER BEHAVIORS 163

Chapter Seven
MICROCOMPUTER TECHNOLOGY AND INSTRUCTION 197

Chapter Twelve
DEVELOPING LEISURE AND RECREATION PROGRAMS   352

Chapter Thirteen
DEVELOPING CAREER AND VOCATIONAL EDUCATION
   PROGRAMS: TRANSITION FROM SCHOOL TO WORK   373

PREFACE

As this book goes into production, the field of special education is at a critical crossroads, one very different from those of the past. Questions concerning whether or not we can justify the existence of special education are resurfacing. Some special educators who are proponents of a movement called the *regular education initiative* (REI) believe that the majority of students in our classes can be served best by regular education. Their arguments are based on those used in the past: Special education may be stigmatizing and it is ineffective in remediating academic and behavior problems of students with handicapping conditions.

Opponents of the REI cite the results of research demonstrating that some students with handicaps are less likely to be stigmatized when others know that their behavior or academic problems are a result of their disability. These professionals also believe that the smaller class sizes found in special education and the skill of special educators stand the best chance of remediating the deficits of these learners.

This debate is only one of the many forces for change in special education. The push to return to "basics," with its resulting increased emphasis on competency-based education, is having a significant impact on students with handicaps. In addition, continued litigation between parents and school districts is redefining the parameters under which special education operates.

As professionals in the field, we should look carefully at what is happening to students after they leave special education programs. Fifteen years have passed since the passage of Public Law 94-142—enough time to judge whether or not we have had a positive impact on the lives of students with handicaps.

Unfortunately, the latest research seems to be painting a less than desirable picture for individuals with handicaps. These individuals continue to be either unemployed or underemployed at rates that are disproportionate to those of the general population. Evidence shows that the dropout rate is higher for learners with mild handicapping conditions than for general education students. Therefore, we must ask ourselves whether or not we really are doing something "special."

As the field continues to grow and mature, our effectiveness is linked to our ability to learn from mistakes and make changes in programs that will help students reach their true potential. A solid teaching technology is available that has proven effective in changing the behaviors of students with handicaps. A number of proven assessment strategies for identifying students' strengths and weaknesses are also available.

What is lacking is clear direction regarding what to teach these learners. Until now, special educators have been preoccupied with trying to fit students with handicapping conditions into paper-and-pencil curriculum developed for general education students. Since research results do not seem to support the effectiveness of this approach, it seems time for a change, and that is the main focus of this book.

AUDIENCE AND PURPOSE

The book is intended for use by both preservice and inservice teachers at either the undergraduate or graduate level. Its emphasis is on developing programs to assist learners with handicaps in making successful transitions at all critical stages of their lives.

The most important challenge these learners continually face is integration into community life, regardless of their age. Therefore, the efforts of special educators should be directed toward teaching skills that are readily applicable to a variety of life situations. This book emphasizes community-based instruction as the primary vehicle for teaching academic, communication, social-emotional, and vocational skills to learners with handicapping conditions. Community-based instruction provides learners with the opportunity to see the importance of what they have learned in school in the context of highly motivating activities. These activities also allow students to generalize the skills they have learned to their daily lives.

Teaching Students with Mild and Moderate Learning Problems is unique in the sense that examples of curricula and methods for instruction are interwoven, demonstrating how community-based activities can be implemented in either resource or self-contained settings. These examples are presented not as entities separate from the regular education curriculum but in a way that demonstrates how they work in tandem with what regular education has to offer.

The book also emphasizes program development and methods for teaching *all* learners considered by schools to be mildly and moderately handicapped. These students generally are enrolled in classes for learners with mild to moderate mental handicaps, learning disabilities, and behavior disorders. Examples of all these types of learners are included because the literature in all three areas reveals that the same basic teaching strategies are used with all types of students. Practical reality dictates that special educators will probably teach learners with all of these exceptionalities at some point in their careers. Indeed, many teach them all on a daily basis in classes labeled *interrelated* or *cross categorical.*

Each chapter contains sections titled "Key Concepts," "Idea Files," and "Case Studies." These sections highlight the major preferred practices and most important considerations found in each chapter.

ACKNOWLEDGMENTS

The successful completion of a book cannot be credited to one individual. Special thanks are due to my teachers and friends at Florida State University, Andy Oseroff, Mark Koorland, David Westling, and Jon Bailey, who gave me a solid foundation from which I could grow professionally. Although I have learned much since I left them, it has all been tempered by their instruction.

My thanks to Janet Buffington, who, in addition to her unique ability to translate my handwriting into something readable, acted as an editor and manager, keeping me organized and on task. Her smiling demeanor and cheerful personality (continuing even as I buried her in work) motivated me to get the job done. Thanks also to Denise Backus, for her help in editing parts of the original manuscript and developing the Instructor's Manual; to Ray Short, my editor at Allyn and Bacon, who demonstrated to me that the production and marketing of a book does not need to be a heartbreaking experience; to Linda Zuk, my production editor; and to Ann Mohan, my excellent copyeditor.

Reviews from experts in the field are a valuable service to the author. Again, I must thank Barbara Wolf at Indiana University, who has helped me before, for her insight into the most effective pedagogy for a book. I have used her suggestions throughout. My thanks to Jo Crain, Valdosta State College; Richard Eigenbrook, Dorot College; Arthur Hasbargen, Western Illinois University; Earle Knowlton, University of Kansas; Lois Pence, University of Wisconsin-Oshkosh; and Joe Reid, Grand Valley State College, for their help in reviewing the manuscript in various stages. A very special thanks to Susan Munson, Duquesne University, and Garnett Smith, University of Alabama, for their thorough review throughout the project. Their in-depth knowledge of the field and their insight concerning the hard issues faced by special educators were apparent in all their reviews. The quality of the final product has been enhanced greatly by the ideas they unselfishly shared.

Finally, I would like to acknowledge my wife and son once again. A special thank you to Christine, who reacts to my ideas and refines my thinking about issues in education. She also has been a major source of information concerning skills for improving interpersonal relationships among professionals. On top of all that, she is my best friend and muse. Kevin continually demonstrates to me that I really do not know everything about behavior management. He graciously has been continuing my education on the art of negotiating with children.

CHAPTER ONE

INTRODUCTION

■ During the 1960s and 1970s, life for students enrolled in special education classes was quite different from the way it is in many classes today. Students with handicaps were often isolated from peers who did not have handicapping conditions. They sometimes rode to school on separate buses and ate in the cafeteria at different times.

The curriculum presented to these students was similar to that for their regular education peers except that the peer group moved through it at a much faster pace. Students in special education were presented with laborious, repetitive activities designed to teach them basic reading, writing, and arithmetic skills in abstract, classroom-based activities. They probably did not progress socially and academically at rates commensurate with their actual potential.

Upon leaving school, some individuals labeled as mentally retarded ended up in sheltered settings such as workshops or institutional placements or blended into society at very low socioeconomic levels. The few students who were labeled as learning disabled (LD) entered society at low-level jobs and encountered many barriers to a more successful life. Individuals labeled as emotionally disturbed or behavior disordered by the schools encountered fates similar to those of their counterparts who were labeled mentally retarded. Successful transition from school to life in the outside world was not a planned affair, but seemed to come about only as a result of the coincidence of a unique series of events in a few isolated instances.

During the 1980s, students enrolled in special education programs are beginning to fare differently and their future looks brighter. Professionals are realizing that the curriculum targeted in the 1960s and 1970s did not meet the needs of these students. Although lipservice was given during that period to developing functional activities, these activities were seldom taught outside the school in realistic environments.

Today the emphasis is on developing programs that promote successful transitions at all stages of life by teaching students skills in the context of the community environments where they are expected to use the skills. Academics are not abandoned, but they are taught where students can apply them in a concrete fashion, with materials that are real to the environments of daily life and in the presence of community members who do not have handicaps. Social, communication, vocational, and a variety of other independent living skills are also taught this way, and students of all ages participate.

CHANGES IN SPECIAL EDUCATION

Special education has changed dramatically in the past 15 years. Students with various handicapping conditions who were once excluded from regular education classes and in some cases banned from public schools are now participating alongside their regular education peers. These changes in the field of special education are a result of many shifts in public policy, the consequences of which culminated in legislation mandating a free and appropriate public education for all handicapped children (Public Law 94-142, the Education for All Handicapped Children Act of 1975).

During this period of growth and change, the individualized education program (IEP) was introduced and implemented. Due process procedures were delineated and applied to ensure that the needs of learners with handicaps were being met. Parents and students themselves became more active in program development.

However, these changes in special education have not occurred in a vacuum. The resources required to implement special education programs are considerable, and allocation of these resources requires close coordination and cooperation among all disciplines. Therefore, in recent years there has been an increase in the number of joint decisions between special and regular education concerning placement and service options for students requiring special programming.

Since the passage of PL 94-142, public policy concerning the equal rights of people with handicaps has involved numerous debates and ultimately has been shaped by litigation. Public policy continues to evolve in relation to and as a result of various challenges in the courts. A recent example is the passage of the Education of the Handicapped Amendments (PL 99-457), which amended PL 94-142 to include early intervention programs for infants and toddlers (birth to school age) who suffer from or are likely to experience handicapping conditions.

On the surface, it appears that special education and related fields have met the goals set by litigation and legislation. Certainly the ability of schools to provide a free education to those who in the past were excluded from this basic right has improved a great deal. Unfortunately, the evidence to date is not sufficient to demonstrate that special education programs have provided learners with appropriate curricula and/or interventions to help them reach their potential (Lilly, 1986; Reynolds, 1988). For example, Edgar (1987) found that more than 30% of students with handicaps who are enrolled in special education eventually drop out. These figures surpass estimates of the dropout rates for students without handicaps. Further, Edgar discovered from his sample that students once enrolled in special education are disproportionately represented in the ranks of the unemployed or among those working in jobs below their actual ability. The results of a study by Hasazi, Gordon, and Roe (1985) correspond with Edgar's work.

Interestingly, the findings of these studies also correspond with a number of follow-up studies conducted periodically between the 1930s and 1960s to track students who are educable mentally retarded (EMR) into community life (MacMillan, 1982). It was found that they, too, were largely unemployed or underemployed, generally blending into society on the lowest rungs of the socioeconomic ladder.

One final result of the changes in the field of special education is a reduction in services to a group who appear to have been lost in the shuffle. The growth of interest in and services to students who have learning disabilities and those with severely handicapping conditions corresponds to a lack of interest in and a decrease in services to students with mild mental handicaps (MacMillan, 1988).

Students who in the past fell into the top end of the IQ score range for what was the educable mental retardation category are no longer eligible for special services. Evidence indicates that these students, now served in regular education, continue to fall behind their peers and are socially promoted until they drop out of school. As MacMillan (1988) has stated,

> Students with general academic deficiencies, particularly those from poor families, have proven to be a hard-to-reach group for educators since 1900. Regardless of what we call them or where we teach them, we have been unable to promote dramatic gains in achievement. It would appear that quality education is as elusive today for this group of students as it was in the 1960s. (1988, p. 282)

According to MacMillan, it is time to analyze the curriculum and emphasize teaching these students skills that are relevant to their *successful* integration into the community. This holds true also for students in special education programs or on the fringes of the services we provide.

The hard question being asked by many professionals and parents is one of quality versus quantity: Are we providing the most *appropriate* educational programs to help learners make successful transitions throughout life, or are we providing as many services as possible without particular concern for quality?

In the ensuing sections of this chapter and in Chapter Two, key issues facing all professionals who work with special education students will be outlined. These issues are important because they reflect many ongoing concerns and eventually may effect a change in the focus of special education. They also serve to establish the philosophy of this text, which differs from the traditional special education model of diagnosis and remediation of academic skills in traditional school environments.

The basic theme of the text is that we need to assist learners in making successful transitions throughout life and view them as lifelong learners in the context of their place in society. Therefore, the text places heavy emphasis on community-based instruction (CBI) as the main curriculum thrust of special education programs. In addition, it provides examples of teaching strategies that proved effective across a variety of students who exhibit different handicapping conditions.

This approach is not based on the belief that all learners with mild and moderate handicaps require the same curriculum and teaching strategies. Sufficient evidence exists to demonstrate significant differences across categories of students labeled as mentally handicapped (MH), behavior disordered (BD), or emotionally disturbed (ED), and learning disabled (LD). The pervasive limited cognitive ability of a student identified as mildly mentally handicapped (MIMH), for example, requires that professionals design different curricular options, and it may possibly limit the types of strategies that can be used with this learner as compared to those used with a student with normal cognitive ability who is labeled as learning disabled. Later in this chapter a more detailed discussion will identify the types of students this text addresses and give a more thorough account of the student characteristics that affect programming.

THE DILEMMA OF LABELING AND CLASSIFICATION

The debate continues to rage over the effects that labeling and classification have on students with handicapping conditions. This debate is not new; it has been and continues to be on the forefront of the professional literature. Some argue that labeling helps get services to the students, while others argue that labeling stigmatizes learners and causes the general population to develop negative attitudes toward them (Meyen, 1988).

Clearly, this issue is complicated and it raises some important questions that have not been answered effectively by research. For example, proponents believe that (1) labels allow funding to flow more easily to the categories where the need is greatest because a lack of labels would confuse all data-gathering procedures; (2) nonhandicapped peers may more readily accept the behaviors of students labeled as handicapped (MacMillan, Keogh, &

Jones, 1986); and (3) professionals can better communicate the results of research when the individuals are placed in specific categories. Opponents believe that labeling (1) magnifies an individual's weaknesses; (2) causes teachers to use so-called self-fulfilling prophecies to explain why their students are not making progress; (3) causes students to acquire a negative self-concept; and (4) allows professionals to keep learners out of regular education programs.

These beliefs are examples of the notions that have been tested by a variety of research projects. Unfortunately, the results of research to date are equivocal at best, and they are certainly confusing (Heward & Orlansky, 1988). The studies that were designed to assess the effects of labeling often yielded contradictory results and were notorious for having flaws in their research designs (MacMillan, 1982).

Variability Within Classification Groupings

It may be most helpful to admit that there are some benefits to labeling students, mainly for the purposes of identifying those learners who need services. Problems begin to arise, however, when professionals overrely on classification systems and assume that these systems help them design programs to meet the needs of individual students (Reynolds, 1988).

Variability with classification groupings has been well documented (e.g., Braaten, Kauffman, Braaten, Polsgrove, & Nelson, 1988; Keogh, 1987; MacMillan, 1982). For example, one student labeled as MIMH may score within the acceptable range for MIMH students on a standardized intelligence test but have severe deficits in social and self-care skills, while another learner diagnosed as MIMH may be functioning at the upper ranges in both intelligence and adaptive behavior skills. Similar examples have been identified for students labeled as learning disabled, behavior disordered, and moderately mentally handicapped (e.g., Braaten et al., 1988; Langone, 1986; Poplin, 1981).

Some students with learning disabilities or behavior disorders may learn to cope with their problems, enter college, and obtain advanced degrees. Others may never reach their potential; they may continue to be nonreaders or have great difficulty engaging in satisfactory social interactions. Some students with moderate mental handicaps may become competitively employed and live in a minimally supervised apartment, while others might become wards of the state and reside in institutional placements.

A variety of schemes for using severity levels have been tried over the years with little success. At various times professionals have attempted to label people within categories by qualifying the effects of the disorder as being either mild, moderate, or severe. The best example is within the field of mental retardation, where the subcategories or qualifiers just listed figure prominently into the definition of retardation. These qualifiers are also used in the professional literature to better describe various subgroups of students with learning disabilities and behavior disorders (Reynolds & Birch, 1988).

In addition to the attempts at delineating subgroupings within categories, there has been a movement to apply these subgroup qualifiers across categories. Textbooks have been published, and at least one organization (TASH) has been formed along the lines of a cross-categorical approach (e.g., mildly handicapped, moderately handicapped, or severely handicapped). This approach has proved unsatisfactory to some professionals because they feel it serves to mask the real behavioral differences across handicapping conditions (Poplin, 1981). For example, the primary thrust of The Association for the Severely Handicapped (TASH) is to promote the needs of individuals with severe handicaps, primarily those labeled as severely or profoundly retarded and multiply handicapped (Schmid, Moneypenny, & Johnston, 1977). According to Poplin (1981), the approach causes real problems because it "excludes by definition whole categories of handicapped persons, i.e., learning disabled . . ." (p. 330). Poplin went on to stress that some people with learning disabilities have severe problems that hinder, and in many cases block, successful community integration.

In a sense, Poplin's argument in defense of students with severe learning disabilities is applicable to other learners from other categories. Students with behavior disorders who are enrolled in a self-contained class may have severe problems later on if their inability to form interpersonal relationships hinders them from becoming competitively employed. It could also be argued that students with learning disabilities who, although otherwise able, read on a sixth-grade level have severe problems if lack of reading ability hinders them from their life goal of attending college. Taking this example one step further, students with moderate mental handicaps may also have severe problems if their difficulty in expressing themselves is a barrier to successful community integration. The use of qualifiers such as *mild, moderate,* and *severe* can be misleading because the deficits of individuals are unique to them and their life situations.

Distance to Life Goals

Grey (1981) proposed an alternative to the method of classification used for learning disabilities in a paper supporting the need for increased services for adults with learning disabilities. He pointed out that the liberal use of subgroupings or qualifiers hinders access to appropriate services by masking an individual's real needs. In the minds of some professionals, a person with moderate to severe learning disabilities may not need the same intensity of services as a person labeled as mildly mentally handicapped. Depending on the life goals and ultimate functioning levels of the individuals, these beliefs may not be valid.

A major problem with label, category, or subgroup systems is that they do not provide adequate information for developing programs for any group of learners (Meyen & Skrtic, 1988). For example, teachers who receive students into their classes who are labeled as learning disabled have little idea as to their specific strengths and weaknesses. Also, there are no prescribed curricular options for one group of students to the exclusion of other groups (e.g., students with learning disabilities need academic remediation; learners with moderate mental handicaps need instruction in self-care skills).

This text incorporates Grey's (1981) theme of distance to life goals into the philosophy of community-based instruction. All students have differing needs regardless of handicapping condition or severity level. The common denominator is that all students have the right to live as independently as possible. To accomplish this, professionals must take into account the life goals of the individual when designing academic, social, or vocational activities. Then these activities can be offered in the environments in which the learner is expected to use the targeted skills. Later in this chapter, information will be presented concerning the characteristics of learners with mild and moderate handicaps that support the need for CBI.

CLASSIFICATION SYSTEMS

Given the general nature of current classification systems and the arguments against their use, why do professionals keep using them? The main reason is for administrative purposes. These classification systems do help to organize programs and direct money to where it is most needed. However, it is important for teachers to realize that labels may provide little information to help in designing appropriate program options (Lynch & Lewis, 1988). Good or bad, categorization systems still are used extensively to identify which learners receive special education services and which do not.

PL 94-142 provides definitions that serve as a basis for those programs implemented in every state. Although they are controversial, the most widely agreed upon definitions are included for the various categories of learners emphasized in this book. It is important for teachers to know these definitions, as well as their strengths and weaknesses, because of the central role teachers play in establishing students' eligibility for services.

DEFINITION AND CLASSIFICATION OF STUDENTS WITH MENTAL HANDICAPS

MacMillan (1982) identified three categories of definitions of mental retardation: biological, social, and psychometric. The first category, biological definitions, was influenced by the medical profession and included components such as diseases affecting the central nervous system and incomplete cerebral development.

Proponents of social definitions viewed mental handicaps in terms of societal issues and the effects resulting from the interaction of individuals with mental handicaps and their environments. These approaches were directed mainly at individuals with mild handicaps and attempted to demonstrate that retardation was primarily a function of the environment in which a person lived.

The psychometric definitions resulted directly from the development of intelligence tests. Their ease of administration and the fact that intelligence tests could compare individuals to the so-called normal population made psychometric definitions popular. In these definitions IQ score became the sole determinant for classifying a person as mentally retarded. There are numerous critics of psychometric definitions, particularly because of the adverse effects of such definitions on minority populations, but this has not prevented the approach from becoming popular. In many areas the intelligence test score is still the prime determinant for identification and placement of children in various educational environments.

Definition

The definition adopted by the American Association on Mental Retardation (AAMR) is the one most used by educators and, at the present time, is the most comprehensive. This definition has evolved through a number of revisions over the years, with the last three occurring in 1973, 1977, and 1983. The 1973 definition was incorporated in PL 94-142.

In the 1983 revision of its *Manual on Terminology and Classification in Mental Retardation,* the AAMR defined mental retardation as "significantly subaverage general intellectual functioning existing concurrently with deficits in adaptive behavior and manifested during the developmental period" (Grossman, 1983, p. 11).

The manual also presented additional criteria explaining the following four components of the definition:

1. *General intellectual functioning* is operationally defined as the results obtained by assessment with one or more of the individually administered general intelligence tests developed for that purpose.

2. *Significantly subaverage* is defined as IQ of 70 or below on standardized measures of intelligence. This upper limit is intended as a guideline; it could be extended upward through IQ 75 or more, depending on the reliability of the intelligence test used. This particularly applies in schools and similar settings if behavior is impaired and clinically determined to be due to deficits in reasoning and judgment.

3. *Deficits in adaptive behavior* are defined as significant limitations in an individual's effectiveness in meeting the standards of maturation, learning, personal independence, and/or social responsibility that are expected for his or her age level and cultural group, as determined by clinical assessment and, usually, standardized scales.

4. *Developmental period* is defined as the period of time between birth and the 18th birthday. Developmental deficits may be manifested by slow, arrested, or incomplete development resulting from brain damage, degenerative processes in the central nervous system, or regression from previously normal states due to psychosocial factors.[1]

The concept of adaptive behavior has caused much controversy among professionals in special education (Clausen, 1972). On one hand, professionals believe that a person's ability to function in society is a better measure of competence than an isolated score on a standardized intelligence scale. Conversely, the lack of objectivity currently inherent in the measurement of adaptive behavior may weaken the argument for its use.

When analyzing the skill areas that comprise what is considered adaptive behavior, it is difficult to dispute that these skills are vital for an individual's survival in society. Grossman has classified adaptive behavior into three areas:

During infancy and early childhood in:

1. Sensory-motor skills and development
2. Communication skills (including speech and language)
3. Self-help skills

---

[1] From *Classification in Mental Retardation,* H.J. Grossman. Ed., 1983, p. 11. Washington, D.C.: American Association on Mental Deficiency. Reprinted by permission.

4. Socialization (development of ability to interact with others)

During childhood and early adolescence in areas 1–4 and/or:

5. Application of basic academic skills in daily life activities
6. Application of appropriate reasoning and judgment in mastery of the environment
7. Social skills (participation in group activities and interpersonal relationships)

and

During late adolescence and adult life in areas 1–7 and/or:

8. Vocational and social responsibilities and performances.[2]

Accurate measurement of adaptive behavior is important and yet very difficult. It is especially crucial for borderline cases in which an appraisal of adaptive behavior may be the only criterion standing between a child and the label *mentally handicapped*.

KEY CONCEPTS

Society has moved from isolating retarded individuals in state institutions supporting an "out of sight, out of mind" philosophy to a better understanding of the need to bring people who have mental handicaps back to the community. There are still problems that hinder a smooth transition, but community members in general are becoming more aware of handicapped individuals and their needs.

- Definitions available for classifying a person as mentally handicapped are many and reflect different viewpoints.

- One of the more popular definitions of mental retardation was developed by the American Association on Mental Deficiency (AAMD) and includes psychometric, biological, and social criteria.

- When an overly representative number of minority children are classified as mildly mentally handicapped, it is possible the school systems are relying too heavily on the psychometric portion of a definition (Huberty, Koller, & Ten Brink, 1980). Some intelligence tests used to establish IQ scores have been found to be culturally biased, thus not providing a true picture of a person's abilities.

- Using measures of adaptive behavior allows professionals access to additional information concerning a person's functioning level in the community (Witt, 1980). If a person's adaptive behavior is considered normal, there should be some question as to whether the label *mentally handicapped* is appropriate.

- Measures of adaptive behavior can be subjective, and ratings of the same individual can vary from rater to rater. Professionals aware of this characteristic can approach the significant others in a person's life and gather as much information as possible concerning adaptive behavior. This information may provide a more thorough profile of a learner's ability to function in the environment.

■ ■ ■ ■

[2] Ibid., p. 25.

Classification Systems for Mental Retardation

Over the years many terms have been used to describe the severity levels of mental handicaps. For example, earlier in this century terms such as *feeble-minded, moron, imbecile,* and *idiot* were used to describe people with mild to severe handicaps. Unfortunately, over time these terms began to take on negative connotations, and the characteristics the public visualized when hearing these terms were, at best, unfavorable.

Today, teachers generally come in contact with two different systems for describing the severity levels of mental handicaps. The first system describes people who have the mildest handicaps as *educable mentally retarded* (EMR); those who have middle level handicaps as *trainable mentally retarded* (TMR); and the most severe cases as *custodial mentally retarded.* Some professionals feel that the use of these terms associates negative images with people who have mental handicaps (Koegal & Edgerton, 1982).

The argument focuses on the terms *educable* and *trainable,* specifically relating to ultimate functioning levels. Some professionals believe that people view EMR students as those who can only be educated in the most basic of academic skills. Similarly, TMR students generally cannot be "educated" in the traditional public school sense and instead must be given instruction in skills relating to self-care, basic communication, and other areas needed for a sheltered life. Terms connoting artificial limits for learners may become self-fulfilling prophecies. As educational technology continues to advance, professionals are realizing that older notions of educable and trainable no longer hold true, because learners are now meeting skill levels previously thought impossible.

An alternative system for identifying severity levels that is becoming increasingly more popular in public schools is the one used by the American Association on Mental Deficiency (Grossman, 1983). This system identifies four levels of severity: (1) mild retardation (IQ 50–55 to approximately 70); (2) moderate retardation (IQ 35–40 to 50–55); (3) severe retardation (IQ 20–25 to 35–40); and (4) profound retardation (below 20 or 25). These terms appear to be more general in nature and less related to preconceived educational outcomes. In this way, professionals are encouraged to look at the behaviors of specific students and design programs to meet individual needs. The categories of interest for this text are mild (MIMH) and moderate (MOMH) mental handicaps. (In recent years, the trend has been to avoid using the term *retardation,* which has negative connotations, in favor of the term *handicap.*)

Information pertaining to students with severe mental handicaps is not included because the needs of these learners are great and must be met by multidisciplinary teams, an approach that is beyond the scope of this text.

DEFINITION AND CLASSIFICATION
OF STUDENTS WITH LEARNING DISABILITIES

A continuing controversy in the field of learning disabilities (LD) has focused on the issue of what is an appropriate definition. Although many definitions of LD have been developed, none has been completely accepted by all parents and professionals. The most widely used definition is one developed in 1968 by the National Advisory Committee on Handicapped Children (NACHC) that defines learning disabilities as follows:

> Children with special learning disabilities exhibit a disorder in one or more of the basic psychological processes involved in understanding or in using spoken or written language. These may be manifested in disorders of listening, thinking, reading, writing, spelling, or arithmetic. They include conditions which have been referred to as perceptual handicaps, brain injury, minimal brain dysfunction, dyslexia, developmental aphasia, etc. They do not include learning problems which are due primarily to visual, hearing, or motor handicaps, to mental retardation, emotional disturbance or to environmental disadvantage.

This definition continues to be the one used for legal and funding purposes because it was included, with only minor wording changes, in PL 94-142.

Criticism of the Legal Definition

Almost from the time it was formulated, this definition has been criticized by many notable professionals (e.g., Reid, 1988). A major concern has been that the definition is so broad that it allows for too much variation in criteria for operationalizing it. This lack of clear direction has set the stage for most states to use three major criteria for deciding eligibility of students for LD programs: (1) the exclusion criteria stated in the last sentence of the definition; (2) a need for services beyond those that regular education can provide; and (3) a discrepancy between a student's potential and his or her actual achievement (Heward & Orlansky, 1988).

Of these three criteria, the two that generate the most controversy are the exclusion and discrepancy rules. The term *learning disabled* was originally meant to describe those children whose inability to learn could not be explained by mental handicaps, emotional disturbance, sensory impairment, or poor teaching. If a student's learning problems were not a result of any of those factors, they must be due to a learning disability (Bryan, Bay, & Donahue, 1988).

This reasoning continues to create problems for students, their parents, and professionals. The exclusions principle provides no answers for why the problems are, in fact, occurring (Reid, 1988). Moreover, this provision hampers communication between professionals and sets the stage for different disciplines to use "different tests, standards, and criteria to define this exceptionality" (Reid, 1988, p. 31).

The discrepancy criteria also has caused continued debate in the field. Many professionals have developed a wide variety of statistical methods to measure the discrepancy between achievement and expectancy (McLoughlin & Netick, 1983). In the Summer 1986 issue of the *Learning Disability Quarterly,* The Council for Learning Disabilities (CLD) published a position paper that refuted the validity of discrepancy formulas. Basically, the CLD believes that these formulas tend to focus on a single aspect of learning disabilities, specifically those related to academic performance. In addition, some tests used to establish expected and obtained performance are inadequate in validity, thus allowing eligibility to be established on the basis of weak data. Finally, many underachieving students may perform below their expectancy level for reasons other than a learning disability. For example, many learners with average or above IQ scores may do poorly in academic subjects for motivational reasons. Even when combined with the exclusion criteria, the discrepancy approach seems to create more questions than it answers.

Toward an Improved Definition

Because of the many questions raised by the NACHC definition, representatives from eight professional groups dealing with learning disabilities gathered together to form The National Joint Committee for Learning Disabilities (NJCLD). This group believed that there were a number of weaknesses in the NACHC definition that were carried over to the federal legislation (Hammill, Leigh, McNutt, & Larsen, 1981). There were five major components of debate according to the NJCLD. First, the NACHC definition described only children with learning disabilities, and professionals have recognized that LD is a lifelong problem (Grey, 1981).

A second problem with the NACHC definition centers around the term *basic psychological processes.* This term tended to polarize professionals into those who believed that retraining these processes was possible and those who believed that deficits in these hypothetical constructs could not be retrained or, in fact, may not exist (Reid, 1988).

The third criticism was directed at the inclusion in the federal definition of spelling as a basic deficit area. The fourth criticism centered on the inclusion of obsolete terms such as *minimal brain dysfunction* in the definition; the NJCLD felt that such terms fostered additional confusion. Finally, the NJCLD took issue with the exclusion clause for reasons described earlier in this chapter.

The NJCLD developed a definition that solves some of the problems presented by the one used in the federal legislation. According to this definition,

> Learning disabilities is a generic term that refers to a heterogeneous group of disorders manifested by significant difficulties in the acquisition and use of listening, speaking, reading, writing, reasoning, or mathematics. These disorders are intrinsic to the individual and presumed to be due to central nervous system dysfunction. Even though a learning disability may occur concomitantly with other handicapping conditions (e.g., sensory impairment, mental retardation, social and emotional disturbance) or environmental influences (e.g., cultural differences, insufficient/ inappropriate instruction, psychogenic factors), it is not the direct result of those conditions or influences. This definition recommended to Congress for use by all agencies for research and placement.

KEY CONCEPTS

Hammill and colleagues (1981) outlined the major intentions of the NJCLD.

- *Learning disabilities* is a broad term that includes many disorders grouped under one label.
- The disorders grouped under the label of LD are a result of a variety of causes.
- A learning disability is not just a mildly handicapping condition. Individuals can have severe learning disabilities that require the sort of intensive programming that is often thought of as needed by individuals with more serious conditions such as moderate to severe mental handicaps.

- The handicapping conditions must be a result of problems in one or more areas including listening, speaking, reading, writing, reasoning, or mathematical abilities.

- The learning disorders are intrinsic to the individual and are not a result of poor teaching, economic depression, cultural differences, or other environmental factors.

- Learning disabilities are presumed to be a result of a central nervous system dysfunction. In terms of diagnosis, this presumed dysfunction does not have to be substantiated; however, when the cause is known to be something else (e.g., economic deprivation), the diagnosis of LD is not probable.

- Learning disability can be found in conjunction with other handicapping conditions; however, it is not a direct result of those conditions. It is considered an entity in and of itself.

■ ■ ■ ■

Classification Systems for Learning Disabilities

Although the NJCLD definition of LD appears to be an improvement over other efforts, it does leave the door open to additional areas of concern. One problem concerns the heterogeneity of the population subsumed under the one label of LD (Robinson & Deshler, 1988). Because of the variety of problems exhibited by people with LD, it becomes difficult at times to differentiate between them and other individuals who exhibit similar problems as a result of mental handicaps, behavioral disorders, or other conditions (Algozzine & Ysseldyke, 1983). Therefore, researchers are continuing to pursue a system for identifying subgroups of individuals whose characteristics are similar enough to be classified consistently across large numbers of people.

For example, Lyon (1985) and Lyon and Watson (1981) identified six subcategories of students with LD who exhibit severe reading problems. The groupings ranged from students in subcategory 1, who had severe global language and perceptual deficits, to students in subcategory 6, who evidenced normal profiles but were underachieving due to other than intrinsic causes. Other researchers (e. g., McKinney, 1984) have generally supported the notion of subcategories within the larger population of individuals with LD.

One reason for attempting to classify subcategories of learners with LD or, for that matter, any category of learners, is to differentiate the effects of educational interventions. The aptitude–treatment interaction (ATI) theory, which has been debated for a number of years, purports that certain groups of learners will respond better to specific types of instructional strategies. The research on ATI to date is equivocal and in some cases premature, and it will remain so until more precisely defined and universally accepted subcategories can be developed (Howell & Morehead, 1987; Robinson & Deshler, 1988).

DEFINITION AND CLASSIFICATION OF STUDENTS WITH BEHAVIOR DISORDERS

To date there is no universally agreed upon definition of behavior disorders (Heward & Orlansky, 1988). Individuals who are chronically in conflict with themselves and others have been labeled with a variety of terms. For example, a perusal of the education literature will reveal any of the following terms used synonymously to describe the same group of students: *behavior disordered, emotionally disturbed, socially maladjusted, severely conduct disordered,* and *psychologically disordered.* If students manifest severely abnormal or bizarre behavior, they also may be labeled as autistic or psychotic. In many respects, the problems surrounding the definition of behavior disorders (the term that will be used throughout this book) surpasses those surrounding LD and MH.

There are many reasons for the lack of a clear definition of BD (Braaten et al., 1988). One main difficulty in defining BD is the lack of a reliable and valid measurement system (Whelan, 1988). Measurement systems are affected by cultural norms and opinions of what is appropriate emotional stability.

In addition, there are many different theories that attempt to explain emotional problems. With each theory comes a different set of definitions and accompanying terms. Finally, the major problem affecting the definition of LD and MR also affects the definition of BD: Behavior disorders can exist concurrently with any other handicapping condition, and sometimes it is difficult to determine whether one handicapping condition was the cause or the result of the other (Morgan & Jenson, 1988).

The following definition of emotional disturbance, which was included in PL 94-142, was adopted from the one developed by Bower (1969):

Seriously emotionally disturbed is defined as follows:

  (i) The term means a condition exhibiting one or more of the following characteristics over
       a long period of time and to a marked degree, which adversely affects educational
       performance:
       (a) An inability to learn which cannot be explained in intellectual, sensory, and health
           factors;
       (b) An inability to build or maintain satisfactory interpersonal relationships with peers
           and teachers;
       (c) Inappropriate types of behavior or feelings under normal circumstances;
       (d) A general pervasive mood of unhappiness or depression; or
       (e) A tendency to develop physical symptoms or fears associated with personal or school
           problems.
  (ii) The term includes children who are schizophrenic or autistic. The term does not include
       children who are socially maladjusted unless it is determined that they are seriously
       emotionally disturbed. (PL 94-142, 1975, 163)

Since the inclusion of this definition in PL 94-142, the federal government has amended it once to move autism from the category of severely emotionally disturbed to the category of other health impairments (Heward & Orlansky, 1988; Rizzo & Zabel, 1988).

As with the definitions of other handicapping conditions, detractors of the federal definition of BD believe that it is too vague and leaves too much open to subjective options (Kauffman, 1982). The terms used in the definition (e.g., *to a marked extent, over a long period of time, pervasive, satisfactory*) make it almost impossible to operationalize the definition (Wood, 1985). Behavior disorder is a difficult condition to define because of its relationship to normalization. The problem has its roots in the definition, or lack of one, of *normalization.* Apter (1982) has asserted that most of the behaviors associated with children labeled as BD are normal, to the extent that normal children will sometimes engage in the same behaviors (e.g., cheating, lying, acting aggressively). Similarly, Achenbach and Edelbrock (1981), documented that many normal individuals exhibit problem behaviors at some time during their lives.

The question becomes, What is normal, and by whose standards? Some children steal because their parents steal and have taught them that such behavior is normal and even desirable. When the behavior becomes a chronic problem in school, professionals may label these children as abnormal or behavior disordered.

The key elements in identifying learners with behavior disorders appear to transcend all definitions. The behaviors in question must be extremely different from the current norm in a given environment and must be exhibited by the individuals over a long period of time. Therefore, the target behaviors would be more intense than the norm, occur frequently, and be chronic in nature (lasting over time).

These criteria make sense in terms of behaviors that differ from the norm. The problem surfaces when too much freedom is given to one person in deciding what the norm is. This explains the tremendous importance teachers have in the process of identifying students needing BD services. One teacher might view a student's behavior as deviant whereas another teacher might not. Another teacher's inability to be an effective instructor might cause students to react in what might be considered an abnormal manner.

Both scenarios might result in the teachers' requesting an evaluation of the students for possible BD services. Both requests, unfortunately, probably would be based on false perceptions on the part of the teachers. Therefore, the inconsistencies in the liberal definition, and in fact in all existing definitions, can lead to inappropriate placements if professionals are not cautious. For example, some professionals advocate that the problem must have lasted for at least 4 to 6 months before the criteria can be applied consistently (Morgan & Jenson, 1988). Also, the regular classroom should undergo a complete analysis, and professional assistance for the teacher and target student should be made available before any consideration of removing the learner is made.

Behavior Disorders Versus Emotional Disturbance

The Council for Children with Behavioral Disorders (CCBD) has adopted the position that the term *seriously emotionally disturbed*, as stated in the federal regulations, does not adequately describe the variety of students who would be available for services under PL 94-142 (Huntze, 1985). There were several concerns stated in CCBD's position paper that prompted the change in terminology.

First, CCBD felt that the term *behavior disordered* is more generic and is not related to any particular theory of causation and subsequent intervention techniques. For example, the term *seriously emotionally disturbed* is often related to a psychodynamic approach that stresses the theory that the problem behaviors are a result of internal workings remediated through counseling or psychotherapy.

A second reason for the change in terms is that *behavior disordered* is more descriptive of the students receiving services under PL 94-142 (Huntze, 1985). The majority of these students do not manifest severe behaviors that often connote some type of bizarre display of emotions. Finally, according to CCBD, the term *behavior disordered* is much less stigmatizing than the one in the federal definition.

To date, the change in the CCBD term has had no impact on governmental regulations; however, since the CCBD is the major professional organization in the area of behavior disorders, it seems likely that this term will continue to gain in popularity.

For the purposes of this text, the term *behavior disordered* is used because it refers to the broad range of problems exhibited by students covered under PL 94-142 and because it reflects one of the main instructional approaches that encompasses all the topics included in this text. The main task of teachers is to focus on observable behaviors that are being exhibited currently and require modification. In addition, teachers should give significant attention to helping students develop new behaviors that are not currently in the students' repertoire of responses. This approach helps students acquire the skills needed to interact with peers who are not handicapped. The word *behavior* in BD best highlights this approach, whereas the word *emotional* overemphasizes underlying or internal causes.

Classification Systems for Behavior Disorders

Classification systems are designed to assist professionals in communicating with each other and to assist individuals in getting the services that meet their needs. When classification systems become unnecessarily complex, they invite confusion in placing students and potentially result in branding them with labels that may become stigmatizing. As with LD and MH the classification systems for students with BD are overly complex with little or no link to educational interventions.

The systems that follow represent the major approaches to classifying or developing subcategories in the BD area. Teachers should study these approaches to classification carefully so that they can understand the professional jargon used by other authorities such as psychologists. Only brief overviews will be presented here, primarily to point out the major advantages and disadvantages of each system.

Medical Model

Medicine has had a great impact on the attempt by psychologists and psychiatrists to classify various behavior disorders. The medical model of disease stresses symptom syndromes, a set of symptoms that can be traced to a specific pathology (Rizzo & Zabel, 1988). The symptoms alone do not define the problem or suggest solutions; they merely identify some underlying physical disorder. The *Diagnostic and Statistical Manual of Mental Disorders, Revised* (DSM-III-R), developed by the American Psychiatric Association (APA, 1980), is based on the medical model. The DSM-III-R, a classification system used mostly by mental health professionals, includes 230 diagnostic categories to label various types of individuals exhibiting BD.

One deficiency of the DSM-III-R system is that it is not specifically useful for educators (Heward & Orlansky, 1988). The major problem is the lack of reliability across professionals even with the increased complexity of behavioral descriptions. Epstein, Detwiler, and Reitz (1985), for example, found that it was not uncommon for one licensed health care professional to classify a student in one category while a second professional placed that same student in another category.

This lack of reliability, along with the fact that a given label provides no guidelines for treatment, may inhibit a teacher's ability to design appropriate educational interventions. Because of these weaknesses, some professionals are attempting to develop systems that are more descriptive of specific behaviors that might be modified with certain educational strategies.

Grouping Model

Quay (1975, 1979) and his colleagues collected a wide range of data across hundreds of children with behavior disorders and statistically categorized them into groups or clusters. The first subcategory is labeled *conduct disorders,* which includes disobedient and/or disruptive behaviors, verbal and physical aggression, and temper tantrums. *Personality disorders* constitutes the second subcategory and includes such behaviors as anxiety, social withdrawal, fearfulness, feelings of inferiority, and guilt.

The third subcategory in Quay's system is *immaturity.* Learners who fall into this category exhibit poor attention span, passiveness, daydreaming, and a preference for younger playmates. Finally, the fourth subcategory is labeled *socialized aggression.* It includes such behaviors as gang membership, truancy, and stealing.

Drawbacks of Classification Systems

A problem with both the medical model and the cluster system is that they make it easy for professionals to place a label on a given student. The developers of the systems would probably be the first to attest that this was not their intent. Unfortunately, history shows that whenever society attaches a label to a set of characteristics, people so classified eventually become known by the label and less attention is directed to dealing with the behaviors behind the label.

Many professionals believe that the stigma of being labeled as behavior disordered or seriously emotionally disturbed further handicaps students both in school and in life (e.g., Reynolds, Wang, & Walberg, 1987). This worst-case scenario may not be the case however, since the stigma of having behavior disorders may be attached to students because of their behaviors *before* they are staffed into special education (Braaten et al., 1988; Coie & Kupersmidt, 1983; MacMillan, Keogh, & Jones, 1986).

The main concern regarding classification systems is their lack of usefulness in designing educational programs for learners (Sinclair, Forness, & Axleson, 1985). Labels do not tell teachers what to teach; they do not even provide a clear picture of the types of behaviors students are exhibiting. The trend is to improve and apply systems that are designed to label *behaviors,* instead of labeling the people who exhibit the behaviors.

A growing body of research indicates that specific strategies have been successful in modifying certain types of behaviors. The task, then, is to describe objectively the behaviors exhibited by students and match proven educational strategies to those behaviors. Interestingly, this was and is the intent of the authors who devised the classification systems described earlier; however, their attempts to develop workable systems by categorizing the behaviors under headings (labels) has been misused.

Behaviorally Based Systems

Systems that analyze the behaviors of individuals with BD were developed essentially because of a disenchantment with systems that categorized or labeled people (Whelan, 1988). Instead of using diagnostic labels to assign individuals to specific groups, a behavior analysis system classifies behaviors as either excessive or deficient in frequency or intensity (Walker & Shea, 1988).

Hewett (1968) and Hewett and Taylor (1980) have developed a classification scheme based on the varying levels of competence of behaviors exhibited by students. They believe that obscure psychological terms serve only to confuse the educational process. Instead, they suggest a system that classifies behaviors into six levels of learning competence: attention, response, order, exploratory, social, and mastery.

Hewett and Taylor (1980) have proposed a system whereby each level of learning competence allows professionals to categorize behaviors along a continuum from too little to too much. For example, optimal social behaviors can range from extreme self-isolation (too little), up the continuum to alienating others, and ultimately to more appropriate social skills. In the same category, behaviors can range from inability to function alone (too much), to overly dependent, and finally to appropriate social skills.

According to Hewett and Taylor (1980) all behaviors can be categorized in this fashion by precisely describing their frequency or intensity. This system allows professionals to match a specific behavior or class of behaviors to the setting of curriculum goals and educational strategies. Hewett and Taylor's system is very much concerned with behavior analysis: The key is to focus energies on identifying behaviors that are either excessive or deficient instead of on placing the student in a specific category.

Severity Levels and Behavior Disorders

As with the other categories of exceptionalities described thus far, behavior disorders have at various times been described as mild, moderate, or severe according to the problems exhibited by the BD students. One study that contradicted the three levels of severity was conducted by Olson, Algozzine, and Schmid (1980). The results of this study indicated that teachers of learners with behavior disorders regularly viewed these students as exhibiting behaviors that would fall into two severity levels: mild and severe. Students with mild behavior disorders were viewed as those exhibiting behaviors that would respond to educational strategies implemented in regular classrooms by regular educators. Students with severe problems were viewed as those requiring residential placement with intensive treatment programs.

This study raises some interesting questions regarding teacher perception and actual practice. In reality, the students who could be identified as having mild to moderate BD would be a highly heterogeneous group. Many of these learners could do well in regular education settings with support from good teachers. Others in this group might be too disruptive, at least initially, to participate in regular education activities and might require the more restrictive placement of a self-contained special education classroom. This latter group does not, however, demonstrate behaviors that require residential placement.

The focus of this text is to present preferred teaching strategies and curriculum alternatives for this group of learners. They might be placed in mainstreamed situations with support from special education resource teachers or in self-contained classrooms housed in public schools.

PERSPECTIVES ON LABELING AND CLASSIFICATION

Throughout this section certain patterns can be detected that are common across the categories of LD, BD, and MH. In the literature supporting each of these categorical areas, authors stress that the labeling and classifying processes are necessary for keeping some semblance of so-called administrative order. Since there does not seem to be a better alternative available, these systems may facilitate getting monies to the program areas that need them.

Some authors believe, however, that the negative results of labeling far outweigh any positive effects. They cite research supporting their contention that labeling harms a person's self-concept and causes other people to have erroneously preconceived notions about the individual who is labeled LD, MH, or BD. In some cases, this is probably true.

Conversely, other authors believe that the label itself has little effect on a person's self-concept. They support the notion that students with significant cognitive, learning, and behavior problems have, by virtue of their behaviors or performance, called attention to themselves long before the label is attached. In this sense, the reaction of people to these learners and the fact that they have probably failed at obtaining appropriate social, academic, and/or independent living skills are the reasons for their poor self-concept. These authors also provide research to support their claims, and in many cases they are probably right.

The arguments for and against labeling may be clouding the basic premise of special education. Some students, regardless of labels, need help. They have been unable to keep up with their age peers in academic work or have been unsuccessful in establishing satisfying relationships with people. In some cases, the traditional public school curriculum may not be appropriate for these learners and may not be assisting them in meeting their true potential.

These key points should be the primary concern of teachers. No one would dispute that if students do not meet the criteria for services delineated in PL 94-142, they should not be labeled and placed in special education. When this happens, teachers should voice their opinions loudly to the contrary. For those learners who could benefit from additional services because of their handicapping conditions, teachers should focus on the behaviors that are a result of their conditions. This approach minimizes the concern over how the student is labeled and emphasizes what the student needs.

LEARNING AND BEHAVIORAL CHARACTERISTICS
OF STUDENTS WITH MILD AND MODERATE HANDICAPS

The most important lesson that can be derived from the efforts to classify learners into categorized groups is that each category is made up of many diverse individuals. This is especially true for students with learning disabilities and behavior disorders, because the complex interaction of intelligence and achievement varies a great deal within each group (Gloeckler & Simpson, 1988). For example, some learners with BD tend to score in the slow learner to mildly mentally handicapped range, while others score above average (Heward & Orlansky, 1988; Kauffman, 1985). This does not mean that the students who scored in the MH range are, in fact, mentally handicapped. Instead it may mean that their behavior disorders have acted as a barrier to learning, resulting in poor performance on an intelligence test.

At some point in their lives certain students with LD may have scored in the mild mentally handicapped range on a given intelligence test. These instances do not mean that these students are retarded; rather, their performance may be a result of poor testing techniques. Another reason for these poor performances may be that, at a given point in time, the students' ability to perform on the test was hampered by their learning disabilities.

The key in these instances is that most students with LD and BD have the potential for average or above average cognitive functioning. This would not be the case for students with mild or moderate mental handicaps. These learners do have a pervasive limited cognitive ability and would not demonstrate the same inconsistent ability profile demonstrated by students who have learning disabilities (Keogh, 1988) or behavior disorders (Braaten et al., 1988). Still, within the group of students identified as having mild and moderate mental handicaps the variance of academic and behavioral characteristics is great (Edgar, 1987; MacMillan, 1982).

This difference of ability versus achievement between groups of learners can be confusing. They allow for comparisons to be made by both professionals and parents that may hinder the ability to provide appropriate education for all. For example, the argument that "these kids aren't really retarded" leads some to believe that being learning disabled is a higher status position that being mentally handicapped. Such beliefs only cause dissension among the people who should be using all their energies to help students reach their inherent potential.

The remainder of this section includes a discussion of characteristics that are similar across all learners regardless of traditional categorical placement. At times, some students from any of the categories presented thus far might exhibit these characteristics.

Academic Characteristics

The major characteristic that crosses all categories of learners with mild and moderate handicaps is that they fall significantly behind their nonhandicapped peers in academically related tasks. Deshler and Schumaker (1986) found that by high school many of these learners are *at least* 6 years behind their nonhandicapped age peers in achievement. These gaps can be attributed to a number of characteristics that have been investigated by many researchers over the past 3 to 4 decades.

Learning Skills

Students with mild to moderate learning problems may have difficulty grasping concepts at symbolic or abstract levels. They may learn facts and lists by intensive drill but fail to master higher order skills of inference and association. Similarly, abstract concepts in mathematics such as time, money, measurement, and numerical reasoning may prove difficult.

Students with mild and moderate handicaps have deficits in their use of learning or knowledge acquisition strategies. These deficits can range from a simple lack of study, notetaking, and outlining skills to a more complex lack of awareness that knowledge acquisition strategies are needed and useful.

Over all, these students appear to have deficits in their metacognitive processes. Reid (1988) defined *metacognition* as "both the knowledge about cognition and the regulation of cognition" (p. 14). In reviewing the body of research that investigated metacognition, Reid summarized good metacognitive strategies as involving three major skills: (1) planning, including predicting outcomes, ability to schedule, and forms of trial and error; (2) monitoring, including self-testing, revising, and rescheduling; and (3) checking outcomes, including evaluation of the effectiveness and efficiency of one's efforts.

A majority of research in metacognition has been conducted with students who have learning disabilities. Because of the relatively high level of cognitive abilities of these learners, most of the implications from this body of research apply to them. However, the ability to plan, monitor, and check outcomes can also be taught to students with behavior disorders and mental handicaps in varying degrees, depending on the wide range of their abilities (Gloeckler & Simpson, 1988).

Language

Varying deficits in language ability are common across all categories of learners with handicaps. Some learners may demonstrate difficulties in grammar usage while others may have strong receptive language in the presence of little expressive language.

Language and communication are the cornerstone to all learning and social interaction. Therefore, students handicapped in these areas continue to fall further behind as their age peers progress by obtaining more complex language skills. Most learners with mild or moderate mental handicaps and many with learning disabilities and behavior disorders need intensive training in language and, in some cases, communication skills to allow them to reach their potential in other academic areas.

Memory

Memory problems plague many learners with mild and moderate handicaps. Some researchers have indicated that memory deficits are more prevalent in individuals with handicaps than in their nonhandicapped peers (e.g., Ellis, 1963; 1970); however, others find that these individuals demonstrate no inherent memory problems over the long term (Belmont, 1966; Sternberg, & Wagner 1982; Worden, Malgren, & Gabourie, 1982).

The work involving discrimination learning completed by Zeaman and House (1963) with learners with mental handicaps may provide some insight into possible strategies for dealing with other handicapped learners' memory deficits. One explanation for deficits in short-term memory identified during these research efforts was that the learners generally did not attend adequately to relevant stimuli in the learning task. This problem in paying attention to the task at hand may be directly related to memory problems.

Two aspects of learning theory that have led to strategies for assisting students are called *mediators* and *paired associates*. Mediators involve the use of some memory bridge between stimuli and responses. For example, a common mediator used by some elementary school students involves memorizing the sentence, "My very educated mother just served us nine pickles." The first letter of each word in the sentence represents the planets in the solar system in the order of their positions from the sun (Mercury, Venus, Earth, Mars, Jupiter, Saturn, Uranus, Neptune, Pluto). This memory device helps the student to bridge the gap between information learned and the ability to recall it under specific circumstances (Borkowski & Varnhagen, 1984).

Paired-associate learning involves pairing two words together so that when one word is used as the stimulus the other word will result as the response (MacMillan, 1982). Research results indicate that some learners with handicaps have more difficulty than their nonhandicapped peers in using paired associates for learning (O'Connor & Hermelin, 1963). However, these differences appear to be related to the types of materials used in research. Specifically, when the material is meaningful to the student and concrete in nature (e.g., pictures), students with handicaps can make the associations as well as their peers who do not have handicaps (Spitz, 1966).

Skill Generalization

Paired-associate learning deals with the acquisition of a skill or series of skills; however, once the skills are learned they must be transferred to other situations before they can be useful to the individual who has acquired them. The ability of individuals with handicaps to generalize acquired skills has become an important point of interest among educators.

In the past, many educators assumed that once these students were taught skills in the classroom they would automatically be able to transfer those skills to other settings, where different materials were used or different people were supervising the activity. A number of research efforts have demonstrated that this assumption may not be true (Wehman, Abramson, & Norman, 1977). Since learners with handicaps do not generalize learned skills and knowledge across conditions as well as their peers, teachers may need to be more aware of strategies that can assist these students in transferring training (Stokes & Baer, 1977).

Affective Characteristics

Identifying personality problems and specific affective characteristics associated with mental handicaps continues to be a source of debate among special educators. In the past, some professionals believed that personality deficits were inherent to mental handicaps, finding a tendency among people with mental handicaps to be overly anxious, easily frustrated, aggressive, rigid in thinking and acting, and generally a potential menace to society. Although there appears to be a higher incidence of personality disorders among people with mental handicaps, these disorders may not necessarily be a function of their handicaps (Robinson & Robinson, 1976; Stuckey & Newbrough, 1981). Rather, personality disorders or differences in the affective behaviors of such individuals may be the result of a complex interweaving of the individuals, their families, and the social systems that provide them services (Balla & Zigler, 1979; Hill & Bruininks, 1984; Reiss, Levitan, & McNally, 1982). For example, a child with mental handicaps may not be born with inherent personality problems. Her family, however, may suffer the severe stress that parenting such a child can place on its members. This stress may affect the quality of parent–child and sibling interaction, causing the child to develop personality problems (Crnic, Friedrich, & Greenberg, 1983).

Students with learning disabilities do not appear to exhibit personality problems at rates that are much different from those of the general population. There is some evidence that these learners may be at a greater risk for low social status (Dudley-Marling & Edmiaston, 1985; Gresham & Reschly, 1986); however, there are also some studies in dispute of that claim (e.g., Sabornie & Kauffman, 1986). The same complex interactions of individual, family, and social systems probably affect students with learning disabilities in the same way that these variables affect people with mental handicaps.

Students with behavior disorders, however, do exhibit personality problems that are more intense and last over a longer period of time than would be expected from individuals without handicaps. There are certain affective characteristics that are generic across all categories. These characteristics are included here because they ultimately have a negative effect on a person's ability to learn and they require attention by teachers to minimize their effects.

Overdependency

Researchers have attempted to identify variables that would cause a person with handicaps to develop abnormal affective characteristics. For example, some professionals have felt that as a group, people with mental handicaps appear to be overly dependent on others. When studying institutionalized people with mental handicaps, Zigler and his colleagues found this to be the case (Zigler, 1961; Zigler & Balla, 1972); however, this overdependence did not appear to be caused by the handicaps. Instead, the problem appeared to be related to the social deprivation these people suffered as residents of a large institution. Results of some research studies appear to indicate that close contact with significant others lessens the tendency of people with mental handicaps to be overdependent, thus providing a strong argument for normalizing relationships between these individuals and their families or significant others.

Research appears to support the existence of this same phenomenon with learners who have learning disabilities and behavior disorders (Gloeckler & Simpson, 1988). The term now used is *learned helplessness*, which refers to the same characteristic as overdependency. This behavior involves the manipulation of others to get help on tasks that could have been completed independently by the individual. Students who exhibit this trait tend to blame mistakes on others or on the situation; often they expect to fail.

Disruptive Behaviors

Students with mild and moderate handicapping conditions are often more disruptive than their nonhandicapped peers. There could be many reasons for this. These learners may be frustrated at their unsuccessful attempts to master academic content. They may have poor impulse control, may become confused easily, or may just fail to show common sense.

Whatever the reason, this trait of disruption tends to get such students noticed quickly. Frequent crying and temper tantrums and verbal or physical abuse of other children or teachers are frequent behaviors of some students within all categorized areas.

IDEA FILE

Knowing the affective and learning characteristics of students with handicaps can give teachers a better understanding of how certain instructional techniques can increase the probability that these students will learn. The following ideas are related to research findings that teachers can incorporate into their classes:

- By gradually fading cues and prompts, teachers may help learners come to rely more on their own problem-solving abilities.
- Breaking a task into smaller parts (task analysis) may help to relieve the anxiety exhibited by some learners when facing a new activity.
- Breaking a task into component parts may also reduce the avoidance behavior of some learners.
- Learners can be encouraged to discuss their own strengths and weaknesses regarding a specific task.
- Gradually fading artificial reinforcers (e.g., candy, free time) and allowing more natural reinforcers to take effect (e.g., smiles, a pat on the back) may assist learners in becoming more confident in their internal abilities to control the environment around them.
- Learners will often require a number of repetitions before a skill or set of skills can be learned. An important technique is to vary the activities used to teach these skills, thus minimizing boredom while increasing the students' attention to relevant stimuli.
- Verbal mediators can help students learn new words and concepts (MacMillan, 1972; Milgram, 1967). For example, a teacher who wishes a student to learn the two words *ball* and *box* may construct a sentence that includes the words ("The ball is in the box"). The sentence acts as a mediator by helping the student remember the key words.
- Words and experiences that are familiar to a student can be paired with unfamiliar content to form an association that may help the learner retain the new information.
- Varying the settings, time of day, materials, and people working with a student may facilitate generalization of learned skills (Langone & Westling, 1979; Stokes & Baer, 1977).

■ ■ ■ ■

This chapter has provided a broad overview of several important issues in the field of special education that relate to program development for students with mild and moderate handicaps. Over the past 15 years, the field of special education has grown tremendously, and many services are now offered to students that previously were not available. Unfortunately, there is some indication that the increase in services available for greater numbers of students may not be linked to improved quality of programs.

Part of the difficulty in improving the quality of programs may be related to the problems inherent in identifying and classifying students with handicapping conditions. The problems that result from a lack of agreement in definitions for mental handicaps, learning disabilities, and behavior disorders has led to confusion for teachers and other professionals who attempt to place students in programs designed to meet their needs. In addition, a number of common learning and behavioral characteristics cut across all categorical areas.

One important point highlighted in this chapter is the need for community-based instruction. The reality of daily practice in special education reveals the following important facts:

1. Regardless of their label (LD, MH, BD), students identified for special education differ significantly from their nonhandicapped peers in either one or all behavioral, social, and academic skills.

2. Regardless of definitions (or because of them), the needs of all these learners vary tremendously within categories.

3. Most students with mild and moderate handicaps learn best when information is presented in a concrete fashion (as opposed to an abstract format) and in a meaningful way.

4. The main job of special educators is to help their students become as independent as possible in the communities where they live or will live in the future.

With these considerations in mind, the approach proposed by Grey (1981) is adopted as a starting point for identifying the needs of learners with mild and moderate handicaps. Grey's approach is to view students' needs in terms of their "distance to life goals" (p. 428). This approach allows professionals to look past labels and concentrate on curriculum and instruction. Therefore, the distance to life goals for a nonreading student who wants to go to college might be just as great as for a nonreading student who wants to be a mechanic or one who wants to be mainstreamed into a regular education elementary class. The teacher's job becomes one of helping students set realistic goals and then identifying curricula and instruction geared to meeting those goals. The best setting for helping students set meaningful goals, solve meaningful problems, and learn meaningful skills is the community.

CHAPTER TWO

PROGRAM ALTERNATIVES AND DEVELOPMENT

■ Some professionals may have misinterpreted the philosophy of the least restrictive environment. Basically, it means that learners with handicaps should be educated in environments as close to normal as possible, as determined by each individual's abilities and disabilities. The principle of least restrictive environment was developed to minimize placement of learners in self-contained settings when their current needs do not dictate that type of environment (Leinhardt & Pallay, 1982). Even individuals in residential settings should have educational goals designed to assist them in moving to less restrictive settings as soon as possible.

This principle applies to all learners. For example, a student with mild cognitive disabilities who has the skills to participate in regular classes with support from special educators should be placed there on a full-time basis. Similarly, learners with severe handicaps should not be placed in an institutional program if they can benefit from the experiences of self-contained public school classes. Least restrictiveness emphasizes the fluid nature that special education programs should adopt (McCord, 1983).

NEED FOR FLEXIBLE PROGRAM OPTIONS

Educational options for students in special education historically have been static; once a learner was placed, there generally was little movement from one placement option to another. In contrast to this, the principle of least restrictive environment suggests that a learner's needs are continually changing, and with those changes comes the need to modify program options when and where necessary. Setting program goals designed to move learners on a continuum toward less restrictive environments appears to be a desirable approach.

Rigidity in placement options may also exist within special education program options. Students who have been classified as moderately mentally handicapped may have little chance of being exposed to MIMH program options even if the appropriateness of these options can be demonstrated. Conversely, learners with mild handicaps who could benefit from skills that can be obtained in a prevocational program for learners with moderate handicaps may be excluded from such a program. An important part of the least restrictive environment is the principle of individualization: Where each learner has unique needs, programs are developed to meet those needs. As these principles become accepted, there should be much less emphasis on categorical labeling of students. At present, however, there may still be a tendency to place learners primarily based on category (e.g., LD, BD, MH).

THE REGULAR EDUCATION INITIATIVE

The regular education initiative (REI) is a movement within the field of special education that potentially can have a profound effect on how services are provided for students with mild and moderate handicaps. The REI is essentially a proposition by a group of special educators to merge regular and special education units into one delivery system (Davis, 1989; Marozas & May, 1988). The various opinions of these educators can be placed on a continuum ranging from fairly drastic measures of abolishing special education (Stainback & Stainback, 1984) to more moderate measures of developing an equal partnership between regular and special education (Reynolds, Wang, & Walberg, 1987). The REI movement includes students with mild handicaps (e.g., MIMH, LD, and BD) as well as learners who are not targeted for special education but are receiving some type of service (e.g., Chapter I reading, migrant education).

Rationale for the REI

The basis for the REI was explained by Will (1986) when she delineated the limitations of special, remedial, and compensatory programs that pull students out of regular classrooms to provide them with services designed to help them succeed in the so-called mainstream of the school system.

Proponents of the REI cite a general failure of special programs in helping learners achieve their potential (Heller, Holtzman, & Messick, 1982; Reynolds et al., 1987). They identify the inconsistencies of labeling and classification systems (see Chapter One) as a reason why these students are segregated or become the outcasts of school systems. These educators also support the notion that all students with learning problems require the same type of help. They believe that the forced dichotomy of special and regular education creates an unnecessary rivalry that hinders delivery of the best instruction to the very students who need it most.

The REI assumes that (a) too many students are being identified for special programs and (b) many of these students can be served best in regular classes with in-class support or basic curriculum changes (Kauffman, Gerber, & Semmel, 1988). This may be an oversimplification of the REI; however, REI proponents do believe that sufficient evidence exists to support new models of instruction to provide for students with learning problems in regular classrooms (Hallahan, Keller, McKinney, Lloyd, & Bryan, 1988; Wang & Walberg, 1988).

For example, Reynolds and colleagues have suggested a heterogeneous grouping approach that would include curriculum-based identification systems and the Adaptive Learning Environments Model (ALEM) (Wang, 1980). This model includes the following strategies designed to adapt instruction to any student:

1. A hierarchically organized curriculum emphasizing the instruction of basic skills.
2. A flexible learning environment.
3. A classroom management program that allows for a blend of diagnostic/prescriptive and exploratory activities.
4. A cross-age program that groups learners movement between teams of teachers based on their progress.
5. A high degree of family participation.

Essentially, the ALEM program restructures the entire elementary school curriculum by structuring basic skills into hierarchical units. When students master one unit, they move to the next higher one. The school essentially becomes ungraded, and the students move through the system at their own speed. There is essentially no labeling, so students with significant learning problems receive help based on their level of functioning in the units of instruction, not according to a categorical label.

The ALEM system is based on a logical, common-sense approach that, on the surface, has several points of merit. This may be the basis for its popularity among some educators who have rallied around it as a viable alternative to the separation of special and regular education. As has happened in the past, however, the most logical approach has not always worked. Some professionals have urged caution in adopting the REI too quickly because there is a lack of empirical evidence that its basis, ALEM, is as successful as its developers claim (Fuchs & Fuchs, 1988a, 1988b).

Arguments Against the REI

A barrage of literature has surfaced questioning the validity of the REI (e.g., Braaten et al., 1988; Bryan et al., 1988; Fuchs & Fuchs, 1988a, 1988b; Hallahan et al., 1988; Kauffman et al., 1988; Keogh, 1988). For example, Kauffman and colleagues (1988) argued that two of the assumptions of the REI, specifically the overidentification of students and the failure of the schools to meet their needs, are untrue. They demonstrated that since 1986 there has been a decline in the percentage of the student population receiving special education services. According to these researchers, blaming teachers for the failure of all students is too simplistic and does not adequately explain the complex interaction between teachers and students with significant learning problems.

Hallahan and his colleagues (1988) looked at the REI from a research perspective and found its basis weak. They argued that the efficacy studies used by the REI proponents to prove the ineffectiveness of special education are flawed methodologically and have yielded mixed results. The results of these studies have provided little evidence that more intensive placements such as special education classes should be abolished. Fuchs and Fuchs (1988), in an intensive critique of the ALEM research literature, found enough methodological and analytical flaws to question whether or not this instructional approach has met its basic goals (see also Bryan & Bryan, 1988).

Keogh (1988) has raised an interesting set of concerns regarding the claims that the REI is a logical and common-sense approach. She has questioned whether it is logical to assume that regular educators can take over the program of the students they have already failed to teach. In addition, she has found that few, if any, of the proponents of the REI are regular educators.

The Middle Ground

As with many of the great debates in education, neither side of the REI debate is right or wrong, and both sides have merit. Reynolds (1988), a proponent of the REI, has admitted to the need for "very careful reflection," concerning reforms of special education (p. 355). For educators in the field to remain stagnant will do little good for the students who need the best services. Unfortunately, taking an all-or-nothing stance either for or against the REI probably will not help students either. Instead, special and regular educators should focus on one main issue that has not yet surfaced in the debate.

The REI is based on one unspoken assumption: The emphasis on traditional classroom-based basic skills is the most desirable alternative for learners with mild and moderate handicaps. This assumption seems to be based on the theory that to be more "normal" you have to engage in the same activities as regular education students. The idea that students with handicaps need to be in as much contact as possible with their nonhandicapped peers is accepted by most, and it is assumed to be important to all learners. Structuring this contact under conditions in which students with significant learning and/or behavioral problems must cope with regular academic activities may turn the lofty goals of least restrictive environment and appropriate education into hollow statements.

The proponents of the REI have overlooked two important characteristics of students with mild and moderate handicaps. First, they have a difficult (but not impossible) time grasping abstract concepts taught in relation to traditional public school activities such as paper-and-pencil exercises, basal reading series, and lectures. Second, even if these students do learn some basic skills, (as shown by some ALEM studies and other research efforts), they may never transfer or generalize the skills to daily life.

The main issue that both camps should address is not the physical placement of these learners as much as the need for changes in curriculum and educational interventions. Community-based instruction (CBI) is not a new concept in the professional literature (e.g., Langone, 1986), yet it has not been readily accepted at the grass-roots level in either regular or special education. Students with mild and moderate handicaps can learn academic, social, and behavioral skills in community environments by practicing activities geared to real-life situations. These activities are not necessarily separate from the activities the students would encounter in their regular education programs; rather, under the supervision of the special educator, they can run concurrently with those initiated by the regular educator.

CBI is an approach that defines the word *special* in special education. It is becoming the mainstay in programs for learners with moderate and severe handicaps (Langone, 1986; Nietupski, Hamre-Nietupski, Houselog, Donder, & Anderson, 1988; Snell & Browder, 1986). CBI should also become a mainstay in programs for students with mild handicapping conditions, because the activities emphasized in this approach allow learners to apply basic academic skills to tasks that are concrete in nature through the use of real-life stimuli. These activities also are highly motivating, allowing students to see the need for learning such skills.

The REI has the potential and possibly the momentum to change the physical arrangements of placement from the traditional special education system to the traditional regular education system. CBI has the potential to change either traditional system into a more progressive one that allows students to learn in the settings where they are expected to live, work, and engage in leisure pursuits. The remainder of this chapter presents the types of program alternatives currently available as well as some basic teacher competencies for developing more effective professional partnerships. Students with mild handicaps *may* continue to find their way back into regular education classes for additional part-time or even full-time placement. Regardless of the placement, however, special educators will have to take a more proactive role in developing appropriate curriculum options for these learners.

IDEA FILE

Regular educators are becoming more interested in exploring the use of community-based instructional options for the learners in their classes who are progressing slowly as well as for those identified as being at high risk for dropping out of school. This is evidenced in two examples that have been gaining some national notoriety. The Oglethorpe County High School Project in Lexington, Georgia, has developed a "School Within a School" that allows students identified as being at high risk for dropping out to learn academic skills in relation to activities based in surrounding communities. Similarly, the City of Schools Project, Brooklyn, New York, places students in community settings to learn or supplement their knowledge of academics.

■ ■ ■ ■

BRIDGING THE COMMUNICATION GAP

The number and variety of duties that teachers must perform may cause some to lose sight of the existing continuum of services ranging from preschool to postsecondary. Consequently, learners entering a secondary program who did not receive instruction in career awareness and basic prevocational skills at the elementary level may be gravely disadvantaged in a program designed to instruct them in independent living and vocational skills. Therefore, there is a need for continual contact among teachers across program grade levels as well as between general and special education.

There are some specific suggestions teachers may find helpful in bridging the communication gap between different programs. First, teachers should become thoroughly acquainted with professionals from all other grade levels that students will come from or move toward. For example, elementary teachers could visit the classrooms of both preschool and secondary programs in their catchment area. In addition to visiting those classes for the purpose of observing teaching techniques and materials, the teachers may have the opportunity to coordinate program objectives in a scope and sequence fashion across different levels. Teachers along the continuum should know what skills the students are working on at the various points in their programs. An additional benefit of increased teacher contact can be the coordination of assessment methods. If two teachers have been communicating on a regular basis, a learner entering a new program should not arrive without adequate support data.

Teachers also need to have a good working knowledge of community services such as work stations in industry, recreational opportunities, and emergency funding sources. Beyond knowing of the existence of such services, teachers will need to visit these programs and establish working relationships with the professionals who staff them.

One illustration of this is the case of a 19-year-old learner named Sam who had a moderate mental handicap. Sam was progressing at a satisfactory rate in the areas of functional literacy (e.g., reading menus in fast food restaurants), social skills including interpersonal communication, use of the telephone, and a variety of other independent living skills. Sam was also included in an innovative program allowing him to participate in a variety of vocational education programs with general education students. The primary focus of these vocational program options was to allow Sam time to practice and generalize skills he learned in special education to settings more like community placements. This approach also allowed him to learn basic vocational skills aimed at eventual employment.

At this point, Sam demonstrated that he might be ready for increased community interaction. A teacher in continual contact with available community services (e.g., vocational rehabilitation) would be in a position to identify sites that could accommodate Sam for half the school day, allowing him an additional opportunity to generalize his skills to the natural setting. Where program options such as this do not exist, a closer working arrangement with community-based professionals, employers, and citizens could provide a resource for developing additional placements.

MAINSTREAMING

Students with mild and moderate handicaps can be placed in many different program options ranging from less restrictive to more restrictive in nature. Less restrictive models, generally called *mainstreaming alternatives,* involve placing students with handicaps in contact with their nonhandicapped peers for a majority of the school day. In practice, mainstreaming is a word with many definitions. Some policy statements refer to mainstreaming in a broad sense, allowing all persons with handicaps the right to participate with their general education peers to the maximum extent possible. This definition includes both placement of learners in regular classes and placement of learners in self-contained programs. Other professionals view mainstreaming as a more restricted concept that deals with the delabeling of students who are capable of participating in general education programs (MacMillan, 1982). Students with mild handicaps are the population most affected by mainstreaming. Since Dunn's (1968) famous article questioning the validity of special education there have been major efforts to avoid placement in self-contained classes that some professionals felt created stigmatizing labels and barriers to socialization (Reynolds & Birch, 1988).

The principle of least restrictive environment (LRE), as originally developed in PL 94-142, differs from what has taken place in many mainstreaming efforts. LRE emphasizes that students should be placed in environments that are best suited to their strengths and weaknesses. This differs from the wholesale belief that regular education placement is automatically the best possible alternative for all learners with mild handicapping conditions. The ultimate goal of both LRE and mainstreaming in the broadest sense should be the successful integration of individuals with handicaps with their nonhandicapped peers on an educational and social level. Accomplishing these goals will require more than mere scheduling changes.

As the field of special education moves into the last decade of this century, there appears to be a renewed interest in close inspection of the curriculum in both self-contained and mainstreamed settings. Professionals such as Polloway and Smith are calling for a move away from the "narrow focus on academic and remedial concerns" (1983,

p. 157). The alternative is to develop a curriculum that is community-valid. Community-valid skills are those that allow students to learn and practice skills applicable to community life. For example, a student assigned to a United States government class would not be asked to try and memorize the branches of government. Instead, the student might be taught to call the local office of the senator representing the district and request assistance in obtaining information about changes in Social Security benefits.

IDEA FILE

Some professionals support definitions that are overconcerned with the administrative functions while giving little consideration to the daily instructional problems involved in making mainstreaming a success (Kaufman, Gottlieb, Agard, & Kukic, 1975). For example, some IEP staffings may result in heated discussions concerning how much time a student should spend in the regular class before the student is considered to be mainstreamed. These arguments can misdirect staffing committees (including teachers) and take time from valuable program planning.

Teachers may be in a position to redirect staffing committees into considering mainstreaming as Kaufman and colleagues have termed it—an "instructional approach" (1975, p. 4). Teachers can point out that effective programming in the mainstream primarily involves development of appropriate services. These services include assessment of learner strengths and weaknesses, designing and implementing effective instructional interventions, and monitoring the interventions for success (revising whenever and wherever necessary). The issue is not the quantity of time spent in regular education, but the *quality* of time spent under these conditions. Teachers may look upon themselves as facilitators, directing other professionals toward the more important considerations of successful programming.

■ ■ ■ ■

Mainstreaming allows learners to participate in classes with their general education peers whenever possible. The following sections present descriptions of placement options currently in use for educating students with handicaps. The models range in restrictiveness from those allowing maximum integration to those allowing minimum integration, depending on individual student needs. Techniques will be presented here that are designed to assist teachers in increasing contact between learners with handicaps and their general education peers in all settings regardless of the existing level of integration.

A Model for Consulting Teachers

The consulting teacher model allows learners to participate fully in the regular classroom. The special education teacher has no direct instructional time with the students included in this placement option (Anderson, Martinez, & Rich, 1980; Reynolds & Birch, 1988). This system allows the special educator to be a consultant to general education teachers, assisting them in developing appropriate assessment tools, modifying the curriculum, and identifying effective educational interventions. The general education teachers, however, provide all the direct instruction.

There are several conditions needed for this model to be an effective alternative. First, the special educator must be expert in diagnosing learner deficits and then matching appropriate methods and materials to those needs. This requirement is important since the consultant must be able to provide the regular class teacher with meaningful assistance in the form of ideas, materials, and techniques (Heron & Harris, 1982X; Westling & Koorland, 1988).

Second, in the relationship between the two educators equal importance must be assigned to the roles of each teacher (Rauth, 1981). If the consultant's role is looked upon as being something more important or prestigious than that of the classroom teacher, the relationship may be hindered (Reynolds & Birch, 1977). This consideration is important to teachers who are or will be functioning in this type of instructional environment. An effective change agent (in this case the special educator) should not enter the classrooms of other professionals to "tell" them how to run their programs. Rather, a more effective technique is to present the role of a consultant sincerely as a support service, there to aid an overburdened teacher.

The techniques teachers use to instruct learners may be useful for presenting effective teaching methods to general educators (Idol-Maestas, 1983). For example, inservice providers often try to present new ideas and methods via lectures and discussions; however, there is little evidence that teachers actually transfer this knowledge into practice (Hentshel, 1977). Instead, the consulting teacher may choose to model techniques targeted for use with specific learners (e.g., demonstrating a behavior management technique).

Special education consulting teachers can also become a source of reinforcement for general educators. For example, when general educators incorporate various direct product measurement systems into their programs, the special educator can provide some form of sincere social reinforcement. A statement such as, "I really like the method you used; I never actually considered that possibility," can go a long way with some professionals.

There are many other ways that special educators can reinforce their regular education colleagues for providing the best educational interventions for students with handicapping conditions. One possibility is to start a school newsletter that highlights successful attempts and ideas presented by the regular education teachers who have mainstreamed students in their classes. Also, special education teachers can make available an "idea box" of instructional strategies that regular education teachers can use with their general education students as well as with any students exhibiting learning problems.

Quality is as important as quantity when making contact with regular education teachers. Consulting teachers who are only infrequently available or those who are frequently available but only for cursory visits will probably not provide services that are adequate for a classroom teacher. Contacts should be frequent, preplanned, and organized so that specific objectives are covered during the time available for the meeting. A few minutes at the end of the visit spent planning what is to be accomplished during the next contact may increase the probability that the goals will be met.

A Model for Resource Teachers

Considerable variations exist in resource teacher models among public school programs (Payne & Patton, 1981). This placement option involves enrolling students in regular classes for at least part of the day. The remainder of the school day is spent in a resource center where the special educator provides direct instruction using either remedial or compensatory instructional techniques. These programs vary in form and the amount of time that students participate in regular education programs. For example, in some school districts learners may be enrolled in regular education programs such as physical education, art, and music while receiving all of their academic instruction in a resource center. Conversely, in some districts learners may be enrolled in regular education classes at least half of the school day before they become eligible for a resource teacher's services. The second example is probably the one that best describes a resource program.

A resource room model that has become increasingly popular recently places students who are mildly mentally handicapped as well as those who demonstrate less than severe learning disabilities and behavior disorders in one resource classroom (Gloeckler & Simpson, 1988; Mercer & Mercer, 1985). The combinations of these learners enrolled in any one classroom may vary from including students in all three disability areas to varied combinations of any two categories (LD/MH, LD/BD, BD/MH).

The objectives of a resource room are generally consistent with what many define as mainstreaming. Resource models strive to provide services for those students who, because of learning problems, are currently unable to participate on a full-time basis in the regular classroom. In a sense, this model may be a vehicle to prepare students for entering a consulting teacher model program as soon as possible. The goals of a resource program are to provide individual or small-group instruction based on the learners' deficit areas while developing innovative instructional techniques that can be used with the students while they are in the regular classroom. Many successful resource center programs are currently in operation. Their success can usually be traced to one or two people who are able to put into practice some basic tenets of good programming. Programs that use peer tutors and volunteers are examples of how teachers can increase the efficiency of instructional interventions.

Special educators have the opportunity to develop a plan designed to increase and maintain quality contacts with regular educators. Initially, special educators can assist their colleagues in understanding the principles of curriculum modification, that is, the need to identify specific content that is appropriate for a given learner. This model is quite the contrary of one where teachers assume that learners must be exposed to everything in, say, a particular chapter in an earth science textbook. The resource teacher can assist the regular educator in choosing only those curricular objectives that are appropriate for the student.

From the initial contacts, the resource teacher can foster a relationship allowing each educator to provide suggestions for effective instructional procedures. The probability increases that interventions designed by both teachers and tried out in the resource center will in turn be implemented in the regular classroom. In addition, the resource teacher can develop and implement community-based activities that complement the more traditional classroom-based activities used by the regular educator. For example, regular educators teaching earth science material via lecture and slide presentation would have their work complemented by special educators who assist their mainstreamed students in participating in a community project to retard soil erosion.

IDEA FILE

Special educators have the opportunity to increase and maintain high-quality contacts with regular educators. Resource teachers, in particular, should spend as much time as possible interacting with and supporting the activities of their regular education colleagues. The following ideas might provide teachers with a starting point for increasing contact with other professionals:

- Resource teachers might consider identifying three or four regular educators per month as people to get to know. As an "icebreaker" they might invite them to an afternoon coffee session to share ideas and tell about each other's programs.
- Weekly reports on the students' progress toward certain objectives can be helpful to regular educators whose students are served by the resource teacher.
- Information on weekly reports can include a sharing of ideas targeting effective instructional procedures and identifying aspects of the regular education curriculum that appear to be useful to the students.
- Writing a newsletter to share ideas and teaching strategies and to highlight noteworthy achievements of regular educators as they work with handicapped students can be a good method for resource teachers to become a more integral part of the school.

■ ■ ■ ■

There are learners who, because of the nature of their strengths and weaknesses, require more structured placement than a consulting or resource option provides. These learners range from a small number who have mild cognitive problems to all learners who are classified as having moderate mental handicaps. Also, a small number of students who demonstrate more severe learning disabilities and behavior disorders are enrolled in self-contained classes.

A Model for Teachers of Self-Contained Classes

Self-contained special education classes are designed for learners who can not benefit from enrollment in a regular class. Primarily, these students are unable to keep up with the instructional pace (Payne & Patton, 1981), and heavy emphasis on traditional academic objectives may not meet their needs (Mercer, 1987; Rizzo & Zabel, 1988).

The arguments are numerous both for and against special class (self-contained) placements for learners, with a voluminous amount of research either supporting or refuting the effectiveness of these program options. The following statement by MacMillan (1977) presents a logical philosophy that could be derived from careful analysis of the pros and cons of self-contained public school classes:

To contend that any one administrative arrangement is the best for *all* EMR children, or, conversely, to argue that one is *bad* for all EMR children, is naive and ignores variation in individuals within the population of EMR. (1977, p. 431)

The same, of course, can be said of all learners when considering placement alternatives. One reason why self-contained special education classes have received a bad name may be because in some instances they have been used as a dumping ground. Some self-contained classes may include an overproportional number of minority group members. They also have been known for easy enrollment policies and for presenting almost insuperable barriers to leaving the program once admitted.

Some students with severe educational deficits can benefit from classes with smaller enrollment and curricular options designed for maximum community integration. However, this option should also allow students placed in special classes to have opportunities for participating with their general education peers whenever possible. Learners spending most of the school day in a special class can be integrated into basic remedial programs, nonacademic programs and clubs, lunch, work-study programs, and vocational education classes. These students may benefit by integration into program options similar to these with a particular emphasis on the career and vocational aspects. The use of peer tutors from regular education programs would increase the contact of these learners with classmates from outside special education as well as provide opportunities for the general population to get to know and assist learners with mild and moderate handicaps (Dale, 1979; Langone, 1981).

KEY CONCEPTS

Self-contained special classes can be an acceptable placement option provided the decision is based on information such as the need for more individualization, specific objectives offered in the self-contained class, and identified student strengths and weaknesses that can best be served in a self-contained setting.

- Teachers should continually reevaluate placements and attempt to integrate learners into less restrictive placements as soon as possible.
- Teachers will continually be developing innovative activities that allow students with handicaps high-quality contact with their general education peers and the community at large.
- High-quality contact refers to activities such as integrating learners into vocational education programs, developing work stations in industry, providing instruction in independent living skills in community sites, and developing recreation and leisure programs that include both students with and those without handicaps.

■ ■ ■ ■

PHYSICAL MANAGEMENT OF THE INSTRUCTIONAL SETTING

Instructional environments can be located anywhere teachers decide learning is to take place. Traditionally, professionals have considered the classroom as the area where teaching occurs; however, the trend is now moving toward recognizing community locales as appropriate instructional environments (Landesman-Dwyer, 1981; Nietupski et al., 1988; Schalock, Harper, & Genung, 1981; Snell & Browder, 1986). The concept of arranging the physical environment to facilitate learning is an important aspect of the program development process (Lindsey, 1964; Payne, Polloway, Smith, & Payne, 1981). Arranging the instructional environment goes beyond moving desks and chairs. Other considerations for designing an efficient learning environment include scheduling, developing group and individual activities, using equipment, and developing learning centers.

Arranging the Physical Environment

When arranging the physical environment of the classroom, teachers should develop an overall plan (including diagrams), allowing a maximum use of space while keeping materials centralized to minimize teacher movement. Valuable instructional time is wasted when a teacher has to stop a lesson to retrieve materials in another part of the room. Peter (1975) has suggested that teachers arrange the classroom in relation to the room's fixed features (doors, windows, closets), functional relationships among areas (study sections away from activities producing higher noise levels), and primary pathways (efficient planning of student traffic routes).

The fixed features of a room become important when the requirements of specific activities are considered. For example, an area of the classroom designed for teaching prevocational skills (e.g., assembly line tasks, woodworking) would need a large storage area. The location of this section should be near a closet. Similarly, the section for teaching self-care skills should be located in an area near a sink, bathroom, or shower.

Arranging centers in relation to their functional characteristics is also an important consideration. High rates of activity (group math lesson) versus low rates of activity (individual reading center) should be separated as far as possible. Centers that require sharing materials, such as a library center and study carrels, should be located close together. Figures 2.1 and 2.2 provide classroom floor plans that teachers may wish to use as models.

Planning efficient traffic patterns can save both the teacher and the learners valuable time and steps. For example, an activity requiring students to leave the room at varying intervals to retrieve water from the hallway lavatories might be located near the class entrance. This eliminates the need for students to move through other activities to reach the door. Activities can also be located so that teachers or other supervisory personnel in charge of a number of duties can easily manage those areas without crisscrossing the room. Various learning centers in the room should be located to facilitate orderly movement (Peter, 1975). In an attempt to maintain order, teachers at times may misinterpret this goal and arrange their classrooms in traditional fashions that discourage student movement (Rich, 1980). These efforts may, at best, simulate an environment very different from what occurs in vocational and other community settings. Instead, a classroom should be designed to teach and then allow maximum freedom and responsibility on the part of the students.

Classrooms should be designed to facilitate the teacher's ability to scan the class with maximum efficiency (Hart, 1981). The teacher must have an unobstructed view of all areas of the room at any given time. For example, teachers can train students to react to eye contact as a reminder to return to a task. Thus, an important feature of the classroom structure is to allow maximum eye contact between the teacher and students from any point in the room. There are a number of reasons for maintaining close visual contact with students, the most important being safety. If students engage in unsafe

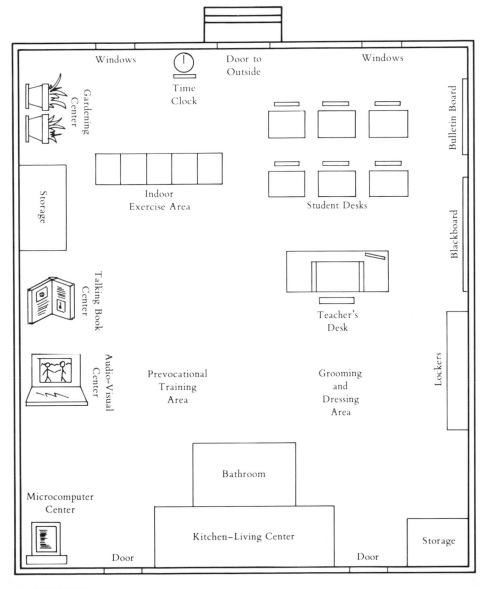

■ FIGURE 2.1
Sample Self-Contained Classroom Floor Plan

activities or are involved in physical altercations, teachers with an unobstructed view may be able to react more quickly.

Scheduling

Developing an efficient time schedule is a valuable skill for teachers. Downtime in the classroom can be a chief contributor to poorly managed programs in which a number of inappropriate behaviors can occur (Laycock, 1980). (*Downtime* refers to times when little or no instruction occurs; students do not know what to do or what comes next.) Consequently, teachers must consider the length of lessons, times of day more appropriate for

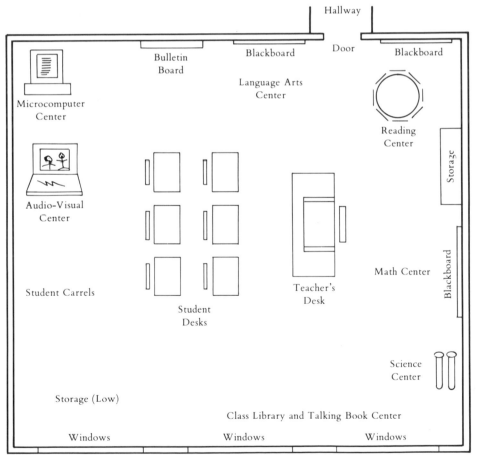

■ *FIGURE 2.2*
Sample Resource Classroom Floor Plan

teaching specific skills, and time blocks for individualized instruction as well as group instruction.

Time schedules can be used as learning tools as well as organizational aids. For example, a teacher may begin by scheduling daily activities consistently so that learners can benefit from the support of a structured environment. Activity in the community, however, does not exist in neatly arranged time blocks. Accordingly, teachers could plan deliberate changes in the schedule over time, thus promoting flexibility in the learners (Hart, 1981). This does not mean schedules should be disorganized so that students are in a continual state of confusion. Rather, planned change allows students to gain skills in dealing with sudden alterations in schedules appropriately and in an orderly fashion. (See Figures 2.3 and 2.4.)

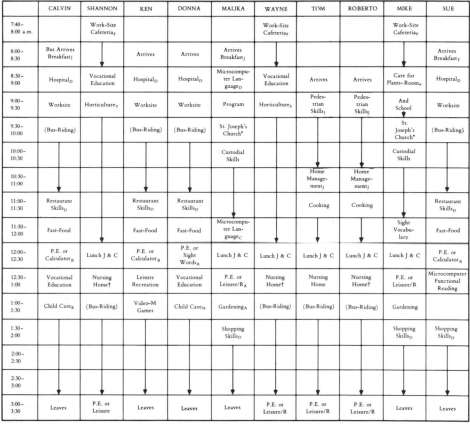

*Attends worksite with Ms. Jones' (Teacher) Group.   †Attends worksite with Ms. Jones' Group.

D = Diane (Teacher)   B = Bonnie (Peer Tutor)   S = Sam (Peer Tutor)   A = Angela (Parent Volunteer)
J = Jim (Aide)   T = Tom (Peer Tutor)   P = Pam (Peer Tutor)   M = Mary (Parent Volunteer)
C = Cathy (Aide)   F = Frank (Peer Tutor)   K = Kay (Peer Tutor)   N = Nancy (Peer Tutor)

■ FIGURE 2.3
Sample Self-Contained Class Schedule

In addition to planning schedule changes as an instructional tool, teachers can design activities to teach learners organizational skills. Teachers can use scheduling as a vehicle for teaching one facet of responsible living. For instance, a higher level goal for students involves obtaining a list of tasks at the start of the day that must be accomplished before the end of school. The learners then develop their own daily schedules around those tasks, keeping in mind the regular daily activities required of the total group. Learners trained in developing such management systems gain an important skill for independent living.

IDEA FILE

First-year teachers may find it difficult to set up their first class schedule. There are many different approaches to scheduling, and teachers should experiment with a number of them until they find one that meets their needs. The following steps may prove helpful for developing a basic schedule:

TIME	MONDAY	TUESDAY	WEDNESDAY	THURSDAY	FRIDAY
8:45–9:00 9:00–9:15 9:15–9:30 9:30–9:45 9:45–10:00 10:00–10:15 10:15–10:30 10:30–10:45 10:45–11:00 11:00–11:15 11:15–11:30 11:30–11:45	Bobby, Lin, Jamal, Karen (Reading) Ricky, Ken, LaRonda, Pam, Deimetris (Written Exp.) Bobby, Lin, Karen, Ken, LaRonda (Math) Tim-Spelling	Juan-Handwriting Telisa, Pam, Jim (Math) Telisa, Pam, Jim, Susan (Shopping Skills Community)	Bobby, Lin, Jamal, Karen (Reading) Ricky, Ken, LaRonda, Pam, Deimetris (Written Exp.) Bobby, Lin, Karen, Ken, LaRonda (Math) Tim-Spelling	Juan-Handwriting Telisa, Pam, Jim (Math) Telisa, Pam, Jim, Susan (Shopping Skills Community)	Bobby, Lin, Jamal, Karen (Reading) Ricky, Ken, LaRonda, Pam, Deimetris (Written Exp.) Bobby, Lin, Karen, Ken, LaRonda (Math) Tim-Spelling
11:45–12:30 12:30–1:30	LUNCH PLANNING PERIOD	LUNCH	LUNCH	LUNCH	LUNCH ....
1:30–1:45 1:45–2:00 2:00–2:15 2:15–2:30 2:30–2:45 2:45–3:00 3:00–3:30	Juan, Bobby, Lin, Ricky, Deimetris (Functional Reading Community) Tom-Reading	Kurt, Kevin, Paula, Sally (Written Exp.) Josh, Peter Diane, Megan (Lang. Arts)	Juan, Bobby, Lin, Ricky, Deimetris (Functional Reading Community) Tom-Reading	Kurt, Kevin, Paula, Sally (Written Exp.) Josh, Peter, Diane, Megan (Lang. Arts)	Juan, Bobby, Lin, Ricky, Deimetris (Functional Reading Community) Tom–Reading
3:30–4:00	Bus Duty Meet With	.... Regular	.... Education	.... Teachers	....

■ FIGURE 2.4
Sample Resource Room Schedule

- Teachers should first decide what lengths of instructional sessions best meet their students' needs. For example, younger learners with shorter attention spans require shorter instructional periods. Some activities may require longer sessions, which may affect the schedule. To start, teachers may wish to divide the school day into half-hour sessions, then adjust the sessions as student need and activity length dictate. (Before dividing the day into sessions, teachers should subtract the times for set activities such as lunch, physical education, art, and recess.)

- Grouping learners is an important part of scheduling (see the next section). The first step in grouping involves the physical management of a given number of students. Teachers can divide the number of students present in the class during a session by the total number of instructional personnel (e.g., teacher, aides, peer tutors). This calculation will give the teacher an idea of the ratio of students to instructors. For example, if there are 20 students in the classroom from 10 A.M. until 10:30 A.M. and only a teacher plus one aide, the ratio is 10 to 1. If the teacher wishes to teach a reading group of six students, the ratio of students to aides increases to 14 to 1. At this point, a teacher may wish to schedule help from a peer tutor or volunteer so that the students not engaged in group work will have adequate supervision while they are working individually or in centers.

■ ■ ■ ■

Grouping Learners

Programming for the individual does not eliminate group instruction. Factors such as dwindling resources and teaching students to work as members of a team make grouping a must. Teachers should consider moving beyond grouping by ability and consider grouping according to the complementary skills of the learners.

Small-group instruction can be implemented in one of two ways, depending on the activity. First, an activity may require that each group member complete a task that contributes to a total group product. For example, a group of students with behavior disorders, learning disabilities, and cognitive deficits can work together to complete a community-based cost comparison activity in local retail establishments. Each student is assigned to identify the prices of certain items that will be collated and analyzed by the group.

The second method of grouping involves meeting the needs of individual students while in the confines of a group, where what the learners share in common are the subject and physical proximity. For example, a group of four students may be working with the teacher on computation objectives. The learners may be at varying levels, requiring the teacher to spend small amounts of time individually directing each student. The primary concern is that the teacher arrange the physical space for delivery of prompts/cues and reinforcers. This arrangement may be advantageous, because the teacher can instruct and direct more learners simultaneously while allowing them to work at their own levels.

Commercially produced materials can be helpful in deciding on how to group learners. A reading program allowing the teacher to work with a more diverse group of students may be more efficient, because the teacher can increase the size of the group. Students with handicapping conditions come to school with many deficit areas and, in a sense, each can use individually designed lessons. Because of their numbers, this would be an improbable task for one teacher, so good commercially produced programs can be invaluable for teaching groups of students who need to learn similar skills.

Individualized instruction that allows a teacher to work one to one with a learner is difficult to schedule. However, this form of instruction should not be overlooked, and short periods of time during the day can be scheduled for it. Teachers who locate their desks in central locations (to maintain maximum visual scan) can call specific students to them for individualized instruction in new skills. The time allotted per student may be minimal; however, if the session is carefully planned, a great deal can be accomplished.

Organizing Classroom Equipment and Learning Centers

Audiovisual equipment, microcomputers, and other instructional aids are available that can be highly effective for use with learners with handicaps. Commercial catalogs are one source for identifying these resources, and another is exhibits at professional conventions. Learners with mild and moderate handicaps have strengths and weaknesses in different instructional modalities, as do all learners, and matching the appropriate equipment to those needs is important. Learning centers are often built around individual themes specified by the portion of curriculum being emphasized. Hence, a classroom may be equipped with centers dealing with such subjects as career education, science, prevocational skills, mathematics, reading, and self-care skills. The efficiency of these centers can be improved if teachers incorporate equipment into them that can be used to individualize instruction. For example, a tape recorder incorporated into a reading center can allow students to practice reading skills using talking books and taped lessons.

Structuring Learning in Community Settings

Hopefully, teachers will be increasing the time they spend in community instruction. Each of the areas previously discussed has implications for developing community-based learning activities. For example, arranging the physical environment would be important for teaching mobility and safety skills to younger learners. In this case, teachers can enlist the aid of law enforcement officials for controlling traffic.

Similarly, when designing community-based activities teachers should consider the need for efficient scheduling and grouping of students. Scheduling problems will have to be worked out on an administrative level in order to make available the necessary personnel. Scheduling the assistance of more able learners to assist the less able ones can provide valuable help. Using teams of students to work on problems or practice learned skills involves careful planning and matching of group members.

Good teachers demonstrate many superior competencies, including those described in this section. They also demonstrate superior qualities in their relationships with people. The following section presents issues and techniques for improving a teacher's professional relationships as well as improving the efficiency of support staff.

KEY CONCEPTS

- Carefully arranging the teaching environment (e.g., classroom, community work sites) increases the probability that learning will occur.

- All space in the classroom should be used efficiently. Traffic patterns should be considered that allow freedom of movement to all areas. In addition, equipment and furniture should be arranged to allow observation of students from any point in the room.

- A well-designed schedule is vital. Teachers need to be able to schedule frequent trips to the community with small groups while scheduling the remainder of the class in school-based activities.

- A small group is the most efficient method of teaching many skills.

- Groups involved in community-based instruction often work well when students with different problems are represented.

■ ■ ■ ■

OTHER TEACHER COMPETENCIES

An interesting phenomenon may occur when groups of teachers from various disciplines gather together for cross-training workshops. Special educators may have a great deal of difficulty describing their specialty areas to others. Regular education teachers generally find this task easier, because most specialize in one or two content areas (e.g., mathematics, science). Special educators, however, are not always specialists in subject areas, and the skills and competencies they possess are much more ambiguous.

There are three broad competency areas in which many teachers are proficient: assessment and diagnosis, curriculum development and modification, and applied behavior analysis. A special educator should be able to use a variety of both normative and criterion-referenced assessment tools (described in Chapter Three) to pinpoint a student's strengths and weaknesses. After the information from these assessment strategies is gathered and closely analyzed, the teacher should be able to identify each student's major strengths and weaknesses.

Special educators should also be proficient in skills related to designing instruction based on student need. They should be capable of breaking down instruction into component parts and expert in monitoring student progress.

Finally, teachers should develop competencies involving behaviorally oriented instructional programs. This system allows teachers to define target behaviors precisely; conduct frequent and accurate measurements of defined behaviors; apply instructional procedures or materials designed to change the students' behavior; measure change; and revise the program where necessary.

The ability to describe these competencies to other teachers is an important starting point for establishing cooperative relationships. For example, a vocational educator teaching a learner with learning disabilities may need help in identifying the learner's academic strengths and weaknesses and matching a module format to those needs. The special educator could provide the competencies of criterion-referenced assessment and curriculum modification to support the vocational educator. Similarly, a special educator may lack the necessary content expertise to develop activities for learners with mental retardation that reflect skills similar to those in industrial settings. A vocational educator can provide the technical expertise, materials, and community contacts needed to develop more appropriate curricular options. Other teacher competencies that appear to be vital to program success involve the ability to use and schedule paraprofessionals, volunteers, and materials to maximize instructional time and the ability to deliver appropriate consequences based on observed learner behaviors (Boomer, 1982; Fredricks, Anderson, & Baldwin, 1977). In addition, special educators may be called upon to provide inservice training for regular educators mainstreaming students into their classes. In any event, before teachers can bring skills and knowledge to a team effort, they first must have a strong grasp of what they can and cannot do.

MANAGEMENT OF OTHER INSTRUCTIONAL PERSONNEL

A problem faced by some teachers is the need for additional classroom personnel. Unfortunately, it is unlikely that there will be large amounts of funds available to hire additional staff in the future. More efficient use of existing personnel may prove to be the best long-term solution. Efficient use of instructional support personnel is much like good teaching; that is, teachers must have clearly stated objectives for what their assistants are to accomplish (Lombardo, 1980). This approach to management is accomplished by devising a written plan for each individual providing instruction for learners. This plan should be developed in a combined effort between the teacher and the assistant, with the assistant providing input into the objectives.

Scheduling other instructional personnel efficiently is the first step toward developing a good management system. Lieberman (1982) has suggested ways to cut down on the travel time of children (thus increasing their learning time) by scheduling their activities closer together in the school. Efficiently managing a volunteer's or paraprofessional's time can involve similar scheduling practices.

Teachers may provide assistants with only verbal instructions, assuming that the assistant can follow through with the task, or they may have more success using techniques such as modeling and prompts to demonstrate what they want the assistant to do. Frequent observations of assistants can provide information for helping them to improve their skills.

Teachers can choose to use additional techniques for managing the effectiveness of other instructional personnel, such as self-charting and public posting (see Chapters Five and Six). Various schedules of reinforcement are also important considerations for managing instructional assistants. Teachers may have more success at improving the effectiveness of their assistants if they provide them frequent reinforcement and feedback concerning the quality of their work.

Scheduling frequent staff discussions is an important consideration for managing other classroom personnel. A 15-minute daily meeting after school to review the day's occurrences is often all the time needed to review and improve instruction. Is is often easier to handle problems when they are addressed as quickly as possible after they occur.

Teacher Aides and Paraprofessionals

A variety of labels are used for individuals paid by a school district to assist teachers. For example, titles such as *teacher aide, teacher assistant, instructional assistant,* and *paraprofessional* are all common terms describing other classroom personnel. Many teachers of learners with handicaps have an aide of some type, ranging from a full-time assistant to varying levels of part-time help. The formal educational requirements for these positions vary from school district to school district; however, the basic requirement is generally a high school diploma.

Paraprofessionals, who often have degrees from community colleges or technical schools, can accomplish a variety of tasks that support the special educator, including managing students, providing basic instruction, and acting as members of the educational team (Goff & Kelly, 1979). Paraprofessionals and teacher aides can be invaluable, and teachers should guard them from being underused or inappropriately assigned tasks that lessen both their effectiveness and efficiency. Teachers can avoid problems by precisely defining the roles of instructional assistants.

There may be some confusion as to whether an aide should perform only non-instructional duties or provide direct teaching to the learners (Peter, 1975). Some teachers may decide to use aides only for noninstructional tasks that in many cases are ones that teachers would not consider doing themselves. This situation can hinder the development of a mutually beneficial relationship between teachers and aides. First, the aides may feel that they are only to do the teacher's "dirty work," possibly resulting in their developing less than effective work habits. Second, by adhering to the noninstructional role policy, teachers may be losing an effective vehicle for providing individual instruction to learners.

Barriers can also exist between teachers and aides if they allow age differences to adversely affect their working relationship. For example, most teachers just entering the field and many experienced teachers have to establish working relationships with aides who are older than themselves. Under these circumstances, teachers may be uncomfortable in a supervisor-subordinate relationship with their aides. This attitude of teachers may result in their providing little concrete direction to assistants, hoping they will find something useful to do. Any requests made by the teacher are made carefully in an effort to avoid hurting the aide's feelings.

An important factor for establishing a good working relationship with an aide is the ability to establish rapport on a personal level and to feel comfortable with the individual (Marsh & Price, 1980). When teachers do not participate in choosing an aide it is necessary to establish a good working rapport on the first meeting day. Greer (1978) has suggested that the teacher firmly establish that the aide is an important part of the educational team, with the stipulation that the aide must "take no independent action, and have no decision making authority" (pp. 3–4). Making these basic facts clear will help set the tone for the future of the relationship.

IDEA FILE

Whether or not aides and volunteers become effective instructors often may depend upon the extent to which teachers train them in the appropriate classroom procedures. For instance, a brief training program and periodic review sessions can assist other classroom personnel in learning skills needed to observe student behavior in a consistent manner.

- The teacher might consider developing a training manual that explains how to deal with certain behaviors and implement specific classroom procedures (Marsh & Price, 1980). This technique can save lengthy discussions while providing the assistant with a guide for times when the teacher is unavailable for help. The manual can be more helpful to assistants if snapshots or drawings are included depicting the teaching technique being explained.
- Assistants may be more willing to implement programs if they have been included in the planning (Hart, 1981). Short daily meetings between teachers and assistants can be a good method for correcting problems and sharing ideas.
- These short meetings should be a dialogue *between* the teacher and assistant, not a one-sided conversation presenting all of the teacher's ideas.
- Teachers should develop daily schedules for their assistants and post them where they can refer to their responsibilities frequently.
- The following is a partial list of appropriate tasks for assistants:
  - ☐ Perform clerical tasks.
  - ☐ Observe, record, and chart student behaviors.
  - ☐ Implement behavioral programs.
  - ☐ Assist learners in academic skill practice or generalization.
  - ☐ Help learners generalize independent living skills to community settings.

■ ■ ■ ■

Volunteers

Volunteers are an often overlooked source of classroom assistance that can potentially provide a wealth of instructional talent. Developing a good volunteer program involves careful planning and scheduling.

Teachers may find it difficult to implement behavior analysis programs because of the need for independent observers. Volunteer parents can assist teachers by learning to monitor the behavior of the target learners. For example, a teacher may ask a parent to participate as an observer in a program designed to increase on-task behavior of a student. The main thrust of the program may only last 2 weeks, allowing the teacher time to evaluate a number of interventions and choose the one that has the most success. The following steps are examples of those that might be used to train the parent in correctly observing the target behavior:

1. If possible, videotape the learner engaged in the behavior. Using the videotape, the parent can practice observing and recording the behavior.

2. When videotaping is not possible, allow the parent to observe the student and practice recording the behavior a number of times before actual data are charted.

3. During either the videotaped or classroom practice sessions, check the progress of the parent by initiating a reliability check at specified intervals (see Chapter Six).

4. When the parent and reliability checker agree at least 80% of the time, begin collecting actual baseline data.

For many behaviors that parent volunteers may be called upon to observe, detailed training such as this may not be necessary. Nevertheless, whether the task requires intensive training or simple instruction, the benefits of the additional help are many.

Parents and other volunteers can also be of immense help in performing a wide variety of other tasks. Assisting in activities such as charting data and escorting learners on community instruction trips are additional suggestions for the use of volunteers. Using parents as classroom assistants has two added benefits. First, the communication between the school and home is enhanced because the parents feel a part of the process and have a vested interest in the program. Second, teachers can make use of this time with parents to instruct them in preferred teaching practices that can be used at home (Gallagher, Beckman, & Cross, 1983). During this time in school parents may become more comfortable with the teacher and provide valuable input into the program.

Besides parents, there are other volunteer resources available in communities. Teachers can approach church groups, service organizations, and specific community members to act as instructional assistants. Take, for example, a local retailer who may assist by allowing learners to practice consumer skills in his or her store. Similar examples could be securing the assistance of salespersons, personnel managers, and bus drivers. The help is available to institute a number of innovative program options if teachers are willing to seek it out and provide the necessary leadership and coordination skills.

IDEA FILE

Following are some general suggestions for more appropriate use of volunteers of all types:

■ Be sure to schedule volunteers to assist when they are needed the most.

■ Keep a master schedule posted to minimize the overlapping of volunteers.

■ When volunteers arrive, be sure that a list of tasks awaits them.

■ Take time to train volunteers in the techniques they are to use and in the rules of the class.

■ Use principles of applied behavior analysis to monitor the actions of volunteers. Observation, public posting, and self-charting are useful techniques to use with these assistants (see Chapters Five and Six).

■ Approach service organizations and church groups, and volunteer your services as a speaker for their meetings. A slide show demonstrating a class in action, followed by a discussion of program goals, is a good public relations tool and may encourage potential volunteers.

■ Carefully interview each volunteer, selecting only those who appear to be dependable, punctual, flexible, and emotionally stable (Lombardo, 1980). Prior to interviewing prospective candidates, teachers should list the qualities they wish the volunteers to have, so they can compare the candidates to the list.

■ Providing a job description prior to interviewing candidates can help candidates to decide whether or not they would like to participate.

■ ■ ■ ■

Peer Tutors

Peer tutoring began to gain widespread acceptance in the late 1970s as increased numbers of students with handicaps were being mainstreamed into regular classes. The results of several studies indicate that peer tutoring can be an effective method for helping students with mild and moderate handicaps acquire specific skills (Dale, 1979; Ehly & Larsen, 1980).

Peer tutors can come from a number of sources both within special education and from general education classes (Morsink, 1984). Tutors from within the teacher's classroom can be the first source of these assistants. Older and/or more able learners can be used in a number of instructional situations. For example, resource room teachers may choose to pair off learners, allowing students who have mastered specific academic skills to help others who have not.

Another alternative is to make use of the talents of students from other special education classes to assist as peer tutors. Programs allowing students with learning disabilities or behavior disorders to participate as tutors for learners with moderate mental retardation are becoming popular. These program options can often present a student the opportunity to learn responsible behavior by helping others if the opportunity to tutor is regarded as a privilege earned by demonstrating predetermined appropriate behaviors.

Most special education classes are now closer to the mainstream of public education than they were in the past. The opportunity exists to incorporate the use of general education students as peer tutors. These general education students can provide excellent assistance in tutoring academic, self-help, and vocational skills. Equally important is the opportunity such options allow for the general population to learn appropriate interactions with learners who have handicaps (Poorman, 1980).

Peer tutors can also be a factor in facilitating better generalization of skills. For example, peer tutors who reside in the same neighborhood as a target learner can assist that student in transferring skills learned in school to the learner's natural environment. Specifically, a peer tutor who has participated in a program designed to teach shopping skills can accompany the student to neighborhood grocery stores and assist in generalizing the shopping skills to new environments.

Teachers may wish to consider the following suggestions for recruiting peer tutors:

1. Teachers must thoroughly plan a peer tutor program, including objectives and types of skills to be targeted, and then present the outline to the school principal. Winning over the administration may stimulate more teachers to participate in the program.

2. Teachers can present this idea immediately to any general education teacher who will be working with these learners. The topic can be approached as a method for taking some of the pressure off the regular education teacher.

3. Teachers can present the idea to other teachers who are club advisors. Parents or cooperative extension agents who are in charge of 4-H programs are also likely sources of help in identifying potential peer tutors.

4. If club advisors agree, teachers can speak to the members, explaining the program goals and presenting information about people who have handicaps. Using slides of special education classes can augment the presentation.

5. Teachers should enlist the support of parents early in the development stages, asking for time during PTA meetings to present the format of the tutoring program.

6. Being careful to adhere to school district policy, teachers can use the media for public relations purposes. A story about the benefits of the peer tutoring program can elicit additional support from the community and other school personnel not currently participating.

7. Teachers should take time to carefully schedule the tutors and train them prior to their contact with the learners, making sure they understand their assignments.

University or College Classroom Assistants

For some teachers, the use of university or college classroom assistants is not a pressing concern. For teachers who do interact with these individuals, however, there are some basic suggestions for effectively using them that may prove helpful. First, student teachers (interns) can be a great asset to teachers, becoming an "extra pair of hands" and providing support to students that might otherwise be unavailable. Scheduling a student teacher's duties should reflect a gradual increase of responsibility, moving from small groups to eventually spending a period of time programming for the entire class.

1. Teachers should make a list of the skills they would like the student teachers to gain during the internship.

2. Teachers can require the student teachers to list the skills they would like to attain during the internship.

3. Teachers and interns should translate both lists into behavioral objectives that are to be completed by the end of the quarter or semester.

4. Teachers can schedule short daily sessions with the student teachers to discuss problems or concerns as well as allowing the interns to contribute ideas to program development.

5. Teachers should define the desired student teacher behaviors operationally and observe/ record/chart those behaviors while the student teachers are implementing lessons (Chapters Five and Six). These techniques will help the interns get a clearer idea of their performance on a daily basis.

Teachers should give serious consideration to evaluating the quality of their contacts with the student teachers' college supervisors. Problems can arise when a college supervisor maintains only a minimum of contact with both the intern and the teacher. This situation is not desirable since the college supervisor presumably has the knowledge to assist the intern in translating the best practices from the college curriculum into daily instructional methods. Therefore, teachers should consider the following points that may help to foster a better professional relationship:

1. At the initial meeting, the teacher can request a list of objectives required by the supervisor and share the list of teacher-developed objectives.

2. The teacher can request that the supervisor visit for at least half of the school day when observing the intern. At the end of the observation a short session can be scheduled to discuss any points of concern with the supervisor and the intern.

3. The teacher can schedule frequent evaluation sessions that allow for a sharing of data among the college supervisor, teacher, and intern.

Developing a professional relationship with another person may not be an easy task. College supervisors are sometimes perceived as being superior to the classroom teacher, an image that can be fostered by either the supervisor or the teacher. Instead, the goal should be to become a team, each providing skills to improve the quality of the student teacher. To accomplish this and other workable professional relationships, teachers must be adept at certain competencies that allow them to be efficient with their own time and assertive enough to accomplish their goals. With these considerations in mind, the following section briefly presents additional competencies designed to assist teachers in developing effective professional relationships.

COMPETENCIES FOR EFFECTIVE INTERACTIONS WITH OTHER PERSONNEL

Effectiveness as a teacher is not restricted to performing skills geared to instructional intervention; it also involves learning skills needed to become better managers. Teachers are increasingly called upon to interact with many individuals. Two areas in which they generally need to improve their skills are assertiveness and time management.

Assertiveness

The ability to be assertive, rather than aggressive, involves a positive approach to dealing with others. Interacting with other professionals may place the special educator in a low power position, that is, accepting the judgments of administrators, psychologists, physicians, and/or parents. How a teacher reacts to these attempts at control can result in either self-denying (nonassertive), assertive, or aggressive behaviors. Unfortunately, if teachers resort to either self-denying or aggressive behaviors it can cause others to ignore the good ideas they may have regarding a student's program. Baer (1976) distinguished between assertive and aggressive behavior by defining assertiveness as those traits that allow people to stand up for themselves and make their own choices. Conversely, aggressiveness is an attempt to enhance one's own position at the expense of someone else's rights. In contrast to either of these approaches, nonassertive people allow others to make their decisions and guide their actions, usually at the expense of their own self-esteem (Alberti & Emmons, 1974; Dyer, 1979). A great deal of stress can be placed on individuals who either continually allow others to dictate to them or alienate colleagues through aggressive actions.

Assertiveness is the ability to state a point of view or make a request in a positive, plain, and strong manner. The key is that the affirmation is made clearly and is based on a well-thought-out set of logical statements. For example, a school psychologist may inform a teacher that his or her findings support the decision to place a student with learning disabilities in a self-contained class. Accepting this judgment without question or vehemently arguing against the placement will probably not bring about a satisfactory conclusion. Conversely, if the teacher practices assertive techniques he or she can calmly but firmly convey to the psychologist agreement or disagreement with the finding, subsequently supporting the teacher's own position with data gathered in the classroom.

The emphasis, then, is on the *delivery* of the message to be conveyed to others. Alberti and Emmons (1970) have presented the following seven suggestions for delivery of an effective message using the components of assertive behavior:

> Eye contact: Looking directly at another person when you are speaking to him is an effective way of declaring that you are sincere about what you are saying, and that it is directed to him;
>
> Body posture: The "weight" of your messages to others will be increased if you face the person, stand or sit appropriately close to him, lean toward him, hold your head erect;
>
> Gestures: A message accented with appropriate gestures takes on added emphasis (overenthusiastic gesturing can be a distraction!);
>
> Facial expression: Ever see someone trying to express anger while smiling or laughing? It just doesn't come across. Effective assertions require an expression that agrees with the message;
>
> Voice tone, inflection, volume: A whispered monotone will seldom convince another person that you mean business, while a shouted epithet will bring his defenses into the path of communication. A level, well-modulated conversational statement is convincing without intimidating;
>
> Timing: Spontaneous expression will generally be your goal since hesitation may diminish the effect of an assertion. Judgment is necessary, however, to select an appropriate occasion, such as speaking to your boss in the privacy of his office, rather than in front of a group of his subordinates where he may need to respond defensively;
>
> Content: We save this obvious dimension of assertiveness for last to emphasize that, although what you say is clearly important, it is often less important than most of us generally believe. We encourage a fundamental honesty in interpersonal communication, and spontaneity of expression. In our view, that means saying forcefully, "I'm damn mad about what you just did!" rather than "You're an S.O.B.!" People who have for years hesitated because they "didn't know what to say" have found the practice of saying something, to express their feelings at the time, to be a valuable step toward greater spontaneous assertiveness.
>
> One further word about content. We do encourage you to express your own feelings—and to accept responsibility for them. Note the difference in the above example between "I'm mad" and "You're an S.O.B." It is not necessary to put the other person down (aggressive) in order to express your feeling (assertive).[1]

Assertiveness training is a vital topic for all teachers. Sources of further information include Fensterheim and Baer's (1975) excellent section involving assertiveness on the job and Gordon's (1974) discussion of teacher communication skills.

---

[1] From *Your Perfect Right: A Guide to Assertive Living* (Fifth Edition). © 1986 by Robert E. Alberti and Michael L. Emmons. Reproduced for Allyn and Bacon by permission of Impact Publishers, Inc., P.O. Box 1094, San Luis Obispo, CA 93406. Further reproduction prohibited.

Time Management

"If only we didn't have all these regulations from the federal and state governments, we could have time to teach." "The principal is driving me crazy with paperwork and extra duties. I wish I could see my class long enough to teach them!" Anyone who has had the opportunity to teach either may have made similar statements or will have heard others voice such complaints. Interruptions in teaching can be frequent occurrences given the many bureaucratic regulations and daily duties of public school personnel. However, teachers should not feel they have no control over the situation. Teachers can control their own time given some basic planning techniques.

There are a number of resources that interested readers can seek out for assistance in time management. Two of the more thorough works are by Lakein (1973) and Applegate (1980), and the following list includes suggestions from both authors. These techniques should also be taught to learners and, in fact, in many cases they are used to change student behaviors.

1. Teachers should sort out their professional and personal goals by making lists. First, a list of what is to be accomplished during the school year, prioritizing the items from most to least important, is needed. Second, a daily list of what needs to be accomplished, by priority, is a valuable tool.

2. Teachers should analyze the work setting, including both the classroom and the school in general. All schools have activities requiring preset times. Teachers can organize their time around these activities by identifying times for uninterrupted work. Also, when interruptions occur (e.g., assembly) lessons that can be shortened can be planned.

3. Teachers can identify the times of the day that they are most productive (e.g., A.M. or P.M.). Accordingly, they can schedule the most important tasks for their peak times. Also, keeping a schedule fairly constant is important. The routine of performing a task at roughly the same time each day helps cut down on indecision. Once a schedule is set, it is reinforcing to cross out the activity upon completion.

4. Teachers should build into their schedules frequent, short periods when there is nothing to do. Daydreaming can be an effective reinforcer when controlled. For example, 2 minutes of daydreaming after completion of an activity can be an effective impetus for beginning the next task. When teachers sit down to accomplish an activity, goals should be set that require a specific period of time or a specific amount of work that must be completed before leaving.

5. Teachers should be assertive and say no. Teachers can't please everyone, so they should be selective of tasks accepted. Some principals, other teachers, and aides are always willing to transfer their burdens onto the shoulders of others. Instead of saying, "I'll do it" or "I'll think about it," teachers can refer the problem back to these people by saying, "What are you going to do?" or "What do you think about it?"

6. Teachers need to delegate authority. Using aides, volunteers, and peer tutors more effectively can accomplish this task.

7. Teachers can battle procrastination through reinforcement. Many teachers use the Premack Principle in reverse, doing something enjoyable first, then working. Unfortunately, this usually results in procrastination. The goal should be to work first and then get a reward. Also, teachers can task-analyze the activity into smaller chunks, reinforcing themselves after completion of each component of the task.

8. Teachers should be flexible when unforeseen interruptions occur, for interruptions are inevitable in schools no matter how good the planning. Before returning to a task, teachers can ask themselves if they should move on to a new task and reschedule the interrupted one.

Conflict Resolution and Negotiation

Special educators will always be in the unique position of having to maintain close contact with professionals from many different fields and community members from many different walks of life. Inevitably, conflict will arise over issues requiring careful negotiation before the program can move forward and benefit the students. For example, conflict may develop in an IEP meeting as to whether or not placement in a regular education first-grade class would be desirable for a student with behavioral disorders. Arguing differences of opinion can be productive when each side uses facts and does not introduce emotional statements such as "You just don't like BD students" or "All you want to do is dump him in my class."

There are two major concerns that should be considered when engaged in conflict: achieving your personal goals and keeping a good relationship with the other person. These considerations drive the appropriate approach to take in an effort to resolve the conflict to everyone's satisfaction.

Gamble and Gamble (1982) proposed some basic principles for managing interpersonal conflicts. The first principle is to recognize that conflicts can be settled rationally. Pretending that the conflict does not exist, withdrawing from the conversation, or finding fault or blaming will not facilitate a productive end to the dispute.

The second principle is that the conflict should be defined. Each participant should ask Why are we in conflict? What is the nature of the conflict? How can each of us feel as though we have won? Participants in the conflict should also check their perceptions, suggest possible solutions, assess the solutions and decide on the best one, and finally try out the solution and evaluate its effectiveness.

The key to any successful negotiation is *not* to approach the discussion with the attitude "I must win and really don't care about the other party" (Maddux, 1988, p. 13). This attitude will usually result in a no-win situation for all concerned. Teachers should enter conflict situations with a win/win attitude, interested in the needs of others and flexible in their approach to the negotiations at hand. In the IEP meeting example, a successful conclusion might have been the development of a plan that found the special educator spending some time in the regular education class when the student was in attendance. This would allow the special educator to help the regular educator set up a general behavior management plan that would meet the needs of the mainstreamed student and the rest of the class.

KEY CONCEPTS

■ Special educators should be competent in three areas: assessment and diagnosis, curriculum development, and applied behavior analysis.

- Teachers must be able to efficiently manage other instructional personnel such as aides, volunteers, and peer tutors.
- Frequent discussions with other personnel can help solve problems before they occur.
- Teachers should not assign only nonpreferred activities to aides and paraprofessionals.
- Programs can often be improved when the opinions of other personnel are solicited.
- Training manuals developed by teachers can be helpful to other personnel in effectively completing their duties.
- Volunteers make excellent behavioral observers. Videotapes representing different types of student behavior can help train volunteers as observers.
- Parents can be excellent volunteer teachers and observers. When parents participate in class activities, teachers can model preferred teaching strategies with the students of the parent volunteers.
- Service organizations and church groups are excellent sources of volunteers.
- Techniques of assertiveness are vital competencies for teachers. Appropriate body posture, eye contact, and gestures are important considerations when converting others to a point of view.
- Teachers can manage their time more efficiently if they list and prioritize their tasks. Breaking tasks down into smaller components can be an effective technique.
- Special educators should practice strategies of conflict resolution to enhance relationships with parents and other professionals.

■ ■ ■ ■

CHAPTER THREE

ASSESSMENT OF LEARNERS WITH MILD AND MODERATE HANDICAPS

■ Educators have at times looked to the field of medicine for a conceptual base on which to develop programs. Consequently, the term *diagnostic-prescriptive* has become popular for describing the relationship between assessment and instruction (Lerner, 1981). *Diagnosis* refers to identifying the reasons why students are failing to learn targeted skills. This process could involve pinpointing factors such as a student's learning style, preferred reinforcers, and the point on a skill sequence where instruction is not leading to student progress.

Prescription refers to the methods and materials teachers choose to use with students based on the strengths and weaknesses identified during the diagnosis phase. Thus, the process of teaching is ongoing and all of the parts are interrelated. A teacher would have a difficult time deciding where to begin instruction without a thorough assessment of the student's present level of performance. Chapter Four, on curriculum design, will introduce the concept of objective-based assessment—measuring learner progress in relation to prestated goals and criteria. The underlying tenets for Chapter Four serve as a basis for this chapter. That is, all students are different, and teachers need to be familiar with these differences in learning styles before appropriate instruction can be developed (Cartwright, Cartwright, & Ward, 1989). Curriculum design and assessment are interwoven, and one process will not necessarily precede the other (Berdine & Meyer, 1987).

The purpose of this chapter is to present teachers with a systematic approach for gathering assessment data that will be useful in program development. Generating assessment data for their own sake—without a clear, concise plan for why the information is needed—may be counterproductive. The main goal, then, is to demonstrate how teachers identify the information that is most important for developing daily lessons.

PROTECTION IN EVALUATION PROCEDURES

PL 94-142 provides comprehensive protection for students with handicapping conditions and their families. One major component of this legislation is the provision of a free and appropriate education in the least restrictive environment for all students with handicaps. A second major component of the law emphasizes the rights of students and their families to appropriate screening and identification procedures to determine (a) whether or not an individual qualifies for and would benefit from special education services and (b) if the individual qualifies for special education, what placement, curriculum, instructional strategies, and services will best meet his or her needs.

This second major component of PL 94-142 has the greatest impact on the initial discussions in this chapter. The general consensus of most professionals is that students who do not have handicapping conditions should not be placed in special education. For example, students who are inaccurately labeled as mentally retarded or behavior disordered may be stigmatized by the label for the rest of their lives. Therefore, procedural safeguards have been built in to PL 94-142 to minimize inaccurate labeling, classification, and placement of students into special education programs—especially students from minority groups who have traditionally been placed in special education in disproportionate numbers.

In addition, PL 94-142 guarantees that, once identified for special education placement, students have the right to have developed for them a program based on the best possible assessment procedures. These safeguards require that a transdisciplinary or multifactored assessment approach be used, combining data gathered by professionals in allied fields to include information such as developmental and cognitive variables, adaptive behavior, medical or psychological information, and information from parents and from observations of community functioning in general (Luftig, 1989).

To accomplish the major components just described, PL 94-142 includes a number of procedural safeguards.

Consent of Parents

The law requires that parents be notified before their child is evaluated for possible special education placement. When school personnel propose to change the classification, evaluation, or educational placement of a child in any way, they must obtain the parents' permission.

If a child is to be singled out and removed from class to be tested by either a psychologist, speech and language specialist, or special educator, parents must be informed in writing in their primary language. This safeguard allows them the opportunity to refute the referral and obtain legal assistance if they deem it necessary.

Nondiscriminatory Assessment

PL 94-142 mandates that the assessment materials and procedures used for placing students in special education be selected and administered in a fashion that is not culturally or racially biased. Historically, many students placed in special education were not handicapped. Their placement was based solely on an intelligence test given to establish eligibility, and these tests were often found to be culturally or racially biased.

To safeguard against this problem, the law mandates that a variety of tests be administered and multiple data sources be explored before determination can be made. The evaluation procedure should include a number of professionals to safeguard against inappropriate administration practices.

Open Access to Student Records

To ensure that parents are provided with all relevant information concerning their child, PL 94-142 mandates open access to their child's records. The law not only allows for access, but also guarantees that the school must provide an interpretation of those records if necessary.

PL 94-142 also allows parents to challenge records that may be inaccurate or misleading. This mandate tends to curb overzealous professionals from making written comments that might not be supportable and could potentially be stigmatizing to the child.

In addition, the school must obtain written consent from the parents before they release a child's records to a third party.

Due Process

All of the safeguards included in PL 94-142 fall under the category of *due process*. Due process means that the rights of students and their families are protected and that educational agencies can take no action without the informed consent of all parties. A number of the components of due process were embedded in the previous discussion: notice of referral and parental consent, information about rights, access to school records, confidentiality of assessment results, and explanation of assessment results.

One important component of due process that directly affects all others is the parents' right to an independent evaluation if they disagree with the results obtained by the school system. If the parents desire an independent evaluation, information concerning where one can be obtained must be provided by the school and the independent evaluation must be free to the parents if the school system cannot prove that its evaluation results were accurate. The school system must consider the results of the independent evaluation in any decisions made concerning the child's program.

Student Support Teams

In an effort to increase procedural safeguards relating to inappropriate placement of students in special education, many states are mandating the development of individual school-based student support teams (SSTs). These teams, made up mostly of teachers and the responsibility of regular education, are charged with the responsibility of reviewing student cases *before* they are referred for possible special education placement. The role of these teams is to suggest instructional procedures, curriculum modifications, or available support services, (e.g., inservice education for teachers, remedial programs) that could keep the child in the regular education program.

A student support team may also be charged with monitoring the progress of the student once the program it designed is initiated. If the student's progress continues to deteriorate, the SST could choose to forward the child's case to the special educators to initiate the referral process outlined in PL 94-142.

GOALS OF ASSESSMENT

For teachers, assessment increases in importance after students are placed. Students who have problems are referred to the school psychologist or psychometrist for in-depth evaluation to determine the most appropriate classroom placement. After the assessment is complete and an IEP meeting is convened, the learner may be placed in a special education classroom.

This is when the teacher's job begins. Formal testing done by the school psychologist is valuable for obtaining general information about the academic and behavioral performance of students; however, this information cannot stand alone. In developing instructional programs, consideration must be given to the unique qualities inherent in each teacher's class (Hammill, 1987). Different professionals have varied styles of teaching, their classrooms have a variety of materials, and their presentation of skills can be disparate. Consequently, any psychologist will find it difficult to predict how a student will react from teacher to teacher if only a formal battery of tests is given in isolation. An alternative is to rely on the assessment of the teachers who know a student best when planning educational strategies.

For example, Norman's general education teacher realizes that Norman continues to fall behind the class in reading. The SST could meet on Norman's case and recommend that his teacher receive some help from the Chapter I reading specialist in designing additional activities for Norman or that he be placed in Chapter I reading. After a period of time designated by the SST, a review of Norman's case might show a continual decline in reading. At this point the SST could forward the case to the special education department, which would follow the appropriate due process procedures. Part of the assessment procedure should be developed by both Norman's regular education teacher and a special educator. Together, they can design and implement a comprehensive assessment package that addresses specific areas delineated as important. The data are then collected by each teacher as designated. Information gathered from these sources can feed directly into developing an effective intervention for teaching the target skills. Using this system, eventual placement into special education may be possible. However, Norman's strengths and weaknesses will need to be identified by the professionals working with him on a daily basis. Transition time should be minimized. Placement into the special education program will be based on data demonstrating that Norman's needs will best be met there.

IDEA FILE

Effective special educators need to be competent in several areas of assessment such as selecting appropriate tests, correctly administering a variety of tests, managing records, interpreting results of assessment, and making sound decisions based on interpreted data (Lund, Schnapps, & Bijou, 1983; McNutt & Mandlebaum, 1980). In addition, special educators must be thoroughly versed in the legal implications of assessment (Bateman, 1982).

Nonbiased assessment is an important principle of PL 94-142 and should assist in reducing overrepresentation of minority children in special education classes (Oakland, 1980). Certain key elements should be carefully observed when assessing students for placement purposes (Marozas & May, 1988).

- ■ Students should be tested using instruments developed in their dominant language (e.g., Spanish-speaking children should be tested by instruments written in Spanish).
- ■ All medical, visual, and auditory problems and problems resulting from emotional disabilities should be explored prior to evaluating students for educational deficits (Gonzalas, 1982).

■ ■ ■ ■

LEVELS OF ASSESSMENT

Assessment is an ongoing process and should not be thought of as merely an end-of-the-week quiz or unit test. Rather, assessment is difficult to separate from teaching. The most effective teachers may be the ones who use a systems approach to assessment. These teachers continually sample whether or not they are making an impact on the lives of their students, constantly probing into the teacher-learner interaction and monitoring

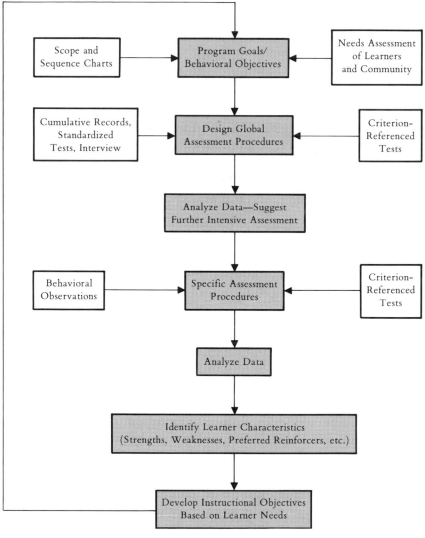

■ FIGURE 3.1
Objective-Based Assessment Model for Classroom Implementation

program effectiveness and subsequent student progress (Scott & Goetz, 1980). To accomplish this, teachers choose from various levels of assessment that vary in intensity and comprehensiveness to assist them in "drawing a picture" of each student's learning style.

Wallace and Larsen (1978) have identified the following three levels of assessment of learning problems:

1. A survey level of assessment resulting in a measure of general classroom performance and initial verification that a problem exists.

2. An intermediate level of assessment involving administration of diagnostic tests designed to further specify areas of difficulty.

3. An intensive level of assessment resulting in a comprehensive evaluation of the learner including specific diagnostic testing and a study of the home, health status, and other factors.

The process of assessment begins with a broad collection of data concerning general learning problems. As the assessment process continues, the data gathered become more specific, gradually narrowing in focus until specific learner strengths and weaknesses are identified. The assessment results also allow teachers to identify the individual needs of students within different learning environments (Zentall, 1983).

As the IEP is developed, it moves from the broad to the more specific. This approach relates to the levels of assessment as identified by Wallace and Larsen (1978) (see Figure 3.1). First, during the survey level, teachers notice that there is a marked difference between a particular student's performance and that of the rest of the class. The difference in learner progress usually shows up in general screening procedures initiated by the school system, for example, by administration of the California Achievement Test (Tiegs & Clarke, 1970), or in classroom activities developed by the teacher. Once it is suspected that a problem exists that will require an extensive change in programming, the teacher begins to gather general assessment data supporting a referral for further analysis (Algozzine & McGraw, 1980). The information gathered at this level (teacher-made tests, behavioral observations, district screening procedures) sets the stage for implementing the second assessment level needed for IEP development. For example, an elementary student is rapidly falling behind peers in learning to read. Although instruction continues, the teacher begins to collect survey data concerning where skill-related problems appear to be occurring. In this case, data reveal deficits in letter recognition and decoding. With this information, a teacher can either seek the assistance of a psychometrist or continue to the next level of assessment independently.

The second or intermediate level of assessment relates to the section of the IEP dealing with the student's current level of performance. Here the teacher gathers data from standardized tests, criterion-referenced measures, and more detailed behavioral observations. These measures can be gathered from different sources such as other teachers, psychometrists, and social workers. However, the teacher who is functioning as coordinator organizes the data for a workable analysis (see Figure 3.2). During this level of assessment, the professional team (teacher, psychometrist, physical therapist, or other professional) attempts to pinpoint specific deficits in all curricular areas. In addition, information relating to student learning styles and strengths and potential reinforcers are gathered mostly as by-products of the general assessment procedures. At this level, an adaptive behavior scale or behavior checklist is administered to pinpoint deficit areas that could hinder learner progress in a workshop environment. Also, learner strengths are identified to further assist in programming decisions. Other pertinent information can also be gathered at this level, including medical workups.

Finally, the last level of assessment results in an intensive and ongoing evaluation of the learner. Gathering information at this level is the responsibility of the practitioners who are involved with the learner on a daily basis and who have the ultimate responsibility for program implementation and revision. This intensive level of assessment involves an ongoing evaluation of learner progress. An important fact to remember is that by law the IEP must be evaluated once a year. This requirement may be "too little, too late." The ongoing monitoring of student performance is the most important assessment task, and this responsibility rests primarily with teachers. By monitoring the student on a daily basis, teachers can measure the effectiveness of their instruction and revise it as necessary.

The levels of assessment demonstrate important features in their relation to the IEP process (refer to Figure 4.2, Chapter Four). As professionals move through the levels, information is gathered in a systematic fashion, moving from broad to specific characteristics. Systematic assessment procedures allow the professional to function in the same manner as a good detective; each bit of information gathered becomes a clue, and enough clues gradually pinpoint a solution. Data gathered at the survey level lead the teacher to apply certain tools at the intermediate level for further clarification. Information gathered at the intermediate level needs further clarification at the intensive level, and the subsequent instructional programming is based on this information. Finally, during the intensive level of assessment, student progress is monitored for feedback into the instructional

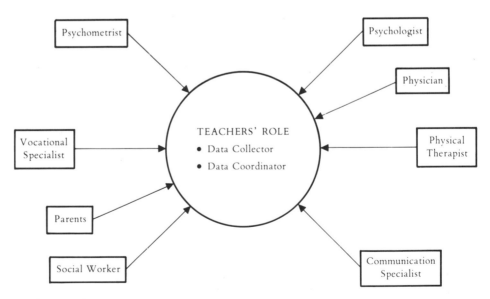

■ *FIGURE 3.2*
Teacher's Role in Assessment Process

system (Wesson, King, & Deno, 1984). The conceptualization of this process of systematically moving from broad to specific assessment data is important. It is the basis of this chapter. Once this concept is understood, the focus shifts to finding the best sources for collecting assessment data.

SOCIAL VALIDITY AND ASSESSMENT

If teachers take a close look at their classrooms, curricula and school systems, they may find that the programs developed for learners with handicapping conditions are isolated from everyday community activities. For example, teachers may present lessons on grocery shopping without allowing the class to visit a market, or they may teach map reading skills in the confines of a classroom. These same problems can be experienced in the assessment process. The psychometrist who administers a diagnostic evaluation of a learner's computation skills in a strange room may not get a true picture of how the student performs in the classroom.

Professionals are becoming more aware that the concept of social validity (Bailey, 1977) requires educational programs to be in the best interest of learners with regard to both their needs and the needs of their community. The related concept of ecological validity (Brooks & Baumeister, 1977) views learners with mental handicaps in complex interactions with their environments. Methods and materials for teaching are developed to instruct the learner in those skills appropriate for community life. Therefore, assessment, if it is to relate to the teaching of community skills, must occur in the learner's natural environments (e.g., home, neighborhood, worksite).

Examples of ecologically valid assessments can be found in the literature related to teaching independent living skills. Behavioral observations and records of learner progress including (a) self-care skills (Fowler, Johnson, Whitman, & Zukotynski, 1978), (b) community mobility (Cortazzo & Sansone, 1969), (c) home and life management skills (Robinson-Wilson, 1977), and (d) leisure activities (Johnson & Bailey, 1977) are made in several settings. The concept of ecological validity would also support programs that allow learners to apply academic skills to everyday living experiences, as opposed to practicing academic skills only in workbooks or on dittoed exercise sheets. The charge is to evaluate student needs accurately. Assessment should be taken out of its traditional confines and applied to the learner-community interaction.

IDEA FILE

Teaching students skills that are directly applicable to both their current and future lives in the community (defined in this text as *community-valid skills*) is an important concept for programming. Consequently, teachers must first decide whether what they want to assess is a basic skill to be taught in isolation from the community (e.g., finding the main idea in a story from a basal reader) or a community-valid skill (e.g., reading a story from a newspaper and identifying the main idea). Younger learners will generally spend more time during the school day working on basic skills in traditional activities. Older learners, however, may be allowed the chance to apply arithmetic, reading, and writing skills to community problems. Teachers may wish to consider the following tips as an alternative approach:

■ Younger students may benefit from increased exposure to community-valid basic skills instruction. For example, when assessing subtraction skills the teacher might present the students with problems relating to the difference in cost among store items such as toys, candy, and books.

■ Teachers may be surprised to find that students can compute how much change they should receive from a soda machine yet cannot compute the same problem when it is presented on a written test. For a more accurate appraisal of certain skills, teachers may wish to enlist the aid of parents or volunteers to monitor student completion of such community-based tasks.

■ As an alternative to writing objectives with traditional academic outcomes, teachers should consider writing the short-term objectives on the IEP in terms relating to community activities. All teaching of basic academic skills occurring during the year would relate to the final community outcome.

Example:
The student will be able to correctly compute the answers to 10 subtraction problems that require regrouping in consecutive places (e.g., 517−358).

Alternative:
The student will be able to locate the prices of used furniture in an ad provided by the teacher and subtract the differences between two couches, two tables, two lamps, and two chairs. The prices included in the ad will require the skills of regrouping in consecutive places.

■ ■ ■ ■

TEACHER'S ROLE IN ASSESSMENT

We live in a society of specialists—in education, medicine, the trades, and other fields. In education, the assessment specialists are school psychologists and psychometrists. Administrators and teachers often refer learners to testing specialists for diagnostic work-ups. Although these professionals can provide useful information, teachers may in fact be the best, most reliable source of assessment data.

There are definite advantages to giving teachers the central role in learner evaluation. These advantages were voiced in 1969 by Smith and Neisworth and are more recently becoming popular with teacher educators (e.g., Choate et al., 1987; Howell & Kaplan, 1980). One advantage is that teachers know their students better than anyone else. This fact is important, especially in light of the credence that psychometricians place on establishing rapport with the learner prior to testing. Teachers generally have a solid rapport and can assess the learner at times and places that are comfortable to both, whereas a professional from outside the classroom is often a stranger with little hope of observing the learner's true performance. In addition, a professional from outside must test the student while adhering to a strict time schedule and subject to availability of testing facilities (Mercer & Mercer, 1989).

A second advantage to having teachers conduct assessment involves the contact they have with students. Teachers are in a position to observe students under varied conditions, including their contact with a variety of peers and others associated with the school. For example, when assessing the social skills of a learner with behavior disorders, a teacher has the option to place the student in different situations where target behaviors can be observed (e.g., in the lunchroom and on the playground). This freedom to alter environments allows teachers to obtain a more global picture of learner behaviors. Similarly, when assessing a student's academic skill problems, a teacher can structure activities testing the learner's ability to apply the target skills to a variety of daily living tasks.

Another advantage of teacher involvement in the assessment process relates to program development and accountability. Teachers are familiar with the program goals and objectives that they have developed themselves. Thus, they are in an excellent position to assess students in relation to those goals. Typically, psychometrists use standardized tests to measure academic skills that may not correlate with the curriculum. For example, studies indicate that the Key Math Diagnostic Arithmetic Test (Connolly, Nachtman, & Pritchett, 1971) omits considerable content (Howell & Kaplan, 1980). Therefore, performance on a standardized test may not relate to items taught in the classroom at a given time. Teachers having knowledge of exact program objectives can assess specific skills that are being required in their classroom. In addition, teachers have the responsibility to develop educational interventions and continually revise those interventions as needed. To accomplish this, there must be a system of continuous measurement of learner progress so that decisions can be made concerning appropriate program revisions.

Teachers should view assessment activities as part of their instructional role. The work these activities entail will pay off in the development of more effective instructional strategies.

DEVELOPING ASSESSMENT COMPETENCIES

The previous section presented a case for teachers acting as the primary evaluators of their students. Obviously, if teachers develop their program objectives and have the opportunity to observe learners in a number of situations during the school day, then they are the most likely candidates to administer appropriate assessment measures to students. What remains, however, is to provide teachers with the competencies they need to measure student behavior effectively. Burnett (1970) identified guidelines for teachers that included the following competencies:

1. Identify useful data from past assessment results and observations.
2. Develop informal assessment measures designed to increase the diagnostic information about learner characteristics.
3. Analyze data once they are gathered.
4. Apply the analysis to designing educational interventions.

In addition to these competencies, teachers should be able to analyze assessment data so that they can have adequate feedback for program revision. These competencies provide the scope for the remainder of this chapter.

OBJECTIVE-BASED ASSESSMENT

The process of evaluating student behavior in relation to criterion-referenced goals is termed *objective-based assessment*. It is the foundation for assessment models described by several authors (Howell & Kaplan, 1980; Howell, Kaplan, & O'Connell, 1979; Smith, 1969; Smith, Neisworth, & Greer, 1978; Wallace & Kauffman, 1978; Wallace & Larsen, 1978; White & Haring, 1980). The process of assessment is dynamic in that it is ongoing and totally interwoven with curriculum design (see Chapter Four). When teachers design program goals and subsequent behavioral objectives, they have actually developed yardsticks by which they can assess student achievement. The highlight of this system is simply the organization and the systematic procedures that it entails.

Teachers begin by identifying the goals and objectives that may be important to learners and then assessing them in relation to those objectives. Using a system of this nature can answer two important questions, namely, What do I assess? and What do I teach? This process involves moving from general learning characteristics to more intensive specific assessment aimed at pinpointing the exact needs of the learner.

KEY CONCEPTS

The process of assessment is one that moves from screening broad learning problems to identifying specific strengths and weaknesses. Teachers play an integral part in every level of assessment and should be active as equal partners with psychologists, psychometrists, and administrators.

■ During screening, the teacher may be the first to recognize that a student is having a problem and refer the student for testing according to district policy. Any information that the teacher can provide the psychometrist (e.g., class work, program objectives) will be helpful.

■ Information regarding present level of performance for the IEP may be most useful if gathered by the student's teachers.

■ Daily monitoring of student progress toward IEP objectives is a must. This monitoring helps the teacher relate the quality of instruction to how the student is doing.

■ Assessment should relate to the activities students will be expected to accomplish in the community.

■ ■ ■ ■

OVERVIEW OF ASSESSMENT METHODS

Standardized Academic Measures

Standardized tests are in wide use in the field of education and are also known as formal or norm-referenced measures. These commercially produced measures require administration by trained professionals, including teachers, and they provide results that allow comparisons between the learner and other students on a national or regional basis. There are various levels of standardized tests (e.g., achievement and diagnostic tests) and methods of administration (e.g., group and individually applied). Therefore, teachers have a choice of which tests they wish to administer based on the information they will yield. This chapter does not include a comprehensive description of available tests, their applications, or their quality. For that information the reader is referred to excellent books by Salvia and Ysseldyke (1985), and Wallace & Larsen (1978). An excellent source for critiques of specific tests is Mitchell's *Tests in Print III* (1983).

Professionals may, at times, inappropriately use group achievement tests to place and subsequently program for learners. Group achievement test results are valuable only for screening for gross learning problems—a process similar to finding a basketball in a medium-sized haystack. In the same light, individually administered achievement tests, although somewhat more appropriate, again only provide broad information concerning learning problems (see Table 3.1). Teachers should not feel that results from these tests are futile. Rather, this level of testing needs to be placed in proper perspective, that is, achievement testing is a method to quickly ascertain general learner problems and suggest more specific diagnostic testing. Under no circumstances are achievement tests sensitive enough to measure daily progess, much less program effectiveness (Witt, Elliott, Gresham, & Kramer, 1988).

Diagnostic tests generally are characterized by their administration to individuals and their testing of more specific skills in designated subject areas. Therefore, subtests on a diagnostic arithmetic test cover cluster goal areas such as basic operations, numeration, time, and money. Similarly, a diagnostic reading test includes subtests covering areas such as word attack, sight vocabulary, and comprehension. These diagnostic tests can provide a global picture (yet one that is more detailed than achievement tests) of a learner's abilities in a particular subject area in a relatively short time. A test of this nature also

TABLE 3.1   *Examples of Commercially Produced Tests That Can Provide Information for a General-Level Assessment of Academic Skills*

Name of Test	Skills Covered	Appropriateness for Students	Type of Reference
Reading			
California Achievement Tests (1979) CTB/McGraw Hill, Monterey, CA	Vocabulary Reading comprehension Math	Grades 1–High School Group Test	Normed
Diagnostic Reading Scales-R Spache (1981) CTB/McGraw Hill Monterey, CA	Oral reading Comprehension	Grades 1–8 Individual	Normed
Woodcock Reading Mastery Tests-R Woodcock (1987) American Guidance Service Circle Pines, MN	Letter identification Word identification Word attack Word comprehension Passage comprehension	Grades K–12 Individual	Normed

TABLE 3.1   (Continued)

Name of Test	Skills Covered	Appropriateness for Students	Type of Reference
Arithmetic			
Key Math-R Connolly, (1988) American Guidance Service Circle Pines, MN	Basic operations Fractions Numeration Word problems Money Measurement Symbols Time Geometry	Grades K–8 Individual	Normed

Stanford Diagnostic
    Arithmetic Test
Beatty, Madden, &
    Gardner (1976)
The Psychological Corp.
Cleveland, OH
	Basic operations
	Decimals
	Fractions
	Percent
	Counting
		Grades 1–High School
		Individual
			Normed

Spelling			
The Test of Written Spelling-2 Larsen & Hammill (1986) Empire Press (Pro Ed.) Austin, TX	Dictated words	Grades 1–8 Individual	Normed
General Achievement			

Peabody Individual
    Achievement Test-R
    (PIAT)
Dunn & Dunn (1981)
American Guidance Service
Circle Pines, MN
	Mathematics
	Reading recognition
	Reading comprehension
	Spelling
	General information
		Grades K–12
		Individual
			Normed

General Diagnostic			

Criterion Test of Basic
    Skills (CTBS)
Lundell, Evans, & Brown
    (1976)
Academic Therapy Pub.
San Rafael, CA
	Reading
	Arithmetic
		Individual	Criterion-referenced

Brigance Diagnostic
Comprehensive Inventory of
    Basic Skills
Brigance (1980)
Curriculum Associates
Woburn, MA
	Readiness
	Reading
	Mathematics
	Language Arts
		Very comprehensive
		All students with
		    academic learning
		    problems
		Individual
			Criterion-referenced

Brigance Diagnostic
Inventory of Essential Skills
Brigance (1980)
Curriculum Associates
Woburn, MA
		Excellent for
		    functional
		    assessment
			Criterion-referenced

allows teachers to use systematic procedures when students first enter their programs. This characteristic of diagnostic tests is valuable, especially when a new student is placed with a new teacher and a quick, relatively reliable technique is needed to profile the learning needs of the student (See Table 3.1).

Master teachers who have in-depth experience with academic evaluation realize that information from an achievement or diagnostic measure has minimal value when the test was administered by another professional. In cases where someone other than the teacher administers a test, various problems associated with standardized testing such as overgeneralization of findings, lack of teaching information, and child/administrator variability become accentuated (Wallace & Larsen, 1978). Therefore, the relative usefulness of these types of evaluations depends on whether or not the teacher can participate with the student in the testing process to view behaviors and become familiar with test content in relation to program goals.

This section has presented some of the more cogent and pragmatic arguments concerning standardized academic testing. Readers will notice the lack of discussion concerning measures of intelligence. This omission was not an oversight, but a planned strategy to make a point. Setting aside all arguments either supporting or refuting the value of intelligence testing, scores yielded by these measures have almost no benefit to teachers in designing educational programs for learners.

The IQ score generated by intelligence tests is an indicator of the relative success or failure of a student in the academically based public school system. Therefore, these scores are used as one of several indicators for initial identification and placement. Programming concerns begin where the identification (screening) process ends. The role of teachers is in program development and in realistically identifying the curricular areas of benefit to learners. With this in mind, the next section is concerned with a general level of assessment of those skills that benefit learners by assisting them in becoming as independent as possible in community living.

Standardized Social Competency and Behavioral Measures

The prevailing goal of many special educators is to teach academic skills by relating them to community living skills. Therefore, the logical connection with social competency, or more appropriately, independent living skills, is evident. Adaptive behavior scales are measures used at the general level of assessment to assess the independent living skills of learners who are mentally handicapped (see Table 3.2). Generally, adaptive behavior scales incorporate various categories such as interpersonal relations and self-help skills, allowing professionals to rate learners on a graduated scale. In order to rate a learner, the professional must either interview someone who intimately knows the student (teacher, parent) or have contact with the learner in observable situations.

The use of adaptive behavior measures constitutes a general level of assessment designed only to identify the global strengths and weaknesses of the target learner. Inherent problems—the high degree of subjectivity in rating, for example—preclude these devices from being useful for specifically monitoring student progress or assisting in program accountability (Childs, 1982). Adaptive behavior scales are also useful in obtaining a

TABLE 3.2 Sample of General-Level Assessment Instruments for Measuring Adaptive Behaviors

Assessment Instruments	Ages Covered by Scale	Reference	Measurement Techniques	Scores Obtained	Primary Use	Content Covered by Scale	Comments
Adaptive Behavior Inventory for Children (ABIC) Psychological Corporation New York, NY	5–11 years	Norm-referenced Good ethnic group representation	Interview	Scaled scores for each category	Classification decisions	Family Community Peer relations Nonacademic school roles Self-maintenance	Self-maintenance category may have some use with young children, especially where group includes diverse ethnic background.
Adaptive Behavior Scales (Institutional and Public School Version) American Assoc. of Mental Deficiency 5201 Connecticut Ave. Washington, D.C., 20015	Infant +	Norm-referenced	Interview and observation	Percentile that rates student against others according to sex, age, ethnic group, educational placement	Classification decisions	Independent function Physical development Language, etc.	Most of the scale not suitable for preschoolers; independent functioning section may be useful.
Balthazar Scales of Adaptive Behavior Consulting Psychologists Press 577 College Ave. Palo Alto, CA 94306	Infant +	Criterion-referenced	Direct observation	Rating on student's ability to complete task quality measure	Programming	Motor skills Language Social/emotional Self-help Independent living Recreation/leisure	Allows teacher a thorough profile on actual skill attainment.
Cain Levine Social Competency Scale Consulting Psychologists Press 577 College Ave. Palo Alto, CA 94306	5–13 years Primarily TMR students	Norm-referenced	Interview	Scaled scores	Classification and programming	Self-help Imitative Social skills Communication	Can be used with young, mildly handicapped children.
Camelot Behavioral Checklist Systems P.O. Box 607 Parsons, KS	Infant +	Criterion-referenced	Interview and observation	Scaled scores	Programming	Self-help Independent travel Motor skills Cognition Social/emotional	Can be useful in identifying large deficit areas.
TARC Assessment Inventory for Severely Handicapped Children H & H Enterprises P.O. Box 3342 Lawrence, KS 66044	3 years +	Criterion-referenced	Observation	Scaled scores	Programming	Motor Language Cognition Self-help	Teacher administers by watching child perform task.
Vineland Social Maturity Scale Educational Testing Service Princeton, NJ	Infant +	Norm-referenced	Interview	Scaled scores	Classification	Self-help Locomotion Communication Self-direction	New version recently on market.

Note. From "Self Help Skills" by J. Langone, 1985. In N. Fallen & W. Umansky (Eds.), Young Children with Special Needs (2nd ed.) (p. 376). Columbus: Charles E. Merrill. Copyright 1985 by Charles E. Merrill. Reproduced with permission of the publisher.

relatively fast assessment of students' severe deficits that hinder independent living. In addition, once a learner's global deficit areas and relative strengths have been identified, the teacher can proceed in identifying appropriate assessment tools that will be more specific in pinpointing areas needing matching interventions.

The same holds true for assessing the behavior problems and social skills of students who may be referred for possible placement into classrooms for students with behavior disorders. For example, teachers or parents may be asked to fill out a behavior checklist such as the Conners Parent and Teacher Checklist (Conners, 1969) or the Child Behavior Checklist and Profile (CBCL) (Achenbach, 1979; Achenbach & Edelbrock, 1983). These assessment systems allow the rater to decide from memory whether or not the behavior has occurred and to rate the intensity or frequency of the behavior (Morgan & Jenson, 1988).

These systems are helpful in identifying the existence of major problems and should highlight the need for additional assessment. The fact that these systems rely heavily on a person's memory and opinion precludes their sole use in placing a learner in special education. In-depth behavioral observation will be needed before more detailed placement and program development decisions can be made.

Sociometric measures can be helpful in establishing some general parameters for a student's program (McConnell & Odom, 1986). Peer nomination, the first type of sociometric measure, allows students to rate each other and establishes the most popular and least popular individuals in a class. Peer rating, the second type, allows students to rate each other on items related to social competence.

These devices are useful in providing screening information, but they cannot and should not stand alone in the placement process. They can, however, provide teachers with a fast way to target important curriculum areas relating to helping students improve their social competence and acceptance.

Curriculum-Based Assessment (CBA)

Curriculum-based assessment is the term for the practice of using nonstandardized instruments to establish the instructional needs of students based on their daily or frequent performance of tasks relating to the curriculum requirements of their school setting (Berdine & Meyer, 1987; Smith, 1989; Tucker, 1985; Wesson, King, & Deno, 1984; Witt, Elliott, Gresham, & Kramer, 1988). The foundation for CBA is geared to the individual needs of each student and the relationship of those needs to the school district curriculum. Therefore, a test that covers science material presented to students in the fourth grade in a Georgia school may be different from one based on the curriculum in a school in Washington. There might be differences in terms of content and in terms of levels of tolerance for what is considered mastery in each system.

CBA does not completely move away from standardized testing; it does, however, limit the degree to which standardization is used. Standardized tests attempt to compare a learner's scores to the scores of learners from a national sample. Some proponents of CBA (e.g., Deno, 1985; Germann & Tindal, 1985; Peterson, Heistad, Peterson, & Reynolds, 1985) have developed systems that compare a student's progress against the progress of other students except that the comparison group remains within the local district. This unique quality of CBA allows for a more objective analysis of students' abilities based on the norms for the areas in which they live (Galagan, 1985).

The results of CBA measures are not used for identification, labeling, or placement of students for special education services (Gickling & Thompson, 1985; Hammill, 1987). Instead, they are used to plan for activities, target instructional strategies, and monitor ongoing student progress. Teachers can easily compare the progress of students with mild and moderate handicaps against their regular education peers by occasionally sampling the regular education students and comparing the results (Marston & Magnusson, 1985).

Blankenship (1985) outlined the steps to implementing a CBA model. The first step involves developing a list of skills presented in the materials selected to instruct the students. This list is analyzed to make sure no important skills have been omitted, and the final list is arranged in hierarchical order.

The next step involves writing an objective for each skill on the list (see Chapter Four) and then developing test items relating to the objectives. What remains is to plan how to administer the CBA.

CBAs designed to pretest learner knowledge provide information concerning skills already mastered and learning style. CBAs designed to posttest learner knowledge provide data required to assess instructional success or failure. This information then enables teachers to redesign educational interventions when needed.

CBA correlates well with the principles of community-based instruction. The strategies used to gather CBA data can be used effectively to analyze student performance in community settings (e.g., observational data, data from permanent products). In addition, CBA allows for the main point of reference to be the local district or, in this case, the local community in which the student resides. Therefore, teaching strategies for consumer-related reading and mathematics skills are reflected in the activities available in a given locale and will vary across communities (Bigge, 1988)

CBA should not be viewed as unsophisticated or unsystematic because it is at times referred to as informal testing. On the contrary, this particular type of assessment can yield the most important and often the most intensive information for program development. At the specific or intensive level of assessment, teachers identify from general information gathered (e.g., formal procedures at the global level) exactly what areas of learning need further scrutiny. Using CBA, the teacher can design very specific measures to assess learner performance based on objectives in a specific area of the curriculum. For example, a teacher may have information on a student with moderate cognitive deficits obtained from administration of a Cain-Levine Social Competency Scale (Cain, Levine, & Elzey, 1963). Data from this measure may indicate that the learner is performing below a designated norm in communication skills. This information is important because it alerts the teacher to initial problems; however, there is generally not enough information provided to make appropriate programming decisions. Therefore, the teacher would then develop objectives specifying the conditions under which the behavior will occur (e.g., When the class is questioned, the student will communicate the need to use the restroom facilities) and with a preset criterion (e.g., successful elimination after each request).

A similar illustration of assessing academic performance of a student with learning disabilities might begin with information from a diagnostic reading test identifying severe deficits in decoding skills (see Table 3.1). The next step is to further assess each of the decoding areas that is suspect by first developing behavioral objectives that relate to each identified skill. An example of an objective that could be used as a basis for intensive assessment might be

> *Context:* Given a printed list of 20 prefixes.
>
> *Outcome:* Student will be able to point to each prefix and say it correctly.
>
> *Criterion:* 18 out of 20 correct.

In this case, the teacher now can develop a test and obtain a measure of student performance based exactly on the objective. Similar objectives can be written for each of the skills within the cluster goal of decoding using various commercially produced scope and sequence charts for guides (see Chapter Four).

The preceding section on CBA was designed to describe how assessment moves from the formal or general level to the informal and more intensive level of measuring learner performance. Within this intensive level of assessment there is an additional method of gathering data that is often the most valuable technique for measuring specified behaviors of learners. Systematic observation allows the teacher to assess the learner's application of skills or identify the lack of such skills in naturalistic settings (classrooms, community environments) on a daily basis. If observation measures are designed and implemented appropriately, reliable information can be gathered that meets the rigorous standards of social validity.

Observation as an Assessment Tool

The foundation for designing a high-quality observation system is the operational definition of the behavior(s) in question. If the behaviors have not been defined in terms that are measurable (i.e., they can be seen, heard, or touched), then the data collected by the system will be questionable (Smith, 1989). The test for defining a behavior is simply this: Can two independent observers record the defined qualities of the behavior and be fairly reliable as to the occurrence or nonoccurrence of the stated qualities at least 80% of the time? This requirement of defining behaviors in observable, measurable terms can be met provided the behavioral objectives for the student are written accurately. That is, if the context, outcome, and criterion are included in the objective, the necessary components for observation will be present.

CASE STUDY

Laronda was a student in Mr. Moss's class who was exhibiting behavior problems. One day in the teachers' lounge Mr. Moss lamented that Laronda was driving him crazy by acting out more and more frequently.

"I know what you mean," said Ms. Barnes. "She's acting out more in my class, too. Why, just yesterday she spent my entire math period passing notes to her friends!" Mr.

Moss looked at her with a puzzled expression. "That's interesting. But when I say she's acting out I mean that she jumps out of her seat during lessons to do things that can wait until a later time."

Listening with interest was Mr. Vader, the school psychologist, who had just finished reading an article about observation and analysis of behavior. "The problem you two are having," he said, "is that you both have different ideas about what the problem is. You need to *operationally define* 'acting out' as a class of behaviors."

After Mr. Vader explained to Mr. Moss and Ms. Barnes that operational definitions describe the behavior in such a way that it can be either counted (number of times the behavior occurred) or times (how long the behavior was exhibited), the teachers set about trying to be more precise. The operational definition they devised would now allow them to assess Laronda's unproductive behavior:

> Acting out occurs when Laronda ceases doing the assigned task either by looking away from her work for more than one minute or by standing and leaving the work area. If Laronda looks away or stands in order to ask a question about her work, it will not be counted as an occurrence of acting out.

■ ■ ■ ■

Another component of systematically observing behavior results in the recording of events other than the behavior itself (Mercer & Mercer, 1989). In order to adequately assess behaviors in relationship to a learner's environment, the teacher must also record events that happen prior to the target behavior (antecedent events) and events occurring after the behavior (consequences). The same criterion of rigor in behavioral definitions holds true in either case. Knowledge of such occurrences is vital when assessing learner behaviors, because teachers can design an intervention more appropriately when they can make decisions based on events that are influencing and interacting with the student in question.

Recording Systems

Once important behaviors have been defined in observable, quantifiable terms, the next step involves designing an appropriate measurement system for collecting the necessary data. Hall (1971) identified five techniques that can be used to record the frequency of defined behaviors: continuous recording, event recording, duration measures, interval recording, and time sampling procedures.

Continuous recording allows the teacher to observe and record in anecdotal format behaviors occurring at a given time. This system requires the observer to state the specific behaviors in an operational format. Continuous recording systems are useful in identifying antecedent consequences that are important for eventual programming. For example, if a middle school student with behavior disorders is engaging in a number of fights while attending mainstreamed classes, the teachers involved first record all the happenings prior to each fight. If there is an obvious cause such as the student's reacting to being called names, the teachers will have a better idea of how to correct the problem. Continuous recording should, in most instances, be a first step because the recording of antecedent events can often lead to a common-sense solution.

A second type of recording system is called *event recording*. This system involves a simple frequency count, noting the occurrence of specified behaviors (Germann & Tindal, 1985). For example, a teacher may record the number of times Jeff pokes his peers during the school day or the number of times Theresa has a temper tantrum.

Duration recording is a useful measurement system for behaviors that do not have a clear onset and termination. That is, teachers come in contact with behaviors that have no discrete reference points, making it impossible to count the number of times the behaviors occurred (e.g., some types of off-task behavior such as daydreaming). When dealing with behaviors of this nature, it becomes necessary to measure the behavior in terms of the length of time that it occurs, noted as duration of occurrence. Theresa's temper tantrum is a behavior that can dictate the type of measurement system used. If the temper tantrums are short and have a clear beginning and end, a simple frequency count could be used. However, behaviors such as this ordinarily do not occur in a nice, concise form. Spontaneous outbursts often occur in varying lengths and intensity, making them difficult to predict. Therefore, a duration measure can be used to assess the length of the occurrence. Subsequent interventions will be designed to shorten the duration of the behavior.

A fourth observation system measures behaviors that are erratic—those that start and stop or continue for long periods without warning. *Interval recording* systems are characterized by establishing a defined period of time (e.g., 10 minutes) and dividing that time period into standard components (e.g., 20-second intervals). Observers can then watch a behavior in relation to each interval and record either of two possibilities: (1) the behavior occurred or did not occur during the interval (frequency), or (2) the behavior lasted for the entire interval (duration). Over the period of 10 minutes in which the behavior is recorded, the teacher can compute the total data, such as the percentage of time that behavior occurred or the total length of time the behavior was exhibited. Information such as this gives the teacher a benchmark to compare the resulting behavior with after the intervention has been implemented (e.g., percentage of intervals when the behavior decreases).

Time sampling, another technique used to measure behaviors, is a method similar to interval recording with one important difference: The observation is not continuous. Teachers may not have the time to watch target learners continually. Instead, teachers may interrupt their schedules occasionally to observe and record certain behaviors. For example, a teacher may look up from a group lesson every 5 minutes to record whether a student working independently is on task. Similarly, a teacher may record behaviors of a group interaction where different students are observed and their behavior recorded every 3 minutes. In either case, this system allows teachers the freedom to perform additional tasks along with the observation process.

Task Analysis and Assessment

Task analysis actually has two uses. First, a task analysis allows the teacher to develop a management system that structures a learning task in a logical teaching sequence. This use of task analysis relates it to curriculum design. Second, task analysis can be a method of assessment when it is used to compare learner progress to specific steps in the instructional sequence. The use of task analysis as an assessment tool is discussed here.

The skill of developing task analyses should be practiced based on the information presented in Chapter Four. If there were a request to analyze the goal of division or the goal of cost comparison shopping, the teacher could develop a breakdown of the steps involved in sequential order from least to most demanding. These substeps, when learned in the same order, would lead the student to perform increasingly more complex tasks. Repeating this process for a specified number of behavioral objectives would result in the learner's being proficient in the given cluster goal area. The relationship between task analysis and assessment will be clarified further in the following paragraphs.

Each step on a given task analysis is the yardstick by which to assess student performance. For example, a behavioral objective under the social skills component of the curriculum might state, "The student will be able to cope with conflict in the regular education class, in the special education class, and in at least 3 community-based instructional sites." This objective is delineated by including the following task sequence:

1. Walks away from peer when angry, to avoid hitting peer.
2. Expresses anger with nonaggressive words rather than physical or verbal aggression.
3. Responds to teasing by ignoring or leaving the setting.
4. Appropriately accepts constructive criticism or punishment for inappropriate behaviors.

Using the objective and its components as an assessment tool, the teacher then merely records how the learner responds at each level of the instructional analysis. Given a task sequence of academic skills, the teacher can follow the same process (see Figure 3.3).

Using task analysis as an instructional tool has become increasingly important to teachers. Once a task analysis of a particular skill area has been completed, the teacher

Goal Area:	Phonetic Analysis—Reading
Cluster Goal:	Student will be able to recognize and read in context words containing consonant variants.
Short-term Objective:	
Context:	Second grade passage to be read orally.
Outcome:	Words, including all consonant variants.
Criterion:	95% of the targeted words must be correctly read.
Subskills:	Soft or hard c
	Soft or hard g
	Silent sound of letter when in kn, wr, gn blends
	Final sounds of gh/f

■ FIGURE 3.3
Sample Task Analysis for One Area of Phonetic Analysis of Reading

has a "blueprint" for assessing behaviors, teaching new skills, and subsequently modifying the program. This flexibility in the task analysis approach also allows it to work well in conjunction with other assessment techniques.

Task analysis is not, however, a casual process. The ability to develop high-quality task sequences involves a logical thought process and the ability to observe the fine details of how a task is completed.

For example, a task analysis of reading comprehension might include basic steps such as identifying the main idea, pinpointing details, drawing logical conclusions, and making inferences. These areas may be broken down further, however, with the se-quenced skills written in behavioral format. The teacher then develops criterion-refer-enced tests or administers a standardized test to gather information on student progress in each of the stated areas. Similarly, a task analysis for teaching a high school student a vocational task related to office work might be broken down into simple duties that are completed in a specific sequence. In any case, the blueprint of the task analysis has been developed, the teacher can include an observation component that allows a trained observer to record student progress.

This section includes assessment techniques that should be used, and in most cases developed, by teachers for collecting assessment data. Data must be interwoven with program development and teaching, allowing the results of assessment to aid the teacher in making appropriate instructional decisions.

Scores can provide valuable information for monitoring purposes, just as a body temperature that is too high or too low can indicate the presence of a health problem. Assessment scores, such as a score from a standardized reading test indicating a deficit area in decoding, can be valuable to a teacher when they are (a) based on preset criteria or (b) used for global assessment purposes. Unfortunately, some teachers may find them-selves totally relying on various test scores. For example, to such teachers grades may have become an end in and of themselves instead of being the monitoring system they are intended to be.

KEY CONCEPTS

- Standardized tests are helpful for identifying severe deficit areas in both academic and social skill areas.

- Standardized diagnostic tests of academic skills are most useful when given by the teacher because the teacher can observe student behavior and error patterns that will have an effect on the student's behavior in his or her classroom.

- Curriculum-based assessment (CBA) can be either commercially produced or developed by the teacher. They are developed from specific objectives, allowing the teacher to compare the student's performance in relation to certain skills instead of in relation to the performance of other students.

- CBAs often provide the most useful information relating to classroom programming because they can be developed with a specific skill area in mind. For example, a teacher working on fractions can develop a CBA that intensively assesses a student in only that area.

■ Observation is a valuable assessment tool, especially when dealing with social behaviors, independent living skills, academic skills that are being applied to community problems, and vocational skills.

■ Task analysis is both an assessment and teaching tool, providing the teacher with a device to monitor a student's performance against a series of subskills. This approach allows the teacher to identify exactly where the student is having difficulty and where to begin instruction.

■ ■ ■ ■

Teachers must analyze learner responses to identify error patterns and areas of strength. This process is opposed to viewing a set of scores as the end product of assessment. Gathering only scores from standardized assessment batteries provides little, if any, useful information for teaching. Conversely, teachers should gather assessment data that allow them to make competent programmatic decisions. The next section of this chapter presents a pragmatic approach to gathering useful data that will assist the teacher in developing effective educational interventions. The format is based on the IEP process, following sequential steps to demonstrate the importance of assessment and the kind of data needed to develop effective programs.

ASSESSMENT AND THE IEP

Initial assessment of learners to establish their present level of performance provides the foundation for future program development. This level of assessment is crucial for identifying the needs of the student where more intensive investigation is necessary. The teacher's responsibility for appropriate assessment of the learner is paramount, and it begins before the IEP meeting convenes. The teacher plays an important part in the data collection and program development process as well as being an advocate for the student.

Present Levels of Student Performance

Information for establishing a student's present level of performance is collected from three sources: cumulative records and an interview of the student, the parents, and past instructors; standardized tests; and criterion-referenced measures (including observation of student behaviors). The information from these sources must be collected and analyzed prior to IEP development if the data are to be of practical use.

First, a careful inspection of cumulative records, followed by an interview, can produce a wealth of information that will point to the next step in the assessment process. Moran (1979), for example, found that cumulative records can yield valuable data such as deficiencies in academic and social areas, age at onset of difficulties, absenteeism, and testing results in comparison to classroom performance. Identifying noticeable deficits in student behavior can save time when the teacher is deciding the types of diagnostic measures to use. For example, achievement test results located in a learner's record may indicate severe problems in reading. This information can save time by alerting the teacher to this area for intensive analysis. Similarly, information from previous adaptive behavior scales and behavioral checklists can pinpoint areas for further inspection without the teacher's having to repeat screening procedures.

The age of onset of learning problems is especially important for profiling academic skills (Moran, 1979). If records show that the student demonstrated problems when entering school (which should be the case for learners with cognitive deficits), the indication is a developmental disability. Learners whose deficits do not appear until later grades, however, generally demonstrate learning problems resulting from sources other than mental handicaps. This data could aid in interpreting poor test results and signal that placement in classes for students with mild mental handicaps would be inappropriate.

Two final indications of the need for more specific assessment are absenteeism and discrepancies between records and classroom performance. Carefully scrutinizing absentee and health records can pinpoint when in a student's career a long illness occurred. This may point to deficits in skills normally taught at that time (Moran, 1979). Absentee and health records can also supply information concerning when during the year certain students may be absent (e.g., in cold weather) and pertinent information concerning vision or hearing, as well as possible medical problems. This level of assessment provides valuable clues to the types of standardized and/or criterion-referenced measures that will be necessary for further analysis.

When information pertaining to student performance on a standardized measure is presented to a teacher, it may have little meaning for program development. Often the most valuable data provided by measures of this nature are not test scores. Rather, the most useful information is what some professionals call by-products of assessment. These by-products are learner characteristics that can only be observed by the astute assessor. Besides the obvious data generated by administering a particular type of test, information such as the following should be noted:

1. *Preferred modality:* Does the student respond better to visual, auditory, or tactile stimuli?

2. *Learning style:* How does the learner respond to unfamiliar questions? Will the learner guess (risk taker) or refuse to answer (failure avoider)?

3. *Information processing:* Does the learner reason through an answer or quickly attempt the first answer available?

4. *Error patterns:* Do there appear to be patterns of errors that occur in specific skill areas?

5. *Reliance on assistance:* Will the learner attempt to work on the solution to a question alone (independent learner), or does the learner demand constant feedback with questions such as "Is this right?" (dependent learner)?

6. *Hierarchy of reinforcers:* What types of initial reinforcers appear to have positive effects on the learner (e.g., smiles, "good job," etc.)?

To obtain such valuable information, the teacher should have first-hand experience with testing the learner. This can be obtained by closely observing the learner while administering standardized measures.

IDEA FILE

Assessing a student's modality preference and whether or not any changes can be effected in identified deficit areas is a highly controversial issue (e.g., Kavale, 1981; Sternberg & Taylor, 1982); however, there appear to be some data supporting the need to identify preferred modalities when assessing academic skill areas (e.g., Kampwirth & Bates, 1980; Tarver & Dawson, 1978).

Learners could probably benefit if teachers could identify their modality strengths, because teachers could then present some information in ways that were easier for the students to grasp. For example, a student with strong auditory perception skills might be allowed to listen to stories on tape while reading a corresponding manuscript.

■ ■ ■ ■

Assessing Skill Areas with Standardized Tests

Standardized tests also provide a quick, relatively accurate measure for assessing skill areas. For example, the administration of several academic diagnostic tests provides a general profile of student strengths and weaknesses in the designated area. These measures then can identify skill areas where more intensive assessment is necessary. The information generated from these measures can also be of sufficient detail to develop objectives for the IEP. However, before the IEP can be translated into an implementation plan, the teacher will have to gather more intensive information. One word of caution: Students may not perform their best when presented with a standardized test (Moran, 1979). Teachers should not underestimate the extent to which a student can perform. Often, a student's performance is less than his or her potential for progress.

Teachers may find it impossible to collect data using standardized tests. In this case a number of less formal measures are available including behavioral checklists, informal reading inventories, and teacher-made tests, among others. The goal of administering these measures is the same as it would be if formal tests were used: to establish a global learning profile of the student.

Constructing the Performance Profile

Before an IEP can be adequately developed, a profile of student performance relating to predetermined goals and objectives is required. Therefore, the standardized and curriculum-based assessment measures administered during this pre-IEP level of assessment relate specifically to those outcomes. Once data have been collected and analyzed relative to goals, it will be time for the teacher, parents, and supporting professionals to meet for detailed program development.

For example, an assessment battery including an intelligence test, achievement and diagnostic measures, and an adaptive behavior or behavior checklist may have been administered for a given student. This information, although valuable for setting parameters for additional assessment, is far too general for use in making programming decisions. To obtain more specific information the teacher may have to coordinate and in some cases implement the following assessment activities:

1. Conduct direct observations and recording of student behavior relating to interpersonal skills in school and in a variety of community environments.

2. Complete measurement of permanent products including the student's completed assignments relating to both classroom and community-based activities.

3. Conduct interviews with community members who have direct contact with the student and can provide information about the student's social interactions or application of academic skills.

Importance of the Teacher's Role

Two crucial points are implicit in the assessment activities listed. First, teachers may feel that coordinating these activities is not part of their job and will result in additional work. This attitude may be difficult to overcome. Teachers need to realize that a process of this nature actually saves time and can result in less work. When learners are placed in a program, the teacher may have to rely on information provided by people they have never met and information about important areas may not be available. The result is that the teacher must perform additional work to assess the learner adequately, and these tasks have to be completed while responsibility for the rest of the class is pending.

The second point involves the pivotal role of the teacher in the assessment process. In each of the assessment activities listed, teacher involvement is vital for two reasons: (1) the teacher can ensure that skills important to the student and related to the classroom are assessed; and (2) the teacher benefits from the knowledge of the specialists and can assimilate data concerning the learner. This last point assists in the development of the more intensive assessment activities needed for program implementation.

The same assessment activities would be applied with learners who have academic learning problems, substituting the use of academically related measures and eliminating or including assistance from other professionals as needed (e.g., vocational educator). Whatever modifications are made, the process is the same, culminating in information used for IEP decisions.

The next step in the assessment continuum occurs after the IEP has been developed and involves the implementation plan, including the instructional objectives. This level of assessment includes the intensive activities that will be used for both judging learner performance and monitoring student progress.

IDEA FILE

Error analysis is a vital component in the assessment process that is becoming more popular with special educators (e.g., Howell & Kaplan, 1980). Essentially, error analysis involves carefully reviewing a sample of errors that a student is making and hypothesizing the cause for the student's mistakes. This approach should be used with both standardized and criterion-referenced measures by recording the stimulus that was presented to the student and the erroneous response given.

The method presented by Howell and Kaplan (1980) is a simple, yet effective one for teachers to use. Their approach is to develop a table such as the one shown in Table 3.3 and record student errors as they occur.

Analyzing the mistakes of learners appears to be a more important end product of assessment than the mere recording of scores. The error analysis allows the teacher to locate a student's current level of performance in relation to a scope and sequence chart and begin teaching from that point.

■ ■ ■ ■

Assessment for Revision: Ongoing Monitoring of Learner Progress

Formative Evaluation

Formative evaluation involves a continual monitoring of student progress. Performance is measured against preset instructional objectives chosen specifically for the individual learner. The assessment tools available to the teacher for this level of intensive inspection of skills include both criterion-referenced tests and behavioral observations.

For a student with moderate mental handicaps, the IEP objectives may indicate that instruction is necessary in all areas of self-help skills (e.g., teaching independent fast-food restaurant skills). The teacher would devise a systematic observation system to record ordering and paying for food; locating and retrieving condiments, napkins, and straws; locating a table; eating appropriately; cleaning off the table; and placing trash in the appropriate receptacle. During the initial assessments the adaptive behavior scales may have indicated a deficit area in restaurant-related skills. A more intensive evaluation involves matching the learner's abilities against the task sequences of these skill areas.

A similar example can be given for assessing an academic skill. Global assessment procedures may have identified a deficit area in fractions, as pinpointed by the Key Math Diagnostic Arithmetic Test (Connolly et al., 1971). From these data and other information (e.g., cumulative records, curriculum-based assessment), adequate behavioral objectives could be written for the IEP. From this point, teachers would devise both

TABLE 3.3   *Student Error Record*

Stimulus	Response	Assumed Cause
195 ×7 1365	195 ×7 735	Cannot regroup in consecutive places.
SHOW BOY	SHOE BY	Does not read diphthongs in context.

criterion-referenced tests based on their instructional analysis and subsequent objectives similar to the following:

Behavioral Objective 1.1

Outcome: 20 numbers including decimals (e.g., 1.75)

Context: Student will be able to correctly write the equivalent fraction.

Criterion: 80%

Instructional Objectives: 1.11 Divide figure into designated number of parts.

1.12 Write fractional parts into which a whole has been divided.

Given a complete instructional analysis of the fraction area (available in a number of scope and sequence charts and commercial teacher manuals), the teacher can intensively assess the learner in relation to the stated objectives. When this step is completed, the teacher will have a profile of the learner's abilities.

Assessment-Instruction Interaction

What occurs in a process of this nature is simply a sequence involving assessment-instruction and so forth. Explaining differences between the two steps is difficult because they are interwoven throughout the instructional process. For example, a teacher instructing learners to buy insurance will be providing the necessary prompts and reinforcers to increase the probability that the students will master each instructional objective. In addition, that teacher will be recording the success rate of the learners for each objective, thereby collecting ongoing assessment data. Similarly, when a teacher administers a short test designed to measure progress in reading comprehension, that teacher will spend time reviewing the test with the learner to reinforce appropriate answers, correct existing errors, and generalize skills to the next step in the instructional sequence. In this case interfacing occurs between assessment and instruction.

Probing

Probing is a technique of assessment that results in an ongoing profile of learner progress. The techniques used to probe learner behavior are tools that have been discussed throughout this chapter: curriculum-based tests and systematic observation. A unique feature of probes that relates directly to the IEP is that they are frequent and, if possible, they should occur daily. This principle of frequent monitoring is important. By definition, students with mild and moderate handicaps learn at a slower rate than their nonhandicapped peers, resulting in less obvious gains. Therefore, frequent probing is important because any gains that are made should be an indication of program effectiveness. Conversely, if no student progress occurs the teacher is alerted to program inadequacy. With frequent probing, ineffective teacher techniques, materials, and/or reinforcers will be identified and modified, thereby reducing the amount of time needed for instruction. With all the extra activities and unseen events that occur during the school day, every minute of instructional time is valuable.

A typical sequence of teaching events usually involves scheduling a short time each day for individualized instruction in all categorical areas. That is, the teacher ensures at least 5 minutes of one-to-one instruction for the student in the academic areas designated by assessment data. Also, the teacher arranges for individual guided practice time on the instructional objective(s) covered during the session. The teacher eventually presents the learner with a probe covering what the student was targeted to learn, attempting to measure whether or not the instruction had an impact. By applying probes of this nature teachers gather information from assessment measures that are sensitive to student progress. Based on data from the probes, teachers subsequently can make decisions as to whether more practice is needed before continuing to the next objective, a revision of the instructional intervention is required, or the skill has been mastered.

Examples of Ongoing Assessment

To illustrate the important points concerning assessment and its relationship to program evaluation and revision, two brief examples concerning both academic and vocational skill areas are presented here. In the first example, an instructional sequence is to be designed to teach subtraction with the final objective that the learner will subtract by regrouping in alternate places. A typical instructional analysis of subtraction might include at least the following instructional objectives:

1.1 *Context:* Given worksheets requiring written answers, student will be able to

Outcome: Correctly compute subtraction problems.

1.11 With no regrouping.

1.12 Regrouping in each of the decimal places.

1.13 Regrouping consecutively.

1.14 Regrouping alternately.

Criterion: Between 80% and 90% per worksheet

Percentages are used as a quality measure of student performance in this instance because the teacher probably will change the number of problems that will be included in each probe. If the number of problems changes from day to day, a measurement system that will allow comparison between daily performances is necessary. In other words, criterion requirements stated in terms of four problems out of five correct or eight problems out of ten correct cannot be compared because the total number is different. However, if they are converted to percentages, the results become 80% and 80% respectively, demonstrating that the learner is maintaining the quality of performance. Figure 3.4(a) presents an example of how an assessment profile in subtraction can be obtained on a student.

The original curriculum-based assessment of the most complicated subtraction problems indicated a severe deficit in that area, which alerted the teacher to begin instruction with simple facts. The first two sessions resulted in a review for the student based on the scores of both probes. Instructional objective 1.13, however, indicated that the student probably was just learning regrouping in each of the decimal places and the current mode of instruction is having no effect. In this case, the teacher might have decided to break down the instructional sequence into finer steps that included each of the separate decimal places. In addition, decisions to add different or additional cues, change reinforcement schedules, and use more modeling could be made to increase the probability of learner success. In any case, these data indicate that the student met the criterion after the program revision was made. Figure 3.4(b) is self-explanatory, demonstrating the eventual learner success at mastering the unit objectives.

A similar example of how ongoing assessment provides teachers with data for program revision can be illustrated by a process for developing vocationally related skills. To summarize the initial steps, both the special education teacher and the vocational

Cluster Goal (1.0): SUBTRACTION

Behavioral Objective (1.1): Given 15 worksheet problems concerning regrouping alternately, student will be able to correctly write the answers.

Instructional Objectives: Given worksheets requiring written answers, student will be able to correctly compute

1.11 Simple facts

1.12 No regrouping

1.13 Regrouping in each of the decimal places

1.14 Regrouping consecutively

Assessment Results:

Objective		Criterion Expected	Criterion Obtained
Preinstructional assessment:	B.O. 1.1	85%	0%
Probes:	I.O. 1.11	100%	100%
	I.O. 1.12	100%	100%
	I.O. 1.13	90%	70%
	I.O. 1.13	90%	70%
Decision to revise instruction:	I.O. 1.13	85%	90%
	I.O. 1.14	85%	80%
	I.O. 1.14	85%	90%
	B.O. 1.1	85%	90%

■ FIGURE 3.4(a)
Sample Assessment Profile—Subtraction

education teacher work together to gather preliminary information about each student's present level of performance. Subsequently, this team of educators provides the IEP participants with suggestions based on their findings as to what goals and objectives would be beneficial for the learners. Once the decision has been made concerning modified placement either in an occupational readiness program or a combination readiness and occupational preparation program, the team applies curriculum modification procedures (see Chapter Four) to develop appropriate instructional objectives. For example, a learner who demonstrates appropriate adaptive behavior and motor skills may benefit from vocational instruction in a horticulture cluster. The following cluster goal and objectives highlight one potential curricular area: horticulture.

Cluster Goal 2.0: Transplanting

Short-Term Objective 2.1: Given any potted plant, with verbal directions to transplant it to another container, student will be able to gather necessary materials and reroot the plant so that at least 98% of the repotted plants survive for a minimum of two weeks.

Sample Instructional Objectives: Given materials and verbal directions, the student will be able to

2.11 Judge whether or not a plant needs watering.

2.12 Sufficiently water a plant.

2.13 Transport potted plants without dropping.

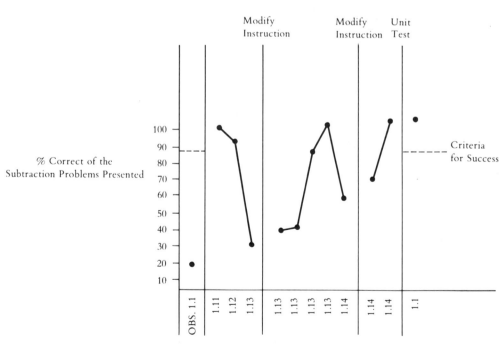

■ *FIGURE 3.4(b)*
Example of a Graph Depicting a Profile of a Student's Progress in Subtraction

2.14 Handle a nonpotted plant without damage.

2.15 Root a nonpotted plant.

Etc.

The objective reflects the content area knowledge of the vocational educator and a technique for assessing contributed by the special educator.

A task analysis format is used in assessing the ongoing performance of the student. Figure 3.5 presents an example of a task analysis including the instructional objectives just outlined. Both educators have contributed to developing this tool. However, once the analysis form has been devised, the vocational specialist can use it to monitor the progress of the learner. As instruction continues, the teacher observes that the student is having difficulty progressing with instructional objectives 2.14 and 2.15. Using this assessment data, the educator team can decide what revisions are needed to increase the probability of learner progress. For example, the data presented in Figure 3.5 should alert the teachers to problems the student is having with controlling fine motor movements. When presented with the delicate task of handling unpotted plants without precise guidance from a teacher or peer tutor, the student damages the plant. In this case, program modification would require introducing additional instructional objectives that would allow the student to practice control of fine motor movements.

This section has described the process of applying ongoing assessment techniques in an effort to monitor student progress for program revision. The two examples presented

Goal Area:	Horticulture								

Cluster Goal: Student will be able to transplant plants.

Short-term Objective: 2.1

Subskills	1 S	2 E	3 S	4 S	5 I	6 O	7 N	8 S	9
Judge whether or not the plant needs watering.	G	G	VI						
Sufficiently water the plant.	G	G							
Transport the potted plants without dropping.	G	G							
Handle an unpotted plant without damaging it.	G	G							
Root an unpotted plant.	G	G							

Code

VI: Student completes task with only verbal instruction.

M: Student completes task with only teacher model.

PP: Student completes task with only physical prompt.

G: Student completes task with only guidance.

■ *FIGURE 3.5*

An Example of a Task Analysis Recording Sheet for Horticulture

provide a basis for understanding the use of assessment data on a continual basis. What remains is to take a step back to view the entire instructional system as a whole instead of daily interventions. To accomplish this task, teachers need to reapply assessment techniques similar to those they used to establish the learner's entry behavior on designated behavioral objectives.

Assessment for Program Effectiveness: The IEP Review

The principle of summative evaluation will be discussed in detail in Chapter Four. Basically, summative evaluation involves gathering information at the completion of the unit that establishes whether student performance matches the preset criteria. The general assessment methods that can be used at this level involve direct product measurement, observational analysis, and learner output. Examples of each of these techniques are presented in Chapter Four. They were also stressed in this chapter. This form of evaluation is essentially a posttest, that is, an assessment based on the behavioral unit objective the results of which are compared with those of a similar measure administered at the program's outset. When the learner entered the system, he or she was assessed in accordance with preset criteria. The results of this assessment delineated what specific objectives were to be the focus of the learner's instructional program. When instruction is completed, the student is presented with the same or a similar assessment measure to note overall progress in the unit of study and to make judgments concerning overall effectiveness of the program.

One more consideration must be addressed during summative evaluation. Generalization and the need to program for it are discussed in a later chapter, but a brief explanation relating to assessment is warranted here. When a learner has successfully completed a unit, the next step in the summative evaluation process is to allow the student to demonstrate those skills under varying circumstances. In this instance, the teacher requires the learner to perform the skill in different settings, under the supervision of different individuals, using alternative materials, and under varying reinforcers or schedules. If the learner fails to accomplish the transfer, the teacher should develop additional program components that will focus on using the learned skills under varied conditions.

KEY CONCEPTS

- ■ Ongoing monitoring of student progress is a vital component of the IEP process and allows the teacher to modify the instructional methods and materials if results indicate that little or no learning is taking place.
- ■ Monitoring a student's daily progress can be done either by using CBAs or by observing student behavior. *Probes*, another term for the frequent monitoring of learner progress, come in many forms. Flashcards, worksheets, workbooks, having students answer questions orally, task analyses for grooming skills, and watching students interact in a group are all examples of probes.

■ Converting the data from probes to chart form may help teachers and students to better follow the learning patterns of the person being charted.

■ *Summative evaluation* relates to assessing the student's performance over a large block of instruction (e.g., end-of-the-unit test). For example, a student working for 2 weeks on the six subskills of subtraction might have demonstrated sufficient progress that the teacher wishes to assess her over a more complicated area. In this case, the teacher may choose to develop a criterion-referenced test including a sample of subtraction problems representing all six of the subskills.

■ Another aspect of summative evaluation vital for assessing learners involves monitoring the generalization of learned skills to community problems. Thus, if the student in the example passed the unit test on subtraction the teacher would devise another measure that tested the student's ability to use the skills to solve a community-based problem (e.g., balancing a checkbook or conducting a cost comparison between two items in a grocery store).

■ ■ ■ ■

CHAPTER FOUR

DESIGNING CURRICULUM

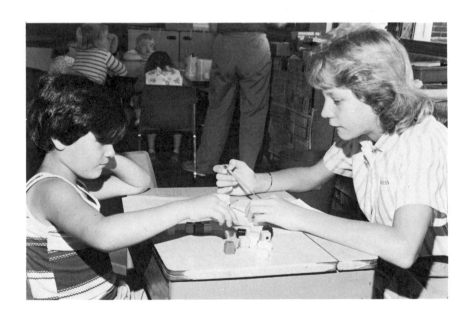

■ Curriculum, as a concept, is not easily or precisely defined. For example, various definitions spark debates over whether curriculum should emphasize the child versus a subject-centered approach, transmission of a culture, or the totality of experiences learners encounter in schools (Tanner & Tanner, 1980). Such issues have generated a number of definitions of what curriculum is (Goldstein, 1981a). Unfortunately, the many definitions of curriculum may confuse the teachers they were designed to help, unless they are seen as valid parts of a dynamic whole.

SELECTIVITY IN CURRICULUM DESIGN

Whatever its definition, a curriculum needs to be flexible enough to meet the needs of a variety of students (Heiss, 1981). All learners, including those with handicaps, need exposure to a wide array of curriculum options. The key to the differences between curriculum development for general education students and that for learners with mild and moderate handicaps is *selectivity*. Skills and objectives chosen for these students should reflect their goal of becoming as independent as possible in both existing and future living environments. Therefore, one definition of curriculum may establish two priority levels in curriculum content: what skills are *essential* for individuals to meet some defined level of independence and what further skills are *desirable* for those individuals to learn, provided they have mastered the essential skills.

Selectivity involves the careful identification of the skills and objectives that must be met by each individual to reach his or her optimal level of independence. Special educators may be in the best position to identify what those select curricular experiences should include, but unfortunately they are relegated to a secondary role in the curriculum design process. A curriculum plan may either be adapted from some other source (e.g., commercially produced curriculum guides) or written without input from the teacher. The resulting product may be a curriculum that is "content redundant" (Cegelka, 1978, p. 187). Content redundancy results when curriculum guides for one area (e.g., urban New York) closely reflect the content of guides from other areas (e.g., rural Texas).

There has been a consistent movement away from what has been termed a watered down curriculum for students with mild handicapping conditions (MIMH, LD, & BD). This movement has resulted in an increase in the number of these learners enrolled in regular education classes with the curriculum remaining the same and only the instructional procedures changing to meet individual needs (Gloeckler & Simpson, 1988; Wang & Walberg, 1988). The assumption here is that the regular education curriculum is the most appropriate option for these learners and that survival in regular education classes should be the primary focus of curricular and instructional development.

Up to a point, this assumption has merit because the foundation of the regular education curriculum includes academically related skills geared towards self-sufficiency and use in daily living environments. The problem arises when survival in the regular class becomes the final goal and the principle of selectivity is forgotten. There is much in the regular education curriculum that is superfluous to basic community independence. Also, many of the activities within the regular education curriculum involve paper-and-pencil tasks. Special educators must take the lead during the curriculum development process by helping to select the most crucial skills for instruction and design or co-design with regular educators curriculum activities that allow students to practice their basic skills in relation to community-based tasks.

A major problem arises when teachers try to follow curriculum guides in which they have had little or no input. The goals included in many commercially produced guides may have objectives that are too broad, too general, or inappropriate for teachers to apply to the unique needs of their students.

CURRICULUM DEVELOPMENT AS A DYNAMIC PROCESS

This chapter depicts curriculum somewhat differently. First, curriculum development is viewed as an ongoing, dynamic process, always in a state of planned change. The goal is learner improvement based on individual needs. Second, the process of curriculum design should be adaptable and applicable to many different subjects and situations (Bigge, 1988). For example, when developing curriculum options for learners with handicapping conditions, teachers may assist in modifying a middle school science curriculum for students with mild handicaps or develop community mobility options for students with moderate handicaps. To match skills to learner needs, the curriculum design process must have a clear-cut sequence of steps that can be applied to a variety of situations.

Finally, the teacher should have a primary role in the design process. At present, some teachers are relegated to a secondary role in identifying appropriate curriculum for students (Budde, 1981). This situation is unfortunate because teachers frequently are the one stable factor in some students' lives. If one goal of special education is to individualize programs for learners, then the person who knows students best as learners and individuals ought to have a primary role in curriculum planning. Accordingly, this chapter focuses on teachers as the coordinators of curriculum design for their students. This does not place the burden of the entire process on teachers, but it suggests that teachers be allowed a leadership role in curriculum design with assistance from other professionals as needed (Gloeckler & Simpson, 1988).

A SYSTEMS APPROACH TO CURRICULUM DEVELOPMENT

Of the three curriculum components that are the basis of this chapter, two require more detailed discussion. A *systems approach* to curriculum views any development project as dynamic and adaptable to many situations (Dick & Carey, 1978; Gagne, 1975). The systems approach involves the application of systematic, clearly designed procedures to a problem or to an identified goal (see Figure 4.1). Some features of this approach set it apart from other techniques.

First, before a problem can be solved or an objective achieved, it must be clearly defined. For example, a group of secondary school special educators are concerned that students with mild and moderate handicaps instructed in their program appear to be unemployed in numbers exceeding the national average. Taken by itself, knowledge of a high unemployment rate among former students probably will not be of much help to the teachers in terms of program development or adjustment. If they were able to define the problem in terms of the following examples, they might have a better understanding of the variables influencing the situation.

1. Many former students appear to have had a skills training sequence that was too narrow. When they lose a job, they do not have sufficient skills to be instructed easily for a new position.

2. Certain former students obtained their first jobs through the work-study coordinator or vocational rehabilitation counselor. After losing a job or when wishing to change jobs, they do not appear to have the necessary job-search skills.

These examples represent only two of the elements that might have been included in the definition of the problem. By beginning with these, the teachers can take an important step toward identifying potential solutions. First, the students seem not to have learned a wide enough array of usable vocational skills, and second, they appear weak in job-search skills.

Once the problem has been pinpointed, the teachers should find it easier to identify possible solutions. One effective method for generating solutions involves a brainstorming session in which each teacher expresses his or her ideas. The following are typical solutions that might be generated in such a session by the secondary school teachers:

1. Develop a scheduling system that gives students the option to spend the first four semesters of high school in four different vocational education clusters. The last four semesters might involve intensive training in one or two clusters depending on observed student interest and aptitude.

2. Work-study or co-op blocks that give students work experience in industry or other community sites might be expanded to include more than one experience.

3. Beginning in the freshman year of high school, students could be given intensive instruction to teach them effective job-search skills. Information should be appropriate for these learners and should be structured to include role playing based on a variety of interview situations. As the secondary program continues, students should be given opportunities to attend interviews in a large number of business and industrial settings.

Once the teachers have discussed these possible solutions, one of two things can happen. The suggested solutions may turn out to be unworkable, requiring a redefinition

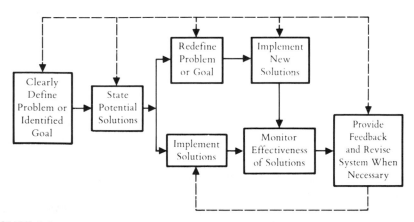

■ FIGURE 4.1
A Systems Approach to Planned Change

of the problem or goal. If the problem or goal has been precisely identified, the solutions are more likely to be appropriate and implementation can occur.

The target problem or goal is then observed under the new conditions, and any changes are monitored. The foundation of the systems approach is the ability to monitor the effectiveness of a set of solutions. A good monitoring system should be able to pinpoint ineffectiveness within the overall plan and indicate possible changes as necessary (Goldstein, 1981b).

For example, one specific technique for monitoring the job-search skills program would be to establish criterion behaviors for a student to demonstrate at each field-based interview. Sample criteria might include neatness of dress and appropriateness to the job situation; ability to ask job-related questions regarding specific duties, salary, working conditions, and fringe benefits; and ability to answer questions concerning past employment. These criteria could be rated on a qualitative scale, with both the teacher and the interviewer rating the student independently to compile a reliable measure of the student's skills.

If such an exercise were implemented at selected points throughout the job-search program, teachers should begin to receive information on program effectiveness. Based on this information, the teachers could make decisions concerning program changes, the last component of the systems approach. If the teachers found that most students were consistently scoring low in asking job-related questions, it might indicate a weakness in the instruction (implementation) component. A revision incorporating more oral communication exercises and three-by-five cue cards that students could carry with them might be needed to improve interview performance. This type of revision is important and reflects a basic philosophy of the systems approach: If something does not work for the students, change it. Changes can be made by redefining problems or goals, stating new solutions, or improving components of existing solutions (see Figure 4.1).

KEY CONCEPTS

The systems approach is very useful for solving problems and identifying program goals in a curriculum. There are four main steps in this approach:

1. Define clearly what is to be accomplished or what situation currently exists.
2. Develop and implement potential solutions based on the definitions.
3. Monitor the progress of solutions.
4. Revise any component of the system as necessary.

■ ■ ■ ■

THE IEP AND CURRICULUM DESIGN

Curriculum design is a two-level process. First, a curriculum can be developed for learners based on their assumed needs and a general set of learner characteristics. A class of learners with moderate cognitive deficits may have annual goals identified for them in areas such as self-care, career and vocational education, language and communication development, and functional academics, among others. This process is used by regular educators to identify curricular options for a group in the content areas (e.g., social studies, science, and commercial and industrial education). Similarly, teachers of students with mild handicapping conditions would identify the skills that would allow these learners to be independent producers, consumers, individuals, and citizens. These broad curriculum areas allow teachers to teach academic skills in relation to tasks that make sense to learners in terms of their ultimate community independence.

The second level of curriculum design emphasizes individual needs in relation to the group. This is the basis for all special education and is highlighted by the development of the individualized education program (IEP). The IEP is a vital requirement of Public Law 94-142 (1975) and includes a number of elements that are best described by the actual text of the law as follows:

> [an IEP includes] (A) a statement of the present levels of educational performance of such child, (B) a statement of annual goals, including short term instructional objectives, (C) a statement of the specific educational services to be provided to such children, and the extent to which such children will be able to participate in regular educational programs, (D) the projected date for initiation and anticipated duration of such service, (E) appropriate objective criteria and evaluation procedures and schedules for determining, on at least an annual basis whether instructional objectives are being achieved.

Basically, these points relate to five components of curriculum design: (1) assessment of learner needs; (2) development of curriculum components to meet those needs; (3) identification of support systems and instructional settings to meet student needs; (4) implementation of program management and time-line components; and (5) development of a program monitoring system. The IEP may be viewed as a management system that assists teachers in providing the most effective and efficient instruction for individual students (Cartwright et al., 1989; Price & Goodman, 1980).

Components of the IEP

The entire system is based on assessment. A profile is developed that gives a clear picture of the learner's current level of performance (Turnbull, Strickland, & Brantley, 1982). Standardized tests, criterion-referenced measures, and behavioral observations can be used to assess student behavior in curriculum areas such as academic and social skills (Mercer & Mercer, 1989). Assessment of a student's strengths and weaknesses is the basis for both instructional design and the IEP. For example, a social or affective goal for some students with learning disabilities might be to enhance their self-regard by increasing the positive self-critical comments they make (Harter, 1983; Meyer, 1983). Once this has been established, a program to increase the target behavior can be developed.

Similarly, the current computation skills of a student with learning disabilities may be assessed by using the Key Math Diagnostic Test (Connally et al., 1971). Both on the IEP and in systematically developed instruction, sampling the learner's entry behavior is vital. The difference between the systems is simply the degree to which assessment is implemented. The IEP assessment level is broad and describes a student's general level of performance, while the process of instructional design continues and the assessment becomes more specific. (See Figure 4.2.)

The second component of the IEP deals with curriculum options stated as annual goals and short-term instructional objectives. Objectives based on the initial assessment are written in performance terms and designate the broad curriculum goals and subsequent objectives that are important to the student. There is an important relationship between this component of the IEP and instructional design. To best understand this relationship, the IEP should be viewed as the document identifying the components of the general curriculum best fitting a learner's needs. Principles of instructional design are then applied to those areas outlined in the IEP to implement the plan for daily teaching.

The third component of the IEP identifies support services needed by the learner to successfully participate in the selected program options. For example, a student with behavior disorders might require the services of a child psychologist once a week or might have to spend 2 hours daily in a psychoeducational service center working on an affective curriculum.

The connection between the IEP and instructional design is a simple one. Students should have the necessary methods, materials, and services they need to succeed. The ultimate goal in both systems is essentially the same: to increase the probability of student progress.

The fourth major area of the IEP is program management. Here, availability of regular education programs in which the student can participate is indicated. Also, the anticipated duration of the program is stated to assist in overall time management and to suggest schedules for goal reevaluation. The systems approach to instructional design relies on organization to ensure a smooth transition between program components.

The final component of the IEP deals with program evaluation and accountability and outlines procedures for ongoing assessment of student behavior. Frequent samples of learner performance, usually in the form of criterion-referenced tests and behavioral observations, are used to measure the program's effectiveness in bringing about the desired change (Bepko, 1981). If the program is not working, the analysis should result in the necessary modifications.

The elements of the IEP not only relate to but actually were developed from the tenets of systems analysis. Each area of the IEP is based on empirically validated components from a number of systems models. For example, Glaser (1962) developed a model consisting of (1) designing instructional objectives; (2) determining student entry behavior; (3) developing instructional procedures; and (4) implementing performance assessment. These four units resemble the components of many systems analysis and instructional design models. The usefulness of a systems approach to designing curriculum is that the model can translate the IEP management plan into objectives and activities used by teachers.

When the systems approach is used, the IEP is not the end of program design. Rather, the development of this plan is only the beginning, the framework. The principles of instructional design are then further applied to develop a more detailed implementation plan. This plan has many labels such as individual implementation plan (IIP), portfolio, student profile, and unit of instruction. Whatever the label, the construction

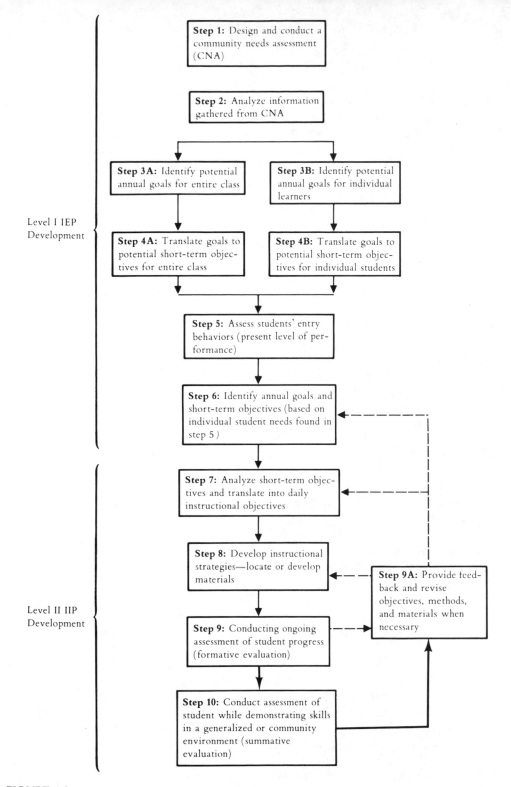

■ FIGURE 4.2
A Systems Approach to Designing Special Education Curricula

of an IIP requires more detailed use of instructional design. In perspective, the IEP is a plan based on the identified needs of individual students that establishes broad curriculum goals and program objectives. The IIP for a target student specifically states day-to-day objectives and intervention techniques to be used.

Developing Effective IEPs

Developing an IEP that is an effective management plan is not a difficult task. Unfortunately, the bureaucracy of public schools may put pressure on teachers to use shortcuts when developing programs (Nadler & Shore, 1980). A number of mistakes may occur if IEP development is looked upon as an arduous task. Table 4.1 presents some possible errors that can be made and alternative steps that may be more appropriate.

APPLYING THE PRINCIPLES OF INSTRUCTIONAL DESIGN: IDENTIFYING ANNUAL GOALS THROUGH THE COMMUNITY NEEDS ASSESSMENT

Teachers generally can choose broad program goals before learners enter the classroom. An appropriate curriculum for learners with handicaps includes goals that emphasize teaching these individuals to live in less restrictive environments (Cronis, Forgnone, & Smith, 1986; Frank, 1983; Siders & Whorton, 1982). The most appropriate goal areas for some young students with cognitive problems may be self-feeding, dressing, communication skills, and participation in leisure activities. Many learners with mild handicaps may profit from the application of complex academic skills (e.g., math word problems, word analysis).

Arithmetic can serve as an example for this process of program goal identification. Arithmetic goals are found in most special education curricula (e.g., functional use of the hand calculator for shopping, measurement in a vocational setting, or counting change to buy a soda). Within the broad program area of arithmetic there are a number of subunits or cluster goals (Schwartz & Oseroff, 1975) such as the basic operations (e.g., addition, subtraction), time, money management, and fractions.

Self-care skills are a second example of a program area. A number of cluster goals can be identified immediately, including dressing, eating, and grooming.

Basic skill areas (reading, arithmetic, writing, self-care) are identified before the student arrives, providing the teacher with an organizational reference for assessment. Teaching students with mild and moderate handicaps requires teachers to go beyond what are considered traditional basic skills and develop programs to teach community mobility, career education, and prevocational/vocational components. The instructional design process begins with establishing this framework for identifying annual goals. It then becomes more specific, with annual goals analyzed into subtasks (Tymitz-Wolf, 1982). At this stage the instruction is individualized by comparing the learner's present performance against these subtasks. This component allows teachers to make decisions about the skills most important for a student's needs (See Figure 4.2).

TABLE 4.1   Potential Mistakes and Solutions When Developing IEPs

Undesirable Practices	Preferred Practices
1. Evaluation information used to establish present level of performance is based only on survey-level norm-referenced instruments. For example, in order to expedite the IEP development process only a Wide Range Achievement Test is administered to establish academic deficits. This test provides only a rough grade-level score over certain academic areas.	1. A thorough assessment process is applied including specific-level tests in each academic area. These tests might include norm-referenced and such criterion-referenced measures as the Brigance Test—where portions pertaining to a given student are administered to obtain a complete picture of, for example, a learner's ability to add and subtract.
2. Present level of student performance is represented only by grade-level scores, e.g., Math 2.6 Reading Recognition 2.2 Spelling 2.3	2. Present level of student performance is represented by a *thorough* list of student strengths and weaknesses identified by the above assessment process (refer to Table 4.8).
3. Annual goals and short-term objectives are taken from a list provided by the school system or obtained from a computer-generated IEP program. Essentially all learners in a class have objectives from that list based on what is being taught in their class at a given time.	3. Annual goals and short-term objectives are tailored for a specific student based on results from an in-depth assessment process. Using this method, students within the same group may have somewhat different objectives based on their needs.
4. Short-term objectives are written in terms that are not measurable, e.g., Understand division. Improve communication skills. Improve mealtime behaviors.	4. Short-term objectives are written in terms that are measurable, e.g., Correctly compute 10 division problems. Orally request free time. Make 10 new manual signs. Use a spoon to place food in mouth.
5. Evaluation procedures consist of retesting student at end of year with a norm-referenced measure, e.g., Fall 1983—PIAT Math 3.2 Spring 1984—PIAT Math 3.3	5. Ongoing evaluation procedures involve the weekly or daily criterion-referenced (teacher-made) tests relating to each objective. When this approach is used, if learning is not occurring a change can be made relatively quickly.
6. Educational services such as time spent in regular classes are based on existing class sizes and which courses are easiest for students to take. Also, once staffed into a regular class, the student has to follow the same curriculum as everyone else.	6. Designating what regular classes are best for a given learner is based on course content and its appropriateness to the student's life. In such cases students might only be staffed into some classes for specific modules when the subjects were deemed appropriate. Where students are placed in classes on a full-time basis, it is done because they are to benefit, not because of an opening in the schedule.

TABLE 4.1 *(continued)*

Undesirable Practices	Preferred Practices
7. One afternoon a week is designated as "IEP day," and schedules of 10-minute sessions are used to develop the document.	7. IEP sessions are scheduled at the convenience of all participants, and ample time is allotted to develop an effective document. Preparation for the IEP can begin before the actual meeting by assigning different tasks to different people. For example, a pool of objectives based on a community needs assessment can be developed from which the committee can choose the ones that are the most appropriate.
8. For expediency purposes, IEP meetings are called at a time when concerned professionals cannot attend, or they are attended by others instead of the teachers who will be in charge of the child (e.g., vocational supervisor attends instead of the agriculture teacher in whose class the learner will be enrolled).	8. The specialists whose impact may be crucial to a given student's IEP (e.g., physical therapist, vocational educator, special educator, or regular educator) take an active part in the development process. For example, if a student is being considered for placement in a vocational education program, the vocational educator assists in developing work samples that can be used to determine the student's present level of vocational performance. These results are used by the vocational educator to develop a pool of objectives for the IEP committee's consideration.
9. Parents are invited to the meeting and presented with standardized test scores and educational jargon in an effort to convince them that professionals know what is best for their children.	9. A volunteer (possibly the teacher who will be working closest with the parents) becomes the family's and student's advocate. This individual meets with the parents prior to the IEP meeting, explaining the assessment results (in terms of strengths and weaknesses, not test scores). Also, the advocate attempts to assist the parents and whenever possible the student to set their goals and express their interests in what they feel is important.

Relying only on what teachers *think* students need, however, may result in a narrow view of curriculum (Morgan, 1981). For example, teaching functional arithmetic in some schools may translate into computing addition and subtraction problems on worksheets. The alternative is to apply the principle of *community validity*, establishing whether or not curriculum content is useful to students. Community validity is a principle that allows teachers to judge the usefulness of certain skills to the lives of learners. If skills are not deemed to be community valid, they are not given a high priority for instruction. For some learners, computing addition or subtraction problems on a worksheet may not be considered a community-valid set of skills. On the other hand, teaching those same skills in the context of making purchases in a grocery store may translate the skills into more valid outcomes.

The method of deciding the validity of potential annual goals or identifying previously unidentified goals is to conduct a *community needs assessment* (CNA). This first step in the curriculum development process (see Figure 4.2) allows teachers and other concerned professionals the opportunity to be more aware of what skills are needed in the home and in other community sites. The information from a CNA assists teachers in identifying actual student needs and establishing priorities for teaching based on those needs. For example, a teacher of students between the ages of 18 and 21 years who have moderate handicaps might visit potential community living options targeted for these students. In any given community, there may be many options ranging from home placement to independent living centers to no community-based group homes.

Each available living option will differ in its features that learners must adapt to, for example, availability of mass transit, relationship to leisure/recreation activities, types of cooking facilities, amount of supervision, and physical layout of the living quarters. These and other environmental features will dictate different annual goals and short-term objectives, which teachers can address while the students are still in school (see Table 4.2).

Sources of CNA Data

The CNA can be a formal project resulting in a published research study or a series of informal observations resulting in information for use by teachers. There are many sources where this information can be obtained. The most important sources are those most

TABLE 4.2 *Sample Questions for Community Interviews*

Parents' Interview (Current Students)

Sample Questions

1. What jobs or self-care tasks would you like your son or daughter to be able to perform independently at home?
2. Are there any academic skills that, if your son or daughter could do them, would be directly usable at home or in the neighborhood?
3. Do you live near any mass transit? If so, what type?

---

*Former Student Interview**

---

1. What training did you receive in school that does not help you in your current job or life in the community?
2. What skills did you have to learn in order to live on your own?
3. Are there any jobs that you would rather do? Why have you not tried to get these jobs?
4. What problems do you have where you live, where you work, or in your places of recreation?

---

*In the case of individuals with moderate retardation, the same information can be gained by directly observing them in their current placement.

affected by the program (e.g., parents, guardians, and current students) (Soffer, 1982). As dictated by PL 94-142, these individuals should be allowed to participate in the program planning process and provide input into the identification of appropriate goals and objectives (Goldstein, Strickland, Turnbull, & Curry, 1980).

Meeting the parents at the IEP meeting and discussing potential curriculum options may not provide the best information. If possible, teachers should consider working with parents by conducting a needs assessment of skills required at home. A teacher might teach a student to cook on an electric stove at school only to find out that there is a gas or woodburning stove at home. Similarly, teaching a student to take a shower if there is only a bathtub at home serves to narrow the scope of the curriculum. Including parents and learners in the community needs assessment provides a wealth of knowledge about the need for specific skills in the natural environment.

There are many other sources of information as well. Graduates of the program and their parents, as well as nongraduates or dropouts, can often provide insight into how well the curriculum is training students to live and work in the community. Employers in business and industry can also provide useful information concerning types of job skills required, trends in employment, current openings, and the possibility of establishing community work sites. This information regarding job requirements can be helpful when establishing objectives for a secondary curriculum. In addition, information concerning the types of jobs available may be of help to elementary teachers who are developing career awareness components in their curricula.

There are other people in the community who can be useful to teachers. For example, neighbors of group homes can often provide insight into what makes adults with handicaps good neighbors and accepted members of a neighborhood. Community agencies, state departments, and university faculty can all provide data useful in establishing the scope of curriculum.

One immediate source of information is teachers from different disciplines, who can identify skills learners will find helpful in mainstreamed environments. In any case, before special educators can consider developing curriculum options, a community needs assessment should be implemented to identify the skills learners need to be as independent as possible in current or future environments.

Gathering CNA Data

Methods for gathering community assessment data include questionnaires, interviews, public meetings, and direct observation. Questionnaires can often reach large numbers of people, providing a large amount of information to those who conduct the survey. However, because it may be difficult to get a significant return, this method may not be practical for teachers. The questionnaire method might be used to better advantage by district-wide curriculum committees.

Interviews will be an important part of any community needs assessment effort. Gathering information from parents, students (both present and those no longer involved in the program), employers, and neighbors are examples of how the interview method can be used. An interview with any community member will be more productive if the teacher plans for it in advance. This advance planning usually involves listing several questions that are pertinent to the person's occupation (e.g., questions to parents will be different from questions to employers) and designing a form so that the data collected can be kept for analysis and future use. Table 4.2 provides two examples of sample questions that may be asked of former students and parents of current students. In each instance the goal of the interview will be to ascertain how well these people are integrating into the community, what skills would be helpful for them to be better integrated, and what skills were taught to them that had very little impact on their lives.

Public meetings can be another form of interview technique. Teachers can attend these meetings and discuss with participants their ideas about appropriate curriculum options. For example, teachers may attend local or state meetings of the Association for Retarded Citizens (ARC), The Council for Children with Behavioral Disorders (CCBD), or The Association of Children and Adults with Learning Disabilities (ACALD). By request, they may be included on the agenda, presenting the group with questions similar to those in Table 4.2.

Other meetings where teachers can gather useful information are advisory board and service group meetings that are held periodically around the community. Vocational educators are mandated by law to develop advisory boards in their service areas. A special educator who has established a working relationship with a vocational educator may be able to attend an advisory board meeting and discuss topics such as the skills needed for students to enter the workforce.

The final, and often most useful, technique for gathering CNA information is direct observation. This technique involves venturing into the community, observing specific skills demonstrated by community members, and recording those skills in the sequence in which they occur. Gathering information in this manner should not be overlooked or underrated. A teacher of secondary learners may, for example, record the duties and skills required of a person who works in a hospital. This recorded information can be translated into objectives and included in the curriculum. Similarly, by riding a city bus and recording the steps required to do so (e.g., communication skills—asking the driver about stops; academic skills—counting out the correct change), teachers can better identify the skills a learner would need to be more mobile. Once identified, these skills can become part of the general curriculum area of community mobility.

Regardless of whether students have cognitive impairments, behavior disorders, or learning disabilities, a majority of these learners can benefit from practicing academic, social, and independent living skills in relation to community-based activities. Innovative teachers can look to insurance agencies for materials and activities that will help support instruction in reading, arithmetic, and social skills development. Banks, post offices, retail establishments, and industrial sites are examples of places where teachers can extend their classrooms to develop new and exciting activities that are designed to support the instruction students are exposed to in their regular and special education classrooms.

There are an endless number of community-based environments that teachers and others can observe and analyze. Table 4.3 provides some of the more important of these. As information is gathered about relevant community environments, a more detailed analysis of each situation will produce a list of specific skills for each area for inclusion in the curriculum (see Table 4.4).

IDEA FILE

Most teachers do not have unlimited time to venture into the community and implement a needs assessment. However, there are a number of other ways to gather a good deal of valuable information.

■ Use volunteers. High school students, college students (if available), community service groups, and parents are all potential sources of assistance.

■ Spend a little time training the volunteers. For example, a high school student whose task is to observe and record the job skills of a hospital orderly will need to know what skills to look for, such as number of communication efforts the orderly engages in, types of verbal directions the orderly must understand, and academic skills needed to perform the task (e.g., reading labels on boxes).

■ Identify one or two environments to observe per week (this number can change depending on the availability of volunteers).

■ Organize information as it is gathered in file folders. For example, an analysis of a grocery store could include folders for adding, subtracting, money management, adaptations for academic skill deficits (e.g., use of calculator), communication skills (e.g., asking where items are located). This information is easily retrieved for later IEP development if it is organized in a systematic fashion.

■ Use the telephone as a quick and efficient method for gathering some types of information.

■ ■ ■ ■

TABLE 4.3 *Analyzing Community Based Environments: Direct Observation*

Environment	Skill Areas
1. Grocery stores	1. Academic skills $\begin{cases} \text{Reading} \\ \text{Math} \end{cases}$ Communication skills Mobility skills
2. Bowling alleys Video game arcades	2. Academic skills $\begin{cases} \text{Reading} \\ \text{Math} \end{cases}$ Communication skills Mobility skills Leisure/recreation skills
3. Home	3. Self-care skills Home management skills Mobility skills Home maintenance skills
4. Restaurants	4. Potential employment outcomes Self-care skills Communication skills Academic skills Eating skills

Analyzing CNA Data

Identification of annual goals for a student's IEP is one result of the information gathered during the community needs assessment. A strict definition of community may be understood to include everything outside the school. The learner's school experience, however, is a large part of his or her life (Kerr, Nelson, & Lambert, 1987). Therefore, the concept of community should also be applied to school activities. For example, a learner who is to be mainstreamed into a science class may be at a disadvantage if someone has not analyzed the situation beforehand. In this instance, the needs assessment may involve having the regular and special educators decide which of the units in the science curriculum would most benefit the learner.

Similar examples of students entering a vocational education class or students eating in the school lunchroom highlight the need for an in-school needs assessment. In the first case, the learner may need a number of adaptations to be successful that, if

TABLE 4.4   Analyzing Community-Based Environments: Direct Observation

Community Environment	Location of Task Completion	Tasks or Skills
1. Grocery stores	Deli	Request two types of cold cuts Use a calculator to figure cost Read names of cold cuts
	Checkout line	Communicate with cashier Place items on counter Pay for items Check returned change
2. Bowling alley	Cashier counter	Ask fees Rent shoes Pick up score sheet
	Bowling ball rack	Choose appropriate size and weight
	Alley	Find correct alley Play game Keep score
3. Home	Kitchen	Wash dishes Make simple meals Clean kitchen
	Bathroom	Practice appropriate grooming and toileting skills
4. Restaurant (fast food)	Counter	Read menu Estimate cost Order; communicate with cashier Pay
	Seating area	Choose seat Eat Clean area

identified, can be programmed into the curriculum by both teachers. The student eating in the lunchroom may require a different set of skills than those needed to eat in an isolated classroom (e.g., choosing among a variety of foods). The teacher who analyzes the lunchroom environment should be alert to these differences and account for them in the teaching sequence. Similarly, students enrolled in regular education classes may require a set of skills that are different from those required in a resource placement. Independent study skills, appropriate behavioral skills in large groups, and increased listening skills, are examples of specific skills that teachers would identify via the in-school CNA.

KEY CONCEPTS

- Annual goals for IEPs are a direct result of a needs assessment conducted for community and school environments.

- By knowing what learners must be able to do at home, on the job, in leisure/recreation situations, and so forth, teachers are in a better position to separate curricular goals and objectives into *need-to-know* and *nice-to-know* categories, teaching the need-to-know objectives first.

- Deciding which annual goals are a best match for individual student needs is not an easy process. However, there are some techniques and criteria that can help teachers make good decisions.

  □ Interview parents and the students themselves, asking for their opinions.

  □ Consider the age of the students and how many years they have left in school (e.g., for an 18 year-old student community mobility may be a high priority).

  □ Decide whether the skill is a necessary prerequisite for other skills (e.g., addition and subtraction skills are required before it is possible to learn division).

  □ Identify any adaptations that may assist students in moving on to more advanced skills (e.g., a student who has not mastered the basic operations may be able to use a calculator to comparison shop).

- Questionnaires, interviews, public meetings, and direct observation are all useful methods for gathering needs assessment data for curriculum development.

■ ■ ■ ■

IDENTIFYING SHORT-TERM OBJECTIVES

Short-term objectives on the IEP are an important concern in two steps of the instructional design process (see steps 4a, 4b, and 6 in Figure 4.2). First, a group of potential short-term objectives identified during the CNA can be used as a guide by which students can be assessed. For example, the analysis of one CNA may identify an annual goal of improving community mobility using public transportation (bus riding). A breakdown of the skills required to meet this goal generates a number of potential short-term objectives.

The teacher now has a guide to assess a student's present level of performance in riding a bus. This step is important. Without a bank of community-valid short-term objectives to use as a guide, the temptation may be to judge the student's performance against academic skills and isolated self-help skills as evaluated by adaptive behavior scales.

The second step in identifying short-term objectives (step 6, Figure 4.2) is to choose those that meet the needs of the individual learner. In this step a group of professionals establishes a student's present level of performance against many potential short-term objectives (see Table 4.5). For a given learner there can be a large number of areas that require attention (each area having a large number of potential short-term objectives); however, it would not be possible to cover all the identified student needs in one school year. Therefore, in step 6 of the process the IEP committee picks those short-term objectives that the learner most needs to accomplish.

Before discussing how the most important short-term objectives are chosen for students, the process of translating annual goals to short-term objectives should be discussed. *Translating* refers to breaking down large units of instruction into smaller, more manageable tasks, a process that has been termed *task analysis*.

Performing Task Analyses

The process of instructional or task analysis may not be as simple as some professionals believe. Teachers are finding that to develop a meaningful analysis they need such resources as knowledge of the content area, ample time, and brainstorming sessions with their peers. Teachers are also finding that although many task analyses are commercially available in the areas of academic and self-help skills, there is still a need to analyze task-specific skills that arise in prevocational cluster areas.

In beginning the process of analysis teachers ask one important question: Do I have the expertise to design a program in the subject area in question? No one is an expert in all content areas. In instances when unfamiliar subject matter is involved, specialists should be consulted. A special education teacher, for example, may not be familiar with

TABLE 4.5 *Examples of the Many Areas That Can Be Assessed Prior to the IEP Development*

Professional	Potential Areas Assessed
1. Classroom teacher	1. Specific-level academic skills (e.g., decoding vowels, reading comprehension: sequence) Street crossing skills (e.g., three community intersections)
2. School psychologist	2. Performance on personality tests Psycholinguistic skills
3. Vocational educator	3. Work samples in agricultural education
4. Speech therapist	4. Articulation of sounds Use or need of alternate communication systems

the intricacies of teaching in the cluster area *decoding* under the program goal of *reading*. The teacher could consult with a reading specialist concerning an appropriate task analysis for this area. By the same token, teachers may not be familiar with some of the basic or more advanced counseling approaches to behavior management (e.g., life-space interview) for use with students exhibiting behavior disorders and how these techniques are used in an affective curriculum. In either case, consultation with appropriate professionals must occur before an effective task analysis can be accomplished.

The technique of instructional or task analysis is used to translate annual goals into short-term objectives (IEP) and later to translate the short-term objectives into daily instructional objectives (IIP or lesson plans). Dick and Carey (1978), Gagne and Briggs (1974), and Gagne (1977) have differentiated between two major forms of instructional analysis that can be useful for teachers: the procedural approach and the hierarchical approach. The procedural approach is used when individual behaviors are taught consecutively to reach a specific objective. The series of behaviors included in a procedural analysis are independent of each other and often can be interchanged. One example of this approach is home dishwashing skills. Some teachers may require a student to wash all the dishes before rinsing, while other teachers may require their learners to wash each dish and then rinse it before moving on to the next step. Each step is independent, and in some cases they can be interchanged depending on teacher decision or student needs (Table 4.6).

The hierarchical approach involves identifying prerequisite skills and placing them in a hierarchical order leading to the desired objective. Academic skills generally lend themselves to this approach, each skill in the sequence being somewhat dependent on the previous skill. The instructional analyses of reading and arithmetic shown in Figures 4.3 and 4.4 were developed by Schwartz and Oseroff (1975) and provide a good example of hierarchical analyses.

Finally, a logical extension of the two approaches is a combination of both. The combination approach, as described by Dick and Carey (1978), is useful when dealing with behaviors requiring a complex set of both psychomotor and cognitive skills. For example, an approach to teaching a community mobility skill such as riding the bus might look like the one shown in Figure 4.5.

TABLE 4.6   *Examples of Task Sequences for Washing Dishes*

Skill Sequence	Skill Sequence
1. Place plug in drain.	1. Place plug in drain.
2. Place dishsoap in sink.	2. Place dishsoap in sink.
3. Turn on hot water (adjust temperature).	3. Turn on hot water (adjust temperature).
4. Place dishes in sink.	4. Place dishes in sink.
5. Wash all dishes and place in second sink.	5. Wash each dish and rinse, placing dish in drainer.
6. Rinse each dish and place in drainer.	6. Drain water from sink.
7. Drain water from sink.	7. Rinse sink.
8. Rinse sink.	8. Dry counter.
9. Dry counter.	

The task sequencing approach a teacher uses depends on the behaviors that are to be taught. A number of resources exist for teachers to gain assistance in developing a workable analysis. For example, appropriate instructional analyses for academic skills can be found in the scope and sequence charts in teachers' manuals and college textbooks (e.g., Choate et al., 1987). Also, commercially available task analyses for independent living skills are plentiful (e.g., the MORE System, Keilitz, Horner, & Brown, 1975) as well as those available for teaching social skills (e.g., *Procedures for Establishing Effective Relationship Skills,* Hops et al., 1978; and *ACCEPTS Social Skills Curriculum,* Walker et al., 1983).

IDEA FILE

There are different ways to use task analyses to develop effective guides for determining what skills to teach and in what order the skills should be presented. Practice in analyzing tasks is the one sure way teachers can become good at developing skill sequences.

■ For analyzing complex tasks, gather a team to participate in analysis. Parents and regular education high school students are examples of people who can be useful in helping the teacher to task analyze a skill. Often, two people riding a bus will be able to analyze the task more thoroughly than one person could. If two people ride the same route at different times and their analyses are compared, a more detailed task analysis will be the product.

■ A stack of 3 × 5 inch cards can be valuable when task analyzing complex skills such as opening and managing a checking account or shopping for groceries. Each step on the task analysis (subskill) can be assigned to one card. The teacher can then spread the cards out over a large table or on the floor and attempt various sequential arrangements until the most appropriate analysis is found. This method prevents the erasures and discarding of paper that are inevitable when an analysis is written in a conventional format. Moreover, as individual learners require modifications in the original analysis, the new substeps generated can easily be added on cards and filed in sequential order. The bus-riding task analysis shown in Figure 4.5 was designed in this fashion. Each skill was placed on a card and moved about until the final sequence was agreed upon by those involved.

■ At a later time, if a skill requires that a complete objective be written, it can be done on the same 3 × 5 inch card.

■ Before using a task analysis with the students, run a trial on other people, for example, a group of regular education students. Mistakes in the original analysis can often be discovered before exposing the target learners to any errors such as steps that are too difficult.

■ If the equipment is available, it may be helpful to videotape certain highly critical community skills such as crossing a busy intersection or engaging in complex social interaction. Videotapes allow practitioners to review and re-review segments in which complex behaviors require close inspection.

■ ■ ■ ■

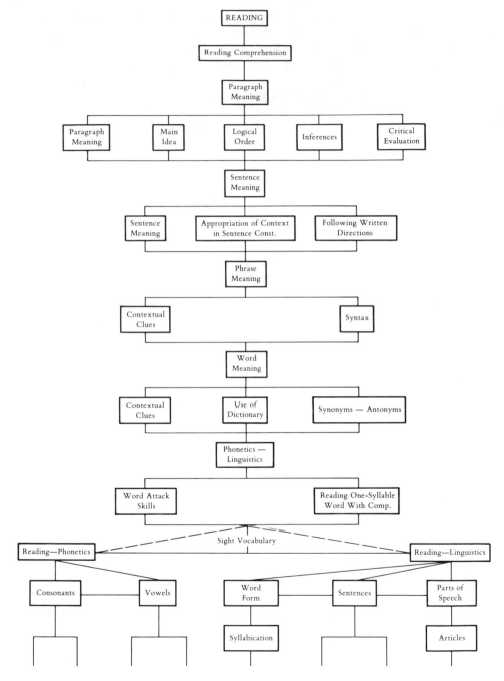

■ FIGURE 4.3

Sample Hierarchical Task Analysis of Reading (From The Clinical Teacher for Special Education by L. Schwartz and A. Oseroff, 1975. Tallahassee: Florida State University.)

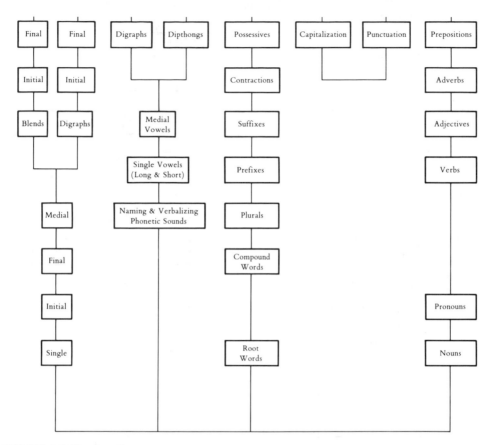

■ FIGURE 4.3 (Continued)

Developing More Detailed Skill Sequences

Whether task sequences can be developed once, for large groups of learners, or must be developed individually according to specific student needs appears to depend on the severity of a student's disability. As the severity level increases, the need to tailor the skill sequence to the individual becomes more important. A task analysis for addition may look markedly different for a learner with a mild mental handicap as opposed to a student with learning disabilities. In the first instance, the skills targeted may involve addition of numbers up to three digits to include a variety of prices in a grocery store with the use of a hand-held calculator. For the student with learning disabilities, the task sequence chosen may be exactly the same as the one used in a regular education curriculum for his or her age group. This example, like all others, must be couched in the principle of individualization. Another student with learning disabilities might require the same task sequence as the student with a mild handicap, with adaptations.

The process of task analysis also becomes more specific when translating short-term objectives (IEPs) for daily instructional use in lesson plans. For example, the task analysis

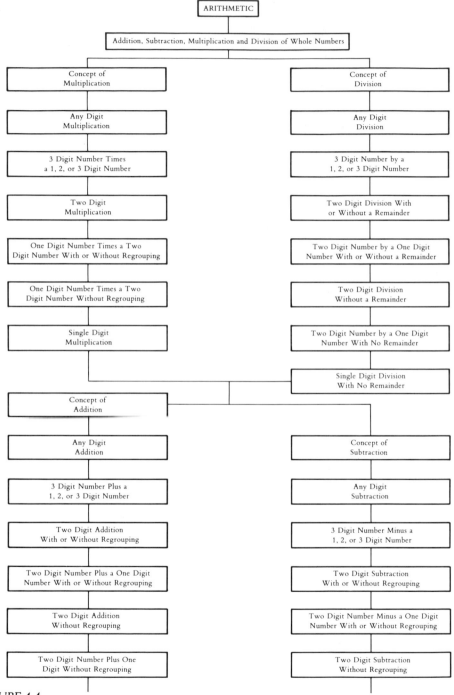

■ FIGURE 4.4

Sample Hierarchical Task Analysis of Arithmetic (From The Clinical Teacher for Special Education *by L. Schwartz and A. Oseroff, 1975. Tallahassee: Florida State University.)*

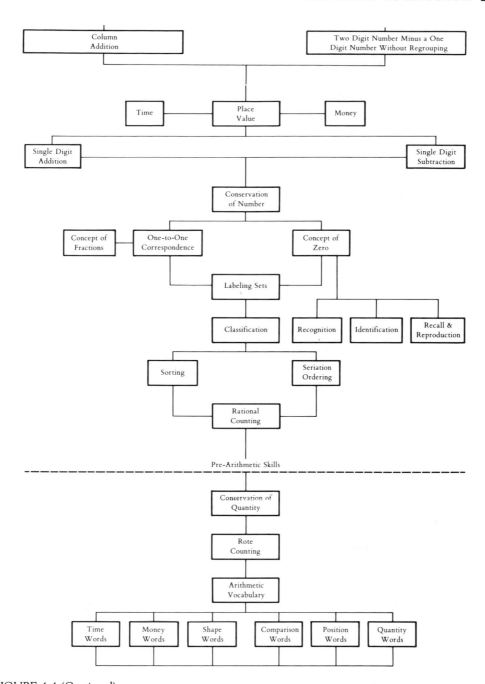

■ FIGURE 4.4 (*Continued*)

of reading presented in Figure 4.3 has a skill area under vowels that requires the learner to pronounce diphthongs. A further breakdown of that area would involve identifying the specific diphthongs (ou, ow, oi, oy, aw, ew). Each diphthong essentially becomes a step in the sequence when the teacher develops objectives. Similarly, a goal of most social skills curricula would involve demonstrating a positive attitude toward self. A teacher might include additional subtasks such as saying thank you when complimented, making positive statements about self when asked, and beginning new tasks with a positive attitude when requested.

SKILL AREA: RIDING A PUBLIC BUS

Task Sequence

1. Walks to correct corner and bus stop.
2. Stands at proper location at bus stop and exhibits appropriate social skills.
3. Identifies bus by reading location or asks driver if this bus goes to the desired location.
4. Boards bus and deposits correct change (two quarters or five dimes).
5. Asks for transfer if desired.
6. Pays for transfer if desired.
7. Finds seat and exhibits appropriate social behavior.
8. Identifies landmarks along route.
9. Gets off at appropriate stop or requests stop by ringing buzzer.
10. Departs bus within 15 to 20 seconds after bus stops.
11. Continues to desired destination.

If transfer is required:

12. Walks to correct corner and bus stop.

13. Stands at proper location at bus stop and exhibits appropriate social skills.
14. Identifies bus by reading location or asks driver if this bus goes to the desired location.
15. Boards bus and hands driver the transfer slip or token.
16. Finds seat and exhibits appropriate social behavior.
17. Identifies landmarks along route.
18. Gets off at appropriate stop or requests stop by ringing buzzer.
19. Departs bus within 15 to 20 seconds after bus stop.
20. Continues to desired destination.

Program for the following uncontrollable variables:

1. Bus never arrives.
2. Bus is late.
3. Driver is rude.
4. Other passengers are rude.
5. No seats are available.

■ *FIGURE 4.5*
Sample of Bus-Riding Task Sequence

KEY CONCEPTS

- Task analyses can be divided into three categories or types: hierarchical (e.g., reading and arithmetic), procedural (e.g., assembly line work in a factory), and combination (e.g., riding a bus).

- The approach that may be the most useful for analyzing community-based skills is the combination approach. Many community situations will require a student to perform both cognitive skills (reading) and psychomotor skills (crossing the street).

- Developing a task analysis is often a *chaining* process whereby each step (subskill) is linked together with the next step (subskill), thereby cueing the learner to perform the next step in the chain. For example, in a factory assembly line task such as assembling an electrical transformer, the completion of each step of the task analysis *signals* the beginning of the next step in the chain.

- Chaining is accomplished by linking subskills together in either a forward or backward fashion. For most learners, a forward chaining approach (e.g., beginning with the first step and continuing through to the last) is the most effective and natural teaching approach. For learners with moderate mental handicaps or for very young learners, however, backward chaining (starting with the last step and working backward) is more effective.

- Some skill sequences can lend themselves to either a forward or backward chaining approach, depending on which works best for a given student. Some students learn to make a bed faster following a forward approach, while some learn faster following a backward chaining process.

- Subskills on a task analysis should be written in measurable terms, and in some cases complete objectives should be written for the subskill (see next section).

■ ■ ■ ■

Writing Measurable Objectives

Behavioral objectives[1] (Gronlund, 1970; Mager, 1975; and others) are similar to yardsticks; that is, they are a device by which to measure student progress. These instructional devices assist teachers in organizing their programs into manageable components for teaching. Objectives should be viewed not as an exercise in futility, but as a method to make teachers' jobs more systematic and easier to manage.

The three components of a measurable objective are outcome, context, and criterion (Schwartz & Oseroff, 1975). The outcome component of the objective is simply a statement describing what learners will do after instruction that they could not do prior to it (Dick & Carey, 1978). This statement is written in behavioral terms so that the teacher can observe the student's performance. For example, the following outcome statements represent possible objectives for learners with mild and moderate handicaps:

- Correctly *writes* the answer.
- *Orally reproduces* vowel sounds.

---

[1] The term *behavioral objectives* is used here in a general sense to include short-term objectives (IEP) and instructional objectives (IIP or daily lesson plans).

- *Manually assembles* the complete set.
- *Orders* a complete meal at a designated restaurant.
- *Accepts consequences* for own actions.

The context component specifically outlines the situation the teacher will structure that will allow the student to perform the behavior identified in the content area. This sets the stage for the conditions of the learning environment. Using the previous examples, the objectives begin to take shape as follows:

Outcome: Student will correctly write the answers.

Context: Twenty written double-digit addition problems with and without regrouping.

Outcome: Student will orally reproduce the sounds.

Context: Taped demonstration of vowel sounds.

Outcome: Student will manually assemble the complete set.

Context: Given a disassembled lawn mower carburetor and screwdriver.

Outcome: Student will independently ride the bus from point A to point B.

Context: Upon request from supervisor, including oral information concerning departure time.

Outcome: Student will order a complete meal consisting of one main course, dessert, and a drink.

Context: Given a limited amount of money and taken to a designated restaurant.

Outcome: Student will accept consequences for own actions.

Context: Reports to teacher after spilling or breaking something.

The final component of a well-written objective involves establishing the criteria for success. Here the teacher considers what criteria must be met before the learner will have adequate skills for continuing to the next step in the learning hierarchy. The teacher can decide whether the criteria can be adjusted up or down to match the learner's strengths or weaknesses. An erroneous conception is that 90% correct is a standard for mastery. This magical number may not be appropriate, based on individual students or on different types of tasks. Conceivably, five different students in the same classroom could be working on the same annual goal and the same short-term objective, yet have varying criteria for success based on their individual needs. Referring to the previous examples, the criteria might be as follows:

Outcome: Student will correctly write the answers.

Context: Twenty written double-digit addition problems with and without regrouping.

Criterion: Eighteen out of twenty correct.

Outcome: Student will orally produce vowel sounds.

Context: Taped demonstration of vowel sounds.

Criterion: 100% correct articulation of all sounds.

Outcome: Student will manually assemble the complete set.

Context: Given a disassembled lawn mower carburetor and screwdriver.

Criterion: 100% correct for all steps on the task analysis.

Outcome: Student will independently ride bus from point A to point B.

  Context: Upon request from supervisor, including oral information concerning departure time.

Criterion: Arrival at point B.

Outcome: Student will order a complete meal consisting of one main course, dessert, and a drink.

  Context: Given a limited amount of money and taken to a designated restaurant.

Criterion: Four out of five trials.

Outcome: Student will accept consequences for own actions.

  Context: Reports to teacher after spilling or breaking something.

Criterion: Each instance an accident occurs.

The measurement unit chosen for each criterion depends on how the data will be recorded. For example, when dealing with academic skills, teachers may wish to use a quality measure such as percentages. As the number of problems or questions changes from day to day, the standard of percentage correct can maintain a relatively stable measure and thereby facilitate charting of progress. Effective criteria can also be measured by rate (number of correct problems per minute), frequency (percentage of correct trials), duration (length of time the behavior occurred), and latency (length of time that passed before the behavior began).

The process of task analysis and the procedure for writing measurable objectives are interwoven. It may be helpful to highlight and expand on the diphthong example from the previous section here. During the *needs assessment* (steps 1 and 2, Figure 4.2) the teacher may have discovered that while attending the third grade regular class (mainstreaming) Joanne is being exposed to reading exercises that are requiring her to decode unknown words—a task which she is having a great deal of difficulty performing. A potential *annual goal* for Joanne might be to *improve her decoding skills when presented with unknown words* (step 3, Figure 4.2).

The arrows between steps 3a and 3b and steps 4a and 4b represent the translation or task analysis of decoding into its component parts. In the case of an academic skill such as decoding, it is likely that task analysis of the skills has already been done and is commercially available (e.g., Stephens, Hartman, & Lucas, 1982). For example, a general task analysis for decoding skills usually includes (1) short vowels; (2) long vowels; (3) initial consonants; (4) medial consonants; (5) final consonants; (6) diphthongs; (7) digraphs; and (8) blends. (For another example, refer to Figure 4.3.) The *translation* that is mentioned in steps 4a and 4b involves writing a measurable objective for each of the eight areas if such objectives do not exist.

Highlighting diphthongs, a possible *short-term objective* might be the following:

Outcome: The student will recognize and pronounce the sounds *ou, ow, oi, oy, aw, er.*

  Context: Thirty whole words on the second- and third-grade levels.

Criterion: Between 80% and 90% accuracy.

In this example, the task analysis was used to identify the steps in decoding, and the teacher then was able to translate the steps into measurable objectives.

A second example, involving a learner with behavior disorders, may help to demonstrate that the process is the same—only the outcomes change. During the needs assessment phase (steps 1 and 2, Figure 4.2), teachers' discussions with Steve's parents and visits to Steve's home have identified the need for increased leisure and recreation skill training. The information from the CNA highlights the fact that Steve, upon returning home from school, spends his entire time in front of the television set. A potential *annual goal* for Steve might be to instruct him in a number of potential leisure and recreation activities found in and around his home and to provide him with a means to communicate his choice from a number of available activities.

The task analysis of this annual goal is more difficult only in the sense that it must be completed on site (at Steve's house) with the assistance of his parents. Potential skills in the task sequence might include the following possibilities (all located in Steve's home): (1) playing a video game; (2) listening to a talking book; and (3) listening to music. As with the example on decoding, the *translation* (steps 4a and 4b) involves converting each of the three leisure activities into potential short-term objectives.

Taking the example of the talking book, a possible *short-term objective* (IEP) might be as follows:

> *Outcome:* Student will select a talking book tape, place tape in recorder, and turn on the recorder.
> *Context:* Selection from 10 talking books.
> *Criterion:* [Selection not critical.] Correct manipulation of tape and recorder.

The selection of tapes is not a critical component of the criterion since the teacher's job at a later stage will be to expose the student to a variety of options. Rather, the crucial criterion is that Steve learn to manipulate the equipment independently or with some adaptation, so that he can make a choice as to whether or not he wishes to engage in this activity.

Using task analysis as the vehicle for moving from potential annual goals to potential short-term objectives is the first level of the curriculum design process. The identical sequence of steps occurs once more when task analysis becomes the vehicle for moving from short-term objectives (IEP) to smaller bits of instruction termed *instructional* or *daily objectives* (IIP or lesson plans).

ASSESSING PRESENT LEVEL OF PERFORMANCE

Assessment and curriculum are complexly interwoven, and separating them into different components may weaken the entire system. For the assessment of a student's present level of performance (IEP) and an ongoing monitoring of student progress (IEP and IIP), several evaluative tools and procedures must be employed. A complete discussion of the assessment process was presented in the last chapter. However, there are several important considerations for curriculum development that are appropriate to discuss here.

Identifying Prerequisite Skills

As teachers are notified of the students they will be teaching, they can begin to identify potential curricula that may be appropriate for these learners. Therefore, global curriculum areas can be identified. This process becomes more systematic as additional data on the students are gathered and present levels of performance are pinpointed. A number of resources and methods are available for accomplishing this data collection.

First, the teacher should inspect each learner's permanent records, noting information such as absentee patterns, time of onset of learning problems, previous test scores, and previous teacher observations (Moran, 1979). Information from records can be valuable in a number of ways. For example, a deficit in crucial basic skills can often be traced to a particularly long absence period at a time when instruction in those skills was being given. Similarly, studying previous test scores often pinpoints discrepancies with current assessment results, indicating possible errors in the testing process, loss of skills, or gains in student abilities.

Teacher observations, if written in behavioral terms and supported by data, can often alert teachers to potential problems that need immediate attention. Teachers must treat observations from former colleagues with caution, however, since in many cases they reflect a subjective opinion. For example, the statement that "Student A is exhibiting extremely violent behaviors" may adversely affect a teacher's expectations of this learner. Conversely, if the statement reads that "Student A lightly punches other students on an average of three times a day," the teacher has data-based facts with which to work. In this case, the possibility of cueing the class to ignore the occurrence may be sufficient to eliminate or decrease the inappropriate behavior.

Effectively identifying student prerequisite behaviors may also minimize unnecessary assessment efforts. Often teachers can judge where to begin intensive assessment with a student when they have analyzed previous records. Consideration of instruction in the academic areas can provide an illustration of this. For example, a student's records may indicate a long absence during one school year. By estimating the skills that were to be taught during that time, the teacher can begin to evaluate the student's proficiency in those skills. The teacher also has the option to return to the most basic skills in the sequence and begin testing there. Beginning at the bottom, however, may result in a loss of time that could be spent in instruction. Inspecting student records is merely a survey method to place the teacher "in the ballpark" when beginning to evaluate student characteristics. Other data collected on a learner's entry behavior assist in establishing a clearer picture of student needs.

Defining Student Behavior Important to Instruction (Learning Styles)

Teachers must be constantly observant of behaviors exhibited by students that can affect learning. As previously mentioned, student records can sometimes alert the teacher to behaviors that may influence performance. The best assessment of these behaviors, however, will generally occur when the student enters the classroom and the teacher can observe various interactions within the environment. For example, a learner with behavior problems who continually taunts other students needs to have these behaviors decreased because they interfere with learning. Similarly, teachers should note affective entry behaviors of students such as task completion, risk taking, and other social behaviors (e.g., cooperation within the group, ability to follow spoken or written directions).

Identifying Potential Reinforcers

At the outset, teachers must begin compiling lists of potential reinforcers that may affect each of their student's behaviors. This process begins by noting whether the learner appears to be reinforced intrinsically or extrinsically. In addition, an important notation would be whether the student relies only upon immediate reinforcement or can tolerate having reinforcement delayed to a later time (an important vocational prerequisite).

Observation is the most useful method for identifying reinforcers for individual learners; however, interviewing the student will often help. Teachers may also have to develop structured situations where the student can be exposed to several reinforcers. Observations can then be made to identify rewards that are most potent for specific learners.

KEY CONCEPTS

The point of assessing student entry behavior is simply to gain an initial understanding of learner strengths, weaknesses, and needs. These data can be collected by analyzing student records (including interviewing parents and past teachers) and observing the learner upon entry into the program.

The collected information is used in two ways. First, an overview profile of the learner is developed using entry behavior data. Initial data (e.g., prerequisite behaviors) are used to place the student in position for the second step, which involves further assessment with standardized and criterion-referenced measures. Pinpointing specific student strengths and weaknesses is discussed in detail in Chapter Three. All entry behavior data assist the teacher in placing students at levels that most appropriately meet their needs.

- Reviewing students' files can be considered one activity in the CNA (steps 1 & 2, Figure 4.2). The information obtained may be of assistance in establishing potential annual goals and short-term objectives.
- Observing student learning styles as well as potential reinforcers can be considered part of the assessment of present level of performance (step 5). This information aids the teacher in deciding what specific goals and objectives are appropriate for a given learner.

■ ■ ■ ■

THE IEP: ANNUAL GOALS, SHORT-TERM OBJECTIVES

After an individual student has been thoroughly assessed and a list of strengths and weaknesses has been generated as a result, the identification of appropriate annual goals and short-term objectives can begin (step 7, Figure 4.2). The information obtained from the needs assessment and the potential goals and objectives generated were used as guidelines against which students' present levels of performance were assessed. By the nature of their disabilities, learners with mild and moderate learning and behavioral problems will have many deficit areas that could be targeted for instruction. However, listing all possible instructional areas on an IEP is not prudent. Rather, the rule is that only those objectives that might reasonably be taught to a student *in one school year* should be included on the IEP. (Tables 4.7 and 4.8 provide examples of IEPs.)

The problem is how to decide which of the potential goals and objectives should be included in the individual's curriculum. One reason for allowing the IEP committee to make these judgments is that the committee is comprised of members (including the students themselves) who should best know the needs of the students. However, there are some criteria that teachers and other committee members can use to judge whether or not goals and objectives are appropriate. The following is a list of criteria that may be helpful in establishing priorities for learning:

1. *Age of the learner:* Beyond a certain age, remediating academic deficits may not be desirable and some form of compensatory skill may be more appropriate. For example, a high-school-age student with mild retardation may learn to use a calculator exclusively to solve mathematics problems encountered in daily living. Short-term objectives involving calculator use (the calculator is included in the context component of the objective) may be more desirable than objectives that reflect practice on math worksheets.

2. *Prerequisite skills:* Priority may be given to those skills that must be mastered before other skills can be learned. A disruptive student may need to learn more appropriate behaviors before he or she can move on to more advanced skills.

3. *Community validity:* The skills should be ones that the students can quickly generalize to the community. Students learning to read sight words, for example, might have better success if the words chosen reflect those they see on a daily basis (e.g., words on menus in fast-food restaurants). Information from the CNA (e.g., opinions of parents) should provide a basis on which to judge the validity of a given skill.

4. *Resource availability:* There may be times when the necessary materials and expertise are not available for teaching a skill. If this is the case, and alternative solutions cannot be generated, the decision to put off teaching the skill (if not critical to the student's life) may be a possibility. For example, if the student is not scheduled to leave the program in the next year, in-school training involving the same subject areas (e.g., cooking, cleaning, budgeting) may be substituted for a placement for training in a community program.

KEY CONCEPTS

- The final product of assessment is the development of a list of strengths and weaknesses that become the foundation for short-term objectives.
- Older students may benefit from learning compensatory academic skills rather than attempting to remediate basic skills.
- Short-term objectives in any curriculum area should reflect some form of relevance to the community.

■ ■ ■ ■

TABLE 4.7 *Sample of IEP*

Name Stephanie W.		Date of Development 4-1-88		
School Chase School		IEP From 8/29/88 to 6/5/89		
Current Placement Chase School		*IEP Committee*		*Signature*
Date of Birth March 10, 1978		Dr. Jones	Principal	
Age 10		Mrs. Barnes	Regular class teacher	
		Ms. Couch	Special education teacher	
		Ms. Smith	Psychologist	
		Mr. & Mrs. W.	Parents	

Special Education and Related Services	*Start Date*	*End Date*	*Responsibility*
Speech and Communication	Oct. 1, 1988	June, 1989	Ms. Ball
Remedial Reading	Oct. 1, 1988	Jan., 1989	Mr. Moss
Resource Room Remedial Help	Oct. 1, 1988	June, 1989	Ms. Couch

Evaluation Data				*Extent of Regular Class Placement*
WISC-R (5-88) Verbal	Performance	Full Scale		60% Regular Education
Kay Math (6-88)				40% Special Education (Resource)
Woodcock Reading Mastery (6-88)				

Present Level of Performance	*Annual Goal Statements*	*Short-Term Objectives*	*Evaluation Procedure*
Strengths: 1. Can sound out consonant-vowel-consonant words. 2. Can read 90% words from Dolch word list Level 1. 3. Can read orally at instructional level from second grade passage. *Weaknesses:* 1. Doesn't know second grade sight words. 2. Cannot decode words with beginning/ending consonant blends. 3. Cannot answer comprehension questions based on main idea, specific details, and sequencing directly stated in second grade passage.	1.0 Student will correctly read out loud all consonants inbedded in the words from a second grade passage. 2.0 Student will read sight words at second grade level. 3.0 Student will comprehend material read at second grade level.	1.4 OUTCOME: Consonant blends (pl, sm, cr, fr, tr, gr, pr, bl, sl, st, sw, cl, dr, br, sp) CONTEXT: When presented in a word (pronounce whole word) CRITERIA: 50 words—90%–100% 2.1 Given Dolch word list, Level 2, student will read words with 90% accuracy. 3.1 Given 100-word passage at second grade level, student will demonstrate recall of directly stated specific details by answering teacher-made questions with 80% accuracy. 3.2 Given a 100-word passage at second grade level, student will answer sequencing questions with 80% accuracy.	50 nonsense words with initial consonant blends. Teacher reads ending, student supplies beginning sound. Probe sheet—20 words w/ initial consonant blends Dolch word list Five teacher-made questions Five teacher-made questions

(Prepared by Tina Kinsley.)

TABLE 4.8 *Sample IEP*

Present Level of Performance	Annual Goal Statements	Short-Term Objectives	Evaluation Procedure
Strengths: 1. Tells time to the hour. 2. Average fine motor skills. 3. Is ambulatory. 4. Has good receptive language. 5. Makes needs known with verbal requests. *Weaknesses:* 1. Has short attention span. 2. Hits others. 3. Has poor self-help skills. 4. Has poor gross motor skills. 5. Has poor posture.	1.0 Student will improve grooming. 2.0 Student will improve home management skills. 3.0 Student will improve vocationally related behaviors.	1.1 OUTCOME: Wash and blow-dry hair with no assistance CONTEXT: Shampoo Blow-dryer Towel Sink (school & home) CRITERIA: 100% of steps on task analysis over 1 month, twice a week 2.0 OUTCOME: Make toast CONTEXT: Toaster Loaf of bread Butter and knife CRITERIA: 100% of steps on task analysis over 5 days 3.0 OUTCOME: Care of plants—transplanting, watering, etc. CONTEXT: Flower garden Vegetable garden (school) CRITERIA: Successfully transplant and care for three house plants over a period of 6 months	See context and criteria for all objectives. Charting of percentage correct steps on task analysis.

CHAPTER FIVE

DEVELOPING INSTRUCTIONAL INTERVENTIONS, PART I: MEASUREMENT SYSTEMS

■ Some teachers mistakenly believe that assessment and program implementation are separate processes. Information from the previous chapters demonstrates that, in some instances, discriminating between assessment and instruction can be an impossible task. Many teachers use assessment probes to provide immediate feedback to the learner. As they administer the probes, they also demonstrate and prompt correct responses, thus combining both assessment and instruction.

Assessment is an ongoing process; it works alternately with instruction in an assess-instruct-assess-instruct format. Data acquired from the assessment probes feed immediately and directly into the instructional system, facilitating program improvements (Scott & Goetz, 1980; Utley, Zigmond, & Strain, 1987). The success of the program is measured by learner progress; therefore, assessment and instructional intervention are virtually dependent upon each other (Walker & Shea, 1984).

The goal of this chapter is to present instructional interventions that are keyed into a continuous assessment system. Chapter content will address current approaches to teaching and focus on behavior analysis, an approach that this author and others feel has the strongest empirical foundation (e.g., Center, 1989; Sailor & Guess, 1983; Snell, 1983; Wallace & Kauffman, 1978). A large body of the literature regarding individuals with handicapping conditions demonstrates the extent of operant procedures and the success they have had with this population (Repp, 1983; Walker & Shea, 1988).

APPLIED BEHAVIOR ANALYSIS

Many research studies attempt to measure changes in the behavior of learners while they are members of a group. For example, a statistical research design might be used to measure whether or not a new reading program will be useful for teaching a group of learners, with success indicated by increasing student scores on standardized reading tests. By choosing participating students based on specific characteristics of a larger group, the researchers hope to generalize their findings to the identified population. Therefore, if the target group of students has increased its reading scores, the generalization is that this program may be effective with the larger group.

The current trend appears to be moving away from the traditional method based on group norms because these norms are seen as inappropriate for teaching learners with mild and moderate handicaps. These students differ significantly from group norms in both academic and social behavior. Statistical methodology that uses mean scores to represent the total group's behaviors serves only to point out the deviance between these learners and the general population, a deviance already known to exist. Public Law 94-142 states that learners need an educational program that is individually designed to match their strengths and weaknesses. Therefore, a measurement system that can analyze the learner as an individual and not as a member of a group is desirable.

A Technology for Teaching

A desirable technology for teaching includes a system that identifies the needs of individual learners, applies behavioral techniques to meet those needs, and uses measurement systems that monitor progress frequently. A system that meets these criteria has been developed from years of operant conditioning research paired with the principles of systems design (Lovitt, 1976). Applied behavior analysis (ABA) is a process that is best conceptualized by focusing on the word *applied*. As used here, it refers to the systematic application of operant conditioning principles designed to improve learner behaviors (Sulzer-Azaroff & Mayer, 1977). ABA should not be confused with behavior modification, which is a narrower approach that refers to only the operant procedures themselves. Applied behavior analysis, on the other hand, includes a number of components needed for comprehensive program development such as observing, measuring, and changing the behaviors of learners in their daily environments (Bailey, 1977).

A perusal of the literature will identify a great number of research endeavors demonstrating the effective use of ABA principles with learners who have a variety of handicapping conditions (e.g., Polloway & Polloway, 1980; Schilling & Cuvo, 1983). Problems can arise, however, when these well-documented programs are not completely understood and/or are inappropriately implemented by practitioners. This situation is unfortunate since the techniques of ABA can be very useful (Evans, Evans, & Schmid, 1989).

Components of ABA

A classic article by Baer, Wolf, and Risley (1968) described several characteristics of ABA that can provide special educators with a powerful tool for changing learner behavior. First, an ABA program must be *applied;* that is, it must be relevant to the learner for which it was designed.

The concept of "applied" has taken on the added dimension of social validity, supporting the study of behaviors important to individuals and the environments in which they live (Wolf, 1978). Programs guided by this philosophy are not concerned with comparing learners with others. They are concerned with modifying behaviors to improve the quality of a person's life.

A second characteristic of ABA programs is that they are what Baer and colleagues termed *analytic.* Establishing that the teaching procedure used is in fact altering the behavior of the learner is the essential component of the analysis phase. A clear cause-effect relationship must be established between the instruction given and the learner's behavior. A teacher introducing a positive reinforcer to a learning setting may expect that the reinforced behavior is strengthened. Conversely, if the reinforcer is removed from the learning setting the teacher might expect the behavior to decrease.

A third area delineated by Baer and colleagues (1968) involves the behavioral aspects of ABA, emphasizing Skinner's (1953) discussion of measuring observable behaviors. ABA concerns itself with behaviors that are operationally defined so that an accurate measure can be obtained of how often or how long they occurred. Once the definition has been established, more than one observer should be able to view the behavior concurrently, and the observers should be reliable among themselves concerning the measurement.

Finally, the procedure used to change the behavior must be described in a systematic fashion (Baer et al., 1968). Precisely describing procedures used to change the behaviors of learners allows others to use the techniques elsewhere. Clearly outlining instructional procedures also provides teachers with opportunities to analyze certain portions of their approach that prove to be ineffective.

When a behavior is targeted for change, any change that occurs must be deemed effective. That is, the change in behavior must be great enough to be of practical significance to the learner (Bailey, 1977). This point is related to the concept of *social validity* mentioned earlier. Wolf (1978) delineated three criteria for social validity:

1. The social significance of the goals. Are the behavioral goals really what society wants?

2. The social appropriateness of the procedures. Do the ends justify the means? That is, do the participants, caregivers, and other consumers consider the treatment procedures acceptable?

3. The social importance of the effects. Are consumers satisfied with the results? All the results, including any unpredicted ones? (p. 207)

Social validity should be a major concern in developing programs for learners. All aspects of the curriculum must be of practical use to the consumer (student). Using the concept of social validity as a guide, teachers will seek input from the learner (where possible), parents, significant others, and the community at large. Making program judgments without such input carries the risk that skills will be taught in isolation with little or no carry-over into the learner's out-of-school daily activities.

A final point relating to the effectiveness of ABA involves the generalizability of program results (Baer, Wolf, & Risley, 1968; Bailey, 1977). Practitioners should develop instructional procedures that teach students to generalize new skills to different situations, times, and people, and while using alternative materials. Hoping the skills learned will be generalized to other situations is not enough (Stokes & Baer, 1978). Teachers must consciously program for generalization if they wish it to occur. ABA techniques lend themselves as tools available to teachers for programming the transfer of newly learned skills to community living.

KEY CONCEPTS

- Applied behavior analysis (ABA) is a systems approach that includes application of behavioral principles (e.g., fixed-ratio reinforcement schedules; time out from positive reinforcement); replicability of the procedures used to change behavior; evaluation of the effects of the procedures on behavior; and change in procedures when evaluation results demonstrate that a change is warranted.

- ABA programs differ from traditional techniques of analyzing change in learner behavior primarily because ABA systems involve direct, frequent measurement of behavior as opposed to infrequent standardized testing procedures.

- The measurement strategies imbedded in ABA systems are analogous to formative and summative evaluation procedures discussed in Chapter Three. As formative evaluation tools, these procedures enable teachers to monitor student progress daily and make changes in instructional strategies or materials as necessary. As summative evaluation tools, they enable teachers to determine whether or not the students have met the criteria of the objective upon completion of instruction.

- An important concept imbedded within ABA programs is social validity (Wolf, 1978). Social validity is a guideline for designing ABA programs that requires that the behavioral procedures used be designed with the best interests of the student in mind. In the field of special education, one way to interpret social validity is to apply instructional techniques that assist the learner in becoming as independent as possible.

■ ■ ■ ■

Identifying Behaviors Targeted for Change

If the foundation of a newly built house is weak, the structure will not stand the test of time. Starting with an inappropriate definition of learner behaviors is an example of a weak foundation that can adversely affect an educational program. Teachers who do not specify and define the behaviors they wish to change may set the stage for eventual failure of the programs they design.

All objectives in a curriculum can be defined so that the behaviors involved are observable; that is, they can be seen, felt, and/or touched to establish a record of occurrence or of quality. For certain behaviors, an observable definition may require timing the behavior to determine the length of occurrence. Teachers should describe *precisely* what they want the learner to do. Statements such as "He annoys me" or "He can't read" do not communicate what changes in behavior the teacher would like to see occur.

All effective programming is built on objectives. The quality of these objectives and whether or not they include the necessary components (see Chapter Four) dictate the success or failure of the intervention (Polloway, Payne, Patton, & Payne, 1985). Therefore, if the objectives are written in measurable terms the first step of the design has been successfully completed. White and Haring (1980) have suggested viewing behaviors in terms of physical movements. They believe that all objectives targeted by practitioners as being "teachable" require the learner to demonstrate some type of movement during or after instruction has occurred. For example, if a learner is asked a question, the expected answer may require the movement of lips to produce the necessary sounds. Likewise, when the learner is presented with an arithmetic problem, the movement might be a written response. White and Haring (1980) defined a movement as "any change in the position of the body" (p. 12). Teachers may find it difficult to visualize a learning situation for students in which the student would not be required to move in some physical way. In all curricular areas, learners are required to move to demonstrate a skill (or sequence of skills) and to demonstrate the application of some knowledge that has been learned. Therefore, if teachers can describe the movement of the learner when defining a particular behavior, they essentially have written the main part of an objective.

The precision of movement definition varies among different behaviors. For example, the out-of-seat behaviors of Brenda may be easily counted because her movements away from her chair are obvious and distinct. Jeff's out-of-seat behaviors, however, may not be as clear, requiring a more complete definition of the movement before an accurate measure can be obtained. White and Haring (1980) provided three questions by which teachers can judge the precision of their movement (behavioral) definition:

1. Does the definition allow for more than one type of movement to occur?
2. Are all the behaviors in a class equally acceptable or important to us?

3. Would two or more people be able to agree exactly as to when an instance of the desired movement has occurred, how long it occurs, and when it stops occurring? (p. 13)

A closer inspection of these three criteria suggests a number of implications for classroom teachers. First, in instances in which there may be a number of ways a behavior can be exhibited (e.g., different learners might exhibit different types of verbal resistance), the teacher must precisely describe the behavior(s) so that there is no debate as to which form of the behavior is acceptable. On the other hand, if it is not critical, for example, whether students compute addition problems using their fingers or using counting sticks, this also should be stated.

Expanding on the second example, the best way to clarify the type of academically related skill that the teacher wants to reinforce is to label each objective as one that builds either accuracy, fluency, or automaticity (Howell & Morehead, 1987). For students who make many errors, instruction to improve accuracy will be warranted. For those who make few errors but are slow to complete their work, improving fluency is the main thrust of the objective. Finally, when emphasizing the use of a learned skill in order to generalize it to other problems or situations, the teacher would stress automaticity as the purpose of the objective.

A second implication for teachers involves making decisions concerning the importance of certain behaviors. A behavior considered appropriate by some teachers may be deemed inappropriate by others. Therefore, any nuance that could lead to potential disagreement should be defined adequately.

A study by Rhode, Morgan, and Young (1983) highlighted the need for adequate definitions when attempting to measure the instructional gains of learners. The authors provided six students identified as behavior disordered with assistance in controlling their inappropriate behaviors. They then emphasized a self-evaluation procedure that allowed the learners to monitor their own progress. These procedures were generalized to each student's resource room placement.

In order to verify the success of the program both in the special class and in general education class placement, the authors carefully defined the target behaviors so that independent observers could rate student progress and be reliable in measuring behavior change. Table 5.1 includes these operational definitions and is an excellent example of operational definitions that can be either counted or timed and can be agreed on by different observers.

CASE STUDY

Mr. Moss and Ms. Tree were having coffee in the lounge and discussing Waldo, a student who was causing trouble in both of their classes.

"I just don't know what to do, Palma," said Mr. Moss. "Waldo is driving me crazy! He's hyperactive and swears in class. On top of all that, his academic functioning is poor. Why, he never understands the answers to questions!"

TABLE 5.1   *Operational Definitions of Behavior*

I. Appropriate Classroom Behavior	II. Inappropriate Behavior
1. *Attend*—The student is looking at the teacher when the teacher is talking or presenting information to the individual or class, looking at materials in the classroom that have to do with the lesson, or looking at a peer who is presenting related academic information to the class. Attending behavior is characterized by eye contact with (and head and body orientation in the direction of) the appropriate classroom objects (teacher or task).	1. *Talking Out*—The student speaks without permission or interrupts the teacher and another student who are talking to each other.
2. *Work*—The student is engaged in or is completing teacher-assigned tasks. Work responses are characterized by nonverbal, motor movements if a written response is required. If the student is reading, progressive eye movement and page turning are evidenced.	2. *Out-of-Chair*—Movement of the student from his chair when not permitted. Such movement may include leaving the chair to open the window, remove items or threaten to remove items from the teacher's or other students' desks, name-calling, and moving around the room.
3. *Volunteer*—The student raises his hand to offer information or otherwise offers an appropriate response related to the ongoing academic activity in response to a teacher's question or suggestion.	3. *Modified Out-of-Chair*—Movement of the student from his chair with some part of the body still touching the chair (excluding sitting on feet).
4. *Reading Aloud*—The student is observed to be orally reading during the reading period or when asked to do so by the teacher. The student can be reading any form of printed material ranging from books, charts, blackboard, or word cards.	4. *Noise*—The student creates any audible noise other than vocalization.
5. *Answering Questions*—The student will answer questions when called on to do so by the teacher.	5. *Rocking*—The student lifts one or more of his chair legs from the floor while he is seated in his chair.
6. *Asking the Teacher a Question*—After raising his hand to gain teacher attention, the student asks the teacher a question when she calls on him.	6. *Noncompliance*—Failure by the student to initiate the appropriate response as requested by the teacher.
7. *Other*—The student exhibits appropriate classroom behavior as determined by classroom rules in operation in the classroom.	7. *Aggression*—The student makes movement toward another person so as to come into contact with him, whether directly or by using a material object as an extension of the hand.
	8. *Other*—The student clearly violates school or classroom rules or engages in behavior which prevents him from engaging in learning tasks and which are not otherwise specifically defined. Such behavior must be determined by the rules in operation in students' classrooms. Examples of such behavior may include engaging singly in activities or tasks not approved by the teacher or related to the assigned academic tasks (i.e., combing hair, writing on desk, looking at or handling objects within the immediate area surrounding the student's desk or work area, not appropriate to the academic task at hand).

Ms. Tree looked concerned, and after some thought she said, "Pete, the problem we're both having with Waldo may not be so much Waldo but the trouble we have defining what he does! My professor in this course I'm taking says that we have to define Waldo's behaviors operationally before we can develop procedures to change them."

"Oper . . . what? I said he was hyperactive, swears, and doesn't understand questions," exclaimed Mr. Moss.

"*Operationally defined* means that we define his behaviors in terms of movements," said Ms. Tree. "For example, *hyperactive* might be defined as the number of times Waldo leaves his seat during a 20-minute lesson. *Swearing* might be defined as the exact words you identify as disruptive and the number of times Waldo says these words during a given period of time."

"Palma, those definitions sound reasonable, but what do we do for understanding?"

"Now, Pete, calm down. We can define understanding in terms of the percentage of correct answers Waldo gives during an oral question-and-answer period!"

Suddenly Mr. Moss's eyes lit up. "I see what you mean, Palma. By defining the behaviors more precisely we can each attempt to change them in our classes and know we are working on the same things!"

"That's right Pete. Furthermore, we could come into each other's classrooms, watch Waldo's behaviors, and compare the results to see how reliable our system is."

"Palma you're brilliant!"

■ ■ ■ ■

Finally, the best test of the precision of a definition is whether or not independent observers can simultaneously record and agree on the occurrence or nonoccurrence of the behaviors (Sparzo & Poteet, 1989). For the most part in classroom situations the teacher's judgment concerning behaviors will suffice; however, some learners exhibit behaviors that are difficult to measure. In these instances a second, or at times more than two observers, will be required. For example, an accurate measurement of off-task behavior or temper tantrums may require a reliability check by two independent observers. Likewise, recording the duration of a student's temper tantrum may require an accurate measure to count the number of minutes it lasts. Measuring the subtle changes in a behavior of this type requires that teachers establish the accurateness of the measurement system by employing additional observers and comparing their results.

For the purpose of defining behaviors, it may be necessary to structure situations in which they occur as frequently as possible. These situations are important for learners, who require many trials to learn a specific task. If a behavior is defined so that it may only occur once or twice a day, it may not be sufficient for teaching purposes. For example, this consideration is important when teaching students with behavior disorders nonviolent alternatives to fighting. To have sufficient opportunities for instruction, a teacher may need to structure the behavioral definitions and the environment to provide frequent opportunities for the practice of appropriate behaviors. If the teacher waits for natural occurrences of these behaviors, they may be sporadic and infrequent.

DEVELOPING EFFECTIVE MEASUREMENT SYSTEMS

Developing a precise behavioral measurement system is a vital first step for all teachers. Such measurement systems provide a means for analyzing the effectiveness of an ABA program (Sulzer-Azaroff & Mayer, 1977). Measures used to track the progress of students under specified behavioral conditions are required as a component of the IEP (individualized education program). There are a number of techniques of behavioral measurement available to classroom teachers that can be grouped into two categories: (1) direct measurement of permanent products and (2) observational recording of transitory learner behaviors (Cooper, 1981; Sulzer-Azaroff & Mayer, 1977).

Measures of Permanent Products

A measure of a permanent product is a desirable and highly effective method for assessing learner progress. This measurement system allows the teacher to evaluate a product that the learner has generated by demonstrating behaviors that the teacher has targeted for change. Examples include the number of mathematics problems computed, pages read, items assembled, glasses broken, and floors mopped. Unfortunately, even though most teachers use permanent product measures, some do not use them in a systematic fashion, possibly losing valuable learners progress data. Cooper (1981) has summarized a number of techniques that teachers can use to assess permanent products. These techniques have been discussed by a number of different authors (e.g., Bailey, 1977; Sulzer-Azaroff & Mayer, 1977) and have been validated by research (e.g., Johnson & Bailey, 1977).

Frequency and Rate of Behavior

The first technique actually includes two methods, each a mathematical function of the other: measuring frequency of behavior and measuring rate of behavior. Obtaining the frequency at which a behavior occurs involves taking a count of that behavior. For an accurate count, the behavior must be discrete (with a clear beginning and end) and the length of the session must be kept constant. For example, using a frequency measure of a permanent product a teacher could count the number of correct arithmetic problems completed in 10 minutes or the number of pine tree seedlings a student correctly planted in 1 hour. Using permanent products is a desirable technique because it allows the teacher to return to the completed products and compare the progress with newly completed tasks.

Rate is a function of the frequency count. It is used when the time needed to complete a product is variable. For example, a teacher may require a learner to work on 20 problems for 10 minutes one day, 15 problems for 7 minutes the next day, and so forth. In order for the measure to remain standard, a rate of correctly completed problems is divided by the total number of minutes the learner had to complete the task. The result yielded by this method will be the number of correct problems the learner produced per minute (see Figure 5.1).

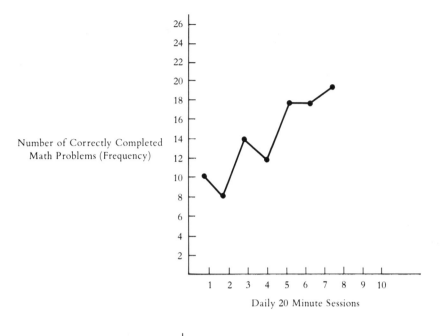

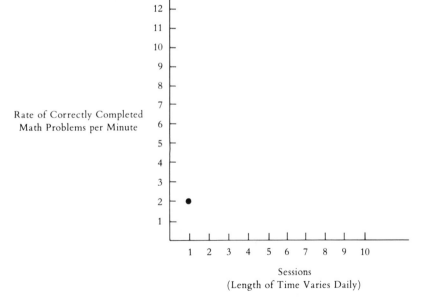

■ FIGURE 5.1
Two Charts Depicting the Frequency and Rate of Correctly Completed Math Problems

Measures involving rate of permanent products can be tremendously useful to teachers. Rate lends itself to measurement of efficiency, a vital prevocational and vocational skill. In many instances, the speed at which workers can correctly complete tasks is a requirement for job success. Using rate as a classroom measure introduces students early to the need for efficiency in their work. In addition, the use of rate as a measure can be an efficient method for data collection. Students can be taught to monitor their own time by recording when the task was completed, thus freeing the teacher from constant supervision.

Percentages

One technique of measurement that allows the teacher to follow learner progress across varying numbers of completed tasks is calculating the percentage of correctly completed products. Percentages are computed by dividing the number of units the learner completed correctly by the total number of units presented. The use of percentages lends itself to monitoring progress in academic skills and is the technique most used by teachers to award grades. There is a problem, however, in using percentages only for grading purposes. Percentages as quality measures have more utility when they are charted, allowing the teacher and learner to obtain a picture of progress made on specified objectives (see Figure 5.2). All basic skills can be monitored using percentages, including the quality of a learner's writing skills, oral communication skills (when a taped permanent product is retained), and computation and reading skills.

There have been a number of research efforts demonstrating the utility of percentages as a measure of ongoing assessment of student permanent product data (Cooper,

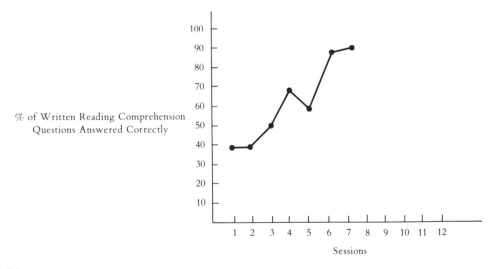

■ FIGURE 5.2

Chart Depicting the Percentage of Written Comprehension Questions Answered Correctly During Seatwork Sessions

1981; Lovitt, 1976, 1978). Cooper (1981) has suggested that percentages are a most effective measure when they reflect relatively large numbers of units. For example, a learner who answers three out of ten items correct reflects a 30% accuracy rate. On the following day the same student might correctly complete four out of ten items for a 40% accuracy rate, resulting in a 10% improvement. However, in such cases teachers should not make hasty judgments about results of their teaching. The use of percentages with a small number of units tends to generate spurious results, thereby requiring a longer period of time before judgments about the success of teaching techniques can be made. Referring to Figure 5.2, the reader will note that between any 2 days in sequence, the learner's progress will have increased or decreased by a minimum of 10 percentage points. However, when these data are put into perspective for the entire 8 days, a steady pattern of improvement is demonstrated. Generally the larger the number of permanent products (e.g., mathematics problems, reading questions), the more sensitive the system will be to fluctuations in performance. Percentages can be useful for probes with a small number of assessment units if the data are considered over longer periods of time after patterns of progress are established.

Number of Trials to Completion

Other techniques for evaluating permanent products are deviations of or used in conjunction with frequency/rate and percentages. Cooper and Johnson (1979) and later Cooper (1981) discussed four variations, two of which are particularly relevant. First, for some learners who are mildly to moderately handicapped, prevocational skills are the main curricular area. In instances where steps or tasks are identified for student completion, a measurement system would be used that records the number of trials needed for the student to learn each step. For example, a high school student may be learning to disassemble, clean, and assemble a carburetor from a lawnmower. For each step in the process, a number of trials will be needed before the learner will master that step and move on to the next one. If the instruction is effective, the teacher will expect to see a gradual reduction in the number of trials needed for the student to successfully complete each step (refer to Figure 5.3). Since the student requires fewer trials to criterion, the data would indicate an improvement in fine motor skills, ability to follow certain directions, and so on.

Task Analysis

A final technique for measuring permanent products is task analysis. A student learning to add numbers follows a set of steps ranging from column addition with no carrying to carrying in alternate places. Taking the example of the carrying in alternate places, the learner must actually perform a multiple-step operation depending on the number of place values in the problem. Each of the steps the learner successfully completes can be counted and charted. The technique of analyzing task complexity can be extremely useful when teaching writing skills. The number or percentage of correctly formed letters is an example of the utility of this technique.

IDEA FILE

The use of permanent products as a measure of learner progress continues to increase in popularity among teachers. These techniques have a wide range of uses and often are limited only by the teacher's imagination. The following is a short list of examples of how some teachers have used permanent products and how researchers have used these techniques to validate their experimental procedures.

- Hansen (1979) used electronic sensing devices to count the frequency of bedwetting instances for two children.
- Neef, Iwata, and Page (1980) monitored the cumulative number of words students learned to spell correctly.
- Martin, Pallotta-Cornick, Johnstone, and Goyos (1980) used the mean number of units correctly produced to monitor any improvements in work production rates for clients in a sheltered workshop.
- Wood and Flynn (1978) developed 15 criteria for appropriate room cleaning and used them to measure any improvements in room cleanliness exhibited by boys reinforced to complete the tasks.
- Espin and Sindelar (1988) used the written products of students with learning disabilities as the source to evaluate the remediation of written errors of grammar and syntax.
- Mastropieri, Emerick, and Scruggs (1988) used grades on science examinations as an indicator of student success in using mnemonic strategies to learn science concepts.

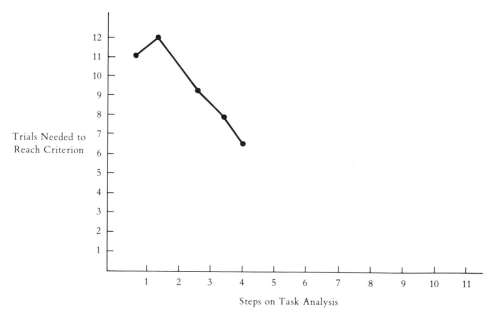

■ FIGURE 5.3
Trials to Criterion in Task Analysis

Other Examples

■ Match-to-sample, where a student completes a task by copying the design of a model provided by the teacher (e.g., student attempts to copy a pegboard design provided by the teacher).

■ The number of times in a taped conversation with a peer that the student states his or her point of view.

■ The number of square feet of floor space that a student mops.

■ ■ ■ ■

With the availability of videotape equipment such as portable cameras, teachers can now record the completed product on film so a more in-depth observation can be made at a later time (Bailey, 1977). Pictures of a task can be taken at various points along the way, so that a record is kept of the learner's progress. Also, teachers could videotape a play session or role-playing activity and later analyze student behaviors. Research has been conducted on the use of videotaping for instructional purposes; however, the use of this technology for observational purposes and to assist teachers in task analysis merits further study.

Portable video cameras can be a very effective instructional tool for use in community-based activities. For example, a teacher could film students in their roles as consumers when exchanging items at a department store customer service office. The taped segment could be used in two ways. First, the teacher could analyze the segment as assessment data to determine the students' progress (e.g., appropriately express reasons for returning the item) and make judgments concerning whether or not further instruction is necessary. In addition, the taped segment could be used during classroom instruction as a method of feedback to students.

Direct Observational Recording of Behaviors

Many learner behaviors do not result in the completion of a permanent product and therefore require different measurement systems. These behaviors involve what Sulzer-Azaroff and Mayer (1977) termed *transitory events;* that is, behaviors that must be observed under natural environmental circumstances to make it possible to count or time whether the behavior occurred or did not occur. For example, behaviors in this category that are often exhibited by learners include temper tantrums, name calling, sound utterances, out-of-seat behavior, off-task behavior, compliance, smiling, and initiating conversations. Measuring these and other behaviors requires the use of live observers. In any case, transitory behaviors do not result in permanent products by students but rather in behaviors that can be categorized as either discrete or transient.

Measuring Discrete Behaviors

Discrete behaviors have a clear and distinct beginning and end (onset and offset). Teachers who use task analyzed curriculum components have in fact identified discrete behaviors. Therefore, when teachers define a behavior operationally, it can be termed discrete if there is no doubt when the behavior started and when it stopped. If a student asks a question, this can be considered a discrete behavior. Conversely, if a student with learning disabilities daydreams during independent seatwork, it may be difficult to determine a clear distinction of the beginning and end of the episode.

Two methods can be used to measure discrete behaviors: event recording and duration recording (Alberto & Troutman, 1983; Bailey, 1977; Cooper, 1981; Sulzer-Azaroff & Mayer, 1977; Walker & Shea, 1988). Event recording involves a count or tally of the number of times that a specific behavior occurs within a designated period of time. The teacher can choose either frequency, rate, or percentage to use with event recording. For example, a teacher may record the number of words that a young student can repeat in 10 minutes (frequency), or convert the system to record rate simply by dividing the total number of words said correctly by the total time. The percentage of words said correctly by the student can be determined by dividing the number of correct responses by the total number of words presented. The choice of whether to use frequency, rate, or percentage depends on the task to be taught; some tasks lend themselves better to one type of measurement technique than to either of the others.

There are a number of event recording techniques teachers can use to obtain accurate data. Probably the most efficient and unobtrusive technique is to use a wrist golf counter. Teachers (or other observers) can keep this device with them at all times, keeping their hands free to engage in other activities. Additional devices or techniques for collecting event data might include transferring pennies from one pocket to another, making tallies with a pencil on a recording sheet, and the like. It is up to the teacher to choose the most appropriate techniques given the target behaviors and the environment in which the data are being gathered.

The second method for recording discrete behaviors involves taking a measure of duration (length of time). This method allows the teacher to time the length of a specific behavior with the goal of either decreasing or increasing the length of time that the behavior occurs. For behaviors for which approximate measures will suffice (e.g., length of time to complete an assignment), teachers can use a wristwatch or wall clock. However, if a duration measure is to be accurate, a precise definition of the discrete behavior must be available, and for this there is no substitute for a stopwatch. Teachers will find that both a stopwatch and wrist counter are vital tools for monitoring and changing the behaviors of their students. Figure 5.4 shows examples of two types of recording sheets that teachers can use for recording discrete behaviors.

Event recording does not lend itself to recording behaviors that occur at high rates (e.g., interruptions during class). Therefore, teachers should be able to develop observational systems to collect data that, when charted, will provide an accurate picture of those fleeting behaviors. Research in applied behavior analysis has provided time sampling procedures that use intervals of time as the basic unit of measure for recording these fleeting behaviors.

Measuring Transient Behaviors

Transient behaviors include movements exhibited by learners that occur at varying intensities and varying times of the day. These behaviors often do not have a predictable pattern associated with their occurrence or nonoccurrence. Behaviors such as sporadic temper tantrums, rocking, sudden utterances, and other types of fleeting movements that do not have a clear onset and offset require a recording system that can "capture" the essence of the behavior. Interval recording systems take a standard block of time such as a 20-minute reading lesson and break down the total time into smaller, discrete time intervals. This allows teachers to analyze the components or patterns that are being exhibited by learners and attempt to alter the patterns of behavior (Cooper, 1981).

Continuous Observation Systems. Bailey (1977) has classified interval recording systems into two categories. The first category includes techniques known as *continuous observation.* These methods require that the teacher or other observers watch the learner continuously and record the specified aspects of the target behavior for the entire interval. For example, a teacher who is interested in increasing the self-initiated social conversation of a student with behavior disorders might choose to observe the student for 10 minutes during a physical education class. Since self-initiated utterances are fleeting behaviors, the teacher can break down the 10-minute period into forty 15-second intervals. The teacher would then observe for the entire 10-minute session, recording some aspect of the behavior during each of the forty intervals (see Figure 5.5).

Student: _____KEVIN_____   Observer: _____MR. PETE MOSS_____

Behavior: _____INTERRUPTING OTHERS DURING INDEPENDENT SEATWORK ACTIVITIES (FREQUENCY)_____

Observation Times: _____DAILY 9AM – 9:30 AM_____

3/26/84	3/27/84	3/28/84	3/29/84	3/30/84	4/1/84	4/2/84	4/3/84
ℍ III	ℍ I	ℍ IIII	ℍ	ℍ I			

Student: _____JAMAL_____   Observer: _____MR. PETE MOSS_____

Behavior: _____LENGTH OF TIME ENGAGED IN AN INDEPENDENT LEISURE ACTIVITY (DURATION)_____

3/26/84	3/27/84	3/28/84	3/29/84	3/30/84	4/1/84	4/2/84	4/3/84
3 MIN. 10 SEC.	3 MIN.	4 MIN. 5 SEC.	3 MIN. 5 SEC.	5 MIN.			

■ FIGURE 5.4
Examples of Event Recording Sheets

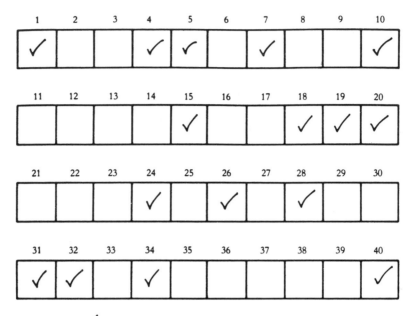

$\checkmark$ = Self-Initiated Social Conversation

Each interval is 15 seconds, total 10 minutes

$$\frac{16 \text{ Intervals Where Behavior Was Observed}}{40 \text{ Total Intervals}} \times 100 = 40\%$$

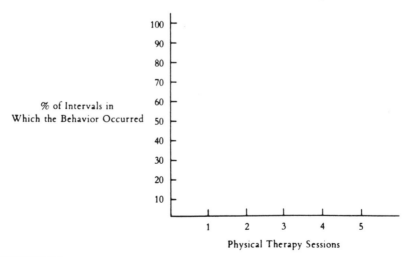

■ FIGURE 5.5
Partial Interval Recording System Plus Charted Data

There are two different methods for developing continuous observation systems that are especially useful for classroom teachers. These methods have been discussed by many authors (e.g., Bailey, 1977; Cooper, 1981; Hall, 1971; Sulzer-Azaroff & Mayer, 1977). First, the *partial interval recording system* allows the observer to record a response if the response occurred during any portion of the interval. In the example just given, if the learner made a sound any time during the interval that interval would be scored (see Figure 5.5). This system allows the teacher to record a percentage of intervals during which the learner initiated social conversation, thus providing an estimate of the current level of this behavior. Subsequently, the teacher might design a program to increase the number of utterances emitted, and this would be represented by an increase in the percentage of intervals in which self-initiated social conversation occurred. The use of percentages results in a type of quality measure, allowing the teacher to judge whether and when patterns of improvement occur.

Partial interval systems have a weakness that can be minimized with some preplanning. When behavior occurs at high rates (e.g., more than one talk-out per interval), the data recorded will not be representative of the actual number of behaviors if only the first occurrence is marked. Any additional occurrences are lost (not counted) until the following interval. The simplest solution to this problem is to shorten the length of the intervals. In many cases this modification will decrease the probability that more than one occurrence of the behavior will be exhibited during any interval. Rapidly occurring behaviors may require teachers to use an event recording system if a discrete definition of the movement can be developed.

A second method of continuous observation in an interval recording system involves observing whether or not the target behavior was emitted for the entire interval. This *whole interval recording system* allows the teacher to mark the interval only when the student engages in the behavior for the entire length of the interval. If the behavior ceases at any time during the interval, that block is not scored (see Figure 5.6). For example, the deteriorating work habits of a learner may have become a concern to her teachers. Karen may be demonstrating alarmingly long periods of time when she engages in some type of off-task behavior. After a behavioral definition has been established delineating what constitutes off-task behaviors, her teachers can set up an observation system using a whole interval approach. By totaling up the numbers of the intervals that Karen has engaged in these behaviors and multiplying by the length of time of one interval, the teachers can obtain a conservative estimate of the length of time she stayed off-task.

Whole interval recording systems tend to produce conservative estimates of the behaviors they measure. Figure 5.6 demonstrates that parts of the behaviors actually occurred within intervals two, three, and five. Following the rules of using whole intervals, these segments cannot be recorded, and yet some behaviors did occur. This characteristic of whole interval systems is not necessarily a weakness; instead it can be considered a strength when certain behaviors are being recorded.

Sulzer-Azaroff and Mayer (1977) have pointed out that to select a valid measurement system professionals must match the characteristics of the system to the characteristics of given behaviors. Therefore, since whole interval systems tend to be more conservative (they underestimate) and partial interval systems tend to be more liberal (they overestimate), considering how they affect the recording of behaviors is important.

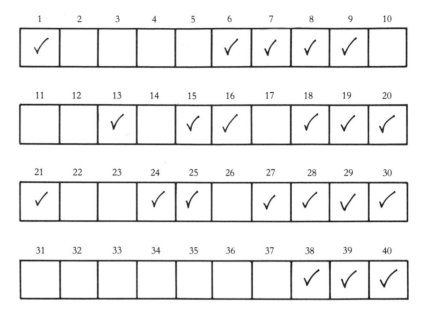

1	2	3	4	5	6	7	8	9	10
✓					✓	✓	✓	✓	

11	12	13	14	15	16	17	18	19	20
		✓		✓	✓		✓	✓	✓

21	22	23	24	25	26	27	28	29	30
✓			✓	✓		✓	✓	✓	✓

31	32	33	34	35	36	37	38	39	40
							✓	✓	✓

✓ = Scored only when behavior occurs for the entire interval.
Each interval is 15 seconds, total 10 minutes

```
  21 Intervals Scored              5.15 Minutes
× 15 Seconds per Interval      60 ) 315
  315 Seconds                        300
```

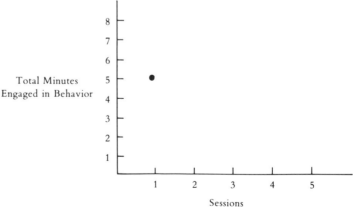

■ FIGURE 5.6
Whole Interval Recording System Plus Charted Data

For example, in Karen's case any eventual reduction in her off-task behavior would actually be less than what is presently occurring. It might be more efficient to redefine the behavior so that the amount of time Karen engages in on-task behavior is recorded. An observation of on-task behavior using the conservative method would estimate slightly less time engaged in the activities than was actually occurring. When attempting to increase these behaviors, a slightly conservative estimate would show more improvement than is actually being charted. One general rule of thumb would be to use more conservative methods when an increase in behavior is required and more liberal measures when a decrease is desired (Sulzer-Azaroff & Mayer, 1977; Wolery, Bailey, & Sugai, 1988).

IDEA FILE

Teachers will find that the methods of direct observation are extremely useful for measuring student progress in community-based activities. For example, teachers might use frequency, rate, or percentage to measure the progress learners are making in completing consumer-oriented cost-comparison problems in community grocery stores. Teachers might also choose to record transient behaviors on site via partial and whole interval systems while students are engaging in community-based vocational activities. Examples would include the use of appropriate social cues, both physical (e.g., gesturing) and vocal.

Momentary time sampling techniques work well when teachers are monitoring several groups of students in a large community environment. For instance, when instruction is occurring in a mall and three small groups of students are in different locations under the supervision of an aide and two volunteers, the teacher can move from group to group recording on-task behavior, appropriate social interactions, and so forth.

■ ■ ■ ■

Momentary Time Sampling. Another interval recording system, momentary time sampling, allows teachers to record the occurrence or nonoccurrence of target behaviors only at the end of prespecified time periods. As a result, teachers using momentary time sampling systems are free to participate in other activities while they are collecting data on a target behavior. For example, a teacher interested in obtaining a representative sample of how often young students participate in cooperative activities with other children could use this approach (see Figure 5.7). The instructor may wish to observe the children during a free play period but not waste valuable teaching time by observing them continuously.

The teacher could choose to break up the hour into twelve 5-minute intervals, observing the learners only at the end of each time period and recording whether or not a cooperative interaction is taking place at that time. This system allows the teacher to interact with other students without abandoning the applied behavior analysis program formulated for the target learners. With momentary time sampling systems, teachers can either use fixed time periods or observe learners at random intervals. In either case, if teachers are able to gather a sufficient number of data points (observations of the behavior), this system can be efficient and practical.

Inherent in all behavioral observation systems is a chance of error from recording more or less of a behavior than is actually occurring. Therefore, teachers should consider some type of system that checks whether or not observers are seeing what is intended. This system of checks, called *reliability of measurement,* is easy to use in classrooms. It will be discussed in the next section.

KEY CONCEPTS

- Permanent product evaluation is easy to use because obtaining these data does not interfere with the class schedule. Teachers can evaluate the products after the students complete the assignment.
- By writing good objectives with clearly stated criteria, teachers can easily evaluate a completed product based on the preset criteria.
- Frequency, rate, and percentage are three measures that can be used to evaluate permanent products.
- By task analyzing the steps needed to complete permanent products (e.g., assemble a lawn mower carburetor), teachers can monitor students' progress toward the final objective.
- Observational recording systems are used to measure behaviors that do not result in a permanent product.
- Discrete behaviors are those with clear beginning and ending points (e.g., brushing teeth, catching a ball).
- Event recording differs from permanent product evaluation only in the sense that discrete events occur and can be observed yet do not necessarily result in a lasting product (e.g., toothbrushing). Event recording can also use measures such as frequency, rate, and percentage.
- Duration recording involves recording the length of time a student engages in a targeted behavior. Latency is similar to duration because it involves a length of time; however, this measure is used to record the length of time that elapses *before* a student engages in a behavior (e.g., length of time before students pick up their toys after a request by the teacher).

10′	20′	30′	40′	50′	60′
0	+	+	0	+	0

+ Engaged in activity at end of interval

0 Not engaged in cooperative play activity at end of interval

■ *FIGURE 5.7*
Momentary Time Sampling at 10-Minute Intervals

■ Transient behaviors are fleeting, leaving no predictable pattern for when they occur or for how long (e.g., student quarrel). Interval recording systems artificially break down larger blocks of time into discrete units in an effort to "capture" the fleeting response.

■ Partial interval recording systems are used to record a response if it occurs at any time during the interval. If there is a chance that the behavior will occur more than once during an interval, the length of the intervals should be shortened. Data resulting from a partial interval system can be graphed using frequency of intervals in which the behavior occurred or percentage of intervals in which the behavior occurred.

■ Whole interval recording systems are used to get a duration measure of a behavior. The teacher marks an interval only when the behavior has occurred for the entire interval. A count of the number of scored intervals multiplied by the interval length results in an estimate of the total time a student was engaged in a behavior.

■ Momentary time sampling allows the teacher to record behaviors if they occur at the end of an interval (e.g., whether Tommy is on-task at the end of each 5-minute interval). This system is less accurate than the others, but it does allow the teacher to sample behavior while engaged in other activities.

■ ■ ■ ■

ESTABLISHING RELIABILITY OF MEASUREMENT

The best test of a measurement system's accuracy is whether or not it allows two or more people to simultaneously observe and consistently record the occurrences or nonoccurrences of the behavior. Interobserver reliability checks should produce a figure demonstrating that the observers agreed a minimum of 80% of the time.

A number of methods exist for establishing reliability among observers. However, for the purpose of most classroom teachers the point-by-point method and its variations appear to have the most utility. Interobserver agreement is reported in the form of percentage of agreement and disagreement among the various observers (see Figure 5.8). When the data gathered by two or more observers are compared using the simple formula given in Figure 5.8, the reliability percentage should be greater than 80% before the teacher can feel comfortable that the measurement system is accurate. Moreover, to increase the accuracy of the reliability estimate, it is important to compare each interval and note whether or not observer agreement occurred. This point-by-point method tends to be more conservative and accurate, lending additional support to the quality of the measurement system.

The importance of establishing good reliability estimates should be evident. If teachers fail to check the accuracy of their measurement systems, they can never be sure that they are obtaining an accurate count of learner behavior (Repp, Nieminen, Olinger, & Brusca, 1988). Bailey (1977) has outlined a number of steps for enhancing the effective use of interrater reliability checks:

1. Observers must share the same vantage point.
2. Observers should not be able to view each other's scoring.
3. Observers must be using exactly the same interval.

4. Observers should not communicate with each other.
5. Observers, if possible, should be unaware of checks. (pp. 111–116)

It may not always be possible to institute these procedures. However, being aware of the potential problems may limit the damage done to reliability estimates. For example, the first two steps can be handled easily by using room dividers and other partitions located in many classrooms. The third step can easily be arranged by making a simple cassette tape that has been pretimed with a recorded voice stating "Interval one . . . , interval two . . . ," and so forth. The observers can be hooked in to the tape recorder via inexpensive single-ear receivers and plug-in jacks. The fourth and fifth steps can usually be handled simply by the teacher's monitoring of the situation.

IDEA FILE

One disadvantage inherent in the use of applied behavior analysis systems is the need for assistance when implementing such programs. A majority of behavioral programs should require only the efforts of the teacher, who can implement the intervention and quickly record the data. At times, however, programs become more complicated, especially when teachers are attempting to monitor and change transient behaviors of their students. The following suggestions may help teachers design and implement more sophisticated programs.

■ Teachers should locate and train a pool of volunteer observers who are available when needed. Parents, members of church groups, and members of community service groups can be good sources of volunteers.

■ Another source of potential observers is students enrolled in either high school or postsecondary vocational child care classes. Teachers of these classes often look for activities to increase their students' contact with children.

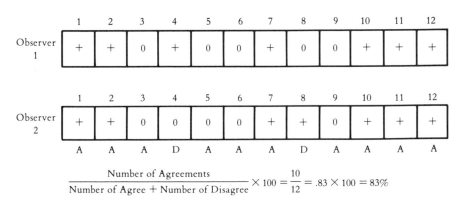

■ FIGURE 5.8
Point-by-Point Reliability Formula

- Teachers who have developed a good peer tutoring program also will have a ready pool of observers for recording data.

- Whenever possible, teachers should help students learn to record their own behaviors. This technique affords learners some measure of control over their lives and helps them to take more responsibility for their actions. Self-charting can also become a behavior modification procedure, helping students keep track of frequency, duration, or intensity of their behaviors.

■ ■ ■ ■

Finding and Training Observers

No standardized procedures exist for training observers. As with all the components of applied behavior analysis, the foundation for training observers is the behavioral definitions, and concise, operational definition of movements will make training observers easier.

Once the behaviors have been outlined and defined, the next step is to locate potential observers who are available during the times needed for observation, are interested in the class, and are reliable enough to meet with the teacher for training sessions (Bailey, 1977). Reliable, well-prepared observers are invaluable; however, there are times when even the most conscientious volunteers cannot attend a session. To avoid losing data, substitute observers should be available.

The length of training sessions varies from teacher to teacher. However, all sessions should allow ample time for practice. The mechanics of manipulating data sheets, tape recorders, and/or stopwatches while attempting to observe a learner can cause a loss of data. Initial sessions should allow observers to get a feel for the target behavior(s) either from the teacher's discussion and modeling of the behavior(s) or from viewing a videotape of the student exhibiting the movement(s). The latter technique is preferred when the behavior is resistant to change and video equipment is available.

More than one observer may be necessary (especially when the teacher cannot act as a reliability checker), and it is best to train all observers at the same sessions. This allows them to ask questions and discuss the behaviors simultaneously. Additional sessions allow for practice in coding the behaviors. Observers who are trained with video equipment should practice their skills in the natural setting at least once before the actual data collection sessions begin. Trial runs tend to iron out many problems that are unforeseen during training sessions.

Developing Data Recording Sheets

The efficiency of a data recording sheet is vital to both the teachers and any other observers gathering data. A cluttered, poorly designed sheet causes confusion and adversely affects the reliability of the measurement system. Therefore, a primary concern of the teacher is to design a recording sheet that will facilitate observation.

A coded sheet minimizes the amount of writing required of the observer, thus simplifying the system. Figure 5.9 demonstrates how it is much simpler to mark through a predetermined code than it is to remember the codes and write them down. When an interval system is employed, the observation sheet would include boxes representing each interval. A simple check mark would be made in the box if the behavior was observed during that interval.

Bailey (1977) has suggested that an efficient observation sheet should contain three sections: (1) descriptive information; (2) observation boxes; and (3) a scoring and reliability summary of the data. The demographic data on the top of the sheet provide a reader with all information needed to understand when and how the data were gathered. This section is part of the teacher's management plan, allowing for the original data to be filed for later use.

Observational boxes were explained previously; however, equally important is the data scoring and reliability summary. This information minimizes confusion at later dates concerning who the reliability checker was or what the scores were for a particular day or session.

ESTABLISHING A BASELINE: ONE TOOL OF ASSESSMENT

Traditional assessment procedures attempt to measure a learner's present level of performance with standardized instruments such as diagnostic arithmetic or reading tests. The scores obtained from these tests establish a point of reference, allowing a comparison for later test samples. The information presented in Chapter Three suggested that these scores may not be sensitive enough to monitor the progress of learners with mild to

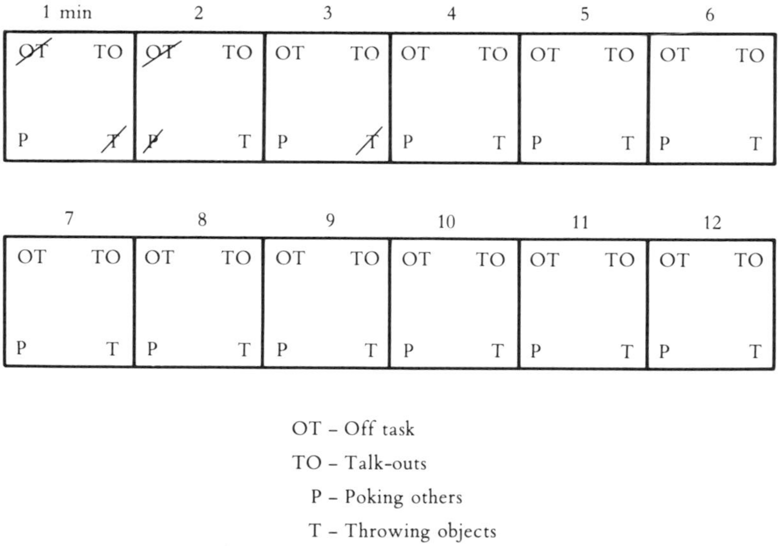

OT – Off task

TO – Talk-outs

P – Poking others

T – Throwing objects

■ *FIGURE 5.9*
Example of a Coded Data Sheet Within Intervals

moderate handicaps. The techniques of direct measurement, on the other hand, provide a way to visualize learner progress.

Establishing a baseline involves recording data that reflect student behaviors prior to the application of instructional techniques and materials or changes in the physical environment. These data can reflect permanent products (e.g., number of syllables pronounced correctly), discrete movements (e.g., getting out of a seat), or transient behaviors (e.g., rocking) and can all be charted to form a baseline.

Establishing a baseline of learning behavior is a vital component of the applied behavior analysis process; however, problems that can occur during baseline may adversely affect the gathering of a representative sample of learner behaviors. Professionals agree that it is best to gather repeated measures of a behavior over a period of several days or, in some cases, more than 1 week. Data that have been charted provide teachers with the best indication of when a truly representative sample has been obtained. For example, a teacher interested in modifying Kathy's sudden talk-outs may find that these behaviors had alternately high and low rates of emission. In this case, it would probably be wise to continue baseline observation longer. Figure 5.10 presents a chart of Kathy's baseline for talk-outs. Note that during the first week (sessions 1–5), the number of talk-outs recorded was unstable. In this instance, the teacher was wise to extend the baseline over the next 4 days in order to obtain a clearer representation of Kathy's behavior. Of course, not all the behaviors exhibited by learners will stabilize over time. When they do not stabilize, teachers can take an average of the behaviors and use that as a point of reference for possible changes occurring after intervention (see Figure 5.10).

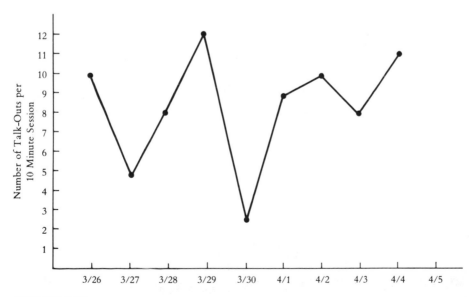

■ FIGURE 5.10
Chart of Kathy's Talk-Outs—Baseline

CHARTING STUDENT PROGRESS

One goal for teachers should be to make instructional techniques more effective. Accomplishing this goal will require teachers to monitor student progress carefully and relate any progress to the intervention. This functional relationship between what the teacher does (e.g., use of behavioral procedures, materials, or media) and subsequent student behavior was discussed earlier. A key point, however, is that student behavior should occur as planned or it will be necessary to alter the behavioral procedures.

The methods used to measure student progress should be designed to monitor the behaviors of individuals. Often data will be more useful if they are converted into graphic forms that allow teachers to see the patterns of behaviors as they occur. The old saying that "one picture is worth a thousand words" has definite implications for charting the behaviors of learners with mild to moderate handicaps.

Line Graphs

Line graphs are drawn using two axes on graph paper, with the horizontal axis (abscissa, or x-axis) representing the times the behavior was observed and the vertical axis (ordinate, or y-axis) representing the amount of behavior that will be charted. Figure 5.11 provides examples of line graphs for monitoring behaviors. These graphs provide teachers with a method for frequent, easy-to-use checks of their students.

Cumulative Graphs

Cumulative graphs are an excellent way to monitor behaviors that occur at low rates by providing the user with a view of the upward trend of the response. To use a cumulative graph, the teacher adds the number of occurrences for the present session to those of the previous session.

For example, a resource teacher may wish to chart Maria's tardiness for class. Since Maria can only be late once each day, the use of a line graph would not be helpful because it would not demonstrate a pattern (e.g., a line fluctuation between zero and one occurrence). A cumulative graph, on the other hand, will allow the teacher to establish a pattern of Maria's behavior (see Figure 5.12). The teacher defined the target behavior as crossing the door's threshhold after the class bell has rung. On the first day Maria was late, and the teacher recorded this on the chart. Days two and three were also late days for Maria, requiring her teacher to add the first occurrence to the second (scoring a 2 for day two) and the third to the first two (scoring a 3 for day three). For days four, five, and six, however, Maria was on time. This required the teacher to add zeros (representing no occurrences of late behavior) to day three.

The cumulative graph is a helpful tool for teachers because it allows them to monitor the patterns of behaviors occurring at low rates and pinpoint the exact times the behaviors occurred. In the example given, the teacher's goal will be to plot a straight line that will represent Maria's getting to class on time.

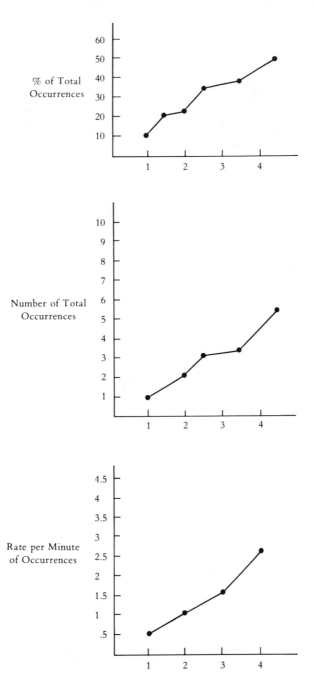

■ FIGURE 5.11
Basic Line Graphs

Ratio Graphs

Ratio graphs are becoming popular for charting behaviors occurring at high rates (e.g., handwaving) or for cases in which the numbers of possible occurrences from session to session vary sufficiently that charting percentages would not be useful. (e.g., Monday a student gets 18 out of 20 math problems correct, or 90%, and Tuesday he gets 48 out of 50 correct, or 96%—a difference of six percentage points when the student could have missed the same two problems.)

In these instances, teachers could choose to use ratio graphs, charting the rate per minute of their students' behaviors (Figure 5.13). These charts allow a great deal of variability, charting behaviors up to 1,000 per minute. A form of applied behavior analysis called *precision teaching* (White & Haring, 1980) uses ratio charts for improving academic skills, social behaviors, and any other response that can be converted into rate.

Single-Subject Designs

The charting methods used for establishing a cause-and-effect relationship between student behaviors and the interventions used by the teacher are called *single-subject designs*. The designs provide teachers with tools for judging the success of their teaching techniques and materials.

The first step in using single-subject designs is to gather *baseline* data. These data reflect the student's behavior *before* the teacher attempts to make any changes. Taking baseline data is important because the teacher will compare the student's behavior *after* the intervention has been applied. When single-subject designs are used appropriately to

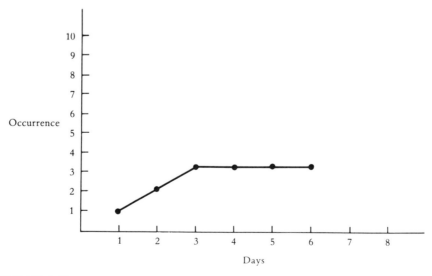

■ *FIGURE 5.12*
Cumulative Graph

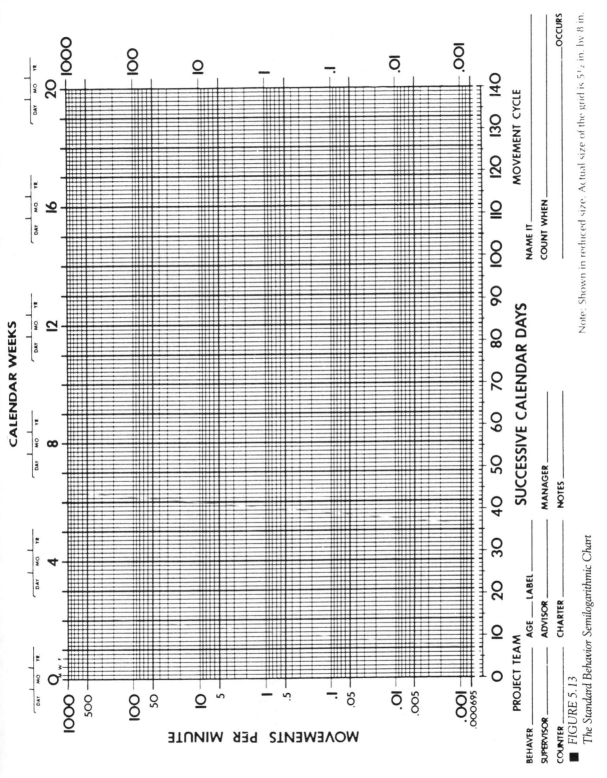

CALENDAR WEEKS

MOVEMENTS PER MINUTE

SUCCESSIVE CALENDAR DAYS

MOVEMENT CYCLE

PROJECT TEAM

BEHAVER		AGE	LABEL		NAME IT
SUPERVISOR		ADVISOR			COUNT WHEN
COUNTER		CHARTER		MANAGER	
				NOTES	OCCURS

Note: Shown in reduced size. Actual size of the grid is 5½ in. by 8 in.

■ FIGURE 5.13
The Standard Behavior Semilogarithmic Chart

control other variables, any changes in the student's behavior might be attributed to the intervention.

The most basic of the single-subject designs is the *A B design*. This design is easy to use because it only requires the teacher to collect data during two phases: the baseline and after the intervention. For example, Ramon has been having a great deal of trouble

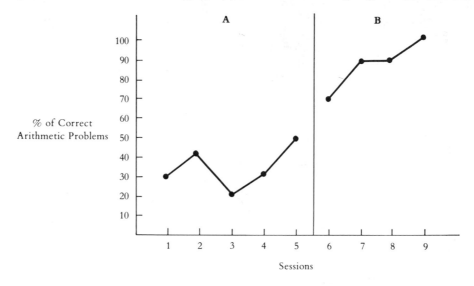

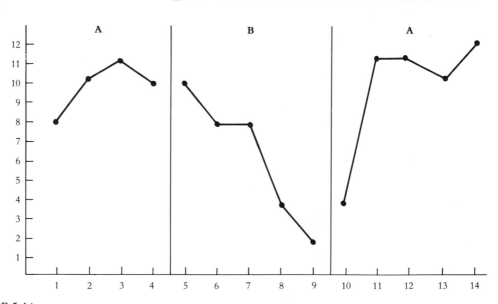

■ FIGURE 5.14
Examples of A B and Reversal Designs

completing his arithmetic worksheets with any degree of success. After analyzing his errors, Ms. Barnstorm suspects that Ramon is not discriminating between the various operational signs ($+$, $-$, $\times$, $\div$). She first records his scores for five trials, and then after the fifth trial she begins to color code the signs on his worksheets (Figure 5.14). In this case, the intervention (color coding the signs on the worksheets) may have been a help to Ramon, since the data indicate a rapid improvement after the treatment phase began.

The *reversal design* is a technique used to assess the causal relationship between interventions and behaviors by following four steps: (1) taking baseline data; (2) applying the intervention; (3) returning to the baseline phase by removing the intervention; and (4) returning once again to the intervention phase (Figure 5.14). The control exerted by the reversal design is based on the belief that the intervention is controlling the behavior. Therefore, when the intervention is removed the behavior should return to its normal rate.

The example of the reversal design in Figure 5.14 shows the measurement of the effects of ignoring on the unproductive behaviors of a student. In this example the teacher counts the number of times that a student requests assistance from others. The teacher, who had previously stopped all her activity to help the student, now ignores each incident and praises the student for attempting the task before requiring assistance.

The numbers of requests dropped during the treatment phase, suggesting that the teacher's ignoring and praise technique was working. Further evidence that the treatment was effecting the decrease in the target behavior occurred when the teacher discontinued this intervention. When the intervention was not in place, the target behavior returned to higher levels, and it decreased again when the teacher began to ignore and praise.

Multiple-baseline designs are used to analyze the effects of an intervention on behaviors that are difficult to reverse. For example, if a student learns to add single-digit numbers because of a teacher's intervention, the removal of the intervention does not guarantee a reversal since the behavior has been learned. Therefore, most academic behaviors are not easily measured with reversal designs.

Multiple baselines have also been used to measure behaviors that it would be considered unethical to reverse. If a student's headbanging is controlled by using a pleasant stimulus such as light or sound, the procedure should not be reversed to prove that the treatment is effective, because the student might injure himself.

When using the multiple-baseline design, the teacher applies the intervention at different times across different settings, individuals, or target behaviors. The first example (Figure 5.15) demonstrates how a teacher uses a multiple-baseline across different settings. The resource teacher wishes to demonstrate that the use of chapter outlines developed by regular education peers might affect the test performance of a mainstreamed student. Baseline data on the student's performance on semiweekly quizzes in science, social studies, and health education are taken by the regular educators for 2 weeks. Volunteer students in the science class then begin providing the target learner with chapter outlines the week before each quiz.

During this intervention the teacher continues to monitor the student's performance in social studies and health, where no outlines are used. After 2 weeks of using outlines in science, the teacher introduces them to the social studies class and then 2 weeks later to the health education class. As the baselines in Figure 5.15 indicate, the outlines appear to have assisted the student in improving his grades in all settings.

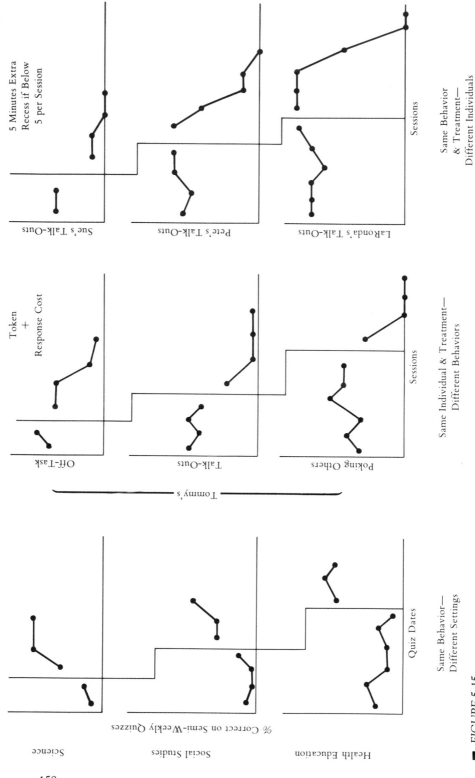

■ FIGURE 5.15
Examples of the Different Uses for Multiple-Baseline Designs

Multiple baselines have a great deal of utility because they can also measure the effects of interventions on more than one individual or on more than one behavior of the same individual. Figure 5.15 provides examples of each of these variations.

Multiple-probe designs are a variation of multiple-baseline designs. One difference is that continuous (daily) measurement of the target behavior(s) is not required when gathering baseline data. This variation is useful because it is less time consuming than multiple baselines and provides a reliable estimate of student progress.

The major difference in the multiple-probe design is that data are collected at various points in the project as opposed to having baseline data gathered continuously (daily). These data, gathered at various intervals, are called *probes*. Specifically, data are collected continuously during each baseline only prior to implementing each separate intervention.

Using the same example as that provided for the multiple baseline, the resource teacher who wanted to monitor the effects of daily chapter outlines on a student's progress in three academic subjects might also have chosen a multiple-probe design (Figure 5.16).

In this example, the teacher records the student's semiweekly test scores for each subject area (Probe I). She then introduces the chapter outlines (possibly provided by a regular education peer tutor) for science and continues to monitor semiweekly scores for this subject. The other two subjects are ignored temporarily, thus saving some time in the monitoring process.

During each probe phase, data are gathered for all subject areas, but data are only gathered for the subject area when the chapter outlines are first being introduced (see Figure 5.16). As the chapter outlines are introduced to a new subject area (e.g., social studies), they continue to be used in the previous academic area (i.e., science). This design helps teachers gather useful data for making decisions about instructional interventions without requiring continuous data collection across all baselines.

Changing-criterion designs can be extremely useful to teachers as a tool to help motivate students toward a desired goal. In a strict experimental sense, baseline data are collected on a behavior and an intervention is introduced that is designed to move the behavior to a predetermined criterion level. When that criterion is met a new one is set, and so on, until the actual goal for the behavior is met. The main element for demonstrating experimental control is the variability of the criterion (either up or down) and the behavior matching the preset criterion.

Figure 5.17 is an example of how a changing-criterion design might be used to monitor the out-of-seat behavior of a student in a self-contained class for students with behavior disorders. The intervention consisted of providing the student with 10 minutes of extra time working in the class-owned community garden each time he matched or went below the preset criterion for that phase. The teacher opted to raise the criterion up in Phase 4 as an extra measure of experimental control.

For general classroom use when rigorous experimental control is unnecessary, teachers may omit the phase that moves the behavior back toward the original baseline (e.g., Phase 3, Figure 5.17). The utility of this design is that it allows students to see progress that is being made gradually. This feature is very important when considering the learning styles of students with mild and moderate handicaps.

For example, some learners with behavior disorders, learning disabilities, and mild mental handicaps become extremely frustrated when faced with what seems to them as an insurmountable task. A teacher can use the changing-criterion design to demonstrate to these learners that their improvement toward criterion is gradual and should not be expected to occur immediately.

Figure 5.18 provides an example of a changing-criterion design that targets a gradual improvement of a student's reading comprehension skill as measured by short,

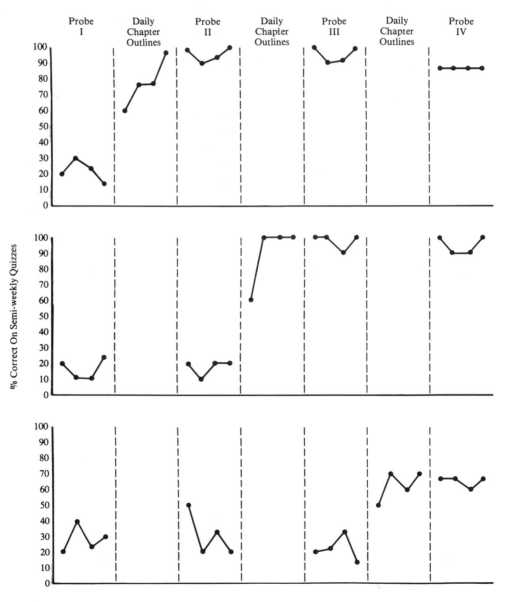

■ FIGURE 5.16
Example of a Multiple Probe Design

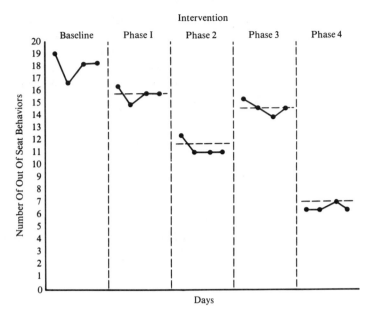

■ FIGURE 5.17
Example of a Changing Criterion Design for Monitoring Out-of-Seat Behaviors

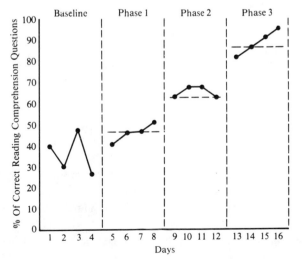

■ FIGURE 5.18
Example of a Changing Criterion Design to Measure Improvement in Reading Comprehension Skills

daily probes. Changing-criterion designs can also act as reinforcers for students who see the preset criterion as a challenge and attempt to meet the new goals. Initially, the teacher might incorporate an additional reinforcer into the program that the students can earn if they meet or exceed the preset criteria on any given day. Eventually, the reinforcer can be faded out, and for many learners the chart will take on reinforcing characteristics.

KEY CONCEPTS

A system of monitoring student performance is a vital component of ABA programs. This system usually results in charting student behaviors, making it easier to *see* slower learning rates and to discover problems with interventions.

■ Line, cumulative, and ratio graphs do not allow teachers to establish a cause-and-effect relationship between their intervention and student behaviors. These graphs do, however, allow for a relatively simple way to monitor student progress.

■ Single-subject designs are methods of charting that allow teachers to experimentally verify the cause-and-effect relationship between teaching strategies and student behaviors.

■ A B designs are the easiest to use and the least rigorous in terms of experimental control. The "A" represents the baseline phase, during which the teacher measures the target behaviors before any intervention occurs. The "B" represents the intervention phase, which is a measure of the target behavior after the intervention is applied. Any subsequent changes *might* be attributed to the intervention.

■ Additional phases can be added to the A B design if the teacher wishes to try more than one intervention on the same behavior (e.g., A B C D E . . .).

■ Reversal designs are more sophisticated than A B designs because they require a return to baseline, attempting to prove that without the intervention the target behavior will return to the previous levels. This design becomes more powerful as the number of reversals increases (e.g., A B A B . . .). Reversal designs cannot effectively measure acquired behaviors (e.g., academic skills) and should never be used to reverse behaviors when ethical questions are of concern (e.g., self-injurious behaviors, aggressive behaviors).

■ Multiple-baseline designs have great potential for use in classrooms for retarded learners. They can be used to measure the effects of teaching strategies on a student's behaviors across different settings. These designs can also measure the effects of teaching strategies across more than one individual (e.g., token reinforcement on the student's completion of homework assignments). Finally, multiple baselines can be used to measure the effectiveness of a treatment across more than one behavior of an individual (e.g., ignoring and praise on Pam's out-of-seat, talking, and note-passing behaviors).

■ Multiple baselines establish experimental control by successively applying the treatment at different intervals to different baselines.

■ Multiple-probe designs, a variation of the multiple baseline, eliminates the need for continuous (i.e., daily) measurement.

■ Changing-criterion designs help students and teachers see a gradual improvement toward a desired goal.

■ ■ ■ ■

CHAPTER SIX

DEVELOPING INSTRUCTIONAL INTERVENTIONS, PART II: TECHNIQUES FOR CHANGING LEARNER BEHAVIORS

■ Teachers may fail to realize the utility of behavioral teaching strategies, and they also may fail to recognize exactly what they do in the teaching process. Some lesson plans describe in great detail what the student will do, but they present no description of what the teacher does during the instructional process. Lovitt (1976) stated that a crucial element of applied behavior analysis (ABA) teaching programs is that all teaching procedures must be replicable. For example, a typical description of a teacher-learner situation might be that the teacher will present the learner with a discrimination task that, if successfully completed, will be reinforced. Unfortunately, this statement's lack of precision makes it impossible to understand or analyze what variables are occurring, which makes it impossible to judge the effectiveness of instruction. A replicable description might state that the teacher will model the discrimination task in conjunction with verbal directions, subsequently following the model with a graduated guidance procedure. Each time the learner correctly completes the task, a social reinforcer (e.g., smile) and a verbal reinforcer (e.g., "good job") are presented.

Along with behavioral strategies, there are two other categories of strategies that teachers can use to guide students with mild and moderate handicaps toward exhibiting more appropriate behaviors: counseling approaches and cognitive behavior management strategies. These strategies require the same replication and measurement that are traditionally associated with operant procedures. For example, some teachers of students with BD use one or more aspects of the life space interview (LSI) to assist their students during crisis situations (Morse, 1959). This counseling strategy helps teachers and learners establish communication during a crisis (e.g., fights, temper tantrum) and explore the situation surrounding the incident.

The key is to describe, in terms that are as exact as possible, how the LSI will progress so that other professionals such as regular educators can use the same procedures. It would be appropriate to share these strategies only after they had proved to be effective with the learner. In this instance, the teacher might have been recording incidents of fighting using an AB design to monitor progress (decrease in fights) after the LSI had been instituted.

USING A VARIETY OF STRATEGIES

To some professionals, it is shocking to mention behavioral (operant) procedures and counseling and/or cognitive behavior management approaches in the same chapter. Historically, these approaches have been viewed as incompatible, with each camp extolling the many disadvantages of the other while listing their own positive, long-lasting effects on the individuals they serve.

Unfortunately, these philosophical battles may force teachers into one specific camp and hinder them from obtaining other skills that can be extremely useful for helping students. This chapter provides information that will allow teachers to gain entry-level skills in using a variety of procedures for changing learner behavior. The focus of the chapter is to demonstrate a link between the procedures and provide examples of how they can be used concurrently to assist learners in obtaining and exhibiting more socially acceptable behaviors.

COUNSELING PROCEDURES

Learners with mild and moderate handicapping conditions have many psychological and physical needs that, if not met, can result in the manifestation of inappropriate or socially unacceptable behaviors. Many problems between teachers and students that often escalate into major incidents do so because teachers overlook or fail to understand the basic needs of students.

Maslow (1970) has long been recognized for his theory of self-actualization. Basically, Maslow believed that individuals must have certain physiological and psychological needs met before they can reach self-actualization. He theorized that when these basic needs are not met for school-aged children, the likelihood of inappropriate behavior will increase.

From a common-sense standpoint, Maslow's ideas do answer some of the questions concerning the inappropriate behaviors of some learners. For example, students need to have basic physiological needs met before they can be expected to learn. School breakfast and lunch programs have gone a long way toward helping hungry students. However, students whose parents do not provide appropriate supervision or establish specific bedtime rules may be attending school with far less sleep than they need.

Along with physiological needs, learners have a need for safety and security. Aside from the basic safety and security issues surrounding physical abuse, students need to feel safe from psychological abuse from peers and teachers. This issue will be a key component in a later discussion on the counseling strategies for behavior management.

Maslow also addressed the need to belong and the need for affection, as well as the need for self-respect. Finally, students need to see the relevance of activities presented. Irrelevant activities may be the root of many behavior problems.

One need stands out in terms of its effect on the ultimate relationship that is established between teachers and learners: All people have the need to feel in control of their lives. This need for *power* varies among individuals, but generally those who feel little control over what is happening around them tend to engage in some type of unacceptable behavior ranging from withdrawal to aggression.

Many teachers perceive students' attempts to control their own lives as a threat to their authority. This is unfortunate because the natural process of a child's claim to his or her life is a desirable development.

Understanding the needs of students may not directly change inappropriate behaviors, but such understanding may serve to temper how teachers react. The reactions a teacher exhibits can serve to minimize a tense situation or exacerbate it, possibly causing it to escalate out of control. For example, understanding that middle school learners need to socialize with their peers can direct teachers into avoiding unnecessary conflicts. Providing 2 to 3 minutes at the beginning of an instructional session allows students time to catch up on their social happenings. This short time period might serve to decrease the probability of outbreaks later in the session.

IDEA FILE

Sharing power with students in a more democratic fashion need not result in classroom anarchy. On the contrary, it allows students to feel ownership in the program, which can decrease instances of inappropriate behavior. The following list presents some suggestions for allowing students to participate in the governing of their lives:

■ Daily roundtable sessions can be conducted on group business, problems, and other issues, which can be discussed and for which solutions can be developed.

■ Students can negotiate, discuss, and vote on important class rules, reward systems, and possibly *mild* fines for violations of rules.

■ Students can participate in identifying community sites where instructional activities can be developed.

■ Students can help develop the class schedule and assist in room arrangement and decor.

■ Students can help identify the skills they will learn, and they can participate in evaluating the success of the program.

■ ■ ■ ■

IMPROVING COMMUNICATION WITH STUDENTS

A barrier that often arises between teachers and their students involves either a lack of communication or an inappropriate form of communication. Haim Ginott (1971), in his book *Teacher and Child,* observed that teachers cannot control what students say during the communication process but they can control the messages they send back to students. He believed that the most important part of classroom discipline is the teacher's own self-discipline (Charles, 1989). Basically, the thrust of Ginott's philosophy was to demonstrate to teachers how they can help or harm the way students view themselves. When they verbally attack students, either intentionally or unintentionally, they set the stage for reprisals in the form of misbehaviors or withdrawal.

Ginott advocated using what he called *congruent communication,* a method of speaking to students that outlines what is happening without attacking the student personally. This form of communication invites cooperation instead of demanding it, and it also eliminates sarcasm and personal attacks from the teacher's verbal repertoire regardless of student provocation. In addition, Ginott pointed out that labeling with caustic statements such as "You're always causing trouble!" only serves to exacerbate existing problems.

As an alternative, Ginott suggested the use of "sane messages" and "I" statements as a preferred method for communication. Sane messages are a means to simply describe what is happening without making a personal attack on any one student. For example, a teacher might say to the class "We must respect the feelings of other shoppers and be as quiet as possible" as a sane response to misbehavior during a community activity. This statement is different from "Jamar and Robert be quiet! You two are always a nuisance!"

"I" statements allow teachers to demonstrate that they are human and express feelings of anger without verbally attacking the student. Statements such as "I get angry when other people cannot concentrate on their jobs because of too much noise" conveys a better picture of the problem. Using "you" statements, such as "you are noisy," directs the problem toward one student, which invites retaliation or a continued reinforcement that "you are bad."

Many authors have supported the notion that improved communication between teachers and students results in improved student behaviors (e.g., Charles, 1989). Improving communication and treating students the way we want others to treat us is merely a use of a most powerful teaching tool: modeling. Gordon (1974), in his book *Teacher Effectiveness Training,* argued that when teachers use adverse tactics such as ordering, threatening, preaching, criticizing, and ridiculing they are actually modeling socially unacceptable behaviors that become roadblocks to further communication.

Similarly, Glasser (1969, 1985) observed that teachers can help students make good behavioral choices through improving communication and sharing responsibilities that allow students more control over their lives. There are many other examples of authors whose theories support the need for universal communication as a preventive measure in classroom management (e.g., Center, 1989; Webber & Coleman, 1988). They all have one basic principle in common, namely that teachers can be good models or bad models in terms of personal discipline, and only they can choose which they wish to be. If they choose to be bad models, they should accept the fact that student misbehavior will occur.

COGNITIVE BEHAVIOR MANAGEMENT

A number of behavior management approaches that have arisen from social learning theory and cognitive psychology have become more popular in recent years (Mann & Sabatino, 1985). These approaches, categorized as *cognitive behavior management,* blend the theories of cognitive, affective, and behavioral researchers to develop strategies for changing behaviors through cognitive means (Harris, 1988).

Basically, cognitive behavior management procedures attempt to modify and control behavior through cognitive change. Learners are taught to use strategies for imaging, thinking, adjusting attitudes, and using inner language to involve more appropriate behaviors (Meichenbaum & Asarnow, 1979). Hobbs, Moguin, and Troyler (1980) have categorized cognitive behavior management strategies into the following three types:

1. *Self-instructional training.* Students are taught verbal coping strategies that they repeat to themselves in problem situations (e.g., "Okay, what do I care if he calls me 'retard'! I can do a lot of good things! Smile and walk away").

2. *Problem-solving techniques.* Students are taught to repeat to themselves the steps required or the strategies needed to complete the task successfully (e.g., "First, find the coded price sticker under the first item, then look for the cost per unit, ounces, for example, and write it down. Next, find the sticker under the second item, find the cost per unit and write it down. Now choose the one that costs *less* per unit").

3. *Cognitive modeling.* Students are taught to model a peer or teacher who verbalizes the things that the student will imitate. This strategy is used to teach the students the first two techniques.

Meichenbaum and Goodman (1979) outlined a training sequence that can be used readily to teach learners with mild and moderate mental handicaps, learning disabilities, and behavior disorders. First, the teacher uses cognitive modeling to teach the student the cognitive strategy. Second, the teacher overtly guides the student through the task with verbal prompts and additional cues as necessary. Third, the teacher fades the prompting of self-guidance, encouraging the student to whisper the instructions while completing the task. Finally, the student uses covert self-instruction by performing the task using covert self-speech (silent speech).

The results of a number of research studies have demonstrated the effectiveness of cognitive behavior management strategies with students who have mild and moderate handicapping conditions. For example, Hallahan, Marshall, and Lloyd (1981) taught three students to self-monitor their on-task behavior during reading lessons. A tape recorder cued the students at certain intervals to ask themselves "Was I paying attention?". After a period of time, the recorded cues were faded and a visual prompt, the statement on the blackboard, remained. All three students made significant improvement in their on-task skills.

As previously mentioned, traditional approaches to behavior management tend to separate counseling/communication approaches, cognitive behavior management, and operant procedures as incompatible styles that cannot be used together. In practice, this view discourages professionals from using many useful tools. An eclectic approach allows teachers to use procedures that work with some students and not others. Also, such an approach allows teachers to combine strategies that may make any one strategy more powerful.

For example, the use of polite communication and improved listening skills may enhance the effectiveness of a token reinforcement system (to be explained later in this chapter). Similarly, pairing a cognitive behavior management strategy with a tangible reinforcer during the beginning stages of training may speed up the desired results by increasing the student's motivation.

In any case, the key to accurate measurement of student progress is important regardless of the strategies used. If a teacher chooses to institute Glasser's (1969) reality therapy in the classroom, it is important to measure changes in the student's behaviors reliably (see Chapter Five). The results of such measurement activities allow teachers to make informal judgments concerning program effectiveness.

APPLYING BEHAVIORAL TEACHING STRATEGIES

Before the appropriate instructional procedure can be chosen, teachers must decide what effects they wish to have on student behaviors. To begin the process, it may be helpful to categorize the behaviors targeted for change. A simple procedure is to view behavior change in one of four ways: (1) increasing (accelerating) new or existing behaviors; (2) decreasing (decelerating) inappropriate behaviors; (3) maintaining existing behaviors; and (4) generalizing learned behaviors (Evans et al., 1989; Kysela & Hillyard, 1978; Snell & Smith, 1978; Sulzer-Azaroff & Mayer, 1977). All behaviors of learners should fall into one of these categories. Behavioral procedures (teaching strategies) are designed to change behavior in one of these four ways.

REINFORCEMENT

Technically, reinforcers are stimuli that, when applied as a consequence of a behavior, increase the probability that the behavior will reoccur. The principle of reinforcement is relatively easy to understand, and that may be one reason why it has been misused. When the principles of primary reinforcement became popular among educators, there was a rather abrupt increase in the use of sweets (candies) to modify the behavior of learners. At times these sweets were administered in an unsystematic manner, and at times they were not contingent upon the target behavior but rather a series of behaviors. As children began to catch on to the system, these sound behavioral principles became known as bribing and ultimately took on a negative image among some teachers—a situation analogous to blaming the hammer for pounding a nail in crooked.

At least a decade has passed since the push to use edible reinforcers, but some of these same problems may still be evident. Changes have occurred in the type of edibles that are used, but not in the quality of use. Recent visits by the author to some classes for young learners with mild mental handicaps found that candy has given way to sweet cereal, or in more health-oriented programs apples and raisins. Although these changes may be appropriate, they will need to reflect a more systematic and precise use of the principles of reinforcement before desired changes in behaviors can occur.

A variation of the old saying that "one person's bread is another person's poison" can represent the basic foundation of reinforcement. Reinforcers that may be highly preferred by one learner may have little or no effect on others. Similarly, an event that may appear to be punishing to one person may, in fact, be reinforcing to others. These two examples illustrate why some teachers may have problems when using reinforcers. A first step for teachers is to incorporate techniques and/or observations designed to establish a hierarchy of reinforcers for each learner as part of their assessment strategies.

IDEA FILE

Many students have little experience with a wide variety of reinforcers. For example, a student who has never heard jazz music will not choose jazz records as reinforcers. Teachers can better assess a learner's hierarchy of reinforcers by exposing the student to a wide variety of potentially pleasant experiences. This assessment technique is called *reinforcer sampling.* It can be implemented in two ways.

First, teachers can observe students engaging in normal daily activities. The activities, materials, and other individuals most frequently approached by each learner can be considered reinforcing.

A second technique is to structure situations in which students can be exposed to different activities, materials, and individuals, noting which ones appear to be preferred (sometimes called a *reinforcer menu*). The reinforcers for each student are then ranked in terms of preference. Also, teachers can talk to the students, their parents, and siblings to establish other potential reinforcers.

In its own right, community-based instruction can be highly reinforcing for many students. Similar to basic physiological and psychological needs, students have an educational need to see the relevance in what they are being asked to learn. CBI is a highly reinforcing way to help students see the relationship between academic and social skills training and real-life events.

■ ■ ■ ■

Positive Versus Negative Reinforcers

Positive reinforcers are consequences that, when paired with behaviors, cause an increase in or strengthen the rate of response. If the behavior does not increase or maintain itself after a specific consequence has been applied, that consequence is not a positive reinforcer. Negative reinforcers also increase or maintain the behavior they are connected with; the difference is that negative reinforcers are aversive consequences which when *removed* from the situation cause the behavior to increase. Negative reinforcers are frequently used by teachers. When a teacher tells a student that she must complete her workbook activities before she can go with the rest of the class to recess, the teacher is using negative reinforcement. The aversive consequence of missing recess will be removed when the student completes her assignment. Some teachers use academic work as negative reinforcers, which may cause students to dislike their assignments.

Negative reinforcers resemble punishers only because they may stimulate adverse side effects in the student. In the example just cited, the danger is that the student will come to dislike workbook activities and attempt to avoid them. The misuse of negative reinforcers may be partially responsible for student dislike of academic tasks. Negative reinforcers are different from punishers in their effect on behaviors. Negative reinforcers tend to increase behaviors, whereas punishers tend to decrease behaviors. A reinforcer, then, serves to increase or maintain the level of a behavior.

Effective Use of Reinforcers: Relationship to Behaviors

Teachers can enhance the effectiveness of their positive reinforcement systems by precisely defining the behaviors they wish to reinforce. This step relates to the important principle of *immediacy of reinforcement;* that is, a poorly defined behavior makes it difficult to present the reinforcer immediately following that behavior. Moreover, an imprecisely defined behavior may result in the teacher's inadvertently reinforcing the wrong behavior.

For example, a teacher wishing to reinforce a learner for "appropriate verbalizations" needs to define the kinds of verbalizations that are considered appropriate. Otherwise, utterances such as curses and screams may be reinforced by mistake. Similarly, if a behavior has not been defined in a manner identifying a clear beginning and ending, such as the completion of an assembly task, the teacher may fail to reinforce the behavior as soon as it is completed.

Levels of Reinforcers

Positive reinforcers are enhanced when teachers match the most effective reinforcers to specific learners. Therefore, teachers should understand a reinforcer hierarchy (MacMillan, 1973; Snell & Smith, 1978) and how the levels of primary, secondary, and generalized reinforcers affect students.

Edible reinforcers are powerful tools for use with learners if not abused or overused. The use of nutritious foods such as fruits and vegetables is desirable. However, teachers should be aware that satiation may occur if a specific food item is used too often. Overuse of reinforcers should be avoided at all costs. Edibles should be distributed in small quantities and should always be paired with a social reinforcer (e.g., a smile, a pat on the back). For instance, younger children may respond better to a small quantity of a reinforcer (one raisin or one piece of unsweetened cereal) paired with a *very* enthusiastic delivery ("Great job" or physical contact such as a pat on the arm).

Tangible reinforcers are the next level of the hierarchy. They include items such as toys, comic books, colored pencils, and free time. Teachers may look negatively upon tangible reinforcers because of excess cost or problems associated with presenting such reinforcers in conjunction with the behavior (Sulzer-Azaroff & Mayer, 1977). Tangible reinforcers do, however, improve the learning of some students and are generally most effective when used in conjunction with a token system.

Tangible reinforcers alone can be used effectively if two points are kept in mind. First, more complex behaviors merit more expensive rewards. In other words, you would not present a learner with a record album for completing one math assignment. Instead, the album may be contingent on a series of complex behaviors, such as using math skills appropriately in a number of community settings. Second, it may be wise to use tangible reinforcers that have many parts (Sulzer-Azaroff & Mayer, 1977). In this way, a student can earn, for example, a different crayon for each completed task, culminating in the presentation of a coloring book when the sequence of skills is combined to produce a completed task. This technique eliminates the possibility of using up potent reinforcers early and not having additional tangibles that are as effective for the remaining sequence.

The third step in a positive reinforcer hierarchy involves the use of token reinforcers. Token reinforcer systems are characterized by allowing students to earn points for specific behaviors that can be "cashed in" at a later time for various tangible reinforcers. In classrooms, group homes, workshops, community-based training sites, or on-the-job placements, token economy systems can be an effective tool for changing the behaviors of learners. Token systems may be the best available tool for teaching learners to defer reinforcement. In many ways, these systems are effective methods of simulating work-for-pay situations.

The final step in a positive reinforcer hierarchy involves approval (praise) by significant others. Social reinforcers, such as smiles, verbal praise, a pat on the back, or a handshake are the types of reinforcers teachers should work students toward. The utility of social reinforcers lends strong support for their use because of their ease of application and the extent to which they are available in the natural setting. If the primary goal is to assist learners to be as independent as possible, the use of social reinforcers becomes an important program component. Therefore, it is important to pair social reinforcers with each presentation of edible, tangible, or token reinforcers. The goal is to fade the primary reinforcers gradually and allow behaviors to come under the control of social reinforcers.

In general, it is best to use the highest level of reinforcer that works with a learner and move on to the next highest level as quickly as possible. For example, a teacher would not choose to use edibles for a learner with a moderate mental handicap if tangible reinforcers proved to be effective. Likewise, the teacher would attempt to move the learner promptly to the next higher level of a token economy. This effort moves the learner closer to more natural contingencies.

Additional Considerations for Using Positive Reinforcement

Maximizing the effects of reinforcers requires that students have a clear indication of the conditions for reinforcement. For example, if a student is to be reinforced after completing a certain number of tasks or at a certain time of the day, the delivery of the reinforcers and the conditions must remain constant.

Deprivation of reinforcers is an important concept to consider when using edible reinforcers. Martin and Pear (1978) have defined deprivation as the time period that precedes any teaching in which the learner has not come in contact with the reinforcer. For example, presenting an edible reinforcer soon after a student's lunch period probably will minimize the strength of the reinforcer. Training sessions should be scheduled to allow a reasonable gap between when the student has eaten and when edibles are used as reinforcers.

Severe conditions of deprivation are unethical (Martin & Pear, 1978). Under *no* circumstances should teachers develop programs that incorporate intensive deprivation conditions such as eliminating a student's breakfast and lunch so that edible reinforcers will be more powerful. Natural deprivation that is part of a student's daily schedule is a more appropriate option. For example, a teacher may wait until just before a learner leaves school to present instruction for which edibles are reinforcers. In this case, there has been a reasonable length of time since the lunch period, and the potency of the reinforcer is increased.

Using highly preferred activities to strengthen the response of nonpreferred ones is another form of reinforcement, known as the *Premack Principle*. Students often will engage in a behavior that otherwise has a low probability of occurring provided that they are then allowed to engage in behaviors that have a high probability of occurring (Premack, 1959). Parents and grandparents have for ages found this principle to be effective when they have told children, "Finish your chores and then you can go out and play."

Teachers can find many uses for the Premack Principle (e.g., "Finish your arithmetic and you can have extra recess time."). However, the failure to use this approach to reinforcement systematically can cause it to be less than effective. When using preferred activities it is important to establish firm conditions under which the behavior is to be reinforced and to use preferred activities sparingly.

KEY CONCEPTS

- A positive reinforcer is a stimulus that, when paired with a behavior as its consequence, either maintains the behavior at the current level or increases the probability that the behavior will reoccur.

- Positive reinforcers will be most effective when their presentation is *contingent* upon the production of the target behavior and is administered *immediately* following the behavior in question.

- Negative reinforcers *are not* punishers, because they tend to increase the behaviors they are paired with while behaviors paired with punishers tend to decrease. The key to understanding how negative reinforcers influence behavior is based on the concept of removal of an aversive stimulus or escape from one. If the teacher pairs the removal of an aversive stimulus with an increase in a desired behavior, a negative reinforcer has been used.

- Using counseling strategies such as listening closely to students and taking a relaxed, unassuming approach may be more reinforcing than an aggressive, demanding posture.

- Negative reinforcers should be used with caution since they can trigger aversive side effects in some students. Some students become aggressive when presented with an either/or choice, and they can also learn to dislike the desired behavior if they perceive that it caused them to be subject to the aversive consequence.

- Positive reinforcers that can be used with learners fall into four categories: edible, tangible, token, and social reinforcers. Each of these can be powerful tools for behavior change if not abused or overused.

- Students should have a clear indication of the condition under which they will be reinforced.

- Satiation results when a student is overexposed to a given reinforcer and its effect is severely weakened. This is especially true with edible reinforcers.

- Deprivation or the space of time between meals can either strengthen or weaken the effects of edible reinforcers. For example, using edibles after lunch tends to weaken their effect.

- The Premack Principle is a powerful tool for change. Highly preferred activities are used to strengthen the responses of less preferred ones.

■ ■ ■ ■

STIMULUS CONTROL: INCREASING NEW OR EXISTING BEHAVIORS

Antecedent stimuli are a set of events preceding behaviors that have a profound influence on the direction those behaviors will take. A stimulus is any one or a set of events, objects, or changes in the environment that results in a change in a learner's behavior (Miller, 1980). In an instructional setting, stimuli exist that may increase the probability that a student's behavior will reoccur in the presence of those events, objects, or changes in the environment. For example, a teacher's saying to the class, "Let's get ready for lunch" increases the probability that activities will cease, materials will be returned to their places, and students will begin washing their hands.

Identifying and analyzing antecedent stimuli that trigger learner behaviors is a most important teacher responsibility. Teachers may fail to see the cause-and-effect relationships between what they do and how learners react, and the relationship between the behaviors of learners and their effects on other students can also be easily overlooked. This section presents strategies of stimulus control, that is, techniques for increasing the probability that a learner behavior will occur in the presence of certain stimuli and not in the presence of others. Stimulus control through a systematic arranging of antecedents is a technique for teaching learners with mild to moderate handicaps to discriminate among environmental events.

Discriminating Among Environmental Events

Historically, some professionals have felt that individuals with handicapping conditions had a deficit in the ability to discriminate, that is, the ability to detect differences in objects, events, and behaviors needed to respond appropriately in different situations.

The use of systematic and precise instructional strategies for teaching appropriate discrimination skills appears to remediate some of these deficits (Westling & Koorland, 1979). For example, a nonhandicapped infant is apt to pick up subtle cues from its mother as she prompts the baby to babble—a behavior that brings immediate reinforcement. An infant who has developmental delays, with some degree of sensory deprivation or other problems, may not pick up on these cues. Over time, reinforcers for the parents tend to decrease as the baby fails to generate responses, and this exacerbates the problem. Conversely, parents of these infants should *increase* their talking and babbling in order to help the infant to begin discriminating among sounds.

Differential Reinforcement

The procedure for teaching learners to exhibit certain behaviors in the presence of specific stimuli while inhibiting responses in the presence of others is called *differential reinforcement*. This strategy involves reinforcing a learner under certain conditions and not under others. For example, each time a student is about to enter the bathroom, the teacher points and says, "Mike, you're going to the men's room." If the teacher reinforces Mike when he enters the room, Mike should respond to the sign "Men," discriminating between the different bathrooms. The term for a stimulus occurring prior to a behavior that will be positively reinforced upon its occurrence is *discriminative stimulus* (S^D). For example, if a teacher wishes to have a learner change assignments, the teacher may press a low-frequency buzzer, reinforcing the learner only when the change is made. Over a number of trials the buzzer will become the S^D, increasing the probability that in its presence the learner will appropriately change assignments.

Two other ways to use differential reinforcement for stimulus control include choosing not to reinforce a learner's response when it occurs in the presence of a stimulus ($S^\triangle$) or choosing to punish a response when it occurs in the presence of a stimulus (S^{D-}). Teaching learners to discriminate appropriately, then, involves either positively reinforcing, ignoring, or punishing behaviors when they occur in the presence of specific stimuli. Teaching learners with mild to moderate handicaps requires precision in identifying the stimuli important for control purposes and also in correctly reinforcing those stimuli once identified.

Teachers should consider a number of points before developing programs aimed at bringing behaviors under the control of environmental stimuli. First, the stimuli chosen by the teacher (e.g., verbal directions, events) must be clear and distinct. Stimuli can be identified adequately when teachers make a written list designating the condition under which the behavior should occur as well as what conditions are inappropriate.

Students must know exactly what the S^D involves, along with the target response expected and the method of reinforcement. This communication can be enhanced by posting and referring to specific rules (Martin & Pear, 1978). The use of verbal directions by teachers must be concise. Teachers may have a tendency to combine a number of verbal directions with no clear beginnings and endings to their requests (Langone, Koorland, & Oseroff, 1987). For learners who have auditory processing problems, such directions may increase confusion.

Teachers must find a way to clarify S^Ds for learners who have difficulty comprehending rules and verbal directions. Clarifying S^Ds can be accomplished by developing distinct cues to catch the learner's attention. The teacher can also schedule several opportunities for the learner to come into contact with the designated stimulus. This allows the teacher to guide the behavior and subsequently reinforce it, structuring a number of pairings of the discriminative stimulus and behavior to allow additional reinforcement.

Choosing and appropriately applying the best reinforcement procedures for each learner is vital. Some learners do not respond to what are considered appropriate reinforcers such as social praise. As a result, teachers can become frustrated in their efforts to change behavior.

CASE STUDY

"S^D, S^D, S^D, who does this nut from the university think we are, physics professors?" exclaimed Betty. "This inservice course was supposed to teach me to teach my kids, and all she's doing is talking about discriminative something or other!"

"Now don't get all worked up, Betty. Dr. S. Control has some good ideas," said Gene. "Remember, the examples she used to teach academic skills were very good and made me realize that my behaviors have a tremendous influence on how the kids will react."

Betty asked, "Well, explain to me how all this mumbo jumbo is going to help me teach reading."

Shaking his head, Gene stated, "One example of an S^D is when you ask your kids to pick out the words you read them that begin with a certain sound. When students identify a correct word you reinforce them with social praise. That's an example of a discriminative stimulus that will increase the probability that they'll get the right answer when you read the words aloud."

"OK, I understand how that can be useful, but what's this $S^\triangle$ and S^{D-} stuff?"

"$S^\triangle$s are easy to remember because you ignore a wrong answer, providing no reinforcer, and redirect the student toward the correct choice. S^{D-}s are used very infrequently because they involve punishing a response in the presence of a given stimulus. Dr. Control told us that punishers have many bad side effects and may not be worth using."

Betty looked relieved. "When you explain it, I can understand how discriminative stimuli can be more helpful if I use them more precisely and am careful about whether or not I reinforce or ignore my kids' responses. Does that mean that everything I do affects how my kids will respond?"

"Just about," answered Gene. "Verbal instructions, models, prompts, written cues, and guidance are all considered discriminative stimuli."

"Now I understand," said Betty. "I can't wait until our next cocktail party, when I can impress my wise-guy science teacher neighbor with my new technical vocabulary! By carefully using S^Ds I'll get him talking about what I want to talk about for a change."

"The idea, Betty, was to use S^Ds to be a better teacher, remember?" asked Gene.

"Oh, yeah, that too!"

■ ■ ■ ■

Implications for Teaching

Stimulus control involves action by the teacher that is either direct, such as a physical prompt, or indirect, such as a written cue. The goal of arranging antecedent stimuli is to increase the probability that the desired learner outcome will occur. First, teachers must be more aware of the quality of the verbal directions they use with learners since, with the constant action and interaction occurring within classrooms, verbal instructions can become confusing.

IDEA FILE

- The teacher should get the student's attention before presenting the instruction. A rule of thumb would be to have the learner look at the teacher's face just prior to and during the verbal direction. (Langone et al., 1987).
- Verbal instructions should have a clear onset and offset. Also, in most cases one verbal direction should be presented at a time. When it is necessary to provide more than one instruction at a time, there should be a distinct pause between directions. (Langone et al., 1987).
- Verbal directions should be sequenced in the order in which the student is expected to perform them (Sulzer-Azaroff & Mayer, 1977).
- In many cases teachers should speak slowly, using sentences with appropriate vocabulary and simple word combinations (Snell & Smith, 1978).
- Teachers should determine whether or not the target response is in the learner's repertoire (Sulzer-Azaroff & Mayer, 1977) so that the instruction given is not beyond the student's present functioning level.
- Teachers should assess whether or not the verbal direction is, in fact, an effective discriminative stimulus (Sulzer-Azaroff & Mayer, 1977). Teachers may erroneously assume that instructions have been in the presence of a behavior long enough for the response to be adequately reinforced.

■ ■ ■ ■

Verbal Directions

Verbal directions are the most sophisticated of stimulus control procedures. The ability to live independently requires that individuals be able to respond appropriately to the verbal instructions and requests of others. Conversely, there might be times when a person would be responding appropriately to a verbal instruction by not responding at all, for example, if a peer were to instruct him to shoplift. In either case, the ability to discriminate and act on verbal directions is an important competency for learners. Nevertheless, some learners with mild to moderate disabilities have inadequate or no skills for being able to follow directions alone (Dunlap, Koegel, & Burke, 1981). Consequently, teachers initially must pair verbal directions with other techniques of stimulus control, eventually getting the learner to respond to verbal instructions alone or, in most cases, to environmental stimuli that trigger the need for them to perform certain behaviors (Richman, Reiss, Bauman, & Bailey, 1984).

Modeling

Modeling is an important teaching tool. Unfortunately, some individuals demonstrate a severe deficiency in their ability to model the behaviors of others (Whitman & Scibak, 1979), and teachers do not appear to use modeling techniques to their fullest advantage (Langone et al., 1987). The result may be the loss of a valuable teaching technique.

Modeling involves demonstrating a sequence of skills as a complete set or simply demonstrating isolated steps in a sequence. The learner watches the demonstration and is then required to imitate the desired responses.

IDEA FILE

- Teachers should always get the student's attention prior to each step in the modeling procedure (e.g., Neef, Walters, & Egel, 1984). One suggestion is to direct the learner's view toward the task being modeled (e.g., hands in an assembly task) (Langone et al., 1987).

- Teachers should combine clear, concise verbal directions with the modeling procedure (Langone et al., 1987).

- A model must be carefully chosen. Learners tend to model more readily the behaviors of others who have characteristics similar to their own (e.g., same-sex models), and they will also model the behaviors of others they deem prestigious. Therefore, teachers should point out the similar characteristics of the model and use class leaders as models in a peer tutoring process (Sulzer-Azaroff & Mayer, 1977).

- Teachers should keep the modeling process as simple as possible. If an instructional analysis has been designed properly, the teacher follows the sequential steps from the easier to the more difficult (Martin & Pear, 1978).

- Teachers can use effective reinforcement procedures to reinforce correct modeling behaviors of learners. Learners tend to imitate more readily when the models have been reinforced for their behavior (Sulzer-Azaroff & Mayer, 1977).

- Teachers should choose models who are familiar to the learner and allow the models to demonstrate competence in the behaviors they are to demonstrate (Sulzer-Azaroff & Mayer, 1977).

- Teachers should always model the behaviors from the same direction that the learner is required to perform the task. This minimizes any left to right confusion (Langone et al., 1987).

■ ■ ■ ■

A variation on modeling procedures that is very effective in teaching prevocational skills to learners is called *match-to-sample modeling*. This technique involves teaching the learner to follow a completed task matching the steps to a completed duplicate sample.

For example, when students are being taught to complete a circuit board assembly, using a completed unit as a sample helps by serving as a reference to the pattern. Similarly, when students are practicing map-reading exercises somewhere in their community, a teacher might issue a color-coded example that serves as a model for them to complete the exercise. Such match-to-sample materials can be developed for many skills, including classroom-based mathematics assignments and cost-comparison shopping exercises in a grocery store.

Physical Prompts

Physically prompting a learner by using gestures or building written cues into instructional materials is a technique of stimulus control. For example, a teacher may *point* to an object and request that the student pick it up. Similarly, when teaching reading comprehension skills a teacher may underline key words in a paragraph in order to cue the student to the main ideas of the passage. In each case, the teacher systematically attempts to direct the learner's attention to some relevant stimulus of the task.

IDEA FILE

- Teachers should always use a clear verbal direction with each prompt and cue, following the rules for verbal directions stated earlier in this chapter (Langone et al., 1987).
- When using cues embedded in activities and materials, teachers should make sure the cue is distinct enough in color, shape, or size to direct the learner's attention to the key aspects of the stimulus (Westling & Koorland, 1979).
- Teachers should order prompts and cues in a hierarchy from the most natural to the most artificial (Sulzer-Azaroff & Mayer, 1977). For example, when requiring a learner to discriminate between two different colors of transistors, the most natural prompt may be to point in the direction of the desired color. The most artificial prompt, then, may be to push the desired transistor closer to the student, facilitating the choice of that object.
- Teachers should not overuse any prompt or cue that encourages the learner to become overly dependent on it (Sulzer-Azaroff & Mayer, 1977). A general rule of thumb is to fade the prompt or cue as soon as possible.
- Teachers can use a combination of prompts and cues as required by student needs, carefully fading one element of the combination at a time (Fisher & Zeaman, 1973). Initial teaching of a skill may require the use of two or more artificial prompts and cues, for example, pointing as well as increasing the size and changing the color of the stimulus. However, when fading the cues, the teacher should gradually fade one cue, then another, and so on.

■ ■ ■ ■

Using physical prompts and cues as teaching procedures can be highly effective when applied systematically. Gold (1972), in his now famous bicycle brake study, demonstrated the effectiveness of using color cues in teaching a complex assembly task to learners with cognitive deficits. Similarly, Lovitt (1978, 1984) has demonstrated in a number of research projects the utility of prompts and cues in teaching academic skills to individuals with learning disabilities.

Physical Guidance

The concept of antecedent events is concerned with using a teaching procedure that ensures learner success. Physical guidance involves carefully guiding the learner through the desired task by shadowing the student's movements. For instance, golf pros often shadow a beginner's movements by standing behind the student, placing their hands over the student's grip on the club, and guiding the student through the swing. Likewise, when teaching a psychomotor skill, the teacher can guide the learner through the task by manipulating the learner's hands, arms, or legs. Physical guidance can be subdivided by degrees. The first degree, called *graduated guidance*, involves partially guiding a learner through a task. The second degree, *total guidance*, involves completing the entire task while manipulating the learner's movements (Foxx & Azrin, 1973). Total guidance is designed to ensure the learner's success by guiding the learner through the entire task. This procedure allows for immediate and frequent reinforcement because the student completes the desired task on each trial.

The second degree of guidance gradually directs the learner through the task using varying amounts of hand pressure (Foxx & Azrin, 1973). Graduated guidance may in some cases have more utility for teachers than a total guidance procedure. This technique uses only the amount of force necessary to direct the student toward the desired goals. That is, if a learner resists a teacher's direction, the teacher should use enough force to counteract the opposition. The amount of force used to begin the student's movement will be minimal, increasing only as the need arises (Foxx & Azrin, 1973). For example, when teaching cursive writing, the teacher may assist students by gently touching their writing hands in the direction that the pen should go to complete the letters.

IDEA FILE

Whether a teacher decides to use total or graduated guidance depends on the needs of the learner.

- If a learner is very passive (e.g., limp hands), or if a learner simply resists a teacher's efforts at total guidance, the teacher should use the graduated technique (Foxx & Azrin, 1973).
- Teachers should develop a teaching setting that is relaxed and comfortable, thereby increasing the probability that the learner will resist teacher direction only minimally (Sulzer-Azaroff & Mayer, 1977).
- Teachers should use clear, simple verbal directions with each attempt at guidance (Langone et al., 1987).
- Teachers should fade guidance to a touch or shadow the learner's movement from a short distance away as soon as possible (Foxx & Azrin, 1973).

■ When fading the guidance, teachers should use a smaller degree of the original procedure, such as touching the wrist, the elbow, and finally the back (Snell & Smith, 1978).

■ ■ ■ ■

One technique of presenting the antecedent events (teacher behaviors) is to do so in hierarchical fashion. The hierarchy generally proceeds from giving the most sophisticated S^D of verbal directions to modeling, then physical prompts/cues, and ending with the lowest level of guidance. PROJECT MORE, developed at the University of Kansas, sequences teacher behaviors in this hierarchy and suggests that teachers follow this pattern when teaching skills to learners with moderate cognitive disabilities (Lent & McLean, 1976). The important point is that the level of antecedent teacher behavior used is dependent on learner needs. Information gathered during the assessment process (see Chapter Three) should help the teacher decide the level of S^D that a student comprehends. The teacher begins the instructional presentation by gradually fading each of the lower levels until the student can function under modeling and eventually with only verbal directions.

KEY CONCEPTS

■ Increasing the probability that behaviors will occur and reoccur can be accomplished more efficiently by pairing some form of antecedent stimulus with a consequence following the behavior. Essentially, the teacher provides learners with some type of prompt or cue designed to stimulate the desired responses. If the desired behavior occurs, the teacher positively reinforces it, increasing the probability that it will reoccur when the original prompt or cue is given.

■ Teachers can choose to positively reinforce, ignore, or punish behaviors that occur after antecedent events. Once these events begin to have control over the behaviors, they become *discriminative stimuli* (S^D).

■ Using S^Ds is a method of helping students discriminate between conditions when behaviors may be appropriate or inappropriate. For example, ringing a bell in the classroom may signify that it is time to engage in a noisy game.

■ The most common S^Ds used by teachers are verbal instructions, modeling, physical prompts, visual or auditory cues, and physical guidance.

■ All teachers use S^Ds. The skill is in using S^Ds consistently and precisely across different situations. For example, if a teacher asks a student to complete his mathematics assignment—sometimes punishing him for failure to do so and sometimes ignoring him when assignments are unfinished—she sends mixed signals to the student. It then may become a game, with the learner trying to see if he can "get away with it" when she asks him to do his work.

■ Fading is an important concept that involves the *gradual* removal of less desirable prompts so that behaviors will eventually come under the control of more natural S^Ds (e.g., verbal instructions).

■ ■ ■ ■

Developing New Responses: Shaping and Chaining

Shaping is a strategy designed to develop behaviors not currently in a student's repertoire of responses. The teacher first identifies some response related to the target behavior. The next step is to reinforce any changes in behavior (no matter how minor) until those changes begin to resemble the desired outcome.

For instance, Michael, a student with behavior disorders, lacks many basic social interaction skills. Consequently, he tends to be the scapegoat for other students. Michael's teacher ascertains that he has no assertive conversational skills and that this may be contributing to the problem. Using modeling (both by herself and by peers) and roleplaying, she begins to teach Michael skills such as standing erect, making eye contact, and making statements with little emotional response (e.g., crying). Along with this instruction, Michael's teacher structures scenarios in community environments where a volunteer who is known to Michael approaches him and asks him why he has done something wrong. The *shaping* procedure surfaces here when the teacher reinforces a successive approximation that Michael exhibits in this situation. If he forgets or fails to exhibit any desired behaviors, the teacher can prompt them or revert back to modeling the appropriate responses. The teacher selectively reinforces movements that get closer to the target (*successive approximations*) while discontinuing reinforcement of those approximations when they are no longer useful (*extinction*). The result is a procedure that can be used successfully to develop new academic, language, social, self-care, and vocational behaviors in learners.

Learners with mild handicaps may have a great deal of trouble dealing with large numbers of stimuli presented at one time. Students who are mainstreamed into regular classes for academic subjects often find it difficult to complete assignments involving many parts (e.g., 25 arithmetic problems or 15 reading comprehension questions). Shaping can be a useful technique for helping students gradually be able to complete larger units of work.

For example, out of 25 arithmetic problems, Cassius generally can only complete about 5. His teacher will reinforce him for any improvement over 5 and continue to reinforce him only for improvements over the preceding level. (Improvements may at first consist of writing down one more problem than the original 5, but not completing the answer.) Gradually, the teacher should begin to note an increase in Cassius's completion rate until over time he will meet the target of 25 problems. The quality of his work can be addressed at the same time or after the quantity of work has improved.

IDEA FILE

- Teachers need to be specific in defining target behaviors. General classes of behaviors are too difficult to keep track of when deciding on successive approximations (Martin & Pear, 1978).
- Teachers should carefully identify the most appropriate starting point (Sulzer-Azaroff & Mayer, 1977). In some cases, the point at which shaping begins may only be minimally

related to the target goal. However, choosing behaviors that occur more often increases instructional time.

■ As the learner's behavior becomes more refined, teachers should withhold reinforcement for those behaviors that have become obsolete. (This procedure is called *extinction*). Teachers can reinforce the new approximations of the behavior, extinguishing them in the same fashion when they are no longer useful.

■ Teachers should preset a desirable criterion for each approximation that the learner must reach before continuing to the next approximation (e.g., 70–80% of the trials).

■ When extinguishing undesirable behaviors, teachers may want to rethink their goal and instead try to decrease the frequency or intensity of the behavior (e.g., talking to friends in class).

■ ■ ■ ■

Chaining

When teaching learners a variety of community-based self-care, vocational, and academic skills needed for independent living, the procedure of behavioral chaining can be a valuable tool. The chaining procedure is an essential component of the task analysis process. It involves reinforcing a series of simple sequenced learner behaviors that, when combined, form more complex behaviors. The simple behaviors are in the learner's repertoire before teaching begins; however, they need to be linked together in a sequenced pattern before the complex behavior can be performed.

Chaining can be applied as a forward or backward procedure. For example, when teaching most leisure and recreation skills that require psychomotor skills, either forward or backward chaining may be used. A teacher might choose to teach one student to fish by beginning with baiting the hook, while another student might require more immediate reinforcement in all the steps completed up to, but not including, putting the line into the water.

CASE STUDY

Bill was a high-school-age student with learning disabilities who spent two periods a day in a resource room and the remainder of the day in mainstreamed regular as well as vocational education classes. Mr. Hansom, the resource teacher, discovered that Bill was having a particular problem in his consumer education class in keeping up with the class assignments and grasping the material.

Mr. Hansom approached Ms. Adams to ask her about the problem. "I just don't know what to do Mr. Hansom. Bill tries hard but he can't see the total picture of anything I teach. For example, just yesterday I taught a lesson about the importance of choosing a place to live based on individual and family needs, and when I assigned the homework Bill just looked at me with this blank look on his face!"

"Tell me more about the assignment," said Mr. Hansom.

"Well, I asked them to look in the "For Sale" and "Rental" sections of the newspaper and pick a place to live based on a net income of $1,000 a month for a family of four," answered Ms. Adams.

"I have an idea," claimed Mr. Hansom. "Why don't we develop *successive approximations!*"

"Please, Mr. Hansom, watch your language!"

"No, no, Ms. Adams, you misunderstand me. What I mean is that we can break down the large assignment for Bill and reward him for each step he completes toward the desired outcome."

Ms. Adams and Mr. Hansom worked out the following steps, each a successive approximation toward completion of the desired assignment.

- Bill will locate a home based on its accessibility to mass transit (because he doesn't have a car) and where his job is located.
- Bill will locate a home based on the number of bedrooms needed for him and his wife plus their two boys. He will also take into account the available storage space and size of yard.
- Bill will decide whether or not the school is close enough to their home so he or his wife can walk the boys to and pick them up from school.
- Bill will decide whether or not rental or mortgage costs are in line with their monthly budget based on the proportion of 30% of their total budget (using a calculator).
- Bill will judge whether or not any restrictions to tenants would be undesirable (e.g., no pets).

With this list of successive approximations in hand, Ms. Adams now reinforces Bill each time he completes a "mini-assignment." After he completes all the steps, she will give him another assignment that combines all the approximations at one time.

■ ■ ■ ■

The procedure of backward chaining may be a more appropriate technique for teaching skills that require immediate completion and those that reinforce the learner when the last step in the chain is finished. Teaching young learners to dress is one example in which the completion of the last step first allows students to see the completed task early in the teaching sequence. A second advantage for using the backward chaining procedure was demonstrated by Martin and Pear (1978) in an example of teaching a girl with moderate retardation to make her bed. The last step of the chain is to pull the bedspread over the pillow at the head of the bed. When the backward chaining procedure is applied, each step in the chain, when sufficiently reinforced, eventually becomes an S^D, serving as a cue to the next step.

Teachers have the option to use either forward, backward, or a combination of chaining procedures depending on the learner and the skill to be taught. However, it is important to be aware that when used inappropriately or in an unsystematic and inconsistent fashion, chaining can be a frustrating event for both teachers and students.

IDEA FILE

- Field testing the task analysis with other people such as teachers, aides, general education students, and parents before applying it with learners can improve the teaching sequence.
- Teachers should make sure the steps are taught in proper sequence so that each step in turn becomes a discriminative stimulus (Martin & Pear, 1978).
- Teachers should move slowly through the steps, being sure one step is thoroughly in place before moving on to the next step. (The criterion component of each instructional objective or step on a task analysis becomes the guide.)
- Teachers should use clear, distinct verbal directions; models; prompts; and guidance when teaching each link of the chain (Sulzer-Azaroff & Mayer, 1977).
- As external prompts and cues become obsolete, teachers should fade them, leaving the natural S^{D}s that are inherent in the task.
- Teachers should be cognizant of areas where shaping can be incorporated into the teaching strategy. If there are links in the chain that are weak and not firmly in place in the student's repertoire, shaping will be helpful in strengthening those skills (Sulzer-Azaroff & Mayer, 1977).
- At any level of the chain, teachers should require the student to perform *all* the steps learned up to that point (Martin & Pear, 1978).
- Teachers should identify and use reinforcers that are effective with the target learner.

■ ■ ■ ■

Increasing Behaviors: Token Economy Systems

Token economy systems, a form of reinforcers, are so complex in design and implementation that they can easily be misused and rendered ineffectual. However, the literature concerning token economies demonstrates a great many successes with these systems, supporting their *potential* value when they are designed carefully and implemented with a great deal of consistency.

Token economies are based on the same principles as our economic system; that is, we perform specified tasks for artificial incentives (money), and in turn we use money in exchange for our choice of goods and services. For educational purposes, tokens or points are earned by learners for exhibiting appropriate behaviors as negotiated between the teacher and students. The learners can then exchange these tokens or points for tangible reinforcers such as free time, preferred activities, and comic books. The effectiveness of token economies depends on the learner's ability to understand a system of delayed gratification. A system of this nature can prove useful with many learners.

If token economies are scorned by some practitioners as being ineffective, it may be due to an unsystematic use of the technique. Research on token economies demonstrates that these systems have been quite effective in improving the academic skills (Bijou, Birnbrauer, Kidder, & Tague, 1967), prevocational task completion (Repp, Klett, Sosebee, & Speir, 1975), and self-help skills (Thomas, Sulzer-Azaroff, Lukeris, & Palmer, 1977) of learners.

IDEA FILE

- Teachers should present tokens to learners immediately after the task has been completed (reinforce small steps at the beginning, gradually increasing the requirements necessary for earning tokens). However, teachers should set a minimal period that a learner has to wait before the tokens can be cashed in for the backup reinforcers.

- Backup reinforcers must be reinforcing to the students. Establishing a fair price list stating the cost in tokens for each reinforcer is a must. This price list should be in proportion to the actual cost of the items (Martin & Pear, 1978) or reflect the importance that the students place on the item (e.g., free time being a highly preferred activity).

- Once the price list has been set and the rules of immediate reinforcement developed, it is vitally important that teachers *be consistent* in the delivery of tokens and the procedures for allowing tokens to be cashed in. Making exceptions to set rules will, more often than not, destroy the effectiveness of a token system.

- Teachers should be sure to obtain an accurate baseline of the target behaviors (Martin & Pear, 1978). Ongoing data are just as necessary as in any other behavioral program for establishing whether or not the token system is working.

- Teachers should keep an accurate, up-to-date recording system. Systems can become unmanageable if teachers lose track of who has how many tokens and who purchased what items. Data of this nature will be valuable when revising the program.

- Teachers should identify people who can be of assistance in monitoring the program. Aides, parent volunteers, and regular education students, among others, can assist teachers in implementation, record keeping, and program management.

- Teachers should use tokens that cannot be counterfeited (Martin & Pear, 1978). In many instances, a points system that allows both the teacher and the student to keep a record of points earned may be more efficient for classroom purposes.

■ ■ ■ ■

To be effective, token economies must be consistent and systematic. These programs are best implemented in an open atmosphere where administrators, parents, and significant others are kept abreast of occurrences and progress. Complicated token systems are generally devised for settings that encompass the learners' entire day, such as residential or vocational settings; however, in many classrooms token systems can involve earning points for the completion of a specific activity (e.g., a mathematics assignment). These points can be cashed in at a later time for preferred activities.

A technique that often works well in conjunction with token systems is called *contingency contracting.* Learners react well to this approach, which spells out in contractual form what is expected of the student and what the teacher's role will be (Welch & Holborn, 1988). After the teacher and the learner agree to the stipulations, they both sign the contract. This technique works well for some students and not for others. Yet, when used properly, it allows learners to take responsibility for their actions and make decisions concerning the behaviors they wish to demonstrate. The teacher should always keep the original contract in a safe place, allowing the student to have a copy. At times, a learner who has not met the stipulations of the contract, and thus fails to receive the reinforcement, may destroy the document. After a "cooling off" period, the student may wish to reenter the agreement, which will necessitate only making a new copy of the document (Homme, 1969).

This section has provided teachers with suggestions for developing new behaviors or increasing existing ones. There are occasions, however, when teachers will need to apply techniques for decreasing the inappropriate behaviors of learners. These techniques, designed to reduce the frequency and intensity of target behaviors, also require planning and systematic application. Inconsistent application of these techniques not only renders them ineffective but also has negative side effects related to punishing contingencies. Therefore, it is crucial to develop programs that not only are effective for reducing inappropriate behaviors but also are consistent in their use.

DECREASING INAPPROPRIATE BEHAVIORS

Teachers should use a positive technique for behavior reduction first, applying aversive consequences only if the positive methods fail to have an effect (Barton, Brulle, & Repp, 1983). There are a number of positive methods that can be used to reduce behavior which are classified as techniques of *differential reinforcement* (Deitz & Repp, 1983; Martin & Pear, 1978; Sulzer-Azaroff & Mayer, 1977; Wolery, Bailey, & Sugai, 1988).

Differential Reinforcement Techniques

Differential reinforcement of low rates of behavior (DRL) allows the teacher to reinforce a learner who is emitting a behavior less than a predesignated amount during a certain time period. For example, while at a work station in vocational education, Ralph continually stops work to ask passers-by whether or not his work is all right. In this case, the teacher may inform Ralph that if he only stops work to ask this question five times or fewer during a 1 to 3 hour session, he will be allowed to work on a preferred activity at the end of class. Ralph's teacher has decided that it would be best if Ralph seldom asked the target question; however, *for now* five times or fewer is an acceptable level.

In addition to the DRL technique, teachers have the option to apply a *differential reinforcement of other or zero behaviors* (DRO). This procedure involves reinforcing learners only after there are zero responses emitted during a specified time period. In Ralph's case, the teacher may decide that after he has decreased the number of target responses, he is now ready to eliminate the behavior entirely. To accomplish this goal, the teacher would reinforce Ralph only if there were zero inappropriate questions asked during the 1-hour session.

A third technique for reducing behaviors using positive methods is called *differential reinforcement of incompatible behaviors* (DRI). Essentially, this procedure involves reinforcing a response that is incompatible with the target behavior. For example, students with behavior disorders who admit to having trouble with thoughts about hitting others when they are angry can first be taught to use "private speech" that lists the steps of more assertive behavior and then be reinforced for using it. The thoughts resulting from their private speech may be incompatible with the less desirable ones.

A final technique is termed *differential reinforcement of alternative behaviors* (DRA). This procedure is similar to DRI except that the teacher reinforces behaviors that are substitutes for the target response. For example, a teacher might show a student how to work out with weights in the gym and reinforce the student for doing that instead of becoming overly anxious and engaging in destructive behaviors. Another example would be to reinforce students with behavior disorders for writing letters of complaint to the teacher instead of talking back and cussing. The main thrust of the DRA procedure is to teach students more socially acceptable ways of dealing with stress.

IDEA FILE

Differential reinforcement procedures generally take longer than aversive approaches to bring the target behaviors under control. However, the use of these procedures often leads to long-lasting effects because the students are learning new behaviors to compete with or supplant the undesirable ones.

- Differential reinforcement procedures can be used in conjunction with full sessions or intervals, depending on the frequency of the target behavior.

- Full sessions take a large block of time (e.g., 30 minutes), with the student being reinforced at the end of the session.

- Interval approaches take the session and divide it into equal parts (e.g., 30 minutes divided into 1-minute intervals) with students reinforced at the end of each interval.

- A full-session DRL (differential reinforcement of low rates of behavior) might be used for a less frequent behavior, reinforcing the student if he or she exhibits the behavior less than the preset criteria during the 30-minute session.

- An interval DRL can be used for behaviors that occur frequently, thus allowing the student more chances for reinforcement. For example, a student who leaves her seat about 30 to 50 times in 30 minutes would have little chance for reinforcement if the teacher targeted 20 incidences. However, if the teacher used 1-minute intervals and reinforced the student if she left her seat once or less, she might be able to keep the incidences at 30. The next step would be to lengthen the interval to 2 minutes, reinforcing her if she left her seat once or less during that interval.

- The lengths of intervals should not be set arbitrarily. Interval lengths should be set only after baseline data have been taken and analyzed. Teachers can choose interval lengths that best fit the student's needs and the characteristics of the target behavior.

- Full sessions and intervals can also be used with DRO procedures (differential reinforcement of other or zero behaviors).

- There have been a number of research efforts proving the effectiveness of differential reinforcement procedures, including the following applications:

  □ Controlling the activity level of learners (Edelson & Sprague, 1974).

  □ Reinforcing low rates of misbehavior (Dietz & Repp, 1973; 1974).

  □ Training staff members (Repp & Dietz, 1979).

  □ Reducing self-injurious behavior (Rose, 1979; Tarpley & Schroeder, 1979).

☐ Reducing stereotypic behaviors (Harris & Wolchik, 1979).

☐ Reducing inappropriate verbalizations using DRO (Konczak & Johnson, 1983).

☐ Reducing aggressive behaviors (Knapczyk, 1988).

■ ■ ■ ■

Aversive Consequences

Unfortunately, positive approaches for decreasing inappropriate behaviors do not always work with different learners or at different times with the same learner. In cases such as these, teachers have the option to apply aversive consequences. Various punishers range in level of severity, and teachers should always use the least severe methods such as response cost, time out, and overcorrection. The most severe of the aversive techniques (corporal punishment) results in too many negative side effects and should be governed by an advisory committee of parents, administrators, and teachers (McDaniel, 1980; Rose, 1983). Aversive techniques such as electric shock are beyond the realm of the special education practitioner and are governed by human rights committees and other qualified professionals.

Response Cost

Response cost is the levying of fines on reinforcers, withdrawing specified amounts that are contingent upon certain offenses (Walker, 1983). For example, if a student is fined 20 tokens for fighting, a response cost procedure has been applied. As with all behavioral procedures, a systematic application is needed if response cost is to be effective. When confronted with an inappropriate behavior that has not been previously targeted and explained to the learner, some teachers may be inclined to include it in the program. In this case, a teacher identifies a misbehavior and levies the fine before the student is informed of the response cost contingency. For a response cost system to be effective, the rules of the system must be clearly stated and understood by the learner in advance of its application and then consistently applied for each occurrence. Generally, response cost systems are used in conjunction with some form of a token economy.

IDEA FILE

■ Teachers should make sure learners have an adequate reinforcer reserve before implementing a response cost system. Fines are less effective when students have very little to lose.

■ Whenever possible, teachers should allow learners to have input into developing the rules and fixing the fine lists in accordance with the severity of offenses.

■ Teachers should develop a rule poster with accompanying fines. Learners should demonstrate that they understand the rules and what the consequences are for breaking those rules (Sulzer-Azaroff & Mayer, 1977).

■ Teachers should not design systems in which learners can become bankrupt too easily. Building in opportunities for the learners to earn back some reinforcers for acts of restitution (e.g., picking up the blocks that were kicked across the room) makes a system more positive and fair.

■ Teachers may find it helpful to review some examples of response cost systems that have been used in research efforts, for example:

☐ Modifying rule-violation, off-task, and academic behaviors (Iwata & Bailey, 1974).

☐ Controlling unproductive behaviors of boys (Phillips, Phillips, Fixsen, & Wolfe, 1971).

☐ A group response cost system (Salend & Kovalich, 1981).

■ ■ ■ ■

Problems will occur when response cost programs are implemented. Some students will refuse to hand over point cards or tokens when they are given their initial fines. A careful recording system can minimize this by demonstrating that the teacher's records are the accurate count of how many tokens a learner can spend. Response costs can themselves result in emotional outbursts or aggressive behaviors. Sulzer-Azaroff and Mayer (1977) have suggested downplaying this problem. Fines should be levied with little discussion and fanfare, and when necessary the emotional outburst itself can be fined.

Time Out from Positive Reinforcement

Time-out procedures involve removing the student from the source of reinforcement or removing the source of reinforcement from the student. The mistake made by some teachers is to assume that their classes are reinforcing to students and that removing the students from class is a punishing consequence. In fact, some learners may prefer to be somewhere else if faced with activities that they perceive as having no relevance to their lives. To be effective, time out must be based on the removal of reinforcers known to work for a particular learner. Time out ranges in complexity from simply turning away from a student (ignoring) to physically removing the student to a neutral room (Harris, 1985).

Time out is a powerful technique for reducing behavior and should be used with great care. Parents, administrators, and significant others must be included in the decision-making process before programs of this nature are implemented (Nelson & Rutherford, 1983). However, if less intense reductive measures are ineffective, time out can be used.

Misuses of Time Out

Time out may be one of the most misused of the behavioral procedures, and this problem is especially noticeable in public school programs. Television and newspaper accounts of students forgotten in locked rooms until after school hours and of students spending over half of the school day in time-out booths are becoming more prevalent. Some instances of this misuse are a result of a lack of understanding of the basic principles of this technique on the part of regular education teachers and administrators. The problem may be compounded further if the special education teacher is assigned as a monitor for the time-out booths.

The responsibility to help their regular education colleagues understand about the appropriate use of time out from positive reinforcement rests with the special educators, since they may be the only professionals in the school with any behavior management training. First, everyone needs to realize that the strategy is termed *time out from positive reinforcement*. If there is little in the classroom that is positive for students (i.e., activities, content, and teacher behaviors toward students), removal of students from the classroom may actually *reward* them.

Second, time out, by nature, is a highly restrictive procedure and should be used only after all else has failed. This requires teachers to evaluate what or how they are teaching and attempt to improve communication before such a restrictive procedure is implemented. In addition, a variety of positive behavioral procedures (e.g., DRA) are available that may be used first and probably would serve to head off the exclusion of a learner from class.

IDEA FILE

- If a time-out room is to be used, there should not be any reinforcers in that room (e.g., toys, books, view from window). However, the room should be comfortable in temperature and well lighted.

- There should be no locks on the door to the time-out room. If the teacher must hold the door shut, the wrong procedure is being used.

- For best results, a time-out room should have an observation window so that the learner can be monitored for injurious or self-stimulatory behavior. If either type of behavior occurs, the teacher should try another procedure (e.g., overcorrection—described in the next section).

- When escorting a learner to a time-out area, the teacher should refrain from all conversation except a brief statement of the misbehavior (e.g., "No throwing blocks").

- If the learner has to be forceably dragged to time out, the teacher should use another procedure.

- Time-out areas should be as close as possible to the teaching setting. This minimizes potentially reinforcing occurrences such as being seen by friends or other staff while walking to time out.

- A student may engage in crying or temper tantrum behavior while in a time-out situation. In these cases, if the time-out period is to last for 1 minute, wait until the crying or tantrum stops, then time the 1 minute from that point.

- The length of a time-out session should only reflect what is minimally needed to affect the behavior. White, Nielson, and Johnson (1972) found that shorter durations of time out appear to be more effective.

- Time out should never be used in isolation. Merely eliminating a misbehavior without replacing it by reinforcing an acceptable alternative behavior may result in other inappropriate outbursts.

■ Whenever possible, the reinforcer should be removed from the learner instead of the reverse. For example, when working with young learners, the teacher can remove a food reinforcer by simply turning around in the chair for a specified period of time (Smith, Piersel, Filbeck, & Gross, 1983). McReynolds (1969) used this technique when teaching language skills by removing a reinforcer (ice cream) when the learner exhibited other than the appropriate responses.

■ Another, milder form of time out involves asking students to leave the group for a short period of time by turning their chairs around (exclusionary time out). After the time period (e.g., 2 minutes), the teacher would reinforce the student upon his or her return to the group.

■ The following examples of time out from positive reinforcement can be found in the research literature:

□ Removing a reinforcer worn by students if they misbehave (Foxx & Shapiro, 1978).

□ Moving students away from the activity to watch other students receive reinforcers for the correct behaviors (Porterfield, Herbert-Jackson, & Risley, 1976).

□ Use of a time-out room (MacPherson, Cander, & Hohman, 1974).

■ ■ ■ ■

Overcorrection

Overcorrection is another procedure for decreasing inappropriate behaviors. Azrin and Foxx (1971) included in their toilet training program a reductive procedure that required the students to make some restitution for an inappropriate act (e.g., they had to take a bath and wash soiled clothing). Overcorrection is a mild punisher with two distinct variations: restitutional overcorrection and positive practice overcorrection. Restitutional overcorrection involves what Foxx and Azrin (1973) have described as requiring the person to correct the result of the inappropriate behavior by restoring the setting to a level that is better than it was prior to the occurrence of the incident. Students who deliberately spill their milk may be required to clean not only their table but also surrounding tables and the floor.

Positive practice overcorrection varies from restitutional overcorrection by requiring the learner to practice the correct alternatives to the inappropriate behaviors. For example, learners who spill milk would have to practice correct pouring over a number of trials. Overcorrection can involve a combination of many behavioral techniques, including reinforcing alternate behaviors, using verbal instructions, coaxing behaviors through graduated guidance, time out, and feedback to the learner describing the inappropriate behavior. In many cases restitutional and positive practice overcorrection can be used together to achieve the desired result. Teachers should keep in mind, however, that although overcorrection has proved to be quite effective in reducing inappropriate behaviors such as self-injurious behavior (Azrin, Gottlieb, Hughart, Wesolowski, & Rahn, 1975), aggression (Foxx & Azrin, 1972), and classroom disturbances (Azrin & Powers, 1975), it is not a simple procedure to apply.

IDEA FILE

- Teachers should choose alternative or corrective behaviors that relate directly to the inappropriate behavior. For example, if a learner throws objects, then the teacher should choose like objects for the learner to restore to their storage places.

- Teachers should keep talking to a minimum. A teacher should give only the verbal directions that are needed to direct the student's attention to the misbehavior and to the behaviors requiring restitution.

- As with all behavioral procedures, teachers should address all occurrences of the inappropriate behavior immediately. This suggestion requires that the classroom arrangement be such that a teacher, aide, or volunteer is in constant contact with the target learner.

- During the time that a learner is engaged in restitution or positive practice procedures, the teacher should avoid all forms of reinforcement (time out). Further, Foxx and Azrin (1972) have suggested that a short additional time-out-from-reinforcement-phase be extended beyond the time necessary to correct or practice the behaviors.

- Teachers should use appropriate graduated guidance procedures (refer to the earlier section of this chapter) when requiring the student to correct the misdeed or practice an alternative behavior.

- Overcorrection procedures have been demonstrated to work on classroom behavior problems. For example:

    □ Having students recite the correct class rules (Azrin, Azrin, & Armstrong, 1977).

    □ Controlling disruptive classroom behavior by positive practice methods (Bornstein, Hamilton, & Quevillon, 1977).

    □ Positive and negative practice (Durana & Cuvo, 1980).

■ ■ ■ ■

Professionals may find from experience that even mildly aversive procedures have a number of disadvantages. Punishment has been known to cause learner withdrawal, violent outbursts, and negative peer reactions toward the student being punished. Before an aversive program is implemented, teachers should give some thought as to how they will handle these potential negative side effects should they surface. Keeping the suggestions given in this chapter in mind and including parents, other professionals, and administrators in the development process should minimize problems.

KEY CONCEPTS

- Severe aversive stimuli such as paddling often lead to unwanted side effects. Students may become aggressive or withdrawn or attempt to escape the situation when severely punished. Also, if students see teachers punish others severely, they may model those teacher behaviors.

- Students may learn to avoid punishers by not getting caught instead of by omitting the inappropriate behavior.

■ Teachers should try positive differential reinforcement approaches first, before they use mild punishers.

■ DRL techniques (differential reinforcement of low rates of behavior) lower students' rate of responses by reinforcing learners when they emit the behavior at less than a predetermined level.

■ DRO techniques (differential reinforcement of other or zero behaviors) eliminate inappropriate behaviors by reinforcing the students if they do not emit the response within a certain time period.

■ DRI techniques (differential reinforcement of incompatible behaviors) reinforce responses that compete with the unproductive behaviors.

■ DRA techniques (differential reinforcement of alternative behaviors) teach students more desirable alternatives to unproductive behaviors.

■ Response cost is a system of levying fines when students break prespecified rules. It is usually applied in conjunction with token economy systems.

■ Time out may be one of the most abused of the behavioral procedures. It should not be used for long periods of time (e.g., 15 minutes or 2 hours) because it results in the teacher being timed out from the student and probably has little effect on the target behavior (Vandever, 1983).

■ Nonseclusionary (exclusionary) time-out procedures are preferable to seclusionary time-out procedures.

■ Both restitutional and positive practice overcorrection procedures can be effective techniques for decreasing behaviors.

■ ■ ■ ■

GENERALIZATION OF SKILLS

Skills taught in an isolated classroom setting, under conditions different from those in the learner's natural environment, may not be demonstrated by the student in the community setting. Therefore, careful consideration must be given to transferring control of behavior to natural reinforcers.

Intermittent Reinforcement

Initially, teaching skills to learners (acquisition) generally requires reinforcing these students on a *fixed ratio* scale of one to one (i.e., reinforcing the learner after each occurrence of the target response). This procedure is important at the beginning of skill acquisition; however, research results indicate that it is not a durable schedule that will maintain behavior over long periods of time. This schedule of reinforcement is artificial; it does not reflect a true picture of how behaviors are reinforced naturally in the environment. Therefore, once the learner has demonstrated some competence in a skill area, it is best to move to an intermittent schedule of reinforcement that cannot be predicted by the student.

The two schedules that most resemble naturally occurring events are called *variable ratio* (VR) and *variable interval* (VI) schedules. VR schedules allow teachers to reinforce target behaviors on an average of correct responses that cannot be predicted by the student. For example, a teacher may reinforce a student after 5 correct mathematics problems on one day, after 7 correct problems the next day, after 11 correct problems the next day, and so on. The unpredictability of the schedule maintains the behavior.

VI schedules work in much the same fashion except that the reinforcer is dependent on the average length of time the student engages in the target behavior. Therefore, a student may be reinforced for production behavior in a workshop on an average of every 10 minutes with the lengths of the interval varied slightly (e.g., 11 minutes, 15 minutes).

By adding a *limited hold* component to VI schedules, teachers can increase the efficiency of the technique. Limited hold components restrict the length of time after the interval has occurred that the students can receive their reinforcers, thus forcing them to respond quickly. For example, teachers often state that at the end of a 2-minute interval the bell will ring and those students working quietly will receive a token. Adding a 30-second limited hold time period after the bell allows the students to get seated and organized, increasing their chances for reinforcement. In the community, a student may learn to ride an elevator by pushing the button and waiting an average of 2 minutes (VI 2). When the door opens, the student may have 10 seconds of a limited hold to enter the elevator before the door closes (VI 2, LH 10 sec.).

Programming for Generalization

Teaching learners isolated skills and then hoping the skills will carry over into their everyday lives is not a sound educational practice (Stokes & Baer, 1977). Teachers need to consider more sophisticated techniques designed to program for generalization, including activities in their programs that allow students to practice skills across settings, persons, materials, and time (Langone & Westling, 1979). For example, generalization can be increased across settings by allowing students to practice mobility skills on different types of buses or alternate transit systems. The possibilities for innovative generalization training exercises are endless. They include staggering training times, substituting new materials, and increasing the number of different mainstreaming alternatives, among other techniques. Teachers should consider switching to natural reinforcers as soon as possible (Stokes & Baer, 1977).

In their research review, Stokes and Baer (1977) found support for using more than one stimulus at a time to enhance the generalization of target skills. Teachers can accomplish this by using techniques such as simultaneously including two trainers or concurrently training a skill in more than one setting. Using more than one teaching technique during a training session (e.g., ignoring inappropriate behaviors while reinforcing alternate ones) appears to facilitate generalization more than just applying one procedure.

IDEA FILE

Learners may generalize skills across different settings, materials, and time more efficiently if they are accompanied by the same person under all conditions. The use of peer tutors is a highly effective method that continues to gain in popularity and can be used

in resource, self-contained, and community training situations (e.g., Donder & Nietupski, 1981).

■ Before mainstreaming learners into regular or vocational classrooms, teachers should
choose general education students from those classes and pair them with the learners in a
tutoring situation. When the students move to the regular class settings, the peer tutors
accompany them.

■ Peer tutors can be valuable in helping students with handicapping conditions generalize
learned skills to community settings. For example, a teacher might have a peer tutor teach
a student shopping skills in the classroom and then accompany the student to local grocery
stores or help generalize social skills across settings (Shafer, Egel, & Neef, 1984).

■ ■ ■ ■

Another consideration that has important implications for teachers involves using
less structured teaching techniques. The initial teaching of a skill often requires structured
techniques such as prompts, models, and guidance. As the student becomes more competent in the task, the teacher can loosen up the structure of the techniques so that they
are more representative of actual community stimuli (Stokes & Baer, 1977). For example,
a teacher using very precise, slowly presented models for teaching addition skills may
loosen up by speeding up the models or combining two steps at a time after the learner has
reached a certain competency.

CASE STUDY

"Ms. Barnes, Ms. Barnes, may I talk to you?" "Sure Mr. LaMont what can I do for you?"
"Well, the principal said that you were doing your master's thesis on modeling, and I was
wondering if you could help me," said Mr. LaMont. "I have a student this term in my
resource room who's very shy and withdrawn. He's been labeled both behavior disordered
and learning disabled at different points in his life, and I just can't get him involved in
class activities!"

"Well," said Ms. Barnes, "that sounds like an interesting problem. My guess is that
some type of modeling procedure might be helpful, but first we've got to get better
organized if we're going to help your student. Give me until tomorrow and I'll write out
a list of tasks we have to do with a brief description of how modeling might be used."

The next afternoon Ms. Barnes provided Mr. LaMont with the following plan:

1. Define the behaviors you want to improve. For example, if the student is usually alone you
   might want to increase his time actively engaged in a group activity (you need to define
   actively). You may want him to volunteer more or respond more positively to criticism.
   The key is to define what you want.

2. Once you have defined the behavior(s), then you need to establish a baseline. My guess
   is that this student rarely volunteers or *actively* engages in group activities; however, it is
   important to chart this for a couple of days.

3. Once we have the baseline you then can include the student along with one or two other
   students in a situation or activity in which you show (model) them how to work more

actively in the group. You can then let him practice the behaviors you demonstrated in a role-playing session with two other students. During these sessions, while you are reinforcing the other students they also become models for your target learner.

4. Finally, you continue to take data during another class activity and see whether or not the student increases his group participation. If he doesn't, you may need to include your modeling exercise in each group during the day.

■ ■ ■ ■

KEY CONCEPTS

- Many learners with handicapping conditions do not readily generalize skills across people, places, and time.
- Intermittent reinforcement is one method of helping students generalize skills. Essentially, this reinforcement schedule prevents students from predicting when they will be reinforced and thus promotes more durable behavior over time.
- Variable ratio (VR) schedules allow teachers to reinforce behaviors after an *average of correct responses*.
- Variable interval (VI) schedules allow teachers to reinforce behaviors after an *average length of time* that they occur.
- Natural reinforcers improve generalization of skills.
- Peer tutors and a variety of instructors also help students to generalize skills.

■ ■ ■ ■

CHAPTER SEVEN

MICROCOMPUTER TECHNOLOGY AND INSTRUCTION

■ The growth of the educational applications of microcomputer technology is unprecedented in the field of special education. In 1984, Maddux estimated that 160,000 microcomputers were being used in special education classrooms. More recently, Mokros and Russell (1986) reported that 88% of the schools sampled in their survey claimed to be using microcomputers with students with learning disabilities or behavior disorders. As the 1990s approach, these numbers appear to be increasing.

For individuals with handicapping conditions, the applications of microcomputer technology offer opportunities never before imagined, with improvements and new developments occurring almost weekly. The effects of microcomputer technology on the lives of these individuals may best be summarized by the following excerpt from the introduction of *Apple Computer Resources in Special Education and Rehabilitation* (DLM Teaching Resources, 1988):

> It's clear that the personal computer represents something very special to the disabled individual. Not a cure, not something that makes the disability any less real. But an equalizer of sorts. An enabler. A partner like no partner the disabled person has ever had before. (p. ix)

The use of microcomputers allows students with handicaps to be able to communicate, play, work, and generally interact with their environment when meaningful interaction previously may not have been thought possible.

The most inspiring examples of the applications of microcomputer technology have been in the development of devices for individuals with sensory or physical impairments. For example, an individual with a hearing impairment can communicate over the telephone to non-hearing-impaired individuals using a computer with a built-in voice synthesizer. The individual can type a message into the computer and the message is converted to speech via the voice synthesizer over the telephone. When a touch-tone decoder is added to the microcomputer, it can read and display a message spelled out by a non-hearing-impaired person on a touch-tone phone. Development of microcomputer-assisted augmentative communication systems has also made it possible for individuals with severe handicaps to engage in more complex and meaningful interactions with their environment (Iacono & Miller, 1989).

In a more widespread application, microcomputer technology can have a tremendous impact on the lives of students with mild to moderate handicapping conditions. Microcomputers in the classroom can help teachers manage daily tasks such as record keeping and IEP development, or they can be instructional tools, helping students practice learned skills. Computer-assisted instruction has several advantages that can be applied to the instructional needs of many learners (Hagen, 1984). Rupley and Blair (1983) identified six such advantages of microcomputers:

> Enhancing student interaction and motivation.
> Providing immediate feedback.
> Providing record-keeping capabilities.
> Providing needed reinforcement.
> Allowing self-paced instruction.
> Freeing the teacher to work with other students while some students work on the computer.
>   (p. 426)

These advantages have been highlighted by many other authors stressing how microcomputers can promote and supplement learning (Mather, 1988; Wilson, Casella, & Wilson, 1989).

The literature includes many examples of promising applications of microcomputer technology to the learning of academically related skills. Unfortunately, however, there is a paucity of empirically based studies that "investigate [the] authenticity" of approaches and programs (Ellis & Sabornie, 1988, p. 355). For many students with learning problems, promises of the remediation of their deficits via computer technology have not been kept (Hasselbring & Goin, 1989).

This chapter presents information to assist special educators in using microcomputers as an effective and efficient instructional *tool*. In addition, information is presented for helping students use computers as a tool to minimize the effects of their handicapping conditions. Like any tool, microcomputers can be and are being misused in special education. The aim here is to help teachers avoid some of the pitfalls of integrating microcomputer technology into their curricula.

The information presented in this chapter is limited to applications for the majority of learners with mild to moderate handicapping conditions. Therefore, no information is provided concerning adaptive equipment designed to allow individuals with physical handicaps to access computers and none is given about computer-assisted augmentative communication devices. The discussion here highlights the effective and efficient use of computer-assisted instruction (CAI) and computer-managed instruction (CMI). Also included is a short discussion of the applications of microcomputers to computer-assisted management (CAM).

APPLICATIONS OF MICROCOMPUTERS

An analogy used earlier in this text in relation to standardized assessment devices is equally appropriate when related to microcomputers. If a person hits her thumb with a hammer while trying to strike a nail, is it the hammer's fault? This tongue-in-cheek analogy should serve to remind us that, like the hammer, a microcomputer is a tool that can be misused. When this happens, blaming the tool serves no purpose except to divert our attention from the real reasons for failure.

Some professionals have questioned whether or not the gains made by students are worth the time, money, and effort needed to integrate computers into the curriculum. They cite some research efforts that demonstrate that student gains in learning while interacting with computers are far less than expected. These opinions can be misleading without a careful review of the quality of the research efforts that are being cited to support these notions.

An increasing body of research literature describes results that indicate a different perspective. These studies suggest that the failure of students to learn while interacting with computers appears to be linked both to poor instruction, delivered by poorly designed software, and to poor teaching strategies that fail to link the computer-assisted instruction to the rest of the curriculum (Block, 1988; Hasselbring & Goin, 1989; Marozas & May, 1988). For example, having students spend hours alone in front of the computer while the teacher does other things relegates the computer to the role of babysitter and probably offers little in the way of meaningful instruction. Similarly, teachers who allow students to use the computer only after they have earned the right with good behavior fail to see its role as a "learning partner" with other daily instructional activities.

The role of the special educator in terms of microcomputer applications is becoming that of "technologist," a professional who can effectively use microcomputer technology to promote and enhance student learning. To assume this new role, teachers must understand the general applications of microcomputers in educating students with mild to moderate handicapping conditions.

Computer-Assisted Instruction

Computer-assisted instruction (also referred to as computer-based instruction [Hasselbring & Goin, 1989]) is the most logical application of microcomputer technology and the most direct in terms of helping students improve knowledge and skills, develop fluency, learn to solve problems, and generalize skills to new situations (Behrmann, 1988). Although it is the most commonly used application of computers in education, it has also been the most criticized over the years (Hasselbring & Cavanaugh, 1986).

Most of the criticism of CAI has revolved around poor-quality software that, at times, resembles ditto sheets in the form of computer programs. Another criticism has been that this form of instruction has been used by teachers as something to keep students busy, with no relationship to the daily curriculum. Both of these criticisms have been valid, but they should not hinder teachers from recognizing the power and effectiveness of CAI when it is used appropriately, with high-quality educational software based on sound principles of instructional design.

CAI provides a number of advantages that can directly improve the skills of students with mild to moderate handicaps. Microcomputers can provide students with immediate and meaningful feedback while the teacher is engaged in other tasks. Computers can also monitor student performance and provide the teacher with an analysis of progress and a summary of skills not yet mastered. Using certain software packages, CAI can integrate graphics, sound, and examples to reinforce specific concepts—a highly motivating approach that results in improved learner attitudes (Watkins, 1989). Finally, computers can present instruction in a systematic manner, allowing students to work at their own pace and never getting impatient with students errors (Behrmann, 1988).

Until recently CAI has been identified by the types of software available: drill and practice, simulations, gaming, tutorials, tool applications, and problem solving. Now, however, some professionals believe that this approach to categorizing CAI is outdated. Many current software packages combine any number of the categories mentioned (Behrmann, 1988; Hasselbring & Goin, 1989; Wilson et al., 1989). Hasselbring and Goin (1989) have proposed that CAI can be classified more functionally by basing it on the four stages of learning: acquisition, fluency (proficiency), maintenance, and generalization (p. 153).

IDEA FILE

Successfully integrating CAI into the overall curriculum is a must if students are to receive the maximum benefits that can be obtained from this type of instruction. Using Hasselbring and Goin's (1989) four categories as a base, the following suggestions should assist teachers in using CAI appropriately in the classroom:

- Drill-and-practice software is not appropriate for use when students are still acquiring a skill or a set of skills. These activities cannot be used as a substitute for teaching basic concepts (Hannaford, 1987; Hofmeister, 1983).
- Hasselbring and Goin (1989) have suggested using computer-based tutorial software to assist instruction in basic skills during the acquisition phase. Tutorial software provides frequent corrective feedback and reinforcement when presenting new material.
- Once students have acquired target skills, they must improve their fluency in the use of these skills. Improving fluency, or the rate at which students can automatically complete the basic skills, leads to mastery of more advanced skills (Torgeson, 1984). At this point drill-and-practice software becomes valuable in helping students speed up their use of these skills while also improving their overall quality (Tobin, 1988). The important point to remember is that drill-and-practice software is not appropriate for use with learners who have not yet acquired the basic skills and concepts of a task.
- As with all instruction for students with mild to moderate handicapping conditions, the skills learned through a combination of teacher strategies and computer-assisted instruction must be consciously generalized to community-based activities. CAI assists students in acquiring and becoming more fluent in the basic skills; however, application to daily living problems is best handled by activities in environments such as retail establishments, court clerk offices, and restaurants.
- LOGO is a computer program that acts as a learning environment, allowing students to learn basic computer programming, mathematical thinking, and problem-solving skills. There are many components of LOGO, but the one that is used most often with students who have mild handicaps is Turtle Graphics. Basically, this component allows students to create geometric designs by programming the turtle (a small, triangular graphic) to move around the screen. Weir and Watt (1981) have asserted that using LOGO helps students improve their fine-motor skills and short-term memory, as well as their directionality, and obtain a sense that they control the actions of the computer. LOGO is a fine program that will certainly teach students new skills; however, there is no empirical evidence that it teaches problem-solving skills that can be used in daily life.
- Simulation software is becoming increasingly available for use in special education classes. Generally, this type of software is not specific to any one curriculum area but stresses understanding of a process by applying rules to specific problems (Tobin, 1988). Simulations can allow students to experience some real-life events that cannot easily be recreated in the classroom. Examples include such events as being an airline pilot, traveling in space, conducting science experiments, running for political office, and being part of a wagon train in the frontier era.
- Simulation software can be most useful to students if teachers keep two important considerations in mind. First, some students may overrely on trial-and-error (guessing) strategies to complete a simulation and therefore not gain the full benefit of the software (Bransford,

Stein, Delclos, & Littlefield, 1986). This can be remedied by close teacher supervision. Students with handicaps will not automatically gain problem-solving skills by themselves. Teachers should interact with them periodically to model and prompt problem-solving behaviors and point out relevant information provided in the simulation. This suggestion applies for all CAI used by teachers.

The second consideration is that students may actually learn more from interacting with the simulation software while working in groups. Group interaction promotes social and communication skills while allowing students to learn the team-related skills (cooperation) needed for the group to solve the problem.

■ ■ ■ ■

Computer-Managed Instruction

Computer-managed instruction helps teachers become more efficient in handling the daily paperwork and record keeping inherent in the role of special educator. In addition, CMI can assist teachers in developing IEPs and monitoring student progress as well as diagnosing and assessing student strengths and weaknesses.

Computer-based word-processing programs can facilitate a teacher's communications with parents and other professionals and provide an efficient mechanism for storing, filing, and retrieving data. Word-processing programs can be helpful in a number of ways. Teachers can generate letters and forms that require frequent changes (dates, places) with little effort. These programs also allow teachers to quickly enter information such as class lists and schedules that can easily be edited when necessary. Finally, word-processing programs can be of tremendous help in collating and storing data obtained from the community needs assessment. Information relevant to environments in the community where instruction (e.g., resources, subenvironments, task sequences) will occur can easily be entered and stored. Subsequently, teachers can use these programs to list community-based behavioral and instructional objectives by curriculum area for retrieval during IEP development.

There are a number of computer-generated IEP programs available commercially. Basically, these programs allow teachers to pull objectives from a list and transfer them to a template form of the IEP. Some programs are keyed to a specific standardized or criterion-referenced assessment device. Once the teacher enters the student's data, the program will retrieve precoded objectives based on the student's assessment profile.

Computer-generated IEPs can be a tremendous timesaver and can improve the overall quality of IEPs if used correctly. However, teachers should keep in mind two important considerations. First, generating a list of objectives from only one assessment device can be less than effective. A student's program should be the result of multiple attempts to access strengths and weaknesses. An overreliance on only one instrument may miss important gaps in the student's learning profile.

Second, commercially produced IEP packages cannot reflect objectives specific to every community and the unique environments in each locale. Probably the best result will be a combination of commercially produced packages and objectives developed from each teacher's community needs assessment. It is important for teachers to choose IEP packages that will allow input from specific word-processing programs so that they can transfer their selected community-based objectives into the commercially produced IEP template.

Data-based instruction has long been the goal of special educators, and with the advancement of computer-based monitoring programs this task becomes much easier. Computer-based monitoring programs allow teachers to store, graph, and analyze academic, social/emotional, and other behaviors of students (Hasselbring & Goin, 1989; Stephens, Blackhurst, & Magliocca, 1988).

Hasselbring and Hamlett (1984) have developed a computer-based monitoring program called AIMSTAR. This program allows teachers to develop student data files that include information about the instructional program and store performance data relating to a student's program. For example, a teacher could store Jamar's performance data on the number of correct cost-comparison shopping problems he solved during one community-based instructional session. The teacher could also include in the data file the amount of time it took Jamar to complete the task. Upon demand, the program would generate a graphic representation of Jamar's progress (similar to the ones presented in Chapter Five) depicting his progress in rate or movements per minute. The AIMSTAR program assists teachers by recommending changes in the program when appropriate.

In addition to their use in monitoring student progress, computers can be used earlier in the program development process to assist professionals in diagnosing and assessing students' strengths and weaknesses (Lick & Little, 1987). Computer programs are now available to assist in the scoring and analysis of many standardized tests. In addition, some programs are available that allow the students to take the test directly on the computer with little assistance from professionals. Such programs offer the potential of minimizing some of the time-consuming tasks required of special educators and allowing them to spend more time in teaching and instructional development.

Computer-Assisted Management

Computer-assisted management is not directly a concern of teachers, and therefore only a brief description of this area will be presented here. Administrators of special education programs are finding CAM programs to be of great assistance in the accountability requirements of federal, state, and local agencies (Lahm & Levy, 1985; McClellan, 1985). These programs provide administrators with the means to store, organize, and use large quantities of data for decision-making purposes in a highly cost-effective manner (Marozas & May, 1988).

For example, software programs exist that assist in scheduling, grading, managing grants and projects, establishing student tracking systems, writing budgets and financial reports, and a host of other effective and efficient management approaches. Two systems mentioned in the previous section, computerized IEPs and computer-assisted assessment, are also helpful to administrators.

KEY CONCEPTS

- The growth of microcomputers in special education is unprecedented.
- Students with mild and moderate handicapping conditions can benefit greatly from increased interaction with microcomputers to improve their cognitive skills, increase their functional community survival skills, and learn to use their leisure time more productively.

- Unfortunately, the promises of the great effects that microcomputer technology would have on the lives of these learners has not been fulfilled.

- This technology may be misused when computers are used as "babysitters" to keep students busy. Also, teachers sometimes err when they rely on computer programs as a student's sole source of instruction in new concepts and skills.

- Computer-assisted instruction provides students immediate and meaningful feedback and reinforcement while it continuously monitors their performance. Computer software can assist students during the acquisition, fluency, maintenance, and generalization phases of learning.

- Computer-managed instruction assists teachers by minimizing many time-consuming tasks (e.g., data analysis and graphic monitoring of student progress) while allowing them to make informed decisions about program changes.

- Computer-assisted management assists administrators in a more cost-efficient and effective approach to meeting the daily federal, state, and local requirements relating to special education programs.

■ ■ ■ ■

HARDWARE

By this time, most teachers will have had at least some experience with microcomputers in an educational setting. Interestingly, some teachers still avoid using CAI and CMI, making statements such as "Computers scare me," "I'm just not a technical person," and "I never was good in math, and using computers requires a lot of knowledge in math." Such statements indicate the lack of knowledge concerning microcomputers that still exists among some special educators.

The inaccurate belief that computers are something mystical, understood by only a few, may be a major barrier for some teachers. This section presents a brief, nontechnical overview of how computers work and how software allows computers to carry out their tasks. Before beginning, it might be helpful for the reader to reflect a moment on the role of computers in the classroom. Microcomputers can be extremely helpful tools when teaching students who have learning problems. They are relatively simple to use and will do only what they are instructed to and no more. In most cases, the quality of the software dictates whether or not a computer is difficult to use and will complete the desired task.

A microcomputer system can carry out four functions: accept input, process the information placed in the system, and either store the information once the processing is complete or provide some type of output. The last two functions are not an either/or proposition, because the computer can provide some type of output upon request and store the same information for retrieval at a later time.

To input information (communicate with the computer), the user employs a keyboard similar to a standard typewriter keyboard. This method is still the most common for entering information; however, other methods exist for people with physical disabilities (e.g., voice-entry terminals and large, touch-sensitive keyboards). Other devices are available that work in conjunction with a keyboard to simplify entering data. For example, a mouse is a device connected to the computer that controls the movement of the cursor (a flashing dot on the monitor's screen that indicates the location where the input will be placed).

After the information is entered, the computer processes it in system unit. The system unit actually consists of three components: the central processing unit (CPU), read only memory (ROM), and random access memory (RAM). The CPU is the heart of the machine; it includes the parts (microprocessing circuits) that allow the computer to complete its task. ROM is the permanent memory of the unit that remains when it is switched off. This memory component is preprogrammed at the factory and contains information critical for the computer to run.

RAM is temporary memory that is manipulated by the user. This memory component is the user's workspace; it allows the user to store instructions temporarily, using programs and software that the computer accesses to complete the desired task. RAM also stores information temporarily until it can be stored permanently by other devices.

RAM is the most important part of the system unit for teachers to understand because they directly influence what the computer accomplishes by using it. For example, if a teacher wishes to send home a letter to parents, the teacher turns on the computer and, upon direction, "loads" a word-processing program into RAM. Once the program is activated, the teacher is allowed space in RAM to create the letter (or any other document). When the task is complete, the teacher can print out the letter or store it using another device. When the computer is turned off, the letter is erased from RAM.

Another example of the use of RAM involves developing IEPs by means of the appropriate software. Activating the program allows the teacher to manipulate a shell (blank) IEP and either type in objectives or choose some from a list provided by the program. Upon completion of the document, it must either be stored on a floppy disk or hard drive or printed out before the computer is turned off so it will not be lost.

The amount of RAM a computer has can differ from machine to machine. The term used to denote the amount of information that is temporarily stored in RAM is K or *kilobytes*. One K of memory means that RAM for that computer can store up to 1024 letters, numbers, or symbols. Therefore, 128 K of memory can store about 128,000 characters. The key point to remember is that software programs require a certain amount of RAM before they can be used. If the total capacity of RAM is used to load the software program, no space is available for work. For example, if a word-processing program requires 256 K and the capacity of the machine's RAM is only 256 K, no memory will be left for the user to create documents. Similarly, if a mathematics software program requires 256 K and the RAM for a particular machine is only 128K, the program will not load. Generally, this is the most technical information a teacher needs to be aware of when using computers.

External storage can be accomplished by using either cassettes or disks. Cassette storage is cumbersome and has become outdated. Disk storage uses three types of devices: 3½ inch floppy disks, 5¼ inch floppy disks, and hard drives. Software programs provide directions on how to store information to the disk, and the type of device used is dictated by which comes with or is added on to the machine.

The output component of a microcomputer allows the user to see information once it is processed by the system unit. Microcomputers output information in two major ways, but other forms of output are available for people who have sensory handicaps. Monitors resemble a television screen displaying text and graphics for immediate feedback to the user. The information displayed on the monitor's screen and stored in RAM is not permanent. The user can choose to have a hard copy printed via the link to the system's printer or have the information stored on disk. Printers are a necessity for teachers because they provide copies of students' work for additional analysis and for sharing with other professionals or parents. The quality of printers varies. The type most often used in schools is the dot matrix printer because of its speed and ability to reproduce graphics (Stephens et al., 1988).

IDEA FILE

Stephens and colleagues (1988) have suggested six rules for handling floppy disks that should be posted and taught to students:

1. Handle the disk only by its label.
2. Keep disks away from magnets.
3. Keep the disk in its envelop when not in use.
4. Keep disks at comfortable temperatures.
5. Be careful not to bend disks.
6. Never remove a disk while the red light is on. (pp. 221–222)

In addition to these suggestions, teachers should consider the following rules for protecting microcomputer systems:

1. Never keep plants near a computer. There is a risk of spilling water on the system when plants are watered.
2. Avoid keeping the system in direct sunlight for long periods of time.
3. Avoid placing the computer on an enclosed shelf that restricts the flow of the unit's cooling fan.
4. Many computers are stored on moveable carts, and teachers should avoid stretching cords across areas where the students walk.
5. If a computer is used in a carpeted area, an antistatic device should be used.

■ ■ ■ ■

SOFTWARE EVALUATION

Computer software provides the computer with the instructions necessary for it to complete the desired functions. For example, the computer requires instructions before it can operate a spelling program or an IEP development program. Teachers are rapidly becoming aware of the fact that not all software programs are created equal in terms of quality, ease of use, and adaptability to a variety of instructional situations. Therefore, teachers are spending more time attempting to locate information for judging software programs (Malouf, Morariu, Coulson, & Maiden, 1989). The ability to judge and choose software programs that match the needs of their students may be one of the most important emerging competencies for special educators.

The ability to evaluate software is not as difficult as some teachers may think if they have a good understanding of the basic principles of learning and related principles of good instructional design (Test, 1985). Thorkildsen and Reid (1989), for example, found that the quality of instructional sequencing (i.e., the steps in which the material is presented) appears to be more important than the number of corrective or remedial loops included within a program. As most special educators know, a teacher's ability to analyze a task for presentation in a logical, sequential fashion increases the probability of learner success. With this basic understanding of instructional design and the learning style of students with handicaps, teachers can look for software that presents content in a sequence consistent with their general curricular objectives.

One general rule for evaluating software is that the reviewer should not be swayed by an attractive package with a number of laudatory comments and promises of what the software will do. Companies selling software are in the business to make money and will use a variety of advertising ploys to sell their products. Slick graphics, sound, and advertising strategies sometimes serve to mask poorly designed instruction. Teachers who are aware of this possibility will be in a better position to make informed judgments about the software they choose.

Test (1985) identified three important considerations in evaluating software that are based on research relating to instructional design and learning theory. First, the software should provide antecedent stimuli that set the stage for the type of responses the students will be required to make. Second, the software should allow students many opportunities for making the desired responses. Finally, the software should provide systematic consequences to include reinforcement and performance feedback.

These three criteria, all based on empirically validated research, may be better understood by applying an example. A teacher reviewing software packages for use as part of a spelling program would look for one that introduces lessons by helping the student complete a preinstructional activity. This use of antecedent stimuli models the desired terminal task for the student. The more desirable packages also allow the student the opportunity to respond in a fashion similar to the skill being taught. Hasselbring and Goin (1989) provided an example of this criterion in their choice of a spelling program that allows the student to type the correct spelling of a word instead of requiring the student to choose the correct spelling from a computer-generated list.

A more desirable software program would include frequent opportunities for students to spell the similar words with frequent practice in spelling previously presented words. The number of new words presented would be limited, and frequent reinforcers and information about student progress would be provided. Finally, good programs provide a component that analyzes student errors and provides the teacher with a permanent record of student progress throughout the program.

IDEA FILE

Software reviews are becoming more prevalent; however, teachers should not take favorable reviews at face value. In a sense, teachers should review the reviews, asking themselves whether reviewers have provided enough information about certain critical areas outlined in this chapter and elsewhere.

Many software evaluation forms are available, and some are better than others. One suggestion is for teachers to obtain a copy of the evaluation form developed by Test (1985). Test divided his form into three sections: program presentation, student response, and consequences/feedback. Each section includes a number of questions for teachers to answer while trying out the software program. A small sampling of these questions is presented here. Teachers who obtain the entire form will have a highly useful tool for making informed decisions about software purchase and use.

Program Presentation

■ Is it personalized? The program should ask for and use the student's name (Test, 1985, p. 38).

■ Does it present information in a logical sequence? A unit on checking accounts, for example, would not be in logical order if it tried to teach students to balance a checkbook before they learned to fill out the register (Test, 1985, p. 38).

Student Responses

■ Are sample responses presented to the student? A model response can save unnecessary questions while allowing the student to operate programs without assistance (Test, 1985, p. 43).

Consequences/Feedback

■ Is corrective feedback specific enough to allow students to remediate incorrect answers? Many programs show students the correct answer, but, according to Test, they would be more useful if they included a brief explanation of why the student's answer was correct or incorrect.

The article by Test provides many insights into the development of more effective software based on the principles of learning. It should be a required reading for all teachers who use microcomputers.

■ ■ ■ ■

MICROCOMPUTERS AND THE CURRICULUM

Computer-assisted instruction can play a pivotal role in helping teachers provide more effective instruction to learners with mild to moderate handicaps. However, professionals must consciously plan for how CAI will correlate with curriculum content and behavioral objectives for specific students (Panyan, Hummel, & Jackson, 1988). Without such careful planning, it is likely that the use of CAI will result in what Hofmeister (1982) referred to as "instructional fragmentation" (p. 120). Hofmeister used this term in referring to situations in which CAI is applied in a random fashion, with little or no consideration given to the student's IEP or the general curriculum.

For example, a teacher borrowed a new software program in mathematics and decided that Monte, a student with severe deficits in this subject, was to work a half hour a day with the program. This teacher did not ask some critical questions, such as whether or not the program was a tutorial, which would fit Monte's needs, or drill and practice, which might only serve to confuse him. This is an example of instructional fragmentation because the teacher did not analyze whether or not the program correlated with Monte's IEP objectives in mathematics. The teacher also failed to determine whether or not the program correlated with the curriculum content currently being presented in class activities. This is another example of Hofmeister's concept of instructional fragmentation.

The key is to carefully plan for a match between the curriculum (what is being taught), the student (identified strengths and weaknesses), and the type of CAI best suited to the situation (Bigge, 1988). This section provides information regarding the use of CAI as it relates to the major areas of the curriculum. The first subsection provides information about the current state of the art for merging computer instruction and videos for teaching a variety of skills to students. These technological advances transcend all curriculum areas, and during the next decade they will have a much greater impact on the instruction of students with handicaps.

Interactive Videodiscs

Laser videodisc technology suggests to some a highly complex, costly, and future-oriented approach that is beyond the capability of schools, both in knowledge and affordability (Hofmeister, 1989). But, as Hofmeister stated, "such first impressions are far from the truth" (1989, p. 52). The cost of videodisc systems continues to decline while the technology continues to improve.

Laser videodisc systems use a safe, low-power light to focus on a disc, reflecting the information stored on the disc back to a sensor. The technology is basically the same as that used in home compact disc players. The bits of information collected by the sensor can then be shown in rapid succession to create motion on a television monitor or can be shown in still-frame sequences that stay on the screen, allowing the teacher to explain or elaborate a point (Carnine, 1989).

One major advantage of this technology is the amount of information that can be stored on a 12-inch videodisc. Up to 54,000 individual high-resolution color frames can be stored on one side of a disc. These frames can be combined to show motion (similar to a movie on a home videocassette recorder), or one frame at a time can be shown (e.g., a painting in a museum). A second advantage of this technology is its speed. Using a videodisc player, a teacher can move anywhere on the disc in a few seconds. This has tremendous potential in terms of instruction. The flow of the lesson does not have to be interrupted as it does with the slow forwarding and reversing that is required of VCR players.

Laser videodisc players can be used in a stand-alone mode or they can be linked to a microcomputer. Both modes provide teachers with powerful instructional tools. In a stand-alone mode the videodisc player is linked to a television or monitor and is controlled by a remote control keypad pad similar to a remote control device for a television or VCR.

A teacher working with groups of students can present information about a variety of science concepts and enter the sequence on the videodisc that either reviews each concept or presents supplementary information (e.g., a picture of a rock formation or an actual experiment being conducted). Application exercises can be programmed at the end of each sequence. The remote control device allows the teacher to move about the group freely to gather information concerning student progress or provide individual assistance (Carnine, 1989).

There are many advantages to using the videodisc as an instructional partner. The videodisc allows the teacher to stop, scan, and step forward or backward frame by frame in seconds. These functions can be accomplished while the teacher is explaining or clarifying information for the students. In addition, information on videodiscs can present "experiments and demonstrations that are difficult or expensive to conduct in classroom situations" (Carnine, 1989, p. 527). Also, various motivating effects can be included in the program to capture and hold the attention of the students.

When the videodisc player is interfaced with a microcomputer it can serve as a more expensive but highly effective type of CAI (Hofmeister, 1989). As with all CAI programs, students can work with the computer to learn new skills or practice old ones. The difference is that the program contains instructions to access various sequences on the videodisc to support or explain a concept.

A variety of videodisc courseware is available to teach academic skills. Courseware that has been developed using a sound base of learning theory and instructional technology can be a useful supplement to instruction for many learners with mild handicapping conditions. Carnine (1989) and his colleagues have developed and field-tested videodisc courseware that covers core mathematics and science concepts. It is based on the mastery learning approach combined with direct instruction strategies explained elsewhere in this text. Basically, each program allows students to orally answer questions posed by the narrator of the program. Students are also required to write answers after explanations, and those explanations are replayed if a certain percentage of the students continues to have difficulty with the concept. Quizzes are presented frequently throughout, and remedial explanations are presented when appropriate. Use of these programs allows teachers the opportunity to assess learner progress frequently and retrieve remedial explanations to assist them almost instantaneously.

The use of videodisc courseware seems especially applicable for students with learning disabilities who are mainstreamed in regular education core subject areas (Miller & Cooke, 1989). These programs have been used to successfully teach fractions (Lubke, Rogers, & Evans, 1989) and a variety of other subjects, from earth science to mastering ratios and word problems (Carnine, 1989).

IDEA FILE

The Minnesota Educational Computing Corporation (MECC) maintains a directory of available videodiscs. Some of the videodisc courseware described here can be obtained from Systems Impact, Inc. Addresses are given below.

MECC	Systems Impact, Inc.
3490 Lexington Avenue, N	4400 MacArthur Boulevard, NW
St. Paul, MN 55126	Suite 203
1-800-228-3504	Washington, DC 20007
	1-800-822-4636

■ ■ ■ ■

CAI, Reading, and Written Expression

CAI can be of great value to students who have significant deficits in reading and written expression skills (Balajthy, 1989). CAI cannot replace good teacher-student interaction, but it can supplement this interaction and provide students with a means to practice skills taught by the teacher. The word-processing capability of computers allows students with poor handwriting, grammar, and spelling ability to get their ideas and experiences on paper. This allows teachers to develop reading and written expression activities based on the experiences of the students, a highly motivating approach.

Reading software in general should provide interesting activities that allow students to practice both reading and writing (Balajthy, 1989). These programs should not only provide structured drill and practice, but also allow for students to create stories. This second approach helps reading come alive for students and provides them with a more active role in the process of learning to read. The following is a partial list of sources of software for reading and written expression:

AppleWorks
Apple Computer, Inc.
10260 Bandley Drive
Cupertino, CA 95014
Apple II series

Bank Street Filer
Scholastic, Inc.
PO Box 7501
2301 East McCarty Street
Jefferson City, MO 65102
Apple II series, Commodore

Bank Street Speller
Scholastic, Inc.
Apple II series

Bank Street Story Book
Mindscape
3444 Dundee Road
Northbrook, IL 60062
Apple II series, IBM-PC, Commodore 64

Bank Street Writer
Scholastic, Inc.
Apple II series, IBM-PC, Commodore, Atari

Compu-Spell
Edu-Ware Services
PO Box 22222
Agoura, CA 91301
Elementary

Deadline
Infocom
125 Cambridge Park Drive
Cambridge, MA 02140

Apple II series, Macintosh, Atari, Commodore, IBM-PC, TRS-80, and others

English Achievement
Microcomputer Workshops
225 Westchester Avenue
Port Chester, NY 10573
Apple, Commodore, IBM-PC, TRS-80

Essential Idioms in English
Regents/ALA
2 Park Avenue
New York, NY 10016
Apple II series

First Categories
Laureate Learning Systems
1 Mill Street
Burlington, VT 05401
Preschool–Adult

Grammar Mastery
Regents/ALA
Apple II series

Hitchhiker's Guide to the Galaxy
Infocom
Apple II series, Macintosh, Atari, Commodore, IBM-PC, TRS-80, and others

Kermit's Electronic Story Maker
Simon & Schuster Computer Software
 Division
1230 Avenue of the Americas
New York, NY 10020
Apple II series, Commodore 64

MicroSpeed Read
CBS Software
1 Fawcett Place
Greenwich, CT 06836
Apple, Commodore, IBM-PC

Milliken's PreWrite
Milliken Publishing Co.
1100 Research Boulevard
St. Louis, MO 63132
Apple II series

Milliken's Word Processor
Milliken Publishing Co.
Apple II series

The Newsroom
Scholastic, Inc.
PO Box 7502
2931 E. McCarty Street
Jefferson City, MO 65102
Apple II series

Past Tense Present Tense
Computer Courseware Services
300 York Avenue
St. Paul, MN 55101
Elementary

PFS File
Scholastic, Inc.
Apple II series, IBM-PC

PlayWriter Series
Woodbury Software
127 White Oak Lane
CN 1001
Old Bridge, NJ 08857
Commodore 64, Apple series, IBM-PC
Separate disks for *Adventures in Space, Tales of Me, Mystery!,* and *Castles and Creatures*

Puzzler
Sunburst Communications
39 Washington Avenue
Pleasantville, NY 10570
Apple II series, IBM-PC, Commodore 64

Quill
D. C. Heath
125 Spring Street
Lexington, MA 02173
Apple II series

Quizit
Regents/ALA
Apple II series

Sensible Grammar
Sensible Software
210 South Woodward
Suite 229
Birmingham, MI 48011
Apple II series

Sensible Speller
Sensible Software
Apple II series

Sentence Combining
Milliken Publishing Co.
Apple II series

Steps to Comprehension
Educational Publishing Concepts
PO Box 715
St Charles, IL 60174
Grades 1–8

Story Machine
Spinnaker Software
125 First Street
Cambridge, MA 02139
Apple II series, IBM-PC

Story Maker
Sierra On-Line
Coarsegold, CA 93614
Apple II series

Story Maker: A Fact and Fiction Tool Kit
Scholastic, Inc.
Apple II series

Story Tree
Scholastic, Inc.
Apple II series, IBM-PC, Commodore 64

Tank Tactics
Data Command
329 East Court Street
Kankakee, IL 60901
Grades 4–6, remedial reading and spelling

That's My Story
Learning Well
200 South Service Road
Roslyn Heights, NY 11577
Apple II series

Tinker Tales
Compu-Tech
240 Bradley Street
New Haven, CT 06510
IBM-PC

Vocabulary Baseball
J & S Software
14 Vanderventer Avenue
Port Washington, NY 11050
Apple II series

Vocabulary Mastery
Regents/ALA
Apple II series

Winning with Phonics
Wise Owl Workshop
1168 Avendia de las Palmas
Livermore, CA 94550
Grades 4–8, remedial reading instruction

Wizard of Words
Computer Advanced Ideas
2550 Ninth Street
Suite 104
Berkeley, CA 94709
Grades 2–8

Write a Character Sketch
Minnesota Educational Computing Corp.
 (MECC)
2520 Broadway Drive
St Paul, MN 55113
Apple II series

Write a Narrative
Minnesota Educational Computing Corp.
 (MECC)
Apple II series

The Writing Adventure
DLM Educational Software
One DLM Park
Allen, TX 75002
Apple II series

Zork
Infocom
Apple II series, Macintosh, Atari, Commodore, IBM-PC, TRS-80, and others

CAI and Arithmetic

CAI can be used in arithmetic instruction for tutorial, drill-and-practice, and gaming applications (Kinzer, Sherwood, & Bransford, 1986). In general, CAI can best be used when it augments the teacher's instruction; therefore, it is important to carefully select software that matches the objectives targeted for instruction.

At times the tutorial software provides instruction and can be used independently of the teacher. For students with mild to moderate handicaps, however, interacting with these programs without teacher assistance can lead to problems. The best instruction for these students would combine teacher-centered activities, CAI, and daily living activities presented in the community. The following is a partial list of arithmetic and mathematics software packages and where they can be obtained.

*Academic Skill Builders in Math: Set-Ups for
 the Adaptive Firmware Card*
DLM Teaching Resources
1-800-527-4747 TX
1-800-442-4711

Academics with Scanning: Math
Washington Research Foundation
(206)633-3569

Arithmetic 1, 2, and 3 with Speech
Life Science Associates
(516)472-2111

Fay: That Math Woman
Didatech Software, Ltd.
(604)299-4435

First Shapes
First Byte, Inc.
(213)595-7006

Fun With Math
Access Unlimited-Speech Enterprises
(713)461-1666

Job Survival Series
MCE Inc.
(616)345-8681

Kennedy Handi-Math Program
Kennedy Memorial Hospital for Children
 Education Department
(617)254-3800 Ext. 189

LogicMaster
Dunamis, Inc.
(404)932-0485

LogoLearning with Numbers
J B Software
(408)996-9630

Math Disk
Washington Research Foundation
(206)633-3569

Math Power Program
Instructional/Communications
  Technology, Inc.
1-800-225-5428

Math Scan
Barry R. Ankney
(309)248-7447

Math Scratchpad I
Zygo Industries, Inc.
(503)297-1724

Math Scratchpad II
Zygo Industries, Inc.
(503)297-1724

Mathtalk
First Byte, Inc.
(213)595-7006

Mouse Math
Ballard & Tighe, Inc.
1-800-321-4332 CA
(714)990-4332

Trace Math Aid
Computers to Help People, Inc.
(608)257-5917
(608)257-1270 (TDD)

Voice Math
Voice Learning Systems
1-800-531-5314
(213)475-1036

Other Applications of Computers

The field of special education changes rapidly. New developments including teaching strategies, technological advances, and curriculum alternatives are available almost weekly, and keeping up with these developments is a Herculean task. Computer networking via electronic bulletin boards allows teachers to keep in touch with the latest developments in the field and share information with other professionals.

To access bulletin boards, the user dials a telephone number with a device called a *modem* (a device linked to the computer that allows it to communicate with another computer over the telephone lines). The user can then retrieve electronic information from the bulletin board or place information on the board for others to retrieve. The cost of most bulletin boards includes only time spent using the telephone lines and, for some, a start-up fee and monthly charge. The most common bulletin board for special educators is Special Net (1201 16th Street, NW, Washington, DC 20036). This service is available through subscription and allows users to access special education information on more than 30 bulletin boards. Information can be obtained about a variety of topics such as early childhood special education, pending legislation, computer applications in special education, current research, and legal issues.

KEY CONCEPTS

- ■ Microcomputers are relatively uncomplicated tools that can improve teaching effectiveness and efficiency.
- ■ Microcomputers are designed to accept input, process information, store the information, and provide some form of output.

- Random access memory (RAM) is the user's temporary workspace; it is erased when the machine is turned off or otherwise loses power.

- Read only memory (ROM) is permanent memory built into the computer at the factory and includes instructions the computer needs to complete its basic functions.

- The amount of RAM a computer has differs from machine to machine and dictates the programs that can be run by the machine and the amount of space available to create documents.

- Software provides the computer with instructions to complete a variety of functions.

- Software evaluation requires an ability to match principles of learning against the instruction presented by the program.

- The quality of the sequence (task analysis) used to present the material is the basis of more effective CAI software.

- Attractive packages or accompanying laudatory comments and promises about the software do not necessarily reflect its usefulness.

- Software should present antecedent stimuli to catch the learner's attention or set the stage for the instruction.

- Software should also allow students many opportunities to make the desired responses. In addition, software should provide systematic consequences and performance feedback.

- The software evaluation form presented by Test (1985) provides teachers with an effective method for making informed decisions when choosing software for use in their classes.

- Instructional fragmentation can occur if teachers do not carefully match CAI programs to their curriculum objectives and the needs of their students.

- Interactive videodiscs can provide teachers with a powerful instructional tool: the ability to present students with experiments, situations, and demonstrations that are difficult to conduct in classroom or simulated activities.

- Laser videodiscs can be used in a stand-alone mode or while interfaced with a computer.

- Laser videodiscs allow teachers to retrieve information instantaneously from any part of the disc without interrupting the flow of the lesson by rewinding or fast forwarding.

- Videodisc courseware based on the principles of learning has been found to be highly effective in teaching learners with mild handicaps difficult academic and content area subjects.

- Software designed to be a part of a total reading program should provide drill and practice, but it should also allow readers the opportunity to create their own stories.

- Electronic communication via computers allows teachers the opportunity to stay current by accessing information from bulletin boards set up by various professional organizations.

■ ■ ■ ■

CHAPTER EIGHT

TEACHING FUNCTIONAL READING AND WRITTEN EXPRESSION

■ Instruction in reading and other language arts skill areas has been given considerable attention in most curricula for students with mild and moderate handicaps. Both special and regular educators have come to realize that traditional approaches to teaching reading and language arts, when used alone, may be ineffective for students with learning handicaps (Paris & Oka, 1989). Over time, unsuccessful teaching procedures may cause students to lose enthusiasm for reading and result in poor attitudes and general loss of motivation.

When this happens, it compounds the original effects of the learning problems, and the cycle of the poor reader becomes seemingly unbreakable (Weisberg, 1988). Motivation for learning to read and use language arts skills in a functional manner is an important place for teachers to begin. Developing motivating reading activities such as games or computer-assisted instruction is important, but it should not be the entire focus of the special education classroom. Using community-based instruction is a major way to motivate students to read and write more effectively. Teachers are finding many ways to teach reading and language arts skills in environments other than traditional classroom settings (Wesson & Keefe, 1989).

BASIS FOR READING AND LANGUAGE ARTS INSTRUCTION

Reading and language arts programs for students with learning problems should be developed according to individual needs. For example, a high school student with behavior disorders might need assistance in reading in the content areas and require help with learning new strategies to gain knowledge from his science assignments (Mastropieri, Emerick, & Scruggs, 1988). Two other students who have learning disabilities and mild mental handicaps, respectively, might require instruction in reading comprehension (Pany & McCoy, 1988). In each case, these students may need help in generalizing reading and written expression to life situations.

The basis for developing reading and written expression activities for any capable learner is the *functionality* of the skills being taught. For example, one learner may be able to read on a third-grade level using a basal book, but may not be able to read and follow the directions accompanying a power tool. Other learners may be able to read cautionary words when they are presented in the classroom, but may not be able to act appropriately in community situations when confronted with the same words.

The major reason for teaching learners reading and language arts skills is that these skills can help them to be more independent in home, work, leisure/recreation, and other community environments. If some professionals have not been successful in teaching these students useful reading and language arts skills, it may be due to their use of general education curriculum approaches presented at a slow rate (Blanton, Sitko, & Gillespie, 1976). The academic curriculum for regular education, although accurate in scope and sequence of skills (i. e., the order in which skills are generally learned), generally does not emphasize application of the skills to community problems and situations.

Special educators can use basically the same scope and sequence of reading and language arts skills, but the diagnosis of reading deficits and the methods of instruction must be more precise than those used with nonhandicapped students. Also, special educators should combine the teaching of the basic skills with the immediate application of those skills to community situations (e.g., finding words in the community that are examples of certain decoding rules).

This chapter provides an overview of the preferred practices for teaching reading and written expression skills to learners with mild and moderate handicaps. As with the other chapters in this half of the text, the material will be presented in terms of the curriculum development process discussed in Chapter Four. Readers may wish to return to that chapter and review Figure 4.2 before continuing to the next section.

READING AND WRITTEN EXPRESSION: THE IEP

Steps One and Two: Conduct the Community Needs Assessment

Conducting a CNA allows teachers to place reading and written expression skills in the context of the community. The information gathered during this exercise should help in designing long-term goals that reflect application of basic skills to activities in home, vocational, leisure-recreation, and other community environments. Conducting a CNA may also assist teachers in finding volunteers and community sites where academic skills can be practiced in more natural settings (e.g., shopping malls, employment offices).

Table 8.1 presents a partial list of community settings where reading and written expression skills may be used and practiced. Once these settings have been identified, teachers can organize the information into subenvironments, depending on the type of skills required (Brown et al., 1979). For example, the reading and written expression skills

TABLE 8.1 *Partial List of Potential Community Environments Where Students Can Use Reading and Written Expression Skills*

Community Environment	Related Reading and Written Expression Skills
Fast-food restaurants	Reading sight words from an over-the-counter menu
Family restaurants	Reading sight words from an individual menu
Grocery stores	Reading sight words on store items Reading sight words on signs Writing checks
Employment agency	Reading job notices Filling out forms Developing a resumé
Public library	Locating and reading books and magazines Listening to and visually following talking books Researching information about various topics and summarizing it in writing
Home	Reading a newspaper Reading directions for assembling items, cooking, and cleaning Writing letters and cards Writing expressively for pleasure

what different from those required for filling out an application. Both of these settings may be located at an employment agency, yet they can be considered separate subenvironments.

Tables 8.2 through 8.4 provide examples of how the CNA process can be applied within the school to identify functional skills needed by students to succeed in mainstream settings. These skill areas are as important to learners as the environments and skills taught outside the school. However, a total program for teaching reading should not favor either in-school or out-of-school activities; it should be a blend of both.

Step Three: Identify Potential Annual Goals

Potential annual goals for reading and written expression can be identified on two levels. The first level deals with the basic skills identified in scope-and-sequence charts, while the second identifies the application of these skills to the community. Based on skills listed in Figure 4.5 and on skills suggested by other authors (Bender & Valletutti, 1982; Mercer & Mercer, 1985; Radabaugh & Yukish, 1982; Stephens, Hartman, & Lucas, 1982), the following is a partial list of potential annual goals that could be set at both levels. This list should provide teachers with starting points for developing their own reading and written expression curricula.

TABLE 8.2 *Example of a CNA Gathering Device for Mainstreamed Middle or Junior High School Students*

Analysis of CNA Results:

Skill Areas Tapped	Specific Skills
Reading	Read list of scheduled classes: Course name, teacher's name. Read list of assignments and comprehend directions. Read titles of textbooks.
Mathematics	Tell time to the hour and minute on a wristwatch and a school clock. Be aware of the passage of short periods of time between classes. Develop a work schedule for home. Recognize room and locker numbers.
Speaking	Generate questions for clarification or explanation of assignments.
Writing	Record due dates for assignments. Record directions for assignments. Prepare written assignments accurately and edit them.
Self-Management/Organization	Organize materials: a notebook for every course and pencils. Have a pocket in notebooks for assignments. Tape a copy of the class schedule on the front of each notebook. Stack books and notebooks in order of class schedule in locker.
	Designate a work area at home. Keep all necessary supplies available. Post a list of assignments in the work area. Monitor task completion according to a time schedule. Designate an area near the morning exit to store books and assignments.

Prepared by Susan Munson, Duquesne University

READING

Decoding

1. Identifies and pronounces blends commonly found in words at the first-, second-, and third-grade levels.
2. Identifies and pronounces consonants when found in the initial, medial, and final positions in words.
3. Identifies and pronounces both short and long vowels in words.
4. Identifies and pronounces digraphs and diphthongs in words at the first-, second-, and third-grade levels.
5. Identifies and pronounces root words, prefixes, and suffixes.
6. Identifies rhyming words and decodes words with the same pattern.
7. Recognizes endings: *s, es, ed, ing.*
8. Identifies compound words.
9. Identifies plural endings, irregular plurals, and *'s* possessive.
10. Uses vowel digraphs correctly.
11. Decodes silent *k* in *kn* (know).

TABLE 8.3   *Examples of a Task Sequence Involving Reading Skills Generated from the CNA in Table 8.2*

Environment: Middle or junior high school
Task to be completed: Managing time, assignments, and materials

Procedures for Gathering Information:
  Method: (a) Direct observation
            (b) Interview
  Source of Information: (a) Competent student
                          (b) Teacher, student

Location of Task Completion	Specific Skills Performed
Locker	1. Read schedule of classes and rooms.
	2. Take books, notebooks, assignments, and pencils for classes until able to return to locker.
Hallways	3. Walk to classroom during allotted transition time before late bell.
	4. Recognize classroom number.
Classroom	5. Enter room and take assigned seat.
	6. Get materials ready for class.
	7. Submit homework assignments due.
	8. Record due date and directions for next assignment.
	9. Ask teacher for clarification/explanation.
	10. Gather materials and leave for next class.

Complete steps 3–10 until able to return to locker for next set of materials.

Locker	11. At end of day, review assignments list and take necessary materials home.
Home	12. Place materials in designated work area.
	13. Review directions and make list of the order for assignment completion.
	14. Complete assignments, check for accuracy, cross off the list.
	15. Place assignments in correct notebook for the next day.
	16. Put books in designated place so they will be remembered the next morning.

Prepared by Susan Munson, Duquesne University

12. Decodes silent *gh* (through).
13. Recognizes and uses words that signal relationships (*and, or, except, but, especially, such as*).
14. Uses context clues to derive meaning from unfamiliar words.
15. Uses root words, prefixes, and suffixes to derive the meaning of words.
16. Recognizes and pronounces a variety of functional community-valid words using a whole-word memorization approach.

Comprehension

1. Demonstrates the meaning of a wide variety of words.
2. Locates and describes the main idea of a story and can recall details.
3. Follows written directions.
4. Sequences events in logical order.
5. Makes basic inferences and evaluations.
6. Relates printed words to objects or actions.
7. Follows printed directions ("Find the boy's house").
8. Reads to find information.
9. Predicts events in a story.
10. Skims for information.
11. Makes judgments from given facts.
12. Recognizes the stereotyping of people in stories.
13. Draws logical conclusions.

TABLE 8.4 *Example of a Task Sequence Involving Reading Skills Generated from the CNA in Table 8.2*

Environment: Library
Task to be completed: Locate reference material for a writing project
Procedures for Gathering Information:
  Method: Direct observation, interview
  Sources: Self-performance, librarian
Analysis of Specific Skills:

Location of Task Completion	Specific Skills Performed
Main area	1. Enter library and select a worktable. Walk/talk/work quietly.
Reference desk	2. Ask librarian how to find information on topic.
Card catalog	3. Look for topic in card catalog for subject, author, or title.
	4. Read summaries on cards.
	5. Write down call numbers of books/periodicals that relate to topic.
Bookshelves	6. Read signs/map to determine where books/periodicals are located according to call number.
	7. Find area and locate desired books.
	8. Take books to work table.
Worktable	9. Read books and record information (make a reference card for each book). (Photocopy sections if desired.)
	10. Do not reshelve books when finished.
Circulation desk	11. Present library card/sign-out book (name, address, phone).
	12. Return book on due date.

Prepared by Susan Munson, Duquesne University

14. Selects an appropriate title after reading an untitled selection.
15. Recognizes that characters change as a story develops.
16. Summarizes main ideas and selects facts to support main ideas.
17. Identifies and recalls story facts and significant details.
18. Identifies the point of view in a selection.
19. Identifies the influence of setting on characters and events.
20. Recognizes elements of characterization (presentation of characters, completeness of characters, function of characters, and relationships with other characters).
21. Proves a point with factual information from the reading selections.
22. Identifies the basic elements of a news story (who, what, where, when, why, and how).
23. Demonstrates the meaning of words by acting appropriately when confronted with a wide variety of community-valid vocabulary (e.g., "danger," "push").
24. Follows some written directions with adaptations.
25. Makes basic inferences and evaluations based on listening comprehension skills.
26. Locates basic information about subjects using source books, manuals, encyclopedias, dictionaries and other reference tools.
27. Uses maps to arrive at intracommunity and intercommunity locations.
28. Assembles objects using written directions.
29. Demonstrates reading skills used in a variety of home, work, leisure/recreation, and other community settings.
30. Demonstrates the meaning and acts appropriately when confronted with a wide variety of community-valid skills.
31. Locates, reads, and acts appropriately in relation to key words found in the context of recipes, menus, directions on labels, and the like.

WRITTEN EXPRESSION

Spelling, Handwriting, Composition

1. Spells consonant and vowel sounds correctly both out of context and in the context of words.
2. Spells a variety of phoneme/grapheme groups both out of context and in the context of words.
3. Uses dictionary location skills in spelling.
4. Demonstrates match-to-sample manuscript writing skills (e.g., use of visual models).
5. Demonstrates match-to-sample cursive writing skills (e.g., use of models).
6. Arranges words in logical order to form sentences.
7. Writes simple answers to questions.
8. Dictates a story.
9. Writes a short paragraph.
10. Demonstrates the correct use of punctuation.
11. Establishes a preference for either left- or right-handedness.
12. Draws familiar objects using the basic strokes of manuscript writing.
13. Uses writing paper that is standard for manuscript writing.
14. Uses correct writing position of body, arm, hand, paper, and pencil.
15. Writes clear, legible manuscript letters at a rate appropriate for ability.
16. Arranges work neatly and pleasingly on a page (i.e., uses margins and paragraph indentions and makes clean erasures).
17. Writes from memory all letters of the alphabet in cursive form.
18. Uses cursive writing for day-to-day use.
19. Maintains and uses manuscript writing for charts, maps, and labels.
20. Reduces size of writing to proportions of letters that an adult would use.

21. Writes imaginative stories in which ideas and feelings are expressed.
22. Writes simple thank-you notes using correct form.
23. Builds ideas into paragraphs.
24. Correctly sequences ideas in sentences.
25. Makes simple outlines with main ideas.
26. Uses correct form and mechanics in writing invitations and business letters.
27. Compiles a list of books read, including the title and author of the books and their subjects.
28. Writes a brief story in response to a community-based activity.
29. Organizes writing by sticking to one subject and striving for a continuous thought flow.
30. Writes from a point of view that is consistent with the intention.
31. Spells own name and names of significant others correctly.
32. Spells correctly a variety of community-valid sight words.
33. Dictates directions and explanations of witnessed events.
34. Writes name, address, and other personal information.
35. Fills out employment, bank, and other applications.
36. Writes brief letters of complaint.
37. Writes personal letters.
38. Lists activities that need to be accomplished.
39. Records brief directions.
40. Records notes concerning job descriptions or community activities.
41. Carries a card containing personal information and can transcribe the information onto other forms.

These examples of goal statements are a starting point for teachers, who may add to the list as dictated by the needs of their students.

Step Four: Translate Goals into Potential Short-Term Objectives

For goals to be translated into potential short-term objectives, the student outcomes must be described in measurable terms. Teachers have two choices concerning the types of objectives they wish to write in relation to academic or basic skills. First, objectives can be written in a traditional fashion, reflecting skill performance in classroom activities. For example, the following objectives represent two classroom-based skills.

Outcome: The student will locate an answer in the body of a story, reading it as proof to a question asked by the teacher.

Context: Story chosen from basal reader (second-grade level).

Criterion: 5/5.

Outcome: The student will write basic explanations to questions asked by the teacher.

Context: Oral questions asked by the teacher.

Criterion: Explanations must include relevant details and sequential ordering of ideas. Product judged by the teacher.

The second approach involves restructuring the objective by either using community-valid materials or requiring the student to perform the skill in a community environment. In this instance, the objectives can be altered to reflect the following:

Outcome: The student will locate an answer in the body of a story, reading it as proof to a question asked by the teacher.

Context: Stories from newspaper articles.

Criterion: 5/5.

Outcome: The student will write basic explanations to questions asked by an employment counselor.

Context: State and private employment agencies.

Criterion: Explanations must include relevant details and sequential ordering of ideas. Product judged by teacher and employment counselor.

A rule of thumb concerning the type of objectives to write generally concerns the age or functioning level of the students. Older or higher functioning students should move quickly toward practicing reading and written comprehension skills in community environments using community-valid materials.

Younger children would also participate in frequent community instruction, but not on the same scale. The key is to help students see the need for developing these skills and to generalize skills taught in the classroom to community activities in which they will most likely be used (Dever, 1989).

Short-term objectives that describe skills related to natural environments help teachers structure activities that provide students with practice in reading and written expression under conditions (e.g., with certain materials or certain people) they will be confronting when they are not in school. Following are examples of additional long-term goals and short-term objectives that allow for instruction in both reading and written expression. These examples are presented in a different format from the previous ones to allow the reader a choice of approach for objective development.

Goal: 1.0 *Student will demonstrate appropriate health habits.*

Objective: 1.3 Student will demonstrate knowledge of proper nutrition and weight control to include the following subskills:
Subskills
Lists components of a balanced daily diet.
Practices exercise and weight control.
Uses scale to monitor weight.
States appropriate weight for height and body frame.
Suggested Sites
County extension office
Fitness center
Health department

Objective: 1.4 Student will demonstrate the appropriate prevention and treatment of common illness to include the following subskills:
Subskills
Gets proper amount of rest and sleep.
Practices basic sanitary habits.
Suggested Sites
Health department
County extension office

Goal: 1.0 *Student will demonstrate appropriate health habits.*

Objective: 1.1 Student will demonstrate appropriate dressing skills to include the following areas:

☐ Climate and weather

☐ Color and pattern coordination

☐ Fit of clothes

☐ Components of appropriate attire

☐ Dressing for occasion

☐ Basic clothing care

Suggested Sites
County extension office
Local department stores
Local discount stores

Objective: 1.3 Student will demonstrate knowledge of proper nutrition and weight control to include all of the following skill areas:

☐ Dangers of fad diets versus balanced nutritional diets

☐ Consulting medical doctor or health clinic about dietary problems

☐ Importance of exercise and weight control

☐ Use of scale for monitoring weight

☐ Appropriate weight for height and body frame

☐ Safe use of nutritional supplement

Suggested Sites
County extension office

Goal: 11.0 *Student will demonstrate knowledge of various postal services.*

Objective: 11.1 Student will demonstrate different methods of mailing letters and packages, including the following:

☐ Registered mail

☐ Certified mail

☐ Express mail

☐ Federal Express

☐ United Parcel Service (UPS)

Suggested Sites
Post office (2)
UPS office

These examples of community-based objectives should not culminate in a one-shot field trip such as going to the county cooperative extension office after several classroom lessons on weight control and nutrition (objective 1.3). Instead, the teacher and students, in small groups, should attend programs offered by the county agent and gather pamphlets and support materials on a regular basis. Activities that include reading and written expression could be built around these programs and materials.

Similarly, the objective relating to postal services (objective 11.1) could stimulate activities in a variety of post offices located within the school district. Conceivably, elementary school students might engage in post-office-related activities twice a month, middle school students three times a month, and high school students weekly. The object of this approach is to teach all necessary skills in every local post office and maintain those skills over long periods of time. This approach will stimulate many new classroom-based reading and written expression activities.

Minimum Competency Testing

Many states have initiated minimum competency tests that students must pass at various points in the school curriculum in order to move on to the next level. Students must pass such a test before they can receive a high school diploma. Minimum competency testing has a distinct disadvantage for students in special education, because the requirements and the testing conditions may prevent many of them from receiving a high school diploma.

Although minimum competency testing is not directly related to assessing entry-level skills, the effects of these measures are felt in the curriculum development process within special education. Some teachers may be overemphasizing these tests and building their curricula entirely upon the test objectives. This approach can be a major setback for students with mild and moderate handicaps, because it puts emphasis on paper-and-pencil activities, the types of activities that have been a continued source of frustration for these learners.

The objectives that are the foundations for the various minimum competency tests can be useful to special educators, provided they can translate them into community-based activities. Once the basic skills and concepts are learned, teachers can more easily show students how to master them in paper-and-pencil testing situations. The following are an objective and an example from a second-grade minimum competency test for reading (Georgia Board of Education, 1975):

Skill Area: Inferential comprehension

Objective 4: The student recognizes implicitly stated main ideas, details, sequences of events, and cause and effect relationships in the context of academic materials or everyday situations.

Examples for Objective 4:

Susan did not close the gate to the yard when she left for school. When she got home, Freddy was gone. Meg and Robert came over to help her find her dog. Susan looked behind the garage. Meg and Robert looked in the yard. They walked around the block. On the way back to Susan's house, Robert looked in the neighbor's dog house. "There you are, Freddy!" Robert said.

Implicit main idea — Which is the best title?

√(A) The Lost Dog
(B) Susan and Meg
(C) The New Dog House
(D) Susan's Day at School

Implicit detail — Which is the dog's name?

(A) Meg
√(B) Freddy

| | (C) Robert |
| | (D) Susan |

Implicit sequence — Where is the last place someone looked?
- (A) at school
- (B) in Susan's yard
- ✓ (C) in the dog house
- (D) behind the garage

Implicit cause and effect — Why wasn't Susan's dog in her yard?
- ✓ (A) Susan left the gate open.
- (B) Her friends took care of him.
- (C) The neighbors played with him.
- (D) Susan didn't close the door to the garage.

Instead of relying only on paper-and-pencil tasks, the teacher might develop a series of activities to be implemented in a local pet store. During these activities the children would participate in minor prevocational tasks such as assisting in cleaning the pet cages. The teacher could discuss with the students various "what if" topics (e.g., "What if we accidentally left this cage open?") and even demonstrate what happens when the cage door is left open.

Over the course of this community experience (spanning several weeks or months, with periodic visits to the store), the students could begin writing their own stories and questions that they could practice answering.

Once the community becomes the classroom, teachers can develop many such activities that link concrete experiences to basic skills such as reading for implicit details, sequence, and cause and effect as tested by the question in the example.

One further example demonstrates the link between reading objectives and minimum competency tests. The following is an indicator and subsequent example from a high school test (Georgia Department of Education, 1985):

Skill Area: Problem solving

Indicator 11: The student recognized relevance of data in the context of academic, everyday, or employment materials.

Examples for Indicator 11:
Luke, Maria's friend who is a mechanic, offered her this information:

1. The Elan is as well-constructed a car as you'll find anywhere.

2. The Elan has great looks and handles well on the highway.

3. Compared to other compact cars, the Elan may be a little more expensive.

4. Compared to other makes, fewer Elans come through my shop for repairs.

Relevance of data — Maria doesn't have much money to spend on upkeep and repairs for a car. If she wants to buy an Elan, which statement provides the most useful information for her decision?
- (A) 1
- (B) 2
- (C) 3
- ✓ (D) 4

There are many places in the community where the skills required by this indicator can be taught. The best example is an auto dealership. Although the topic is not the crucial part of this indicator, automobiles are highly motivating for high school students and activities built around them can be exciting. Teachers and students can visit dealerships and gather literature that can be used as reading materials. Salespeople can be contacted as resources for knowledge, and they can assist in community-based role-playing situations. The students can ultimately write their own questions regarding scenarios they have developed that help them practice choosing the relevance of written data.

KEY CONCEPTS

- Placing artificial boundaries on groups of students may either hinder the growth of some or set unrealistic goals for others. Therefore, one yardstick to measure whether or not a set of skills is appropriate for a given learner is to judge the functionality of the skills in relation to life in the community.

- Reading and written communication skills can often be taught most effectively in relation to a person's role as a consumer, worker, citizen, and individual.

- A community needs assessment for reading and written expression skills involves a careful examination of the types of behaviors important for community integration. For example, a teacher may analyze a number of grocery stores to identify words a student must know to become an independent shopper.

- Potential annual goals allow the teacher to establish an appropriate scope and sequence of skills for presentation to the learner.

- Potential short-term objectives are subskills that lead to mastery of one or more goals. Because they are measurable, teachers can use these objectives as yardsticks against which a student's present level of performance is compared.

- Whenever possible, short-term objectives should reflect the application of academic skills to community-valid activities.

■ ■ ■ ■

Step Five: Assess Student Entry Behaviors

Before teachers can adequately develop teaching techniques designed to improve reading and written expression skills, a thorough analysis of each learner's strengths and weaknesses must be conducted (Ekwall, 1985). When a new student enters the class or prior to a student's placement in special education, teachers will conduct a survey-level assessment pinpointing general deficit areas. Teachers have available a wide range of commercially produced tests that provide information on reading level, decoding, reading comprehension, word usage, spelling, handwriting, and other areas (see Table 3.1, Chapter Three).

Specific assessment of reading and written expression skill levels involves proving that what has been found at the survey level is, in fact, true (Howell & Kaplan, 1980). In addition, specific-level assessment information allows teachers to pinpoint the exact areas where deficits are occurring (Meyers & Lytle, 1986; Rupley & Blair, 1983). For example, a teacher may discover that a student is having difficulty on the passage comprehension subtest from the Woodcock Reading Mastery Test-R (Woodcock, 1987). An analysis of the student's responses on this subtest may provide some clues concerning specific problem areas; however, no one commercially produced test can be expected to provide thorough coverage (Witt et al., 1988).

The teacher's job is to look at a scope-and-sequence chart for comprehension and then use a commercially produced criterion-referenced test or develop teacher-made tests that will answer the question, "How does the student fare on each reading comprehension subskill?" One commercially produced criterion-referenced test that appears to be gaining in popularity is the Brigance Diagnostic Inventory of Basic Skills (Brigance, 1977). This instrument is thorough, and it can provide the teacher with a complete breakdown of how the student performs in areas such as recall of facts, main idea, inference, drawing conclusions, and all subskills of reading comprehension.

Teachers can also perform specific-level assessment by using more informal methods such as teacher-made tests, graded word lists, and informal reading inventories (e.g., Woods & Moe, 1985). The key is that, whatever area the teacher is interested in testing, the items used are based on objectives from a scope-and-sequence chart.

Whether information is gathered from survey or from specific levels of assessment, its value depends on how it is used by teachers. The best information concerning a student's present level of performance is obtained when an error analysis is conducted. This

TABLE 8.5   *Error Analysis Chart Including Examples of Reading and Written Expression Problems*

Stimulus	Student Response	Assumed Cause for Problems
hat	hot	Substituted medial vowel
learn	learned	Changed word ending
grown	gown	Omitted letter
pave	pmave	Added letter
was	saw	Reversed letters in word
cake	sake	Poor sound discrimination—consonant variant
balloon	ballon	Poor sound discrimination—digraph
pout	put	Poor sound discrimination—dipthongs
The boy went to the store and then to the movies. Where did the boy go first?	To the movies	Inappropriate sequencing of events
Writing	Writeing	Improper formation of derivatives
I'm going to the barn.	im going to the barn	Improper use of punctuation and capitalization
The boy ran home.		Spacing problems when writing manuscript letters

task, discussed in Chapter Three, involves recording the response the student should have made, the response that was actually made, and an assumed cause for the error (Howell & Kaplan, 1980). An error analysis can provide the teacher with the specific data needed to develop appropriate teaching strategies (See Table 8.5).

IDEA FILE

Following are suggestions for developing a sequence of tasks to obtain a reading profile of a learner:

■ Gather multiple samples of reading passages of varied lengths and organize them at different grade levels (Beals, 1989). (You may need to conduct a readability sample of the passage to establish its grade level. Consult any reading textbook for readability formulas needed to accomplish this task.)

■ Using either standardized or criterion-referenced methods, establish the easy, instructional, and frustration levels (grade equivalency) of a student. Establishing these levels makes it easier to locate materials for future use (e.g., for instruction and leisure reading).

■ Gather commercially produced graded word lists or develop your own that can be used to assess the sight vocabulary or the "out-of-context" word recognition skills of learners. Organize these according to grade levels.

■ Obtain scope-and-sequence charts in reading and translate the goal statements into behavioral objectives. A correctly written behavioral objective will dictate how the skill will be assessed (Stephens, Hartman, & Lucas, 1982).

■ Use more than one method to sample a particular reading skill. For example, Howell and Kaplan (1980) suggested sampling reading comprehension by applying four survey assessment techniques: questioning, paraphrase, the cloze procedure, and the maze procedure. The use of only one procedure severely limits the quality of information received by the teacher (Howell & Morehead, 1987).

■ Periodically practice recording student responses so that the loss of information will be kept to a minimum. When a student is reading a passage aloud, the teacher should have a copy of the passage, marking both the stimulus and the actual response made by the learner (e.g., stimulus = "b a t t l e," response = "b o t t l e").

■ Perform an error analysis as the data are collected. Howell and Kaplan's (1980) system, presented in Chapter Three, is a good example. Organize data into a column for the *stimulus* (what the student should have read), a column for the *response* (what the student's actual answer or response was), and a column for assumed causes (what the teacher thinks the problem is). A system along these lines assists the teacher in organizing data for decision making.

■ ■ ■ ■

The reading ability of most learners with moderate handicaps can best be assessed using activities that relate to independent living skills. Most of these students appear to learn best when presented words in the context of everyday community activities (Snell, 1983). The assessment approach dictated by this system involves asking students to read high-utility words commonly found in the community. The question teachers should answer is whether the words chosen should be presented out of context (e.g., on flash-cards) or in community situations. Some students may not be able to read the word "McDonalds" when it is presented on a flashcard, but they may recognize the word when it is seen in the presence of its discriminative stimulus, the "Golden Arches."

Since a large majority of words most important to these students are functional to community life, assessment should occur, as often as possible, in community-based activities. For example, a teacher could have a predetermined list of words commonly found in grocery stores. During a trip to the store the teacher could point out key words to learners, asking them to read each word. After each trial the teacher would record whether or not the word was read correctly.

CASE STUDY

"Mr. Jackson, could you do a reading workup on Robbie? He's next on the waiting list for possible placement, and we need a reading level on him."

"Now Mrs. Root," said Mr. Jackson, "I know as the special education coordinator you have to expedite matters. It's just that reading levels alone provide insufficient information about Robbie's present level of performance. If he's having enough trouble to be considered for placement, then I can tell you without a test that he will be reading far below his peer group!"

"Well, what do you suggest?" said Mrs. Root.

"First, I would administer the Woodcock Reading Mastery Test-R for two pieces of information. This diagnostic test will tell me not just one reading level but Robbie's easy, instructional, and frustration levels so we can choose the most appropriate materials for him.

"If I observe Robbie closely while he takes the test, I can learn a great deal about his learning style. For example, if he's not a risk-taker, it will show up in his reluctance to answer questions. Also, when I score the test, I'll isolate his errors and analyze them so that I can make decisions about what to do next."

"You said 'first.' How long will this assessment last?" frowned Mrs. Root.

Mr. Jackson tried his most disarming smile. "Not long. The second phase involves a close inspection of the areas of concern that show up on the Woodcock. If I find an indication of serious deficits in decoding, I'll want to use a more detailed criterion-referenced test to pinpoint the exact deficit areas, for example, an inability to blend consonant-vowel-consonant. When I'm done I'll be able to write a fairly detailed list of Robbie's strengths and weaknesses in reading."

"Well, it certainly is thorough, but it sounds like a lot of time and energy when you can just give a quick achievement test."

"It will take longer," sighed Mr. Jackson, "probably about 3 to 4 hours. The result, though, will be a solid workup that allows us to design the best reading program for Robbie. Besides, the time invested now will save time later, because it'll be much easier to program for Robbie once his strengths and weaknesses are known."

"Hmm," said Mrs. Root pensively, "save time later. OK Mr. Jackson, I like the idea. Grab your Woodchuck Test!"

"No, no, Mrs. Root, that's W O O D C O C K!"

■ ■ ■ ■

Assessment of written expression can actually encompass several areas including mechanics of writing, handwriting, and spelling (Cohen & Plaskon, 1980; Hammill & Poplin, 1982). Specific-level assessment of written expression can cover areas such as capitalization, punctuation, written composition, and creative expression (Mercer & Mercer, 1985; Moran, 1983; Smith, 1989). Written samples of the student's work can be obtained and analyzed for errors in the same areas (Poteet, 1980; Weiner, 1980).

Specific-level assessment of handwriting involves analyzing samples of the student's writing assignments. (Student writing samples can be used to assess written expression, handwriting, and spelling.) The ability to write legibly is the functional goal; therefore, assessment of a student's handwriting can encompass six areas: letter formation; letter size, proportion, and alignment; spacing; line quality; slant; and rate (Graham, 1983; Mercer & Mercer, 1985, 1989).

Spelling is closely related to reading, and much of its specific-level assessment information can come from reading exercises completed by the students. An analysis of spelling errors should result in a clustering of words related to certain patterns. For example, Polloway and Smith (1982) identified several error patterns such as adding unneeded letters to words, omitting letters, reversals, mispronunciations, and final consonant changes.

Microcomputer software now exists that can assist teachers in analyzing student spelling errors. Hasselbring and Crossland (1982) and Hasselbring and Owens (1983) have developed programs that present learners with a word list given via a computer-driven cassette recorder that allows the students to type in their version of the words. The computer then scores the responses and provides the teacher with a printout listing the student's mistakes and the types of errors made.

PROGRAM IMPLEMENTATION

Identifying and Analyzing Short-Term Objectives

Short-term objectives are easily identified if a thorough list of student strengths and weaknesses has been delineated. The short-term objectives relate to the list of weaknesses, where each weakness can become the content for an objective. For example, a student who has a deficit (weakness) in the use of digraphs might have a corresponding objective such as the following included on his IEP:

Outcome: The student will read both in- and out-of-context "ch" as an ending sound.

Context: Flashcards with words including "ch" or with only the "ch" written on the card.

Criteria: 10/10 different words.

10/10 times "ch" is presented independently.

In this case, the analysis of this short-term objective would be a list of words with the "ch" ending (e.g., "lunch" or "watch").

Another example might be for a learner who, when assessed, was unable to read any words on various fast-food menus. A corresponding short-term objective might be as follows:

Outcome: The student will read five basic words from a fast-food menu.

Context: At three different restaurants that primarily serve hamburgers.

Criterion: 100% of the trials.

The task sequence of this objective would also be the listing of the key words, for instance, "hamburger," "fries," "cola," "ketchup," "cheese."

Developing Instructional Strategies

A major consideration in teaching reading and written expression is basing the instruction on each student's needs. Because of their strengths and weaknesses in auditory, visual, and kinesthetic modalities, different students may require programs that meet specific learning styles. This is contrary to the approach some teachers take when they include all students in one reading series. For example, some learners may continue to fall behind in a mainstream situation if the teacher uses only one basal series. The series may require good auditory perception skills on the part of the learner, a problem area for many students with learning problems. Teachers should review many possible approaches and programs, deciding which individual program or combination of them is the best match with each student's needs.

Phonetic Analysis Approach

The phonetic analysis approach involves recognizing new words by identifying sounds when presented with their corresponding printed symbols, sometimes called the grapheme (symbol)-phoneme (sound) relationship. Phonetic analysis (word attack or decoding) is one of the chief and most useful methods for teaching nonhandicapped students. Basically, students are taught that letters representing sounds can be blended together to form new words, an approach termed "cracking the code."

Unfortunately, the auditory perception deficits suffered by many learners with mild and moderate handicaps make instruction by this method a difficult task. Learners can use decoding skills to learn new words, but they generally require additional methods (Kirk, Kliebhan, & Lerner, 1978). These learners can acquire decoding skills if they are presented in small doses using words that are controlled and follow set rules (Chall, 1967).

IDEA FILE

A number of ideas for teaching decoding skills can be found in a variety of reference books. The following list is a representative sample to help teachers begin their idea file.

- Decoding training can begin after the student can discriminate among environmental sounds and some letter sounds.

- Decoding skills taught out of context should be generalized immediately to reading words in sentences.

- The sounds of initial consonants can be paired with pictures of objects whose names begin with the same sound (e.g., b = bat).

- Before new words or stories are introduced, the new sounds that are included should be highlighted. Color coding new sounds may help the students associate the sound with the color. Once the sound has been learned, the color can be faded.

- Introducing rules to learners often confuses them and hinders them from using their decoding skills. Using color coding is a better way to show how the blend shows up in different words.

- For some students, decoding may have a lower priority than comprehension. Howell and Morehead (1987) have provided examples showing that the inability to decode words does not always preclude comprehension.

- Organizing the sounds and blends into groups with similar characteristics can help learners generalize at a faster rate. For example, "an" and "at" can be paired for presentation showing the student that by changing an initial consonant new words can be formed (e.g., "pan," "tan," "man").

- Learners may have difficulty blending individual sounds to form a word even if they recognize the sounds. They sometimes "break down" on the first sound or syllable and repeat it many times. The Language Master™ may be helpful in helping students overcome this problem by allowing them to see the sounds printed on a card and hear the model pronounce the blends. Color cues can also be added to the cards to facilitate learning.

■ ■ ■ ■

Basal Reader Approach

Basal readers are major components of many reading programs. Teachers like basal series because they are structured, have organized teacher manuals listing objectives and supplemental activities, and are self-contained in the sense that all necessary materials needed to conduct the lessons are generally included. There are also several disadvantages of basal readers, as noted by Mercer and Mercer (1989). Using basal readers in a preset fashion limits a teacher's willingness to develop innovative activities. Also, basal series are designed for group instruction, and although they are efficient, they tend to overshadow the needs of the individual.

Language Master is a trademark of Bell & Howell, Inc.

One major disadvantage of using basal readers involves the scope of material presented in a given lesson. Many basal series present multiple objectives within one lesson with some practice on the objectives in subsequent lessons. For learners with mild and moderate handicapping conditions, especially those trying to keep up with a group in a mainstream situation, too many objectives in a presentation may be overwhelming. Basal readers can be an effective teaching tool if teachers emphasize one or two objectives and develop many different types of supplemental activities. These supplemental materials allow students the variety of practice they need on fewer objectives. As the objectives are mastered, new ones can be added to the list.

This approach adds another dimension to basal readers by using only those parts of the lessons that relate to the target objectives. Group instruction can and should be used, except that grouping is based on similarity of objectives across students, not on reading level. Grouping can also be flexible, changing as the students begin to master objectives.

Language Experience Approach

The language experience approach attempts to stimulate language as an impetus for teaching reading. In this system, the student's experiences are used as the basis for the reading material. Students who can write put their stories on paper, and those who are unable to write present their stories orally to be transcribed by others. As teachers begin involving their students in more community-based activities, these students will have more experiences to share.

Linguistic Approaches

Linguistic approaches emphasize phoneme/grapheme relationships and minimize any comprehension skills in the early stages of instruction (Marsh, Price, & Smith, 1983), stressing the student's ability to see patterns across groupings of words. Many linguistic programs use a whole-word approach, clustering words that are similar in structure. Students learn not separate sounds but words based on similar spelling patterns. For example, a student who learns the word "cat" can use that word as a model for identifying similar words such as "bat" and "fat."

Some basal series use linguistic exercises in their overall approach. Linguistic exercises may prove to be difficult for many learners with handicaps because of the stress on auditory perception skills and the assumption that students will begin to perceive relationships on their own (Kirk et al., 1978). Learners who have difficulty transferring knowledge or skills across situations will probably have a great deal of difficulty with this approach.

Teachers will find linguistic approaches useful if they closely monitor student progress and provide ample direction in the form of frequent prompts and cues built in to the materials (e.g., "man," "pan," "tan").

Remedial Reading Approaches

One common characteristic of learners with mild to moderate learning problems is they generally have not progressed well in programs that have used one of the developmental approaches to reading instruction. Approaches that rely too heavily on auditory perception skills or do not allow adequate practice on fewer skills will provide difficult obstacles. Remedial reading approaches attempt to teach skills in a format matching the learning characteristics of the students to specific strategies.

Basically, remedial reading approaches include some, all, or varied combinations of the following features:

1. They allow repeated practice (overlearning) of skills spread out over a longer period of time, helping learners with long-term memory deficits retain the material better.
2. They include cues in the material that assist the learner in focusing attention on the relevant stimuli of the task.
3. They include a more thorough scope and sequence, allowing learners to master easier skills before moving to more difficult material.
4. They provide learners with immediate feedback concerning their responses and shape correct responses when errors are made.
5. They include opportunities for students to practice learned skills under varying conditions to promote generalization.
6. They incorporate the use of antecedent teacher behaviors such as modeling or prompting to increase the probability of correct student responses.
7. They incorporate a variety of techniques allowing students to practice skills using visual, auditory, and tactile modalities.

Remedial approaches are specialized and should be matched to the strengths and weaknesses of each learner. Remedial approaches in the resource room may not be appropriate if they conflict with the primary instruction in the regular education classroom. However, for learners whose reading program is the responsibility of the special educator or in cases where regular educators are convinced a change is needed, remedial programs can be an asset.

DISTAR Reading Program

The DISTAR Reading Program (Englemann & Bruner, 1974, 1988) is a highly structured program emphasizing decoding skills. This program includes activities emphasizing left-to-right orientation and sequence, blending tasks that stress spelling by sounds (e.g., "say it slow" then "say it fast"), and rhyming tasks that demonstrate relationships between sounds and words.

The DISTAR program uses several of the instructional techniques previously mentioned. Students receive immediate corrective feedback and are given both tangible and social reinforcers for appropriate responses. Also, this program provides ample repetition, with mastery required before movement to new skills can occur.

The DISTAR approach has proved to be very effective with some children. The key elements of this program appear to be its structure, continuous feedback, and systematic reinforcers. By providing these elements in all reading activities, teachers may be able to effect greater gains in reading among their students.

Peabody Rebus Program

The Peabody Rebus Reading Program (Woodcock, Clark, & Davis, 1979) is a unique system because it uses pictures instead of words during initial instruction. These pictures, called *rebuses,* introduce readers to a basic vocabulary of 35 words that, when used in stories, allow them to learn and practice several basic reading skills.

As students increase their rebus vocabulary, the program moves them into a transition phase, pairing the rebuses with the printed words they represent. Over time, the rebuses can be faded as students learn the words without need of the picture cues.

At the completion of the Rebus program, students should have developed skills necessary to succeed in beginning basal programs. This system may provide help to students who have gained little or no reading skills at younger ages. The technique of pairing pictures with printed words can also be carried over to basal readers with some additional work by the regular and special education teachers.

Hegge-Kirk-Kirk Remedial Reading Drills

The Remedial Reading Drills (Hegge, Kirk, & Kirk, 1965) is a program designed to remediate the severe deficits in decoding exhibited by some elementary-age learners. This program helps students to establish sound-symbol association, closure, and the left-to-right orientation in reading words.

The authors do not present this program as being self-contained or separate from other programs (Kirk et al., 1978). Conversely, they see the Remedial Reading Drills as an attempt to help students learn the skills necessary to use basal readers. The program first presents activities that allow for practice in associating sounds with the consonants, vowels, and blends that commonly occur in beginning basal readers. The activities allow for immediate practice in saying sounds in the context of words. Subsequent lessons introduce more complex blends and uncommon sounds.

This method has been successful with learners who have failed to learn to read (Marsh, Price, & Smith, 1983). The strength of the program appears to be its highly structured approach and the opportunity it provides for the students to immediately generalize the decoding skills to words commonly found in their reading books.

Functional Whole-Word Approach

For many students with moderate handicaps, learning to read through traditional approaches such as phonetic and basal readers may not be a realistic goal. This does not mean that these learners cannot acquire useful reading skills. The approach to teaching reading skills must be redefined and expanded beyond what was once thought possible for these students.

Functional reading has been defined as a student's actions or responses resulting from reading printed words (Brown & Perlmutter, 1971). The key to teaching functional reading skills is the teacher's ability to observe the student's actions as they relate to words read. For example, a learner who reads the word "bread" on a shopping list and then selects a loaf of bread in the store has performed an observable behavior that was a result of her reading the printed stimulus. *Functional* is the key word, and it is related to the concept of community validity. Words targeted for instruction must be functional because the ability to read them allows learners to become more independent in community-living activities (Snell, 1983).

The approach that has been most successful in teaching functional reading skills is called the *whole-word approach*. This method involves pairing pictures with corresponding words, using both auditory and visual modalities (Sidman & Cresson, 1973). The difference between this approach and the Rebus approach described earlier involves the words used during instruction. The whole-word approach teaches words that have immediate application to the community. The Rebus system teaches words that are immediately applicable to beginning readers, and it also teaches additional skills related to reading stories.

Functional reading involves two distinct outcomes: identifying and reading the word and performing the related task. Learners must be able to master both outcomes before their reading skills can be considered functional. For example, teaching a learner to read and say the phrase "Turn on the water" is nonfunctional until the student learns how to turn on the water. When teaching some learners, both aspects have to be taken into account.

In addition, functional reading involves identifying words that are needed by students to actively participate in community activities. Teachers can cluster words according to specific activities (e.g., words encountered in grocery store shopping) or technical vocabulary related to potential employment outcomes (e.g., words encountered when engaging in custodial skills).

KEY CONCEPTS

Two categories of approaches are available for teaching reading skills: developmental or remedial. Developmental approaches include basal reading programs, phonetic analysis or decoding programs, language experience programs, and linguistic systems. Remedial approaches used after reading problems surface include the DISTAR Reading Program, the Edmark Reading Program (Bijou, 1977), the Peabody Rebus Reading Program, the Hegge-Kirk-Kirk Remedial Reading Drill, and the functional whole-word approach.

■ Basal reading programs can be an excellent source of structured reading activities. However, some learners will have a difficult time keeping up with the lessons because too many objectives are covered per lesson and the number of opportunities for practice may not be sufficient.

■ Approaches that emphasize cracking the code, such as phonetic and linguistics systems, may also discourage learners if presented in a traditional fashion. These approaches rely heavily on auditory processing skills, an area in which many learners have deficits.

■ Language experience techniques can be used effectively; however, the learners will need to be involved in many interesting activities so they will have the requisite experiences for discussion. This approach is not a total program, but it can be helpful as a source of supplemental activities.

■ Remedial reading programs have helped learners make great gains. However, they can also be confusing to learners if used in conjunction with the developmental approaches.

■ ■ ■ ■

IMPLEMENTING INSTRUCTIONAL STRATEGIES

Deciding what to teach students based on their needs is a major portion of the programming effort. Younger students have an excellent chance to become independent readers if teachers can match an appropriate program to their needs and head off their learning of inappropriate reading habits. As they grow to adolescence, their programs should become increasingly more functional, providing opportunities for them to apply their reading skills to community activities such as reading the newspaper, job applications, and recipes.

Some students need to begin reading functional words as soon as they master the ability to complete the related task. For example, once a learner learns to wash dishes, he can begin to learn words relating to dishwashing (e.g., "soap," "sponge," "towel").

Direct Instruction and Reading

Regardless of the approach chosen by the teacher, the common denominator affecting student success or failure is the quality of organization and presentation of materials. *Direct instruction* is an approach that includes a series of instructional strategies designed to increase the probability of student success. Specifically, with direct instruction, teachers use a "consistent practice of demonstration, guided practice, and feedback" (Gersten, Woodward, & Darch, 1986, p. 18). These controlled presentation approaches are paired with specific principles of instructional design as presented in Chapter Four. They have been thoroughly tested and proved effective (Chou-Hare & Borchardt, 1984).

Direct instruction can best be summarized by a paragraph excerpted from a 1985 report to the National Commission on Reading (Anderson, Hiebert, Scott, & Wilkinson, 1985):

> Direct instruction needs to be distinguished from questioning, discussion, and guided practice. Direct instruction in comprehension means explaining the steps in a thought process that give birth to comprehension. It may mean that the teacher models a strategy by thinking aloud about how he or she is going about understanding a passage. The instruction includes information on why and when to use the strategy. Instruction of this type is the surest means of developing the strategic processing that was identified earlier as characteristic of skilled readers. (p. 72)

The components of direct instruction are a blend of instructional design and the operant procedures of modeling, prompting, guided practice, and frequent positive teacher feedback. This approach stresses teaching students to think by instructing them in rules and concepts, how to apply these rules and concepts, and gradually fading unnecessary assistance while helping them to generalize learned skills to new situations (Mathes & Proctor, 1988).

Originally developed by Siegfried Engelmann and Douglas Carnine, this teaching process has seven major components (Gersten & Carnine, 1988). These were expanded from a list produced by Gersten and associates (1986). First, teachers provide instruction in a systematic and explicit step-by-step format. The exact reading behavior required is modeled extensively if the step-by-step format is not possible.

Second, students must reach mastery of a skill before the teachers begin instruction on the next skill. Third, teachers must develop systematic procedures for correcting the errors students make. The fourth step is to fade teacher-directed activities to independent work.

The fifth step in the direct instruction model involves the use of systematic guided practice across a wide variety of examples. Sixth, a cumulative review is provided after sets of skills are completed. Finally, teachers use instructional formats that anticipate possible errors and correct for them prior to their occurrence.

Direct instructional procedures in reading need not be restricted to the use of classroom-based materials. Figure 8.1 provides an example of how a teacher might use these strategies to help students master the skill area of problem solving, indicator 11, presented in the earlier section on competency-based testing.

IDEA FILE

- When learners receive their primary instruction in the special education class, the teacher may wish to use a remedial program as the main thrust. These programs provide more practice over smaller chunks of instruction and give the students more feedback. In addition, they often include visual cues that assist learners who have auditory deficits.

- At least two options exist for students mainstreamed for their reading program. In conjunction with the IEP committee, the regular and special educator may decide not to use the more traditional approaches until the learner has gained a certain number of skills. For example, the Rebus program could be used for a designated period of time, after which the student would have gained sufficient skills to enter a basal program.

- Another option is to assist the regular teacher in adapting the basal system to meet the learner's needs. The regular teacher would need to be convinced that only one or two objectives should be targeted for a learner at one time. When the student masters those, he or she can move on to the next set of objectives. For example, if a lesson covers six objectives, the student would be required to do the activities related to one or two targets.

- Choosing only parts of lessons for one or two students means these learners will be required to do more independent work while the regular education teacher finishes with the rest of the group. Because some learners are not always the best independent workers, peer tutors can be used liberally to assist these students in completing their tasks (Cooke, Heron, & Heward, 1983).

■ Independent workers may be engaged in activities requiring them to read stories that may be slightly above their easy reading level. When this occurs, regular education teachers can have the stories tape-recorded by other students. (The special educator may wish to have this done as a service to mainstreamed students and a help to the regular education teachers.) The independent workers can then listen to the story while they are reading it.

Environment: Local Car Dealership
Subenvironment: Showroom
Resources: Assistant Manager

Verbal prompts	1. Teacher:	Listen carefully. This is a rule.
Specifically stated rule		People who want to sell you a car may not tell you all the information you need to know to buy the best car you can afford.
Verbal prompt	2. Teacher:	Watch and listen to this example.
Modeling	3. Assistant Manager:	Hi, can I put you into a new car today?
	Teacher:	Yes, I'd like a car that's inexpensive, with good gas mileage to go back and forth to work.
	Assistant Manager:	Economy is OK, but remember a car is an investment. If you buy a little more car with a bigger engine it'll last longer.
Probe	4. Teacher:	OK. Is the salesman helping me buy the car I need?
	5. Students:	Yes.
Correction procedures	6. Teacher:	No. Remember, people who want to sell you a car may not tell you all the information you need to know to buy the car you can afford.
Redirection to important points	7. Teacher:	Listen. I want a car that's inexpensive, with good gas mileage. The salesman says a car is an investment and he suggests it will last longer if it has a bigger engine. A bigger engine costs more and gets poorer gas mileage.
	8. Teacher:	Does a bigger engine cost more or less?
	9. Students:	More.
	10. Teacher:	Does a bigger engine get better gas mileage?
	11. Students:	No.
Guided practice; fading of assistance	12. Teacher:	Great. Let's try the scene again, with each of you getting a chance to play my part. I'll help you if you don't quite use the right words.
	13. At this point, each student practices.	
Cumulative review and generalization	14. Teacher:	Now let's read a short passage written by an auto manufacturer and see if it tells us all we need to know to buy a car.

■ *FIGURE 8.1*
Examples of Direct Instruction Applied to a Community-Based Activity

■ Special educators can help regular education teachers and mainstreamed students by modifying materials to meet the students' needs. For example, the reading level of material can be reduced by rewriting. This technique allows students to study the content on their own reading levels. Additional materials that accomplish this task for teachers are being produced commercially.

■ ■ ■ ■

Techniques for Teaching Decoding

It can be easier to teach decoding skills to students with reading deficits if teachers locate exactly where the skills have broken down in relation to a task analysis. A student who cannot decode words with consonant blends will have difficulty moving on to more difficult skills. Once the teacher has identified the area where the breakdown has occurred, instruction can begin at that point.

Teachers should not overemphasize activities designed to teach decoding skills. By the nature of their disability, students with mild and moderate handicaps have a great deal of trouble learning to read by using traditional approaches to "cracking the code." This generalization is not meant to imply that exercises designed to teach these skills are not beneficial. Evidence suggests that intensive programs using methods of direct instruction work when they follow a prespecified and consistent sequence of task analysis, sound production, and blending (Reid, 1988).

The alternative to gearing the majority of instruction toward teaching phonetic analysis is to help students see the value of reading in terms of comprehending the material presented. This stresses reinforcement of the meaningfulness of the reading process (Mercer & Mercer, 1989; Polloway, Patton, Payne, & Payne, 1989). Therefore, the following list of suggestions may be helpful for teachers if they use them in relation to reading activities that stress understanding what is read.

1. To combat attention and auditory processing problems (Felton & Wood, 1989), some learners may need to spend some time practicing saying and identifying sounds/blends while they listen to a tape-recorded activity via earphones. Visual stimuli should be presented in conjunction with the auditory exercises (Blackman, Burger, Tan, & Weiner, 1982).

2. Using pictures of visual cues can assist learners in remembering a specific consonant or vowel sound as well as various blends. For example, pairing initial consonants with pictures whose names begin with the same consonant helps to cue students to remember and pronounce the sounds (e.g., S = picture of a snake).

3. Learners may have trouble generalizing the application of rules to many different situations; however, they may be able to use a model as a guide for decoding words that have similar sounds and blends. For example, one rule for words that end in a consonant plus "ble" is that the consonant usually begins the last syllable. The word "table," an example of this rule, could be taught to the student using picture cues and then could be used by the students as a model for decoding similar words such as "able" and "cable."

4. Initial sounds can be taught by placing the letter on one side of the page and several words that begin with the sound on the opposite side of the page (e.g., b = __ all, __ at, __ end, __ ent).

5. Instruction in auditory discrimination may be an important part of learning the decoding process for some students. Activities that allow students to practice discriminating among sounds are important. Some learners may benefit from practicing auditory discrimination exercises using *good quality* headphones, tape recorders, and tapes. Some learners with auditory processing deficits can better discriminate among relevant stimuli when all other stimuli are reduced and the key words are isolated. The headphone exercises can gradually be faded out of the instructional system to be replaced by similar exercises conducted in a group activity.

6. Context clues and the ability to use them are an important extension of word attack skills (Allington, 1980). The use of sentences from which phrases or single words are omitted helps students learn to look for context clues. For example, the sentence "I am going *(home, house, help)* after school" can be presented and the student required to fill in the blank. The difficulty some learners have in attending to relevant stimuli hampers their ability to decode the meaning. Color coding the context clues or the actual answers in a number of model sentences may provide valuable assistance to these learners, helping them to retain the skill as the color codes are gradually faded (Singh & Singh, 1984).

7. Helping students see the structural analysis of words (e.g., compound words, prefixes, suffixes) can be accomplished by color coding or including pictures or symbols depicting the meaning of, for example, common prefixes.

8. Some learners may perseverate or hesitate on one letter or blend. Helping students see whole syllables can assist them in decoding words. Any technique that allows the student to pay attention to a syllable as a unit may be helpful (e.g., making one syllable larger and one smaller or using different colors for different syllables).

IDEA FILE

Microcomputers can be a great asset in teaching reading (Beltz, Detwiler, & Grant, 1983). For example, CAI can be used to provide students with varied practice activities reinforcing the basic skills in decoding and comprehension. The many practice exercises that have always been necessary and boring can now be presented in a highly motivating fashion.

There is software available that allows students to practice phonics, context clues, and syllabication activities (Goldenberg, Russel, & Carter, 1984). Also, there are a number of programs currently on the market that allow learners practice in content area reading exercises (Criscoe & Gee, 1984).

Computerized study guides are available to assist students in specific context areas such as social studies (Hofmeister, 1989; Horton, Lovitt, Givens, & Nelson, 1989). In addition, CAI for sight word recognition has proved to be a highly successful method (Torgesen, Waters, Cohen, & Torgeson, 1988).

The following lists provide representative samples of computer software programs available to assist in teaching reading. These lists were adapted from Criscoe & Gee (1984) and Hagen (1984). Both sources contain an excellent description of the materials as well as complete addresses, prices, and in the case of software, the computers that will accept the programs.

Periodicals

The Book of Apple Software. Los Angeles: The Book Company.
Educational Technology. Englewood Cliffs, NJ: Educational Technology Publications.
International Software Directory. Fort Collins, CO: Imprint Software.
TRS-80 Educational Software Sourcebook. Fort Worth, TX: Radio Shack Educational Division.

Software

Descriptive Reading. Freeport, NY: Educational Activities Incorporated.
First Words. Burlington, VT: Laureate Learning Systems.
Language Arts Skills Builders. Allen, TX: Developmental Learning Materials.
PAL Reading Curriculum Packages. Aurora, CO: Universal Systems for Education.
Reading Comprehension Games. Roslyn Heights, NY: Learning Well.
Reading Skills Series. Glenview, IL: Scott, Foresman Electronic Publishing.

■ ■ ■ ■

Techniques for Teaching Reading Comprehension

Helping students to get "hooked" on reading can be an important first step in teaching reading comprehension skills. Learners with a history of reading failure may find it stressful to be placed in a situation where reading is required. Two important tasks that teachers should accomplish are pinpointing the student's independent or instructional reading level and finding age-appropriate or high-interest material on the target level.

Reading to students is an important motivation technique. Some students come from homes where reading is not stressed. Students who witness others reading for pleasure may be more apt to try it themselves. Setting aside small portions of the school day for reading the students a continuing story is one technique to foster more interest in reading.

Finally, many learners who have severe reading deficits can be helped by talking books, which can be useful in teaching them some comprehension skills and generally increasing their interest in reading. An extensive talking book library should be a part of many classes, and it can be obtained by asking volunteers to tape books and stories. Choosing people who do not have pronounced accents and using good-quality tapes and recorders lends to the effectiveness of this method.

The following are suggestions for methods and activities that may be helpful in teaching reading comprehension:

1. Understanding basic vocabulary is an important initial step in improving comprehension skills. Helping students develop branching trees by clustering words according to association is one technique to improve word comprehension (Baumann & Johnson, 1984). For example, the word "ball" can be associated with "catch" and "throw." As students begin to learn words in clusters, these words become cues for other associated words.

2. It is important to teach learners vocabulary words that lend meaning to a paragraph by describing when things occur. Mercer and Mercer (1985) have suggested that initially teachers should present words such as "to begin with, next, after that, and finally" (p. 301), helping the students to follow the organization of the story.

3. The ability to identify key words and main ideas in a sentence or paragraph is an important skill. Color coding words or underlining main ideas can help direct students' attention to relevant stimuli. Whenever artificial cues are used, they should be faded from the instruction as soon as they are no longer necessary (Bruno & Newman, 1985).

4. After students read stories, teachers can provide them with phrases that describe what the story was about (Englert & Lichter, 1982). After a number of trials, teachers can provide multiple phrases, requiring the students to choose the one that best fits the story.

5. Teaching learners the thinking process that accompanies reading comprehension may help them to grasp some more difficult skills. Stauffer (1969) has expressed the belief that questions asked by the teacher (e.g., "Can you prove it?" help stimulate interest in reading comprehension because they require students to support answers with information from the text (Wood & Mateja, 1983). Students can also generate their own questions prior to reading the passage (Cohen, 1983).

6. Having students role play the characters in stories may help them pay more attention to the details of the text (Jenkins, Stein, & Osborn, 1981). For example, a student might silently read a sentence such as "Jimmy was sad" and then act out how Jimmy felt. This technique can be used with more difficult material and longer stories.

7. An instant camera can be an aid in teaching comprehension skills. Pictures can be taken of students participating in various activities. The pictures can accompany the sequence of the events, and students can practice placing the pictures in the appropriate sequence based on the story. An adaptation of this technique is to number the pictures and then place the same number next to the corresponding sentence.

8. Prompting students during comprehension practice (e.g., setting the stage for the story, providing questions prior to reading, verifying story ideas) is another technique that may help students improve their skills (Rupley & Blair, 1983).

9. Kann (1983) developed a method called *repeated readings* that requires a student and teacher to read a passage aloud together several times. This method is a version of the neurological impress method that is designed to improve the fluency of learners who tend to get stuck on sounding out words phonetically. Neither the repeated readings method nor the neurological impress method claims to improve comprehension per se; however, the students do seem to improve their oral expression and confidence. These techniques should be used in conjunction with other reading comprehension activities (Bos, 1982).

10. Teachers can develop story frames to assist students in organizing the information presented in a reading passage or story. Fowler (1982) presented five tasks for developing story frames that can focus on plots, locations, characters, and times: (1) identifying the problem of the story; (2) writing a paragraph about the problem; (3) deleting unnecessary words that mask the problem; (4) designing cues to help students focus on the problem; and (5) modifying the frame for other passages. The frames are essentially outlines that include written cues that direct student attention to the important areas of the passage (e.g., "The name of the troublemaker is . . . ") (Moldolfsky, 1983). Teachers can read a passage and show the students how to use a frame, eventually allowing them to use the frames independently.

11. Teachers should cue learners about the content of a passage or story prior to instruction or reading (Wilson, 1983). Some learners tend to have poor experiential backgrounds, and this can adversely affect their ability to comprehend subject matter. Teachers can help by providing students with information about the story before reading begins.

12. An increase in language comprehension can directly impact a student's reading ability (Mann, Cowin, & Schoenheimer, 1989). Community-based activities expose learners to a variety of experiences that can become the base for language development activities.

IDEA FILE

Professionals are beginning to recognize the need to provide students with significant reading problems as alternatives to instruction in decoding. E. D. Hirsch, Jr. (1987) in *Cultural Literacy,* has stressed the need for more instruction in skills designed to teach students the basic information needed to thrive in the modern world.

Teaching learners to be culturally literate implies teaching the *meaning* of words instead of just teaching them to read words with little or no meaning. More accurately, it stresses teaching the meaning of certain important words and phrases that allow the reader to converse with others and to understand what they read. The following list is a brief example of the words and phrases included in an extensive appendix developed by Hirsch and his colleagues:

1776	phobic
abolitionism	phrase
abortion	pie in the sky
absenteeism	a pig in a poke
Achilles' heel	the pill
acid rain	refugee
active voice	right angle
as the crow flies	sexism
balance of power	subpoena
P. T. Barnum	symbol
bee in one's bonnet	touch and go
the best things in life are free	vaccine
bite the bullet	war on poverty
botulism	yuppie
chain reaction	zoning

Of course these selections are only a small sample of the exhaustive list included in Hirsch's book. Many of the words in the list would not be useful to most students with mild and moderate handicaps and, therefore, would not be taught or would have a very low priority. Teachers can supplement the list with words that may not fit the definition of cultural literacy but are important for students to be able to read and understand in their roles as consumers, citizens, producers, and individuals.

A word of caution: Any lists of functional words can best be taught in relation to community-based activities. For example, the meaning of colloquialisms such as "a pig in a poke" can best be taught when embedded in an activity taking place in a local retail store.

■ ■ ■ ■

Techniques for Teaching Content Area Reading Skills

The move to mainstream learners into classes with their regular education peers has created new problems for teachers. As these students move up through the grades, their participation in content subjects (e.g., science, social studies) requires them to absorb material via traditional methods such as reading textbooks and taking notes on teacher lectures.

Unfortunately, the reading skills of most learners with mild and moderate handicaps are far below the reading levels of many content area textbooks. Teachers must use innovative methods to teach these students the desired content skills by circumventing their reading deficits. New materials are being developed that cover the content subjects on lower reading levels (e.g., Project Life School, Fearon Publishers). These materials can be a great help and can be used to supplement other basic techniques.

1. Teaching students key vocabulary in content area lessons can assist them in comprehending class lectures and scanning more difficult reading materials. These words can be taught using sight word techniques such as pairing the word with a corresponding picture.

2. Having peers tape record chapters can provide learners with another modality for covering the assignments. Peer tutors can also assist learners in studying for tests or completing assignments.

3. Teaching good study and note taking skills can be a great help to mainstreamed learners. Criscoe and Gee (1984) have suggested teaching the "survey, question, read, recite, review" approach. Basically, students are taught to survey the material briefly, locating the main points. They then convert the main points to questions that may help to increase their comprehension. At that point, they read until they can answer each question, recite the answers and finally review after all questions have been answered.

4. Regular education peers can take notes for mainstreamed students who are unable to listen and write at a fast pace. Another approach is to provide the learner with a tape recorder to record lectures. The study techniques listed in (3) can also be used when studying from taped materials (Maheady, Harper, & Sacca, 1988).

5. Use of memory aids is an important set of skills for learners. Criscoe and Gee (1984) have suggested five categories of memory aids: (1) poetic devices—"thirty days hath September"; (2) associations—"*ie* in p*ie*ce is a p*ie*ce of p*ie*"; (3) grammatical devices—acronyms, coined words; (4) linking techniques—linking words to form a mental image; and (5) location techniques—visually "walking through" the exercise (pp. 251–255).

6. Many learners may not perform well on content area tests because of their deficits in reading (Bruno & Newman, 1985; Swanson, 1988). Special educators could assist regular education teachers in developing alternate projects that assess students' knowledge yet do not rely solely on reading ability (Wilson, Majsterer, & Southern, 1989). For example, students may be required to obtain the phone numbers of community agencies and legal aid services, calling each to gather information about how they can help with legal problems. This project might be assigned in lieu of a test covering information about a state's legal system.

7. Providing learners with an outline of the subject matter they are about to read helps them anticipate what to look for in their reading (Bean & Peterson, 1981). Special educators can develop these outlines by asking the content area teachers what topics in the readings

are considered most important. Partially completed outlines can be provided for students to complete (Roe, Stoodt, & Burns, 1983). This technique also helps students discriminate the important points in the reading.

8. Computer programs are available for many content area subjects that help students who have reading problems learn the content (Horton, Lovitt, & Slocum, 1988).

IDEA FILE

There are many resources available that provide suggestions for teaching techniques and activities. The following is a partial list:

Baumann, J. F., & Johnson, D. (1984). *Reading instruction and the beginning teacher*. Minneapolis: Burgess.

Bender, M., & Valletutti, P. (1982). *Teaching functional academics*. Baltimore: University Park Press.

Criscoe, B., & Gee, T. (1984). *Content reading*. Englewood Cliffs, NJ: Prentice-Hall.

Devine, T. (1980). *Teaching study skills*. Boston: Allyn and Bacon.

Hammill, D., & Bartel, N. (1984). *Teaching children with learning and behavior problems* (3rd ed.). Boston: Allyn and Bacon.

Lovitt, T. (1984). *Tactics for teaching*. Columbus, OH: Charles E Merrill.

Lucas, J. (1978). *Ready, set, remember*. White's Creek, TN: Memory Press.

Mercer, C., & Mercer, A. (1985). *Teaching students with learning problems* (2nd ed.). Columbus, OH: Charles E. Merrill.

Polloway, E. A., Payne, J. S., Patton, J. R., & Payne, R. A. (1985). *Strategies for teaching retarded and special needs learners* (3rd ed.). Columbus, OH: Charles E. Merrill.

Radabaugh, M., & Yukish, J. (1982). *Curriculum and methods for the mildly handicapped*. Boston: Allyn and Bacon.

Schulz, J., & Turnbull, A. (1983). *Mainstreaming handicapped students* (2nd ed.). Boston: Allyn and Bacon.

Wiederholt, J., Hammill, D., & Brown, V. (1983). *The resource teacher: A guide to effective practices* (2nd ed.). Boston: Allyn and Bacon.

Young, M. N., & Gibson, W. B. (1962). *How to develop an exceptional memory*. Hollywood: Wilshire.

■ ■ ■ ■

Techniques for Teaching Community-Based Reading Skills

The techniques for teaching community-based reading skills are the same as those used for teaching other reading skills. The uniqueness of this approach involves the functionality of the targeted words (Polloway & Polloway, 1981). Recipes, newspapers, job applications, safety words, menus, and street signs are representative of vocabulary that can be considered functional. The approaches used to teach community-based skills can be the same as those used to teach decoding and comprehension.

1. Classic studies by Dorry and Zeaman (1973, 1975) provided evidence that pairing vocabulary words with pictures, *slowly* fading the pictures when they were no longer needed, was a powerful technique for teaching reading using the whole word approach (Worrall & Singh, 1983).

2. This instructional approach can be strengthened when words are presented in clusters organized by their common characteristics (Domnie & Brown, 1977). For example, teachers may teach as a cluster words that are commonly found in fast-food restaurants.

3. Pictures paired with written directions such as recipes can be a successful method for teaching learners functional reading (Hargis, 1982; Robinson-Wilson, 1976; Staples, 1975).

4. Matching to sample is a technique that helps students discriminate among words by matching a word to a stimulus provided by the teacher (Taylor, Thurlow, & Turnure, 1977). For example, a student matches a card with the printed word "danger" to a similar card presented by the teacher.

5. Having students imagine or visualize a situation or picture in conjunction with a word may help them remember the word (Gickling, Hargis, & Alexander, 1981).

Techniques for Teaching Written Expression Skills

Skills in written expression can be viable curricular goals for most learners. Activities that foster letter writing skills, note taking, and in some instances creative writing can help these learners become more independent.

1. The microcomputer can be a tremendous help to learners practicing written expression. Word-processing packages (e.g., BANK STREET WRITER™ from Broderbund Software, Inc.) can assist learners who previously have found writing too difficult because of severe deficits in handwriting, spelling, punctuation, and other skills. Using microcomputers, which are fun and easy to use, these learners can now complete work they once considered tedious (Graham & MacArthur, 1988).

2. Providing students with a list of words they can use to form sentences can be a meaningful exercise for those who lack an adequate vocabulary.

3. Providing students with uncompleted sentences that they are required to finish by supplying the main idea can help them complete their thoughts. The procedure would be to gradually fade the numbers of words provided by the teacher (Mercer & Mercer, 1985).

4. For students whose experiences are limited, organizing groups to share ideas for a story can be a helpful way to generate content. Teams of students can work together to polish the story on the microcomputer.

5. Graham and Miller (1980) have supported teaching manuscript writing to exceptional learners. Manuscript appears easier to master than cursive; however, it is less versatile. The best practice may be to match the technique best suited to each student.

6. Hagin (1983) has suggested an approach that combines both manuscript and cursive writing. Manuscript letters are connected using waves, pearls, wheels, and arrows. Students practice at the chalkboard and on acetate sheets placed over printed models.

7. Commercially produced methods for teaching cursive writing may provide teachers with an effective, structured program (e.g., Barbe, Lucas, Hackney, Braun, & Wasylyk, 1984; Thurber, 1986).

8. Reading and spelling are so closely related they should be emphasized together as much as possible. For example, students can identify words in their readings that have been difficult for them to spell, and underline these words whenever they occur.

9. Learning phonetic rules that relate to spelling certain words can benefit students by helping them generalize to new situations. Dropping the "y" to add "ing" to certain words or the "i before e except after c" rules are the most common examples.

10. Helping students visualize the spelling of words and using multisensory approaches have been successful methods for improving the spelling of some learners. Fitzgerald (1951) developed a method that allowed students to look at the word, say the word, visualize the word, and then write the word without use of a stimulus. Fernald's (1943) method allowed students to trace with their fingers words written with crayon or cut out of sandpaper.

11. Presenting functional words that students frequently come in contact with allows additional opportunities for correct spelling.

12. Many learners will always have trouble spelling; therefore, they should be taught how to locate and use the many excellent spelling reference books available that are often easier to use than a dictionary. Also, if students have access to microcomputers, they can be taught to use word-processing software that either locates or locates and corrects misspelled words in written expression.

13. Newcomer, Barenbaum, and Noding (1988) found that visual reminders were more powerful prompts than verbal ones for assisting students in story production exercises. Visual reminders blend nicely with community-based activities because they allow students to picture what they are writing about. A teacher can facilitate this by taking photographs of some activities to be used later as reminders when the students are producing stories in the classroom.

14. Rakes and Choate (1989) recommended that teachers emphasize students' efforts more than their products. The main goal is to get students to write more, and an overemphasis on grammatical errors initially can detract from this goal. Rakes and Choate have suggested that proofreading can be done as a group, using an editor's proofwriting format.

15. Time spent at the local newspaper (more than a one-shot field trip) can help students improve their writing skills. Teachers can develop activities around a reporter's day and incorporate into their lessons strategies that reporters use to write articles. Seeing the reporters use the strategies and hearing their explanations can help students when attempting to use the techniques themselves.

KEY CONCEPTS

■ When teaching decoding skills to learners it is important to pay close attention to auditory processing deficits. Having students use headphones to listen to sounds while pronouncing them may be helpful because outside distractions are minimized and they can hear their responses directly.

■ Pairing picture cues with sounds, color coding, drawing arrows, and underlining are all useful techniques for helping learners attend to the important properties of stimuli.

■ Reading aloud to learners frequently, especially when a story is spread over a number of days, can help build a more positive attitude toward reading.

- Using the talking book approach may help students improve their comprehension skills and assist them in learning new concepts presented in books they may not be able to read independently.

- Peer tutors can be helpful in all areas of teaching reading. They can be especially helpful to learners who are unable to read content area texts while they are enrolled in mainstreamed classes.

- Pairing pictures with words and clustering words based on common characteristics can aid in teaching functional reading skills.

- Word-processing software for microcomputers can be a helpful aid for teaching written expression skills.

■ ■ ■ ■

TEACHING FUNCTIONAL MATHEMATICS

■ Teaching students mathematics has long been a priority of special educators. Traditionally, learners with mild handicaps were expected to learn rote arithmetic skills at about the third-grade level. Less able learners were thought to be able to count basic groups of objects and add and subtract simple numbers.

Fortunately, research efforts have provided evidence that these students can learn more advanced mathematics skills. For example, Lancioni (1982) used nonhandicapped peer tutors to teach abstract problem solving to elementary school students. Smeenge, Page, Iwata, and Ivancic (1980), in an applied behavior analysis study, demonstrated the effectiveness of using a task analysis for teaching measurement skills.

NEED FOR FUNCTIONALITY

The studies just cited are representative of the many that can be found in the literature. Proof exists that students can learn complex arithmetic skills in controlled situations. Why, then, do teachers find this curriculum area so difficult to teach? A partial answer to this question may be found in the outcomes teachers choose for their learners (Bartel, 1982). Arithmetic programs that require students to demonstrate their competence in arithmetic by practicing only paper-and-pencil activities may not be providing them any reason to learn.

The thrust of teaching arithmetic to learners with mild and moderate handicaps has been to move away from teaching these skills out of context and toward teaching them as functional skills (Schwartz & Budd, 1983). Schwartz and Budd defined functional mathematics (arithmetic) as "uses of mathematics needed for vocational, consumer, social, recreational and homemaking activities" (1983, p. 322).

Vitello (1976), after numerous studies of how students who are mildly retarded learn arithmetic skills, posited that these learners have considerable problems comprehending arithmetic concepts that involve symbols and abstract notions, the types of problems presented on many paper-and-pencil activities. Studies that have attempted to teach functional arithmetic skills generally have met with success, possibly because the symbols automatically are presented in a more concrete, highly motivating form (Eich, 1981; Frank & McFarland, 1980; Sarber & Halasz, 1983; Trace, Cuvo, & Criswell, 1977).

The underlying theme throughout this text has been to emphasize the importance of functionality in skills taught to learners. Functionality involves identifying those skills that have a high probability of use in community settings (Bott, 1988). Often the skills identified as community-valid resemble skills listed in a traditional arithmetic scope-and-sequence chart. For example, a teacher may want to teach her secondary students how to use fractions and percentages. At this stage she has two choices: (1) to teach these skills using worksheets, blackboard exercises, or other classroom activities or (2) to teach these skills in relation to how they are used in everyday life (e.g., household budgets, recipes). These two choices may not be mutually exclusive; however, in some instances, teachers do teach arithmetic skills out of context instead of blending classroom activities and community exercises into a worthwhile unit (Oberlin, 1982; Wiggins & Behrmann, 1988).

This chapter presents some of the key methods for teaching arithmetic skills effectively. Most students can learn at least *some* arithmetic skills provided the skills are meaningful for their independence. This statement coincides with the current emphasis on viewing arithmetic not as merely mastery of basic computational skills but as mathematics and the *application* of computational skills to life problems (Cawley, Miller, & Carr, 1988). Cawley and associates have argued that achieving competence in basic computational skills is important if students are to solve daily living problems and determine what is truthful and what is not in everyday activities.

Readers should refer to two important charts presented in Chapter Four before proceeding in this chapter. The first is Figure 4.2, which presents the curriculum development process this chapter will follow. The second is Figure 4.5, which presents a scope-and-sequence chart for arithmetic skills. All community-based activities in arithmetic can be based on the skills presented in this chart.

ARITHMETIC: THE IEP

One practice used when developing IEPs is to list a series of arithmetic skills from a scope-and-sequence chart that are about at the student's grade level. Although this practice may be technically acceptable, it may not be in the best interest of the learner, because the skills listed may not be functional in terms of the learner's present and future needs. An alternative is to write the short-term objectives for the IEP including outcomes that are community valid.

For example, one type of outcome for a coin equivalency objective might be that the student will discriminate among quarters, dimes, and nickels. An alternative might be that the student will identify the coins necessary to purchase a soda from a vending machine. Further examples of this approach will be presented later in this chapter. The key issue involves the ability of teachers to actively seek out the types of activities needed for skills to become functional. This task requires teachers to conduct a thorough community needs assessment.

Steps One and Two: Conduct the Community Needs Assessment

The process of conducting and analyzing the results of a CNA (see Figure 4.2) helps keep teachers constantly aware of the functional uses that academic skills have in society. More important, the CNA allows teachers to identify situations and places in the community where they can bring their students to practice the skills they learn.

Students generally will learn best if the skills presented are ones they are most likely to use frequently. For example, sorting coins in an attempt to learn names or equivalencies may not be as realistic as choosing coins to operate a vending machine. By conducting a CNA, teachers can identify the daily uses that students have for arithmetic skills.

Arithmetic skills have a variety of applications in a person's life roles. These skills are important to a person as a consumer, home manager, worker, and family member. Teachers may wish to develop their CNAs around these roles, attempting to identify the types of skills students need to be more independent in these areas, where these skills can be practiced, the types of realistic materials needed, and community members who can help by either being part of the program or providing resources. Table 9.1 provides an example of some areas that a CNA in mathematics might cover. These skills have been identified as ones that hinder adults with handicaps from making successful transitions to the community (Smith, 1988).

Step Three: Identify Potential Annual Goals

Potential annual goals for mathematics can be identified on two levels: those typically found in scope-and-sequence charts and those that are applications of arithmetic skills to community activities. Figure 4.5 provides one example of a scope-and-sequence chart of mathematics goals. The following list of examples is not inclusive, but it should provide teachers with a model for developing their own arithmetic curriculum. Bender and Valletutti (1982); Mercer and Mercer (1989); Radabaugh and Yukish (1982); Silbert, Carnine, and Stein (1981); and Stephens, Hartman, and Lucas (1982) have provided additional examples of scope-and-sequence charts for arithmetic.

Arithmetic

1. Matches the correct numerals with pictured sets of objects.
2. Says the correct numbers when presented with sets of objects up to 10.
3. Writes numbers from 1 to 100 when directed.
4. Writes numbers that either precede or follow a given number up to 100.
5. Writes the words "odd" or "even" when presented with numbers up to 10.
6. Orders objects based on their positions, first through tenth.
7. Identifies place values up to the hundredth place.
8. Writes numbers up to the hundredth place when presented with oral stimuli.

TABLE 9.1 *Partial List of Potential Community Environments Where Students Can Use Arithmetic Skills*

Community Environment	Related Arithmetic Skills
Fast-food restaurants	☐ Calculating change and cost of items
Grocery stores	☐ Cost comparison shopping ☐ Calculating change and cost of items
Banks	☐ Managing a checkbook ☐ Obtaining change ☐ Cashing paychecks
Various worksites	☐ Telling time ☐ Liquid and solid measurement
Home	☐ Cooking involving measurement ☐ Developing a family budget ☐ Other activities involving measurement (e.g., woodworking)

9. Memorizes basic addition and subtraction facts from 0 to 10.
10. Computes one-digit plus one-digit numbers and two-digit plus two-digit numbers without regrouping.
11. Computes one-digit plus one-digit numbers and two-digit plus two-digit numbers with regrouping.
12. Computes one-digit minus one-digit numbers and two-digit minus two-digit numbers without regrouping.
13. Computes one-digit minus one-digit numbers and two-digit minus two-digit numbers with regrouping.
14. Memorizes basic multiplication facts.
15. Computes two-digit times two-digit numbers both with and without regrouping.
16. Memorizes basic division facts.
17. Computes three-digit divided by two-digit numbers with and without borrowing.
18. Relates the words *minuend, subtrahend,* and *difference* to sum given addend, and missing addend.
19. Memorizes basic subtraction facts from 0 to 9.
20. Names the differences between 3-digit (3D) and 2-digit (2D) numbers with no regrouping.
21. Names the differences between 3D and 3D with double regrouping.
22. Computes 2D × 1D without regrouping.
23. Computes 2D × 2D with regrouping.
24. Finds missing factor.
25. Computes division facts with 1 as divisor.
26. Estimates 3D ÷ 1D and computes 3D ÷ 1D.
27. Estimates 3D ÷ 2D and computes 3D ÷ 2D.
28. Separates regions into subregions that are equivalent.
29. Models, on the number line, equivalent fractions.
30. Generates sets of equivalent fractions.
31. Compares fractional numbers.
32. Computes sums of mixed numerals, no regrouping, same denominator.
33. Computes differences between two fractions with like denominators without regrouping, then with regrouping.
34. Computes product of whole number × unit fraction, product.
35. Computes quotient of whole number ÷ nonunit fraction.
36. Demonstrates the proper care and maintenance of a variety of pocket calculators.
37. Uses a variety of pocket calculators to compute daily living problems requiring addition, subtraction, multiplication, and division (e.g., discriminating between similar items in a grocery store based on a price per unit).
38. Compares objects on the basis of length (e.g., longer vs. shorter).
39. Measures in linear units a variety of objects relating to home living and vocational settings.
40. Compares linear metric units to customary units.
41. Compares weight of objects using a balance.
42. Weighs a variety of objects found in home-living and vocational settings.
43. Compares metric units of weight to customary units.
44. Measures liquid and dry volumes in a variety of home-living and vocational settings.
45. Compares liquid and dry metric units to customary units.
46. Measures temperature in a variety of home-living and vocational settings.
47. Compares temperature using metric units and customary units.
48. Interprets the symbol for percent (%) as a fraction and as a decimal.

49. Rewrites fractions or decimals as percents.
50. Solves word problems requiring percents.
51. Identifies coins.
52. Demonstrates the value of coins.
53. Computes money problems. Uses addition and subtraction to compute money problems involving making change for various coin denominations.
54. Identifies currency.
55. Demonstrates the value of currency.
56. Makes change for currency.
57. Uses addition and subtraction to compute money problems involving making change for various currency denominations.
58. Successfully uses money in a variety of transactions.
59. Computes sales tax for a variety of objects.
60. Uses coins and currency (up to $10) in a variety of transactions.
61. Uses coins to successfully obtain goods from a variety of vending machines, mass transit ticket machines, and other devices.
62. Successfully uses adaptive shopping methods (e.g., the dollar plus technique, Nietupski, Certo, Pumpian, & Belmore, 1976).
63. Names days of the week and months and knows the year.
64. Indicates times of the day by naming activities occurring (e.g., supper time).
65. Uses the calendar to locate dates and manage activities.
66. Tells time using a conventional or digital clock by the hour, half hour, quarter hour, and minute.
67. Understands time in relation to vacations, holidays, and weekends.
68. Estimates time involved to complete various tasks around the home and in vocational settings.
69. Practices the principles of good time management.
70. Understands time zones in the United States.

This list includes goal statements that teachers can use as a base, adding to the list as necessary. The list is not rigid. The goals chosen should ultimately be based on the needs of the individual, meaning that any student may benefit from any of the skills included on the list.

Step Four: Translate Goals into Potential Short-Term Objectives

As teachers strive to develop IEPs that include skills that are more valid to the community, the outcomes of the short-term objectives should reflect this shift in philosophy. For example, a classroom-based objective might include the following outcome:

Outcome: The student will correctly complete word problems involving the ability to make change up to $5.

Context: Paper-and-pencil activities in blocks of 20 minutes.

Criterion: 95% of the presented problems correct.

Keeping the outcome similar, the example can be modified to represent a short-term objective that may be more functional to the learner:

Outcome: The student will correctly compute the change that should be received up to $5 while purchasing items in five different community businesses (use of a calculator).

Context: (1) A meal in a fast-food restaurant.
(2) Bread, milk, eggs at one large grocery store.
(3) Soda, candy at one small grocery store.
(4) A newspaper and magazine at corner stand.
(5) Light bulbs and assorted items at a grocery store.

Criterion: In each instance the student will have computed the correct change to be received prior to entering the checkout line.

A short-term objective such as this one may take months or the entire school year to achieve. Teachers can design a number of classroom activities that will help the student reach this final objective and also develop activities that allow the student to practice the skills in the community. The advantage to writing short-term objectives for arithmetic in this fashion is that it allows the teacher and students to keep on track, concentrating on the ultimate functionality of the skills.

There are different forms for writing objectives, and teachers may prefer using another approach. The following are examples of outcomes and contexts of community-based objectives (minus the criteria). A discussion of potential activities linked to each will follow each example.

GOAL: 1.0 *Elementary school student will demonstrate proper knowledge of handling and spending money.*

OBJECTIVE: 1.1 Student will demonstrate proper knowledge of handling and spending money to include the following subskills:
Subskills
Recognizes names and values of all U.S. currency.
States relationship of monetary equivalents (e.g., 10 pennies or 2 nickels equals 1 dime).
Reads and writes money amounts using symbols and decimals.
Computes total cost on purchases.
Makes change on purchases less than or equal to $5.
Uses money to make actual purchases.

GOAL: 2.0 *Student will demonstrate a proper knowledge of liquid, solid, and linear measurement.*

OBJECTIVE: 2.1 Student will demonstrate knowledge of linear measures to include the following subskills:
Subskills
Introduces vocabulary (key words/abbreviations).
Lists and identifies English/metric tools (ruler, metric stick, etc.).
Computes measurements of objectives using linear tools with accuracy (e.g., $1/4$, $1/2$, $3/4$).
Estimates linear measures to lengths appropriate for task (e.g., length of pencil, width of desk, height of door).

OBJECTIVE: 2.2 Student will demonstrate knowledge of liquid measures to include the following subskills:

Subskills

Introduces vocabulary (key words/abbreviations).

Lists and identifies English/metric units and tools for liquid measures (e.g., cups/pints, pints/quarts, milliliters/liters, liters/cubic centimeters).

Measures liquids (e.g., within 1 ounce, 1 gallon).

Estimates liquid measures to amounts appropriate for task (e.g., to the ounce for mixing orange juice).

GOAL: 3.0 *Student will demonstrate proper knowledge of shopping (e.g., groceries, clothing, transportation, household items).*

OBJECTIVE: 3.1 Student will discriminate between items to be purchased (comparative shopping) on the basis of all of the skill areas to include the following subskills:

Subskills

Discriminates between items based on prices and comparable products (e.g., fast-food chain vs. grocery store, generic vs. name brand).

Discriminates between items based on nutritional value of groceries.

Goal 1.0 and objective 1.1 are relatively easy to teach in many community environments. Goal 2.0 and objectives 2.1 and 2.2 may require more imagination in identifying appropriate instructional sites. For example, a teacher might bring students to the kitchen in a nursing home to participate in cooking activities that incorporate measurement and fractions. Similarly, participating in an activity related to the work done by a small building contractor who is adding a room on to a house helps students see the relationship of linear measurement and daily living as well as practice the skills themselves.

GOAL: 3.0 *High school student will demonstrate proper knowledge of shopping (groceries, clothing, transportation, household items).*

OBJECTIVE: 3.4 Student will demonstrate a proper knowledge of buying on credit to include all of the following areas:

Subskills

☐ Credit limits in relationship to income.

☐ Importance of credit rating.

☐ Mechanics of credit card use.

☐ Safe use of credit to avoid fraud.

☐ Interest calculations.

☐ Terms of unconditional credit plans.

OBJECTIVE: 3.5 Student will demonstrate a proper knowledge of dealing with high pressure sales to include all of the following areas:

Subskills

Distinguishes real from "convinced" necessities (e.g., "You need a million-dollar life insurance policy").

Distinguishes real necessities from luxuries.

Uses assertive principles in sales situations (e.g., knows how to say no).

GOAL: 4.0 *Student will demonstrate proper knowledge of paying utilities and using postal services.*

OBJECTIVE: 4.1 Student will list the following reasons for paying utilities promptly:

☐ Maintaining good credit.

☐ Avoiding late charges.

☐ Maintaining continued services and/or avoiding loss of deposit.

OBJECTIVE: 4.2 Student will locate and/or travel to all utility offices, including gas, electric, telephone, water/sewer, etc.

OBJECTIVE: 4.3 Student will locate and recite pertinent features of each utility bill, including amount due, due date, and address for payment.

GOAL: 6.0 *Student will demonstrate proper knowledge of securing housing (e.g., apartments, houses, mobile homes, and other real estate).*

OBJECTIVE: 6.1 Student will demonstrate a proper knowledge of searching for housing, including all of the following areas:
Subskills
Reads key related vocabulary.
Locates sources of housing.
Makes a list of important questions.
Uses telephone to make inquiries.

OBJECTIVE: 6.2 Students will determine the appropriateness of housing for needs, including all of the following areas:
Subskills
Compares cost of living to overall budget.
Evaluates location of house in relation to mass transit, work, recreation, schools, safety, etc.
Evaluates size of living unit in relation to need.
Evaluates property in terms of proposed length of residence.
Lists restrictions on property owners (e.g., no pets, etc.).

Buying on credit can be useful but problematic for students once they reach adulthood. Understanding about credit, its uses, and abuses is an important topic for middle school and high school students. Applying basic computational skills to these problems can help students understand these concepts. For example, frequent trips to storefront loan companies to gather information on interest rates, payback clauses, and fines can provide students with valuable experience in computing the *real* cost of borrowing money. Similarly, activities in utilities companies can help students obtain data for use in budgetary exercises that apply computational skills to real-life problems. The experiences gained from these activities in the community serve as a link between the abstract and the concrete.

Minimum Competency Testing

As discussed in the last chapter, minimum competency tests are required by many states before students can move to higher grades, and they are eventually required for graduation with a high school diploma. For many students enrolled in special education, the crunch comes at the high school level when it may make a difference, vocationally and educationally, if they can meet the requirements and receive their diploma. Some students with learning disabilities and behavior disorders may be candidates for postsecondary programs that require a high school diploma.

The problem surfaces when teachers use these tests as the sole basis for curriculum development and attempt to develop only paper-and-pencil activities as their mechanism to teach the skills. Because of a history of continued failure with these activities, the chances are that sudden progress in these subjects will not be possible.

A more desirable alternative would be a variety of activities that combine community-based tasks, microcomputer simulations (see Chapter Seven), and finally some paper-and-pencil activities to generalize the skills to a test-taking situation.

For example, following are an objective (indicator) and two examples from a high school minimum competency test for mathematics:

Skill Area: Problem solving

Indicator 13: The student organizes data into tables, charts, and graphs in the context of academic tasks, everyday tasks, or employment activities.

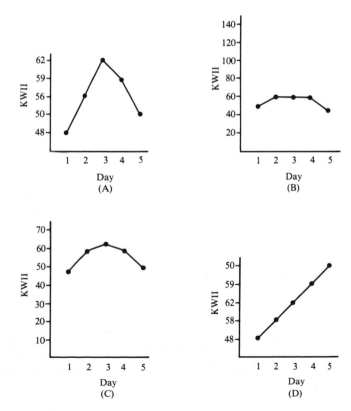

Determines
information

Sam is driving a truck and sees a sign that says the underpass has a clearance of 13'2." Which does Sam need to know about his truck to avoid problems in clearing the underpass?
(A) Contents of the truck
(B) Height of the truck
(C) Size of the motor
(D) Weight of the cargo

In the first example, teachers might design a series of activities that allow the students to chart the electricity usage of some homebound elderly individuals. The students and the teacher could help these individuals identify ways they could curb their usage, charting any subsequent improvement.

The second example can be enhanced with the inclusion of some concrete examples. A teacher might contact a truck rental agency that would allow students to conduct measurement exercises with the trucks. The teacher could cover the warning labels a truck has posted, and students could compare their figures to the labels when uncovered (immediate feedback). On subsequent trips to the community, students could note the height requirements of various overpasses and discuss which of the trucks could be driven under each overpass. Alternative results could be discussed. Computer-assisted instruction is also available that allows students additional practice on a variety of mathematics concepts (e.g., Lubke et al., 1989; Miller & Cooke, 1989).

KEY CONCEPTS

- The results of research studies indicate that learners with mild and moderate handicaps can learn more complex arithmetic skills than previously thought possible.
- Teachers may find it difficult to instruct many learners in arithmetic if they present the material out of the context of real-life activities.
- The movement by special educators is toward teaching arithmetic skills in the context of functional activities, allowing students to practice skills in community environments.
- An important task for teachers is to locate a scope-and-sequence chart of arithmetic skills and relate them to how they will be used in community activities.
- A community needs assessment (CNA) allows teachers to identify places in the community where their students can practice functional arithmetic skills and people from the community who can provide help and resources to their program.
- Annual goals can reflect skills taught and practiced in traditional classroom fashion (e.g., paper-and-pencil or blackboard activities) or skills taught in a more functional manner.
- Because many learners with handicapping conditions have trouble generalizing learned skills, teachers cannot be certain that arithmetic skills learned in the classroom will be used in community activities. One solution to this problem is to write short-term objectives in a form that allows learners to demonstrate that they can use their skills in functional ways.

■ ■ ■ ■

Step Five: Assess Student Entry Behaviors

Survey-Level Assessment: Achievement Tests

Identifying the arithmetic strengths and weaknesses of learners is an important step in matching the best instructional techniques to their needs. Standardized assessment measures of arithmetic skills can be a useful beginning point for obtaining survey-type information (Algozzine & McGraw, 1980).

Commercial achievement tests are used frequently by school systems and provide data in the most general sense concerning student progress over a longer period of time (e.g., 1 school year). Some information such as grade levels and general deficit areas can be obtained from these tests: however, they are not sensitive enough to pinpoint specific learning problems (see Table 9.2).

Survey-Level Assessment: Diagnostic Tests

Diagnostic tests of arithmetic are more thorough because they deal with only one subject, whereas achievement tests attempt to measure a number of academic areas (e.g., arithmetic, reading, spelling, general information). These tests tend to provide more information from each of the subskill areas of arithmetic such as word problems, operations, fractions, time, and money.

Standardized diagnostic arithmetic tests (Table 9.2) are useful as a quick method of pinpointing the areas where a student's primary deficits exist. These tests do have weaknesses, however, which require teachers to gather more information at the specific level of assessment. For example, Goodstein, Kahn, and Cawley (1976) found that on the Key Math Diagnostic Arithmetic Test the skills included were logically sequenced but there were large gaps between the objectives represented by test items. The problem is that teachers might list on an IEP the objectives that a student misses on a diagnostic test, thus ignoring the large gaps in the learner's skills.

Another problem with many standardized tests is that they test items represented by abstract or semiconcrete concepts. The test scores of many learners who function at a concrete level may not reflect the skills they have actually obtained. For example, a student may not be able to compute the answer to the problem 8 + 6 when presented in a test item, whereas that same student may be able to tell you she assembled 14 products, 8 of one type and 6 of another.

The weaknesses of standardized diagnostic arithmetic tests do not render them useless to teachers. When used properly, these tests can provide teachers with a fast estimate of where more intensive assessment is needed. For example, a teacher may discover that Betty has scored significantly below average on a measurement subtest and yet scored about average in all other areas. This information should alert the teacher to the need for additional assessment of Betty's measurement skills. Additional specific-level assessment would come in the form of either commercially produced or teacher-made criterion-referenced tests.

Specific-Level Assessment: Curriculum-Based Tests

Curriculum-based tests rely heavily on a teacher's or someone else's ability to task analyze the skills of interest. A task analysis of linear measurement might resemble the following set of steps:

1. Indicates whether objects of different lengths are longer or shorter.
2. Indicates three objects of different lengths as being either long, longer, longest, or short, shorter, and shortest.

TABLE 9.2   *Common Commercial Achievement and Diagnostic Tests of Mathematics Skills*

Test	Areas Assessed	Grade Levels
California Achievement Tests California Test Bureau McGraw-Hill Monterey, CA	Computation Concepts Applications	1–9
Metropolitan Achievement Tests Harcourt Brace Jovanovich New York, NY	Numeration Geometry Measurement Problem solving and operations	3–9
Peabody Individual Achievement Tests American Guidance Service Circle Pines, MN	Matching and recognizing numbers Geometry	K–12
SRA Achievement Tests Science Research Associates Chicago, IL	Concepts Reasoning Computation	K–12
Fountain Valley Teachers Support System in Mathematics Zweig Associates Huntington Beach, CA	Numbers and operations Geometry and measurement Application Sets Problem solving	K–8
Key Math Diagnostic Test-Revised American Guidance Service Circle Pines, MN	Content Operations Applications	K–6
Sequential Assessment of Mathematics Inventory (SAMI) Charles E. Merrill Publishers Columbus, OH	Mathematics language Ordinality Measurement and geometry Computation Work problems	K–8
Stanford Diagnostic Mathematics Test Harcourt Brace Jovanovich New York, NY	Numeration Computation Applications	K–12

ENRIGHT DIAGNOSTIC
  ARITHMETIC INVENTORY
  OF BASIC SKILLS®
Curriculum Associates
North Billerica, MA
	Basic facts
	Skill placement
	Wide range achievement
	Basic skills test
		K–8

3. Explains the use of a ruler.

4. Measures lengths to the nearest inch and records measurement.

5. Measures lengths to the nearest half and quarter inches.

6. Correctly converts inches to feet and feet to inches.

7. Explains the use of a yardstick and notes that a yard is 36 inches or 3 feet.

8. Correctly converts feet to yards and yards to feet.

9. Correctly converts inches to yards and yards to inches.

10. Measures various lengths using either a conventional ruler, a yardstick, or a tape measure.

A curriculum-based test on linear measurement would assess the learner's ability on all 10 of these areas, measuring performance against preset criteria. Continuing with the previous example, the teacher discovered Betty's assumed deficit in measurement. Using the task sequence as a guide, he develops problems representative of the 10 areas for linear measurement. Betty's performance on these problems should provide a much clearer picture of her strengths and weaknesses in this area.

Both the Brigance Diagnostic Inventory of Basic Skills (Brigance, 1977) and the Brigance Diagnostic Inventory of Essential Skills (Brigance, 1980) are commonly used examples of commercially produced criterion-referenced tests. These tests cover arithmetic skills from kindergarten through twelfth grade levels and provide teachers with a list of objectives for IEP development that is more thorough than those found in standardized tests.

Teachers may find that with some learners they still need to assess certain areas using their own task sequences as a guide. This will be especially true as teachers move more toward teaching functional, community-based skills. For example, if the goal is to teach students the use of arithmetic for comparison shopping in a local grocery store, commercially produced tests could not provide a valid task sequence for that situation. In this instance a teacher-made test based on a teacher-developed task sequence would be more appropriate.

Error Analysis

Assessment activities become most useful when teachers translate the data into a form that allows student error patterns to emerge (Howell & Morehead, 1987). Error analysis allows teachers to pinpoint the computational mistakes being made by students and interpret reasons for the mistakes. A thorough error analysis goes beyond obtaining a score on a standardized test or a grade on a weekly quiz. Error patterns can only be found by carefully analyzing each mistake a student makes, looking for answers to two basic questions: "(1) What is the nature of the error?; (2) What are the most likely causes of the error?" (Wiederholt, Hammill, & Brown, 1983, p. 197).

Learners are often consistent in the mistakes they make, either because they have never learned the rules for completing the problems or because the rules they have learned are being applied in the wrong fashion. Identifying these error patterns is the first step in choosing the instructional strategies to correct the problems. Many error patterns exist in arithmetic, the most common being the four presented by Roberts (1968): (1) using the wrong operation, e.g., student adds when he should multiply; (2) making an obvious computational error, e.g., student adds 2 + 6 = 7; (3) using a defective algorithm, e.g., student cross-adds columns; and (4) providing a random response, e.g., student guesses at the answer using no logical pattern.

Howell and Kaplan (1980) believed that the four areas presented by Roberts did not provide enough examples of common error patterns. They developed a chart based on work from Englehardt (1977) that provides a more complete system of error patterns. Their chart is presented in Table 9.3.

Error patterns can be established by collecting data from three basic sources: (1) mistakes made on problems from standardized tests; (2) mistakes made on problems from commercially produced or teacher-made criterion-referenced tests; and (3) mistakes students are in the process of making (Ashlock, 1982). The first two sources of errors can be obtained by teachers in the form of permanent products that can be analyzed without having the student present.

TABLE 9.3   *Common Error Patterns*

1. Basic fact error.	Use of untrue simple number sentences.	(a) $5 + 2 = 6$ (b) $6 \times 8 = 52$	
2. Incomplete or defective algorithm.	(a) Use of predictable but incorrect procedure.	(a) $\begin{array}{r} 25 \\ 4\overline{)208} \\ 20 \\ \hline 008 \end{array}$ and	$\begin{array}{r} 26 \\ 7\overline{)434} \\ 42 \\ \hline 14 \end{array}$
	(b) Use of the correct procedure with an omitted or added step.	(b) $\begin{array}{r} 68 \\ +7 \\ \hline 1386 \end{array}$ and	$\begin{array}{r} 47 \\ +5 \\ \hline 962 \end{array}$
3. Grouping errors.	Failure to place digits in proper column as required in regrouping.	(a) $\begin{array}{r} 86 \\ +47 \\ \hline 1215 \end{array}$ (b)	$\begin{array}{r} 47 \\ \times 9 \\ \hline 42 \\ 36 \\ \hline 78 \end{array}$
4. Inappropriate inversion.	(a) Reversal of a step in an algorithm. (b) Reversal of place values.	(a) $\begin{array}{r} 52 \\ -17 \\ \hline 45 \end{array}$ (b)	$\begin{array}{r} 35 \\ \times 3 \\ \hline 141 \end{array}$
5. Incorrect operation.	Use of the wrong operation.	(a) $\begin{array}{r} 4 \\ +2 \\ \hline 8 \end{array}$ (b)	$\begin{array}{r} 100 \\ -74 \\ \hline 174 \end{array}$
6. Identity and/or zero errors.	(a) Confusion of zeros and ones. (b) Failure to understand the concept of zero.	(a) $\begin{array}{r} 5 \\ \times 0 \\ \hline 5 \end{array}$ (b)	$\begin{array}{r} 10 \\ +5 \\ \hline 6 \end{array}$

From *Diagnosing Basic Skills* (p. 248) by K. Howell and J. Kaplan. Copyright 1980 by Charles E. Merrill Publishers. Reprinted by permission. The authors based this chart on information from "Analysis of Children's Computational Errors: A Qualitative Approach" by J. M. Englehardt. 1977. *British Journal of Educational Psychology, 47,* 149–154.

The third source is an important one that is often overlooked by teachers. Asking a student to compute a problem while explaining to the teacher the process being used can provide excellent information about the nature and causes of the error.

Error analysis is a technique that teachers use as "educational detectives," analyzing clues to solve some of the severe learning problems of their students. A high-quality error analysis involves following some simple steps. Howell and Kaplan (1980) have listed six steps that provide a good framework for identifying error patterns in arithmetic:

1. Collect an adequate behavior sample by having the student do several problems of each type in which you are interested.
2. Encourage the student to work, but do nothing to influence the responses the student makes.
3. Record all the responses the student makes, including comments.
4. Look for patterns in the responses.
5. Look for exceptions to any apparent pattern.
6. List the patterns you have identified as assumed causes for the student's computational difficulties (pp. 250–251).

Organizing the data collected from a student's work requires a system that is simple, keeping the information in a systematic format. One of the better systems was developed by Howell and Kaplan, classifying data by the categories *stimulus, response,* and *assumed causes.* Table 9.4 provides an example of an error analysis chart for additional problems. Charts such as the one shown in Table 9.4 are most valuable when the teacher watches how the students compute answers to problems and then asks the students to explain how they arrived at the finished product. The information from these informal observations is recorded in the column labeled "Teacher Observations" and is used to provide a more thorough analysis.

CASE STUDY

"Hi, Bob. How's life for the fifth-grade teacher?"

"I've been better, Anne. Some days I can't seem to make teaching work. I guess I don't have the patience you special ed teachers were born with!"

"Give that old myth about special educators having tons of patience a break, Bob. We have no more or less than you regular educators! What's wrong?"

"Well, I have this kid in my class who keeps falling farther and farther behind in arithmetic. He's staffed into a resource class part of the day with one of your colleagues, but he won't give me any concrete suggestions about what I can do!"

"Well, Bob, interpersonal relations are not my strong suit, so I can't give you suggestions for dealing with the kid's teacher. However, if you tell me the types of mistakes the kid is making I may be able to give some instructional tips."

"Mistakes? What do you mean by types of mistakes? I give my students arithmetic problems and then record their progress by percentage of answers correct."

TABLE 9.4 *Sample Error Analysis Chart*

Problem Presented	What the Child Writes	What the Child Says (Oral Interview)	Error Analysis Teacher's Hypotheses	What the Teacher Does Next
7 −3	7 −3 2	7 take away 3 = 2.	Doesn't know number fact.	Present same problem in another form (rule out random error). Check other subtraction facts. Provide practice with physical objects, worksheets, number line, flashcards, games, etc. Retest before going to more difficult subtraction.
15 −6	15 −6 11	6 take away 5 is 1; 1 stays the same.	Faulty algorithm; doesn't understand integrity of minuend and subtrahend; doesn't know number fact.	Check further to see if child always subtracts smaller number from larger. Review addition and subtraction at enactive and iconic level (Bruner) with one-digit numbers, then two-digit. Have child respond orally before returning to written form.
85 −3	85 − 3 52	3 from 8 is 5; 3 from 5 is 2.	Problem worked left to right; problem with place value (subtracting ones from tens).	Review place value at the enactive, iconic, and symbolic levels; provide practice with subtraction algorithm in simpler two-digit problems.
85 −9	85 − 9 86	The 8 goes down here; then you have to change the 5 to 15, then subtract 9 from 15.	Problem worked left to right; doesn't understand effect of regrouping ones on tens.	Provide experience with place value—manipulating bundles of straws (1's, 10's, 100's), pocket chart, or Stern materials; then provide workbook pictorial practice. Finally, rework symbolic problem.

Problem Presented	What the Child Writes	What the Child Says (Oral Interview)	Error Analysis Teacher's Hypotheses	What the Teacher Does Next
91 − 83	91 −83 1	Since you can't take 3 from 1, the answer is 1; also because 8 from 9 is 1.	Problem in regrouping: possible problem in number fact.	Review place value (tens and ones); perform several problems of this type on the pocket chart, or with Cuisenaire rods. Provide successful experience on problems of this type before returning to numerical form.
523 −284	523 − 284 249	This 2 (in tens place) should be 12, that makes this 5 a 4. Now 12 − 8 = 4 and 4 − 2 = 2. To take 4 away over here (ones column) you make the 3 to a 13; 13 − 4 = 9; change 12 to 11.	Sequence is the problem here. The child performed all the steps correctly but in the wrong order.	Practice right-to-left sequence in problems not involving regrouping. Use place-value box or chart to show why sequence affects results.
300 −157	300 −157 053	You have to get ones from the three because there aren't any here (pointing to 0's); 3 take away 2 makes the 3 a 1. Now we have 10 ones, and 10 tens, and we can subtract.	Relationship of empty sets of ones to tens to hundreds a problem. Child doesn't understand conversion from one unity to another.	Provide child with experience in converting tens to ones and hundreds to ones. (It might be very effective to use dollars, dimes, and pennies first; then use the paper-and-pencil mode). First provide practice using only tens and ones, together, then hundreds and tens together, then hundreds and ones together, finally conversions involving all three units in one problem.

From Donald D. Hammill and Nettie R. Bartel, *Teaching Children with Learning and Behavior Problems*, Third Edition. Copyright © 1982 by Allyn and Bacon. Reprinted with permission.

"That may be the reason why you can't pinpoint this kid's problem! If you have the student's paper in that stack you're correcting, I'll show you what I mean. For example, here the student has missed four subtraction problems on this assignment. The first problem gives us a clue to at least one of his deficits."

"Note what the student's answer was. It leads me to believe that he hasn't grasped the relationship of zeros in the ones, to tens, to hundreds. He still can't convert from one column to the next."

"By analyzing this problem instead of just marking it wrong, we have gathered information that may lead us to a solution for this deficit."

"OK Anne, you've got my attention. What's the solution?"

"Well, one possibility is to allow the student to practice converting tens to ones using concrete objects such as real money. As he practices with the objects, have him also put the problem and answer on paper. The next step would be practicing hundreds to tens and so on until he consistently gets the idea. If you follow these procedures with a representative sample of the kid's mistakes you should get a pretty good error pattern, allowing us to make some assumptions about remedial techniques."

"Anne, I can't tell you how much this helps. If I can ever do you a favor just ask!"

"Well there is one thing you can do for me, Bob. How about letting me mainstream one of *my* students into your class? Wait, Bob, don't faint!"

■ ■ ■ ■

Step Six: Assess Community-Based Mathematics Skills

Hopefully, many teachers of elementary- through high-school-age students will assess both their entry behaviors and their later progress toward using mathematics skills in community settings. All learners will benefit from as much practical use of skills as possible. Therefore, arithmetic assessment for these learners may best be accomplished in more realistic settings.

Using money, telling time, and measuring are the arithmetic skills most useful to learners. As teachers increase the time spent in community-based instruction, the opportunity to assess these skills in daily living activities increases. For example, a teacher wishing to see how a student reacts when asked to purchase a soda from a machine needs to structure a situation in which the student has access to a soda machine. This information is important because some students who are not able to count change in the classroom may be able to purchase a soda from a vending machine.

Vocational training sites in the community are also examples of where mathematics skills can be assessed. Students working in a nursing home might need to have some time-telling skills to know when certain jobs need to be completed. In this instance, teachers would be interested in two pieces of data.

The first is an assessment of what skills the student had achieved prior to arrival at the work site (e.g., knows that 12 P. M. means lunchtime). The second piece of data is an assessment of the situation for the purpose of developing adaptations that will allow the student to complete the job. For example, if the student could not tell when it was 12 P. M., would an alarm watch set by the supervisor remind the student that at 12 P. M. the trays needed to be delivered to the residents?

There are many more examples of community environments where teachers can directly assess a student's ability to use mathematics skills. Grocery stores are excellent sites for assessing and later instructing skills in basic operations and relationships of cost to units of measure. For example, teachers can develop activities that test students in solving word problems, adding the cost of items on a shopping list, or subtracting the difference between two items of identical size.

The following list of goals includes examples of those that should be taught in community environments. All students with mild to moderate handicaps need to practice the skills related to these and other goals in realistic settings, using real materials, and in the presence of nonhandicapped community members. Elementary-age students should begin learning basic skills related to these areas, with situations and problems becoming more complex as they advance through school.

- Reviews the cost of desired food items at different stores and buys those items where they are most economical.
- Compares the cost of generically labeled food with brand name and store brands and selects the food item that best meets budget and taste preferences.
- Compares the unit prices of food items (price per ounce or pound) and selects the food item that is most economical and best meets personal food quality and quantity requirements.
- Clips discount coupons from daily newspapers, magazines, and store handouts and uses them to purchase desired food products.
- Uses food stamps to purchase needed food.
- Compares the accuracy of store receipts with products purchased.
- Checks the prices of prescription drugs, over-the-counter drugs, and medications at different stores and buys needed items where they are most economical.
- Compares name, store, and generic brands of over-the-counter drugs and medications and selects the one best suited to budgetary needs and quality preferences.
- Compares the sizes and prices of various over-the-counter drugs and medications and purchases the one appropriate to personal needs.
- Compares prices of generic and brand names of prescription drugs and selects the one best suited to budget.
- Checks the prices of clothing at different stores and buys needed items where they are most economical.
- Checks out prices of furniture and appliances at different stores and buys needed items where they are most economical.
- Reviews sale advertisements in newspapers, store handouts, and posters for furniture, appliances, and other items, compares their prices with non-sale-item prices, and purchases desired items.
- Reviews ads for heavy-duty and non-heavy-duty appliances and purchases those most suited to personal needs.
- Reviews monthly bills and statements for accuracy and, after verification, pays bills by the due date.
- Reviews energy-saving hints in pamphlets that accompany fuel bills and, when possible, follows their suggestions.

- Locates transportation schedules, selects an appropriate form of transportation from these schedules, and then plans trips according to time and budgetary constraints.

- Compares utility bills to meter reading in the home for accuracy and as a method of budgeting for future utility bills.

- Reviews bank statements and deposit and withdrawal receipts or notations for accuracy.

- Makes and continuously reviews a weekly and monthly budget.

- Compares the various interest rates of banks and other lending agencies and institutions for buying on time and selects the one that best meets personal financial needs.

- Establishes a savings program.

- When paying cash is not the best option, selects an appropriate credit card and purchases goods and services that are within a projected personal budget and within credit limits.

- When paying cash is not the best option, draws a check to pay for foods and services.

- Reviews the information on tax forms and arranges for them to be completed and filed on time.

PROGRAM IMPLEMENTATION

Identifying and Analyzing Short-Term Objectives

Once teachers have pinpointed a student's strengths and weaknesses, identification of short-term objectives becomes the next logical step in the instructional process. Knowing a student's strengths helps to identify instructional procedures that may be helpful. A student's weaknesses, on the other hand, can become the content for a short-term objective. For example, a student may demonstrate a severe deficit in addition and subtraction skills. An analysis of the student's errors may pinpoint two areas where the deficit appears most severe: carrying in addition and regrouping (borrowing) in subtraction. Short-term objectives for these areas may resemble the following:

Outcome: The student will correctly compute addition problems involving carrying.

Context: Written problems with paper and pencil. Written problems with calculator.

Criteria: 10/10 with paper and pencil. 10/10 with calculator.

Outcome: The student will correctly compute subtraction problems involving regrouping (borrowing).

Context: Written problems with paper and pencil. Written problems with calculator.

Criteria: 10/10 with paper and pencil. 10/10 with calculator.

Analyzing these objectives for a clearer picture of the subskills is the next step. Skills needed to master the addition and subtraction objectives might be sequenced as follows:

1.0 Addition short-term objective

   1.3 Carrying from ones column

   1.4 Carrying from tens column

1.5 Carrying consecutively from column to column

1.6 Carrying alternately skipping columns

2.0 Subtraction short-term objective

2.3 Borrowing in the tens and ones columns

2.4 Borrowing in the hundreds and tens columns

2.5 Borrowing consecutively

2.6 Borrowing alternately

Analysis of short-term objectives generally occurs after IEP development, when the teacher is ready to begin instruction. This procedure allows teachers to organize the skills they wish to teach and keep track of the skills mastered by the student (see Table 9.5).

KEY CONCEPTS

- Survey-level assessment of mathematics skills may best be accomplished by using standardized diagnostic tests (e.g., Key Math).
- These instruments provide a fast, fairly reliable estimate of a student's general deficit areas.
- The major weakness of standardized diagnostic tests is their limited sampling of skills. The problems included in these instruments are only representative samples of an area and cannot provide an in-depth analysis of the student's deficit areas.
- Specific-level assessment of arithmetic may best be accomplished by using either commercially produced (e.g., Brigance) or teacher-made criterion-referenced tests or by direct observation of the student's skills in community settings.
- For most learners, it is important to assess mathematics skills both in the classroom and in the community.

TABLE 9.5   *Partial Management System for Monitoring Students' Completion of Arithmetic Short-Term Objectives (Numbers Coded to a Master List)*

	1.3	1.4	1.5	1.6	2.3	2.4	2.5	2.6
Bobby	X	X	X		X			
Jovan	X				X			
Susan								
La Ronda	X	X	X		X	X		
Michael	X				X			
Tamara	X	X	X	X	X	X	X	X
John								
Andrea	X							
Phil	X	X						
Sara	X	X	X		X	X	X	
Jamie	X				X			

X = Successful mastery of objective based on criteria located on student's IEP.

- Error analysis involves determining the nature and possible cause for the types of errors students make.

- Error patterns can result from a number of causes. Most noticeable are choosing inappropriate operations, using a defective algorithm, making computational errors, having language problems, and using random responses.

- Error patterns can be analyzed using information from standardized and criterion-referenced tests and homework assignments, watching the student complete a task, and asking the student how the problem was completed.

- Assessment of a student's mathematics skills should be as functional as possible. For example, instead of testing a student's knowledge of measurement on paper, a teacher might structure a situation in which the student has the opportunity to measure during a cooking activity.

■ ■ ■ ■

Developing Instructional Strategies

Students' strengths and weaknesses refer to the learning characteristics they exhibit. Generally, learners with mild and moderate handicaps have problems focusing their attention on specific stimuli, discriminating among stimuli, remembering facts, grasping abstract concepts, and generalizing skills to new situations. Because these learners as a group are heterogeneous, individuals could have problems in all or some of these areas, and assessment procedures should help by pinpointing what areas are important to each student. Instructional strategies will either help to remediate the deficit or help the student circumvent the problem.

Curriculum materials can be purchased commercially, made by the teacher, or obtained in the community through donations (e.g., practice check-writing packages obtained from a bank). Whether materials are purchased commercially or developed by the teacher, consideration should be given to what techniques are used to help students overcome their deficits.

For example, students with deficits in attention and discrimination may benefit from materials that use color coded key elements, for example, having all the operation signs ($+$, $-$, $\times$, $\div$) in different colors. This technique helps the students focus on the correct operation by directing their attention to the relevant stimulus while helping them discriminate among operations. A similar technique might use arrows plus color coding to help students direct their attention to the appropriate algorithm.

Understanding abstract concepts can be a formidable barrier for many learners, and mastering mathematics content requires the ability to reason and make complex associations. This problem may be exacerbated if mathematics skills are only presented in rote fashion. They may learn the operation but not know the related concepts (e.g., adding numbers versus adding sets of objects).

Cawley and his associates (Cawley, 1978; Cawley et al., 1976; Cawley & Vitello, 1972) have suggested a process for teaching mathematics that addresses the issue of concept development as opposed to teaching rote skills. The model, called the *interactive unit approach*, emphasizes the importance of teacher-pupil interaction. The teacher is required to present the material to the student in four ways: (1) constructing an activity that allows the students to do something; (2) presenting a picture or objects to represent the target concept; (3) saying something, using language to explain the concept; (4) writing something, using written symbols to support the concept (Sedlak & Fitzmaurice, 1981).

Each of the four teacher actions requires a corresponding action by the student. For example, a teacher may use a ruler to demonstrate how to measure the length and width of a table. In the process of measuring the table, the teacher also explains what he or she is doing and then writes down the figures that represent the final product. The student is then asked to repeat the process.

Other authors have highlighted the approach of Cawley and his associates as one that has excellent potential for students having learning problems in mathematics (e.g., Schulz & Turnbull, 1983; Sedlak & Fitzmaurice, 1981; Smith, 1974). The approach has been incorporated into a program entitled Project Math, which will be discussed in the next section. The format of the program allows students to use all of their input modalities to process the content. They *see* the teacher perform the task, *listen* to the teacher explain the task (concept), *do* the task themselves, and finally, *say* what they have done (explain the concept).

The techniques of Cawley and his associates have the added benefit of assisting students with poor memories to remember basic facts that are vital in mathematics. Those learners, who have short-term memory deficits, may benefit from the multiple opportunities to learn a skill or concept. The *doing* component of the interactive approach may help to reinforce students' memorization of basic facts by allowing them to manipulate objects related to the task or concept (e.g., using blocks to learn addition facts to 10).

Some learners may have great difficulty memorizing basic facts regardless of the techniques used. In these instances, memory aids may be helpful, allowing the student to get past the basic facts and complete more advanced tasks. For example, a student having difficulty learning to tell time might have access to a small notebook that shows pictures of clocks depicting the time by the hour and half-hour with the appropriate notation. This same approach can be used with measurement conversions (e.g., 1 foot = 12 inches), money (e.g., 50 cents = 2 quarters), basic arithmetic operations facts, and multiplication tables. Some learners can spend countless hours memorizing their multiplication tables and still have difficulty remembering them. If they were allowed to refer to a reference table, they might be able to apply the skill to daily living activities.

Teachers must be careful to use mathematics terms consistently. Some learners can easily become confused when many terms describing the same process are used. Schultz and Turnbull (1983) presented an example of teachers who might use the terms "regrouping, renaming, and carrying to refer to the same concept" (p. 264).

For some students, learning traditional mathematics skills may not be the most realistic approach. The goal for these learners is to get them involved in more realistic or community-based activities as soon as possible. Therefore, it is important to use instructional techniques designed to allow students to circumvent their mathematics deficit and participate in activities. This approach, called *designing instructional adaptations,* allows students to cope in situations where their lack of ability would normally exclude them.

The most obvious adaptation is to design more activities and structure more opportunities for students to learn to use calculators (Russell, 1982). Calculators have increasingly become a need instead of a luxury in our society, and learners can be taught to use them to their advantage. For example, a learner with moderate cognitive disabilities at the middle school level might have a great deal of trouble learning her basic operations.

However, this same student could be taught how to use a calculator to compare the prices between two items based on certain characteristics of the items (e.g., weight).

Many students can benefit from increased instruction in the use of calculators for completing daily living exercises (Koller & Mulhern, 1977). By the time students are in high school, continued drills in basic mathematics skills may be counterproductive. Instead, activities such as balancing a checkbook, maintaining a budget, and computing taxes can all be taught using the calculator as an adaptive tool.

CASE STUDY

Ms. Joseph, the director of special education, opened the meeting by stating, "We're here today to see if we can identify ways to increase the numbers of students with handicaps served by vocational education."

Turning pale, Mr. Barnes, the director of vocational education, grunted, "Now, Ms. Joseph, we've been round on this subject before. I thought we agreed that your students don't have the necessary prerequisites to benefit from our programs. Namely, they can't read, write, measure, and tell time!"

"Granted, Mr. Barnes, our students do have severe learning problems. However, we think we have a solution to the problem. Mr. Adams, our lead teacher at the high school, has an idea and I'd like him to explain it. Jim, I'll turn it over to you."

"Well, folks, we realize that some of our students are just not getting the basic skills they need through traditional classroom instruction," said Mr. Adams. "Yet, they have the abilities to perform many of the tasks you teach in your vocational classes, if we can figure out how to get past the academic deficits!"

"Well, I'll be dogged if I can see how a kid can be a part of my carpentry class if he can't measure," said Mr. Rule.

"Our goal for some kids may not be entry-level employment, Mr. Rule. We may be only working on ways to help them apply their academic skills in more functional ways. For example, one of our students having trouble with learning linear measurement skills might have a set of samples of commonly cut boards labeled by their sizes. Then, when asked to cut 10 boards measuring 6 feet 6 inches, for example, the student can refer to the sample and either use it to mark the new boards or measure the sample to remind him where 6 feet 6 inches is on the ruler. Over time, we feel he will begin to learn how to measure because he is engaged in a functional, highly motivating task. The added benefit is that our students get valuable training in work-related behaviors, vocational skills, and job sampling!"

"Hmm, I guess I can see what you're getting at," said Mr. Barnes, "but who is going to come up with these ideas?"

"That's the role of our special educators," said Ms. Joseph. "They will work closely with your people and develop a list of potential adaptations."

"Well, heaven knows we have enough regular students who have trouble computing and working with numbers," said Mr. Rule. "Maybe we can use some of these adaptations to help them! I say let's give it a try!"

■ ■ ■ ■

Programmatic Approaches

A number of commercially produced mathematics programs are available. Many of these programs are based on sound educational principles that gear instruction to the perceived needs of learners with handicaps. For example, some provide opportunities for learners to practice skills using multiple modalities. They also provide frequent feedback to the learner and many opportunities to practice the same skill. The following sections present brief descriptions of selected mathematics programs and materials.

DISTAR Arithmetic System

DISTAR Arithmetic (Engelmann & Carnine, 1972–1976) is similar to the DISTAR Reading Program in that it is highly structured and sequenced, with the lessons designed for small groups. The arithmetic skills targeted for instruction cover skills generally taught in kindergarten through third grade. DISTAR I emphasizes ordinal counting, basic addition facts, basic subtraction facts, and simple word problems. DISTAR II presents more advanced addition and subtraction problems, basic multiplication facts, money, measurement, time, and fractions. DISTAR III continues to provide more complex addition and subtraction problems, multiplication, and division, as well as more complex story problems.

The DISTAR system has proved to be highly effective for teaching rote skills to younger, lower income children (Sedlak & Fitzmaurice, 1981), and it may be effective for use with some younger students with mild to moderate handicaps who require consistency and structure. Unfortunately, it does have some weaknesses that teachers must compensate for with additional activities.

Sternberg and Fair (1982) have noted that the DISTAR program does not provide activities that allow students to practice skills in situations relevant to their lives. In addition, the program emphasizes rote skills development over development of mathematics concepts. As students grow older, DISTAR may become less appropriate because of its lack of functional mathematics content.

Project Math

Project Math, developed by Cawley and his associates (1976) is a comprehensive developmental program for teaching kindergarten through sixth-grade level mathematics skills. This program is based on the "interactive unit approach" (refer to the section on "Developing Instructional Strategies"), allowing learners to practice skills using the "do, see, and say" techniques. Cawley's (1977) approach was to develop a mathematics curriculum that would allow nonreaders to learn the skills while using as many modalities as possible.

Project Math presents activities in patterns, geometry, sets, numbers, measurement, and fractions. This program is highly flexible, allowing students to use a number of options for presenting answers while encouraging teachers to be creative when presenting questions.

Project Math has proved to be effective with many learners. Its major advantage is its relevance, because the program includes activities designed to apply mathematics skills to daily life. Project Math also provides opportunities for students to practice divergent thinking, and problem solving is stressed throughout the program.

The major disadvantage of Project Math appears to be that the program was developed to be self-contained and not supplemental to other programs. Therefore, students mainstreamed into a regular class using another program may be difficult to place into the Project Math sequence of activities.

Essential Math and Language Skills Program

The Essential Math and Language Skills Program (EMLS) (Sternberg, Sedlak, Cherkes, & Minick, 1978) was designed to present skills in a developmental sequence, stressing concept attainment and then skill training. Activities from the EMLS program cover six areas, including sets and operations, numbers and operations, patterns, part-whole relationships, spatial relationships, and measurements.

The relationship of the skills presented by the EMLS program to daily life is developed by presenting realistic examples. Concepts are presented in conjunction with concrete examples, and students must show that they have grasped the concept before skills are practiced.

A major advantage of the EMLS program is its flexibility. For example, teaching strategies are outlined, but the teacher has a choice of which ones to use based on student need. Also, the program lists a number of potential student responses for each objective, allowing for more divergent thinking on the part of the student.

Real Life Math

Real Life Math (Schwartz, 1977) is a program that presents role-playing activities, allowing students to practice applying mathematics skills to daily living activities. Specifically, the program presents simulations of banking transactions, bill paying, and other business-related skills.

KEY CONCEPTS

- Instructional strategies directly relate to a student's strengths and weaknesses. These strategies should be designed to help students focus attention, discriminate, improve memory, understand abstractions, and generalize skills.

- Color cues, arrows, underlining, and highlighting are examples of methods to assist students in focusing their attention and discriminating among stimuli.

- Cawley's model, called the *interactive unit approach*, helps learners understand abstract concepts by allowing them to see a model perform the task, practice the task with concrete and semiconcrete objects, verbally rehearse the task, and finally complete the task using only the abstractions.

- Project Math incorporates Cawley's model into a self-contained, commercially produced mathematics program.
- Teachers must use mathematics terms consistently.
- All students should be well versed in the care and use of calculators.
- A number of commercially produced mathematics programs are available that incorporate several preferred teaching strategies. When reviewing materials, important questions such as the following should be considered:

  ☐ Does the program allow for practice using multiple modalities?
  ☐ Does the program provide the learner with frequent feedback?
  ☐ Do the program materials use color cues, arrows, etc.?
  ☐ Is the program self-contained, or are other materials needed?
  ☐ Is the program flexible, allowing for teacher input?
  ☐ Does the program incorporate community-related activities?

  ■ ■ ■ ■

Other Programs and Materials

Accent/Consumer Education
Chicago: Follett Publishing Company

Cuisennaire Rods
New Rochelle: Cuisennaire Co. of America

Developmental Learning Materials for Math
Dallas: Developmental Learning Materials (DLM)

Learning Skills Series: Arithmetic
New York: McGraw-Hill

Mathematics in Daily Living
Austin: Steck-Vaughn Co.

Money Matters
Hayward, CA: Janus Book Publishers

Pacemaker Arithmetic Program
Belmont, CA: Fearon Publishers

Sullivan Programmed Math
New York: McGraw-Hill

Target Math Series
Johnstown, PA: Mafex, Inc.

IDEA FILE

Microcomputers provide students a highly effective way to practice and retain mathematics skills (Bratt, 1983; Burns & Bozeman, 1981; Hofmeister, 1983). Students who have been bored by or turned off to mathematics may now be motivated to practice skills by computer that they might shun in paper-and-pencil format.

Many teachers are familiar with the microcomputer's potential for providing learners with fun activities for drill and practice. Companies are increasingly marketing new software to assist students in this area, and for many learners drill and practice is a key goal. However, microcomputers can be used to a greater advantage.

Goldenberg, Russell, and Carter (1984) identified the following three additional uses of the microcomputer for teaching mathematics skills.

1. Provides educational games that allow learners to interact with graphs and models showing mathematical concepts.

2. Provides tools for helping students organize, record, and visualize information.

3. Provides activities allowing students explore mathematics in ways not possible using conventional instruction.

Teachers should be aware of the power a microcomputer can have for helping children learn problem-solving skills (Hill, 1983). For example, some experts have traditionally felt that students with mental handicaps inherently had poor problem-solving skills. However, with the advance of computer-assisted instruction, some professionals are finding that these students can solve problems previously not thought possible.

LOGO is a computer language that offers a new medium for students to learn self-expression, control over the environment, and a means to positively interact with computers (Hagen, 1984). Basically, the philosophy of LOGO is to allow students to create images independently instead of reacting to a prepackaged program.

LOGO works by using "turtle graphics," in which a cursor appearing on the computer screen is controlled by the student. The "turtle" (cursor) can be moved forward, back, right, or left, with distances traveled by the cursor controlled by numbers added to the command. Students use the turtle to create geometric designs, and often the design is limited only by the student's imagination. Hagen (1984) has suggested that by working with LOGO students begin to develop the ability to sequence events more logically in an atmosphere where there are no right or wrong answers.

If used the way it was intended, LOGO has a great potential for assisting students to learn problem-solving skills. Children as young as 3 and 4 years old have had great success with LOGO, so it would appear that many students with handicaps might benefit from interaction with this software.

Collins and Carnine (1988) conducted a study designed to examine the efficiency of different versions of a computer-assisted program to teach reasoning skills. One of their major findings was that the CAI package that deleted nonessential vocabulary in word problems was most effective in helping students learn word problems.

Hagen's (1984) book is an excellent resource for locating suggested software and publishing companies. The following is a partial list of software available to assist in teaching mathematics skills.

Basic Math Competency Skill Drills
Freeport, NY: Educational Activities, Inc.

Edufun Series
St. Louis, MO: Millilan Publishing Co.

Micro Series
Lowell, MS: Hayden Book Co.

■ ■ ■ ■

IMPLEMENTING INSTRUCTIONAL STRATEGIES

Once teachers have identified the content they wish to teach and the setting where instruction is to take place, the remaining task is to match appropriate methods and materials to the needs of the students. Methods for teaching mathematics skills can take many forms. For example, one method is to model the skills used to calculate an addition problem. Other methods are to provide examples of precompleted problems (match-to-sample) on student worksheets, underline key components of an algorithm, color code, or use arrows to note directionality.

Methods for teaching mathematics skills generally will have three major goals. The first is to assist students in understanding the concept of the skill being taught. The second is to direct the student's attention to the relevant aspects of the task. The third is to increase a student's motivation to complete the assigned tasks.

Some students who find mathematics difficult to conceptualize may require tangible reinforcers at the outset to assist them in completing assigned tasks. Token reinforcement systems (see Chapter Six) and other types of operant procedures have proved successful in teaching mathematics (e.g., Lovitt & Curtiss, 1968; Lovitt & Esveldt, 1970; Lovitt & Smith, 1974).

In a sense, teaching functional mathematics skills can be considered a method in itself. A student may be showing little or no success in learning to solve fraction problems on paper. When the teacher alters the approach and teaches fractions in conjunction with cooking skills, the student may demonstrate marked improvement. The functionality of the skill can then be considered a teaching technique.

Techniques for Teaching Operations

Teaching operations (addition, subtraction, multiplication, and division) can be a frustrating experience for special educators. This frustration may occur when teachers attempt to teach the operation before the student has a full grasp of the concepts involved. Therefore, teachers should be certain that students have a good grasp of place values and number to object sets before presenting problems dealing with operations.

1. Have students practice with concrete objects such as blocks or straws, placing some in "ones" piles and some in "tens" piles (Sander, 1981). Students can practice placing 10 blocks in the "ones" pile and then placing one block to *represent* the 10 in the "tens" pile. For each skill teachers wish to present, they should consider moving their students from the concrete to the semiconcrete and eventually to the abstract level (Reisman, 1982). Therefore, this activity can be repeated using marks on paper in place of blocks (semiconcrete) and finally using numbers in place of either objects or written cues (abstract) (Thornton, 1979).

2. Performance cues (Morsink, 1984) should be used extensively with learners to help them remember the steps in the operation. For example, a teacher might choose to use colored dots, each dot signifying one of the successive steps in subtracting with regrouping (Bellamy, Greiner, & Buttars, 1974; Brown & Bellamy, 1972).

3. Marsh, Price, and Smith (1983) presented an interesting method of helping students add and subtract using a semiconcrete technique. They suggested an activity in which

teachers color code dots on numbers representing their properties. The students then use the dots to count out the answer to the problem.

4. Precision teaching (White & Haring, 1980) advocates the use of timed exercises as a technique to improve the performance of learners. Children are generally competitive and enjoy trying to "beat" the number of correct problems they can compute per minute. (Additional information about rate can be found in Chapter Five.) Prillaman and Abbott (1983) have found that using timed exercises can improve the ability of learners to memorize basic facts (e.g., $6 + 2$ or 5×6).

5. Multiplication facts are often most difficult for some students to learn (Cowan, 1978). If many methods of instruction have been tried with little success, the teacher should consider allowing the student to carry a multiplication table for use in community activities. These wallet-size tables are often given free by banks.

6. Mercer and Mercer (1985) suggested the following trick to teach the difficult-to-learn 9s table. First, the student subtracts 1 from the multiplier and places that number in the 10s digit of the answer. The next step involves adding to the number obtained in step 1 until 9 is reached.

$$
\begin{array}{ll}
9 \times 7 = \underline{63} & \qquad 9 \times 8 = \underline{72} \\
\underline{-1 + 3} & \qquad \underline{+1 + 2} \\
\quad 6 \quad 9 & \qquad \quad 7 \quad 9
\end{array}
$$

7. Ogletree and Ujlaki (1976) developed an approach for teaching multiplication allowing students to use motor responses such as clapping, stepping, and chanting paired with the actual operation. For example, students would clap, step rhythmically, and chant the basic times tables. A similar technique was later used with the other operations (Ogletree, 1977).

8. Learning centers allow students to interact with semiconcrete materials depicting various mathematics concepts or functional mathematics applications (Broome & Wambold, 1977). For example, Ashlock (1982) presented a game that incorporates chips whose colors represent various place values. Games such as this can be incorporated into a learning center allowing students to practice mathematics concepts in a less demanding, more enjoyable setting.

9. The pocket calculator is an effective aid for learners who continue to demonstrate severe deficits in basic operations (Mulhern & Koller, 1977). Students should learn basic care of pocket calculators and how to use them in a variety of situations. Colored marks can be made on the calculator to highlight various signs or cue the learner to the type of operation needed. Calculators that also provide a hard copy printout are now available at relatively low prices. These units can be very helpful to learners because the printout demonstrates the entire operation instead of just providing the answer.

10. A mini reference book can be developed for students that translates common vocabulary and phrases found in word problems and daily living tasks into operational functions (e.g., "which is cheaper" = subtract; "gives to another" = add).

11. Strategies used to teach basic operations must be applied consistently to each area (Goldman, 1989). For example, if color coding is used to highlight the operation signs for addition, the same system should be used for subtraction, and so on. In addition, if a particular memory technique was used to assist a student in one area of mathematics, it should be generalized to other areas.

12. Multiplication and division require students to memorize a large number of facts and may not be used often in daily living activities (Polloway, Patton, Payne, & Payne, 1989). The emphasis in teaching these skills must be on applications to community-valid problems with the assistance of calculators. An overemphasis on memorization may serve only to detract from problem solving and ultimately become a distasteful experience for students who struggle to memorize times tables.

13. Speed drills when solving problems using basic operations can actually motivate students to beat their best time (Enright, 1989). These drills can be used in conjunction with problems the students write for each other based on situations they have discovered in grocery stores, comparing the rents of apartments, measuring electricity consumption, and similar activities.

14. If students show the ability to memorize basic facts, then they can be assisted by using a number of CAI products that allow for practice using graphics and sound for reinforcement. The ability to slow down the speed of presentation is important when choosing such materials.

Techniques for Teaching Time and Money

Teaching the ability to tell time accurately and use money both efficiently and effectively are high-priority goals for most learners (Brock, 1979). These skills, more than some others, require intensive training in relation to community and daily school activities. Whenever possible, teachers should start by using concrete events or tasks that students can associate with the skill (e.g., 12 P. M. is lunchtime; 50 cents will buy a soda from a vending machine). Most learners will associate both time and money with concrete events. They can learn to compute time and money problems at the semiconcrete level and eventually move to more abstract activities such as budgeting and time management (Thurlow & Turnure, 1977).

1. Reisman (1982) suggested using a circular number line to help students remember the relationship between minutes and hours. Number lines have also been successful in teaching money skills (Frank, 1978).

cessful in teaching money skills (Frank, 1978).

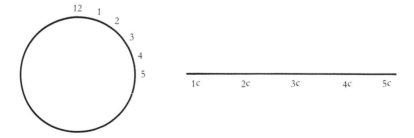

2. Students can develop a time log, pairing drawing of certain times with a common activity.

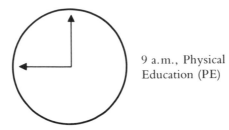

9 a.m., Physical Education (PE)

3. Standard clocks can be paired with digital clocks for as many activities as possible.

4. For some learners, telling time to the minute may not be an appropriate goal. Snell (1983) reported a procedure developed by O'Brien at Southern Illinois University that taught learners to tell time by the quarter hour and then say, "it's about" to the nearest 15 minutes.

5. Mercer and Mercer (1985) have suggested the use of money cards to teach making change. Teachers can develop a card that helps students estimate the amount of change they should receive. For example, a student shopping with $5 can carry a card with five circles, each representing $1. If the student spends $3.50, the student marks three circles and part of a fourth, leaving one whole and part of one circle left. This cues the student that $1 and some change should be received in return for the $5.

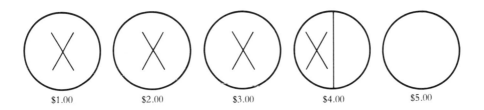

$1.00 $2.00 $3.00 $4.00 $5.00

6. Task analyzing time-telling and presenting students with single small steps has proved to be effective (Barcott, 1973). For example, a first step is counting minutes on a clock. This must be mastered before a student can move on to the next step of counting minutes by fives (Finkel & Zimmerman, 1976).

7. Bellamy and Buttars (1975) successfully taught students to count change by first teaching them rote counting skills. Although these skills were not taught in functional settings, the methods of task sequencing and use of picture cues to help the students match coin equivalents proved to be successful.

8. Paying younger students with real money for classroom activities can be an effective prerequisite to teaching more advanced money management skills (Langone, 1981). As students gain these skills, more advanced ones (e.g., checkbook, banking) can be taught using larger amounts of money (Orr, 1977). Money for these activities can be obtained from donations and class money-making projects.

9. Wheeler, Ford, Nietupski, Loomis, and Brown (1980) presented a comprehensive program designed to teach learners to use calculators when shopping. Basically, the skills were task analyzed and translated into objectives that would allow students to practice the skills in natural settings. Students were taught to label, locate, and obtain a variety of grocery items. In addition, they were taught to use pocket calculators to add the total amount for the nontaxable food items they obtained and subtract the total from the amount of money they carried. These skills were taught using cues and correction procedures such as modeling, verbal correction with direct and indirect cues, gestural cues, and pictorial cues. Similar techniques have proved successful in other studies (Smeets & Kleinloog, 1980).

10. Chaining subskills together to form more complex coin equivalency skills has also proven effective (Trace, Cuvo, & Criswell, 1977). Students were taught to link behaviors such as locating the vending machine, selecting an item, and choosing the appropriate coins. Similar techniques involving chaining, cueing, and reinforcement have also been successful in teaching coin equivalency (e.g., Borakove & Cuvo, 1977; Lowe & Cuvo, 1976).

11. Students appear to learn money skills faster when the objectives are paired with naturally occurring contingencies. For example, programs to teach money skills have been successful when paired with other independent living skills such as eating at restaurants (van den Pol et al., 1981) and shopping skills (Nietupski, Certo, Pumpian, & Belmore, 1976).

12. Mercer and Mercer (1989) have suggested using cardboard regions for demonstrating decimals in money problems. For example, graph paper may be used to show the relationship between $1.00, 10 cents, and 1 cent.

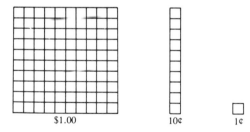

13. Money cards have been demonstrated to be a helpful aid for students involved in community shopping skills instruction. Money cards such as the one shown here have been suggested by a number of authors as a useful adaptive tool for students with mild and moderate learning problems (e.g., Mercer & Mercer, 1989; Polloway et al., 1989; Usnick & McCoy, 1987).

					$5.00 Money Card								
Purchase													*Change*
3.00					$	$	$	$	$				2.00
.20	10	10	10	10	10	10	10	10	10				.70
.05	1	1	1	1	1	1	1	1	1	1			.05
$3.25													$2.75

14. Both time and money are best taught in community settings. For example, some grocery stores have allowed students to practice checking out items at a cash register closed to the general public. The teacher or aide acts as the cashier and students can practice paying, making change, or writing checks. This activity allows for money to be reused. Sites in the community where the students are learning vocational skills and work-related behaviors are excellent environments to learn time-telling skills. Students can make schedules of the workers they observe, pairing the items listed with drawings of time in a standard and digital display.

15. Teach students to play Monopoly®. This game allows students to buy and sell real estate, make change, and practice budgeting in an atmosphere of fun.

Techniques for Teaching Measurement

Teaching measurement skills to learners can be facilitated when a majority of instruction involves activities that allow students to manipulate objects. Therefore, activities such as cooking and those related to vocational tasks lend themselves to measurement instruction (Schwartz & Budd, 1983).

1. Volume, weight, and linear measurement may best be taught using as many concrete materials as possible (Polloway, Payne, Patton, & Payne, 1985). For example, when changing measures or comparing weights, the use of actual materials may help the students grasp the concepts of more and less, heavier and lighter.

2. Activities that allow students to explore novel materials or activities that result in a product may help students learn the skills for functional use. For example, Aiello (1976) allowed students to use tools while learning the metric system. Similarly, Miller (1978) taught metrics to students while constructing projects in a shop class.

3. Having students constantly compare metric measurements with English measurements helps them to at least be able to compare units visually (Sengstock & Wyatt, 1976). The basis for teaching metrics is to be sure the students have thoroughly learned the English system before the comparison process is taught (Etlinger & Ogletree, 1978).

4. Students appear to learn measurement skills best when they are paired with activities that interest them. Therefore, measuring objects found around the home and measuring in relationship to cooking appear to be highly motivating methods for teaching (Marpet & Prentky, 1974).

5. Color coding and pictorial cues can be effective for teaching measurement skills. They are also effective adaptations for assisting students in learning more advanced home management and vocational skills if they have not been able to learn to measure. For example, a learner may be able to participate in an agricultural vocational education class learning the skills of a feed lot hand if color coding is used to help him learn to mix cattle feed (Langone & Gill, 1984).

6. Using students' own weight is a good way to introduce them to metrics. A scale that provides weight in kilograms helps them see the relationship between this unit of measure and pounds (Polloway et al., 1989).

7. Mercer and Mercer (1989) have suggested using a Language Master to assist students in learning linear measurements up to 6 inches. Drawing lines on Language Master cards and

Monopoly is a registered trademark of Parker Brothers.

recording, on the tape, the length of the line in English and metric units allows students to first measure the line and then check their answers by comparing them to the taped answers.

Techniques for Teaching Problem Solving

There is a direct correlation between a person's ability to solve word problems and that individual's ability to read (Smith, 1989). For students with reading problems, irrelevant information in word problems (excess words) can adversely affect their ability to compute the correct answer (Englert, Culatta, & Horn, 1987). Students should be taught to eliminate excess words, identify the critical information needed to solve the problem, identify the appropriate operation, and estimate before computing whether or not the answer is

TABLE 9.6 *Example of Community Needs Assessment of Environment Where Instruction Can Occur for Reading and Mathematics*

Environment: Eat-n-Park Restaurant
Task to be completed: Order dinner from menu and eat dinner
Procedures for Gathering Information:
  Method: Direct observation
  Sources of Information: Observed a competent teenager eating dinner
Analysis of Specific Skills:

Location of Task Completion	Specific Skills Performed
Hostess counter	1. Read sign "Please wait to be seated." 2. Respond to hostess question "How many will be eating?" 3. Walk to booth or table. 4. Thank hostess for menu.
Booth or table	5. Read menu/listen to waitress describe specials. 6. Decide on order. 7. Estimate total cost of order with tip. 8. Wait for turn to place order. 9. Give waitress the selected order and respond to waitress questions (e.g., size). 10. Converse with dinner companions. 11. Thank waitress when dinner is served. 12. Place napkin on lap and select correct utensils/condiments. 13. Eat dinner using proper manners. 14. Look at bill and leave adequate tip.
Cashier	15. Select appropriate currency and coins and give to cashier. 16. Respond to cashier's questions. 17. Check for correct change received. 18. Exit from restaurant.

Prepared by Susan Munson, Duquesne University

reasonable (Smith, 1989). Metacognitive strategies are particularly useful for helping students organize their thoughts and outline a given procedure for approaching certain word problems (Reid, 1988; Wong, 1987).

1. Motivation for solving word problems and an understanding of how word problems are constructed can be enhanced by allowing students to gather community-based data and then write their own problems representing the different types of data collected. For example, a group of students might gather data on the electricity usage of homebound elderly individuals living in their own homes. The students could develop various problems that demonstrate ways less electricity might be used. They could trade problems and practice solving them. This technique can be used across a wide variety of consumer-related situations.

2. Key words in a problem can be color coded, with these prompts gradually faded. Students themselves should be taught to underline key words and cross out irrelevant ones.

3. Polloway and associates (1989) have suggested that students be taught to diagram important information included in the problem and demonstrate the operation(s) required.

4. Word problems should be presented in a simple to more complex fashion (Mercer & Mercer, 1989; Usnick & McCoy, 1987).

KEY CONCEPTS

■ Methods for teaching mathematics skills should help students understand the concepts and motivate them to succeed.

■ Token reinforcement systems have been successful in motivating students to succeed in mathematics.

■ Functional or community-related mathematics skills are themselves highly motivating to students.

■ Students should begin with concrete activities, moving to semiconcrete and then on to abstract activities.

■ ■ ■ ■

CHAPTER TEN

DESIGNING INSTRUCTION FOR INDEPENDENT LIVING AND SOCIAL SKILLS

■ Living in the United States brings people in continual contact with the word *independence* and, more specifically, the concept embedded within that word. Unfortunately, in a country whose leaders and citizens pride themselves on their ability to be independent, there exists a segment of the population that has never enjoyed the freedom from control by others. Citizens who have handicaps are often relegated by society to a position of dependence, relying on others for their daily existence. Many individuals with mild and moderate handicaps integrate into the community at the low end of the socioeconomic scale. In a sense, it can be argued that these individuals, living at or below the poverty level, also have their independence severely curtailed.

This chapter presents two major areas that are so closely related that in most instances one is merely a subset of the other. *Social skills* are the behaviors (both verbal and nonverbal) that people use to interact with others (Morgan & Jenson, 1988; Smith, 1989). Generally, these interactions are both reinforcing and beneficial to all parties concerned if they are a result of behaviors deemed socially acceptable. *Independent living skills* (ILS) are the larger class of behaviors required by people to engage successfully in a variety of events necessary for community integration. Teaching social skills is a necessary part of all instruction in independent living skills.

Unfortunately, programs designed to teach independent living and social skills either have not been emphasized in classes for students with mild and moderate handicaps or have been taught mainly using out-of-context, simulated activities. ILS have been given more attention in classes for students with moderate mental handicaps and minimal attention in classes for students with mild mental handicaps (Polloway et al., 1989) and behavior disorders (Center, 1989; Gallagher, 1988). Even less attention has been given to these curriculum areas in classes for students with learning disabilities, since the traditional view has been that these conditions are primarily academic in nature (Mercer, 1987; Poplin, 1981).

Interestingly, the newest proposed definition of learning disabilities offered by the Federal Interagency Committee on Learning Disabilities includes social skills as a possible area of difficulty (National Institute of Child Health and Human Development, 1987). In any case, educators are now calling for an increased emphasis on specific instruction in independent living and social skills for all students in special education and a deemphasis on skills that target only graduation criteria or basic skills mastery (e.g., Smith, 1989; Smith & Edelen, in press).

The importance of teaching these skills is twofold. First, most students with mild to moderate mental handicaps, behavior disorders, and some with learning disabilities have deficits in social skills, and these deficits can severely affect their successful integration into both the school and community mainstream. Downplaying instruction in these skills can only place additional barriers to learning more advanced academic skills (Alter & Gottlieb, 1987). Second, the broader area of ILS (aside from their obvious value in terms of community survival and integration) can provide exciting and realistic activities for teaching academic, general cognitive, and language and communication, as well as social skills.

For example, Schuler and Perez (1988) have made a case for using social integration activities as the basis for teaching metacognitive or thinking skills. Some prominent theorists now believe that students with learning disabilities and mental handicaps have deficits in metacognition (lack of the effective use of problem-solving abilities) and that students with behavior disorders have deficits in recognizing the effects of their behaviors on events and the behaviors of others (Kneedler & Hallahan, 1981; Reid, 1988; Rizzo & Zabel, 1988). With the growing emphasis on cognitive behavior modification, Schuler and Perez (1988) have called for increased instruction in social cognitive skills (part of social integration) as a more effective and natural approach than applying instruction in self-regulatory skills only to academic areas such as reading and mathematics.

This chapter focuses on the design and implementation of programs for teaching ILS. Because students with mild and moderate handicapping conditions make up a highly diverse group with diverse needs, a variety of skill areas are included. The skills and suggested instructional methods are to be introduced and practiced primarily in community-based environments and are based on the process approach emphasized in the first half of this text.

DESIGNING THE ILS CURRICULUM: THE IEP

Step One: Conduct the Community Needs Assessment

The CNA is an important first step in developing ILS programs. This task helps practitioners identify the types of ILS that may be required of learners; the specific community characteristics that will require program adaptations (e.g., lack of a mass transit system); and the community's resources in the form of people, instructional sites, and materials. At this first level of curriculum development, the task is to analyze the environments where the students live or may live in the future in relation to each of the areas in an ILS curriculum. Students' living arrangements (e.g., in a group home or independent community apartment), where they work or spend their leisure time, and any other environment where social skills are needed may be important.

There are a number of tools that can be used to gather CNA data, including questionnaires, interviews, and observations. Gathering information about ILS is generally best accomplished by going out and *observing* the environments in which students are or will be functioning. For example, a student taught to cook using an electric stove will have obvious problems if his parents have a gas stove at home. Similarly, another learner who was taught to find grocery items in one store may have little hope of finding those same items in another retail establishment.

The first step in organizing the CNA is to list under each of the areas of interest the potential environments where students may be expected to demonstrate these skills (see Table 10.1). This step helps identify the environments that will eventually require a task analysis. Using parents, other teachers, and community members as resources, this first step can often be accomplished by sitting down and brainstorming ideas.

The second step involves taking each of the environments identified in Table 10.1 and deciding in which locations within each environment the desired skills will be demonstrated. (See Table 10.2.) Students learning to eat at restaurants would be required to demonstrate a number of skills in different locations in a restaurant (e.g., communication with waiter and cashier, eating skills at table). For other learners, the location for teaching appropriate manners while eating in school may simply be the cafeteria.

TABLE 10.1 *Identifying Potential ILS Environments and Skill Areas*

Self-Care	Home Management	Community Mobility	Consumer Education	Sex Education
Eating	Present home	*Walking*	Grocery stores	*Hygiene*
at home	Future home	in neighborhood	Supermarkets	home
at school		downtown		
in fast-food restaurants	With relative	in different neighbor-	Neighborhood stores	*Interpersonal relationships*
in restaurants		hoods		community functions (e.g., dances)
	Independent apartment	in shopping areas	Department stores	home
Dressing and grooming at home	Menu planning	*Bicycle riding*	Shopping centers or malls	*Family counseling*
in independent apartment	Home and yard maintenance	in neighborhood		hospital community education programs
for social situations	Measurement skills	downtown	Insurance companies	day care centers
for vocational situations		in different neighbor-	Auto sales	parenting skills
	Budgeting	hoods		family nutrition
		in shopping areas	Appliance stores	
		Using mass transit		
		intracity bus		
		intercity bus		
		taxis		
		subways		
		Using automobiles		
		driver training across different community locations		
		carpooling		

Each environment can be broken down into what Brown and his colleagues (1979) have called "subenvironments," defined as locations within the main community environments that demand different skills. In the examples just cited, the communication with the waiter in a restaurant requires somewhat different skills from those required in paying the cashier. Thus, the location of the tables in the restaurant would be considered one subenvironment while the location of the cashier would be another.

Step Two: Analyze CNA Information

CNAs are important because ILS are often unique to different communities. Shopping in a grocery store in Georgia can be different in some ways from shopping in a store located in New York. Those differences may be great enough to confuse some learners, thus requiring a separate analysis of each environment. Similarly, two different homes in the same town may have enough different stimuli to confuse learners who have been taught in only one location. For example, teaching the home management skill of dishwashing may be noticeably different for the student whose home has a dishwasher as compared to one whose home does not have that appliance.

A second category of information obtained from the CNA involves identifying potential community resources. Table 10.3 presents one example of how community resources for consumer education can be identified. In this example, both people and places are the targeted resources. An actual CNA would list names of people and places unique to each community. For instance, some learners may find it difficult to deal with high-pressure sales tactics and may buy things they either do not need or cannot afford. A teacher can find a volunteer salesperson who is willing to help learners develop strategies to negate those tactics. The salesperson might attend class and participate in role-playing activities, followed by visits to the store and practice in the community setting.

TABLE 10.2   *Identifying Locations for Task Completion: Home Management*

Environment:	Home
Skill Area:	Home management
Skill #1:	Eating
Locations:	Kitchen
	Dining room
	TV room (snacks)
Skill #2:	Mowing lawn
Locations:	Front yard
	Back yard
Skill #3:	Entertaining guests
Locations:	Living room
	Kitchen
Skill #4:	Minor repairs (e.g., broken window)
Location:	Front entrance

Step Three: Identify Potential Annual Goals

Annual goals are a direct result of information discovered in the CNA. ILS goals should reflect the real needs of learners to become independent or semi-independent people. Step three is an attempt to identify all *potential* annual goals that *may* benefit students. Identifying specific annual goals comes later and is based on assessed student needs.

An unlimited number of potential annual goals can be associated with ILS. The types of annual goals written depend on the individual situation of each teacher and the students in a given community. The potential annual goals listed here are examples that teachers might choose to use as starting points in developing their own ILS curricula.

General Social Skills

1. Listens carefully to others.
2. Maintains eye contact.
3. Uses correct tone of voice.
4. Takes turn talking.
5. Uses polite words.
6. Follows rules.
7. Assists others.
8. Touches the correct way.

TABLE 10.3   *Identifying Locations for Task Completion: Community Mobility, Walking*

Environment:	Neighborhood
Skill Area:	Walking
Skill #1:	Using sidewalks
Skill #2:	Street crossing
Skill #3:	Reading signs
Skill #4:	Using landmarks
Locations:	All sidewalks within two blocks of student's home Four-corner intersections with traffic light Four-corner intersections with control signs (e.g., Stop, Yield) Four-corner intersections with no control
Environment:	Downtown
Skill Area:	Walking
Skills #1–4:	Same as above
Locations:	All sidewalks downtown Four-corner intersections with traffic light Four-corner intersections with control signs (e.g., Stop, Yield) Four-corner intersections with no control Five-corner intersections with traffic light Crossing at bus stops

9. Gives appropriate positive and negative feedback.
10. Accepts criticism.
11. Resists peer pressure.
12. Engages in give and take with others.
13. Improves inappropriate behaviors of others.
14. Shares with others.
15. Offers assistance to others.
16. Accepts appropriate authority.
17. Introduces self and others.
18. Expresses feelings.
19. Expresses concern and affection.
20. Acts assertively.
21. Demonstrates social sensitivity toward others.
22. Demonstrates social insight and relates these skills to moral judgments such as identifying appropriate and inappropriate social behaviors.
23. Can communicate socially and understands the subtle nuances of body language in social situations.
24. Demonstrates social problem-solving behaviors.

Self-Care

Eating

1. Demonstrates appropriate table manners.
2. Eats neatly.
3. Orders food in a variety of restaurants.
4. Demonstrates nutritional eating habits.

Dressing and Grooming

1. Chooses clothing appropriate for weather conditions and activity (e.g., job interview).
2. Chooses articles of clothing that match each other in color, style, and design.
3. Bathes and showers in a number of different facilities.
4. Uses an electric razor appropriately.

Home Management

1. Demonstrates the ability to paint interior and exterior parts of a house.
2. Can clean a house appropriately.
3. Can do basic landscaping tasks.
4. Demonstrates the ability to plan and cook balanced meals.
5. Stores unused food properly.
6. Demonstrates the ability to care for infants and young children.
7. Can choose and call a repair person for appliance and home repairs.

Community Mobility

1. Can successfully use all forms of public transportation (both inter- and intra-city).
2. Can learn to drive a car safely and obtain a driver's license.
3. Demonstrates ability to negotiate all types of street corners as a pedestrian.
4. Demonstrates the ability to read and follow city, state, and interstate maps.
5. Demonstrates the ability to get from home to work, home to leisure/recreation activities, and so forth independently.

Health and Sex Education

1. Understands sexual functioning.
2. Understands the use of a variety of contraceptives and their relative effectiveness.
3. Identifies symptoms of venereal disease and can seek out treatment.
4. Understands the effects of AIDS, how it is transmitted, and the best protective measures that can be taken.
5. Understands the birth process.
6. Can read and follow directions on medicine containers.
7. Knows basic first aid.
8. Maintains basic cleanliness.

Consumer Education

1. Can handle high-pressure sales techniques appropriately.
2. Demonstrates ability to lodge a complaint against unfair selling practices, product failure, or warranty agreements that have not been met.
3. Can seek assistance from consumer affairs offices at the state and local levels.
4. Can develop and follow a budget.
5. Seeks an advocate to assist against unfair sales practices, etc.
6. Can conduct a basic cost comparison.
7. Discriminates between store brands and national brands if the store brands are cheaper.

Step Four: Translate Goals into Potential Short-Term Objectives

Annual goals are written in general terms. The next step is to translate annual ILS goals into potential short-term objectives that are measurable and can be used to assess the student's present level of performance. The *translation* requires that the skill areas of interest be converted into a form that includes the *outcome* or skill, the *context* under which the skill will be assessed, and the *criterion* against which the student will be evaluated.

For example, a short-term objective might look like the following:

Outcome: The student will appropriately order a meal, eat the meal, and pay the cashier.

Context: Three different restaurants.

Criterion: 100% of the crucial steps on the restaurant task analysis.

In this example, after task analyzing the skills required to be successful in the target restaurants, the teacher can then assess the student against the stated criterion. For the purpose of assessing present level of performance, the teacher may have assessed the student in only one restaurant. The other two would be used to generalize the student's skills across different settings at a later date.

The following are examples of some ILS short-term objectives. Short-term objectives should be written in relation to community-valid skills.

General Social Skills

Outcome: The student will use polite words and take turns talking.

Context: When dealing with service personnel in restaurants, employees in retail establishments.

Criterion: During each appropriate instance as observed and judged by the teacher.

Self Care

Outcome: The student will wash and blow dry hair with no assistance.

Context: At home and at school.
Three different shampoos and containers.
Two different types of blow dryers.

Criterion: Successful completion of all steps on the task analysis.

Home Management

Outcome: The student will wash and dry clothes with no assistance.

Context: At home.
At school.
Two different makes of washers and dryers.

Criterion: 100% completion of task analysis.

Community Mobility

Outcome: The student can successfully move from home to work using the subway.

Context: Subway system.
Pay station.

Criterion: Arrival at destination within 20 minutes of leaving home.

Consumer Education

Outcome: The student can lodge a complaint to the appropriate person at a department store.

Context: Torn shirt or pants.
Uses a card on which notes were made previous to the meeting.

Criterion: Successfully states all points written on student "complaint card."

Health and Sex Education

Outcome: The student can match the names of contraceptives with corresponding pictures and can list them in order of relative effectiveness.

Content: Pictures and flashcards.

Criterion: 100%

Step Five: Assess Student Entry Behaviors

In some instances, inappropriate tools for assessing ILS may be used. Teachers may use adaptive behavior checklists as the sole determinant of present level of performance. The use of adaptive behavior checklists (e.g., Vineland Adaptive Behavior Scales-R, Sparrow, Balla, & Cicchetti, 1984; AAMR Adaptive Behavior Scale, Nihira, Foster, Shellhaas, & Leland, 1974) is appropriate as a screening device and to get input from parents. However, they fall into the realm of *survey-level assessment,* and their information should be treated as general data requiring more specific analysis.

The Brigance Inventory of Essential Skills (Brigance, 1981) includes some areas that can be useful for screening certain independent living and social skills (Taylor, 1989). The following are some subareas covered by this criterion-referenced test: metrics, which allows the teacher to assess understanding of and ability to apply metrics; money and finance; travel and transportation; food and clothing; and oral communication and telephone skills.

There are a number of rating scales and checklists available that can help teachers initially identify major deficit areas in social competence. For example, a teacher might choose to use the problem behavior checklist from the *Getting Along with Others Curriculum* (Jackson, Jackson, & Monroe, 1983) to generally identify a student's problems with peers. These checklists provide teachers with a starting place that leads to more intensive assessment.

Sociometric measures provide some information regarding how students rate the popularity of other students. The information obtained from these measures lacks specific information for program planning, but when used with other measures of social competence they can provide useful information that allows the teacher to develop a more specific method of assessment (Kerr & Nelson, 1989).

For example, a teacher noting the results of a sociometric measure and a behavior checklist targets one of Bobby's problem areas as calling others names. This piece of information cues the teacher to the need for a more specific level of assessment that will measure the intensity of the problem. In this instance, direct observation of Bobby with his peers may provide data demonstrating that Bobby calls others names on an average of two to three times during an instruction period. This information can be used as a benchmark against which an instructional program can be measured.

Teachers can develop their own assessment devices, which often will be more useful and meet the criteria for specific-level assessment. Use of the task analysis as an assessment tool reflects actual materials found in the school or community setting, which makes this approach more realistic to the student and teacher. Continuing with the example just cited, Bobby's teacher may decide to try to decrease his name calling by teaching him to make positive remarks to a team member while engaging in a joint grocery shopping exercise. As part of the task analysis developed to teach cost-comparison shopping, the teacher may build into the steps the opportunity to compliment a partner for finding the correct prices. After a number of trials on this instruction, the teacher can observe Bobby in situations similar to the baseline phase to see whether or not his name-calling behavior has decreased.

IDEA FILE

Kerr and Zigmond (1984) developed a school survival skills questionnaire that provides teachers with an instrument for quickly assessing skills that regular educators deem important for students to be successful in their classes (reprinted in Kerr, Nelson, & Lambert, 1987, pp. 88–89). Knowing the skills that will help students be more successful in their mainstream placements provides special educators with the opportunity to target these skills for instruction prior to the students' entry into the regular education program.

For example, the Kerr and Zigmond survey instrument gives teachers the opportunity to rate the importance of skills such as "turns in work on time," "can calm down someone who is upset and angry," "has a sense of humor," "writes so people can read," and "offers help when a person has a problem." In addition, this instrument gives teachers the opportunity to rate what they consider the intensity of potential problems such as "is late to class," "gives back talk to teacher," "cannot take notes," and "does not belong to group, club, or team."

Administering this questionnaire to regular education teachers who will be working with students with mild to moderate handicaps is one component of survey-level assessment that socially validates important skills to be taught, thereby increasing students' chances for success in mainstream environments. This questionnaire and others like it can help special educators further individualize their curricula.

This same approach should be used by special educators during the community needs assessment. Employers, neighbors, store managers, and employees, for example, should be polled for their opinions concerning appropriate social skills for specific environments.

■ ■ ■ ■

To assess social skills effectively, teachers must keep in mind that students often do not act appropriately because they lack one or more of the prerequisite skills or selection strategies necessary for them to demonstrate appropriate social alternatives (Howell & Morehead, 1987). When students lack these prerequisites or are unable to select what strategies are most appropriate in certain social situations, no behavior management program can be expected to change their behavior.

Howell and Morehead's system for assessing social behaviors stresses the need to carefully ascertain whether or not various prerequisites exist before attempting to decrease inappropriate social behaviors. For example, if a student frequently hurts others, simply establishing the frequency of these incidents and applying aversive consequences will not achieve a permanent solution to the problem (i.e., the student's more positive interactions with peers). Instead, the teacher should analyze the situation to see whether or not the student has the prerequisites to these behaviors. In this case the teacher will want to know whether the student knows that he is supposed to touch other students without hurting them and can recognize when he is hurting another student (Howell & Morehead, 1987).

Once the teacher has established these prerequisites to the ultimate target behavior, he or she can structure a situation in which the student can verbalize answers to such situations or act out how he reacts to each instance. If the teacher establishes that the student does not have these prerequisites, the strategy would be to teach them in an attempt to eliminate the undesirable responses instead of merely punishing the misbehaviors.

PROGRAM IMPLEMENTATION

Identifying Short-Term and Instructional Objectives

The decision as to what goals and objectives are to be included on a student's IEP is based on two sources: the assessment of present level of performance and the community needs assessment. The CNA (discussed earlier) generates information such as parent and community opinions concerning what skills are important. These can be used as guidelines for choosing specific objectives.

Since the short-term objectives on the IEP cover longer periods of time, it is necessary to break these objectives down into more manageable units of instruction (instructional objectives or subskills) that can be taught on a daily basis. Once again, the tool that assists teachers in accomplishing this step is the task analysis. The key to developing effective task sequences for ILS lies in the validation of the skill breakdown. Specifically, teachers should consider validating their task analyses by allowing others who specialize in an area to review the document.

For example, Johnson and Cuvo (1981) had a home economics professor and a graduate student who specialized in foods and nutrition review their task sequences in cooking. To further validate their work, they also consulted cookbooks and community members who were cooking specialists.

The principle of community validation can easily be transferred to other areas of ILS. For example, developing a task sequence for crossing a high-traffic, controlled intersection can be accomplished by videotaping others crossing the street or simply by observing and carefully recording the steps it takes to cross the street safely.

Specialists in sex education, drug abuse, consumer affairs, and many other areas can all be of service when validating skill sequences or teaching units. The result of the CNA conducted for independent living skills should be a series of task analyses reflecting skills needed to master tasks in a variety of community environments. For example, the following short-term objective on a student's IEP might result in the task sequence shown in Table 10.4:

Outcome: The student will successfully ride a public bus with no teacher assistance.

Context: From the bus stop in front of the school on Baxter Street to the mall on Broad Street.

Criterion: 3/3 attempts.

For some students, each step on the task sequence (Table 10.4) might become part of an instructional objective. One example might be Step 2: Stands at the proper location at the bus stop and exhibits appropriate social skills. The teacher would take this step and identify the specific social skills required (e.g., greet other waiting passengers; engage in

TABLE 10.4 *Sample II.S Section of an IEP*

Present Level of Performance	Annual Goal Statements	Short-Term Objectives	Evaluation Procedures
Strengths 1. Can eat independently in a number of community settings. 2. Chooses the correct clothes for weather and working conditions. 3. Is able to ride city buses independently. 4. Demonstrates appropriate pedestrian safety.	1. The student will be able to make a complaint to a store manager appropriately.	1.1 *Outcome*: Student will say and demonstrate the five steps for being assertive in a consumer situation. *Context*: Role playing and three community stores—complaints ranging from poor service to clothes exchange. *Criterion*: 100% demonstration of all steps.	Generalization of skills monitored in home and home management house. Bar graphs representing the application of each step of assertiveness.
	2. The student will be able to plan and cook nutritionally balanced meals.	2.1 *Outcome*: Student will plan on paper meals (breakfast, lunch, supper) for five consecutive days. Also, student will purchase the necessary groceries and correctly cook each meal. *Context*: Requisite materials, home living center. *Criterion*: Adequate completion of all steps on checklist.	Meal planning and preparation for one week—checklist.
Weaknesses 1. Does not demonstrate assertiveness in consumer situations. 2. Is unable to plan and cook nutritious meals. 3. Cannot mend torn clothing or sew on buttons.	3. The student will be able to mend clothing and sew on buttons.	3.1 *Outcome*: Student will mend tears in pants seams and knees and in shirt seams and elbows. Also, student will sew on five different-size buttons. *Context*: Home economics lab, assorted shirts and pants, thread, needles, scissors. *Criterion*: Satisfaction of home economist.	Task analysis for each sewing and mending task.

300

social conversation while waiting for bus; allow passengers on arriving bus to exit before attempting to enter; allow older passengers to enter bus first). Depending on the needs of the students, these skills might be learned while they are imbedded in the overall task sequence and could be practiced as part of the sequence. For other students, the skills will need to be taught and practiced alone before moving on to the next step in the task analysis. In these cases, Step 2 becomes part of an instructional objective in its own right:

Outcome: The student stands at the proper location at the bus stop and exhibits appropriate social skills.

Context: The bus stops in front of the school on Baxter Street.

Criterion: 5/5 attempts independent of teacher assistance.

KEY CONCEPTS

- A community needs assessment helps determine the types of independent living and social skills students need to be independent in their current and future environments. A CNA can help identify the skills needed by the student to prepare food at home (currently) and at an apartment (future).
- Potential annual goals and short-term objectives are identified as a result of asking "What are the skills learners need to function independently in community environments?"
- Students' entry behavior is assessed by comparing their performance against the outcomes, contexts, and criteria of the potential short-term objectives.
- Deciding which short-term objectives are to be included on a student's IEP is the job of the IEP committee. The criteria for deciding which objectives to teach first vary. A general rule of thumb is to choose those objectives which have an immediate impact on the student's level of independence.
- Once the IEP section concerning independent living skills is developed, the teacher uses the process of task analysis to identify the subskills that will be used as instructional guidelines on a daily basis.

■ ■ ■ ■

Developing Instructional Strategies

Teaching students with mild and moderate handicapping conditions independent living and social skills requires a blend of some classroom instruction (e. g., commercially produced instructional programs, role playing) and community-based activities. Instruction in ILS in community environments provides a natural opportunity for students to learn and practice social skills in relationship to the general public. These activities also allow teachers to help students generalize the skills they learned in classroom activities to daily living skills in the community (see Table 10.5).

Social Skills Programs

There are a number of commercially produced programs or published approaches that teachers might find beneficial to support their community-based activities. The work by Weller and Buchanan (1988) is an excellent resource for detailed descriptions of a variety of programs that can be used for teaching some independent living and social skills. The programs briefly discussed here are representative of a larger group that are available.

ACCEPTS Social Skills Curriculum. Walker and colleagues (1983) designed a curriculum for instruction in social behavioral competencies. In this curriculum, 28 skills are organized in 5 major categories: classroom skills, basic interaction skills, getting along, making friends, and coping skills. The program includes a placement test; instructional procedures; daily lesson scripts; a videotape that provides examples of skills; a description of behavioral techniques for teaching the skills; and role-playing probes for measuring progress.

ACCEPTS has been field tested with students who have handicaps, and the results have been encouraging. The social skills learned by the students did carry over to other situations during the school day (e.g., the playground). Unfortunately, these gains did not last over time. This finding suggests the need for a systematic attempt to allow students practice in the skills across a variety of community settings where natural reinforcers are more likely to maintain gains.

Social Skills Group Training Program. Hazel, Schumaker, Sherman, and Sheldon (1982) described a program for teaching social skills to adolescents with learning disabilities. The skills are taught in small groups over a 10-week period and include (a) starting conversations, (b) following directions, (c) negotiating, (d) coping with peer pressure, and (e) giving and receiving positive and negative feedback. The methods used in this program involve group meetings in which the social skills are introduced, described, discussed, and modeled. Students verbally rehearse the steps and then role play using the skills.

PEERS Program. Hops and associates (1978) developed the Procedures for Establishing Effective Relationship Skills (PEERS) program for socially withdrawn, younger students. This program is designed to increase the amount of time children interact in a positive

TABLE 10.5   *Examples of Community Resources Identified from CNA Analysis*

Skill Area	People/Sites/Materials	Skills	Resources/Tasks
Consumer education	Salespersons	Practice with high-pressure sales techniques	Permission to develop training sites
	Store managers Church groups		Volunteers to be used as trainers
	Service organizations		
	Large supermarkets Small neighborhood stores	Cost comparison shopping	

fashion with peers and is implemented simultaneously in both regular and special education classrooms. Included in the program are descriptions of strategies for teaching specific social skills and establishing a peer-pairing arrangement, a point system for implementation during recess, and a self-reporting system.

The uniqueness of the program lies in the emphasis it places on having the student with handicaps practice social skills with a peer who is not handicapped. Students are required to practice social skills daily with different classmates.

Your Life Your Feelings: Growing Up and Understanding. The Utah Association for Retarded Citizens developed a program designed for parents to teach their children about sexuality. There are a number of sex education programs available, and their elements all closely resemble each other. This program is comprehensive in that it addresses attitudes concerning the sexuality of people with handicaps as well as the mechanics of sex education.

The program was originally designed for people with mental handicaps, but its organization and thoroughness make parts of it appropriate for use with all students. Teachers can use the organization of the topics and information provided and gear the presentation to the specific level of the audience.

Living Poor with Style. This book was written by Callenbach in 1972 and is an excellent resource for teachers in the area of consumer education. Although out of print, the book is still available in many libraries and is worth the search to obtain it. Many teachers may not be well versed in strategies for getting the most for the least cost; they must develop these skills themselves before teaching them to students. Callenbach's book provides the reader with concrete and relatively inexpensive methods for coping with the problems of daily living. For example, in a chapter on housing, methods are described for finding and obtaining public housing and handling situations such as getting rid of household pests (e.g., rats and fleas) and avoiding common household materials that can be hazardous to health.

More recent self-help books are also available, and teachers should search libraries and commercial bookstores for additional resources.

Most students with mild to moderate handicaps will need assistance in either learning or refining their meal-time behaviors in public situations. The following list provides some suggestions for program activities and instructional interventions.

IMPLEMENTING INSTRUCTIONAL STRATEGIES

Techniques for Teaching Appropriate Eating and Table Manners

1. At times, teachers will need to develop behavioral programs designed to eliminate disruptive behaviors during mealtime (e.g., stealing food, stuffing mouth, eating with fingers). In cases such as these, time out (removing the food) has been shown to be an effective method for changing the behaviors (Barton, Guess, Garcia, & Baer, 1970; Riordan, Iwata, Finney, Wohl, & Stanley, 1984).

2. During the entire process, all data should be recorded and charted to monitor program success. For instance, if a learner is exhibiting a disruptive behavior such as throwing his

food, the teacher using a verbal reprimand plus time out for 2 minutes (removal from the group) would keep a record of the instances of food throwing. If the number of instances of the target behavior stayed the same or increased over a reasonable period of time, a change in the intervention would be required.

3. A problem may arise when teachers assume that once a student has learned a skill the skill will be maintained in the presence of the food as a reinforcer. O'Brien, Bugle, and Azrin (1972) found that this is not always the case. In their study a child who had been taught to eat properly reverted to eating with her fingers. The researchers had to incorporate various motivational procedures—in this case stopping the incorrect response while rewarding the correct one—in order to maintain the learned skill. Teachers should plan frequent probes even after the skills have been learned, monitoring the behavior over time.

4. Restaurant eating skills should be taught in the community. Marholin, O'Toole, Touchette, Berger, and Doyle (1979) were successful in teaching adults with moderate cognitive disabilities how to travel to, order a meal, and eat at McDonalds. Van den Pol and colleagues (1981) had similar success in teaching students to eat in fast-food restaurants and then generalizing those skills to other restaurants (see Table 10.6). Normalizing mealtimes by using family-style dining has improved the eating behaviors of some students (Wilson, Reid, Phillips, & Burgio, 1984) and should be more in common in school cafeterias.

5. Teaching students to discreetly watch others eat before they begin helps them develop coping skills for new situations. For example, a student may watch others start with their salads or use a particular spoon for the soup and then model their behavior. This can be highlighted by teaching students to say to themselves before beginning, "Watch others eat."

6. Teaching students to eat before they go grocery shopping helps curb impulse buying.

Techniques for Teaching Dressing and Grooming Skills

For younger learners, the state of the art of teaching basic dressing and grooming skills is fairly sophisticated. For example, Project MORE (Ferneti, Lent, & Stevens, 1974), originally developed at the University of Kansas, provides task analyses for a large number

TABLE 10.6 *Sample of Eating Task Sequences*

SKILL: RESTAURANT (FAST FOOD)

Task Sequence

1. Choose food items from menu.
2. Pay cashier appropriate amount.
3. Check change.
4. Pick up order.
5. Choose seat.
6. Eat appropriately without bothering others.
7. Place waste in garbage.
8. Use restrooms if needed.

√ = Complete
− = Incomplete

of these skills along with recording sheets for monitoring student progress. For the program to be effective, teachers must apply it in a systematic manner.

A teacher may choose to develop the task sequences based on the setting, materials available, and the individual needs of certain students. As with all task analyses, the skill sequence is developed best by watching someone perform the target skill. Tables 10.7 and 10.8 are examples of grooming task analyses.

Suggestions for Instruction

1. Teachers can program for generalization by allowing students to practice dressing and grooming skills in different locations and with a variety of materials (e.g., school locker rooms, bathrooms, different makes of electric shavers).

2. Because fashions and preferred color combinations change frequently and may differ across geographic locations, it is important to validate these norms frequently (Nutter & Reid, 1978). Nutter and Reid found it was possible to teach appropriate clothing color combinations by using simulation activities and actual clothing.

3. Teaching students to ask others "What should I wear?" will help them feel less conspicuous in various social settings.

4. Posting lists of requirements for clothing coordination next to students' mirrors (sometimes paired with pictures) and teaching them to compare their images to the lists helps them dress in a more acceptable fashion.

IDEA FILE

- Oversize clothing assists younger students in learning the skills of dressing without the constriction of tight clothing.

- Color coding is a valuable technique for teaching individuals to choose coordinated wardrobes. Clothes can be hung in the closet next to tabs of certain colors corresponding to colors marked on the label of the article. For example, pants and shirts that coordinate well in color, style, or design can have a blue mark on the label. The same color can be placed on a tab hanging on the closet rack. All pants and shirts with the blue mark are hung next to the corresponding tab for easy retrieval. Over time, the color codes can be faded.

■ ■ ■ ■

Techniques for Teaching Home Management Skills

Home management as a curriculum area has generally received some attention (evidenced by the number of living centers included in classrooms for students with moderate mental handicaps, but it has failed to become a daily program option for learners. In recent years, recognition of home management skills as a crucial component for independent living has begun to surface (Dyer, Schwartz, & Luce, 1984). Hence, an increasing number of field-tested programs are becoming available to assist teachers in designing effective instructional programs in this area.

TABLE 10.7 *Sample Task Analysis of a Short-Term Objective*

SKILL: SHAVING

Outcome: Student will independently shave himself.

Context: Electric razor, in four different settings.

Criterion: Smooth to touch of teacher.

1. Get razor out of storage area.
2. Take razor out of box.
3. Remove plastic cover.
4. Take plug out of box.
5. Plug cord into razor.
6. Plug razor into socket.
7. Turn on razor.
8. In an ear-to-chin motion: shave left side of face.
9. Shave right side of face.
10. In an upward motion: shave under chin.
11. Shave below lower lip.
12. Turn off razor.
13. Feel face for any unshaven areas.
14. Reshave if necessary.
15. Unplug cord from socket.
16. Unplug razor from cord.
17. Press button with right hand. Remove top with left hand.
18. Take brush out of box.
19. Clean razor head.
20. Return brush to box.
21. Replace top.
22. Replace plastic cover.
23. Put razor in box.
24. Wind cord around hand.
25. Put cord in box.
26. Store razor.

(Prepared by Tina Kinsley)

TABLE 10.8 *Sample Grooming Skill Sequence*

SKILL: HAIR WASHING AND BLOW DRYING

Task Sequence

1. Get shampoo, towel, dryer, and comb.
2. Kneel at tub or stand before sink.
3. Unscrew cap from shampoo bottle.
4. Pour capful of shampoo.
5. Set shampoo and cap on side of tub (or sink).
6. Turn on hot and cold water.
7. Adjust faucet to desired (warm) temperature.
8. Wet hair.
9. Pick up capful of shampoo.
10. Apply to hair.
11. Scrub with fingers (lather).
12. Rinse hair.
13. Squeeze water out of hair with fingers.
14. Turn off water.
15. Get towel.
16. Dry hair with towel.
17. Put cap on shampoo.
18. Comb hair.
19. Get dryer.
20. Plug cord into socket.
21. Turn on dryer.
22. Dry top and front.
23. Dry back.
24. Dry left side.
25. Dry right side.
26. Turn off dryer.
27. Unplug dryer.
28. Rewind cord.
29. Put away towel, shampoo, dryer, and comb.

(Prepared by Tina Kinsley)

Some programs designed to teach home management skills address a problem faced by many students, namely their difficulty in developing functional reading skills (see Tables 10.9, 10.10, 10.11). These programs capitalize on the use of pictures to supplement difficult cooking directions and complex recipes (Spellman, DeBriere, Jarboe, Campbell, & Harris, 1978; Staples, 1975). In addition to teaching meal planning and preparation by using pictures, researchers have successfully instructed learners to schedule and maintain an orderly system of housekeeping tasks. For example, Bauman and Iwata (1977) used a self-recording procedure that allowed two males with mild to moderate mental handicaps to monitor their own progress in completing housekeeping chores. Over a period of time, the completion of the target tasks was completely transferred to natural reinforcers such as posting their progress on charts when tasks were completed.

Suggestions for Instruction

1. Small-group instruction has been found to be more efficient and in many cases at least as effective as one-to-one teaching (Brown, Holvoet, Guess, & Mulligan, 1980). There are no set rules governing group size; however, three to four students may be appropriate

TABLE 10.9   Sample Task Sequences for Home Management Skills

---

SKILL: CUTTING FOODS

Task Sequence

1. Take cutting board.
2. Take knife.
3. Take food item.
4. Hold item between thumb and forefinger horizontally.
5. Hold knife handle.
6. Hold knife, edge down.
7. Place knife on right edge of item.
8. Cut in vertical direction.
9. Repeat until 1/4″ from finger.
10. Cut pieces again if necessary.
11. Take container.
12. Place pieces in container.

SKILL: OPENING CANS

Task Sequence

1. Take can.
2. Take can opener.
3. Hold opener with blade on top with right hand.
4. Pull apart handle with left hand.
5. Place blade above rim of can.
6. Hold handle with left hand.
7. Squeeze opener until lid "pops."
8. Turn with right hand.
9. Turn in circular direction once.
10. Remove lid: Do not touch edge of can.
11. Throw lid in trash can.

(Prepared by Tina Kinsley)

depending on the size of the teaching area and safety procedures of the activity. Smith and Meyers (1979) discovered that instruction in telephone skills was more efficient and effective when groups of learners were allowed to practice the skills among themselves.

2. A living center built into the school classroom or in a nearby location in the school is the least desirable training site and should be limited to teaching during the acquisition stage. The most desirable alternative would be to locate homes and apartments within the community where training can occur.

3. All instructional techniques discussed earlier in this text apply to teaching home management skills (e. g., modeling, graduated guidance, physical prompts). For example, Johnson and Cuvo (1981) found that verbal instructions paired with visual cues, modeling, and physical guidance were effective methods for teaching food preparation.

4. The instant camera can be a valuable teaching tool. Students who have trouble reading written directions can follow the sequence of a task by looking at pictures taken by the teacher (e. g., teacher photographs the steps to baking a cake). When such pictures are used as cues for teaching directions or maintaining a schedule, teachers can increase the difficulty of the pictures over time (Snell, 1981; Staples, 1975). For example, a series of steps in cleaning a shower stall or bathtub may, during initial teaching stages, require 10 sequential pictures. Over time, a teacher can gradually reduce the number of pictures by combining steps. The purpose of this approach is to fade the unnecessary cues.

5. Additional color and numeral cues can be helpful. For example, when housekeeping skills are taught using picture directions, the directions may include a numeral in conjunction with the picture. The learner can match the numeral in the picture to the same numeral located in the area of the house or apartment where the task is to be completed. The same technique can be used with color cues, for instance, color coding cooking materials (Spellman et al., 1978).

TABLE 10.10   Sample Task Sequences for Home Management Skills

---

SKILL: WASHING CLOTHES and DRYING CLOTHES

Task Sequences

Washing

1. Open lid.
2. Remove lint tray.
3. Clean lint tray.
4. Return lint tray.
5. Gather clothes.
6. Place clothes in washer.
7. Fill 1 cup with detergent.
8. Pour detergent on clothes.
9. Close lid.
10. Set load size selector.
11. Set temperature selector.
12. Pull out on/off button.
13. Turn right to correct setting.
14. Push in button.

Drying

1. Remove lint tray.
2. Clean lint tray.
3. Return lint tray.
4. Open dryer door.
5. Open washer lid.
6. Remove clothes from washer.
7. Place clothes in dryer.
8. Close dryer door.
9. Set temperature selector.
10. Set time cycle.
11. Press start button.
12. Remove clothes.
13. Fold clothes.

(Prepared by Tina Kinsley)

6. It is necessary to keep precise data on skill acquisition and maintenance. The most useful method for this monitoring appears to be a task analysis sheet, which allows the teacher to record what antecedents were used (guidance, modeling, etc.) to assist the learner in completing each step (Cuvo, Leaf, & Borakove, 1978).

7. The data from these skill sequence sheets can be charted in a number of ways. However, the method that seems to be the most expedient for teachers is to chart the percentage of steps on the task analysis that students successfully complete (Figures 10.1 and 10.3).

8. Another charting method that may yield helpful data involves using the percentage for each level of assistance given by the teacher during one instructional session. This format allows a visual picture of the entire instructional system. If the interventions are successful, the amount of guidance used would decrease while the percentage of steps completed under verbal directions or no assistance increases. If the behavioral monitoring demonstrates that little or no improvement in student performance has occurred, a change in the instructional system is required (Figure 10.2).

9. Cuvo, Jacobi, and Sipko (1981) used a system of least prompts to teach students clothes sorting, washing, and drying skills. For example, the teacher may say to the student, "What's the next step?" in order to prompt the student to complete the next task.

10. Incorporating visual cues into the instructional material can be an effective aid for teaching home management. Cronin and Cuvo (1979), for instance, used marks on fabric to teach students to stitch along a line. Marks on fabric can also show students where to begin and where to end the task. Over time, these material cues are faded as they become unnecessary.

11. Self-charting (allowing students to record their own progress) can be a powerful reinforcer in its own right. Whenever possible, the students should be allowed to record, for example, the number of task sequence steps accomplished without the aid of teacher prompts. Visual improvement on a graph may become a motivator for the student.

12. Group training (five learners) has been found to be successful in teaching telephone skills (Smith & Meyers, 1979). The key to success appears to be the teacher's use of material cues and coping devices such as a card with a person's picture, name, and color-coded phone number (Leff, 1974; 1975).

TABLE 10.11 *Sample Task Sequence for Home Management Skills*

SKILL: CLEANING BATHTUB

Task Sequence

1. Get out cleanser, towel, and sponge.
2. Sprinkle cleanser on bottom of tub.
3. Turn on warm water.
4. Wet sponge.
5. Scrub bottom of tub.
6. Scrub sides of tub.
7. Scrub top rim of tub.
8. Wipe faucets.
9. Rinse sponge.
10. Rinse faucets.
11. Rerinse sponge.
12. Wipe top rim.
13. Rinse bottom of tub.
14. Rinse sides of tub.
15. Turn off water.
16. Wipe faucets and rim with towel.

(Prepared by Tina Kinsley)

14. Matson (1980) found some interesting information when teaching home accident prevention to learners. After verbal rehearsal, the students could not adequately role play the safety steps. This finding strongly implies that the use of class discussion does not guarantee that students will respond in an emergency. Accident prevention and home safety should be taught by doing, in the most realistic setting available. In some instances parents can be encouraged and trained to carry out these aspects of the curriculum. If not, teachers can teach the skills in community homes or home management houses that have been volunteered.

IDEA FILE

- The program options mentioned so far can be accomplished by developing a volunteer training program in the community. A close working relationship with community service organizations, church groups, and local school groups can help by identifying potential training sites and volunteers to help teach the skills and validate the program.

- Teachers can work with local organizations to develop a volunteer group made up of learners who, under supervision, can enter the homes of the elderly and infirm to assist in housekeeping and cooking tasks. The school supervisor (parent volunteer, aide, teacher) can use these opportunities to program for generalization (new settings, equipment, time schedule, etc.), allow for guided practice, or teach new skills and adaptations of old ones.

- Over the next 5 to 10 years, school systems may find it valuable to purchase a home that can be used in ways similar to the Home Economist College programs for home management houses. Learners can culminate their training (or in many cases acquire skills throughout their program) by living for periods of time in the house with other students, learning and/or enhancing their skills in a real life setting.

■ ■ ■ ■

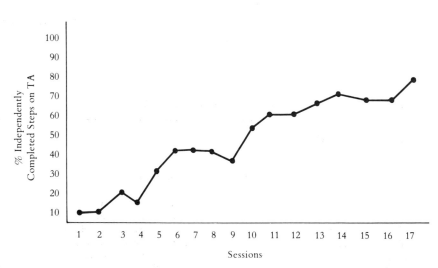

■ *FIGURE 10.1*
Chart of Percentage of Independently Completed Steps

Materials

Many materials are available to assist in teaching home management skills. In most instances, however, the key to finding good materials will be in the teacher's ability to adapt existing equipment. The following are samples of some commercially produced materials that teachers may find useful.

> *Cookbooks.* Some cookbooks are written on lower reading levels and may be more appropriate for students with mild to moderate handicaps. A home economist or county extension agent may be helpful in locating them.
>
> *Recipe picture cards.* Teachers can make cards with pictures that correspond to the steps of a recipe. Examples of this approach can be found in studies by Robinson-Wilson (1977) and Johnson and Cuvo (1981).
>
> *Adaptive telephone devices.* These are material cues to assist in learning to use the telephone effectively. (See *How to Use a Telephone*, Instructo Company, Paoli, Pennsylvania.) Risley and Cuvo (1980) used pictures of emergency personnel (such as firefighters) plus the appropriate phone numbers to teach students how to make emergency calls.

Techniques for Teaching Community Mobility Skills

An area of great importance that directly relates to a person's independence is community mobility. The abilities to obtain and hold a job, participate in leisure activities, and attend to daily needs all depend on a person's being mobile. Unfortunately, community mobility has only recently become a high priority as a curriculum area, and it is often

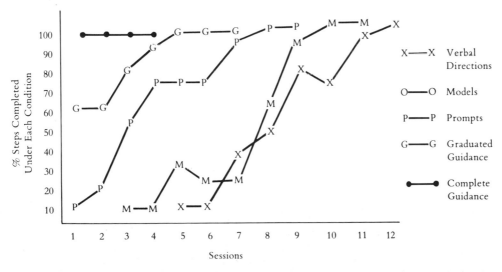

■ FIGURE 10.2
Chart of Teacher Behaviors Required to Elicit Student Response on a Task Analysis for Teaching Manners

confined to adults. The need still exists for an increased emphasis on teaching such skills beginning at the elementary level and continuing throughout the secondary program (see Table 10.12).

In general, there are three major areas of instruction in the category of community mobility: private transportation (bicycle safety, car pooling, and automobile driver training); mass transit; and pedestrian safety. Private transportation has been the category most neglected by researchers.

However, this should not deter teachers from developing appropriate training programs in these skills. For example, with today's gasoline and automobile prices, increased numbers of people are reverting to transportation by bicycle. At the same time, communities are beginning to realize that their road and sidewalk systems are not designed to incorporate this additional traffic. The need to instruct students in safe bicycling skills is imperative.

A similar problem exists in teaching students how to drive automobiles safely. This curriculum area has received attention from some driver training educators who have developed successful programs. However, the main concern in this area appears to be the inability of some students to read drivers' manuals, road signs, insurance forms, and other materials related to driving a car. Teachers can build into their programs behavioral objectives that address these skills.

Developing the ability to use public transportation successfully requires a complex instructional program (see Table 10.13). There are a number of programs that can be used as examples. One of the first programs developed by Cortazzo and Sansone (1969) taught learners to travel on trains, buses, and subways. The interesting component of this program was the comprehensiveness of its approach. It included pedestrian skills, money usage, traveler responsibilities, schedule reading, and safety. The authors developed a system of color-coded cards that could be used by the travelers to seek assistance should they become lost or confused.

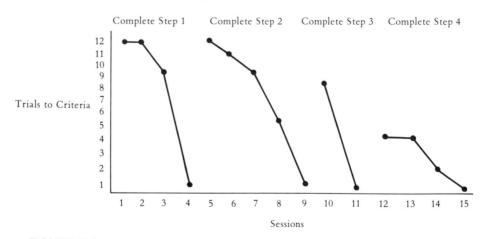

■ *FIGURE 10.3*
Chart of Number of Trials Required for Each Step in a Task Sequence for General Social Skills

A number of more recent studies have demonstrated the use of a behavioral approach to teaching community mobility skills (Certo, Schwartz, & Brown, 1975; Neef, Iwata, & Page, 1978; Sowers, Rusch, & Hudson, 1979). The most interesting and practical approach for teachers involves the technique used in the study by Neef and colleagues (1978). In this study, the learners were taught various bus-riding skills in the classroom, later generalizing them to community settings. The important point to note is that the authors did not rely solely on the lecture method of classroom instruction as many teachers do. Rather, they used a simulated bus and photographic slides that allowed the learners to view and discriminate between correct and incorrect bus-riding behaviors.

Instruction in safe pedestrian skills has been noted more frequently in the literature since Yeaton and Bailey (1978) demonstrated a series of procedures to teach regular education primary school students to cross the street safely. In this study, the authors solved several problems inherent in developing programs of this nature for real-life application. For example, criteria were established for determining how far a car had to be away from the intersection before crossing was permitted. These criteria allowed observers to record the safe versus unsafe behaviors of the students more concisely.

Page, Iwata, and Neff (1976) demonstrated the use of an in-class simulated street intersection to teach safe crossing skills that later were generalized to the community. The interesting point brought out by this investigation was that, overall, there was not a significant amount of time saved by first teaching in the classroom. Further, when they probed for generalization after each skill was taught, the authors discovered that a number of the behaviors required additional instruction. However, the safety factor involved in the beginning stages of instruction was a sufficient reason for beginning it in the classroom. The successful results achieved by Page and colleagues in teaching these beginning skills could possibly be attributed to their use of visual slides that eliminated the need for the student to conceptualize a situation described by the teacher. An additional study by Vogelsberg and Rusch (1979) demonstrated how systematic fading of behavioral procedures can be used to teach individuals with severe handicaps to cross partially controlled intersections.

Safety is an important concern whenever community-based instruction occurs. Sowers, Rusch, and Hudson (1979) included the following safety procedures that might also be considered for use by teachers:

TABLE 10.12   *Sample of Pedestrian Safety Task Sequence*

SKILL AREA: PEDESTRIAN SAFETY

*Task Sequence**

1. Find crosswalk or corner where crossing is safest.
2. Wait at curb and watch signal.
3. When signal to go occurs, look all directions to check compliance of traffic.
4. Cross street while monitoring the status of traffic in all directions.

---

*This sequence is repeated at both controlled and uncontrolled intersections under conditions of heavy traffic, medium traffic, and light traffic. At uncontrolled intersections an additional step should be added for teaching students to judge the speed and distance of cars and then generalize the skill to all other situations.

1. Students carry emergency information cards.
2. Police are apprised of the program.
3. Supervision is highly structured.
4. Parents are included in the program.
5. Observers unknown to students shadow their movements.

Suggestions for Instruction

1. Deciding which, if any prerequisite skills can be taught first in the classroom or on the school campus is an important first step. For example, teaching public bus-riding skills can be initiated in simulated situations by using school buses that are generally available (possibly on request). A bus driver or aide could be recruited to play the part of a public transit worker. In this situation, communication skills, scheduling, money computation, social skills, and the like can actually be prompted or modeled by the instructor, allowing the student to practice under guided conditions.

TABLE 10.13 *Sample of Bus-Riding Task Sequence*

SKILL AREA: RIDING A PUBLIC BUS

Task Sequence

1. Walk to correct corner and bus stop.
2. Stand at proper location at bus stop and exhibit appropriate social skills.
3. Identify bus by reading location or ask driver if the bus goes to the desired location.
4. Board bus and deposit correct change (two quarters, or five dimes)
5. Ask for transfer if desired.
6. Pay for transfer if requested.
7. Find seat and exhibit appropriate social behavior.
8. Identify landmarks along route.
9. Get off at appropriate stop or request leave by ringing buzzer.
10. Depart bus within 15 to 20 seconds after bus stops.
11. Continue to desired destination.

If transfer is required:

12. Walk to correct corner and bus stop.
13. Stand at proper location at bus stop and exhibit appropriate social skills.
14. Identify bus by reading location or ask driver if this bus goes to the desired location.
15. Board bus and hand driver the transfer slip or token.
16. Find seat and exhibit appropriate social behavior.
17. Identify landmarks along route.
18. Get off at appropriate stop or request leave by ringing buzzer.
19. Depart bus within 15 to 20 seconds after bus stops.
20. Continue to desired destination.

Program for the following uncontrollable variables:

1. Bus never arrives.
2. Bus is late.
3. Driver is rude.
4. Other passengers are rude.
5. No seats are available.

2. Yeaton and Bailey (1978) found that a sequence of tactics including verbal instruction on the task, modeling by the teacher, verbal rehearsal by the students (telling what they were going to do), and actual practice of the task by the students was a successful procedure for teaching elementary school students to cross the street. The same or similar procedures have been found successful for learners with mental handicaps.

3. Verbal reminders, which are considered prompts, can be useful for getting students to move on to the next step of the task sequence (Spears, Rusch, York, & Lilly, 1981). These reminders should eventually be faded to allow the learner more independence.

4. Cards can be carried by the learner that correspond to bus destinations displayed on the front of the vehicle (Cortazzo & Sansone, 1969). At this point, the skill of matching is required as opposed to relying strictly on memory. Over time, the cards can be faded when and if they become obsolete.

5. The use of videotapes of actual environmental events can be an effective and efficient method for teaching community mobility skills (Certo, Schwartz, & Brown, 1975). Allowing learners to view, discuss, and compare correct with incorrect responses in any of the skills areas can be useful for later generalization. Teachers should keep in mind, however, that this approach will not work with all learners. Coon, Vogelsburg, and Williams (1981) found that simulated instruction did not work with one client. Mobility skills were only obtained when instruction occurred in the community.

6. For teaching pedestrian safety skills, volunteer drivers can be involved so that various levels of instruction can be introduced under near-actual street conditions. For instance, automobiles with volunteer drivers can be used to allow practice in crossing streets when drivers do not abide by the rules (e.g., failure to use a turn signal which, if used, would alert pedestrians not to cross even if they had the right of way).

7. Driver education is a viable programming option. Special educators should work closely with driver training teachers to adapt the program to the students' needs. The psychomotor skills involved in driving can be handled by the driver training teacher. Academic skill deficits, in particular reading, will be the areas that special educators will address. Material cues (e.g., underlining key words), drill, and peer tutoring may help students learn the rules and regulations for drivers.

IDEA FILE

■ Peer tutoring can be an effective technique for developing community mobility skills. Regular class student volunteers can be trained to accompany the learner on trips into the community for the purpose of generalizing skills, providing the necessary models and prompts, while also recording data on the progress of the student.

■ It can be useful to develop a public relations campaign that includes newspaper coverage of the community mobility activities. A photographic slide package of the activities can be used when speaking to local organizations. Slides of a student's data chart can help the public, and specifically parents, see the utility of monitoring student progress in this fashion.

■ Scheduling community-based activities can be a major barrier to effective programming. Barriers such as lack of transportation to and from the instructional sites can also hinder the implementation of these endeavors. Therefore, an important consideration is to designate one individual (teacher or aide) who is responsible for coordinating the activities. However, the teachers involved will have to convince the administration of the program's worth and should develop the overall plan, listing perceived barriers as well as potential solutions.

■ If the situation is such that total community instruction is not feasible, a solution to the problem can be found in the technique used by Page and colleagues (1976), who used frequent community probes after the initial instruction on street-crossing skills was completed in the classroom. That is, students may learn a set of skills (e.g., starting across the street within a period of time after the "walk" sign is activated) and meet criterion in the classroom setting. Subsequently, the instructors would bring the students to a community site in order to observe whether or not the skill had generalized and, if not, prompt for the skill. The important point is that if it is not feasible to carry out the entire instructional sequence in a community setting, frequent probes and review sessions can be initiated in the natural environment (Snell, 1981).

■ ■ ■ ■

Techniques for Teaching Consumer Skills

One area only minimally addressed in the literature involves teaching learners with mild and moderate handicaps the skills they need to be effective consumers. The current focus appears to be on teaching specific skills that can be applied to consumer needs (e.g., telephone skills, budgeting, coin equivalency). More programs should be made available that teach advanced skills such as comparison shopping, warranty rights, and dealing with hard-sell tactics. Teachers should begin consumer skills early in the elementary program, to be continued throughout the secondary program.

One basic area of consumer programming involves the ability of younger students to learn basic money handling skills. A series of studies by Cuvo and his associates taught learners such diverse skills as coin summation (Lowe & Cuvo, 1976), coin equivalency (Trace, Cuvo, & Criswell, 1977), and change computation (Cuvo, Veitch, Trace, & Konke, 1978). These studies emphasized a behavioral approach that combined the procedures of task analysis, modeling, prompting, and in some cases physical guidance. An interesting technique in the coin equivalency study was the use of a vending machine to return incorrect coin combinations. The natural reinforcer of obtaining the dispensed object when correct coin equivalencies were used was an added feature.

One of the more comprehensive programs for teaching complex skills such as budgeting, checkbook management, and bill paying to students with mild mental handicaps was developed by Orr (1977). The foundation for the program was a fictitious paycheck received by each student with amounts based on the minimum wage. From their paychecks, students were taught to budget their take-home pay to meet daily needs. In addition, a token system for preferred classroom activities, including a built-in response cost for inappropriate behaviors, was included in the program. Over all, the author found the program to be successful with the target learners, who went on to develop a banking system for check cashing and a bookkeeping system to monitor expenditures. However, a program of this nature becomes truly functional to learners when the skills they learn in the classroom can be applied to independent living situations. Consequently, the next logical step for such a program would be to develop activities that allowed for guided practice in community settings and under realistic conditions (see Table 10.14 and Figure 10.4).

For many students with learning disabilities and some with behavior disorders who will be attending postsecondary technical schools and college, it will be important to teach consumer skills related to these environments. Teachers should extend their community needs assessment to these environments and gather information on paying tuition, applying for loans and financial assistance, and using bookstore services. This information can then be translated into activities that can be taught on site for learners who will be making these transitions.

Suggestions for Instruction

1. It is important to teach learners proper dress and presentation so that they do not significantly stand out from other consumers (Cleland, 1978). This is especially important in areas such as consumer skills, color coordination of clothes, and grooming. One technique for accomplishing this is to analyze the skills people use in consumer situations and the clothing they wear. For example, a person making a complaint to the telephone company may gain more consideration by dressing neatly and eliminating any aggressive language from the interview.

2. The calculator has gone beyond being a convenience for many people. Students with learning problems can be taught extensive use of the calculator for solving everyday living problems. Accordingly, it is important to teach learners the care and maintenance of the unit as well as the importance of keeping one with them in situations where needed (Wheeler, Ford, Nietupski, Loomis, & Brown, 1980).

3. Community volunteers are vital to these programs. In particular, experts in sales techniques who can assist in teaching learners to resist unscrupulous sales tactics are a must (Cleland, 1978). For example, students would benefit from instruction on how to discourage salespersons either by phone or in person (see Table 10.15).

TABLE 10.14 Sample Banking and Budgeting Skill Sequence

SKILL: BANKING AND BUDGETING

Task Sequences

1. Receive paycheck and check for accuracy.
2. Use budget organizer sheet to identify priorities.
3. Balance budget.
4. Open savings account and make deposits and withdrawals as necessary.
5. Open checking account and make deposits and withdrawals as necessary.
6. Maintain and balance checking account.
7. Pay bills using checks.
8. Borrow money when necessary and choose the best lending rate of interest.
9. Purchase money orders.
10. Purchase travelers checks.
11. Understand credit cards and their use.
12. Account for credit purchases in budget.

4. Consumer education is for all learners. Some learners with mental handicaps would benefit from instruction on how to ask cashiers whether they have rung up the right price or given back the correct change. Others might learn to comparison shop by telephone. One instructional strategy that works well with all learners is to teach them to ask the cashier, at least once during the checkout process, whether he or she has rung up the correct price for an item. Today's computerized cash registers make it difficult to monitor the computation of many items, and this technique will cue the cashier to be more careful to punch in the correct price.

5. Managers of retail businesses such as grocery and drug stores can be helpful in developing instructional sites in their stores. These sites can be used to maximum effectiveness if the students are taught at times when business is slow, allowing cashiers and stock personnel to participate in instruction.

MONTH

Rent			Food		
Garbage			Gas		
Savings			Drug Store		
Car Loan			Spending		
Cable			Lunch		
Electric			Recreation		
Water			Haircuts		
Gas			Eating Out		
Telephone					
Master Charge					
Pet Supplies					
Food					
Child Care					
Doctor					
Prescriptions			TOTAL		

TOTALS:

Checking
Monthly
Cash _____

DATE: _____

MONTHLY/PERIODIC

Insurance:

Subscriptions:

Other:

Total Income

■ *FIGURE 10.4*
Example of a Budget Organizer

6. It is important to identify situations where consumers are most often cheated and simulate those events using community volunteers. For example, a cashier at a community instruction site can be told to purposely give the student the incorrect change. The teacher can then step in to model the appropriate behavior to exhibit under those circumstances.

7. A technique mentioned earlier in this section involves teaching money usage in real-life situations. Trace and associates (1977) used vending machines to provide feedback and natural reinforcement to students learning coin equivalency. Vending machine skills must be taught on many machines before students will generalize the skills independently (Sprague & Horner, 1984). Langone (1981) suggested that more real-life activities can be programmed into the classroom, for example, having students pay for preferred activities out of money given to them at the beginning of each school day. Students' lack of success in using money may be related more to the realism of the activities provided than to an inability on the part of the learners.

8. A procedure that appears successful in teaching some consumer skills is called *verbal rehearsal.* Students can learn to say the steps of the skill sequence at least once before they attempt an independent trial. The instructional strategy is for the teacher to model the procedure by verbalizing each step and having the students repeat the verbalization before they begin the procedure.

9. Students who have poor long-term memories benefit from learning to write or type notes on cards before they attempt a task. For instance, students who have learned to be more assertive in consumer affairs situations (warranty rights), may still find it helpful to write down the points they wish to make before they talk to the store manager. (See Chapter Two for techniques of assertiveness training.)

10. Generalization will not just happen, except in rare instances. If learners are taught to comparison shop in one grocery store, volunteers can assist them in practicing those skills in other stores that are representative of the businesses in a given community.

TABLE 10.15   *Sample Skill Sequence for Telephone-Related Skills*

SKILL: USE OF TELEPHONE AND TELEPHONE BOOK

Task Sequence

1. Demonstrate appropriate use of both rotary and touch tone telephones (dialing).
2. Demonstrate ability to use special features on different telephones (redial).
3. Demonstrate the ability to plug and unplug telephone into wall jack.
4. Demonstrate use of a variety of public telephones.
5. Demonstrate ability to buy a telephone based on the most features for the cheapest price and after consulting a consumer testing service for durability of equipment.
6. Demonstrate the ability to locate emergency, service, and business numbers in telephone book.
7. Demonstrate the ability to locate telephone numbers and address in the telephone book using guide words and dictionary-related skills.
8. Demonstrate the ability to locate business sections in the telephone book.
9. Demonstrate the proper use of conversation skills using the telephone for a variety of business-related or social calls.

IDEA FILE

Contact the local cooperative extension agent in charge of home economics. This professional can be an excellent resource for program development. Funded through a cooperative effort by federal, state, and local governments, the extension service provides pamphlets and other resources that can be used by teachers for developing curriculum activities. Students can be instructed in the services that the local extension agents can provide them, and they can be given practice in using those services.

■ ■ ■ ■

Materials

Some of the most helpful materials for students are those developed by teachers to help them in coping with daily life problems. One way to begin developing such materials is to look for methods of adapting the task to a particular student need. Identifying the adaptation often becomes apparent during the task analysis phase.

For example, students with moderate cognitive problems who cannot read basic sight vocabulary or compute the basic operations of arithmetic will require some type of adaptation to complete a shopping skill sequence. Nietupski, Certo, Pumpian, and Belmore (1976) came up with one possibility when they developed a portable shopping aid. This material assisted students by sequencing pictures in the order they were found so the student could match the picture to the actual item for selection. The portable aid had a number of adhesive strips (each representing $.50) next to each item, depending on the cost of the item (e. g., soup ☐ = $.50 or less, hot dogs ☐ ☐ = between $.50 and $1.00). The students were taught to remove the adhesive strips and place them on the designated spaces at the top of the aid. Ten spaces were allotted (equivalent of $5.00), so the students would know when they reached their maximum expenditure.

Some professionals have mistakenly assumed that students with mild disabilities automatically become effective consumers. Unfortunately, this has not been the case. In a study to identify the shopping patterns of individuals with mild mental handicaps, Williams and Ewing (1981) found that these adults demonstrated that they could shop independently; however, items were often chosen with little regard to nutritional value or cost comparison but were often chosen on impulse.

Materials for teaching consumer skills can take much the same form in terms of adaptation, but they may not need to be as precise. Matson (1981) taught learners to stay within a predetermined budget by using a shopping aid that grouped items by cost so that they would know when they had reached their spending limit. The examples presented here can be models for other materials that teachers can develop to help students become better consumers (see Figure 10.4).

Techniques for Sex Education

Sexual behavior of citizens with handicapping conditions is still a topic that professionals would rather avoid. Therefore, in some programs the topic is either completely ignored or relegated to discussions concerning basic biological information. The most difficult consideration for teachers in developing a sex education program is not whether a program of this nature is important, but whether or not the individual teacher is capable of dealing with the subject matter (given his or her own feelings and beliefs). A perfectly acceptable stand for some teachers to take is that they do not feel they can teach this content area; however, they will find someone else who can be successful in developing and implementing a program.

Ingalls (1978) suggested that a comprehensive curriculum option for providing sex education includes the following topics: anatomy of both sexes: sexual techniques; contraception; venereal diseases; acquired immune deficiency syndrome (AIDS); pregnancy; and homosexuality. In addition, Schulman (1980) suggested that sex education should be expanded to include methods of communication between individuals, caring for others, trusting, and respecting one another's privacy. There are comprehensive curricula existing that cover those areas, but teachers should not begin instruction without first laying the necessary groundwork.

Assessment of sex-related skills takes a different format from all other curriculum areas. The goal of assessment is not necessarily to identify the student's skill or knowledge; rather, it may be to identify what information the student wishes to know. Accordingly, teachers may consider developing some type of questionnaire that students can respond to either in writing or orally.

Payne, Polloway, Smith, and Payne (1981) developed an interesting assessment device that included 24 questions students might be interested in having answered. The topics ranged from "What are wet dreams?" to "What are the safest forms of birth control?" and "Is it easy to be a good mother?" (p. 316).

Observation can be a useful tool for establishing the present level of performance for some areas related to sex education. For example, a student's ability to care for a baby can be observed in a structured setting such as a day care center. A student's ability to socialize appropriately with others can also be observed under structured conditions.

Suggestions for Instruction

1. Requesting that administrators appoint a committee of professionals, parents, and select community members with the charge of developing the foundations for programs in sex education is a first step. A committee of this nature should be led by someone who is competent in some area of sex education, for example, attitude awareness. This group leader can be a teacher, administrator, parent, or outside authority who has been trained to deal with these topics.

2. Examples of topics that the committee must deal with are attitudes toward sexual expression, community attitudes, and marriage and parenthood (Schulman, 1980).

3. Under the guidance of the committee, volunteer teachers and parents should be chosen who will receive additional training and will eventually teach the content to the learners.

4. As much information as is available concerning sex education should be gathered.

5. The units of instruction to be included must be determined depending on learner need. Payne and associates (1981) suggested six possible units, including awareness of self; understanding maturity and puberty; interpersonal relationships; sexual responsibilities and relationships; sex and marriage; venereal disease; and AIDS.

6. Teachers should avoid judgmental statements that reflect their own values. Information should be presented in direct answers to questions, providing honest and realistic information.

7. Role playing and the use of puppets can be effective methods for teaching some aspects of sex education. For example, Schulman (1980) suggested using puppets to teach role identification and appropriate behavior. Students can write and produce their own puppet shows in relation to family scenes and dating. Similarly, role playing can be an effective method to continue to improve a student's ability to exhibit appropriate behaviors.

8. Polloway, Patton, Payne, and Payne (1989) have suggested that students be encouraged to identify and discuss acceptable patterns of social interaction for their grade level. Students should be encouraged to observe the interactions of others (e.g., holding hands, kissing, petting) and describe how they and others (e.g., parents, ministers) view these social responses.

9. Students should participate in many community-based activities that allow them practice in the use of family planning services and other social service organizations that provide assistance in this area.

OTHER CONSIDERATIONS AND GENERAL STRATEGIES FOR TEACHING SOCIAL SKILLS

Teaching students with mild and moderate handicaps self-control or self-regulatory strategies is vital for their successful integration (Edwards & O'Toole, 1988). Because of their reinforcement histories, interactions with others, and cognition problems, these students often perceive life events differently from the way the general population does. Specifically, these students may demonstrate an *external locus of control,* which causes them to believe they have little control over what happens to them (Bos & Vaughn, 1988). Similarly, these students may demonstrate a *learned helplessness,* which manifests itself in the belief that there is no relationship between what they do and their impact on their surroundings (Reid, 1988). Teachers need to use specific strategies to assist students in overcoming these deficits. Examples of such strategies follow:

1. Fade external reinforcement and use more statements such as "How do you feel about the job you've done?" or "You should be proud of yourself" to help students learn to reinforce themselves internally.

2. Cue students to see the relationship between their efforts and completed products.

3. Encourage students to make positive statements about their work and downplay any negative statements.

Students with mild to moderate handicaps have a tendency to choose less socially acceptable responses from skills that may be in their repertoire, have trouble discriminating social cues, and generally have trouble taking into account the thoughts and feelings of others (Gilliam & Scott, 1987; Goldstein, 1987; Keilitz & Dunivant, 1987; Lovitt, 1989). The literature related to teaching social skills to individuals with special needs describes the use of three major classes of instructional procedures.

First, *descriptive procedures* have been used to help students understand the inappropriateness of their actions (Lovitt, 1989). Teachers simply explain what the students did wrong and clearly describe what the appropriate alternatives are. Teachers also reinforce peer models for demonstrating the appropriate behaviors, subsequently reminding the target students how to exhibit the behaviors and reinforcing them when they behave appropriately.

Modeling, the second procedure, which has been mentioned throughout the chapter, is an effective procedure for teaching all independent living and social skills. When used extensively and paired with other strategies, modeling can help students learn appropriate alternatives to many inappropriate behaviors currently in their repertoire.

Finally, a combination of *rehearsal and feedback procedures* is used to help students learn and use various social skills with the aid of cognitive behavior management procedures (Lovitt, 1989). Students typically verbally rehearse the skill steps until they know them from memory. Teachers provide the students with feedback about their performance and reinforce them for learning the steps of the strategy and using the strategy in a social situation (Trupin, Gilchrist, Maiuro, & Fay, 1979). A number of these approaches have been developed and tested, including self-regulatory lessons (Kerr, Nelson, & Lambert, 1987) that assist students in remembering responsibilities for class preparedness (see Table 10.16 and Figure 10.5).

■ ■ ■ ■

IDEA FILE

Substance abuse continues to be a growing problem in America's schools, and students with handicaps are affected along with the general student population. Kerr and her colleagues (1987) have stated that substance abuse is "a symptom of basic social and psychological problems" (p. 244) and should be treated within that context. They have suggested a number of elements that should be included in a successful school prevention program.

Initially, the school system should have a clearly delineated policy describing how teachers and administrators will deal with substance use and prevention while in school. Also, each grade level should have a drug education curriculum that is "simple, brief, and presented in a nonjudgmental style that emphasizes the concern of the teacher for the student's physical and psychological welfare" (Kerr et al., 1987, p. 245).

In addition to these elements, teachers should learn more about drug problems in their locale and about community service agencies, experts, and other resources. Finding out more about these situations can become part of the ongoing community needs assessment.

Substance abuse programs should involve families as well as students and should provide both one-to-one and group counseling (Kerr et al., 1987). Kerr and her colleagues also have suggested developing a peer-group counseling approach that fosters support groups and positive role models. Readers are encouraged to consult the work of Kerr and colleagues (1987) for a more detailed discussion of potential school intervention strategies for dealing with this problem.

■ ■ ■ ■

Day *Monday, September 18*

Objectives	Activities	Materials	Evaluation
Students will correctly identify the words locker and hallway	Teacher will introduce lesson to students by taking a walk from the classroom through the school. Hallways and lockers will be pointed out and labeled by the teacher as they are passed. On the return trip, students will be encouraged to identify by pointing to hallways and lockers when the teacher says, for example, "show me the lockers" or "where is the hallway?" Higher level students will be asked to label these terms when the teacher asks, for example, "What do we call this?"	check list	Teacher will record students' responses on the check list
Students will identify 2 purposes that lockers serve	Teacher will lead the students to the end of one hallway at 10:25. She will explain that classes are about to change, and that students will see what people do with lockers. She will tell the students to remember at least 2 things they saw people put in or take out of their lockers. After observing, the class will return to their classroom where they will discuss what they saw. Each student will state the 2 items he/she saw being taken out or put into lockers. Teacher will lead the class to the conclusion that lockers are places for students to keep the items they don't need immediately, but will need at other times during the school day. Students will be encouraged to discuss other things they saw, such as students using locker mirrors, reading notes left in lockers, etc.		
	Students will look at pictures of items the teacher holds up, and the class will discuss whether the items could fit or belong in a school locker. Teacher will guide the discussion around meeting criteria for size and usefulness in school setting.	item pictures	
	Students will divide in small groups and look through magazines for pictures of items appropriate for placing in a locker. Each group will find at least 6 items (more if time allows) and then will tell the class why they chose each item.	magazines scissors	Teacher will record 2 correct responses from each student during this activity.
	Teacher will close the lesson by asking students to describe a locker—where it is and what we do with it. She will tell the class that, tomorrow, the students will get their own lockers, and will have to search through the school to find which ones they are.		

■ FIGURE 10.5
Procedure Used to Teach Students About School Lockers

TABLE 10.16   Plan for Teaching a School Survival Skill

Program Description:	Using a school locker
Program Objective:	Given a locker number and its combination, students will locate, open, and close it independently within 2 minutes on 5 consecutive occasions and will maintain this skill throughout the school year.
Domain:	Other community
Environment:	Public school
Subenvironment:	Cherry Street School hallway
Students:	Robert, Louis, Tina, Chad, Eddie
Task Analysis:	1. Locate correct locker.
	2. Turn dial clockwise 3 rotations.
	3. Turn dial clockwise so that arrow points at first number in combination.
	4. Turn dial counterclockwise 1 complete revolution.
	5. Turn dial counterclockwise until arrow points at second number in combination.
	6. Turn dial clockwise until arrow points at third number in combination.
	7. Grasp locker handle.
	8. Lift up.
	9. Pull locker door open.
	10. Add or remove items from locker.
	11. Push locker door closed.
	12. Turn dial clockwise.
Possible Modifications:	Steps 1, 3, 5, and 6 may be completed by memory, or a card with locker number and combination may be used.
	Steps 2, 3, 4, 5, 6, and 12 may be accomplished in any of the following manners:
	(a) With one hand in a twisting motion.
	(b) With thumb and two fingers in opposing up/down motion.
	(c) With hands in opposing up/down motions.
Incidental Objectives:	1. When other students are present, students will:
	• Take turns at locker.
	• Make their way appropriately through crowds.
	• Initiate and respond to appropriate social conversation.
	2. During the instructional phase, students will:
	• Follow verbal directions.
	• Make eye contact with teacher.
	• Imitate fine-motor movements.
	3. Students will identify and use in context the following words and phrases:

open	coat
close	lunch
turn	snack
books	pencil
hat	paper
hall	right
locker number	left
locker	

4. Students will locate the position of a given number between two written numbers (e.g., 47 is between 45 and 50).

Instructional Strategies:

Vocabulary will be used in verbal discussions and directions and will be taught specifically using group and individual work, progressing from match-to-sample to verbal labeling. Task will be taught using backward chaining. Teacher will perform and model all initial steps with verbal explanation. Student will perform last step until criterion (2 consecutive correct performances) is met, then will perform last 2 steps, and so on.

Appropriate social interactions will be discussed and role-modeled in the classroom. Students will be verbally reminded to act appropriately prior to going out in the hall, until criterion (5 consecutive sessions with no inappropriate behavior) is met.

TABLE 10.16   (Continued)

Generalization will be encouraged through enrichment activities involving different locks and lockers in different locations.

Intervention Strategies:
The goal of this unit is for students to use their lockers independently. During the instruction phase and, when required, during the maintenance phase, the teacher will intervene when students have failed after 3 seconds to proceed to the next step of the task analysis. The intervention will be least-to-most intrusive, beginning with verbal instruction, then to modeling, then to physical prompt, then to physical guidance, using only as much intervention as is needed to complete the step.

A time-delay procedure will be used with vocabulary acquisition. Students will be shown or told the correct response after a 4-second delay.

Inappropriate behavior will be treated by giving verbal instructions for an appropriate behavior and using the same least-to-most intervention when a correct response has not begun within 5 seconds.

Reinforcement:
Specific verbal praise, accompanied by eye contact and smiling, will be provided when students initiate the next step in the task analysis, respond correctly to a request to point to or name a vocabulary word, or behave appropriately in the hallways, regardless of the intervention used. This reinforcement will be faded gradually in frequency. Students will be reinforced naturally when they open and obtain items from their lockers.

Maintenance:
Initially, students will attempt this task analysis only during a specific instructional time during the school day. Later students will use the lockers at the conventional allowed times specified for all students in the school: before the first bell, before and after lunch, and before getting on the bus. The teacher will initially stand near the lockers, then at the end of the hall, and then will remain in the classroom. The teacher will ensure maintenance of this skill with time allowed weekly for locker cleaning.

Assessment:
Students' performance of each step on the task analysis will be assessed initially, during the instruction phase, and during the maintenance phase using the chart shown in Figure 10.4. Data collection will include what, if any, intervention is needed to complete a step. This will take place for the preassessment, daily for the instruction phase, and weekly during the maintenance phase.

Knowledge of basic unit vocabulary will also be preassessed with an oral naming test. Data collection will include this preassessment, periodic probes during the instructional phase, and a posttest.

Uncontrollable Variables:
This task analysis may be disrupted by a wet or too-crowded hallway, a jammed locker, or the inappropriate behavior of other students or teachers.

Resources:
Cherry Street School hallway, lockers, written locker numbers and combinations (on cards), teachers and aids, peers. Items to go in lockers: lunch or snacks, coats, backpacks, hats, decorations (mirrors, stickers, magazine pictures, etc.). Items for vocabulary development: actual items and pictures of the vocabulary words.

Prepared by Susan J. P. Vizurraga

KEY CONCEPTS

- ■ Home management skills range from cooking and cleaning to budgeting and parenting skills. The best settings for teaching these skills are community environments such as volunteer homes in neighborhoods surrounding the school.

- ■ Community mobility skills include private transportation, mass transit, and pedestrian safety.

- ■ Learners need to be taught appropriate consumer skills.

■ ■ ■ ■

CHAPTER ELEVEN

TEACHING COMMUNICATION SKILLS

■ The ability of individuals to communicate with others is a prime determinant of their successful community integration. It would be a difficult task to identify daily activities for which the use of some level of language and communication was not necessary. Therefore, some professionals believe that a person's ability to communicate should be gauged by the demands placed on that person in community activities.

Children without handicaps acquire language and the ability to communicate naturally. Unfortunately, many children with mild to moderate handicapping conditions do not fare as well. These learners may exhibit a wide range of language disorders spanning a range from difficulty with simple sound production to complex problems in sentence processing or processing information stored in the memory (Bernstein & Tiegerman, 1985). Regardless of any external labeling system, problems with language and communication affect students with mental handicaps, learning disabilities, and behavior disorders. These problems can adversely affect how these students perform in academic subject areas, social interactions, and vocationally related activities.

Because the scope of potential language disorders is wide and the types of disorders are complex, high-quality interventions require close working relationships among speech/language clinicians, special educators, and any regular education teachers who might work with individual students. Speech/language clinicians can assist by helping diagnose specific problems and providing guidance to teachers about methods for measuring daily progress. They also provide valuable help in identifying the variety of communication demands placed on students in community environments.

Special and regular educators develop activities and implement instructional strategies designed to remediate the problems or learn to compensate for them. These activities are implemented in a variety of environments, including the classroom (regular educator) and many community environments (special educator), so students can generalize new skills to daily living activities.

Speech, language, and communication skills must be an important program component for all learners. The interaction between speech/language, and communication is a complex one; for the purposes of this chapter, the emphasis will be on the "communicative functions" or pragmatic aspects of language development (Reid, 1988, p. 141) instead of the more traditional approach of structuring words and then learning rules for organizing words into sentences. The emphasis on communication skills must be a major effort, interwoven throughout the curriculum (Kaczmarek, 1985). For many learners, a half hour or an hour of language class will not provide the necessary skills for community integration.

Students must learn to use language for the purposes of expressing their intentions, improving their social interactions, and enhancing their cognitive processes (Gloeckler & Simpson, 1988; Marvin, 1989; Reid, 1988), and the emphasis on communication as a major determinant of successful social and emotional competence is an important concern. The need for instruction in communication may in itself be a good reason for increasing community-based instruction.

The basis for developing an effective program to teach communication skills lies in understanding the interactions between the speaker and the listener. In any conversation there must be a give-and-take relationship for the interaction to be a productive one. These attempts to communicate can provide teachers with a great deal of insight into the types of problems some students face. For example, when conveying the events of a sand-lot baseball game, Antonio might have trouble retrieving the appropriate words to describe the action: "I ran fast to, you know, get (catch) the thing (ball)." Morgan has developed fairly sophisticated language and vocabulary for his age. Unfortunately, he has many problems applying the rules of social conversation. His ability to read the body language of others is poor; consequently he does not perceive when people have trouble understanding him. He often misinterprets their signals and blames them for not understanding.

In each of these examples, the key is the student's use of language to communicate with others. Any communication (or lack of it) can become information for program development by teachers. The best places to structure events that require communication are in community environments.

ISSUES IN LANGUAGE AND COMMUNICATION INSTRUCTION

Language, Speech, and Communication

A first task is to clarify the differences among language, speech, and communication. Some professionals use the terms synonymously; however, there are differences in meaning as well as interrelationships among these areas.

Schiefelbusch and McCormick (1981) provided a succinct discussion of the three areas. First, they described language as the "abstract and complex" system that allows the individual to "understand and express intentions" (p. 109). Therefore, language includes both the ability to provide information about events, objects in the environment, and people and the ability to deal with abstract concepts at different levels (grammar and syntactic rules).

Once the different levels of language are mastered, an individual must develop a system for transmitting ideas, needs, and so forth. Speech is a response or output mode that relies on the individual's ability to vocally produce the sounds needed to express those ideas and needs. However, speech is not the only mode for expressing a message. Alternate modes for transmitting language are communication boards with graphic symbols, manual signing or gesturing, writing, or any combination of these.

Finally, communication involves social interactions whereby individuals share some type of information, but not necessarily by means of complex systems of language rules (Reid, 1988; Sailor et al., 1980). Each area of language, speech and communication has important implications for learners depending on their specific needs. The question to be asked, then is Which area should the teacher emphasize: language, speech, communication, or any combination thereof? This question has fostered many debates among professionals in the field of language development.

Approaches to Instruction in Language and Communication

There are a number of issues stimulating the thinking and subsequent practice of professionals developing programs for language deficient learners. The first issue involves whether individuals with mild to moderate handicaps learn language differently from their nonhandicapped peers or whether they learn language in the same manner but at a slower or delayed rate (Schiefelbusch & McCormick, 1981). Research findings tend to support the delayed language theory; however, there are some professionals who believe that the language of some people with handicaps is different from that of the nonhandicapped population.

The theories of delayed language development versus differences in language development originally were applied to individuals with cognitive deficits. A similar dichotomy of views appears to exist among theorists in the field of learning disabilities (Swanson, 1982). For some individuals with learning disabilities, problems with language and communication may revolve around "forming verbal abstractions and performing the logical operations required in complex language situations" (Wiig & Semel, 1984). These deficits in language may lead to further complications in perceiving and interpreting information (Lovitt, 1989; Mercer, 1987).

A second issue concerns the appropriateness of developmental language theory versus behavioral intervention models (Sailor et al., 1980). Developmental theorists believe that learners with severe language problems must be guided through a series of activities that correspond to normal language development. Therefore, providing these learners with instruction in communication skills before they have mastered such cognitive prerequisites as functional object use and the ability to separate themselves from objects (Sailor et al., 1980) decreases the probability that these students will demonstrate intentional language use (Reichle & Yoder, 1979).

Conversely, other researchers believe that there is a paucity of data-based evidence demonstrating that these learners exhibit deviant language structure when they are not taught the cognitive prerequisites (Guess, 1980; Guess, Sailor, & Baer, 1978). Instead, these researchers support the notion that functional communication can be taught to learners who have not mastered the cognitive prerequisites, with no harm to their development of more complex language usage or generalization of language skills.

Both issues have important implications for teaching communication. Adhering to the deviant or different theory of language may influence a teacher to view these learners as being unable to obtain any normal language usage. This approach may serve to bias practitioners against emphasizing language development, especially for learners with more severe problems. Subscribing to the delayed language theory, however, may influence teachers to increase their emphasis on communication skills, shifting the focus to increasing the quantity of language experiences for learners and bridging the gap that the language delay has created.

The issue of developmental versus behavioral approaches may force some professionals into adhering to one approach over the other. Some teachers may believe that all students should master all cognitive prerequisites before being taught functional language skills, while others subscribe solely to an approach that ignores developmental milestones.

Excellent language and communication systems have been developed that are based on different theoretical viewpoints. The important question is not whether one theoretical approach to teaching communication is better than all the others, but whether one approach meets the needs of a given learner at a specific point in time. Instruction in prerequisites may be important for some learners, while teaching functional communication may be important for others.

TEACHING COMMUNICATION SKILLS: THE IEP

Steps One and Two: Conduct the Community Needs Assessment

Understanding how communication skills are used in daily living activities is important for teachers. First, the communication skills students need to interact with others must be identified. Second, teachers should identify situations and areas in the community where learned communication skills can be practiced. Both types of information can be gathered by implementing a community needs assessment (CNA).

For example, teachers may be interested in the topics their students discuss when engaged in leisure activities. Once identified, these topics can be incorporated into role-playing lessons designed to improve the quality of communication in social skills situations.

Similarly, teachers may wish to identify the types of communication skills needed by students in several nonpaid work training sites. Once identified, these skills can be incorporated into their daily instructional activities (Halle, 1982).

The point of these examples is to stress the importance of analyzing the communication demands that either are currently being placed on students or will be placed on them at some time in the future. School is an important environment, and certainly a part of the CNA will take place there. Analyzing the communication demands placed on students in mainstreamed classrooms, on the playgrounds, in the cafeteria, and in extracurricular activities should be a first step. For example, a special educator and a regular educator would want to work together to identify the exact communication skills that are to be required of LaTonya when she participates in a general science class. They may identify skills such as (a) listening to and understanding questions asked by the teacher; (b) answering questions in a socially acceptable and grammatically correct fashion; and (c) developing and presenting a short oral report. With these major goals in mind, the teachers can now informally assess LaTonya's abilities as they relate to these goals and begin to develop strategies to teach any skills that are absent and remediate problems that are found to exist.

Zeroing in on only the school as an instructional environment leaves out the many more functional environments where LaTonya can learn and practice communication skills in situations that are highly motivating. For instance, banks, retail establishments, businesses, service agencies, leisure/recreation environments, utilities, and daily living environments provide many opportunities to develop activities that weave together the teaching of academics, consumer skills, social skills, and communication skills into one integrated unit of study. The CNA is the method used for identifying these sites, activities within the sites, and human and material resources.

Step Three: Identify Potential Annual Goals

There are many annual goals in communication skills that are potentially applicable to learners with handicaps. These goals can range from complex interpersonal speaking skills to simple gestures for enhancing communication. Although assessment data are required to pinpoint the goals and objectives appropriate for individual students, teachers can develop a list of potential goals to help them organize their subsequent assessment strategies.

The following list of annual goals is a representative sample. The key is to design activities based on these goals and their subsequent objectives both in school and, more important, in the context of community-based activities.

1. Demonstrates understanding of common sounds.
2. Imitates simple sentences.
3. Discriminates between singular and plural nouns.
4. Says phrases that have correct noun/verb agreement.
5. Discriminates present tense verbs from other tenses.
6. Completes tasks when orally directed.
7. Answers oral questions with correctly spoken sentences.
8. Gives oral directions involving places and task completion.
9. Asks for directions or help.
10. Converses in social situations.
11. Converses in consumer situations.
12. Demonstrates the ability to decode the nonverbal behavior of others.
13. Uses appropriate nonverbal behavior to communicate intent or mood.
14. Uses appropriate skills in conversation such as opening and closing, turn taking, appropriateness of topics, and staying with a topic.
15. Can tell a story and share events.

Step Four: Translate Goals into Potential Short-Term Objectives

Once teachers have identified the goals they wish to work with, their next step is to translate them into measurable objectives. The technique is the same as the one described in other chapters. To develop a measurable objective the teacher must include the outcome, context, and criterion.

Outcome: The student will rewrite sentences using the present verb tense.

Context: The student will be given five sentences that include either past or future verb tenses.

Criterion: 100% correct.

Outcome: The student will orally answer questions that commonly are asked in social situations.

Context: Questions asked by teachers, friends, and new acquaintances, such as, "How are you?" "What music do you like?" "Where do you go to school or work?"

Criteria: Student will maintain eye contact when answering, maintain appropriate social distance, and occasionally ask a return question.

Outcome: The student will produce the sounds "ma" and "da" by imitating the teacher.

Context: Stimulus provided by the teacher.

Criterion: 5/5 trials.

Short-term objectives are most effective when written in a form that will allow the student to perform the skill in a natural setting. For example, the second objective listed here could include a sentence in the Context section explaining the need to ultimately test this skill in actual social situations. The objective essentially remains the same, with the only change occurring in the context.

Outcome: The student will use appropriate skills in conversation such as openings and closings, turn taking, appropriateness of topics, and staying with a topic.

Context: The student will engage in a conversation with an employee of Jones's Pet Store while practicing prevocational skills. The topics of conversation (chosen by the teacher) will vary and will be initiated by the employee.

Criteria: The student will meet each of the six criteria listed on the teacher's checksheet. The employee will rate the conversation independently using the same checksheet, and the student must meet the six criteria.

KEY CONCEPTS

- A major criterion for the successful integration of learners who have handicapping conditions into the community is their ability to communicate.

- Communication is much broader than speaking. Communication is any technique learners can be taught to use to convey their needs and feelings to others (e.g., gestures, body language, communication, and oral speech).

- A major goal for learners with communication problems is to refine their communication to improve the quality of their independence.

- Some professionals subscribe to a developmental approach to language instruction, while others support a behavioral model. Both approaches have merit and are appropriate for different learners based on their needs. Generally, younger students as a group may be best suited for instruction in developmental prerequisites. Older students may require a more functional method that immediately allows them to interact with their environment.

■ ■ ■ ■

Step Five: Assess Student Entry Behaviors

Assessment of communication deficits should have the same basic goals as would assessment of any set of skills. Screening for learners with communication problems is a primary concern. Establishing the learner's present level of performance is an important second step. This step covers a broad area including identification of present and future communication needs.

An assessment system also monitors student progress, one means of judging program success or failure. Therefore, assessment of a student's communication skills should be ongoing so that judgments can be made as to when and if changes are needed. Ongoing assessment procedures serve to monitor a learner's communication skills in a variety of settings, not just in the classroom.

During the assessment phase, when the primary goal is to pinpoint learner entry behaviors, speech/language pathologists are valuable partners to classroom teachers. These professionals are experts at analyzing deficits in phonology, morphology, syntax, semantics, and pragmatics, and can provide the necessary expertise for developing a complete profile of a student's strengths and weaknesses.

Methods of Assessment

Miller (1978) identified four categories of language assessment procedures: standardized tests, developmental scales, nonstandardized tests, and behavioral observation. Standardized language tests have been normed on large groups of children. As with all norm-referenced instruments, the information obtained can be useful when analyzed with caution. Teachers using standardized language tests do so properly when the results are used for survey-level analysis leading to additional assessment of specific areas (Taylor, 1989). There are a number of commercially produced language tests that are appropriate for obtaining survey-level assessment information. Table 11.1 presents a partial list of these tests.

Information from commercially produced language tests is valuable for identifying major problem areas. For example, the Test of Language Competence (TLC) by Wiig and Secord (1985) has a subtest entitled "Making Inferences." A student might read two statements such as the following:

Mother was happy to have a turkey and all the trimmings in the house.
    The family was disappointed when they had to eat at a restaurant on Thanksgiving Day.
(As reported in Taylor, 1989, p. 303)

The student then must choose two of the following sentences that *might* pinpoint why the family had to eat Thanksgiving dinner out:

1. The mother got sick with the flu.
2. Mother forgot to buy the turkey.
3. Most people think Thanksgiving dinner is always better at a restaurant.
4. Mother burned the turkey by cooking it too long.

Developmental scales are based on normal language development observed over time by professionals. Various stages of development are identified by developmental milestones that generally occur at predictable points in a person's life. These scales provide the means to compare a learner's development to normal development. Developmental scales are checklists that either can be administered to parents by asking them whether their children exhibit a given set of skills or can be given to students by structuring tasks for them and observing whether or not they can complete the tasks for their age level.

Like other standardized tests, developmental scales can be a valuable tool for screening purposes. Developmental scales provide excellent information about the broad deficit areas, but more in-depth analysis will still be needed to determine preferred communication modes and generalization of skills (Bricker, 1983; Luftig, 1989).

Nonstandardized tests, as described by Miller (1978), can be modified to meet the needs of students not requiring the rigid administration procedures of standardized tests. Teacher-made tests fall into this category and are often based on objectives covering areas such as elicited imitation, comprehension, sound production, and free speech analysis.

Teachers can devise nonstandardized or informal exercises that test their students' abilities in the areas of phonology, semantics, morphology, syntax, and pragmatics. An excellent technique is to tape record samples of a student's speech and analyze its quality based on these categories. Table 11.2 provides examples of some common errors students might make that can alert teachers to the need for developing remediation activities.

The last category, behavioral observation, deals with direct measurement of learner behavior and includes useful techniques for teachers, especially when it is important to

TABLE 11.1   *Common Commercial Achievement and Diagnostic Tests of Language Skills*

Test	Dimension of Language Measured	Grade/Target Population
Assessment of Children's Language Comprehension Consulting Psychologists Press Palo Alto, CA	Identifying pictures with multiple verbal elements	Preschool–Elementary
Clinical Evaluations Charles E. Merrill Publishers Columbus, OH	Phonology Morphology Syntax and semantics	K–12
Goldman-Fristoe Test of Articulation American Guidance Service Circle Pines, MN	Articulation	Over 2 yrs. old
Goldman-Fristoe-Woodcock Test of Auditory Discrimination American Guidance Service Circle Pines, MN	Phonology	Over 4 yrs. old
Environmental Language Inventory Charles E. Merrill Publishers Columbus, OH	Semantics	1–30 yrs. old
"Let's Talk Inventory" for Adolescents Charles E. Merrill Publishers Columbus, OH	Pragmatics	9 yrs.–Adult
Peabody Picture Vocabulary Test-Revised American Guidance Service Circle Pines, MN	Receptive vocabulary	2–Adult
Test of Adolescent Language (TOAL)-2 Pro-Ed Austin, TX	Vocabulary Syntax	11–18 yrs. old
Test of Early Language Development Pro-Ed. Austin, TX	Content and form	3–7 yrs. old
Test of Language Development (TOLD) Pro-Ed. Austin, TX	Vocabulary Syntax Phonology	4–9 yrs. old

assess the generalization of communication skills to community settings. This system defines in measurable terms the exact movement that the learner will engage in (e.g., number of requests in social situations) and records the occurrences of the behavior(s) in varied settings. (Review Chapter Five for a more detailed discussion.)

Areas to Assess: Considerations for Teaching

What communication skills should be taught to individual students is one of the more difficult questions that teachers face. Unfortunately, the answer to it may often be based solely on whatever commercially produced program is available in a given classroom. A teacher may find it easier to compare the learners' skills to the criteria of the program, fitting each student somewhere into the scheme of activities presented in the teacher's manual. Learners with communication deficits require a far more intensive assessment system geared to their particular needs. Therefore, teachers may wish to consider additional techniques for gathering the types of information needed for specific learners.

Phonemes are the most basic unit of language, consisting of sounds that, when combined with other sounds, form words. Analysis of a student's ability to produce phonemes can be accomplished by collecting stimuli (e.g., pictures or objects) that contain target sounds and using them to elicit the student's speech. For example, if the student says "pall" when shown a ball, the response on the sound "b" can be scored as incorrect.

Morphemes are the smallest parts of language that have meaning; they include root words, prefixes, and suffixes. Many teachers informally assess this area by using open-ended sentences, as in the following example:

The man *drives* the car.

The man is the _____. Answer: *driver*.

Specific-level assessment of syntax (rules of grammar) can take both written and oral form. An effective approach is to tape record samples of a student's conversations and analyze them for the grammatical rules of interest. Semantics, which involves the meanings of words and their relationships to other words, can be assessed using the same language samples obtained for the syntax analysis.

TABLE 11.2   *Examples of Form and Syntax Error Analysis*

Stimulus	Student Response	Assumed Causes for Problem
You	"OO"	Phonology (expressive)—consonant
Go get the tool.	Go to the pool.	Phonology (receptive)—discrimination problem
He walks to school.	He walk to school.	Morphology—omits progressive verb tense
Bobby's ball	Bobby ball	Morphology—omits progressive marker
He drives the car.	He drived the car.	Morphology—substitutes past for present tense
Where is the ball? The ball is on the floor.	Ball floor	Semantics—problems with subject location

Specific-level assessment should go beyond classroom-based analysis of the phonemes, morphemes, and syntax commonly tested with workbook or worksheet formats. The most important information for helping these learners become more independent involves semantics and pragmatics (the use of language in a given context such as learning the rules for taking turns in a conversation). This information can best be gathered during structured observations in community-based activities. For example, situations can be structured so that teachers can observe students following directions, understanding the meaning of concepts related to life activities, understanding humor, and understanding multiple meanings (Bos & Vaughn, 1988). Similarly, activities can be developed that provide opportunities for observation of students using correct grammar in daily life situations, using appropriate words to convey meanings, and staying on the topic during a conversation.

CASE STUDY

"OK kids, today we begin spending time working as volunteers at Memorial Hospital. We will be coming here twice a week for the next few months and spend about 2 hours each visit," said Ms. Napoli to her group of six students enrolled in a middle school resource room class. "As we talked about in class, I've worked with your other teachers to schedule this block of time so that we can learn and practice a number of different skills at places where you might work someday, or, like the hospital, go as a patient when you need help."

"Luis, what are some of the things we will be learning here?"

Luis replied; "How to work good."

"That's right," said Ms. Napoli, "good work habits. Anyone else?"

"I know Ms. Napoli," Maggie replied, "We're gonna learn math and reading."

"That's exactly right, Maggie. We are going to practice using math and reading skills in work and other life situations. The best thing to remember is that we are also going to learn and practice behaviors that will help us get along with others and good communication skills, which include talking and listening."

After the class had been on site at the hospital for 2 weeks, Dr. O'Toole, the principal of the middle school, visited to observe Ms. Napoli's program.

"Well Nicole, how's your community-based program going?"

"Great, Barbara, the kids are really enthusiastic and, for once, eager to learn!"

"Explain to me again, Nicole, what you are trying to accomplish. Give me an example I can use in case the superintendent or a board member asks me about the program."

"OK, Barbara, let's take Luis as the example. He has trouble with both his receptive and expressive language. Tests given to him in school identified his major deficits, but we can never be sure of what those results mean in terms of his ability to communicate with other community members. So I've structured a number of situations in which hospital employees will strike up conversations with Luis while I'm in the area observing. Sometimes I use a tape recorder that Luis can't see, and sometimes I informally make written notes. Luis is working in food services today, helping deliver trays to patients. He works with a hospital employee in a two-person team. Let's go and watch for a while, and I can show you what I mean."

"The way I want this program to run, Barbara, is that the kids will work in one sub-environment just long enough for them to learn and practice tasks required by various jobs, and then they will move to a new subenvironment where I'll teach them the new skills. The subenvironments here are large enough that I can keep all six in one area, and then we move as a group to a new subenvironment. This system allows me to be there to teach the skills by modeling, guiding, and so forth, and I can handle any unexpected situations as they arise. My professor in college called these 'teachable moments,' because they allow me to teach students about social, vocational, or any other situation that might come up that I couldn't plan for, at the time it happens."

"Here comes Luis and his partner. What I'm watching for is whether or not Luis provides his listener with enough information during a conversation. His test results don't specifically address this area, and I've noticed his tendency toward this problem. If I observe the problem occurring three times while Luis talks to his partner, I'll begin instructing him and eventually teach the hospital employees how to work with him in ways to prompt more effective conversational skills."

"Nicole, I'm a little confused. Isn't the main goal for being here to teach the kids how to work in a hospital?"

"Actually, Barbara, for middle school kids, teaching entry-level vocational skills is not my main concern. I'm more interested in teaching them effective social skills and advanced language and communications skills. Also, I want them to be able to apply math, reading, and written expression skills to everyday life activities. These are my main areas of concern, because they may, in fact, be the most important factors in determining whether or not these kids will someday be successful on the job and in other facets of life. The beauty of this approach is that it also allows me to teach career awareness to the kids."

"Well you sold me, Nicole. Now it's my job to sell the superintendent and the board. Sounds to me like the best approach is to convince them that all you're doing is moving your classroom into the community."

"Well put, Barbara, you have mastered the advanced language skill of using the most appropriate words to convey the concept!"

■ ■ ■ ■

Measuring Communication Behavior

Up to this point, the discussion has emphasized the "what" to assess at both the survey and specific levels. The various methods of assessment were touched upon earlier; however, teachers may now benefit from additional suggestions concerning the application of one specific technique. Specific-level assessment provides the most useful information for program development. This information is gathered via criterion-referenced instruments or behavioral observations, and the decision concerning *what* to assess affects how the information will be gathered.

For example, behavioral observations may take the form of tape recording a learner's verbalizations to judge the quality of sound formation, observing and recording the number of times a student makes a need known through gestures, and timing the length of time a student engages in a conversation with another individual. Hart and Risley (1968) used time sampling to measure the occurrence of spontaneous speech of preschool learners.

The first step is to decide what communication behavior(s) to increase in the student's repertoire. The following sections present program components (e.g., prerequisite skills, functional language, use of adjectives) constituting a list of potential communication behaviors. For now, a few examples may provide a basic indication of how behavioral observation can be used to assess communication behaviors.

1. A simple counting of the number of increasingly complex word pairs that a learner can imitate, for example, preposition and noun (in cup).

2. Interval recording, whereby the teacher records the number of time intervals in which the learner spoke.

3. The number of commands or questions to which a learner responds correctly.

4. A count of the number of times the learner checks to see whether or not the listener is attentive and understands (Simon, 1985).

5. A count of the number of times the learner requests additional information in an effort to understand the directions.

These examples are all based on a common factor. The target behavior can be identified by some type of physical movement by the learner. White and Haring (1980) have provided an excellent discussion of learner movements and how to assess them as functional skills. As teachers and other professionals decide about what they want to know concerning the student's communication abilities, the next step is to translate the *what* into a movement that can be observed and recorded. For example, if the communication question involved asking a co-worker for assistance when trouble occurs on the job, the physical movement would be the actual request and a situation could be structured allowing a teacher to observe and record the occurrence or nonoccurrence of the target response.

The areas of assessment presented in this section provide the boundaries for "what" to evaluate. Translation of these assessment goals into movements by the learner is necessary to provide the "how" to assess. Once this translation is completed the teacher can then observe and record the number of occurrences or the length of time the target behavior occurs.

KEY CONCEPTS

- The main techniques for assessing language skills are standardized tests, developmental scales, nonstandardized or criterion-referenced tests, and behavioral observation.

- Students' language development can be adequately assessed at the survey level using commercially produced tests. Their ability to communicate effectively in social or other community situations will have to be assessed using direct observation and samples of their communications.

■ Specific-level assessment is an intensive analysis of each deficit area identified in the survey-level assessment of a student's communication skills.

■ ■ ■ ■

This information can target any area of language (e.g., phonology, syntax, pragmatics) and can best be observed and recorded in either structured or informal situations while students are engaged in community-based activities.

PROGRAM IMPLEMENTATION

Techniques for Teaching Prerequisites to Communication

Teachers generally are interested in targeting the skills important to a specific learner. A majority of students will be able to produce vocalizations; therefore, a portion of these learners' programs will be devoted to teaching improved verbal behaviors.

A major concern among professionals centers around the teaching of prerequisite skills of language. Most agree that for younger learners who have not yet obtained the basic verbal behaviors, teaching verbal prerequisites is essential (Bricker, 1983; Bricker & Dennison, 1978; Bricker, Ruder, & Vincent, 1976). Others argue that there is little evidence to support the need to teach prerequisites before more advanced language structures (Guess, 1980).

As with many issues in education, there may not be an absolute answer to this debate. A combination approach establishing each student's present and future communication needs, tempered with teaching basic skills where warranted, can provide more than one option for the student.

When dealing with younger learners or those with moderate cognitive disabilities who have not begun to vocalize effectively or who vocalize poorly, the following suggestions may assist teachers in the program development process:

1. Bricker and Dennison (1978) suggested six generic procedures for teaching prerequisite language skills:
   a. Observe the learner in the classroom, home, and community in order to note general functioning level.
   b. Use a systematic assessment program that includes identification of entry behavior, a continuous monitoring system, and follow-up assessment.
   c. Operationally define the target behaviors (e.g., will grunts be counted as vocalizations?).
   d. Specify the length of each training session and decide beforehand the number of instructional trials to be covered in one session.
   e. Develop activities that allow students to generalize the skills they have just learned.
   f. Use small groups for communication training; stimulation among learners should facilitate the activity.
2. Bricker and Dennison (1978) and Bricker, Dennison, and Bricker (1976) suggested providing instruction in on-task behavior before getting into other skill areas. Devany, Rincover, and Lovaas (1981) began their program by teaching the skill of following

instructions first and dealing with the off-task behaviors as they occurred. In either case, the approach to take usually depends on the learner. For example, one student may continually stare at the wall. In this case, the first task would be to teach the student to look at the teacher. Another learner may occasionally leave his or her seat, prompting the use of a behavioral program to control that behavior while the student is being taught imitation skills.

3. The student's ability to imitate the teacher is an essential skill for language training (Jones & Robson, 1979). Devany and colleagues (1979) suggested that instruction in discrimination appears to be the best alternative for teaching learners to imitate either gestures or vocalizations of sounds.

4. The techniques of chaining and shaping have proved to be quite effective in teaching imitation skills. Initially, the teacher will want to reinforce all vocalizations during a session, attempting to increase the overall number. Also, the teacher should reinforce the student for looking at the teacher's face, in particular the lips (Devany et al., 1979). This action will facilitate imitation in later stages of the program.

5. To increase vocalization, some learners will have sounds like grunts or cooing targeted while others have consonants or vowels targeted (Bricker & Dennison, 1978). What skills are targeted depends on where the student is presently functioning.

6. As the learner increases the number of vocalizations produced during the session, the teacher gradually will attempt to get him or her to begin matching the teacher's vocalizations. At this point, the teacher reinforces only those vocalizations that the learner makes immediately after the teacher produces some verbal behavior.

7. Over time, only those verbalizations that sound like the teacher's verbal stimuli will be reinforced. This shaping of the student's response will serve to gradually improve the quality of responses.

8. Another important program component for teaching prerequisite communication skills is teaching the learner to imitate motor skills. Bricker and Dennison (1978) advocated beginning with teaching the learner to imitate actions that are familiar; for example, the teacher begins by imitating a movement made by the student. After a number of trials in which the student has initiated the movement, a chain of movements should be established (e.g., the teacher provides the stimulus and the student responds).

9. The next step in this process is to teach the learner to imitate actions (movements) that are currently unfamiliar (Bricker & Dennison, 1978). To accomplish this, the teacher identifies a number of motor movements not frequently initiated by the learner (e.g., a complex arm movement or the shaking of a rattle). For students who are not able to imitate more complex motor tasks or tasks that are simple but unfamiliar, a series of teacher behaviors ranging from minimal to intensive intervention can be applied. For instance, a teacher can move from verbal direction and modeling ("move your arms like this") to verbal direction, modeling, and complete physical guidance. Subsequent sessions would fade the more intensive techniques (e.g., total guidance) until the student can imitate from the model provided by the teacher.

10. An additional technique for improving the learner's ability to imitate the sounds produced by others involves choosing sounds that allow the teacher to physically prompt the student through the task (Devany et al., 1981). An example is the "p" sound, which the teacher can demonstrate by touching the learner's lips, prompting them to stay closed, and modeling the air flow through the lips. As the student masters sounds, new ones are added to the repertoire.

11. Teaching students to imitate sounds may begin with sounds that are already in their repertoire, then move to sounds unfamiliar to them (Bricker et al., 1976). For some learners, an acceptable approach may be to teach them to imitate words they come in contact with in daily social or vocational situations.

12. Once students have learned to imitate basic sounds, additional prerequisite skills generally involve labeling objects (including discrimination between objects), using objects in the context of language (drink from the cup), using prepositions (under), and using pronouns (my ball).

Implementing a Prerequisite Training Sequence

Teaching the prerequisites to verbal communication is an important program component. The success of such efforts, however, may depend on whether or not certain considerations have been addressed. One consideration is to monitor student progress closely by maintaining an ongoing error analysis. For example, a teacher may require a student to imitate the word "shoe" (stimulus). If the student's response is "to," the teacher can analyze the answer and establish a probable cause (misplacement of tongue). Once the teacher and speech pathologist have analyzed the requirements of correct tongue placement, they can develop a prompt for the correct response. When teachers analyze the sounds students are making, they improve their chances for developing an effective system of shaping successive approximations. Error analysis of communication skills may best be accomplished by taking tape recorded samples of learner responses. Sounds made by a student can be played back many times to analyze components that could be shaped into more meaningful utterances.

Charting student responses works well in conjunction with error analysis. Using charting to monitor the daily progress of learners provides an actual picture of each individual's strengths and deficit areas. For example, a young learner targeted for an increase of verbalizations may be cued to imitate the teacher's stimulus "ba." In this instance, the teacher charts the percentage of trials on which the student correctly imitates the sound "ba." The objective may be that the student will imitate the sound correctly over 100% of the trials. Using the chart shown in Figure 11.1, the teacher can make instructional decisions concerning any necessary program changes. By analyzing these data, the teacher notes that the student appears to be leveling off during sessions three, four, and five. Consequently, in order to increase the probability of additional success, a change in the instructional strategy may be necessary, for example, guiding the student by gently pressing his or her lips together.

Including parents as teachers is a second important consideration of implementing successful prerequisite programs. One basic disadvantage of teaching prerequisites is the amount of time it takes to teach many of these skills to some learners. Parents can provide the additional help needed to teach these skills, and they can also provide the natural reinforcers that are a vital component of language programs (Guess, 1980).

Success in incorporating parents into the instructional program depends on the ability of teachers to provide them with the necessary skills for instructing their children at home. Parents should be invited to participate in a number of classroom sessions, allowing time for the teacher to model the appropriate instructional techniques, correction procedures, reinforcer applications, and charting. Whenever possible, the teacher can accompany parents to their home, assisting them in setting up a schedule and site, and generally seeing that the instruction transfers over to the natural setting. As the student's program becomes more complex, the teacher can assist the parents by demonstrating how to implement the instructional procedures in places such as grocery stores and restaurants (e.g., teaching the phrase "I want").

A final consideration in teaching prerequisites involves the use of functional versus simulated materials. Some teachers may find it easier to teach communication skills such as labeling and object use by incorporating pictures and/or replicas of the objects into their programs. To some extent, commercially produced language programs foster the use of both of these stimuli. The question of whether or not simulated materials are realistic enough to foster daily language development in learners is important. At the present time, for example, the efficacy of using plastic fruit versus real fruit is still in question. However, the goal is to get learners functioning in the community as quickly as possible. Therefore, it may be more reasonable to teach communication skills using realistic materials.

Using Commercially Produced Language Programs

Many fine language programs are available for use with students who have mild to moderate language problems. These programs have been used with success and allow teachers to follow a structured approach that monitors student progress. Good teachers go beyond the scope of commercially produced programs, developing activities that allow students to practice learned skills while involved in the community.

For example, students may be working on skills involving grammatical rules using the Fokes Sentence Builder Kit (Fokes, 1976) Teachers can extend these lessons by

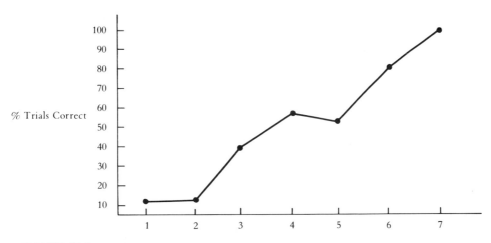

■ FIGURE 11.1
Chart to Monitor Student Progress on Increasing Sound Imitation of a Kindergarten Student

TABLE 11.3 *Common Commercial Language Development Kits*

Name (Author of Kit)	Target Population	Type of Approach	Comments
Developmental Language Lessons 1 and 2 (Mowery and Replogle, 1977, 1980)	Language delayed; other handicapped	Spontaneous language use in structured setting	Emphasis on remediation for syntactic structures in 8 grammatical categories derived from Laura Lee's DDS test. Provides formal/informal diagnosis.
Developmental Syntax Program Revised Edition (Coughran and Liles, 1979)	Ages 3–10 who need syntactic remediation	Elicited response from pictures	Addresses syntactic errors in articles, negations, possessive pronouns, etc.
DISTAR I, II, III (Engleman and Osborn, 1970, 1973, 1975)	Preschool up	Drill and repetition; task analytical imitation and reinforcement	Highly structured and organized. Emphasis on expressive aspect of language. Moves from the familiar and simple to the more complex. Instructional groups based on performance levels. Heavy use of question-answer form of instruction—Teacher: "What's this?"—Pupils: (together) "That's a pencil!" Appears successful in teaching specific responses to specific stimuli; less adequate in generalizing to other situations.
Fokes Sentence Builder Kit (Fokes, 1975)	Learning disabled, deaf, hard of hearing, borderline to mild mentally retarded	Cognitive-psycholinguistic stimulative	Highly structured. Unique design for teaching syntactic rules and structures, but not as rote responses. WHO, WHAT, IS DOING, WHICH, WHERE.
Fokes Sentence Builder Expansion	Same	Same	Adds 3 grammatical categories WHOSE, HOW, WHEN.
GOAL: Language Development—Games Oriented Activities for Learning. (Karnes, 1976a)	Normal to moderately handicapped	Developmental; stimulative	Highly structured. Based on Illinois Test of Psycholinguistic Abilities model. Lessons in game format. Criteria for mastery of each lesson not predetermined.
Karnes Early Language Activities (Karnes, 1976b)	All mentally handicapped	Developmental; stimulative	Downward extension of GOAL (see above). 200 model lessons. Provides instructional ideas only; actual items must be supplied by user.
Language Rehabilitation Program Levels 1 and 2 (Hain and Lainer, 1980)	Aphasic; mentally retarded; hard of hearing		Emphasis on development of verb form. Cards depict familiar scenes, emphasis on retrieving sentences previously known by aphasics.

344

TABLE 11.3 (Continued)

Name (Author of Kit)	Target Population	Type of Approach	Comments
Monterey Language Program (Programmed Conditioning for Language) (Gray and Ryan, 1972)	All children needing help on language	Behavioral; operant	Highly structured. User must be trained and certified by distributor. Includes pre- and posttests, placement tests, branching provisions, specific criteria. Good data showing effectiveness, including transference.
MWM Program for Developing Language Abilities (Minskoff, Wiseman, and Minskoff, 1972)	Ages 3 to 11 with evidence of language deficits	Developmental; stimulative	Rationale is based on the model of the Illinois Test of Psycholinguistic Abilities. Comprised of a teacher's guide, inventory, manual, and materials. Provisions for diagnostic screening; remediation for weak areas according to model. Activities sequenced by difficulty level.
Peabody Language Development Kits (L. M. Dunn, J. O. Smith, & L. Dunn, 1981; L. M. Dunn, L. Dunn, and J. O. Smith, 1981; L. M. Dunn, Horton, & J. O. Smith, 1981; L. M. Dunn, J. O. Smith, & D. Smith, 1982)	All children	General developmental; stimulative	Purpose is to stimulate oral language, heighten verbal intelligence, and enhance school progress. Overall language stressed. Attractive and motivating. Kits contain manual, lessons, manipulative materials, reinforcement chips, and picture cards. Group instruction format. Research showing effectiveness is inconclusive.
Project MEMPHIS (Quick, Little, and Campbell, 1973)	Mild to severely handicapped	Developmental	Emphasis on language for verbal and nonverbal communication. 260 lesson plans based on three steps: planning, implementing, evaluation.
SYNPRO (Syntax Programmer) (Peterson, Brener, and Williams, 1974)	All ages with mild problems	Operant; drill	Can be used by professionals or aides. Provides a highly structured way of programming syntactic strings.
Visually Cued Language Cards (Foster, Giddan, and Stark, 1975)	Normal to profoundly retarded	Stimulation of functional language	Consists of five series of picture cards. Related to Assessment of Children's Language Comprehension Test. May be used at home or school.
Wilson Initial Syntax Program (Wilson, 1973)	Those with syntax problems, especially TMR	Stimulation; Chomskyian	Emphasis on improving receptive syntactic skills. Can be used by teacher aides.

From Donald D. Hammill and Nettie R. Bartel, *Teaching Children with Learning and Behavior Problems*, Third Edition. Copyright © 1982 by Allyn and Bacon. Reprinted with permission.

structuring activities in community retail businesses where students can practice asking clerks who, what, where, and how questions. Bartel and Bryen (1982) have constructed a chart describing the most widely used language development kits. This chart is produced in Table 11.3.

Techniques for Teaching Functional and Advanced Language Skills

Regardless of whether students have been labeled by their school districts as having mild to moderate mental handicaps, learning disabilities, or behavior disorders, they will all benefit from instruction in advanced language skills. Language and communication are useful if they assist persons in interacting with others in their environment. The probability of communication success should increase if the advanced language skills are tied to naturally occurring events that are reinforcing to the learner. Consequently, advanced language skills should be taught within the context of daily life events of the students.

Devany and colleagues (1981) described a program that leads the learner from prerequisite skills to mastering the receptive and expressive use of four skill areas: Prepositions (in, under, on, above); pronouns (my, his, I am); time-related concepts (last, before); and yes-no concepts ("Is this a ball?" "Yes"). The remainder of the program involves teaching conversational skills ("How are you?" "I am fine."), as well as grammatical skills such as past tense and plurals.

Mittler (1976) has identified a series of seven kinds of questions that can be used by teachers to stimulate functional use of advanced language skills:

1. Labeling (nouns): "What is this?" "A cup."
2. Labeling (verbs): "What are you doing?" "Running."
3. Two-choice questions: "Is this a ball or a bat?"
4. Open-ended questions: "What would you like to do?"
5. Facilitating questions: "What happens next?"
6. Rhetorical questions: "Can you tell what this is?"
7. Maintenance questions: "What happened then?"

Questions one and two are designed to teach basic skills of communication, while question three involves teaching discrimination skills. Questions four and five assist learners by allowing them to respond to a larger field of stimuli and begin to translate their thoughts into expressive responses. The last two kinds of questions are designed primarily to keep the learner communicating as much as possible.

The types of advanced language skills mentioned previously are fairly common skills found in many language programs (e.g., Spikman & Roth, 1984; Watson, 1981). For example, the Guess, Sailor, and Baer (1978) program includes skills that are clustered under four content areas: persons and things; actions with persons and things; possession/color; and size/relation and location. Identifying the kinds of skills that would benefit a learner may not be the most difficult job for the teacher. Instead, how to teach those skills once identified may be the area that requires attention.

The answer to this dilemma can be found earlier in this chapter and in other chapters of this text. Whether it be Bricker and Dennison's (1978) program to teach prerequisites; Devany, Rincover, and Lovaas's (1981) system for teaching advanced speech skills; or Guess, Sailor, and Baer's (1978) approach to functional communication, the common denominator involves the teacher's ability to effectively arrange antecedents to the learner's behavior. In addition to the arrangement of antecedents, the rate of student success is tied closely to the effectiveness of the consequences following the targeted behavior (Leonard, 1983).

IDEA FILE

Microcomputers can be a tremendous asset to learners attempting to improve their communication skills. Currently available software can help students improve their grammatical structure. Hardware components such as speech synthesizers now allow students to practice speaking skills using computer-produced speech as a model. (Samples are presented below.) Hagen (1984) has provided the most complete list, and readers are encouraged to study her excellent book on microcomputers for special education.

Computer Assistance Language Program. Minneapolis, MN: Sysdata International.

Language Arts Skill Builders, Allen, TX: Developmental Learning Materials.

Lessons in Syntax. Beaverton, OR: Dormac.

The Microcomputer. Englewood Cliffs, NJ: Scholastic Software.

■ ■ ■ ■

At this point, readers should review the suggestions for teaching prerequisites to communication presented earlier in this chapter. The suggestions for teaching those skills are equally applicable to the instruction of more advanced skills. Following are additional points that teachers may wish to consider when implementing programs designed to increase the functional and/or advanced language skills of learners:

1. Devany and colleagues (1981) suggested that when teaching prepositions, teachers should first instruct learners in the receptive use of the word and then move to instruction in the expressive use. After three or four prepositions can be understood by the learner, instruction can begin in the expressive use of those same words.

2. Devany and colleagues also discussed a technique they call *stimulus rotation*, minimizing the possibility that the learner will "parrot" a response instead of actually learning the concept or word. Using this technique, the teacher presents one stimulus ("in," for example, "Put the ball *in* the box"). The teacher works with the student until the student can perform the task in relation to a prespecified criterion (e.g., five out of five trials). At that point, the teacher switches to a new stimulus such as "over" until the learner meets the established criterion. This system continues by introducing new stimuli; however, the element of stimulus rotation also continues by randomly reintroducing words for which the student has previously met criterion. This technique continues until the student responds correctly on the first trial.

3. A common error made by some teachers is the unsystematic use of antecedents designed to maximize student response. Teachers may find it helpful to write down the sequence of antecedents they wish to use before the lesson begins. For example, complete manual guidance may be needed initially to get the learner to put the ball *in* the box. During subsequent trials, however, less intense antecedents can be implemented such as partial guidance, prompting using touch and pointing, or modeling. The important point here is that the teacher must use the level of antecedent that is right for a learner and that the antecedents must be applied in a systematic fashion (e.g., partial guidance until student reaches criterion, then pointing, etc.).

4. The type of antecedent that the student is working under should be recorded to monitor progress. For example, a chart might reflect that the learner required 10 trials using partial guidance before he or she met criterion for putting the ball *in* the box. Similarly, the same learner may have met criterion for putting the ball *under* the table after 5 trials using touching combined with a pointing gesture.

6. Fading is an important procedure that works in conjunction with the application of antecedent events. Gradual fading from one antecedent event to the next allows learners to generalize their responses to the new teacher behaviors. Fading can also be used as a *fade-in* procedure. When teaching a word such as "in," it may not be possible to include the entire sentence ("Put the ball in the box") if it confuses the learner. Rather, the teacher can begin by saying just the word "in" while prompting the desired response. During later trials, the remainder of the words in the sentence can be gradually faded in to the presentation (Devany et al., 1981).

7. Real objects should always be used when teaching communication skills, and whenever possible teachers should start by choosing objects that have a functional use that can also serve as a reinforcer to the learner (e.g., a cup that can provide the learner with a drink of juice).

8. Teaching advanced/functional communication skills can be as time-consuming as teaching the prerequisites to language. Therefore, an important task for teachers is to organize and instruct parents, volunteers, and peer tutors to assume some of the responsibility for teaching the skills targeted in the student's communication program.

9. Many activities should be developed for which the sole objective is to get students to express themselves orally (Mercer & Mercer, 1985). For example, filmstrips and films that are not narrated can be used to generate discussions among students (Semel & Wiig, 1982).

10. Culturally different students should be encouraged to express themselves as much as possible. Teachers should not pass judgment on the quality of their use of English, but should provide an appropriate model (Polloway, Payne, Patton, & Payne, 1985). For example, Polloway and Smith (1982) provided an example of how teachers can be good language models for students without singling them out. If a student says "Dese car look good," the teacher can model by saying, "Yes, these cars do look good" (p. 84).

11. Cognitive behavior modification strategies help students use more appropriate language skills in a variety of situations. Self-talk, for example, helps students learn to use language to think. The teacher can model the use of self-talk in relation to a number of community-based tasks. For instance, a teacher might verbalize, "I'm going to say to the salesperson, 'Excuse me, I need some help finding the right size.'" He would then model by making the actual request, subsequently guiding the students through the same process. Eventually he would teach the students to self-talk silently.

Self-talking should not be limited only to what a person is doing. Teachers can also demonstrate how self-talk can be used for describing what they are thinking and for reviewing rules as well as strategies for engaging in a variety of social interactions, vocational activities, and consumer tasks (e.g., "What face movements and body language do I look for to see whether Jenny's paying attention to me? Are her eyes looking at me? Is she yawning? Are her fingers tapping?").

12. Teacher modeling may be one of the most important instructional strategies for developing language and communication skills. For example, teachers can model how more information can be expressed ("These cars on the lot can help us get to work, they can also help us to have fun, get help, etc.") and how ideas can be expressed in more complex ways ("That building is tall; it's also higher than the rest, and it looks enormous next to the building over there").

13. Visual imaging can help students use more advanced language and communication skills. With this technique, students are taught to visualize images of objects, social situations, and other events before they retrieve them for use in conversation. The more participation students have in a variety of community-based activities, the more opportunities they have to develop images related to actual events. Teachers can cue these events as reminders for the students, who can practice in role-playing situations how to use them to enhance communication skills.

For example, Malcom is reminded to visually imagine himself going through each step it takes him to fish (taught to him as a leisure/recreation skill earlier in the year). He then practices telling his friend Nikki about his latest fishing trip. This same approach can be used to teach students how to use word association to help them retrieve words and how to cluster words in categories. All of these skills are easier to teach when the teacher and students participate together in a variety of community-based activities.

14. Sometimes teachers are not the best models for appropriate listening skills (DeHaven, 1983; Mercer & Mercer, 1989). In all situations, with students and when interacting with community members in the presence of students, teachers must model giving the speaker their full attention by maintaining eye contact and responding with appropriate sounds (e.g., uh huh; yes), and body language (e.g., nodding head).

15. Teachers should embed a number of cues into their verbal instructions (Alley & Deshler, 1979). For example, a teacher might say "This is important," or "Please listen carefully." As students begin to learn better listening skills, these cues can be faded. At the outset, however, pairing such cues with voice fluctuations and body language can help learners act on them.

Techniques for Promoting Generalization of Communication Skills

As with teaching all skills, a systematic program must be developed to enhance generalization of these skills and increase the probability that the students will be able to use them in daily life.

The first step in helping students generalize newly acquired skills is fairly simple. Initially, the numbers of stimuli in a class should be increased to assist learners in generalizing across materials. For example, when teaching "Put the ball in the box," a number of different sizes, colors, and textures of balls can be used. This technique is essential when teaching the labeling of objects, for example, cups that come in many different sizes.

Another important aspect in programming for generalization involves structuring opportunities for students to practice newly learned communication skills in as many settings as possible and with as many different people as possible. Communication skills cannot be generalized when they are taught in a daily half-hour language session. Instead, when a learner acquires the skill to communicate a need such as "Want cookie," then the opportunity should be provided for the learner to make the request in the cafeteria and at home.

In Chapter Six, the work by Stokes and Baer (1977) involving preferred techniques to promote generalization was discussed. Warren, Rogers-Warren, Baer, and Guess (1980) applied five of the principles from the Stokes article to the teaching of communication skills:

1. Teach sufficient exemplars. Using this procedure, teachers would expand the number of examples that a student would be exposed to until the student was able to generalize the skill to new stimuli. Teaching sufficient exemplars relates to the previous discussion on applying new materials, settings, and persons. For example, students have been taught to expand action verbs into nouns by adding the *er* suffix (e.g., play-player, sing-singer) (Baer & Guess, 1971, cited in Warren et al., 1980). A mean of four or five examples was required before the students could generalize the skill to new verbs.

2. Program for common stimuli. The types of antecedent events used in the original instructional setting can be transferred to additional settings to increase the probability for generalization of the learned skill. For example, if a teacher uses modeling to teach a series of gestures to students, then those same models can be used on visits to community sites to assist the learners in using the gestures in the new settings.

3. Employ a "teaching loosely" approach. This approach requires the teacher to systematically vary stimuli and formats for instruction (Warren et al., 1980).

4. Use contingencies that can be predicted consciously or unconsciously by the student. The basis for this approach centers around the use of intermittent schedules of reinforcement so that the learner is reinforced for communicating in a more natural fashion.

5. Use intrinsic reinforcers and consequences that occur naturally in the environment when programming for language generalization (Bos & Vaughn, 1988; Vogel, 1983). At the outset of instruction, extrinsic reinforcement is important for establishing behaviors (e.g., "I like the way you explained that concept"). After skills have been established, it is important to help learners see how language is a way to control the environment. For example, after instructing the students on the important criteria for renting an apartment (on site in the community), the teacher might ask them who can repeat the five major points. After Bobby successfully states the points, the teacher refrains from the typical social reinforcement but instead says, "Now we know what to look for when we go inside one of the apartments." Upon entering a model apartment the teacher can ask Bobby to point out any important features related to the criteria he outlined (e.g., number of bedrooms versus requirements of family) and explain their significance.

KEY CONCEPTS

■ Preschool and some elementary-age learners will need instruction in developing prerequisites to communication.

- Care must be given to identify a learner's present and future communication needs.
- Some learners will need intensive instruction in skills involving imitation (the ability to model others).
- Parents are important teachers of language/communication skills and should be encouraged to participate in the program.
- Using real life objects and activities whenever possible, may be more appropriate than pictures or replicas for teaching communication skills.
- Learners may react best to one of the better commercially produced language programs. Teachers can choose a program based on the needs of their learners and availability of programs.
- Skills learned by students engaged in activities included in commercial programs should be generalized as soon as possible to social and other community activities.
- Peer tutoring and role playing can be effective methods for teaching communication skills and can assist learners in generalizing skills more rapidly if their peers accompany them to other social activities.

■ ■ ■ ■

CHAPTER TWELVE

DEVELOPING LEISURE
AND RECREATION PROGRAMS

■ A perusal of textbooks presenting information on curriculum and instructional methodology in special education should serve to point out that the major emphasis continues to be on the remediation of academic deficits. This emphasis parallels the practice in public school special education programs, where the approach for students with mild handicapping conditions (i.e., MMH, LD, BD) is to keep them as close as possible academically to their peers who do not have handicaps.

During the past decade, the emphasis on teaching leisure and recreation skills to students with moderate to severe mental handicaps has grown. Researchers and practioners have discovered that these skills are essential for the successful integration of these individuals into the community as well as adding to their general satisfaction and well-being. In addition, professionals have found that by using leisure and recreation skills as the curricular vehicle, they have increased success in teaching social, communication, self-care, and basic academic skills (e.g., telling time, using money, measuring, reading) to students with moderate to severe handicaps.

Unfortunately, this approach has not gained the same popularity for use with students with mild handicapping conditions such as MMH, LD, and BD. This is surprising, considering some of the major problems these learners face. For example, most students with behavior disorders have a great deal of difficulty expressing themselves through language (McDonough, 1989) and acting appropriately in social situations (Center, 1989; Rizzo & Zabel, 1988).

Similarly, professionals working with students who have learning disabilities are becoming more aware of the need to address the social skills deficits of these individuals specifically (Vaughn, Lancelotta, & Minnis, 1988). Baum, Duffelmeyer, and Geelan (1988) noted that resource teachers working with students with LD targeted approximately 40% of them as needing social skills intervention; yet few, if any, of these students were receiving attention in this area. More recently, Blackbourn (1989) discussed the need to program specifically for generalization across many settings when teaching social skills to students with mild handicapping conditions.

Teaching leisure and recreation skills to all students has benefits beyond their use as a vehicle for developing social and communication skills. A leisure and recreation focus also provides a highly motivating way to teach basic academic skills. The most obvious examples are related to mathematics, as teachers use leisure/recreation skill development to instruct students in the use of time (e.g., scheduling leisure events, arriving on time to the movies); money (e.g., paying for and making change when attending a sports event, budgeting money for fishing equipment); and measurement (e.g., linear measurement and woodworking projects, volume and cooking projects).

A less obvious use of leisure/recreation skills to teach academics involves activities for teaching reading, written expression, and general cognitive and language skills. Chapter Eight described activities that allow students to write their own stories based on community activities, developing advanced reading and written expression skills in the process. Both their motivation level and the number of stories they produce increase when some of their experiences are based on leisure and recreation activities.

Finally, development of leisure and recreation skills is particularly important to students with mild to moderate handicaps who come from impoverished backgrounds (i.e., a high percentage of students with mild cognitive deficits). There are many characteristics that distinguish the "haves" in society from the "have nots," but one unique difference is the limited access that people from impoverished backgrounds have to leisure and recreation activities (Dawson, 1988). To improve the quality of life for these students while at the same time designing activities that enhance the teaching of social, communication, self-care, and academic skills, leisure and recreation skills should become a major area of instruction at every level of special education.

RATIONALE FOR TEACHING LEISURE/RECREATION SKILLS

Program designers must decide on the relative importance of spending instructional time teaching leisure and recreation activities (Ball, Chasey, Hawkins, & Verhoven, 1976). The answer may lie in analyzing the needs of learners with mild to moderate handicaps. This approach becomes particularly important when considering that many individuals will spend a large portion of their day engaged in nonwork activities (Cheseldine & Jeffrie, 1981). Unfortunately, the freedom to visit community recreation facilities, blend in with the other patrons, and learn the skills necessary to become participants is not easily attainable for many people with handicaps. Since this is the case, these learners need to be taught the appropriate skills before they can become active in recreation activities (Voeltz & Apffel, 1981).

There are other reasons for assigning importance to teaching leisure/recreation skills. Some people may believe that these skills are acquired incidentally, but this does not appear to be true for either the general population or learners with handicaps. As students become more independent in the community they probably will not automatically make better use of their leisure time. On the contrary, they will in some cases require intensive instructional efforts in order to learn leisure/recreation skills (Wehman, 1978).

Many learners with mild to moderate handicapping conditions have a limited experiential base, and this may be a final rationale for building leisure/recreation skills into the total curriculum package. For example, if a student is given the opportunity to do anything he or she wants during a given period of time, will watching television be a consistent choice? The point here involves excessive exposure to one or a small number of leisure activities. Television is not inherently bad; however, if it is the only option that a learner is exposed to, this form of entertainment may lead to a more passive existence (Katz & Yekutiel, 1974). The goal for professionals, then, is to expose students to a broad base of activities in order to enhance their social acceptance (Eichenbaum & Bednarek, 1964; Frith & Mitchell, 1983; Lathom & Eagle, 1982; McDaniel, 1971; Voeltz, Wuerch, & Wilcox, 1982).

There are two aspects to leisure/recreation programs: exposure and teaching new skills. If the quality of an individual's work life is linked closely to the quality of his or her leisure and recreation pursuits, then the need to incorporate these options in the educational curriculum becomes more important. This chapter presents the basic curriculum areas of leisure and recreation activities. In addition, strategies are included for assessing abilities to perform skills in these areas and techniques for teaching such skills.

LEISURE AND RECREATION SKILLS: THE IEP

Steps One and Two: Conduct the Community Needs Assessment

The idea of assessing leisure/recreation skills may be a difficult concept for some individuals to grasp. People generally think of leisure skills as relaxing or having fun—thoughts that do not readily relate to assessment. Assessment of leisure/recreation skills, however, is a vital component of a program, and when it is implemented with some forethought it should not interfere with the enjoyment of the activities themselves.

The first step in the assessment process is to conduct a community needs assessment (CNA) to gather information concerning the types of activities available in a specific community or a larger geographic area (Dever, 1989) and to classify these activities according to the chronological age interests of various individuals (Kleiber, Larson, & Csikszentmihalyi, 1986; Mobily, 1989). An initial task is to canvass a cross-section of community members to identify their leisure/recreation activities. For example, a secondary school teacher may sample students by age level from the high school, recording the activities they enjoy. Similarly, the CNA can be expanded to other members of the community in order to develop a better picture of the leisure trends across a broader base of people (Jendreck, 1988; Voeltz, Wuerch, & Bockhout, 1982).

The reason for establishing community validity when choosing leisure/recreation skills for a curriculum is twofold. First, a host of activities can be introduced to learners similar to those other students the same age consider enjoyable (see Table 12.1). This consideration helps teachers develop a more realistic attitude toward the kinds of skills to include in their programs.

Second, a CNA helps to pinpoint local resources by geographic location. For example, individuals on one side of town may bowl more than individuals in another area because of the bowling alley's location. Similarly, an electronic games arcade may be located within walking distance of home for some individuals, making it a potential source of recreation that is easily accessible. Program developers must be thoroughly aware of the types of leisure and recreation activities available in a given community and in specific locations within the community.

IDEA FILE

There are a number of techniques for assessing leisure and recreation opportunities. The following are suggestions for developing and implementing a survey designed to identify community-valid activities.

1. Community volunteers, parents, general education peers, and educational support personnel can assist in gathering CNA information. These surveyors can begin by using the telephone and visit selected sites during the later phases of program development when activities must be analyzed.

2. As a method of efficient organization, data can be clustered according to similar properties. For example, when high school students are sampled to find out how they spend their leisure/recreation time, the information can be organized by age and geographic location of the student's home. Another example might be to cluster identified activities in categories such as paid or unpaid and group or individual.

3. A filing system can be developed based on this cluster system, allowing teachers to keep a record of vital information about each activity and community site. If a bowling alley has been identified, pertinent information might include the name and phone number of the manager, hours of operation, transportation required for attendance, equipment needed, and whether the equipment can be rented or must be purchased.

4. Recreation specialists in the community should be contacted. Often the parks department has at least one person who coordinates community programs. These individuals can be a vital resource for helping teachers to develop a thorough community analysis.

TABLE 12.1   *Community Needs Assessment of Leisure/Recreation Skills*

Skills Involving a Group	Skills Involving the Individual	Resources
Softball league+	Bowling*	Mr. Jones, Manager AJAX Lanes
Stage craft—local theater group+	Film Viewing*	
Street basketball+	Raising a dog or cat*	
Dance classes*	Fishing*+	
Martial arts classes*	Maintaining an aquarium*	Ms. Barnes, Tropical Fish Enthusiast
Group camping trips*+	Birdwatching*+	
Volunteer work at a nursing home+	Sewing*+	Ms. Smithe, Coordinator Parks Department Recreation Program
	Photography*	
Travel with groups*		
	Reading*+	
Card games*+		
	Listening to music*+	
	Swimming+	Mr. Felton, Director YMCA
	Auto maintenance and small engine repair*+	
	Gardening*+	Mr. Paine, Owner Karate School
	Card games*+	

+ No cost
* Cost

5. The list of potential leisure/recreation skills presented by Bigge (1982) can provide a good frame of reference for beginning the survey (see Step Three).

6. Identified activities can also be classified according to the age-appropriateness of the task. For example, some activities may be more appropriate for individuals over a certain age while others may be more appropriate for children.

■ ■ ■ ■

Step Three: Identify Potential Annual Goals

A complete leisure and recreation curriculum provides a continuum of skills beginning with the basics of learning how to play and continuing through advanced leisure skills (e.g., intricate hobbies). Accordingly, curriculum options involving these skills should be incorporated into programs for learners at all levels. The first task for teachers is to identify the curriculum areas they wish to incorporate into their programs. Bigge (1982) has identified the following 13 areas that provide an excellent base for a varied program:[1]

1. Arts: film viewing, film making, painting, textiles, photography, ceramics, art appreciation (e.g., Burmeister, 1976).

2. Cognitive/Mental: jigsaw puzzles, crosswords, anagrams, other word and number puzzles, electronic games and puzzles, knowledge and word games.

3. Crafts: woodworking, metalworking, sewing, leather, jewelry.

4. Drama: performance, stage craft, theater appreciation, affective learning activities (mime skits), (e.g., Maynard, 1976).

5. Games: group games, card games, board games.

6. Hobbies: collections, cooking, auto maintenance, food appreciation (gourmet, wine tasting, etc.).

7. Literature and Poetry: reading, writing, discussion groups.

8. Movement and Dance: body awareness through movement, perceptual-motor training, dance (social, folk, fad, modern, jazz, tap dance appreciation).

9. Music: vocal (performance, instruction), instrumental (performance, instruction, composition, music appreciation) (e.g., Schulman, 1980).

10. Outdoor: camping, hiking, boating, fishing, animal care, environmental awareness (e.g., Bundschuh, Williams, Hollingworth, Gooch, & Shirer, 1972; Elium & Evans, 1982).

11. Social Service: volunteer work.

12. Sports: individual sports (golf, bowling, skiing, swimming) (e.g., Seaman, 1973; Sinclair, 1975), team sports (basketball, volleyball, softball, hockey, water polo).

13. Travel and Tourism: community exploration, local travel, organized tours, independent travel. (pp. 338–339).

[1]From *Teaching Individuals with Physical and Multiple Disabilities* (2nd ed.) by J. L. Bigge, © 1982 Merrill Publishing Company, Columbus, Ohio.

This list of leisure and recreation activities is presented as a foundation for program development. Undoubtedly, teachers will be able to add to it depending on their own experiences and the geographic location in which they live. For example, activities such as martial arts training, roller and ice skating, and snow skiing can also be viable alternatives for students.

Professionals should be wary of imposing their value systems on students. When reading a list of potential leisure or recreation activities teachers may tend to be paternalistic in choosing what they think is appropriate or inappropriate. For example, activities such as recreational hiking, judo, or horseback riding may be eliminated because someone other than the individual considers them to be too dangerous or inappropriate in some other way. Teachers can follow certain safety precautions that are task-specific; that is, different leisure activities will require different precautions. Precise planning and effective teaching procedures can minimize the chance for injury and allow learners with skill deficits the same opportunities available for any other participant.

The potential annual goals identified by teachers can be generic across handicapping conditions. For example, skills necessary for attending a local movie can be appropriate for all learners. The differences in the goals will depend on the skills students realistically can obtain. The following examples of potential annual goals are written in generic fashion so that teachers can modify them based on the needs of their students:

1. Identifies all available local community recreation facilities.
2. Demonstrates proficiency in the use of community recreation facilities.
3. Participates in group recreation activities.
4. Demonstrates skills in a variety of independent leisure activities.

IDEA FILE

Leisure and recreation skills can be an excellent vehicle for teaching academic skills to students in a highly reinforcing fashion. A variety of examples are presented throughout this chapter. The following examples are additional ways that academic skills can be taught in relationship to leisure activities:[2]

- Reading the directions for crafts such as model building or needlepoint.
- Acting a part in a school or community play, which can enhance reading skills.
- Using sports activities (e.g., baseball cards, newspaper reports of games, attendance at events) to compute win/loss or batting and pitching averages.
- Keeping stamp collections that are tied to dates and historical events.
- Playing board games that can develop reading and mathematics skills.

■ ■ ■ ■

[2]Provided by Dr. Garnett Smith, University of South Alabama, and Dr. Patricia Edelen-Smith.

As with independent living skills, leisure/recreation tasks are excellent ways to increase contact between learners with mild to moderate handicaps and their nonhandicapped peers. Therefore, programs that actively encourage integration of these learners from preschool throughout the school grades should be encouraged. Leisure/recreation activities are natural vehicles for professionals to use to go beyond encouragement and actually *teach* techniques for more effective social integration. The most natural activities for teaching these skills do not always occur during the school day (e.g., Little League, 4-H, Saturday skating groups, after-school events). However, teachers must be ready to work with others (e.g., 4-H leaders) on a consulting basis to help them successfully integrate students with handicaps into their programs.

KEY CONCEPTS

- Traditionally, leisure and recreation skills instruction has not been given much consideration in public school programs beyond physical education classes.
- The thrust of the normalization movement is to increase meaningful contact between individuals with handicaps and their nonhandicapped peers. Leisure and recreation activities can be a natural vehicle for encouraging this contact.
- Many learners will not acquire leisure/recreation skills incidentally. These learners can acquire some skills on their own; however, their repertoire may be limited. Other learners must be taught the skills before they can be expected to participate actively.
- Identifying leisure/recreation skills should be based on the age of the students.
- A community needs assessment allows teachers to identify activities engaged in by their students' nonhandicapped peers. Also, teachers can identify activities by their location or whether they fall into categories such as paid/nonpaid or individual/group.
- A CNA can also help teachers locate people in the community who are willing to volunteer assistance.
- Bigge's (1982) list of 13 leisure and recreation curriculum areas can be an excellent base for developing annual goals. For example, a teacher could easily convert the outdoor activities suggestions into a number of goals, for example, "Demonstrate the skills necessary to fish from the bank of a river."

■ ■ ■ ■

Step Four: Translate Goals into Potential Short-Term Objectives

Annual goals must be translated into potential short-term objectives before an efficient assessment can be made of student strengths and weaknesses. These potential objectives are particularly important in the leisure and recreation area because standardized tests of these skills are either unavailable or inappropriate (e.g., a standardized test would be inappropriate for measuring ice skating skills). Therefore, most of the assessment techniques for leisure/recreation skills will involve using task sequences and direct observation of student performance on the subskills.

Before these task sequences can be developed, teachers should identify specific outcomes for students. Potential short-term objectives allow teachers to pinpoint those outcomes, developing task sequences based on the objectives. For example, a potential goal might be: "Demonstrate the basic skills needed to ice skate." A resulting potential objective of this goal might take a form similar to the following:

Outcome: The student will be able to pay for skate rental, put on skates, start, stop and skate along the perimeter of the rink.

Context: Local skating rink.

Criteria: The student will fall safely.
The student will avoid collisions.
The student will make one complete turn around the rink without assistance.

Once this objective has been written, teachers have a guideline for developing the skating task sequence that can be used to gather assessment data.

Step Five: Assess Student Entry Behaviors

Task analysis is one of the most important tools for professionals developing leisure/recreation programs (Wehman & Schleien, 1980). Breaking down a leisure/recreation activity into component subskills is the most desirable method for obtaining assessment information about any given learner.

Basically, there are two methods for obtaining a series of task sequences. First, many have been developed by recreation specialists. The second approach involves more work on the part of program developers; however, it opens up a wider variety of activities. This task-analytic approach involves observing a person in the process of performing a set of subskills and recording the steps in order of occurrence. Of course, there are different ways to do many tasks, but a careful analysis can identify the subskills most needed to complete the entire activity.

Fishing can provide an example for developing a task analysis. Probably the most favorable beginning point would be to identify one fishing activity that is less complicated than the rest. Fishing from the bank of a river, lake, or pond should provide a representative set of fishing skills that are not too advanced. Observation of a small number of people fishing may result in the following basic task analysis:

1. Locate a suitable site to obtain bait.
2. Locate a container for the bait.
3. Dig for bait (earthworms).
4. Place the worms in the container.
5. Locate and bring a fishing pole and equipment.
6. Identify an appropriate site for fishing.
7. Bait the hook (pole with no reel).
8. Cast the line into the water.
9. If the fish takes the bait, pull in the fish.

10. Use a net to hold the fish.

11. Remove the fish from the hook.

12. Place the fish in a container with ice.

This set of subskills is merely a representative sample. Certainly, different people approach the task in different ways. However, these subskills do provide a measure against which student strengths and weaknesses can be judged.

The key to effective use of a leisure/recreation task analysis as an assessment tool is to choose appropriate variables by which student performance will be measured. These variables relate to specific behavioral characteristics such as how often the behavior occurs or the length of time that it occurs. In addition, some skills may require a measure of quality of performance (e.g., percentage of parts of a model airplane correctly assembled). Provided that the behaviors are defined in terms of physical movements by the student, observation procedures should enable the teacher to assess student participation and progress.

For example, Johnson & Bailey (1977) developed an observation system to evaluate the leisure activities (puzzles, card games, painting, weaving, and rug making) of women with mental handicaps. In this study the authors identified the important characteristics of each task such as the number of knots completed on a rug or the inches of fabric woven. Other task-appropriate behaviors were also defined for observation purposes (e.g., dipping brush in paint, cutting yarn). Once these characteristics of the skills were identified, the individuals could be assessed for such behaviors as length of time engaged appropriately in the activity as well as a product measure (number of knots completed).

Another method for using a task analysis for assessing leisure/recreation skills involves identifying the antecedent behaviors a teacher uses to involve the student in the skill. For example, in the task analysis presented for fishing, the third step involves digging for bait such as earthworms. Helping a student successfully complete this step may require the teacher to use partial guidance plus verbal instruction. A coding system can be developed for recording the teacher behavior required to assist the student for each step on the task sequence. The task analysis can be placed on a recording sheet similar to the one shown in Figure 12.1.

Generally, the system of recording chosen will depend on whether the skills being taught have been learned and need to be generalized to other situations or are not presently in the student's repertoire. For example, a learner who has never fished would require various levels of teacher assistance to accomplish the task. On the other hand, if the learner were able to complete the entire sequence of skills, then the measurement system would be subject to change. The teacher might wish to record the length of time that the learner stayed on the task of fishing (duration) or even the number of fish caught in a certain period (frequency or rate).

Organizing Assessment Data

In previous chapters, charting was discussed as a method to organize data and monitor the ongoing progress of the learner. Charts can also be a valuable tool for assessing leisure/

VI: Verbal instruction
M: Model
PP: Prompt
PG: Partial Guidance
G: Total Guidance

Session 1

1. Locate site.	VI
2. Locate container.	VI
3. Dig for bait.	PG
4. Place worms in container.	PP
5. Locate and bring pole and equipment.	PP
6. Identify site for fishing.	M
Etc.	

■ *FIGURE 12.1*
Task Analysis Recording Sheet with Teacher Behavior Codes

recreation skills. As with all behaviors, the efficiency of the charting procedure used depends on the characteristics of the student's responses. For example, the behavior targeted for change may be the length of time a student engages in appropriate toy play. A potential charting procedure for that activity is depicted in Figure 12.2.

More advanced behavior analysis designs can be used to monitor student progress in leisure skills. A student who has acquired the skills necessary to participate in a number of community-based recreation activities may not have obtained the necessary task-specific skills. If a teacher is interested in seeing how a particular instructional technique would work across three separate activities (e.g., bowling, tennis, and pinball), a multiple-

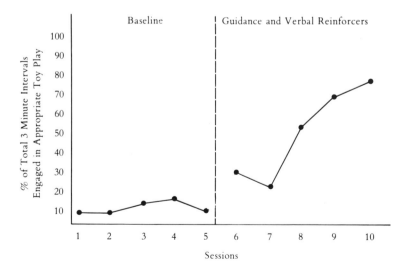

■ *FIGURE 12.2*
Chart Monitoring the Length of Time a Student Engages in Toy Play

baseline design may be appropriate for measuring potential changes in behaviors. Figure 12.3 is an example of how a teacher attempted to increase the number of steps completed according to criteria on a task analysis for each of the three activities.

One technique for organizing assessment information that complements charting procedures is to conduct an error analysis. This procedure follows the same format discussed previously. Teachers can list the verbal stimulus that indicated what the student was to perform, the response (movement) that the student actually exhibited, and the assumed cause for the inability of the student to successfully complete the skill.

For instance a learner might be engaged in a unit designed to teach dog combing and brushing skills as a part of pet care. A simple task analysis for this activity would be similar to the following:

1. Locate a soft brush, a slicker brush, and a comb.
2. Comb out the dog's beard or the area around the mouth.
3. Use the slicker brush for snarls around the mouth.
4. Comb out the dog's back, sides, and rear.

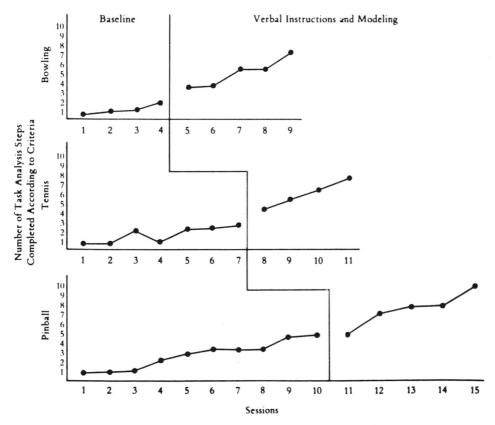

■ FIGURE 12.3
Examples of Multiple Baseline Across Settings Design for Monitoring Student Improvement Over Three Leisure Skills

5. Comb out each leg and paw.
6. Use the slicker brush for snarls.
7. Comb out the chest and stomach area.
8. Use the slicker brush if necessary.
9. Soft-brush the entire coat.

At the outset, the student would probably have difficulty with most of the skills sequenced in this task analysis. However, during the initial assessment the kinds of errors the learner makes are a vital piece of information.

Step 2, combing out the dog's beard or around the mouth area, involves being able to hold the dog's mouth closed with one hand while manipulating the comb with the other. (At the beginning of the task, a further skill is to be able to identify and use the side of the comb that has larger spaces between the teeth.) In this instance, the verbal stimulus would be: "Hold the dog's mouth closed with one hand." The response might simply have been that the student did not or could not comply. The student in question might have had a motor problem with the hand needed to complete the task. Therefore, the teacher now has some information to work with in order to begin teaching the skill. One possibility might be to use a brace on the learner's arm, while another adaptation might be to design exercises for increasing motor control and hand and arm strength.

An error analysis sheet is a tool for organizing assessment data so that it is useful for program development. Organizing data in this fashion allows the teacher to get a better picture of what variables are hindering the student from acquiring the skills necessary to complete the task.

Assessing Leisure/Recreation Preferences

The ultimate goal of a program to teach leisure/recreation activities should be to teach the individual how to participate in a variety of activities. Another goal is to teach students how to decide which activity is best for them to engage in at a particular point in time. Once these goals have been realized, the learner is better able to decide which activity to approach.

Teachers may wish to consider two approaches to assessing leisure/recreation preference. The first approach is to assess the initial preferences of the learner. Using this approach, the teacher structures varied situations in which a learner is allowed to approach desired activities or objects while the teacher observes. This approach allows instruction to begin with the student's preferred choice.

The second approach is a follow-up evaluation designed to measure students' preferences after instruction, when they have gained the ability to engage in a host of activities. This assessment activity allows the teacher to gather information as feedback into the program, which may result in changes in teaching techniques, curriculum activities, and materials.

Students are allowed to make choices without having the teacher's biases enter into the picture. For example, a learner might be taught to cross-country ski. However, after a number of trials the student might decide that she does not like the prolonged exposure to cold weather. Teachers must avoid attitudes that result in statements such as "We taught you to ski, now you *will* participate."

Helping students become more independent involves teaching them a variety of skills and allowing them to choose what they like best. Assessing leisure/recreation preferences allows teachers to observe the kinds of activities the learner chooses, not the activities chosen *for* the learner.

The key to choosing appropriate leisure/recreation activities based on students' preferences is the number of activities in which they have gained a set of basic skills. For example, students with mild to moderate handicaps might not have hit golf balls at a driving range. However, after a number of sessions of instruction in requesting change from the attendant, using money to purchase balls from the machine, and displaying courtesy toward other patrons, as well as the basic skills of hitting the balls with some amount of success, some of these learners might enjoy the activity enough to do it on a regular basis.

KEY CONCEPTS

- Task analysis in conjunction with direct observation of student performance may be the most appropriate format to assess leisure and recreation skills.

- Task sequences are available from recreation or adaptive physical education specialists. Generally, developing leisure and recreation task sequences that are specific to a community may provide the most useful tools for teachers (e.g., a task sequence for bowling can be different for two different bowling alleys).

- The criteria for completing a task or the characteristics of the task will become the units of measurement for assessing student performance. For example, the length of time a student engages in a card game or the number of activities a student samples may provide a measure of abilities or preferences.

- The level of teacher intervention (e.g., modeling, physical guidance) can be used as a criterion for measurement. As a student improves in the performance of a task the need for physical guidance by the instructor is likely to decrease. The amount of physical guidance required during an instructional period can be an effective measure of student progress.

- Charting assessment data is a method for organizing and evaluating the information gathered and for demonstrating progress toward objectives.

■ ■ ■ ■

PROGRAM IMPLEMENTATION

Prerequisites to Developing Leisure Skills

Many preschool-age learners will need instruction to help them improve their prerequisites to obtaining leisure/recreation skills. The developmental lag experienced by some learners may limit them to the very basics of learning to play. The need to learn to play is easily noted in younger children with behavior disorders, who may need program options that will enable them to develop those skills.

For example, Sherburne, Utley, McConnell, and Gannon (1988) structured a play situation to teach preschool students with behavior disorders to play with less violence and fewer aggressive themes. They used a combination of exclusionary time out and verbal prompting to decrease the aggressive play while simultaneously increasing more acceptable play behaviors among these learners.

Playing with Toys

Playing with toys is much more than a diversion for children. It can be an important educational activity, allowing children to improve their fine-motor skills while indicating their cognitive functioning (Wehman, 1979a). In addition, playing with toys allows children an excellent opportunity to learn appropriate social interaction. A child's ability to play independently in a constructive fashion is a desirable skill that helps both professionals and parents (Wahler & Fox, 1980). Finally, teaching children independent play skills can be considered a prerequisite to more advanced independent work skills. In fact, play is often considered the work of children. Unfortunately, some learners have not learned to participate appropriately in either structured or unstructured toy play.

Wehman (1977a; 1979a) has been active in the development of toy play programs for learners. During the course of his work, he has identified six levels of a developmental sequence adapted from work in general child development. Exploratory play is the first level. It involves behaviors ranging from awareness of an unfamiliar stimulus to investigating the stimulus and determining whether or not it is safe for interaction. A child's ability to explore the environment and seek out new stimuli is a very basic, yet vital component of toy play.

The second level described by Wehman (1979a) is independent play. This state finds the child playing alone for longer periods of time while interacting in an appropriate manner with objects. Some professionals suspect that successful independent play is a prerequisite for more intricate leisure skills.

Parallel and associative play are the next two levels described by Wehman. Parallel play finds children interacting with objects independently, but they are involved in the activity close to other children. Associative play allows children to become involved with others on a limited basis. For example, two children playing independently with trucks may occasionally make eye contact to see what the other is doing.

Cooperative play is the next stage; it involves close interaction among children, often with a group goal in mind. Cooperative play includes activities such as team sports, games, object construction, and telephone conversations.

Children have the best opportunity to interact socially with their peers at the cooperative play level. However, at this level initial instruction by adults is also vital. Communication, sharing, and acceptance of others are all cooperative play skills that can be taught.

The final stage discussed by Wehman (1979a) involves symbolic play. This area includes dramatization and imaginative play and can be considered a higher order form of play. Activities that are representative of symbolic play include use of puppets, doll play, and skits. Wehman has found that symbolic play is an excellent format for concept formation.

Children learn the skills at various levels and progress through each, building upon the skills learned at the previous step. Most children learn by watching models, either other children or adults. However, some learners do not imitate well and will not necessarily demonstrate the types of toy play activities described by Wehman. Careful attention by educators to teaching the various levels of toy play will at least increase the probability that these students can gain some of these prerequisites to more advanced leisure skills.

- Young students may need instruction in the prerequisites to obtaining leisure and recreation skills.
- Appropriate use of toys and appropriate levels of play can both be annual goals for some learners.

Identifying and Analyzing Short-Term Objectives

Choosing the right leisure and recreation short-term objectives for an individual has one consideration not pertinent to other curriculum areas. If parents approve of the targeted skills and the student has the physical capabilities, then a primary concern may be exposure to the skills. Individuals with mild to moderate handicaps may be exposed to a variety of activities less often than their nonhandicapped peers, and therefore less able to make choices concerning preference. Also, some leisure/recreation skills require some degree of ability before the activity can be undertaken.

For example, some people may not enjoy snow skiing until the basic snow plow technique is mastered. Once some basic skills are mastered, an individual may still choose not to participate in the activity (e.g., "Why did I learn to ski? I really don't like being out in the cold and snow"). The short-term objectives chosen for a student's IEP should provide for exposing the student to a variety of activities, teaching some of the basic skills, and then allowing a choice of the activities preferred.

Developing Instructional Strategies

Methods and adaptations for teaching leisure and recreation skills to learners with handicaps is an area marked by new and innovative approaches. Professionals in special education and recreation are continually striving to improve upon existing procedures for teaching varied types of skills. Consequently, skills previously thought impossible for these learners have now become part of their repertoire.

The technology to teach such skills has been demonstrated in a number of research efforts (Johnson & Bailey, 1977; Wehman, 1977b, 1978). Apparently, what remains is for teachers to become interested.

IMPLEMENTING INSTRUCTIONAL STRATEGIES

Structured Versus Unstructured Activities

Some teachers believe that students will grow socially if left to participate freely in group or individual leisure activities with no interference from adults. In these situations, the children involved teach each other the many socially acceptable ways to engage in activities, or the individual alone explores new and different methods of amusement. Unfortunately, for learners to engage in these unstructured approaches they must first have mastered basic prerequisite behaviors. Conversely, an approach that may facilitate learning of recreation skills is to develop activities that move the individual from a structured setting gradually toward an unstructured one (Lagomarcino, Reid, Ivancic, & Law, 1984).

Some teachers provide specific times each day when the learners in their classes can engage in free-time activities. This free time is often contingent upon the student's behavior (e.g., if you're good you can have 10 minutes of free time). Students who have not learned appropriate play behaviors or who cannot use free time wisely will tend to engage in repetitive activities with no objective. For example, some learners might be observed wandering among toys or play activities. Recess time in elementary school is another example of a situation in which some learners never get involved with a purposeful activity. To some extent, this lack of purposeful intent is appropriate if the students have been taught the skills needed to participate and then choose not to at a given time.

Teachers should consider treating free time as a learning experience and schedule these sessions as if they were teaching an academic skill (Orelove, 1982). Depending on the functioning level of the students in question, initial activities and instructional interventions will probably require a good deal of structure. The tasks that the teacher has analyzed for assessment and instructional purposes will provide the structure necessary to convert free time into more meaningful experiences. Then, as students gain the skills to actively participate in a number of games or engage in the appropriate use of toys, nonstructured free time can become a time of choice for their enjoyment.

Techniques for Teaching Leisure and Related Social Skills

Socially relevant skills may best be taught if they are interwoven throughout other components of the program (Gaylord-Ross, Haning, Breen, & Pitts-Conway, 1984). Leisure and recreation activities provide a natural setting for instructing learners in appropriate social responses. Social skills range in difficulty from simple greetings (e.g., "Hello") to more complex ones such as discriminating when it is appropriate to hug friends. Other skills include respecting the social distance of others, accepting and giving criticism, carrying on discussions, requesting items or information from others, and maintaining appropriate self-care skills.

When developing task sequences for learning leisure/recreation skills, teachers should include subskills relating specifically to socially appropriate behavior. For example, a task sequence designed to assist in teaching playground skills could include subskills such as taking turns, requesting a turn, and carrying on simple conversations with others. It could also involve learning social skills such as controlling anger when activities are contested (Kolko, Dorsett, & Milan, 1981).

Another example is teaching students to engage in a variety of activities at a local YMCA or YWCO. Teaching these students the skills needed to play in a "pick-up" basketball game, lift weights, swim, attend aerobic dance classes, or play Ping Pong can be expanded to include more complex social skills. Requesting assistance from the locker room attendant, dealing with an argument during a game, and praising others for their good play are all examples of social skills that can be taught during leisure/recreation activities.

Proper arrangement of conditions, materials, and teacher behaviors that precede the student's targeted response may dramatically increase the probability that the response will be in line with prestated criteria. Appropriate use of consequences, contingent upon the learner's response, will also improve the chances that the targeted behaviors will either increase or decrease as the teacher wishes. These two basic principles of teaching have been cited throughout this text, and they are equally applicable to teaching leisure/recreation skills.

Arranging antecedent events to teach leisure skills can range from varying the types and numbers of activities available to matching the most appropriate model to the student's need (Wehman, 1979b). In a number of studies, Wehman and his colleagues have discovered, for example, that the proximity of toys to the learner can account for whether or not the student will engage the objects. In other words, the closer the leisure materials are to the student the greater the chances are for "activity" and "spontaneity in recreation sessions" (Wehman, 1979b, p. 79).

There also appears to be some support for materials preference as a factor in learning leisure skills. Wehman (1978) discovered a definite rank-order preference for certain toys and games among learners with more severe handicaps. If teachers can discover what particular materials appear to be motivating to a target learner, the chances for teaching skills associated with those objects should be greater (Foxx, McMorrow, & Schloss, 1983).

Finally, an important set of antecedent events involves the appropriate application of certain teacher behaviors. The quality of verbal instructions, models, physical prompts or cues, and manual guidance procedures can greatly enhance student learning (Neitupski & Svoboda, 1982). For example, children often learn more effectively from models of similar ages; therefore, teachers may wish to use peer models to teach leisure/recreation skills (Schleien, Certo, & Muccino, 1984).

Consequences, when properly applied, can produce remarkable changes in student behavior. Depending on whether the behavior is targeted for increase or decrease, tangible, social, or negative reinforcers can be effective. Punishers would only be used as a consequence in extreme cases for behaviors that can cause injury to others (e.g., hitting another child with a toy) and only after thorough review by the IEP team. However, most behaviors, such as engaging in the task or learning certain skills, will respond to tangible or social reinforcers. The same rule holds true here as it does for other skill areas: Match the reinforcer to student preferences and apply it immediately after the behavior occurs.

IDEA FILE

There are a number of excellent resources that can help teachers by providing additional examples of leisure and recreation programs and teaching strategies validated by research. The following is a representative sample of topics and authors that may provide additional ideas:

Leisure curriculum for students with mild handicaps (Frith, Mitchell, & Roswal, 1980)

Instruction in dance skills (Glover, 1979)

Leisure skills as enrichment exercises (Horner, 1980)

Using modeling and social reinforcement to teach leisure skills to learners with mild handicaps (Schleien, 1982)

Leisure skills curriculum and methods (Wehman & Schleien, 1981)

Leisure skills curriculum (Wuerch & Voeltz, 1982)

Prompting play skills to increase social interaction (Capone, Smith, & Schloss, 1988)

Increasing play behavior in integrated and segregated settings (Eposito & Koorland, 1989)

Increasing expressive language skills of students with behavior disorders through play (McDonough, 1989)

Improving social skills and peer acceptance in social situations for individuals with learning disabilities (Vaughn, Lancelotta, & Minnis, 1988)

Decreasing violent or aggressive theme play among children with behavior disorders (Sherburne, Utley, McConnell, & Gannon, 1988)

Teaching elementary school children with learning disabilities to generalize social skills across multiple social situations (Blackbourn, 1989)

■ ■ ■ ■

ADAPTATIONS FOR LEISURE ACTIVITIES

The majority of learners have the physical capabilities to participate in most recreational activities, requiring only minimal adaptations on a temporary basis. For those who have motor or other problems, however, more sophisticated adaptations will generally be needed before active participation in a wide variety of activities can be realized.

Generally, the types of adaptations required are specific to the activity and to the student's needs. Therefore, specific adaptations that will work in all instances are rare. Teachers working with parents, community specialists, vocational education instructors, and recreation therapists will find that problems of adapting materials can often best be solved in brainstorming sessions or by contacting other professionals around the world who may have generated ideas or devices.

For example, maintaining a tropical fish tank can be a relaxing leisure activity for some learners. However, there are many details such as water temperature that must be judiciously cared for if the fish are to be healthy and thrive. A community member interested in this hobby can become a valuable resource. An individual who has studied the care of tropical fish may be of help in obtaining or designing a water thermometer with large numbers if the student has trouble reading a regular instrument. Community specialists may also provide ideas for adapting other equipment, for instance, an extension to the regulating switch of a fish tank heater so that it can be used by a person who has motor problems.

Bigge (1982) presented a number of case studies that can be used to stimulate innovative activity modifications by teachers, parents, and others. A good example can be found in Bigge's description of adapting photography equipment to meet the needs of a learner with physical handicaps. In this instance, the 35-millimeter camera was mounted on a tripod and sighted by a person aiding the student. The camera was operated by means of a 20-foot bulb cable release, allowing the student to activate the camera by pressing the bulb release with his thigh.

In a similar example of equipment and activity modification, Bigge (1982) discussed a program of therapeutic horsemanship developed in England during the 1960s that began with participants mounting a dummy horse to teach balance and a feeling for the riding position. The program allowed the participant to move through a series of activities, initially riding double with a trainer and eventually riding alone. Adaptive equipment included the use of special handholds, mounting ramps, safety stirrups, and a number of other adaptations. Of course, the horses included in a program of this nature would require special training.

The process of conceptualizing and developing adaptive equipment for different activities is not an easy one. However, if the modification means that individuals can participate in activities previously barred to them, it is well worth the effort involved.

PHYSICAL EDUCATION

An increasing number of physical education teachers are working with mainstreamed students. This increase in trained professionals means that more appropriate support services for classroom teachers are available. Physical education provided once or twice a week probably will not have a significant effect on the general health or recreational skill attainment of a learner (Moon & Renzaglia, 1982). A more intensive program will require close contact between special and physical educators so that practice in a number of skills can continue daily under the supervision of the classroom teacher.

Some learners suffer from overweight, poor health, or a generally lethargic demeanor. They would probably benefit from a rigorous exercise program such as jogging, swimming, weight lifting, or aerobic dancing. Classroom teachers may wish to suggest such options to their physical education counterparts. There are probably many instances in which programs of this nature would be more beneficial to the student's physical makeup and vocational potential than an adapted game would be.

KEY CONCEPTS

- Short-term objectives should be chosen to expose learners to a wide variety of activities appropriate for their chronological age group.
- Once they have been taught some of the basic skills of the target activities, the students can be allowed to choose whether or not they want to continue participating.
- Behavioral technology assists students in acquiring leisure skills previously thought to be beyond their capacity.
- Leisure/recreation skills should be considered an important part of the curriculum and should be scheduled for instruction in much the same fashion as academic activities.
- Learning social skills in relation to leisure/recreation activities can be important for all students. Learners can benefit from acquiring complex social skills while engaged in highly motivating activities.
- Antecedent behavior techniques such as modeling and guiding can be highly effective when used to assist learners.
- Consequences, in particular social reinforcers, are a necessary component of teaching leisure and recreation skills.
- Adaptive equipment may be necessary for some learners. In these instances it may be best to contact an adaptive physical education specialist and physical therapist for advice.

■ ■ ■ ■

CHAPTER THIRTEEN

DEVELOPING CAREER AND VOCATIONAL EDUCATION PROGRAMS: TRANSITION FROM SCHOOL TO WORK

■ The United States is a work-oriented society. The perceived worth of individuals is often based on their ability to be productive members of a group (usually defined by participating in some type of remunerative employment). Society also places values on specific jobs, attaching various status levels to different occupations. For instance, some people may view sanitation workers as occupying a lower status position than teachers, regardless of the fact that in some cases sanitation workers earn more money than teachers. As a result of these societal views, two factors may affect career and vocational education programs for learners with mild to moderate handicaps: (1) to enhance their worth in society, they must work; and (2) to increase their status in society, they must work at higher status jobs.

In spite of its stringent requirements dictating a person's worth, society traditionally has done little to assure learners with handicaps a place in the nation's workforce. Federal efforts continue to provide the primary impetus for program development by attempting to involve business and industry and by funding projects designed to improve the technology for teaching vocational skills (Ford, Dineen, & Hall, 1984). Unfortunately, these efforts have not been widespread at the local level (Brolin, 1983; Langone & Gill, 1985), and individuals with handicaps are not being represented adequately in the workforce. A Senate subcommittee (February, 1986, as cited by Rusch & Phelps, 1987) presented data that painted a less than desirable picture:

■ Of all Americans between the ages of 16 and 64 who have handicaps, 67% are not working.

■ If an individual with a handicap is working, that person is 75% more likely than a nonhandicapped person to be employed part time.

■ Of all these individuals who have handicaps and are not working, 67% say that they want to work.

One question that must be asked is whether or not all learners with handicaps must become part of the competitive workforce. This question is not difficult. Perhaps the best approach closely relates to the principles of Public Law 94-142 dealing with the least restrictive environment. All individuals with handicaps should be assisted in becoming part of the competitive workforce to the fullest extent possible. Accomplishing this may require developing innovative program options such as sharing and applying systematic educational technologies to teach the job skills.

A second question involves whether or not these individuals can and should be working at higher status jobs. This question again is based on individual abilities and the quality of educational programs available. Substantial evidence exists from cases documented by the National Association for Retarded Citizens that individuals with mental handicaps excel in many different and complex jobs (Payne & Patton, 1981). In some cases, professionals may need to redefine the term *employment* and identify nontraditional job possibilities instead of settling for obvious prospects such as custodial and dishwashing jobs.

Certainly the types of employment possibilities available to individuals with mild mental handicaps, learning disabilities, and behavior disorders in a highly technological society should be directly related to the quality of programs designed to instruct them. As

The author thanks Douglas Gill for his suggestions on and critical analysis of this chapter.

professionals become effective at providing meaningful instruction and long-term services, the status of jobs available to these individuals should rise.

As with any worthwhile program development effort, the first step is to establish a philosophy including the principles on which the program will be based. In the past decade, professionals have spent considerable time formulating such principles. The topic of career education has been emphasized in recent years, especially in its applicability to individuals with handicaps (Brody-Hasazi, Salembier, & Finck, 1983; Cook, 1983). Some of the issues involved in using career education as a foundation for programs are presented in the next section.

CAREER EDUCATION

Career Versus Vocational Education

Career education and vocational education are not synonymous terms. One way to conceptualize the two program areas in relationship to each other is to envision vocational education as having a narrower mission. Career education is broad in scope, involving such areas as work attitudes, career awareness, and remunerative as well as volunteer employment and is closely related to all subject areas of the curriculum (Hursh, 1982; Jesser, 1984). Vocational education deals specifically with occupational preparation. It is tied specifically to needs in the nation's workforce and is a component of a career education program (Clark, 1982). For example, one component of career education deals with a person becoming familiar with the many job opportunities in agribusiness, whereas vocational education may be concerned with teaching a student the skills necessary for becoming a feedlot hand on a large commercial cattle ranch.

Although career and vocational education are different in scope, they are not independent areas of the curriculum (Mori, 1979). Career and vocational education are interwoven, each enhancing the other in all areas. One important distinction between the two curriculum areas, however, involves their emphasis on specific age levels of learners.

Vocational education, being narrower in focus, generally involves secondary and postsecondary learners. On the other hand, career education is related to students' programs throughout their school career. An effective educational program for students should incorporate principles of career education from preschool through the secondary program and into postsecondary programs where possible (Gillet, 1983; Polloway et al., 1989).

What Is Career Education?

During the early 1970s, the movement to elevate career education to a more prominent position in the school curriculum began to gather support (Phelps & Lutz, 1977). Marland (1971, 1974) presented a number of career education principles, including the importance of schools in preparing students for careers, the relationship between career education and all curriculum content areas, the importance of teaching work attitudes as well as exposure to career alternatives, and the need to incorporate career education into curricular options for all age levels. Since Marland's initial presentation, other professionals have expanded on the concept of career education to include not only a person's vocational role, but also family roles, citizenship roles, and, in general, the skills required for daily life in society (Brolin & Kokaska, 1979; Super, 1976). The expansion of career education continues to have a great effect on the educational curricula of all learners with mild to moderate handicaps.

The expanded view of career education can accommodate the needs of all individuals with handicaps regardless of their age, disability, or severity level (Cegelka, 1981). For example, career education should become an integral component in all programs for students with behavior disorders, including instruction in affective skills related to a work personality (Center, 1989; Siegel, 1988; Smith, 1989).

What does career education consist of as it relates to educational program development? Basically, career education can best be viewed as having two components: a job-oriented approach closely linked with vocational education (Phelps & Lutz, 1977) and a life-centered approach closely linked to independent living skills (Brolin, 1989; Brolin & Gysbers, 1979; Kokaska & Brolin, 1985). The first component allows learners to become aware of potential employment outcomes, levels of training within each, and the duties required of individuals undertaking a particular career (Fell, Rak, & Klien, 1982). As students continue through school, career exploration activities allow them to sample experiences and tasks associated with particular types of jobs. Finally, career preparation involves the vocational education component, teaching a learner entry-level job skills in a specific area.

Job-Oriented Approach

Throughout the school curriculum, the learner can participate in awareness, exploration, and preparation activities in relation to the following 15 occupational clusters. (These 15 occupational clusters represent 20,000 job titles located in the *Dictionary of Occupational Titles, 1977*).

Agribusiness and natural resources	Hospitality and recreation
Business and office occupations	Manufacturing occupations
Communications and media	Marine science
Consumer and homemaking occupations	Marketing and distribution
Construction	Personal services
Environmental occupations	Public services
Fine arts and humanities	Transportation
Health occupations	

A thorough career education program allows students to become familiar with aspects of employment in the 15 cluster areas as well as relating academic skills and work attitudes to the requirements of specific jobs.

Life-Centered Approach

A second and equally important component of career education is the competencies required for life-centered goals relating to specific occupations. Brolin and his associates (Brolin, 1989; Brolin & Kokaska, 1979) developed a comprehensive curriculum framework that includes skills under three areas: daily living skills, personal-social skills, and occupational guidance and preparation. This approach is based on the belief that career education includes not only paid employment but also volunteer work, appropriate use of leisure time, use of community resources, and independent living skills (Hoyt, 1977). A broad approach includes all learners in career education programs regardless of their handicapping condition.

Brolin's three areas of curriculum separate program options, but the components are interwoven with all other curriculum areas (e.g., academic skills, physical education). The basis for this career education approach relates to the emphasis of this text on teaching community-valid skills.

Brolin (1989), Brolin and Kokaska (1979), and Kokaska and Brolin (1985) have identified 22 competencies in daily living, personal-social, and occupational areas that potentially can be included in a life-centered curriculum. For example, daily living skills include competencies relating to family finances, home management, caring for children, and leisure-recreation time. Personal-social skills include the application of problem-solving skills, interpersonal skills, and socially responsible behaviors. Finally, occupational guidance and preparation include development of skills directed to potential employment, both paid and unpaid.

These broad competency areas need to be developed into more specific areas. Brolin (1989) has presented the framework for this competency analysis by identifying 97 subcompetencies. Interestingly, various states across the country are beginning to follow suit by developing competency-based education programs including skills that *all* learners need in order to survive in community environments. Therefore, one trend in education is to emphasize skills readily applicable to daily living.

Career education is not completed when a student leaves secondary school. Professionals are becoming more interested in increasing the roles of postsecondary technical schools and community colleges in the lifelong learning process of individuals with handicaps (Brolin & Elliott, 1983).

VOCATIONAL EDUCATION

Vocational education has not always been used effectively in developing programs for learners with handicaps. This lack of appropriate use has created a major barrier to the successful transition of learners with mild to moderate handicaps (Okolo, 1988) from school to the world of work. This problem is unfortunate because vocational education programs may be the single best link school systems have for translating academic skills into work-related behaviors (Ryan, 1988).

One reason for this lack of a more appropriate use of vocational education as part of transitional programs for learners with handicaps may be the lack of support of vocational educators by special educators. This will be discussed in detail in the following sections, but for now it seems appropriate to look at a situation that may contribute to the cause of the problem. In general, special educators at the school level are lacking a basic understanding of the services provided by vocational education and the goals that drive those services (Rau, Spooner, & Fimian, 1989).

The National Commission on Secondary Vocational Education (1984) has outlined five goals that are the basis for secondary vocational education programs: (1) employability skills; (2) acquisition of personal skills and attitudes related to work; (3) broad and specific occupational skills and knowledge; (4) communication and computational skills and technological literacy; and (5) the basis for lifelong learning and planning for a career. Vocational educators accomplish these goals through their school-based vocational programs, community-based work experience programs (cooperative programs), and extracurricular student organizations (Hasazi & Cobb, 1988).

To develop a better working relationship with vocational educators, special educators must change their views concerning what constitutes a high-quality program for students at the secondary level. Many current programs do not stress a curriculum that emphasizes and operationalizes a true vocational and career-oriented approach. As Retish (1989) has stated, "No matter how confident we are that we are teaching what employers want, the lack of employment for the disabled indicates we are pursuing an incorrect path . . . " (p. 37).

To accomplish the difficult task of increasing employment for individuals with handicaps, it is important to develop unique program options such as community-based instructional programs in which classes are located in business and industry (Retish, 1989). In addition, school-based activities should be less academically oriented and provide students with increased opportunities to participate in vocational education programs.

What Is Vocational Education?

Vocational education involves the teaching of entry-level job skills in any of the following seven major program areas: agriculture education; marketing and distributive education; health occupations education; home economics education; business and office education; industrial arts and technology education; and trade and industrial education. Each of the major areas is divided into subcategories; for example, home economics can include child care, food services, and clothing. Therefore, a large number of skills across the seven program areas potentially can be taught by vocational educators. In order to narrow down the number of options presented by any one vocational program area, professionals stay in close contact with their local job market so that courses reflect the types of employment opportunities available. For instance, one part of a state may have a concentration of one particular type of industry, creating a need for specific job skills. A vocational education program should be geared to those needs.

Before the series of legislative mandates of the 1970s, students with handicaps were almost never included in regular vocational education classes. Vocational educators who were interested in working with these learners would do so in classes usually comprised only of these students. In 1976, the new vocational education regulations (PL 94-482) were written to coincide with the Education for All Handicapped Children Act (PL 94-142). With this legislation came increased funding to stimulate the development of new vocational program efforts for learners with handicaps.

The most recent amendments to earlier legislation reaffirm and strengthen the rights of individuals with handicaps to have access to high-quality vocational and transitional programs (Gaylord-Ross, Siegel, Park, & Wilson, 1988). For example, the extension of the Education for All Handicapped Children Act (PL 98-199) provides for federal contracts and grants that fund programs in training, research, and demonstration in the areas of secondary education and transitional services to students who are handicapped. This act reinforces the commitment to increase access for these individuals to vocational education.

The Carl D. Perkins Vocational Education Act, PL 98-524 (1984) amends the Vocational Education Act (PL 88-210) by expanding the opportunities of individuals in vocational education programs. These amendments stress the need for additional service and assessment provisions to include the assessment of vocational interests and abilities of individuals with handicapping conditions (Feichtner, 1988). These amendments also allow for setting aside funds (10%) to be used for meeting the needs of students with handicapping conditions who are enrolled in vocational education programs.

Interest has been stimulated among professionals for developing appropriate program options; however, the actual number of learners with handicaps participating in these programs appears to be minimal. Students included in vocational education classes are generally considered to have mild handicapping conditions. There appears to be a trend toward providing services to students with learning disabilities, with less attention given to those with mild mental handicaps and behavior disorders. With an increase in cooperative relationships developing between special and vocational educators and better quality support being provided by special educators, these students should receive more attention. In addition, the value of vocational educators as consultants for program development with students who have moderate handicaps will be realized.

Quantity Versus Quality

The effort of teachers to increase the number of learners with handicaps in vocational classes is a real concern. On the other hand, an increase in the *quantity* of program options available may not affect the general employability of these learners over the long haul. Consequently, practitioners should consider addressing problems that adversely affect the *quality* of program development. Identifying a common denominator among high-quality vocational education programs is the first task. This task requires teachers from special and vocational education to cooperatively plan and implement effective program options. Albright and Preskill (1981) discovered that of the sampled vocational educators who had students with handicaps in their classes, fewer than half were ever consulted during the IEP development process. Furthermore, once these students were enrolled in vocational education, only 13% of the instructors sampled had contact with other practitioners (e.g., special educators) who could provide instructional support.

A primary concern of special education teachers should be to develop effective working relationships with vocational educators. These working relationships go beyond cooperative agreements among special education, vocational education, and vocational rehabilitation specialists and the surface roles they define. Teachers can informally implement, on a daily basis, strategies that result in a reciprocal rather than a cooperative relationship. This way, each teacher in the team benefits from the skills of the other. Teacher training programs can help professionals gain these competencies by providing activities that include representations from special education, vocational education, and rehabilitation (Clark, 1984).

KEY CONCEPTS

■ Teachers should be concerned initially with three factors that may have an adverse effect on the ultimate employability of learners with handicaps:

1. Very little, if any, attention is being given to career-related or specific prevocational skills prior to secondary programs.
2. Only a small percentage of vocational educators are included in the IEP development process.
3. The percentage of vocationally related objectives on IEPs is, at best, minimal (Pyecha, 1979). These factors should provide the special and vocational educator team with a jumping-off point for developing a sound philosophical program base.

■ Career education and vocational education are separate program components. Vocational education is a part of career education, and it attempts to teach entry-level job skills in a variety of employment areas.

■ Career education is broader in scope than vocational education, including awareness and knowledge of many different employment areas and learning good work habits. This area has been expanded in recent years to include students' roles as family members, individuals, and citizens.

■ Legislative efforts have mandated increased enrollment of students with handicaps in vocational education classes.

■ An increase in the number of high-quality vocational education programs will require a closer working relationship between special and vocational educators.

■ ■ ■ ■

PROGRAMMING FOR TRANSITION

Some people mistakenly equate transition with programs emphasizing only school-to-work programs for secondary-school students. On the contrary, transition is a lifelong process that should be a part of a student's program from birth (Ianacone & Stoden, 1987). For example, preschool-age children with handicaps who are moving into kindergarten should have transition plans developed for them to help make the move easier, with little ground lost between programs. Such transition plans should assist individuals throughout life whenever major program changes are necessary.

A related issue is the question of whether or not transition programs should emphasize only employment-related issues and behaviors (Will, 1984). Halpern (1985) presented an excellent argument for the development of a transition model that would include all of an individual's life roles. He pointed out that, even with the best support for successful transition to work, individuals with handicaps could fail in society without support and instruction in the other areas of their lives (e.g., leisure time). In any case, there are a number of barriers to the successful transition of such individuals throughout life, and teachers must be aware of these in order to avoid some of the problems that may adversely affect their students.

Factors Affecting Successful Transition

Some teachers may have a misconception of what skills are important for individuals to be successfully employed in competitive jobs. Elementary school teachers, for example, may believe that what they teach has little effect on later employability. Similarly, high school teachers may see little relationship between their program and the programs available after their students leave school.

In reality, all skills that students learn from preschool programs on can affect their eventual success on the job and in other areas of their lives. Social skills, the ability to communicate, the ability to dress and groom appropriately, and the enjoyment of leisure time can affect whether or not individuals with handicaps will be successfully integrated into the workforce. This may be because teachers do not understand that a total curriculum, functional in nature, from preschool through adulthood, is directly linked to successful transition.

Over the years, a number of classic follow-up studies have been conducted that attempted to ascertain the correlates that can predict successful transition into the workforce. For example, a comprehensive study by Hasazi, Gordan, and Roe (1985) tracked 462 students across nine school districts in Vermont from 1979 to 1983. The findings supported a number of conclusions that can be made for students with mild handicapping conditions. Most important to this discussion are the findings that graduation from high school, participation in vocational education, and a work history involving part-time jobs were the best predictors of successful transition into the workforce. Similar results were found in studies in the state of Washington (Edgar, 1987) and in Florida (Hudson, Schwartz, Sealander, Campbell, & Hensel, 1988).

The variables that appear to affect job success and their relationship to the school curriculum should be of particular importance to teachers. The amount of time that students participate in tasks related to work, either in vocational education classes or in community worksites, seems to determine eventual success. This seems logical and straightforward, yet there does not appear to be a strong relationship between these functional activities and the actual content included in special education classes (Edgar, 1987). The first step may be to restructure the content of special education programs and target employment as a high-priority goal (Hasazi & Clark, 1988), emphasizing this goal not only in high school, but from entry into the school program.

Transition in Elementary School Programs

Transition occurs during two major time frames and has two major components: (1) transition from program to program, such as the elementary student moving on to a middle school placement and (2) transition from school to work. The first component is relatively basic and calls for a planned and cooperative effort between all concerned professionals to help their students move successfully between programs. For example, for the student moving to middle school, both teachers and administrators at each level should spend time committing a plan to paper that will assure that the student continues a program at the middle school that is consistent with and continues to build upon his or her elementary school program. This team planning would occur both within special education and between special and regular educators.

The second component of transition is more germane to this chapter. As previously stated, transition from school to work actually begins in the early school years. It requires a planned effort to develop activities that help students learn skills to assist them in meeting their work-related potential once they reach secondary and postsecondary programs.

For example, one of the barriers to successful employment of a number of students with handicapping conditions is their poor work attitude. This is a common complaint among special and vocational educators as well as rehabilitation specialists. For students who come from economically depressed areas, a so-called "welfare mentality" may be entrenched. Their only role models in relation to work behaviors may be relatives and friends who see few, if any, advantages to holding down a job. For these students, a high school program to teach good work habits may be too little and too late.

Building a positive work attitude should start in the elementary school and go beyond such surface activities as holding class discussions and reinforcing students for jobs around school. This author has worked with several school districts in setting up arrangements with local businesses that allow students to learn and try out some basic work skills in jobs in actual community environments. The goal is to expose the students in elementary school to at least one potential employment outcome representing each of the 15 occupational clusters per year for 5 years (75 potential jobs).

These activities provide teachers with the opportunity to pair students with good vocational role models in the community in an effort to offset the effects of poor models in their neighborhoods. They also allow teachers to teach positive work habits (e.g., staying on task) in situations that are real to students whose learning styles often require hands-on, concrete experiences. Finally, such activities allow teachers to incorporate instruction in academic skills into real-life activities. Of course, the thrust of the total curriculum is to teach independent living and leisure/recreation skills in community environments. These activities allow students to continue learning and practicing other skills, such as communicating with people who are not handicapped, that also impact on potential vocational success.

Transition in Middle School Programs

At middle school age, students with handicaps can begin to increase their time engaged in functional, community-based activities (Wehman, Moon, Everson, Wood, & Barcus, 1988). The number of potential employment outcomes in which the students can engage increases, allowing for more in-depth training in actual work-related tasks. Enrollment in middle school industrial arts and home economics programs can be helpful for increasing contact with nonhandicapped peers as well as teaching such skills as safety around tools, basic home maintenance, and family living skills.

Job-finding skills can be introduced and practiced at the middle school level, continuing into the high school program. Some students with MMH can begin a dialogue with rehabilitation specialists to learn about their services. Such early contact also helps these professionals begin to plan for services that will be needed when these learners reach high school. Also, teachers can begin instructing students on other methods of finding jobs, allowing the students to begin practicing interviewing skills in local business settings.

Transition in High School Programs

At the high school level, transition from school to work does not overshadow all other curriculum components, but it should become an equal partner. Transition to family life and successful enjoyment of leisure time require equal attention, particularly since the skills learned in these areas directly affect success on the job.

During the high school years the transition program for students with handicaps should involve three major areas: enrollment in vocational education programs, instruction in community-based environments, and paid part-time employment. Participation in vocational programs allows students to continue learning and practicing job-related skills in the presence of individuals who do not have handicaps. In addition, as students get more familiar with the advanced skills introduced in these programs they are actually learning job-entry-level skills required by business and industry.

The second component, community-based instruction in all other curriculum areas has been explained throughout this text and does not need to be repeated here. The third component, paid part-time employment, allows students to establish a work history while they continue practicing appropriate job-related behaviors. These programs are most effective when teachers or school employment specialists periodically spend time on the job with students in order to reteach or reinforce the target skills. Since students left to their own devices can learn inappropriate behaviors from inattention or from co-workers, frequent instructional visits and close contact with their supervisors can help them avoid potential problems (Test, Keul, & Grossi, 1988).

As students move closer to leaving school, teachers need to begin establishing a working relationship with professionals from any agency that might have a positive effect on their successful transition (McLoughlin, Garner, & Callahan; Okolo & Sitlington, 1988; Sileo, Rude, & Luckner, 1988). Szmanski and King (1989) have stressed the importance of including the rehabilitation counselor in the transition process during the early stages of program development for each student. In most instances the requirements for successful transition should be identified when the student enters high school, and the rehabilitation counselor's input can be helpful at this point in the program development process. This increased collaboration among schools and other community agencies helps ensure the student's transition to an appropriate postsecondary program (Neubert, Tilson, & Ianacone, 1989) and also establishes the responsibility for each component of the student's program (Bellamy, Rhodes, Mank, & Albin, 1988; Wehman, 1988).

An individualized transition plan (ITP) is developed by the school and the appropriate adult-service agencies in consultation with the parents and the student. The ITP might charge the school staff with the initial analysis, placement, and training of the student for a full-time, competitively employed job. The responsibility for monitoring and maintaining the student once he or she has been placed and trained might fall to an adult-service agency follow-up staff. All activities, products, dates of initiation and completion, and identified responsibilities of agencies and staff are delineated on the ITP. The ITP addresses all areas of the student's life including family and life issues, vocational placements, leisure and recreation activities, continuing education, transportation, and any other concerns that may impact on successful transition from school to community living (see Table 13.1).

CAREER AND VOCATIONAL PROGRAMS: THE IEP

Unlike some other areas of the curriculum, developing vocationally related programs requires, from the beginning, close contact among teachers from different disciplines. Before a community needs assessment can be implemented, a program philosophy for a given learner must be agreed upon by those involved in its design. Therefore, two additional considerations must be addressed prior to beginning steps one and two of the curriculum development process.

One question teachers should answer concerns when to begin the cooperative or team effort (Gill & Langone, 1982). In practice, vocational educators included in the IEP development process may not formally meet their special education counterparts until the meeting begins. Professionals who begin working together *prior* to the IEP staffing have a better chance to develop high-quality program options. Professionals attempting to design a program in a 1-hour meeting may develop inappropriate program goals such as "The student will participate in vocational home economics."

The special/vocational educator team must meet informally prior to the IEP staffing in order to complete tasks vital to effective program development. This relationship continues throughout the development and implementation stages. The emphasis, however, should be on the concept of laying the groundwork *before* a formal staffing is convened. The tasks targeted for completion by the dual educator team are activities relating to identifying program goals, including establishing a program philosophy, identifying potential employment outcomes, and assessing present levels of vocational performance.

TABLE 13.1 *Individualized Transition Plan*

Student's Name Nichols Jones   Date of Birth 5-26-72   Residence 145 Saxon Place   Phone 555-4588

Parent/Guardian Fred & Wilma Jones   Address 145 Saxon Place   Phone 555-4588

High School Clarke Shoals   Date of Graduation June 8   School Year 1991   Date of Plan 5-14-89

Participants John Langone, Special Education; Joan Smith, Vocational Education; Parents, Student, Amanda Barnes, Clarke Area Technical Institute; Tom Crisp, Department of Rehabilitative Services; Judy Ross, Clarke Parks and Recreation Department

Major Vocational Transition Components	Activities	Tasks to Complete	Date of Initiation	Date of Completion	Personnel and Agencies
Advanced Vocational Training	School staff will meet with the staff of Clarke Area Technical Institute and discuss the possibility of enrolling Nichols in the child care program at the Technical School after graduation from Clarke Shoals.	Completed report to include specific academic strengths and weaknesses that will impact on Nichols's success in the postsecondary program. This report will include strategies for helping Nichols overcome his academic weaknesses. The report will also include a description of the community-based work experience that Nichols will participate in during his program.	5-20-89	6-20-89	John Langone, Clarke Special Education Parents Student Amanda Barnes, CATI
Vocational Training	Nichols will be enrolled in the vocational education child care program during his senior year of high school (1990–91).	Completed plan outlining the services needed to assist Nichols in completing requirements for this class, to include a description of the peer tutoring program that will be used, study skills required (e.g., tape recording lectures and tape recorded chapters out of text).	Immediately	8-28-89	John Langone, Clarke Special Education Joan Smith, Clarke Vocational Education Parents Students
Vocational Training	School staff and representative from the Clarke Parks and Recreation Department will develop a plan for onsite training of Nichols in a variety of potential employment outcomes. Upon completion of initial training by the special education staff, Nichols will be employed by Parks Department during afterschool hours.	Task sequences of potential employment outcomes Assessment devices of work performance Work schedules	8-28-89	Open	John Langone, Clarke Special Education Judy Ross, Clarke Parks and Recreation Parents Student
Transportation	Special education staff will train Nichols to use the Clarke Bus Authority system. Also, staff will design a program to pass the written component of the driver license test. The road test component will be taught by Nichols's parents.	Task sequences for bus use Training materials for written component of driver's license test	8-28-89	6-8-90	John Langone, Clarke Special Education Parents Student Joseph Mano, Special Education Aide

385

Establishing a Program Philosophy

An important step for special and vocational educators is to establish a sound philosophical base on which to build the learner's program. The importance of identifying ecologically valid reasons for teaching skills to learners was presented in Chapter Four. That discussion is particularly important when considering both career and vocational education program goals.

For example, some professionals may feel the role of vocational education is to develop craftsmen, those who are proficient at high-skill-level employment (e.g., plumbers). This philosophy may create negative attitudes toward enrolling some learners in these programs since the prospect of their obtaining all the high-level skills necessary to be craftsmen is low. Similarly, if elementary-level special educators feel that their students are too young to participate in career education activities (e.g., awareness and prevocational skills), a major stumbling block is placed in the path of later program development.

At the initial level of program development, the following questions must be answered: Why should a given student be enrolled in x program? Why does a given student need to learn these targeted skills? To answer these questions, special and vocational educators must work together to identify what skills are most appropriate, based on three general stages: (1) occupational readiness, the development of those skills that apply to any occupation; (2) occupational preparation, the development of those skills that apply to specific occupations; and (3) occupational enhancement, the development of those skills that apply to an individual job site (Oetting & Miller, 1977). There are other theories of adjustment to employment; however, the Oetting and Miller steps are concise and easily applicable to learners with handicaps. These three guidelines assist teachers in matching the needs of the individual student to some component within stage one and possibly into components of either stage two or stage three, depending on the learner's strengths or weaknesses.

The first stage, occupational readiness, corresponds very closely to the principles of career education, including the curriculum areas of independent living skills, interpersonal skills, leisure/recreation skills, career awareness, career exploration, and prevocational skills including areas such as work attitudes. Any learner, regardless of age or problems, can be included at some stage of a life-centered career education program. When students' skills have reached a level of proficiency identified by both special and vocational educators, it is possible that the philosophical base of the program will stress either occupational preparation or enhancement.

At this point, it may be helpful for teachers to view how the expertise of each professional comes into play when developing a program philosophy for specific learners. When targeting career-education-related objectives, the primary responsibility for program implementation will be in the hands of the special educator. Yet, the technical knowledge of the vocational educator will be vital on a consulting basis. For example, the vocational educator can help to define the types of skills considered as readiness for certain vocational options and under what conditions the skills will be required, while the special educator has the skills required for assessment, instructional, and behavioral intervention with learners. Combining the skills and expertise of both educators will provide a broader base for developing the program philosophy.

KEY CONCEPTS

■ The areas of occupational readiness, preparation, and enhancement are closely related. For many learners they cannot be used as prerequisites for each other. For example, a learner who has not mastered all the readiness skills can often be placed in a vocational preparation option, learning the readiness skills in conjunction with the actual job skills.

■ Horner and Bellamy (1978) cited a case in point where learners having difficulty in obtaining certain prevocational skills could benefit from job training in community work sites.

■ ■ ■ ■

Steps One and Two: Conduct the Community Needs Assessment

One of the more important tasks during the pre-IEP meetings is to analyze the employment needs of the community and match those needs to the program goals of a specific student. A major barrier to identifying appropriate employment possibilities may be an overreliance on traditional jobs (Bellamy, Sheenan, Horner, & Boles, 1980). Most special education teachers may be unaware of the wide range of employment possibilities in their own communities or may not have a working knowledge of what skills are required to be successful at a particular job (Alper, 1981). At the same time, vocational educators may view some students as being unable to learn the skills necessary for becoming skilled laborers. Working as a team can provide insight in two ways: (1) the special educator can provide the knowledge and skills to demonstrate that learners can accomplish complex tasks previously thought impossible, and (2) the vocational educator can provide knowledge of potential employment outcomes as well as contacts in the community for becoming familiar with the skills involved in each job. (At this level the vocational rehabilitation specialist can also be a valuable asset to the team in a consulting capacity.)

A job search should not be limited in scope. Many alternatives should be discussed, including those similar to the ones developed by Brown and his associates (1979). For example, job sharing is one alternative in which two individuals who have moderate to severe problems and complementary disabilities work together to complete one job.

Identifying jobs that currently do not exist should also be a priority. Brown (1981) presented an example of identifying new jobs in a hospital setting. In this instance, the job of a hospital pharmacist was analyzed, and it was found that the pharmacist spent a disproportionate amount of the day performing routine tasks such as unpacking medical items—a decidedly inefficient job for a highly trained professional. Accordingly, an individual with multiple disabilities was trained to perform the unpacking task, eventually resulting in a part-time paid position for the student and increased efficiency for the pharmacist.

There are a number of other alternatives for employment opportunities that can be considered by the dual educator team. One viable alternative may be to identify nonpaid positions such as community volunteers. Volunteering can benefit learners in a number of ways. First, individuals who traditionally have spent their lives engaged in nonproductive activities (e.g., inappropriate social behaviors) can have the opportunity to contribute to fulfilling the needs of others. Second, volunteer positions allow for vocational training in a realistic community environment or for generalizing skills learned in a school program. Finally, a program of this nature helps demonstrate to other community members the skills and hidden potential of these students.

Potential employment outcomes can be gathered during the community needs assessment. The CNA can be designed to gather information on the types of jobs available and sample opinions of community members concerning their needs (see Table 13.2). In addition, parent preferences concerning their students' occupational roles and, whenever possible, the opinion of students in regard to their future should be gathered.

Job Analyses

The first task is to conduct a series of job analyses. These analyses involve becoming familiar with various workers and the daily routine their jobs entail. The person conducting the survey observes the workers, recording what they do. One quick measure of a community's employment needs can be obtained from state labor department statistics;

TABLE 13.2   *Community Needs Assessment Form Listing Potential Employment Outcomes* [1]

Potential Employment Outcome	Subenvironment	Employer
Backing crabs	Crab room	Barns Crab Factory
Custodian	Bathrooms Offices	Barns Crab Factory
Heading shrimp	Shrimp room	Barns Crab Factory
Housekeeping	Patient rooms Halls	Smith's Nursing Home
Housekeeping	Rooms Halls Lobby	Ye Olde Motel
Food wrapper Food server	Dietary	Community General Hospital
Line worker 1	Section A	Commercial Industries
Tire mounting & balance person		Tire World
Feedlot hand	Barn	Miller's Farm
Hostess/assistant manager		The Pizza Place

[1] Items from Glynn County, Georgia, School System

however, additional factors must be considered, such as new jobs or nontraditional employment not included in such reports. The goal is to identify what potential employment opportunities exist under each of the 15 occupational clusters. The potential opportunities are many, ranging from jobs that involve entry-level unskilled qualifications to professional requirements.

The next category of information concerns the background of the workers employed in the identified occupations. Information at this level should include the type of preparation a worker needs for a job and any changes in preparation requirements from employer to employer. Information such as the locations of employment possibilities, transportation requirements, and the type of supervision a worker receives on the job is also desirable (see Table 13.3).

Finally, a complete skill sequence of the job itself is an important requirement. This task is accomplished by recording each skill exhibited by the worker and classifying the skills according to whether they are motor or academic. An activity of this nature allows teachers to visualize how similar skills can be included in a school curriculum. This phase of the process helps identify portions of a person's job sequence that can be completed by a learner with handicaps or whether the job can be completed by two individuals working together (see Table 13.4).

Using Volunteers or Aides to Gather Data

Although the benefits of gathering community assessment information are apparent, the time required to complete the process can become a burden. Teachers have the option to gather this information using other resources. One possibility is to use volunteers such as high school students or members of service clubs. A cadre of community assessors can be trained with only a minimum investment of time. Aides and paraprofessionals can also be taught to identify potential employment outcomes and become adept at gathering information.

TABLE 13.3 *Sample Task Sequence of a Job Including Additional Information and Community Resources* [1]

Environment: Barns Crab Factory
Subenvironment: Crab room
Job: Crabber
Community Resource: Joe Barns (Supervisor)
Special Considerations: Must have transportation to and from work. No bus system available; carpool required.
No special equipment needed.

1. Obtain one crab.
2. Remove back and place in "back" basket.
3. Remove legs and place in "leg" basket.
4. Place body in "body" basket.
5. Repeat process.

---

[1] From Glynn County, Georgia, School System

In most cases, teachers need to become more familiar with what is available in the community because some firsthand observation is necessary for the individual providing direct instruction to students and coordinating the program design. Therefore, teachers and administrators should strive to arrange schedules that will free the dual educator team to explore these areas.

TABLE 13.4 *Sample Task Sequence of a Job Including Additional Information and Community Resources*[1]

Environment: Smith's Nursing Home
Subenvironment: Patient's room
Job: Housekeeping
Community Resource: Ms. Rebecca Melrose
Special Considerations: Change bed when patient is out of room.

1. Take fitted sheet from stack.
2. Unfold sheet on bed.
3. Grasp bottom of sheet with both hands. Pull bottom of sheet to bottom of mattress.
4. Place right corner of sheet over corner of mattress.
5. Place left corner of sheet over corner of mattress.
6. Place top right corner of sheet over corner of mattress.
7. Place left corner of sheet over corner of mattress.
8. Spread out wrinkles.
9. Take top sheet from bed.
10. Unfold on bed.
11. Spread over bed.
12. Grasp bottom of sheet hem and pull to bottom of mattress.
13. Center, straighten, and smooth sheet.
14. Grasp top of sheet to pull to top of mattress.
15. Center, straighten, and smooth sheet.
16. Tuck bottom of sheet under bottom of mattress.
17. Tuck bottom right corner of sheet under corner of bed.
18. Tuck bottom left corner of sheet under corner of bed.
19. Take spread from chair.
20. Unfold spread.
21. Grasp bottom of spread with both hands and pull to bottom.
22. Center and smooth spread.
23. Pull top of spread to top of bed and smooth.
24. Pull top of spread back to twice width of pillow.
25. Take pillow from chair.
26. Place pillow on bed lengthwise in front of body.
   Hold one edge of open pillowcase.
27. Grasp in each hand. Pull pillowcase over bottom of pillow about 4 inches.
28. Pull pillow up against chest, holding it with chin.
29. Shake pillow down into case.
30. Lay pillow at top of bed.
31. Fold spread over pillow.
32. Smooth out wrinkles.

---

[1] From Glynn County, Georgia, School System

IDEA FILE

Approaching employers in the community requires careful planning, combining the talents of many individuals within the school system. In an ongoing project with the Glynn County School System, Brunswick, Georgia, the author found that the best results were obtained when a team representing the school district approached employees. This team can include a variety of members, but generally is best comprised of an administrator and the teachers who will implement the program.

There are no set rules for the size of this team; however, between two and four members should be adequate. The administrator must have the power to commit the necessary resources (e.g., transportation) and be able to discuss issues such as liability. Teachers can provide information such as the skills the students can perform and the techniques that will be used to teach new skills.

Liability is the main issue that people such as school administrators in schools and community members will always raise. Again, there is no specific answer as to how to handle this issue. The approach taken in the Glynn County Schools and elsewhere in the nation is to treat liability for these programs as it is treated in other off-campus school programs such as away football games and cooperative vocational work-study programs. Essentially, the school district is always responsible for the students in off-campus activities occurring during the school day. The community-based instructional programs highlighted throughout this text are viewed as moving the classroom from the school building to the community, thus keeping the liability for the students in the hands of the school district.

In some instances, teachers may need to use their own vehicles to transport students to the site where instruction will occur. One way to handle this is that liability is first covered by the teachers' insurance and anything not covered by personal policies is handled by the school district's policy. A more realistic solution, one that is being used by a number of systems, is for teachers to learn the skills and receive their license to drive small school buses. Systems are finding that the cost of providing buses is minimal if they do not have the additional cost of a driver. These issues should be discussed and settled prior to approaching community employers.

■ ■ ■ ■

Advisory groups can also be a source of information. Most vocational education programs presently have community advisory groups comprised of local employers. Special educators can make use of these resources by attending these meetings with their vocational education counterparts.

For example, a CNA may identify at least 10 potential employment outcomes related to vocational agriculture in a rural location (Langone & Gill, 1984). For each of the 10 employment possibilities, information will have been gathered pertaining to specific job skills, training needs, pay plus benefits, transportation required, and any other considerations necessary to complete the job analysis. At this point the special educator can begin to relate the data to existing curriculum components or those that need to be developed. At the same time, the vocational educator learns more by discussing with the special education teacher the real capabilities of learners in relation to specific jobs. In either case, the goal at this level is to identify jobs and resources available in the community so that the eventual objectives included in the learner's IEP are valid and based on realistic options.

Step Three: Identify Potential Annual Goals

Identifying potential annual goals in vocational areas differs somewhat from identifying goals for academic skills. The annual goals teachers choose relate specifically to the potential employment outcomes or job training sites identified in each community. Figure 13.1 includes a list of potential job sites that may be appropriate for students. From this list and other sources generated by teachers in their own geographic area, annual goals such as the following can be written:

1. Completes all the tasks required of a dietary aide in a nursing home.
2. Completes all the tasks required of a stock person at a local pharmacy.

Many high school learners may participate in vocational education classes. Special educators can meet with vocational education teachers and outline some potential annual goals such as the following (Langone & Gill, 1984):

1. Reads major technical vocabulary words presented in the building trades course.
2. Mixes mortar.
3. Measures to the $1/2$ inch.
4. Completes all the tasks required of a feedlot hand in the agricultural education course.

Step Four: Translate Goals into Potential Short-Term Objectives

Translating goals into potential short-term objectives involves describing in measurable terms what the student is expected to accomplish. This process has been described previously, so only one example is presented here:

Outcome: The student will complete the five tasks comprising the job description of a feedlot hand.

1. Hospitals
2. Churches
3. Community colleges
4. Technical schools
5. Grocery stores
6. Department stores
7. Pharmacies
8. Banks
9. Various industries
10. Pizza restaurants
11. City, county, and state government buildings
12. Various small businesses
13. Nursing homes
14. Private homes of homebound elderly citizens
15. Private apartments

■ *FIGURE 13.1*
Examples of Nonpaid Work Training Sites in a Local Community

Context: At the agricultural class work site.

Criteria: For 5 consecutive days, based on instructor's criteria located on the skill sequences for each task.

Step Five: Assess Student Entry Behaviors

The strategy at the assessment level is to identify a student's current vocational performance. Information concerning the learner's strengths and weaknesses must be gathered prior to the initial IEP staffing. These data relate to vocational goals and objectives. One of the first tasks at the assessment level is for the special educator to demonstrate how target skills in a vocational sequence might be learned without academic proficiency. Here the information from the community analysis is useful because of its documentation of the extent to which academic skills are needed by specific workers. Jobs with high academic qualifications may be discounted if adaptations cannot be made.

Assessing the learner's present level of vocational performance relates specifically to the kinds of skills needed to achieve a target job. Preoccupation with specific academic skills only serves to exclude the majority of learners with handicaps from vocational program options. Instead, the primary goal of the dual educator team is to gather information about students' strengths and weaknesses in order to adapt methods and materials designed to teach designated vocational skills.

Standardized Tests

Standardized vocational assessment batteries generally assess both aptitude and interest. Aptitude tests are used to predict how a person will perform at certain jobs, often resulting in a prediction of success or failure. Vocational interest inventories are designed to sample an individual's preferences for various occupational options over others. There is a place in the overall scheme for standardized instruments such as these; however, at the stages of occupational readiness and preparation they may not provide the best information (Langone & Gill, 1986).

There are a number of reasons why standardized vocational measures may not be the most appropriate way to measure present level of vocational performance. They often include high reading requirements and a bias toward males and people from a middle socioeconomic background (Brolin, 1976; Payne & Patton, 1981). Equally important are the facts that learners with handicaps typically generalize skills poorly and that they have, at best, a limited experimental background.

Since some learners have a great deal of difficulty generalizing skills, the results of tests designed to predict success on a job site may not be useful. The dual educator team is concerned with a student's performance in a given vocational class; therefore, the assessment system should be developed and implemented in that setting.

Similarly, some learners have limited experiences due to the sheltered lives they lead. Results from interest inventories will probably provide only limited information. The learners may answer questions in relation to the way they view popular occupations, usually those seen on television. Questions about a job they have not come in contact with may not yield a response. Accordingly, when designing their assessment options the special and vocational educator team would attempt to arrange observations of the learners in different vocational settings, noting how they react to different jobs.

Techniques for Assessing Vocational Performances

Assessment activities that yield more useful information involve direct measurement of operationally defined prevocational behaviors, information from prior vocational or occupational experiences, results of exploration activities in and among various regular vocational programs, and vocational education performance samples.

First, a list of prevocational skills agreed upon by the dual educator team should be developed and converted into performance objectives. For example, the teachers may decide that a student needs to be able to follow directions, locate basic tools upon request, have the manual dexterity to assemble and disassemble threaded machine parts, and meet minimum requirements in proper dressing and grooming.

The technical expertise (knowledge concerning the specific skills) is supplied by the vocational teacher, whereas the assessment techniques (direct measurements of learner behaviors) are supplied by the special educator. Take, for example, the skills involved in locating basic tools. The vocational teacher can set up the situation by identifying the tools important for the student to be familiar with. At the same time, the special educator can design a simple frequency count tally system and charting mechanism to monitor student progress on the task. Although this is a simple example, it should provide the reader with an idea of how a cooperative assessment may work. Assessment activities can range from simple ones such as the example just given to complicated activities involving the use of machinery or a detailed skill sequence. In any case, the expertise of more than one teacher is needed before the data gathered will be useful.

Whenever possible, a good rule of thumb is to collect multiple samples of a learner's behavior. This can be accomplished by combining skills to form a sequence and then assessing the completion of the sequence by the student in the vocational education class, the special education program, and the community. For example, the dual educator team may decide that an important prevocational behavior is the ability of the students to compare his or her work to a preestablished criterion (quality control). In this case, work activities can be structured in both special and vocational classes as well as in community sites, with the teachers observing the extent to which the student can accomplish these skills under a variety of conditions.

Programs that have exposed students to potential employment outcomes beginning in elementary school will have considerable data collected on work attitudes, aptitudes, and employment preferences by the time the students are ready to leave the school program.

KEY CONCEPTS

■ The community needs assessment assists teachers in locating resources in the community that can take three forms: people to provide technical expertise, locations for job sites, and volunteers to help teach students.

- Special educators, vocational educators, and rehabilitation specialists work together to identify community resources.

- Locating traditional jobs is only one aspect of the CNA. Teachers must look for components of existing jobs that students can learn to perform. This approach, developed by Brown (1981), is similar to his concept of partial participation. Looking for the components of a job that tend to make a worker less than efficient and then teaching the learner to complete those components can be a good selling point when approaching employers, and a good opportunity to begin a training program.

- Volunteer positions are an excellent vehicle for teaching learners vocationally relevant skills.

- Community volunteers such as regular education high school students can be used to help gather CNA information.

- Attending meetings of advisory committees used by vocational educators is one method of meeting employers.

- Potential annual goals and short-term objectives are developed from the information gathered during the CNA.

- Standardized vocational assessment tests are designed to obtain survey-level data. They can provide a general assessment of a student's interests and aptitudes.

- These assessment devices may not provide the best information for learners with handicaps because of the limited experience these students have and the difficulty they have in generalizing skills.

- Task analysis of the target vocational objective may be the best vehicle for assessing the skills of these learners.

■ ■ ■ ■

PROGRAM IMPLEMENTATION

Identifying and Analyzing Short-Term Objectives

Once the initial groundwork has been completed by the dual educator team, a clear picture will have developed of the student's needs (including strengths and weaknesses) in relation to available employment options (either competitive or noncompetitive). At this stage the IEP committee will be ready to convene in order to study the information and make judgments concerning which areas to emphasize in setting objectives and what support services will be required. For example, the special and vocational educator may have identified a number of potential employment outcomes existing in vocational agriculture in their location. After delineating the crucial prevocational skills generic to these jobs and assessing the student's skill performance, the teachers may submit the following annual goal to the IEP committee for approval: "The student will be able to meet performance criteria for entry-level job skills in one or more of the potential employment options in vocational agriculture (listed from the community needs assessment)."

The committee has the option to choose, based on assessment data including parent and student preferences, which of the potential employment outcomes is applicable or advantageous for the learner to pursue. The annual goal might then read, "The student will meet the minimum criteria needed to perform the job of feedlot hand" (Langone & Gill, 1984).

The next phase of the IEP meeting involves developing or approving short-term objectives. These short-term or behavioral objectives are usually available if the dual educator team has analyzed the program goals. Continuing with the feedlot hand example, the student will have to learn such skills as tending cattle, feeding cattle, maintaining facilities and equipment, keeping necessary records, and producing feed. The IEP committee can take these skill areas and convert them into performance objectives.

Developing Instructional Strategies

The next task involves joining the efforts of both teachers to modify the curriculum. This means that the relationship between the teachers must continue beyond the IEP development stage and throughout the implementation stage. Therefore, the teachers should consider developing daily implementation plans that involve teaching specific skills in one class and enhancing the same skills in the other class.

In the feedlot hand example, the learner needs a number of skills to complete this job, including using mechanical equipment to fill feed troughs, providing the proper amount and quality of water, and mixing feeds with additives. Each of these subskills can be analyzed into smaller chunks of instruction. For example, mixing minerals entails locating the appropriate items, determining the correct amounts of each mineral, placing measured minerals in a central container, mixing the minerals, and placing the minerals in a location available to the cattle.

Using this system of parallel teaching (Langone & Gill, 1985), one teacher instructs the learner in areas complementing the skills concurrently being taught by the other teacher. Therefore, if the vocational educator is teaching a learner to mix minerals, the special educator will be teaching the same learner a complementary skill such as mixing various amounts of liquids. Similarly, if the special educator is teaching the use of a calculator for computation skills, the vocational educator can concurrently be teaching the application of calculators to problems within the target vocational sequence.

Special educators should be aware of some specific strategies or activities that may facilitate an effective reciprocal relationship with vocational educators. The following suggestions are designed to enhance the development of appropriate career and/or vocational programs for learners with mild to moderate handicaps:

1. Getting to know as many vocational educators in the school as possible is an important first step. Demonstrating a genuine interest in their programs, including the content of their courses and the types of employment possibilities for which they train their students, can facilitate this relationship.

2. Requesting release time during the school day to observe vocational programs provides a better indication of the types of behaviors learners will require in order to participate in those programs.

3. Asking vocational educators to visit special education classes to observe learners in that setting helps them get a better perspective of the skills of these students. This activity, if carefully structured by the special educator, can also serve to desensitize vocational teachers to various handicapping conditions. This opportunity allows the vocational educator to observe activities and suggest other curriculum exercises reflecting prevocational skills.

4. Requesting vocational educators' assistance in conducting an intensive community needs assessment results in better information. Their role can either be active (making community visits with the special educator) or more of a consulting nature (suggestions concerning whom to contact in the community). In any case, working with a number of vocational educators is necessary for gathering data in a number of occupational areas.

5. Mobilizing classroom aides and volunteers can help in conducting community job analyses. These individuals can obtain information about potential employment outcomes and help translate these skills for classroom instruction.

6. Being more aware of how workers conduct themselves in the performance of their jobs assists in developing curricula. For example, when eating in a restaurant or attending a movie, jotting down the kinds of skills employees in these types of establishments exhibit helps increase awareness.

7. Assisting vocational educators in modifying their curricula may first involve posing clarification questions. For instance, when developing behavioral objectives asking for specifics such as the type of equipment needed to complete a task and the conditions under which the student will perform certain skills is an example. Also, it is important to assist vocational educators in requesting the most appropriate information about a learner. A reading score on a diagnostic reading test may not be an appropriate criterion for success; the ability to read technical vocabulary may be a better indicator of success in a vocational program (Gardner & Kurtz, 1979).

8. Options for overcoming scheduling constraints have to be developed in order for the program to be successful. Career and/or vocational program options, to be effective, must be designed to meet the needs of the student. Therefore, innovative program options such as allowing students to spend time in more than one vocational program, using flexible schedules, will require careful planning.

9. Keeping close ties with vocational rehabilitation specialists will help teachers maintain awareness of technological breakthroughs that may be of benefit in vocational instruction and in finding much-needed resources.

10. Foss, Auty, and Irvin (1989) developed a system to teach employment-related interpersonal skills. The most successful classroom-based approach involved the use of videotapes combined with problem-solving activities in which the students viewed the scenarios and worked with the teachers to create solutions to the problems they viewed.

11. Mank and Horner (1988) reinforced the use of applied behavior analysis, including operant teaching procedures (see Chapters Five and Six), for teaching vocationally related skills.

12. Mithaug, Martin, and Agran (1987) developed an Adaptability Instructional Model (AIM) to teach students skills needed to perform a variety of work-related tasks in different settings. The AIM program includes four components: decision making, independent performance, self-evaluation, and adjustment. The thrust of this program is to teach students with handicaps problem-solving skills in work settings. The activities, which use cognitive behavior management strategies, prepare students to handle five generic problems that are related to most employment opportunities: (1) working on tasks employees may or may not enjoy; (2) earning money; (3) working on tasks that match employees' skills and abilities; (4) completing tasks quickly and accurately; and (5) completing tasks that must be done.

13. One of the more comprehensive secondary program models available, and one that is showing great potential, is the Community Vocational Training Program (CVTP), a

project associating San Francisco State University and the San Francisco Unified School District (Siegel, Greener, Prieur, Robert, & Gaylord-Ross, 1989). The program works with high school seniors with mild handicaps and strives to place them in permanent jobs and postsecondary schools.

The CVTP project includes strategies that have proved effective in other programs. For example, community-based instruction is emphasized. Instructional strategies including task analysis, prompt hierarchies, and direct instruction are used. Social skills training and peer counseling provide students with the skills they need to be more successful in the workplace. In particular, the CVTP project strongly emphasizes the need to analyze the interactions of all relevant individuals in a student's ecosystem (Chadsey-Rusch & Rusch, 1988). For example, more emphasis is placed on matching students who have attitude problems with successful employees who might act as good role models.

The CVTP project views the following as an instructional sequence of skills toward successful transition: (1) attendance, (2) social skills, (3) job-keeping skills, (4) job skills, and (5) job search. Readers are encouraged to seek out the in-depth article by Siegel and colleagues (1989) for a further description of the CVTP project.

IDEA FILE

Pairing learners with handicaps with elderly people who need help to survive in their own homes can be an excellent way to teach vocationally related and life skills while performing a needed service. A program in the Glynn County Schools, Brunswick, Georgia, was developed through the efforts of the author, school district personnel, and eight social service agencies identifying homebound elderly citizens who desperately need assistance with tasks such as yard and housework, cooking simple meals, home maintenance, and paying bills. Teachers from the school district take small teams of learners to the homes of these individuals, teach them the identified tasks, and maintain the tasks during the school year.

A program of this nature has many benefits such as the following:

1. Students are learning meaningful skills that they will eventually need to become as independent as possible within the community.

2. Generalization of skills is facilitated because students are coming in contact with a variety of materials and equipment in many settings (Langone & Westling, 1979).

3. Many related skills can be taught in conjunction with the home management skills. For example, students can also be taught community mobility and functional academic skills while they participate in the program.

4. Community-valid skills are being taught in realistic environments.

5. Public relations for such an effort can open other doors in the community, potentially resulting in additional work sites in business and industry.

6. Students are also learning to help others less fortunate than themselves and to improve their social skills.

Beyond this program, additional efforts are beginning in nursing homes and the local hospital.

■ ■ ■ ■

THE ROLE OF VOCATIONAL REHABILITATION SPECIALISTS

Vocational rehabilitation specialists play an active part in developing and implementing prevocational or vocational program options for learners with mild to moderate handicaps. Vocational rehabilitation professionals can provide special educators with vital consulting assistance in a number of areas such as identifying potential employment outcomes, targeting good work habits and other prevocational skills, locating instructional sites and jobs, becoming familiar with technological advances and adaptive equipment, and developing valid vocationally related activities. Vocational rehabilitation personnel assist special educators by keeping vocational programs in close touch with daily community activities.

Szmanski & King (1989) identified the following nine functions of rehabilitation counselors that can be valuable for use during the transition process:

a. career and psychosocial counseling

b. consultation with special and vocational education teachers, school counselors, and other education professionals regarding the vocational implications of disability and potential educational adaptations

c. coordination of school, family, and community efforts in career planning and preparation

d. job placement, job analysis, job modification and restructuring, and placement follow-up

e. work adjustment counseling

f. coordination of job support services (e.g., job coaches, transportation, personal care attendants) during transition

g. referral to and coordination with adult service agencies

h. specialized planning and links with postsecondary programs and support services for students with disabilities

i. development of individual transition plans (pp. 4 & 5)

Vocational rehabilitation specialists should be consulted in the areas mentioned here before the program has been developed and during the implementation stages.

THE STATE OF THE ART: PROGRAMS FOR STUDENTS WITH MODERATE HANDICAPS

Initially, one of the most formidable barriers to placing individuals with moderate handicaps in community settings is ironically a placement option originally designed to assist in that very task (McLoughlin et al., 1987).

Sheltered workshops were designed to provide these people with a setting where they could be evaluated and instructed in work adjustment as well as vocational skills (Flexer & Martin, 1978). They were designed to provide remunerative work while preparing the client for the eventual transfer to a community job site. Another placement option, called *work activity centers*, is designed for clients with more severe handicaps and provides activities such as leisure/recreation skills and prevocational activities that do not necessarily result in remuneration (Flexer & Martin, 1978).

Unfortunately, in many cases sheltered workshops and work activity centers have become a terminal placement. Because these options have not often proved to be monetarily efficient operations, they provide substandard wages for the workers (Pomerantz & Marholin, 1977). In the final analysis, sheltered work sites may serve mainly to occupy a person's time, often with contracts and activities that have little relationship to realistic vocational employment options. In fact, of the contracts obtained by workshops in a majority of instances, the work is slow-moving and extremely repetitive (Greenleigh Associates, 1975).

Some workshops are run like a business, with the goal of becoming a profitmaking endeavor. These workshops have been successful in these pursuits by using the expertise of volunteer businessmen and women and industrial experts (Bellamy, Inman, & Horner, 1977). There are social problems (e.g., high unemployment rates) that can impede progress in this area. Nevertheless, workshop personnel can overcome these constraints, looking toward the technological advances and investing in equipment to participate in moneymaking products (Flexer & Martin, 1978).

The concept of "sheltered," not the workshops themselves, should be abandoned. Clients can benefit most from programs that allow some instruction in the natural environment. Programs such as workstations in industry should be implemented on a broader scale. Programs such as these allow for the client to be taught on the actual work site in an industrial placement so that instead of the contract being brought to the client, the client is brought to the contract. In areas where industry is not prevalent, other community instruction sites can be found in retail business, private homes, and volunteer placements. For most clients, parts of the day should be spent away from the workshop or activity center, learning skills and generalizing them to the natural environment.

The Supported Work Model

Teaching learners with moderate handicaps vocational skills in realistic community placements appears to be a highly effective and cost-beneficial approach (Hill & Wehman, 1983; Wehman et al., 1982). The approach that appears to provide the most success is called the *supported work model* (Kraus & MacEachron, 1982). This model actually contains all the approaches discussed in this chapter, including all the aspects of the community needs assessment.

In many supported work model programs, teachers accompany small groups of learners to the job sites and teach the target skills in the community setting. Less attention is given to students' obtaining all prevocational skills prior to moving into the community. Instead, teachers take the responsibility for teaching the prevocational and vocational skills simultaneously (Bellamy et al., 1988; Wehman et al., 1988).

For example, during the CNA four job training sites (nonpaid or volunteer employment) might have been identified and secured at the local hospital. The teacher might take a group of four students to the hospital 3 days a week for 2 hours each day, teaching them the skills required to complete those jobs. As these students gradually learn the necessary skills required of their jobs, the teacher can gradually fade her supervision, instructing hospital personnel in how to monitor the students' behaviors.

Supported work options have three main advantages over simulated vocational instruction and sheltered workshops. First, students are taught in community environments using realistic materials where professionals project that they will ultimately work. Second, employers and the community at large have the opportunity to come in contact with these learners and realize their potential as productive citizens. This factor may result in competitive employment opportunities becoming available for these students.

Third, inappropriate social and adaptive behaviors are often controlled more effectively in natural environments (Brown, 1981). More naturally reinforcing contingencies exist in the community, and careful structuring of the program allows teachers to manipulate these contingencies to manage behavior. Also, more appropriate social models are available in the community, whereas one of the major disadvantages of sheltered workshops is the abundance of inappropriate behaviors individuals have to imitate.

Strategies for Instruction

Vocational options for learners with moderate handicaps can improve if teachers apply proven techniques for adequately instructing these learners in occupational skills. These individuals can learn complex vocationally related tasks, a fact proved in a number of research studies (e.g., Bellamy, Peterson, & Close, 1975); Crosson, 1969; Gold, 1972 and 1976). These programs appear to be successful because the strategies employed in teaching complex vocationally related tasks revolve around operant procedures and direct measurement techniques.

IDEA FILE

The three resources listed below are a sample of the many resources available to teachers:

Methods of vocational preparation (Brolin, 1982)

Methods for vocational preparation (Lynch, Kiernan, & Stark, 1982)

Methods for vocational preparation (Weisgerber, Dahl, & Appleby, 1981)

■ ■ ■ ■

Techniques for Developing Vocational Programs

Behavioral principles underlying techniques such as the use of discriminative stimuli (S^D), chaining, and fading were discussed in Chapter Six. Instructional procedures such as task analysis, charting of learner behavior, and programming for generalization have also been discussed in relation to teaching other curricular areas. The trick is to match these instructional strategies and techniques with appropriate vocational content and materials (Rusch & Mithaug, 1980; Wehman, 1980).

Using the procedures of curriculum design, assessment, and instructional strategies previously discussed, teachers should be able to match appropriate techniques to the needs of any given learner. At the same time, however, there are certain unique situations that arise when developing vocationally related programs. The following are suggestions for developing program options for such situations. Some were presented earlier in this chapter; however they are important enough to highlight again. The other suggestions are products of research efforts and classroom-based ideas that may assist teachers in dealing with some basic concerns.

1. Teachers should explore the total range of vocationally related services in the areas where students reside. Visiting sheltered workshops, work activity centers, and rehabilitation evaluation services will provide a clear picture of what lies ahead for the learner while allowing the teacher to establish a network with other professionals.

2. It is important to work closely with professionals from local workshops and rehabilitation agencies. The relationship, once established, may allow teachers to provide input into the daily operation of these program options.

3. A major goal is to assist parents in becoming aware of the many options available to their children in the community. Some parents will, when given alternatives, push for options that are more appropriate than the traditional ones available.

4. Keeping in close contact with community resources is a key task. Gold and Pomerantz (1978) suggested that professionals must develop a close working relationship with business and industry. They also suggested that when approaching members of the business community teachers should use an approach other than the traditional "hire the handicapped because they need our help." Rather, these people should be approached in terms of profit-making or efficiency, pointing out the excellent safety and production record of individuals with handicaps. They should also be made to understand that a capable support system will be available to teach and maintain the learner until the initial strategies can be faded and natural contingencies can take over.

5. Effective techniques used to teach these individuals can also be used to increase productivity of the average worker. This approach can sometimes be used as a selling point for developing work stations in industry programs.

6. Students can learn a large number of vocationally related skills during their school years. Therefore, teachers of young as well as older students should participate in designing vocationally related activities.

7. Prevocational skills are valuable, but if a given learner has not attained certain of these skills they can be eliminated from a vocational instruction program (Horner & Bellamy, 1978). In other words, a learner who may not have mastered all potential prevocational skills and who is old enough to move toward community participation should be taught complex vocational tasks. In many cases, prevocational skills can be taught simultaneously with the vocational preparation, allowing the student to learn both sets of skills in the natural setting.

8. Another important task for the teacher is to work closely with vocational specialists to become more familiar with potential employment outcomes, viable community instruction sites, new and nontraditional jobs, and jobs in which learners can work together to complete skill sequences.

9. The procedures of instructional analysis should be applied to break down complex vocational skills into teachable components (Gold & Pomerantz, 1978; Horner & Bellamy, 1978).

10. Programming for generalization is especially important when teaching prevocational and vocational skills (Langone & Westling, 1979). The more learned skills can be practiced across different reinforcing conditions the better the chance that skill sequences will be usable to the learner.

11. Throughout the program development process, parents should be an active part of the team effort, and their perceptions should be taken into account when activities are developed (Hanline & Halvorsen, 1989).

12. It is important to use realistic materials. Simulation activities are used only as long as necessary and are faded as quickly as possible. For example, the safe use of basic tools may be a more desirable goal than learning to cut with scissors.

13. It is necessary to define the vocationally related behaviors in measurable terms and maintain an ongoing monitoring system. Used in conjunction with a task analysis, monitoring and charting can provide teachers with a thorough assessment system for these learners. For example, Bates, Renzaglia, and Clees (1980) used a changing criterion design to monitor the effect of a self-administered reinforcement system (paying oneself after completion of a prespecified task) had on a student's work behavior.

14. Scheduling teacher time for community instruction should be a joint exercise including all special education teachers in a school. For example, if one teacher is out with five members of his class for part of the day, another teacher could supervise the aide teaching the remainder of his class.

15. High school students, community volunteers, and in some cases employees already at the site can assist at the work site as peer tutors.

16. Crouch, Rusch, and Karlin (1984) provided evidence that co-worker prompts can be an effective teaching strategy to improve vocational skills. In their study co-workers were taught to use verbal cues designed to initiate a set of skills previously learned by the students.

17. Picture cues have proved to be an effective strategy for teaching vocational skills. For example, Fisher (1984) was able to teach learners to assemble complex products using assembly drawings as a guide. Wacker and Berg (1983) got similar results using picture prompts.

18. Some vocational and social skills related to work settings can first be taught in game format and later generalized to actual work sites (Foxx, McMorrow, & Mennemeier, 1984).

19. Food services have become popular in and competitive work sites for learners with handicaps (Brickey & Campbell, 1981). For example, Schutz, Jostes, Rusch, and Lamson (1980) used contingent preinstruction (using verbal cues to remind trainees what tasks they forgot to complete or did not complete correctly) to prepare students for competitive employment in cafeterias.

20. Clarke, Greenwood, Abramovitz, and Bellamy (1980) used summer jobs to teach adolescents advanced vocationally related skills. Sowers, Rusch, Connis, and Cummings (1980) improved the time management skills of individuals by using a system of verbal and picture cues.

IDEA FILE

Turning the community into the classroom involves establishing a number of sites in the community where students go with their teachers to learn, practice, and generalize vocationally related academic and social skills. The sites where these training activities take place will vary widely, ranging from locations in business and industry to hospitals and nursing homes and the private homes of some homebound elderly individuals.

Because of the extensiveness of this training and the number of sites needed, many activities will involve nonpaid or volunteer work by the students. In many instances, nonpaid employment makes sense and can provide these learners valuable opportunities for training. Unfortunately, if not carefully monitored and planned, nonpaid employment situations can cause considerable legal problems for a school district.

For example, an article in the May 13, 1989, issue of *The Atlanta Journal and Constitution* had the following headline: "Moms Cite 'Child Slavery' in Lawsuit Against School." Apparently, two mothers in Detroit are suing the school system for using their children to clean the homes of teachers and principals as part of a job training program that included a housekeeping component.

Situations such as this one are unfortunate and can be avoided if the program is developed carefully, with parent input from the beginning, and with frequent feedback to parents. Above all, potential problems should be eliminated before they occur. One suggestion is for the class to be paid for some work done for private citizens, with the money being used for other community-based activities (e.g., restaurant skills). Another suggestion is to develop instructional sites where higher-order skills are taught instead of tasks typically associated with people who are disabled (e.g., janitorial tasks). In general, there is no substitute for careful planning and close contact between the home and the school through telephone calls, notes on progress, and upcoming schedules of activities.

In 1975, *The Vocational Evaluation and Work Adjustment Association Final Report* outlined six general criteria for job site vocational evaluation purposes. With the exception of number six, these areas also can be used as guidelines for setting up nonpaid work sites.

1. The client is not necessarily paid.
2. Placement on the job is primarily for the client's benefit.
3. The placement will not necessarily result in employment in that job.
4. The employer may not experience any immediate gain.
5. The client does not displace another worker or fill a vacant worker slot.
6. The client's performance is supervised and evaluated by the employer or evaluation staff. (pp. 52–53)

■ ■ ■ ■

POSTSECONDARY OPPORTUNITIES

Increased opportunities for inclusion into postsecondary programs that provide continuing services to individuals with handicaps are becoming more prevalent. Both 2- and 4-year colleges, as well as universities, are increasing their services to individuals with learning disabilities. Noncollegiate programs provided in community colleges and vocational/technical schools are accepting students with handicaps and providing long-term services to help them learn advanced skills in specific vocational clusters.

These programs are similar to those found in secondary schools and include combinations of classroom and laboratory experiences as well as work experience in the community. The major difference between the two programs is the depth of the curriculum they offer. Most secondary vocational programs are designed to provide entry-level skills into the workforce. Postsecondary programs are designed to provide a more advanced and in-depth curriculum. These programs would be ideal for learners with mild handicaps who wish to expand their vocational options. Students graduating from high school can bene-fit from postsecondary services and should have representatives from these programs par-ticipating in their individualized transition plan (ITP) meeting.

Transition Planning

As discussed earlier in this chapter, all students with handicaps who will be leaving school in 3 to 5 years should have an ITP developed for them. This plan specifies the services, activities, and resources that will be needed to increase the probability of successful transi-tion into the community. The development of these plans should involve special and vocational educators, parents, the students themselves, adult service providers deemed important to the transition process, and possibly an employer, if a specific job has been targeted at that time.

An ITP should include all services and activities that will help an individual make a successful transition into all facets of community life. Therefore, activities and services relating to leisure and recreation activities, independent living skills, medical and/or psychological services, as well as vocational needs, would all be included as sections on the ITP. For the purposes of this chapter, Table 13.1 is an example of a vocational compo-nent of the ITP.

KEY CONCEPTS

- The relationship between special and vocational educators goes beyond IEP development into a parallel teaching approach. Teachers teach the same student similar skills under dif-ferent conditions.
- Curriculum modification is an important part of developing vocational programs. The role of the special educator is to help the vocational education teacher identify the points in the curriculum that are most important for the student.
- Identification of nontraditional employment options such as job sharing and parts of jobs that a learner can accomplish is an important component of program development.
- Sheltered workshops are not necessarily the best placement options.
- The supported work model allows learners to participate in paid and nonpaid employment based in community work sites.
- Behavioral approaches including task analysis, arranging antecedent events, controlling consequences, and applying proven principles of behavior have been most effective in teaching work skills.

■ ■ ■ ■

CHAPTER FOURTEEN

DAILY PLANNING AND OTHER ISSUES FOR INSTRUCTION

■ Up to this point, the information presented in this text has emphasized the need to teach, in community environments, the skills that students with mild to moderate handicaps need in order to become more independent. Although the text emphasizes community-based instruction, skill instruction must also be translated into classroom-based activities. Regardless of whether teachers are designing community-based or classroom-based activities, systematic planning and implementation are crucial. Teachers also need to instruct students in methods for improving their study and general learning skills so that they can take full advantage of lifelong learning programs and receive the greatest benefit possible from current programs.

This chapter provides information to help teachers improve their daily planning strategies and presents some important strategies for helping students improve their study skills and general learning behaviors.

DAILY PLANNING: THE INDIVIDUAL IMPLEMENTATION PLAN (IIP)

An IEP is both an ending and a beginning. It is the ending of a process that included many people analyzing the environment and assessing a student's present level of performance and culminated in the development of a set of curriculum goals and objectives based on that student's needs. It is a beginning in the sense of its relationship to the daily teaching strategies that educators use (see Figure 14.1).

Some teachers mistakenly assume that the IEP is the plan from which they must teach. IEPs, by definition, are management plans that cover the entire year. Thus, an IEP would be too general to teach from on a daily basis. The IEP development ends with the committee, and its implementation lies in the hands of the teachers involved with the student. The key word here is *translation* (see Chapter Four)—the ability of the teacher to translate the short-term objectives of the IEP to smaller, more workable components called *instructional objectives*.

Accomplishing the move from IEP objectives to daily instructional objectives requires task analysis. The arrow between steps 6 and 7 of Figure 14.1 represents the task analysis (translation) of the IEP's short-term objectives to the instructional objectives of the individual implementation plan (IIP). The first activity is to analyze and sequence the skills needed by a student to successfully complete the short-term objective. Next, the teacher has the option to convert the steps of the task analysis into objectives that conform to the outcome, context, and criterion format. Some skill areas are complex and require the structure of a written objective (e.g., academic skills such as decoding); other skills areas are fairly straightforward and may not require that an objective be written in standard form.

Establishing Instructional Objectives

The same process as described in Chapter Four is used for task analyzing short-term objectives. It includes the following steps:

1. Use a team to analyze complex tasks.
2. Consult other task sequences if available.

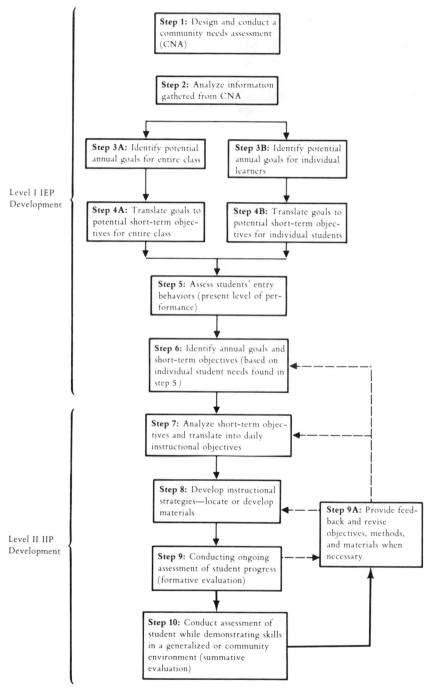

■ FIGURE 14.1
A Systems Approach for Designing Special Education Curricula

3. Analyze the task in relation to existing materials and environment.

4. Match the skill sequence to individual learner needs.

5. Order skills in relation to the next step in the sequence.

6. Decide whether to use a forward or backward chaining procedure if appropriate.

7. Write subskills (steps on task analysis) in measurable form.

In an example used in Chapter Four involving the student's use of diphthongs, the short-term objective was as follows:

Outcome: The student will recognize and pronounce the sounds *ou, ow, oi, oy, aw, ew.*

Context: 30 whole words on the second- and third-grade levels.

Criterion: Between 80% and 90% accuracy.

In this instance, the task analysis is basically complete because the subskills are identified:

1. Pronounce the sound *ou* in context.

2. Pronounce the sound *ow* in context.

3. Pronounce the sound *oi* in context.

4. Pronounce the sound *oy* in context.

5. Pronounce the sound *aw* in context.

6. Pronounce the sound *ew* in context.

At this stage, the teacher can decide whether to convert the skills into the outcome-context-criterion format. No rule of thumb exists to determine whether or not such a conversion is necessary; however, in a general sense the more systematic the objective the more systematic the instruction. Academic skills generally require a systematic approach, and teachers should consider writing objectives that are as concise as possible. Take, for example, the second skill in the example sequence. In its present form, a teacher might forget that there are alternate uses of the vowel diphthong *ow.* A systematic instructional objective for this skill might be as follows:

Outcome: The student will recognize and pronounce *ow* when found in such words as *blow,* and *mow.* The student will also recognize and pronounce *ow* when found in words such as *plow* and *how.*

Context: Five words for each form.

Criterion: 100% for each set.

What remains is to write the instructional objectives for the remaining five skill areas.

Teachers should keep two important considerations in mind when writing objectives. First, in most cases (especially with academic skills), objectives will need only minor modifications to meet individual student needs. Therefore, writing objectives need not be a laborious or never-ending task. With the advent of microcomputers, teachers can routinely store their objectives for instant retrieval when needed.

Second, a well-written objective will provide the teacher with more than just a management statement (Bepko, 1981). It also provides the basis for assessment questions

(Tymitz-Wolf, 1982). For example, in both the instructional and short-term objectives illustrated in the example, the assessment components are clearly delineated (e.g., 30 whole words with 80% to 90% accuracy and five words each form with 100% accuracy).

IDEA FILE

Microcomputers may be the single greatest tool that educators have for teaching students with handicaps. If teachers do not become computer literate over the next 10 years, they may be left behind in the field (Goldenberg, Russel, & Carter, 1984). Throughout this text, examples have been provided of how microcomputers can assist instruction in most curriculum areas. At this point, teachers should consider the use of microcomputers as management tools. As objectives are written, they can be stored on floppy disks and shared among teachers. To do this, a standard coding system must be used. One example of a coding system uses numbers in sequence by assigning a whole number to a goal, the whole number plus a decimal to short-term objectives related to the goal, and so on down to instructional objectives (see Table 14.1). For example:

TABLE 14.1   *Examples of Coded Objectives*

Arithmetic Example

1.0	Annual Goal:	The student will be able to perform the basic operations in arithmetic.
1.1	Short-Term Objective:	*Outcome:* The student will correctly compute addition problems at all levels up to carrying in alternate places.
		Context: 35 problems—written worksheet.
		Criterion: 80%–90%.
1.11	Instructional Objective:	*Outcome:* Add with basic facts 1–10.
1.12	Instructional Objective:	*Outcome:* Add with no carrying (up to two columns).
1.13	Instructional Objective:	*Outcome:* Add by carrying from the 1's place.
1.14	Instructional Objective:	*Outcome:* Add by carrying from the 10's place.
1.15	Instructional Objective:	*Outcome:* Add by carrying from consecutive places.
1.16	Instructional Objective:	*Outcome:* Add by carrying from alternate places.
2.1	Short-Term Objective:	Repeat for subtraction.
3.1	Short-Term Objective:	Repeat for multiplication.
4.1	Short-Term Objective:	Repeat for division.

Reading Example

1.0	Annual Goal:	The student will read orally from a second-grade passage, correctly pronouncing words that include consonants.
1.4	Short-Term Objective:	*Outcome:* Consonant blends (*pl, sm, cr, fr, tr, gr, pr, bl, sl, st, sw, cl, dr, br, sp*).
		Context: When presented in a word (pronounce whole word).
		Criterion: 50 words—90%–100%.
1.41	Instructional Objective:	*Outcome:* *br, cr, dr, fr, tr, gr.*
1.42	Instructional Objective:	*Outcome:* *bl, cl, fl, pl, sl.*
1.43	Instructional Objective:	*Outcome:* *sm, st, sw.*

1.0   Goal

1.1   Short-term objectives (STOs) related to the goal
1.2
1.3
1.4
1.11   Instructional objectives (Os) related to STO 1.1
1.12
1.13
1.21   IOs related to STO 1.2
1.22
1.23
1.24
1.31   IOs related to STO 1.3
1.32
1.41   IOs related to STO 1.4
1.42
1.43
1.44
1.45

■ ■ ■ ■

More commercially produced IEP software hits the market daily. These software packages may be of use to teachers and administrators for managing an IEP data base. Following is a representative sample of companies that market these systems:

Ex-Ed Computer System
71-11 112th Street
Forest Hills, NY 11375

Teaching Pathways
121 East 2nd Avenue
Amarillo, TX 79101

Learning Tools
686 Massachusetts Avenue
Cambridge, MA 02139

Turnkey Systems
256 North Washington Street
Falls Church, VA 22046-45

Screening and Tracking Corp. of America
90 Kent Street
Brookline, MA 02146

The second example used in Chapter Four, concerning Steve's leisure and recreation skills, may be useful in illustrating the translation of IEP objectives to daily instructional objectives. The short-term objective that may have been included on Steve's IEP was:

6.1 *Outcome:* Student will select a talking book tape, place tape in recorder, and turn on recorder.

   Context: Selection from 10 talking books.

   Criterion: Selection (not critical). Correct manipulation of tape and recorder.

One possible task analysis for this short-term objective could include the following skill sequence:

6.11 Requests time at listening center.

6.12 Locates and selects desired tape.

6.13 Removes tape from tape rack.

6.14 Removes cartridge from container.

6.15 Pushes eject button on recorder.

6.16 Places cartridge correctly in recorder.

6.17 Closes dust cover.

6.18 Places earphones on head.

6.19 Pushes play button.

6.20 Adjusts volume and tone as needed.

6.21 Demonstrates use of forward and reverse functions.

6.22 Removes tape and returns to rack (reverse previous steps).

6.23 Steps 1–12 generalized to home environment.

The example illustrates an instance in which a teacher may not need to convert the steps of a task analysis into an outcome-context-criterion format. In its present form, the skill sequence represents an example of a procedural task analysis in which each step is essentially independent of the others and would be taught using a chaining procedure. The teacher generally would expose the student to all the steps during an instructional trial. The subskills are written in such a way that the teacher can record whether or not the subskill was completed by the student. In this case, the subskills are probably precise enough to allow for an accurate appraisal of learner progress. Psychomotor skills (e.g., self-care and some vocational tasks) *generally* can be taught from the task analysis without converting each step to an instructional objective.

Developing Educational Interventions

Educational interventions include a number of components (e.g., strategies for changing behaviors, educational materials, assessment strategies) that, when linked together, increase the probability that the student will learn the skills targeted for instruction. Developing these interventions, more commonly known as *lesson plans,* must be systematic if the students they are designed for are to have a chance to learn the targeted skills (Mercer & Mercer, 1989). Teachers at times confuse a well-designed plan with the plan book that is commonly used in public schools (see Figure 14.2). A lesson plan book would be more appropriately called a lesson plan *schedule* book because the function it serves is to cue the teacher concerning the daily schedule, the location of the students, and the types of activities assigned to the learners. This scheduling procedure is important because it is a quick reference for orderly transitions between activities and events. Lesson plan scheduling should *not,* however, be confused with the more detailed and systematic process of lesson plan or instructional intervention development.

Developing effective instructional strategies (step 8, Figure 14.1) involves a concise, step-by-step process culminating in any one of several formats. Teachers can choose the design that best fits their needs. The necessary components of an implementation plan, however, are basic, including areas that teachers must address if the plan is to work. These plans can be designed for either group or individual instruction because their components will be the same. Group instruction plans may include modifications of materials and teaching techniques to meet a particular individual's needs.

An effective instructional or lesson plan should include, at least, the following components:

1. Demographic information.

2. Annual goal, short-term objective, and instructional objectives.

3. Preinstructional activities.

WEEK OF: 3/21–3/25	MONDAY	TUESDAY	WEDNESDAY	THURSDAY	FRIDAY
Period 1	Reading Group 1 Jim Brian } Workbook Polly } Pgs. 1–3 Kelly } Oral Sam } Reading	Reading Group 1 Jim } Oral Brian } Reading and Polly } Flash Cards Kelly } Workbook Sam } Pgs. 8–9	Reading Group 1 Entire } Reading Group } Comprehen. Test	Reading Group 1 Entire } Read Story Group } Pg. 5– Basal Ans. Ques. 1–10	Reading Group 1 Jim } Flashcards Sam } Brian } Practice w/ Language Master Polly } Oral Kelly } Reading
Period 2	Math Group 1 Entire } Unit Group } Test	Math Group 1 Fractions } Pg. 81 Practice } (Text) # 1–15 Entire Group	Math Group 1 Howie } Seatwork Jerry } Fractions Sheet Brian } Instruct Polly } Add. Jim } Fractions	Math Group 1 Brian } Workbook Polly } Pg. 30 Jim } Howie } Instruct Jerry } Using Fraction Cards	Math Group 1 Entire } Cooking Group } Exercise Fractions in Cooking
Period 3	Reading Group 2 Jeff } Basal Karen } Reader Cindy } Story II Kevin }	Reading Group 2 Entire } Workbook Group } Pgs. 6–8 Individual Testing	Reading Group 2 Jeff } Sight Karen } Vocabulary Cindy } Same as Kevin } Tuesday	Reading Group 2 Entire } Story 12 Group } Oral Comprehen. Questions	Reading Group 2 Entire } Story 13 Group } Workbook Pg. 10
Period 4	Lunch	Lunch	Lunch	Lunch	Lunch
Period 5	P.E. Planning Period	Math Group 2 Play Construction of Shapes Games	P.E. Planning Period	Math Group 2 Entire } Pgs. 50–52 Group } Workbook	P.E. Planning Period
	Math Group 2 Intro. to Basic } Entire Geometry } Group	Art Planning Period	Math Group 2 Have Students Locate and Label Shapes Around School	Music Planning Period	Math Group 2 Entire } Unit Group } Quiz

■ FIGURE 14.2
Example of a Lesson Plan Schedule Book

4. Teacher instructional behaviors.
5. Activity sequencing and student responses.
6. Probes.
7. Generalization activities.

Demographic Information

Demographic information about the students or the group, the teacher's name, and the date of implementation should be included on the top of the form. Although recording this information may seem trivial, it is important for maintaining an overall management system (see Table 14.2). Omitting dates of implementation and student/group descriptors makes it difficult to keep an accurate record of techniques and materials that were tried and who implemented them so that changes can be made when necessary. For example, a teacher instructing a reading group in the use of comprehension skills such as sequencing and main idea may be attempting to use a new instructional strategy of cueing key words in the story by underlining them. During the end-of-the-year IEP review, it would be helpful to be able to refer to previous instructional plans, noting the techniques that were implemented. The demographic data provides information concerning which students were exposed to the techniques, the dates, and so forth.

Goals and Objectives

In addition to demographic data, initial information should include the annual goal, the short-term (IEP) objective, and the day's instructional objectives(s). To save time, a numbered coding system such as the one presented for use with microcomputers provides a quick method for recording goals and objectives (see Table 14.2). For example, an annual goal may involve motor skills, an area that is coded 2.0. One specific short-term objective incorporated in this goal may be to sit in a balanced position for 2 minutes. It can be coded 2.1. Subsequent instructional objectives identified in the task analysis can be coded 2.11, 2.12, 2.13, and so on. When teachers develop their daily lesson plans or strategies, it is simple to use the coding system instead of rewriting the same goals and objectives. The coded numbering system can assist teachers in filing plans for later retrieval.

Preinstructional Activities

Preinstructional activities are devices or techniques that a teacher uses to attract learner attention and increase motivation for an immediate task (Table 14.2). Dick and Carey (1978) have suggested techniques such as cartoons or attractive color schemes to engage student attention. In addition, modeling exactly what the task entails or demonstrating to the learner how the current lesson relates to previously learned skills can have a motivating effect. In any case, teachers should plan how they intend to motivate their students.

For example, Dick and Reiser (1989) suggested distributing brightly colored posters about the room that are related to the upcoming activity. A slide presentation showing

TABLE 14.2 Sample Lesson Plans (Instructional Plans)

Group or Student ___Stephanie, Bob, Jerry, Stacy___

Annual Goal: 1.0 (See Table 3.8)
Short-Term Objective: 1.1 (See Table 4.8)
Instructional Objectives: 1.41, 1.42, 1.43 (See Table 3.6)

Date(s) _____
Generalization: Student, with help from parents, finds 10 words with consonant blends in grocery store.

Preinstructional Activity	Teacher Behavior	Information Presentation and Student Behavior	Materials	Probe
Present pictures of words from story or passage that begin with blends, (e.g., frog, street, grass).	Verbal instructions and prompts: A. As student attempts word, teacher sounds blends as necessary. Model: B. Teacher reads two sentences from passage. C. Demonstrates process for egg carton activity. Cue: D. Underlines blends in words on board or slide.	1. Reads orally from passage. 2. Shake egg carton. Name a word that begins with the blend that the marble lands on.	Pictures Reading passage Egg carton with consonant blends glued to bottom/marble	Laminated file folder: Three columns 1. Pictures beginning with blends 2. Blends 3. Word endings Student matches picture to correct blend to matching word ending.
Student names picture and points to word written on chalkboard or overhead slide.				

(Prepared by Tina Kinsley)

415

other students engaging in a community-based activity is another way to capture the students' attention while introducing the topic. For students engaged in a career awareness unit highlighting potential jobs in agribusiness, a field trip to a farm supply business may provide additional incentives.

Preinstructional activities can also be used to introduce the theme or scope of the lesson. For example, a cartoon may demonstrate to students in a humorous fashion what happens when two people argue. The lesson for that day may concern interpersonal relationships on the job and involve role playing certain vignettes. In this instance, the preinstructional activity is used to set the stage for the activity.

Teacher Instructional Behaviors

One of the most difficult tasks for some teacher educators is to help their students identify the behaviors they exhibit in the classroom. When developing lesson plans, some teachers spend a great deal of time outlining specific behaviors they expect from students, with little or no attention given to what they themselves do. If this is the case, a vital piece of the teaching puzzle that identifies the cause-and-effect relationship between teachers and pupils may be lost. Therefore, antecedent teacher behaviors and their resulting effects on student behaviors must be identified (Table 14.2 and Figure 14.3). For example, some students benefit from fewer verbal directions and more physical prompts. Similarly, a teacher may present a complicated vocational task to a student by using primarily modeling with some verbal directions. Both examples have the common element of pinpointing exactly what the teacher will do to elicit a particular student response.

Antecedent behaviors exhibited by teachers are those that occur *before* the student attempts a task and are designed to increase the probability that the learner will perform the skill successfully (see Chapter Six). In the examples given, verbal directions, models, physical prompts, and various forms of guidance are all considered antecedent teacher behaviors. Also, cues that are built into instructional materials (e.g., underlining key words in a paragraph, color coding two parts of an assembly task) can be considered antecedent events.

Manipulating antecedents in a systematic fashion is the core of the curriculum implementation effort. Knowing *exactly* which antecedents are being used helps the teacher evaluate how they affect the progress of students. For example, a teacher using modeling as the primary antecedent for teaching a complex vocational task may need to know the type of model used (e.g., teacher model vs. peer model) for later analysis. If assessment data indicate that the learner makes too little or no progress, knowing the technique(s) used assists the teacher in changing the instructional strategy. This change or revision of instructional methods and materials directly relates to an upcoming component involving the use of probes.

Activity Sequencing and Responses

Presenting a lesson in an organized fashion helps provide structure, allowing teachers to be more systematic in their presentation and allowing students to be more attentive to the antecedents being delivered. By organizing the presentation, the teacher can better control the instructional setting, intervening as needed. This section of the plan (see Table 14.2) involves listing the steps of the lesson in the order that they are presented to the student. When a task analysis is used as an instructional guide, the steps in the analysis will be the sequence the presentation will follow.

Student responses should be the result of a teacher's manipulation of specific antecedents. In this section of the instructional strategy, teachers list the specific outcomes they hope to elicit from learners. By taking the time to outline the expected student behaviors, teachers can continue to maintain their organizational scheme. When data are reviewed at a later time, all necessary information will be available.

Probes

One important concept for teaching learners with mild to moderate handicaps that was highlighted in PL 94-142 was the requirement for ongoing monitoring of student progress (Bepko, 1981). A common misconception is that "ongoing monitoring" refers to weekly, or worse, semi-yearly or yearly checks. When teaching learners with learning and behavior problems using only weekly or less frequent checks can be a mistake that will be difficult to correct.

An ongoing monitoring system should be continuous (e.g., at least daily, and in some case several times daily), so that problems in the instructional system that are

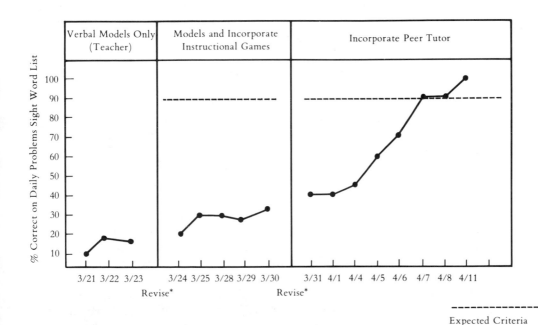

■ FIGURE 14.3
Program Revision Based on Formative Evaluation Data

impeding student progress can be eliminated immediately (Turnbull, Strickland, & Brantley, 1982). For example, if a student who is learning to add on Monday misunderstands a basic concept and practices the mistake all the rest of the week, it will be much more difficult to correct the error.

Probes are one type of formative evaluation that teachers include in their lessons to measure *small* samples of student behaviors. These probing devices relate directly to the daily instructional objectives and can be as simple as a page from a workbook or the teacher's observation of a student cleaning a sink. For example, an instructional objective that was presented earlier in the chapter involved the diphthong *ow* in different context words. The context of the objective involved the student pronouncing the diphthong in five words representing the first context and five in the second. In this case, the probe might involve flashing the 10 cards at the end of the lesson and recording any errors that were made.

Generalization Activities

A common problem faced by some teachers is developing suitable activities that allow the student to practice newly learned skills under different circumstances. When designing instructional strategies, practitioners may overlook a problem faced by many individuals with handicapping conditions. Basically, these students have difficulty in generalizing knowledge and skills to other settings, under the guidance of different persons, or when using alternate materials.

For this reason, teachers must develop a component of their lesson plans to include additional activities that will be used for guided practice. When teaching discriminations among object sizes, the teacher would not stop when the student learned the initial differences in size. Rather, the teacher would vary the number and types of objects as well as requiring more precise discriminations. Similar examples can be noted for teaching most academic skills.

Consider developing an instructional strategy for teaching the basic operation of addition. Traditionally, teachers begin by explaining the basic concept to the student while modeling the target behavior. The student is then instructed to practice the target outcome by completing a predesigned worksheet or a page in a workbook. Unfortunately, instruction and guided practice often end here.

Students in the general population can often transfer what they have learned to daily occurrences outside of the school. Learners with mild to moderate handicaps, however, are not always able to make that transition. Therefore, teachers could delineate activities such as using a grocery store advertisement to work on addition practice or incorporating computation problems into community-based activities. When developing new lessons, teachers must consider alternate activities that allow learners to practice their skills in real-life situations.

Dick and Carey (1978) discussed follow-through activities that essentially are programming for generalization, Such follow-through activities include remediation and/or enrichment materials. These materials are supplemental in that they are gathered by the teacher for possible use by the student (Dick & Reiser, 1989). Therefore, the plan states that they are to be used to assist the learner in guided practice activities (e.g., group projects, activity centers, practice with microcomputers, boardwork, practice in workbooks, instructional games).

Monitoring Student Progress

The process that uses student progress as a measure of program success is called *formative evaluation* (step 9, Figure 14.1). In a strict sense, formative evaluation is a method of field testing units of instruction during the design process to "iron out" difficulties before implementation (Gagne & Briggs, 1974). For example, when developing a task analysis for riding a bus, the teacher would field test the sequence before beginning to train students in this skill area. A formative evaluation of this task analysis might be to have a group of regular education students complete the steps in the sequence, noting any difficulties they might encounter. Subsequent revisions of the task analysis would include corrections based on observed difficulties and feedback from the students who participated in the trial sessions.

However, the principles of formative evaluation can also be applied to daily instruction. Teachers may design instructional components, implement the lessons, and make certain assumptions that the intervention was successful. Subsequently, the instruction will be implemented again in the same or a similar fashion. The resulting transmission of knowledge and/or skills is speculative. By incorporating some type of formative evaluation into their educational programs, teachers can make judgments based on data relative to the efficiency and effectiveness of the instruction. With this information on student performance in hand, teachers can revise their interventions whenever and wherever needed, increasing the probability of student success.

In this chapter, formative evaluation has been presented in the form of daily probes. These daily probes are based on the instructional objective and measure whether or not the learner has met the desired criterion. If the criterion has been met, the teacher can assume that the initial instruction was successful and subsequent guided practice activities can be implemented. The student can then advance to the next objective. Conversely, if the student has not met the desired criterion, the teacher can assume that a revision is needed in the instructional materials and/or techniques. Subsequent alterations in the intervention can be monitored until the desired result is obtained. Chapter Three presented this process in more detail.

Revising Interventions

Historically when learners with handicaps failed the blame for the failure was placed on some inherent quality of the student. Professionals now believe that when learning problems occur energies must be exerted toward matching the appropriate methods and materials to learner needs. Therefore, the principle of revising interventions is critical. Formative evaluation provides teachers with the structured data needed to make decisions about revision (step 9a, Figure 14.1).

The ability to make appropriate decisions concerning changes in the instructional system depends on the ease of analyzing the data collected. To minimize poor decisions, teachers may consider adopting a measurement tool that will help them collapse data into a workable, easy-to-read format.

One tool for information collection is charting data in graphic form (see Chapter Five). Our society is visually oriented, and often a picture of something can aid our understanding. Also, by charting certain learner behaviors, teachers find that they can prevent valuable information from being lost in the daily events of the classroom. When student behavior is charted, a picture emerges that depicts whether or not specific goals are being met. The graphic display presented on the chart should indicate when revisions are necessary. In addition, when the charted behavior is analyzed after a new method or material has been implemented, the data displayed should indicate whether or not more changes are needed.

The cause-and-effect relationship between an educational intervention and learned behavior is the key to the effectiveness of a program. Therefore, a visual display of these relationships can be a useful tool. Figure 14.3 presents an example of how the academic progress of a student can be charted. The criteria expected and the criteria achieved on instructional objectives can be displayed to assist in analyzing learner progress. At the point of continued low performance by the student, the teacher can intervene by revising methods and materials to help the learner master the task. Charted information is also useful for viewing the worth of larger units of study. Analysis of component parts and the unit as a whole is important to establish the value of a program. Teachers can revise any number of program components including teacher behaviors, instructional materials, and the objectives for the program.

Conducting Summative Evaluation

The short-term objectives found on a student's IEP are actually large chunks of instruction that can take many months of time to teach. In many cases, teachers have considered short-term objectives to be those that are the cumulative effort of a unit of instruction. Summative evaluation involves gathering information concerning student performance at the completion of a unit that will assist in assessing the overall effectiveness of instruction (step 10, Figure 14.1).

Three types of data can be compiled for analysis in this final phase of evaluation: direct product data, observational data, and learner input. Measurement of direct products can take different forms such as standardized or criterion-referenced tests for academic skills and completed projects for vocational or leisure skills. For example, a short-term objective for a unit on addition could state:

Outcome: Student will correctly compute addition problems at all levels up to carrying in alternative places.

Context: 35 problems—written worksheet, location: grocery store.

Criterion: 80%–90%.

For many learners, this objective comprises a large unit of instruction that may span several weeks. Subsequent analysis of the objective by the teacher could identify a number of instructional objectives that will be taught daily, leading to the completion of the unit (see Table 14.1). The summative evaluation of the unit, therefore, is simply the testing situation outlined in the short-term objective. The information gathered can then be analyzed, with the teacher noting whether the students have mastered that unit and, if they have, allowing them to proceed to the next unit of instruction.

Another example of a direct product measure is teaching leisure-time activities. A short-term objective may be concerned with a needlepoint project, describing the criteria needed for its completion. Instructional objectives are identified and taught, resulting in a finished needlepoint project. The teacher can then evaluate the project according to the preset criteria, thereby judging the effectiveness of that unit.

Using observational data as a tool for evaluation is a vital component of assessment. As with all techniques of evaluation, observation should be used throughout the system. For example, when teaching self-care skills, the teacher observes the students as they perform the outcomes stated in the short-term objectives (e.g., clothing coordination), carefully noting performance on each of the instructional objectives identified in the task analysis. Similarly, teachers can intervene in (or teach) and subsequently observe the results of programs designed to teach social behaviors. For example, if a student continuously interrupts the conversation of others, the teacher may have to measure by observation the number of occurrences defined as interruptions and design a program to reduce the frequency of that behavior. Subsequent observations of the student's interrupting behavior will provide the teacher with data concerning the effectiveness of the behavioral program.

The final method of gathering summative evaluation data involves obtaining learner input. Professionals should give more credence to the opinions of their consumers. Teachers can sample their students' opinions with interviews or questionnaires. For younger learners, questionnaires that incorporate a choice of happy faces work well (Figure 14.4). Older students frequently respond to "comments" sections on materials that allow them to make statements concerning their value. Learners can often communicate in a brief interview their impressions of certain units. Some people may feel that learners have few opinions worth noting and will progress best when parents and professionals design programs and make key decisions. Paternalistic attitudes such as these are contrary to the current philosophy of helping students with handicaps be as independent as possible. Making an effort to incorporate student feedback into program evaluation is a small step, yet it may well be the first step in instruction for varying degrees of independence.

Additional Summative Evaluation Data

Step 10 of Figure 14.1 indicates a vital component of summative evaluation. This assessment component can be used effectively as the means to observe whether or not students are generalizing skills to community situations. For example, when teaching units on basic operations in arithmetic, teachers will include in their generalization activities tasks that involve some practice with realistic community tasks (e.g., instruction in retail establishments, newspaper ads for grocery stores). The summative evaluation for operations in arithmetic, then, might find students using the basic operations for comparison shopping, vocationally related applications, and other daily living tasks in the community setting. In the case of the bus-riding component of community mobility, the example is simple: The summative evaluation involves observing the students move independently to different parts of the community.

In addition to these community applications, summative evaluations can also include many of the techniques used in the community needs assessment. Specifically, a follow-up of former students allows teachers to rate the relative effectiveness of their curricula and implementation strategies. For example, a problem may be indicated if a large proportion of students with moderate handicaps are leaving a secondary public school program only to enter a sheltered workshop. A situation such as this may be the result of a lack of community instruction sites or a lack of generalization activities built in to daily lessons. In any case, the results from the summative evaluation indicate that the independence of these learners is minimal and further analysis is warranted.

Summative evaluation is the final step in the instructional design process. The techniques of summative evaluation are essentially the same as those used during the formative evaluation process and during initial assessments. In this final evaluation, teachers

1. Was the reading game fun?

2. Do you like the word cards?

3. Does the teacher make you feel good about your work?

■ FIGURE 14.4
Example of Student Feedback

may find it useful to analyze the system as a whole. In this way, additional information that may have been lost inadvertently during ongoing assessment can provide teachers with a more complete analysis of student progress and program effectiveness.

The summative evaluation process is not the end of instruction but part of the cycle of events that continually revises the process and improves upon past efforts. For example, an end-of-unit assessment provides information for improving the unit for future use. This information also suggests changes or adaptations that might be needed in related units.

All of the information in this section was designed to present teachers with preferred strategies to be better classroom and instructional managers. However, regardless of how effectively teachers manage their classes, students will have to be taught to take responsibility for their own learning if they are to be successful in life. To this end, it is important to teach students strategies they can use to take more control of their lives. The following section presents some of the more important self-management skills and strategies that students will need to be successful in both school and community.

STUDY SKILLS AND GENERAL LEARNING BEHAVIORS

Regardless of how good the teacher-student ratio might be in a school district, the amount of time spent in intensive one-to-one instruction is small. Most activities are presented in a small-group format, and during these activities some students are required to work on their own. Independent study is a requirement for students mainstreamed into general education classes, and throughout life individuals who can learn independently have advantages over those who cannot (Emmer, Evertson, Sanford, Clements, & Worsham, 1989).

Teaching students independent study skills and other general learning behaviors relies heavily on the use of cognitive learning strategies (Cherkes-Julkowski & Gertner, 1989). Many students have never been taught how to study and will not pick up these skills incidently (Reid, 1988). Therefore, teachers need to specifically address these skills as they relate to all curriculum areas and to both community-based and classroom activities.

Study Skills and General School Survival Skills

Study skills and general school survival skills refer to a variety of skills necessary for success in any learning situation (Smith & Smith, 1989). They can include anything from arriving to class on time with the appropriate materials to completing assignments on the designated day and paying attention to the teacher. All of these skills are directly related to the good work habits necessary for successful transition to employment. They can be taught in relation to both academic skill areas and career/vocational activities.

The following is a list of the major skills that teachers will want to address:

1. Allots sufficient time to complete an activity.
2. Studies for a prespecified time period before taking a break.
3. Locates a study area conducive to his or her learning style.
4. Uses appropriate notetaking skills.

5. Organizes notes according to a logical scheme.

6. Uses appropriate outlining skills when reading and studying.

7. Underlines or highlights important ideas when reading (or takes notes if it is not appropriate to mark the book).

8. Appropriately uses keys and legends to read maps and tables.

9. Underlines important parts of directions.

10. Organizes ideas before writing them in essay form.

11. Proofreads work when it is completed.

12. Uses short-answer test-taking strategies (e.g., eliminating incorrect choices first, underlining important part of question).

13. Checks test when complete to ensure that all questions are answered.

14. Uses appropriate dictionary and other resource book skills to locate information.

15. Uses appropriate library skills for research and pleasure reading.

16. Establishes a plan to complete all assignments and tasks, including a schedule for completing parts of the larger task.

17. Uses appropriate assertive skills when dealing with others and accepts justified criticism.

18. Uses appropriate time-management skills.

19. Asks for help when needed.

20. Uses cognitive learning skills for facilitating memory and comprehension.

Instructional Strategies

The instructional strategies presented throughout this text are applicable to the list of skills just presented. Some specific examples are highlighted here to give teachers additional help in designing instructional interventions.

1. Peer-mediated strategies have proved highly effective in helping students with mild to moderate handicaps learn and maintain study and school survival skills (Kerr, Nelson, & Lambert, 1987; Pressley, Johnson, & Symons, 1987). For example, peer monitoring can be used effectively to improve both classroom attendance and punctuality. Group contingencies such as additional recess time can be used effectively if teachers do not single out the tardy learners, basing them instead on average time late for the entire class, for example.

2. Self-mediated strategies help students monitor and change inappropriate behaviors (Reid, 1988; Smith, 1989). Watches with alarms, public posting of progress charts kept by the students, and maintenance of an appointed calendar are examples of strategies for self-improvement.

3. Turla and Hawkins (1983) presented a number of excellent ideas for improved time management strategies that can be taught to both teachers and students. For example, students can be taught how to develop and use time logs and action item sheets that prioritize activities to improve their productivity.

4. Contingency contracting can be used to improve a number of study skills (See Chapter Five).

5. Smith (1989) suggested teaching students how to classify, associate, and sequence material using either direct instruction or drill and practice. Classifying allows students to group information into categories based on similar characteristics. Associating helps students see relationships between different knowledge bases. Sequencing helps students put information in order.

KEY CONCEPTS

This chapter has presented the reader with a view of daily planning as a process, that is, a mechanism that is ever changing and relates entirely to individual learners. Viewing curriculum as a process differs from the prevailing view of curriculum as merely a set of outcomes. For example, teachers who practice the process of instructional development are able to assess the needs of any learner, regardless of functioning level, and design appropriate curriculum options for that learner based on identified strengths and weaknesses. Conversely, teachers who perceive curriculum only as a set of outcomes often attempt to identify a preset curriculum, "fitting" the student into established goals and objectives and disregarding individual learner needs.

■ The age of the learner, prerequisite skills needed, community validity of the skills, and the availability of resources to teach the skills are all important considerations when establishing the order in which skills are to be presented to learners.

■ Translating short-term objectives from the IEP to instructional objectives through the individual implementation plan (IIP) is accomplished by using the process of task analysis.

■ Some steps on a skill sequence require the teacher to write out a formal objective including outcome, context, and criterion. Other steps, such as those involving self-care skills, are sufficiently concise (e.g., pick up toothbrush) without a formal objective.

■ Educational interventions are well-designed lesson plans that include demographic information about the learners, goals and objectives for the lesson, preinstructional activities to catch the learner's attention, teacher instructional behaviors, sequence of activities and student responses, probes to monitor student progress, and generalization activities to help students practice new skills under different conditions.

■ Formative evaluation includes trying out lessons on others before the skill sequences are presented to the target learners. This technique helps to resolve problems and increase the probability for learner success.

■ Another component of formative evaluation is included in the implementation of instructional strategies (lesson plans). Probes provide teachers with frequent information about student progress that is used to revise the strategies as needed.

■ Summative evaluation measures student progress over large chunks of instruction and monitors the effectiveness of the curriculum by following student progress in relation to community-realistic tasks.

■ ■ ■ ■

REFERENCES

Achenbach, T. M. (1979). The child behavior profile: An empirically based system for assessing children's behavioral problems and competencies. *Interrelated Journal of Mental Health, 7,* 24–42.

Achenbach, T. M., & Edelbrock, C. (1981). Behavioral problems and competencies reported by parents of normal and disturbed children aged 4 through 16. *Monographs of the Society for Research in Child Development, 46* (Serial No. 188).

Achenbach, T. M., & Edelbrock, C. (1983). *Manual for the child behavior checklist and revised child behavior profile.* Burlington: Department of Psychiatry, University of Vermont.

Aiello, B. (1976). The tool chest: Demystifying the metric system for exceptional children. *TEACHING Exceptional Children, 8,* 72–75.

Alberti, R. E, & Emmons, M. L. (1974). *Your perfect right: A guide to assertive behavior.* San Luis Obispo, CA: Impact.

Alberto, P., & Troutman, A. (1983). *Applied behavior analysis for teachers.* Columbus, OH: Charles E. Merrill.

Albright, L., & Preskill, H. (1981). *An assessment of mainstream and special vocational education involvement in the IEP process and related inservice needs.* Burlington: University of Vermont.

Algozzine, B., & McGraw, K. (1980). Diagnostic teaching in mathematics: An extension of the PIAT? *TEACHING Exceptional Children, 12,* 71–77.

Algozzine, B., & Ysseldyke, J. E. (1983). Learning disabilities as a subset of school failure: The oversophistication of a concept. *Exceptional Children, 50,* 242–246.

Alley, G., & Deshler, D. (1979). *Teaching the learning disabled adolescent: Strategies and methods.* Denver: Love Publishing.

Alper, S. (1981). Utilizing community jobs in developing vocational curriculum for severely handicapped youth. *Education and Training of the Mentally Retarded, 16,* 217–221.

Alter, M., & Gottlieb, J. (1987). Educating for social skills. In J. Gottlieb & B. W. Gottlieb (Eds.), *Advances in Special Education* (Vol. 6, pp. 1–61). London: JAI Press.

American Psychiatric Association (APA). (1980). *Diagnostic and statistical manual of mental disorders* (3rd ed., rev.). Washington, DC: American Psychiatric Association.

Anderson, R. C., Hiebert, E. H., Scott, J. A., & Wilkinson, I. A. (1985). *Becoming a nation of readers.* Champaign, IL: Center for the Study of Reading.

Anderson, R. M., Martinez, D. H., & Rich, H. L. (1980). Perspectives for change. In J. W. Schifani, R. M. Anderson, & S. J. Odle (Eds.), *Implementing learning in the least restrictive environment* (pp. 3–45). Baltimore: University Park Press.

Applegate, J. (1980). Time. In D. R. Cruickshank (Ed.), *Teaching is tough* (pp. 257–300). Englewood Cliffs, NJ: Prentice-Hall.

Apter, S. J. (1982). *Troubled children/troubled systems.* New York: Pergamon Press.

Ashlock, R. B. (1982). *Error patterns in computation: A semi-programmed approach* (3rd ed.). Columbus, OH: Charles E. Merrill.

Azrin, N. H., & Foxx, R. (1971). A rapid method of toilet training the institutionalized retarded. *Journal of Applied Behavior Analysis, 4,* 89–99.

Azrin, N. H., Gottlieb, L. H., Hughart, L., Wesolowski, M. D., & Rahn, T. (1975). Eliminating self-injurious behavior by educative procedures. *Behavior Research and Therapy, 13,* 101–111.

Azrin, N. H., & Powers, M. A. (1975). Eliminating classroom disturbances of emotionally disturbed children by positive practice procedures. *Behavior Therapy, 6,* 525–534.

Azrin, V., Azrin, N., & Armstrong, P. (1977). The student-oriented classroom: A method of improving student conduct and satisfaction. *Behavior Therapy, 8,* 193–204.

Baer, D. M., Wolf, M. M., & Risley, T. R. (1968). Some current dimensions of applied behavior analysis. *Journal of Applied Behavior Analysis, 1*(1), 91–97.

Baer, J. (1976). *How to be an assertive (not aggressive) woman in life, in love, and on the job.* New York: New American Library.

Bailey, J. S. (1977). *A handbook of applied behavior analysis.* Tallahassee: Florida State University.

Balajthy, E. (1989). *Computers and reading.* Englewood Cliffs, NJ: Prentice Hall.

Ball, W. L., Chasey, W. C., Hawkins, D. E., & Verhoven, P. J. (1976). The need for leisure education for handicapped children and youth. *Journal of Physical Education and Recreation, 47,* 53–55.

Balla, D., & Zigler, E. (1979). Personality development in retarded persons. In N. Ellis (Ed.), *Handbook of mental deficiency, psychological theory and research* (2nd ed., pp. 143–168). Hillsdale, NJ: Lawrence Erlbaum.

Barbe, W. B., Lucas, V. H., Hackney, C., Braun, L., & Wasylyk, T. (1984). *Saner-Bloser handwriting: Basic skills and applications.* Columbus, OH: Charles E. Merrill.

Barcott, R. A. (1973). Time-telling instruction in special education classes. *Education and Training of the Mentally Retarded, 8,* 207–211.

Bartel, N., & Bryen, D. (1982). Problems in language development. In D. Hammill & N. Bartel, *Teaching children with learning and behavior problems* (3rd ed., pp. 283–376). Boston: Allyn and Bacon.

Bartel, N. R. (1982). Problems in mathematics achievement. In D. Hammill & N. Bartel, (Eds.), *Teaching children with learning and behavior problems* (3rd ed., pp. 173–219). Boston: Allyn and Bacon.

Barton, E. S., Guess, D., Garcia, E., & Baer, D. M. (1970). Improvements of retardates' mealtime behaviors by timeout procedures using multiple baseline techniques. *Journal of Applied Behavior Analysis, 3,* 77–84.

Barton, L. E., Brulle, A. R., & Repp, A. C. (1983). Aversive techniques and the doctrine of least restrictive alternative. *Exceptional Education Quarterly, 3*(4), 1–8.

Bateman, B. (1982). Legal and ethical dilemmas of special educators. *Exceptional Education Quarterly, 2*(4), 57–67.

Bates, P., Renzaglia, A., & Clees, T. (1980). Improving the work performance of severely/profoundly retarded adults: Use of a changing criteria procedure design. *Education and Training of the Mentally Retarded, 15,* 98–104.

Baum, D. D., Duffelmeyer, F., & Geelan, M. (1988). Resource teacher perceptions of the prevalence of social dysfunction among students with learning disabilities. *Journal of Learning Disabilities, 21,* 380–381.

Bauman, K. E., & Iwata, B. A. (1977). Maintenance of independent housekeeping skills using scheduling plus self-recording procedures. *Behavior Therapy, 8,* 554–560.

Baumann, J. F., & Johnson, D. (1984). *Reading instruction and the beginning teacher.* Minneapolis: Burgess.

Beals, D. E. (1989). A practical guide for estimating readability. *TEACHING Exceptional Children, 21,* 24–27.

Bean, T., & Peterson, J. (1981). Reasoning guides: Fostering readiness in the content areas. *Reading Horizons, 21,* 196–199.

Behrmann, M. M. (1988). How computers work. In M. M. Behrmann (Ed.), *Integrating computers into the curriculum: A handbook for special educators* (pp. 1–28). Boston: College Hill Press.

Bellamy, G., Greiner, C., & Buttars, K. (1974). Arithmetic computation for trainable retarded students: Continuing a sequential instructional program. *Training School Culliten, 704* (4), 230–240.

Bellamy, G., Inman, D. P., & Horner, R. H. (1977). *Design of vocational habilitation services for the severely retarded: The specialized training program model.* Eugene, OR: Center on Human Development, University of Oregon.

Bellamy, G., Rhodes, L. E., Mank, D. M., & Albin, J. M. (1988). *Supported employment: A community implementation guide.* Baltimore: Paul Brooks.

Bellamy, G., Sheenan, R., Horner, R., & Boles, S. (1980). Community programs for severely handicapped adults: An analysis *Journal of the Association for the Severely Handicapped, 5,* 307–324.

Bellamy, T., & Buttars, K. (1975). Teaching trainable level retarded students to count money: Toward personal independence through academic instruction. *Education and Training of the Mentally Retarded, 10,* 18–26.

Bellamy, T., Peterson, L., & Close, D. (1975). Habilitation of the severely and profoundly retarded: Illustrations of competence. *Education and Training of the Mentally Retarded, 10,* 174–187.

Belmont, J. M. (1966). Long-term memory in mental retardation. In N. Ellis (Ed.), *International review of mental retardation* (Vol. 1, pp. 59–74). New York: Academic Press.

Beltz, P., Detwiler, M., & Grant, B. (1983). Computerized reading: Computers enrich your reading program. *Practical Ideas for Reading Teachers, 1* (2), 20.

Bender, M., & Valletutti, P. J. (1982). *Teaching functional academics.* Baltimore: University Park Press.

Bepko, R. A. (1981). The role of evaluation in the development of curriculum. In H. Goldstein (Ed.), *Curriculum development for exceptional children* (pp. 57–70). San Francisco: Jossey-Bass.

Berdine, W. H., & Meyer, S. A. (1987). *Assessment in special education.* Boston: Little, Brown.

Bernstein, D. K., & Tiegerman, E. (1985). *Language and communication disorders in children.* Columbus, OH: Charles E. Merrill.

Bigge, J. (1982). *Teaching individuals with physical and multiple disabilities* (2nd ed.). Columbus, OH: Charles E. Merrill.

Bigge, J. (1988). *Curriculum based instruction for special education students.* Mountain View, CA: Mayfield.

Bijou, S. W. (1977). *Edmark reading program.* Bellevue, WA: Edmark Associates.

Bijou, S. W., Birnbrauer, J. S., Kidder, J. D., & Tague, C. (1967). Programmed instruction as an approach to teaching of reading, writing, and arithmetic to retarded children. In S. W. Bijou & D. M. Baer (Eds.), *Child development: Readings in experimental analysis* (pp. 309–329). New York: Appleton.

Blackbourn, J. M. (1989). Acquisition and generalization of social skills in elementary-aged children with learning disabilities. *Journal of Learning Disabilities, 22,* 28–34.

Blackman, L., Burger, A., Tan, N., & Weiner, S. (1982). Strategy training and the acquisition of decoding skills in EMR children. *Education and Training of the Mentally Retarded, 17,* 83–87.

Blankenship, C. S. (1985). Using curriculum-based assessment data to make instructional decisions. *Exceptional Children, 52,* 233–238.

Blanton, L. P., Sitko, M. C., & Gillespie, P. (1976). Reading and the mildly retarded: Review of research and implications. In L. Mann & L. Sabatino (Eds.), *Third review of special education* (pp. 143–162). New York: Grune & Stratton.

Block, E. B. (1988). Teaching learning disabled students to use computers. In D. K. Reid (Ed.), *Teaching the learning disabled: A cognitive developmental approach* (pp. 416–434). Boston: Allyn and Bacon.

Boomer, L. (1982). The paraprofessional: A valued resource for special children and their teachers. *TEACHING Exceptional Children, 14,* 194–197.

Borakove, L. S., & Cuvo, A. J. (1977). Facilitative effects of coin displacement on teaching coin summation to mentally retarded adolescents. *American Journal of Mental Deficiency, 10*(4), 350–356.

Borkowski, J., & Varnhagen, C. (1984). Transfer of learning strategies: Contrast of self-instructional and traditional training formats with EMR children. *American Journal of Mental Deficiency, 88*(4), 369–379.

Bornstein, P., Hamilton, S., & Quevillon, R. (1977). Behavior modification by long distance: Demonstration of functional control over disruptive behavior in a rural classroom setting. *Behavior Modification, 1,* 369–380.

Bos, C. S., (1982). Getting past decoding: Assisted and repeated readings as remedial methods for learning disabled students. *Topics in Learning and Learning Disabilities, 1*(4), 51–57.

Bos, C. S., & Vaughn, S. (1988). *Strategies for teaching students with learning and behavior problems.* Boston: Allyn and Bacon.

Bott, D. A. (1988). Mathematics. In J. Wood (Ed.), *Mainstreaming: A practical guide for teachers* (pp. 7–21). Columbus, OH: Charles E. Merrill.

Bower, E. M. (1969). *Early identification of emotionally handicapped children in school* (2nd ed.). Springfield, IL: Charles C. Thomas.

Braaten, S., Kauffman, J. M., Braaten, B., Polsgrove, L., & Nelson, C. M. (1988). The regular education initiative: Patent medicine for behavior disorders. *Exceptional Children, 55,* 21–27.

Bransford, J., Stein, B., Delclos, V., & Littlefield, J. (1986). Computers and problem solving. In C. Kinzer, R. Sherwood, & J. Bransford (Eds.), *Computer strategies for education.* Columbus, OH: Charles E. Merrill.

Bratt, M. (1983). Microcomputers in elementary science education. *School Science and Mathematics, 83,* 333–337.

Bricker, D. (1983). Early communication development and training. In M. Snell (Ed.), *Systematic instruction for the moderately and severely handicapped* (pp. 269–288). Columbus, OH: Charles E. Merrill.

Bricker, D., & Dennison, L. (1978). Training prerequisites to verbal behavior. In M. Snell (Ed.), *Systematic programming of the moderately and severely handicapped* (pp. 157–178). Columbus, OH: Charles E. Merrill.

Bricker, D., Dennison, L., & Bricker, W. (1976). Constructive interaction-adaption approach to language training. *M.C.C.D. Monographs (Serial no. 1)*. Miami: Mailman Center for Child Development, University of Miami.

Bricker, D., Ruder, K. F., & Vincent, L. (1976). An intervention strategy for language deficient children. In N. G. Haring & R. L. Schiefelbusch (Eds.), *Teaching special children* (pp. 301–341). New York: McGraw-Hill.

Brickey, M., & Campbell, L. (1981). Fast food employment for moderately and mildly retarded adults. *Mental Retardation, 19*, 113–116.

Brigance, A. (1981). Brigance Inventory of Essential Skills. North Billerica, MA: Curriculum Associates.

Brigance, A. (1977). Brigance Diagnostic Inventory of Basic Skills. North Billerica, MA: Curriculum Associates.

Brigance, A. (1980). Brigance Diagnostic Inventory of Essential Skills. North Billerica, MA: Curriculum Associates.

Brock, G. (1979). Learning money concepts through use of behavior modification. *Education and Training of the Mentally Retarded, 14*, 67–68.

Brody-Hasazi, S., Salembier, G., & Finck, K. (1983). Directions for the 80's: Vocational preparation for secondary mildly handicapped students. *TEACHING Exceptional Children, 15*, 206–209.

Brolin, D. (1976). *Vocational preparation of retarded citizens.* Columbus, OH: Charles E. Merrill.

Brolin, D. (Ed.). (1989). *Life centered career education: A competency based approach.* (3rd ed.). Reston, VA: The Council for Exceptional Children.

Brolin, D. (1982). *Vocational preparation of persons with handicaps.* Columbus, OH: Charles E. Merrill.

Brolin, D. (1983). Career education: Where do we go from here? *Career Development for Exceptional Individuals, 6*, 3–14.

Brolin, D., & Elliott, T. (1983). Meeting the lifelong career development needs of students with handicaps: A community college model. *Career Development of Exceptional Individuals, 7*, 12–21.

Brolin, D., & Gysbers, N. (1979). Career education for persons with handicaps. *Personnel and Guidance Journal, 58*, 258–262.

Brolin, D., & Kokaska, C. (1979). *Career education for handicapped children and youth.* Columbus, OH: Charles E. Merrill.

Brooks, P. H., & Baumeister, A. A. (1977). A plea for consideration of ecological validity in experimental psychology of mental retardation: A guest editorial. *American Journal of Mental Deficiency, 81* (5), 407–416.

Broome, K., & Wambold, C. L. (1977). Teaching basic math facts to EMR children through individual and small group instruction, pupil teaming, contingency contracting, and learning center activities. *Education and Training of the Mentally Retarded, 12*, 120–124.

Brown, F., Holvoet, J., Guess, D., & Mulligan, M. (1980). The individualized curriculum sequencing model (III): Small group instruction. *The Journal of the Association of the Severely Handicapped, 5,* 352–364.

Brown, L. (1981, November). *Curriculum development for the severely and profoundly handicapped.* Workshop presented at the Marc Gold Try Another Way Conference, Charlotte, North Carolina.

Brown, L., & Bellamy, T. (1972). A sequential procedure for teaching addition skills to trainable retarded students. *Training School Bulletin, 69* (1), 31–44.

Brown, L., Branston, M. B., Baumgart, D., Vincent, L., Falvey, M., & Schroeder, J. (1979). Utilizing the characteristics of a variety of current and subsequent least restrictive environments as factors in the development of curricular content for severely handicapped students. *AAESPH Review, 4* (4), 407–424.

Brown, L., & Perlmutter, L. (1971). Teaching functional reading to trainable level retarded students. *Education and Training of the Mentally Retarded, 6,* 74–84.

Bruno, R., & Newman, M. (1985). Modifying content reading to develop comprehension skills in the regular classroom. *TEACHING Exceptional Children, 17,* 208–213.

Bryan, J. H., & Bryan, T. (1988). Where's the beef? A review of published research on the adaptive learning environment model. *Learning Disabilities Focus, 1,* 9–14.

Bryan, T., Bay, M., & Donahue, M. (1988). Identifications of the learning disabilities definition for the regular education initiative. *Journal of Learning Disabilities, 21,* 23–28.

Budde, J. F. (1981). Managing curriculum development. In H. Goldstein (Ed.), *Curriculum development for exceptional children* (pp. 71–88). San Francisco: Jossey-Bass.

Bundschuh, E. L., Williams, W., Hollingworth, J., Gooch, S. & Shirer, C. (1972). Teaching the retarded to swim. *Mental Retardation, 10,* 14–17.

Burmeister, J. G. (1976). Leisure services and the cultural arts as therapy for the mentally retarded individual. *Therapeutic Recreation Journal, 10,* 139–142.

Burnett, R. W. (1970). The classroom teacher as a diagnostician. In D. L. DeBoer (Ed.), *Reading diagnosis and intervention* (pp. 76–92). Newark, DE: International Reading Association.

Burns, P. K., & Bozeman, W. C. (1981). Computer-assisted instruction and mathematics achievement: Is there a relationship? *Educational Technology, 21,* 32–39.

Buros, O. K. (Ed.). (1978). *The eighth mental measurements yearbook.* Highland Park, NJ: Gryphon.

Butz, R. A., & Hasazi, J. E. (1973). Developing verbal imitative behavior in a profoundly retarded girl. *Journal of Behavior Therapy and Experimental Psychiatry, 4,* 389–393.

Cain, L., Levine, S., & Elzey, F. (1963). Cain-Levine Social Competency Scale. Palo Alto, CA: Consulting Psychologists Press.

Callenbach, D. (1972). *Living poor with style.* New York: Bantam.

Capone, A. M., Smith, M. A., & Schloss, P. J. (1988). Prompting play skills. *TEACHING Exceptional Children, 21,* 54–56.

Carnine, D. (1989). Teaching complex content to learning disabled students: The role of technology. *Exceptional Children, 55,* 524–533.

Cartwright, G. P., Cartwright, C. A., & Ward, M. E. (1989). *Educating special learners* (3rd ed.). Belmont, CA: Wadsworth.

Cawley, J. F. (1978). An instructional design in mathematics. In L. Mann, L. Goodman, & J. L. Wriderholt. (Eds.). *Teaching the learning-disabled adolescent* (pp. 201–234). Boston: Houghton Mifflin.

Cawley, J. F. (1977). Curriculum: One perspective for special education. In R. D. Kneedler & S. Tarver (Eds.), *Changing perspectives in special education* (pp. 21–45). Columbus, OH: Charles E. Merrill.

Cawley, J. F., Fitzmaurice, A. M., Goodstein, H. A., Lepore, A., Sedlak, R. A., & Althaus, V. (1976). *Project Math, levels I-IV*. Tulsa, OK: Educational Progress Corporation.

Cawley, J. F., Miller, D., & Carr, S. (1988). Mathematics. In G. Robinson, J. R. Patton, E. A. Polloway, & L. R. Sargent (Eds.), *Best practices in mental disabilities* (Vol. 2). Des Moines, IA: Department of Education.

Cawley, J. F., & Vitello, S. (1972). A model for arithmetical programing for handicapped children. *Exceptional Children, 39,* 101–110.

Cegelka, P. T. (1981). Career education. In J. M. Kauffman & D. P. Hallahan (Eds.), *Handbook of Special Education.* Englewood Cliffs, NJ: Prentice Hall.

Cegelka, W. J. (1978). Curriculum guides for mentally retarded: An analysis and recommendations. *Education and Training of the Mentally Retarded, 13,* 187–188.

Center, D. B. (1989). *Curriculum and teaching strategies for students with behavioral disorders.* Englewood Cliffs, NJ: Prentice Hall.

Certo, N., Schwartz, R., & Brown, L. (1975). Community transportation: Teaching severely handicapped students to ride a public bus system. In L. Brown, T. Crouner, W. Williams, & R. York (Eds.), *Madison's alternative for zero exclusion: A book of readings.* Madison, WI: Madison Public Schools.

Chadsey-Rusch, J., & Rusch, F. R. (1988). Ecology of the workplace. In R. Gaylord-Ross (Ed.), *Vocational education for persons with handicaps* (pp. 234–256). Mountain View, CA: Mayfield.

Chall, J. (1967). *Learning to read: The great debate.* New York: McGraw-Hill.

Charles, C. M. (1989). *Building classroom discipline: From models to practice* (3rd ed.). New York: Longman.

Cherkes-Julkowski, M., & Gertner, N. (1989). *Spontaneous cognitive processes in handicapped children.* New York: Springer-Verlag.

Cheseldine, S., & Jeffrie, D. M. (1981). Mentally handicapped adolescents: Their use of leisure. *Journal of Mental Deficiencies, 25,* 49–59.

Childs, R. E. (1982). A study of the adaptive behavior of retarded children and the resultant effects of this use in the diagnosis of mental retardation. *Education and Training of the Mentally Retarded, 17,* 109–113.

Choate, J. S., Bennett, T. Z., Enright, B. E., Miller, L. J., Poteet, J. A., & Rakes, T. A. (1987). *Assessing and programming basic curriculum skills.* Boston: Allyn and Bacon.

Choate, J. S., & Rakes, T. A. (1989). *Reading: Detecting and correcting special needs.* Boston: Allyn and Bacon.

Chou-Hare, V., & Borchardt, K. M. (1984). Direct instruction of summation skills. *Reading Research Quarterly, 20,* 62–78.

Clark, G. (1982). Career and vocational programming. In E. L. Meyen (Ed.), *Exceptional children and youth* (2nd ed., pp. 144–167). Denver: Love Publishing.

Clark, G. (1984). Issues in teacher education for secondary special education: Time for hindsight and foresight. *Teacher Education and Special Education, 7,* 170–177.

Clarke, J., Greenwood, L., Abramovitz, D., & Bellamy, G. (1980). Summer jobs for vocational preparation of moderately and severely retarded adolescents. *Journal of the Association for the Severely Handicapped, 5,* 24–27.

Clausen, J. A. (1972). QuoVadis, AAMD. *Journal of Special Education, 6,* 51–60.

Cleland, C. C. (1978). *Mental retardation: A developmental approach.* Englewood Cliffs, NJ: Prentice-Hall.

Cohen, R. (1983). Self-generated questions as an aid to reading comprehension. *The Reading Teacher, 36,* 770–775.

Cohen, S., & Plaskon, S. (1980). *Language arts for the mildly handicapped.* Columbus, OH: Charles E. Merrill.

Coie, J. D., & Kupersmidt, J. (1983). A behavioral analysis of emerging social status in boys' groups. *Child Development, 54,* 1400–1416.

Collins, M., & Carnine, D. (1988). Evaluating the field test revision process by comparing two versions at a reasoning skills CAI program. *Journal of Learning Disabilities, 21,* 375–379.

Conners, C. K. (1969). A teacher rating scale for use in drug studies with children. *American Journal of Psychiatry, 126,* 884–888.

Connolly, A., Nachtman, W., & Pritchett, E. (1971). Key Math Diagnostic Arithmetic Test. Circle Pines, MN: American Guidance Service.

Cook, I. D. (1983). Career development for exceptional individuals. *TEACHING Exceptional Children, 15,* 197–198.

Cooke, N., Heron, T., & Heward, W. (1983). *Peer tutoring.* Columbus, OH: Charles E. Merrill.

Coon, M. E., Vogelsburg, T., & Williams, W. (1981). Effects of classroom public transportation instruction on generalization to the natural environment. *Journal of the Association of the Severely Handicapped, 6* (2), 46–53.

Cooper, J. O. (1981). *Measuring behavior* (2nd ed.). Columbus, OH: Charles E. Merrill.

Cooper, J. O., & Johnson, J. (1979). Direct and continuous measurement of academic behavior. *Directive Teacher, 1,* 10–11; 21.

Cortazzo, A., & Sansone, R. (1969). Travel training. *TEACHING Exceptional Children, 3,* 67–82.

Cowan, P. (1978). Teaching the times tables to a hyperactive boy. *Academic Therapy, 13* (5), 569–577.

Criscoe, B. L., & Gee, T. C. (1984). *Content reading: A diagnostic prescriptive approach.* Englewood Cliffs, NJ: Prentice-Hall.

Crnic, K. A., Friedrich, W. N., & Greenburg, M. T. (1983). Adaptation of families with mentally retarded children: A model of stress, coping, and family ecology. *American Journal of Mental Deficiency, 88,* 125–138.

Cronin, K. A., & Cuvo, A. J. (1979). Teaching mending skills to retarded adolescents. *Journal of Applied Behavior Analysis, 12,* 401–406.

Cronis, T. G., Forgnone, C., & Smith, G. J. (1986). Mild mental retardation: Implications for an ecological curriculum. *Journal of Research and Development in Education, 19,* 72–76.

Crosson, J. E. (1969). A technique for programming sheltered workshop environments for training severely retarded workers. *American Journal of Mental Deficiency, 73,* 814–818.

Crouch, K., Rusch, F., & Karlin, G. (1984). Competitive employment: Utilizing the correspondence training paradigm to enhance productivity. *Education and Training of the Mentally Retarded, 19,* 268–275.

Cuvo, A. J., Jacobi, E., & Sipko, R. (1981). Teaching laundry skills to mentally retarded students. *Education and Training of the Mentally Retarded, 16,* 54–64.

Cuvo, A. J., Leaf, R. B., & Borakove, L. S. (1978). Teaching janitorial skills to the mentally retarded: Acquisition, generalization and maintenance. *Journal of Applied Behavior Analysis, 11,* 345–355.

Cuvo, A. J., Veitch, V. D., Trace, M. W., & Konke, J. L. (1978). Teaching change computation to the mentally retarded. *Behavior Modification, 2,* 531–548.

Dale, M. (1979). Peer tutoring: Children helping children. *The Exceptional Parent, 9,* 26–27.

Davis, W. E. (1989). The regular educative initiative debate: Its promises and problems. *Exceptional Children, 55,* 440–446.

Dawson, D. (1988). Leisure and the definition of poverty. *Leisure Studies, 7,* 221–231.

DeHaven, E. (1983). *Teaching and learning the language arts* (2nd ed.). Boston: Little, Brown.

Deitz, S., & Repp, A. (1973). Decreasing classroom misbehavior through the use of DRL schedules of reinforcement. *Journal of Applied Behavior Analysis, 6,* 457–463.

Deitz, S., & Repp, A. (1974). Differentially reinforcing low rates of misbehavior with normal elementary school children. *Journal of Applied Behavior Analysis, 7,* 622.

Deitz, D. E., & Repp, A. (1983). Reducing behavior through reinforcement. *Exceptional Education Quarterly, 3*(4), 34–46.

Deno, S. L. (1985). Curriculum-based measurement: The emerging alternative. *Exceptional Children, 52,* 219–232.

Deshler, D., & Schumaker, J. B. (1986). Learning strategies: An instructional alternative for low-achieving students. *Exceptional Children, 52,* 583–590.

Devany, J. M., Rincover, A., & Lovaas, O. I. (1981). Teaching speech to non-verbal children. In J. M. Kauffman & D. P. Hallahan (Eds.), *Handbook of special education* (pp. 512–529). Englewood Cliffs, NJ: Prentice-Hall.

Dever, R. B. (1989). A taxonomy of community living skills. *Exceptional Children, 55,* 395–404.

Dick, W., & Carey, L. (1977). *The systematic design of instruction.* Glenview, IL: Scott, Foresman.

Dick, W., & Reiser, R. A. (1989). *Planning effective instruction.* Englewood Cliffs, NJ: Prentice-Hall.

Dictionary of occupational titles (4th ed.) (1977). Washington, DC: U.S. Department of Labor.

Domnie, M., & Brown, L. (1977). Teaching severely handicapped students reading skills requiring printed answers to who, what, and where questions. *Education and Training of the Mentally Retarded, 12,* 324–331.

Donder, D., & Nietupski, J. (1981). Nonhandicapped adolescents teaching playground skills to their mentally retarded peers: Toward a less restrictive middle school environment. *Education and Training of the Mentally Retarded, 16,* 270–276.

Dorry, G. W., & Zeaman, D. (1973). The use of a fading technique in paired-associate teaching of reading vocabulary with retardates. *Mental Retardation, 11*(6), 3–6.

Dorry, G. W., & Zeaman, D. (1975). Teaching a simple reading vocabulary to retarded children: Effectiveness of fading and nonfading procedures. *American Journal of Mental Deficiency, 79,* 711–716.

Dudley-Marling, C. C., & Edmiaston, R. (1985). Social status of learning disabled children and adolescents: A review. *Learning Disability Quarterly, 8,* 189–204.

Dunlap, G., Koegel, R., & Burke, J. (1981). Educational implications of stimulus overselectivity in autistic children. *Exceptional Education Quarterly, 2*(3), 37–50.

Dunn, L. (1968). Special education for the mildly retarded: Is much of it justifiable? *Exceptional Children, 35,* 5–22.

Durana, I. L., & Cuvo, A. (1980). A comparison of procedures for decreasing public disrobing of an institutionalized profoundly mentally retarded woman. *Mental Retardation, 18*(4), 185–188.

Dyer, K., Schwartz, I., & Luce, S. (1984). A supervision program for increasing functional activities for severely handicapped students in a residential setting. *Journal of Applied Behavior Analysis, 17,* 249–260.

Dyer, W. (1979). *Pulling your own strings.* New York: Avon.

Edelson, R., & Sprague, R. (1974). Conditioning of activity level in a classroom with institutionalized retarded boys. *American Journal of Mental Deficiency, 78,* 384–388.

Edgar, E. (1987). Secondary programs in special education: Are many of them justifiable? *Exceptional Children, 53,* 555–56.

Edwards, L. L., & O'Toole, B. (1988). Application of the Self-Control curriculum with behavior disordered students. In E. L. Meyen, G. A. Vergason, & R. J. Whelan, (Eds.), *Effective instructional strategies for exceptional children* (pp. 276–287). Denver: Love Publishing.

Ehly, S., & Larsen, S. (1980). *Peer tutoring for individualized instruction.* Boston: Allyn and Bacon.

Eich, J. (1981). Multimodality multiplication for mildly handicapped students. *TEACHING Exceptional Children, 13,* 156–159.

Eichenbaum, B., & Bednarek, N. (1964). Square dancing and social adjustment. *Mental Retardation, 2,* 105–109.

Ekwall, E. E. (1985). *Locating and correcting reading difficulties,* Columbus, OH: Charles E. Merrill.

Elium, M., & Evans, B. (1982). A model camping program for college students and handicapped learners. *Education and Training of the Mentally Retarded, 17,* 241–246.

Ellis, E. S., & Sabornie, E. J. (1988). Effective instruction with microcomputers: Promises, practices, and preliminary findings. In E. L. Meyen, G. A. Vergason, & R. J. Whelan (Eds.), *Effective instructional strategies for exceptional children* (pp. 355–379). Denver: Love Publishing.

Ellis, N. (1963). The stimulus trace and behavioral inadequacy. In N. Ellis (Ed.), *Handbook of mental deficiency* (pp. 134–158). New York: McGraw-Hill.

Ellis, N. (1970). Memory processes in retardates and normals. In N. Ellis (Ed.), *International review of research in mental retardation* (Vol. 4, pp. 40–62). New York: Academic Press.

Emmer, E. T., Evertson, C. M., Sanford, J. P., Clements, B. S., & Worsham, M. E. (1989). *Classroom management for secondary teachers* (2nd ed.). Englewood Cliffs, NJ: Prentice Hall.

Englemann, S., & Bruner, J. (1974). *DISTAR: An instructional system.* Chicago: Science Research Associates.

Englemann, S., & Bruner, J. (1988). *DISTAR: An instructional system* (revised edition). Chicago: Science Research Associates.

Englemann, S., & Carnine, D. (1972–1976). *DISTAR arithmetic, levels I, II, III.* Chicago: Science Research Associates.

Englehardt, J. M. (1977). Analysis of children's computational errors: A qualitative approach. *British Journal of Educational Psychology, 47,* 149–154.

Englert, C., Culatta, B. E., & Horn, D. G. (1987). Influence of irrelevant information in addition word problems on problem solving. *Learning Disability Quarterly, 10,* 29–36.

Englert, C., & Lichter, A. (1982). Using statement-pie to teach reading and writing skills. *TEACHING Exceptional Children, 14,* 164–170.

Enright, B. E. (1989). *Basic mathematics: Detecting and correcting special needs.* Boston: Allyn and Bacon.

Epstein, P. B., Detwiler, C. L., & Reitz, A. L. (1985). Describing the clients in programs for behavior disordered children and youth. *Education and Treatment of Children, 8,* 265–273.

Espin, C. A., & Sindelar, P. T. (1988). Auditory feedback and writing: Learning disabled and nondisabled students. *Exceptional Children, 55*, 45–51.

Esposito, B. G., & Koorland, M. A. (1989). Play behavior of hearing impaired children: Integrated and segregated settings. *Exceptional Children, 55*, 412–419.

Etlinger, L. E., & Ogletree, E. J. (1978). The metric system in EMR curriculum. *Special Children, 4*(3), 61–63.

Evans, W. H., Evans, S. S., & Schmid, R. E. (1989). *Behavior and instructional management: An ecological approach.* Boston: Allyn and Bacon.

Feichtner, S. (1988). Articulation as the conceptual basis for transition. *The Journal for Vocational Special Needs Education, 11*, 19–22.

Fell, G., Rak, C., & Klien, R. (1982). Career awareness and developmental model to prepare the handicapped for employment. *Journal of Career Education, 5*, 263–273.

Felton, R. H., & Wood, F. B. (1989). Cognitive deficits in reading disability and attention deficit disorder. *Journal of Learning Disabilities, 22*, 3–13.

Fensterheim, H., & Baer, J. (1975). *Don't say yes when you want to say no.* New York: David McKay.

Fernald, G. M. (1943). *Remedial techniques in basic school subjects.* New York: McGraw-Hill.

Ferneti, C. L., Lent, J. R., & Stevens, C. J. (1974). *Project MORE: Eating.* Bellevue, WA: Edmark Associates.

Finkel, W., & Zimmerman, K. (1976). Teaching special children to tell time. *Journal for Special Educators of the Mentally Retarded, 12*(3), 181–186.

Fisher, M. (1984). Vocational assembly skills using isometric projection exploded view assembly drawings for mentally handicapped students. *Education and Training of the Mentally Retarded, 19*, 285–290.

Fisher, M. A., & Zeaman, D. (1973). An attention-retention theory of retardate discrimination learning. In N. Ellis (Ed.), *The international review of research in mental retardation* (Vol. 6, pp. 171–256). New York: Academic Press.

Fitzgerald, J. (1951). *The teaching of spelling.* Milwaukee: Bruce Publishing.

Flexer, R. W., & Martin, A. S. (1978). Sheltered workshops and vocational training settings. In M. E. Snell, (Ed.), *Systematic instruction of the moderately and severely handicapped* (pp. 414–430). Columbus, OH: Charles E. Merrill.

Fokes, J. (1976). *Fokes sentence builder.* New York: Teaching Resources.

Ford, L., Dineen, J., & Hall, J. (1984). Is there life after placement? *Education and Training of the Mentally Retarded, 19*, 291–296.

Foss, G., Auty, W. P., & Irvin, L. K. (1989). A comparative evaluation of modeling, problem solving, and behavior rehearsal for teaching employment-related interpersonal skills to secondary students with mental retardation. *Education and Training in Mental Retardation, 24*, 17–27.

Fowler, G. L. (1982). Developing comprehension skills in primary students through the use of story frames. *The Reading Teacher, 36*, 176–179.

Foxx, R., McMorrow, M., & Mennemeier, M. (1984). Teaching social/vocational skills to retarded adults with a modified table game: An analysis of generalization. *Journal of Applied Behavior Analysis, 17*, 343–352.

Foxx, R., & Azrin, N. H. (1973). *Toilet training the retarded.* Champaign, IL: Research Press.

Foxx, R., & Azrin, N. H. (1972). Restitution: A method of eliminating aggressive-disruptive behavior of retarded and brain-damaged patients. *Behavior Research and Therapy, 10*, 15–27.

Foxx, R., McMorrow, M., & Schloss, C. (1983). Stacking the deck: Teaching social skills to retarded adults with a modified table game. *Journal of Applied Behavior Analysis, 16*, 157–170.

Foxx, R., & Shapiro, S. (1978). The timeout ribbon: A nonexclusionary timeout procedure. *Journal of Applied Behavior Analysis, 11*, 125–136.

Fowler, S. A., Johnson, J. R., Whitman, T. L., & Zukotynski, G. (1978). Programming a parent's behavior for establishing self-help skills and reducing aggression and noncompliance in a profoundly retarded adult. *AAESPH Review, 3*, 151–161.

Frank, A. (1983). Formulating long-term goals and short-term objectives for individual education programs. *Education and Training of the Mentally Retarded, 18*, 144–147.

Frank, A., & McFarland, T. (1980). Teaching coin skills to E.M.R. children: A curriculum study. *Education and Training of the Mentally Retarded, 15*, 270–277.

Frank, A. R. (1978). Teaching money skills with a number line. *TEACHING Exceptional Children, 10*, 46–47.

Fredericks, B., & Evans, V. (1987). Functional curriculum. In C. M. Nelson, R. B. Rutherford, Jr., and B. I. Wolford (Eds.), *Special education in the criminal justice system* (pp. 189–214). Columbus, OH: Charles E. Merrill.

Fredericks, H. H., Anderson, R., & Baldwin, V. (1977). The identification of competencies in teachers of the severely handicapped. In P. Mittler (Ed.), *Research to practice in mental retardation* (Vol. 2, pp. 394–430). Baltimore: University Park Press.

Frith, G., & Mitchell, J. (1983). Art education for mentally retarded students: A significant component of the special education curriculum. *Education and Training of the Mentally Retarded, 18*, 138–141.

Frith, G., Mitchell, J., & Roswal, G. (1980). Recreation for mildly retarded students: An important component of individualized education plans. *Education and Training of the Mentally Retarded, 15*, 199–203.

Fuchs, D., & Fuchs, L. S. (1988a). Evaluation of the adaptive learning environments model. *Exceptional Children, 55*, 115–127.

Fuchs, D., & Fuchs, L. S. (1988b). Response to Wang and Walberg. *Exceptional Children, 55*, 138–145.

Gagne, R. M. (1975). *Essentials of learning for instruction.* Hinsdale, IL: Dryden Press.

Gagne, R. M. (1977). *The conditions of learning* (3rd ed.). New York: Holt, Rinehart, & Winston.

Gagne, R. M., & Briggs, L. J. (1974). *Principles of instructional design.* New York: Holt, Rinehart, & Winston.

Galagan, J. E. (1985). Psychoeducational testing: Turn out the lights, the party's over. *Exceptional Children, 52*, 288–299.

Gallagher, J. J., Beckman, P., & Cross, A. H. (1983). Families of handicapped children: Sources of stress and its amelioration. *Exceptional Children, 50*, 10–17.

Gallagher, P. A. (1988). *Teaching students with behavior disorders: Techniques and activities for classroom instruction* (2nd ed.). Denver: Love Publishing.

Gamble, T. K., & Gamble, M. (1982). *Contacts: Communicating interpersonally.* New York: Random House.

Gardner, D., & Kurtz, M. A. (1979). Teaching technical vocabulary to handicapped students. *Reading Improvement, 16*, 252–257.

Gaylord-Ross, R., Haning, T., Breen, C., & Pitts-Conway, V. (1984). The training and generalization of social interaction skills with autistic youth. *Journal of Applied Behavior Analysis, 17*, 229–248.

Gaylord-Ross, R., Siegel, S., Park, H. S., & Wilson, W. (1988). Secondary vocational training. In R. Gaylord-Ross (Ed.), *Vocational education for persons with handicaps* (pp. 174–202). Mountain View, CA: Mayfield Publishing.

Georgia Department of Education. (1985). Georgia criterion referenced tests, objectives and assessment characteristics—mathematics and reading tests. Atlanta, GA.

Germann, G., & Tindal, G. (1985). An application of curriculum-based assessment: The use of direct and repeated measurement. *Exceptional Children, 52,* 244–265.

Gersten, R., & Carnine, D. (1988). Direct instruction in reading comprehension. In E. L. Meyen, C. A. Vergason, & R. J. Whelan (Eds.), *Effective instructional strategies for exceptional children* (pp. 65–79). Denver: Love Publishing.

Gersten, R., Woodward, J., & Darch, C. (1986). Direct instruction: A research-based approach to curriculum design and teaching. *Exceptional Children, 53,* 17–31.

Gickling, E., Hargis, C., & Alexander, D. (1981). The function of imagery in sight word recognition among retarded and non-retarded children. *Education and Training of the Mentally Retarded, 16,* 259–263.

Gickling, E., & Thompson, V. P. (1985). A personal view of curriculum-based assessment. *Exceptional Children, 52,* 205–218.

Gill, H., & Langone, J. (1982). Enhancing the effectiveness of the IEP. *Journal for Vocational Special Needs Education, 4*(2), 9–11.

Gillet, P. (1983). Its elementary! Career education activities for mildly handicapped students. *TEACHING Exceptional Children, 15,* 199–205.

Gilliam, J. E., & Scott, B. K. (1987). The behaviorally disordered offender. In C. M. Nelson, R. B. Rutherford, Jr., and B. I. Wolford (Eds.), *Special education in the criminal justice system.* Columbus, OH: Charles E. Merrill.

Ginott, H. (1971). *Teacher and child,* New York: Macmillan.

Glaser, R. (1962). Psychological and instructional technology. In R. Glaser (Ed.), *Training research and education* (pp. 1–30). New York: Wiley.

Glasser, W. (1969). *Schools without failure.* New York: Harper & Row.

Glasser, W. (1985). *Control theory in the classroom.* New York: Harper & Row.

Gloeckler, T., & Simpson, C. (1988). *Exceptional students in the regular classroom: Challenges, services and methods.* Mountain View, CA: Mayfield Publishing.

Glover, J. M. (1979). The handicapped can dance, two! Four steps to smooth their way. *Parks and Recreation, 14,* 62–66.

Goff, M., & Kelly, P. (1979). The special education paraprofessional and the traditional educational programs process. In E. L. Meyen, G. A. Vergasen, & R. J. Whelan (Eds.), *Instructional planning for exceptional children* (pp. 110–139). Denver: Love Publishing.

Gold, M. W. (1972). Stimulus factors in skill training of the retarded on a complex assembly task: Acquisition, transfer, and retention. *American Journal of Mental Deficiency, 76,* 517–526.

Gold, M. W. (1976). Task analysis of a complex assembly task by the retarded blind. *Exceptional Children, 42,* 78–84.

Gold, M. W., & Pomerantz, D. J. (1978). Issues in prevocational training. In M. E. Snell (Ed.), *Systematic instruction of the moderately and severely handicapped* (pp. 431–440). Columbus, OH: Charles E. Merrill.

Goldenberg, E. P., Russel, S., & Carter, C. J. (1984). *Computers, education, and special needs.* Reading, MA: Addison-Wesley.

Goldman, S. R. (1989). Strategy instruction in mathematics. *Learning Disability Quarterly, 12,* 43–55.

Goldstein, A. P. (1987). Teaching prosocial skills to antisocial adolescents. In C. M. Nelson, R. B. Rutherford, Jr., and B. I. Wolford (Eds.), *Special education in the criminal justice system* (pp. 215–250). Columbus, OH: Charles E. Merrill.

Goldstein, H. (1981a), Conceptual and structural foundations of curriculum. In H. Goldstein (Ed.), *Curriculum development for exceptional children* (pp. 3–22). San Francisco: Jossey-Bass.

Goldstein, M. T. (1981b). Implementing a curriculum field-test model. In H. Goldstein (Ed.), *Curriculum development for exceptional children* (pp. 35–56). San Francisco: Jossey-Bass.

Goldstein, S., Strickland, B., Turnbull, A., & Curry, L. (1980). An observational analysis of the IEP conference. *Exceptional Children, 46,* 278–280.

Gonzalas, E. (1982). Issues in the assessment of minorities. In H. Lee Swanson & B. L. Watson (Eds.), *Educational and psychological assessment of exceptional children: Theories, strategies, and applications* (pp. 375–389). St. Louis: C. V. Mosby.

Goodstein, H. A., Kahn, H., & Cawley, J. F. (1976). The achievement of educable mentally retarded on the Key Math Diagnostic Arithmetic Test. *Journal of Special Education, 10,* 61–70.

Gordon, T. (1974). *Teacher effectiveness training.* New York: P. H. Wyden.

Graham, S. (1983). Measurement of handwriting skills: A critical review. *Diagnostique, 8,* 32–42.

Graham, S., & MacArthur, C. (1988). Improving learning disabled students' skills at revising essays produced on a word processor: Self-instructional strategy training. *Journal of Special Education, 22,* 133–152.

Graham, S., & Miller, L. (1980). Handwriting research and practice: A unified approach. *Focus on Exceptional Children, 13* (2), 1–16.

Greenleigh Associates (1975). *The role of the sheltered workshop in the rehabilitation of the severely handicapped.* Report to the U.S. Department of Health, Education and Welfare. Washington, D.C.

Greer, J. V. (1978). Utilizing paraprofessionals and volunteers in special education. *Focus on Exceptional Children, 10,* 1–15.

Gresham, F. M., & Reschly, D. J. (1986). Social skill deficits and low peer acceptance of mainstreamed learning disabled children. *Learning Disability Quarterly, 9,* 23–32.

Grey, R. A. (1981). Services for the LD adult: A working paper. *Learning Disability Quarterly, 4,* 426–434.

Gronlund, N. E. (1970). *Stating behavioral objectives for classroom instruction.* New York: Macmillan.

Grossman, H. J. (Ed.). (1983). *Manual on terminology and classification in mental retardation* (rev. ed.) Washington, DC: American Association on Mental Deficiency.

Guess, D. (1980). Methods in communication instruction for severely handicapped persons. In W. Sailor, B. Wilcox, & L. Brown (Eds.), *Methods of instruction for severely handicapped students* (pp. 195–225). Baltimore: Brooks.

Guess, D., Sailor, W., & Baer, D. (1978). Children with limited language. In R. L. Schiefelbusch (Ed.), *Language intervention strategies.* Baltimore: University Park Press.

Hagen, D. (1984). *Microcomputer resource book for special education.* Reston, VA: Reston Publishing.

Hagin, R. A. (1983). Write right-or left: A practical approach to handwriting. *Journal of Learning Disabilities, 16,* 266–271.

Hall, R. V. (1971). *Managing behavior I, Behavior modification: The measurement of behavior.* Lawrence, KS: H & H Enterprises.

Hallahan, D. P., Keller, C. E., McKinney, J. D., Lloyd, J. W., & Bryan, T. (1988). Examining the research base of the regular education initiative: Efficiency studies and the adaptive learning environments model. *Journal of Learning Disabilities, 21*, 29–35, 55.

Hallahan, D. P., Marshall, K. L., & Lloyd, J. W. (1981). Self-recording during group instruction: Effects on attention to task. *Learning Disability Quarterly, 4*, 407–413.

Halle, J. (1982). Teaching functional language to the handicapped: An integrative model of natural environment teaching techniques. *Journal of the Association of the Severely Handicapped, 7*(4), 29–37.

Halpern, A. (1985). Transition: A look at the foundations. *Exceptional Children, 51*, 479–486.

Hammill, D., & Poplin, M. (1982). Problems in written composition. In D. Hammill & N. Bartel (Eds.), *Teaching children with learning and behavior problems* (3rd ed., pp. 93–120). Boston: Allyn and Bacon.

Hammill, D. D. (1987). An overview of assessment practices. In D. D. Hammill (Ed.), *Assessing the abilities and instructional needs of students* (pp. 2–37). Austin, TX: Pro-Ed.

Hammill, D. D., Leigh, J. E., McNutt, G., & Larsen, S. C. (1981). A new definition of learning disabilities. *Learning Disability Quarterly, 4*, 336–342.

Hanline, M. F., & Halvorsen, A. (1989). Parent perceptions of the integration transition process: Overcoming artificial barriers. *Exceptional Children, 55*, 487–492.

Hannaford, A. E. (1987). Computers and exceptional individuals. In J. D. Lindsey (Ed.), *Computers and exceptional individuals* (pp. 1–18). Columbus, OH: Charles E. Merrill.

Hansen, G. (1979). Enuresis control through fading, escape, and avoidance training. *Journal of Applied Behavior Analysis, 12*(2), 303–307.

Hargis, C. H. (1982). Word recognition development. *Focus on Exceptional Children, 14*(9), 1–8.

Harris, K. R. (1988). Cognitive-behavior modification: Application with exceptional students. In F. I. Meyen, G. A. Vergason, & R. J. Whelan (Eds.), *Effective instructional strategies for exceptional children* (pp. 216–242). Denver: Love Publishing.

Harris, K. R. (1985). Definitional, parametric, and procedural considerations in timeout interventions and research. *Exceptional Children, 51*, 279–288.

Harris, S., & Wolchik, S. (1979). Suppression of self-stimulation: Three alternative strategies. *Journal of Applied Behavior Analysis, 12*, 185–198.

Hart, B. M., & Risley, T. R. (1968). Establishing use of descriptive adjectives in the spontaneous speech of disadvantaged preschool children. *Journal of Applied Behavior Analysis, 1*, 109–120.

Hart, V. (1981). *Mainstreaming children with special needs.* New York: Longman.

Harter, S. (1983). Developmental perspectives on the self system. In P. Mussen (Ed.), *Handbook of child psychology* (Vol. 4). New York: Wiley.

Hasazi, S. B., & Clark, G. M. (1988). Vocational preparation for high school students labeled mentally retarded: Employment as a graduation goal. *Mental Retardation, 26*, 343–349.

Hasazi, S. B., & Cobb, R. B. (1988). Vocational education of persons with mild handicaps. In R. Gaylord-Ross (Ed.), *Vocational education for persons with handicaps* (pp. 331–354). Mountain View, CA: Mayfield Publishing.

Hasazi, S. B., Gordon, L. R., & Roe, C. (1985). Factors associated with the employment status of handicapped youth exiting high school from 1979–1983. *Exceptional Children, 51*, 455–469.

Hasselbring, T., & Crossland, C. (1982). Application of microcomputer technology to spelling assessment of learning disabled students. *Learning Disability Quarterly, 5*, 80–82.

Hasselbring, T., & Cavanaugh, K. J. (1986). Applications for the mildly handicapped. In C. K. Kinzer, R. D. Sherwood, & J. D. Bransford (Eds.), *Computer Strategies for Education: Foundations and Content Area Applications*, Columbus, OH: Charles E. Merrill.

Hasselbring, T., & Goin, L. I. (1989). Enhancing learning through microcomputer technology. In E. A. Polloway, J. R. Patton, J. S. Payne, & R. A. Payne (Eds.), *Strategies for teachers with learners with special needs* (4th ed., pp. 147–164). Columbus, OH: Charles E. Merrill.

Hasselbring, T., & Hamlett, C. (1984). *AIMSTAR*. Portland, OR: ASIEP Education.

Hasselbring, T., & Owens, S. (1983). Microcomputer-based analysis of spelling errors. *Computers, Reading and Language Arts, 1*, 26–31.

Hazel, J. S., Schumaker, J. B., Sherman, J. A., & Sheldon, J. (1982). Application of a group training program in social skills and problem solving to learning disabled and non-learning disabled youth. *Learning Disabilities Quarterly, 5*, 398–408.

Hegge, T. G., Kirk, S. A., & Kirk, W. (1965). *Remedial reading drills*. Ann Arbor: Wahr Publishing.

Heiss, W. E. (1981). Two models for developing curriculum materials. In H. Goldstein, (Ed.), *Curriculum development for exceptional children* (pp. 23–34). San Francisco: Jossey-Bass.

Heller, K., Holtzman, W., & Messick, S. (Eds.). (1982). *Placing children in special education: A strategy for equity*. Washington, DC: National Academy Press.

Hentshel, D. (1977). Change theory applied to inservice education. *Planning and Changing, 21* (2), 103–114.

Heron, T., & Harris, K. (1982). *The educational consultant: Helping professionals, parents, and mainstreamed students*. Boston: Allyn and Bacon.

Heward, W. L., & Orlansky, M. D. (1988). *Exceptional children: An introductory survey of special education* (3rd ed.). Columbus, OH: Charles E. Merrill.

Hewett, F. M. (1968). *The emotionally disturbed child in the classroom*. Boston: Allyn and Bacon.

Hewett, F. M., & Taylor, F. D. (1980). *The emotionally disturbed child in the classroom: The orchestration of success* (2nd ed.). Boston: Allyn and Bacon.

Hill, B. K., & Bruininks, R. H. (1984). Maladaptive behavior of mentally retarded individuals in residential facilities. *American Journal of Mental Deficiency, 88*, 380–387.

Hill, M., & Wehman, P. (1983). Cost benefit analysis of placing moderately and severely handicapped individuals into competitive employment. *Journal of the Association for the Severely Handicapped, 8*, 30–38.

Hill, S. A. (1983). The microcomputer in the instructional program. *The Arithmetic Teacher, 30* (6), 14–15; 54–55.

Hirsch, E. D. (1987). *Cultural literacy*. Boston: Houghton Mifflin.

Hobbs, S. A., Moguin, L. E., & Troyler, N. (1980). Parameters of investigation of cognitive behavior therapy with children. *Catalog of Selected Documents in Psychology, 10*, 62–63.

Hofmeister, A. M. (1982). Microcomputers in perspective. *Exceptional Children, 49*, 115–122.

Hofmeister, A. M. (1983). *Microcomputer applications in the classroom*. New York: Holt, Rinehart, & Winston.

Hofmeister, A. M. (1989). Teaching with videodiscs. *TEACHING Exceptional Children, 21*, 52–54.

Homme, L. (1969). *How to use contingency contracting in the classroom*. Champaign, IL: Research Press.

Hops, H., Fleishman, D. H., Guild, J., Paine, S., Street, A., Walker, H. M., & Greenwood, C. R. (1978). *Program for establishing effective relationship skills (PEERS)* (Consultant manual). Eugene: University of Oregon, Center at Oregon for Research in the Behavioral Education of the Handicapped.

Horner, R. D. (1980). The effects of an environmental enrichment program on the behavior of institutionalized profoundly retarded children. *Journal of Applied Behavior Analysis, 13,* 473–491.

Horner, R. H., & Bellamy, G. T. (1978). A conceptual analysis of vocational training. In M. E. Snell (Ed.), *Systematic instruction of the moderately and severely handicapped* (pp. 441–456). Columbus, OH: Charles E. Merrill.

Horton, S. V., Lovitt, T. C., Givens, A., & Nelson, R. (1989). Teaching social studies to high school students with academic handicaps in a mainstreamed setting: Effects of a computerized study guide. *Journal of Learning Disabilities, 22,* 102–107.

Horton, S. V., Lovitt, T. C., & Slocum, T. (1988). Teaching geography to high-school students with academic deficits: Effects of a computerized map tutorial. *Learning Disability Quarterly, 11,* 371–379.

Howell, K. W., & Kaplan, J. S. (1980). *Diagnosing basic skills: A handbook for deciding what to teach.* Columbus, OH: Charles E. Merrill.

Howell, K. W., Kaplan, J. S., & O'Connell, C. Y. (1979). *Evaluating exceptional children: A task analysis approach.* Columbus, OH: Charles E. Merrill.

Howell, K. W., & Morehead, M. K. (1987). *Curriculum-based assessment for special and remedial education.* Columbus, OH: Charles E. Merrill.

Hoyt, K. B. (1977). Community resources for career education. *Occupational Outlook Quarterly, 21,* 10–21.

Huberty, T. J., Koller, J. R., & Ten Brink, T. D. (1980). Adaptive behavior in the definition of the mentally retarded. *Exceptional Children, 46,* 256–261.

Hudson, P. J., Schwartz, S. E., Sealander, K. A., Campbell, P., & Hensel, J. W. (1988). Successfully employed adults with handicaps: Characteristics and transition strategies. *Career Development for Exceptional Individuals, 11,* 7–14.

Huntze, S. L. (1985). A position paper of the council for children with behavior disorders. *Behavioral Disorders, 10,* 167–174.

Hursh, N. C. (1982). A career education model of students with special needs. *TEACHING Exceptional Children, 15,* 52–56.

Hudson, B. A. (1987). Adapting computer software and hardware for students with special needs. In J. Gottlieb & B. W. Gottlieb (Eds.), *Advances in special education* (Vol. 6, pp. 171–187). London: JAI Press.

Iacono, T. A., & Miller, J. F. (1989). Can microcomputers be used to teach communication skills to students with mental retardation? *Education and Training in Mental Retardation, 24,* 32–44.

Ianacone, R. N., & Stodden, R. A. (1987). Transition issues and directions for individuals who are mentally retarded. In R. N. Ianacone & R. A. Stodden (Eds.), *Transition issues and directions* (pp. 1–9). Reston, VA: The Council for Exceptional Children.

Idol-Maestas, L. (1983). *Special educator's consulting handbook.* Rockville, MD: Aspen Systems.

Ingalls, R. P. (1978). *Mental retardation: The changing outlook.* New York: Wiley.

Iwata, B., & Bailey, J. (1974). Reward versus cost systems: An analysis of their effects on students and teacher. *Journal of Applied Behavior Analysis, 7,* 567–576.

Jackson, N. F., Jackson, D. A., & Monroe, C. (1983). *Getting along with others: Teaching social effectiveness to children.* Champaign, IL: Research Press.

Jendrek, M. P. (1988). Outdoor recreational needs assessment: The importance of drawing two samples from the community. *Journal of Leisure Research, 20,* 154–161.

Jenkins, J. R., Stein, M. L., & Osborn, J. (1981). What next after decoding? Instruction and research in reading comprehension. *Exceptional Education Quarterly, 2*(1), 27–39.

Jesser, D. (1984). Career education: Challenges and issues. *Journal of Career Education, 11*, 20–24.

Johnson, B. F., & Cuvo, A. J. (1981). Teaching mentally retarded adults to cook. *Behavior Modification, 5*(2), 187–202.

Johnson, M. S., & Bailey, J. S. (1977). The modification of leisure behavior in a half-way house for retarded women. *Journal of Applied Behavior Analysis, 10*, 273–282.

Jones, A., & Robson, C. (1979). Language training and the severely mentally handicapped. In N. Ellis (Ed.), *Handbook of mental deficiency* (2nd ed., pp. 367–400). Hillsdale, NJ: Lawrence Erlbaum.

Kaczmarek, L. (1985). Integrating language/communication objectives into the total preschool curriculum. *TEACHING Exceptional Children, 17*, 183–189.

Kampwirth, T. J., & Bates, M. (1980). Modality preference and teaching methods: A review of research: *Academic Therapy, 15*, 597–605.

Kann, R. (1983). The method of repeated readings: Expanding the neurological impress method for use with disabled readers. *Journal of Learning Disabilities, 16*, 90–92.

Katz, S., & Yekutiel, E. (1974). Leisure time problems of mentally retarded graduates of training programs. *Mental Retardation, 12*, 54–57.

Kauffman, J. M. (1982). Social policy issues in special education and related services for emotionally disturbed children and youth. In M. M. Noel & N. G. Haring (Eds.), *Progress or change: Issues in educating the emotionally disturbed: Vol. 1. Identification and program planning* (pp. 44–73). Seattle: University of Washington.

Kauffman, J. M. (1985). *Characteristics of children's behavior disorders* (3rd ed.). Columbus, OH: Charles E. Merrill.

Kauffman, J. M., Gerber, M. M., & Semmel, M. I. (1988). Arguable assumption underlying the regular education initiative. *Journal of Learning Disabilities, 21*, 6–11.

Kaufman, M. J., Gottlieb, J., Agard, J. A., & Kukic, M. B. (1975). Mainstreaming: Toward an explanation of the concept. *Focus on Exceptional Children, 7*(3), 1–12.

Kavale, K. (1981). Functions of the Illinois Test of Psycholinguistic Abilities (ITPA): Are they trainable? *Exceptional Children, 47*, 496–510.

Keilitz, I., & Dunivant, N. (1987). The learning disabled offender. In C. M. Nelson, R. B. Rutherford, Jr., and B. I. Wolford (Eds.), *Special education in the criminal justice system* (pp. 120–139). Columbus, OH: Charles E. Merrill.

Keilitz, I., Horner, R., & Brown, K. (1975). *Project MORE.* Bellevue, WA: Edmark Associates.

Keogh, B. K. (1987). Learning disabilities: In defense of a construct. *Learning Disabilities Research, 3*, 4–9.

Keogh, B. K. (1988). Improving services for problem learners: Rethinking and restructuring. *Journal of Learning Disabilities, 21*, 19–22.

Kerr, M. M., & Nelson, C. M. (1989). *Strategies for managing behavior problems in the classroom* (2nd ed.). Columbus, OH: Charles E. Merrill.

Kerr, M. M., Nelson, C. M., & Lambert, D. L. (1987). *Helping adolescents with learning and behavior problems.* Columbus, OH: Charles E. Merrill.

Kerr, M. M., & Zigmond, N. (1984). *The School Survival Skills Project: 1983–84 annual report.* Pittsburgh, PA: University of Pittsburgh.

Kinzer, C. K., Sherwood, R. D., & Bransford, J. D. (1986). *Computer strategies for education: Foundations and content-area applications.* Columbus, OH: Charles E. Merrill.

Kirk, S., Kliebhan, J. M., & Lerner, J. W. (1978). *Teaching reading to slow and disabled readers.* Boston: Houghton Mifflin.

Kleiber, D., Larson, R., & Csikszentmihalyi, M. (1986). The experience of leisure in adolescence. *Journal of Leisure Research, 18,* 169–176.

Knapczyk, D. R. (1988). Reducing aggressive behaviors in special and regular class settings by training alternate responses. *Behavior Disorders, 14,* 27–39.

Kneedler, R. D., & Hallahan, D. P. (1981). Self monitoring of on task behavior with learning disabled children: Current studies and directions. *Exceptional Education Quarterly, 2,* 73–78.

Koegal, P., & Edgerton, R. B. (1982). Labeling and the perception of handicap among black mildly retarded adults. *American Journal of Mental Deficiency, 87,* 266–276.

Kokaska, C. J., & Brolin, D. E. (1985). *Career education for handicapped children and youth* (2nd ed.). Columbus, OH: Charles E. Merrill.

Kolko, D. J., Dorsett, P. G., & Milan, M. A. (1981). A total assessment approach to the evaluation of social skills training: The effectiveness of an anger control program for adolescent psychiatric patients. *Behavior Assessment, 3,* 383–402.

Koller, E., & Mulhern, T. (1977). Use of a pocket calculator to train arithmetic skills with trainable adolescents. *Education and Training of the Mentally Retarded, 12,* 332–335.

Konczak, L., & Johnson, C. M. (1983). Reducing inappropriate verbalizations in a sheltered workshop through differential reinforcement of other behavior. *Education and Training of the Mentally Retarded, 18,* 120–124.

Kraus, M., & MacEachron, A. (1982). Competitive employment training for mentally retarded adults: The supported work model. *American Journal of Mental Deficiency, 86,* 650–653.

Kysela, G. M., & Hillyard, A. (1978). Applied behavior analysis and developmental handicaps. In J. P. Das & D. Baine (Eds.), *Mental retardation for special educators* (pp. 178–202). Springfield, IL: Charles C. Thomas.

Lagomarcino, A., Reid, D., Ivancic, M., & Law, G. (1984). Leisure dance instruction for severely and profoundly retarded persons: Teaching an intermediate community living skill. *Journal of Applied Behavior Analysis, 17,* 71–84.

Lakein, A. (1973). *How to get control of your time and your life.* New York: P. H. Wyden.

Lancioni, G. (1982). Employment of normal third and fourth graders for training retarded children to solve problems dealing with quantity. *Education and Training of the Mentally Retarded, 17,* 93–102.

Landesman-Dwyer, S. (1981). Living in the community. *American Journal of Mental Deficiency, 86,* 223–234.

Langone, J. (1981). Curriculum for the trainable mentally retarded—or What do I do when the ditto machine dies? *Education and Training of the Mentally Retarded, 16,* 150–154.

Langone, J. (1986). *Teaching retarded learners: Curriculum and methods for improving instruction.* Boston: Allyn and Bacon.

Langone, J., & Gill, D. (1984). Modifying vocational education curricula to accommodate handicapped learners: Combining the efforts of special and vocational teachers. *The Exceptional Child, 31* (1), 39–45.

Langone, J., & Gill, D. (1985). Assisting the handicapped in becoming productive citizens: Business, industry and education's roles in the parallel teaching approach. *Journal of Career Development, 11* (4), 289–294.

Langone, J., & Gill, D. (1986). Improving the vocational components of the IEP: A partnership between rehabilitation and education. *Journal of Rehabilitation, 52,* 63–67.

Langone, J., Koorland, M., & Oseroff, A. (1987). Producing changes in the instructional behavior of teachers for the mentally handicapped through inservice education. *Education and Treatment of Children, 10,* 146–164.

Langone, J., & Westling, D. L. (1979). Generalization of prevocational and vocational skills: Some practical tactics. *Education and Training of the Mentally Retarded, 14,* 216–221.

Lathom, W., & Eagle, C. T. (1982). Music for the severely handicapped. *Music Educators Journal,* 68(8), 30–31.

Laycock, V. K. (1980). Prescriptive programming in the mainstream. In J. W. Schifani, R. M. Anderson, & S. J. Odle (Eds.), *Implementing learning in the least restrictive environment* (pp. 101–132). Baltimore: University Park Press.

Leff, R. B. (1975). Teaching TMR children and adults to dial the telephone. *Mental Retardation, 13,* 9–11.

Leff, R. B. (1974). Teaching the TMR to dial the telephone. *Mental Retardation, 12,* 12–13.

Leinhardt, G., Bickel, W., & Pallay, A. (1982). Unlabeled but still entitled: Toward more effective remediation. *Teachers College Record, 84*(2), 391–422.

Leinhardt, G., & Pallay, A. (1982). Restrictive educational settings: Exile or haven? *Review of Educational Research, 52,* 557–578.

Lent, J. R., & McLean, B. M. (1976). The trainable retarded: The technology of teaching. In N. G. Haring & R. L. Schiefelbusch (Eds.), *Teaching special children* (pp. 686–726). New York: McGraw-Hill.

Leonard, L. (1983). Speech selection and modification in language-disordered children. *Topics in Language Disorders, 4*(1), 28–37.

Lerner, J. W. (1981). *Learning disabilities: Theories, diagnosis, and teaching strategies* (3rd ed.). Boston: Houghton Mifflin.

Levy, S. A., & Lahm, E. A. (1985). Microcomputers in special education management. In E. McClellan (Ed.), *Microcomputer applications in special education: A training manual for special education teacher educators.* Reston, VA: The Council for Exceptional Children.

Lick, C. M., & Little, T. H. (1987). Computers and mildly handicapped individuals. In J. D. Lindsey (Ed.), *Computers and exceptional individuals* (pp. 61–82). Columbus, OH: Charles E. Merrill.

Lieberman, L. (1982). The nightmare of scheduling. *Journal of Learning Disabilities, 15*(1), 57–58.

Lilly, M. S. (1986). The relationship between general and special education: A new face on an old issue. *Counterpoint, 6,* 10.

Lindsey, O. R. (1964). Direct measurement and prognosis of retarded behavior. *Journal of Education, 147,* 62–81.

Lombardo, V. (1980). *Paraprofessionals in special education.* Springfield, IL: Charles C. Thomas.

Lovitt, T. C. (1976). Applied behavior analysis techniques and curriculum research: Implications for research. In N. G. Haring & R. L. Schiefelbusch (Eds.), *Teaching special children* (pp. 112–156). New York: McGraw-Hill.

Lovitt, T. C. (1978). *In spite of my resistance I've learned from children.* Columbus, OH: Charles E. Merrill.

Lovitt, T. C. (1984). *Tactics for teaching.* Columbus, OH: Charles E. Merrill.

Lovitt, T. C. (1989). *Introduction to learning disabilities.* Boston: Allyn and Bacon.

Lovitt, T. C., & Curtiss, K. A. (1968). Effects of manipulating an antecedent event on mathematics response rate. *Journal of Applied Behavior Analysis, 1,* 329–333.

Lovitt, T. C., & Esveldt, K. A. (1970). The relative effects on math performance of single- versus multiple-ratio schedules: A case study. *Journal of Applied Behavior Analysis, 3,* 216–270.

Lovitt, T. C., & Smith, D. D. (1974). Using withdrawal of positive reinforcement to alter subtraction performance. *Exceptional Children, 40,* 357–358.

Lowe, M., & Cuvo, A. (1976). Teaching coin summation to the mentally retarded. *Journal of Applied Behavior Analysis, 9,* 483–489.

Lubke, M. M., Rogers, B., & Evans, K. T. (1989). Teaching fractions with videodiscs. *TEACHING Exceptional Children, 21,* 55–56.

Luftig, R. L. (1989). *Assessment of learners with special needs.* Boston: Allyn and Bacon.

Lund, K. A., Schnapps, L., & Bijou, S. (1983). Let's take another look at recordkeeping. *TEACHING Exceptional Children, 15,* 155–159.

Lynch, E. W., & Lewis, R. B. (1988). The nature and needs of exceptional people. In E. W. Lynch & R. B. Lewis (Eds.), *Exceptional children and adults: An introduction to special education* (pp. 4–45). Glenview, IL: Scott, Foresman.

Lynch, K. P., Kiernan, W. E., & Stark, J. A. (1982). *Prevocational and vocational education for special needs youth: A blueprint for the 1980's.* Baltimore: Paul H. Brooks.

Lyon, G. R. (1985). Identification and remediation of learning disabilities subtypes: Preliminary findings. *Learning Disabilities Focus, 1,* 21–35.

Lyon, G. R., & Watson, B. (1981). Empirically derived subgroups of learning disabled readers: Diagnostic characteristics. *Journal of Learning Disabilities, 14,* 256–261.

MacMillan, D. L. (1972). Paired-associate learning as a function of explicitness of mediational set by EMR and nonretarded children. *American Journal of Mental Deficiency, 76,* 686–691.

MacMillan, D. L. (1973). *Behavior modification in education.* New York: Macmillan.

MacMillan, D. L. (1977). *Mental retardation in school and society.* Boston: Little, Brown.

MacMillan, D. L. (1982). *Mental retardation in school and society* (2nd ed.). Boston: Little, Brown.

MacMillan, D. L. (1988). Issues in mild mental retardation. *Education and Training in Mental Retardation, 23,* 273–284.

MacMillan, D. L., Keogh, B. K., & Jones, R. L. (1986). Special education research on mildly handicapped learners. In M. C. Wittrock (Ed.), *Handbook of research on teaching* (3rd ed., pp. 686–726). New York: Macmillan.

MacPherson, E., Cander, B., & Hohman, R. A. (1974). A comparison of three methods for eliminating disruptive lunchroom behavior. *Journal of Applied Behavior Analysis, 7,* 287–298.

Maddux, C. D. (1984, January). Using microcomputers with the learning disabled: Will the potential be realized? *Educational Computer,* 31–32.

Maddux, R. B. (1988). *Successful negotiation.* Los Altos, CA: Crisp Publications.

Mager, R. F. (1975). *Preparing instructional objectives.* Palo Alto, CA: Fearon.

Maheady, L., Harper, G. F., & Sacca, M. K. (1988). Peer mediated instruction: A promising approach to meeting the needs of learning disabled adolescents. *Learning Disability Quarterly, 11,* 108–113.

Malouf, D. B., Morariu, J., Coulson, D. B., & Maiden, V. S. (1989). Special education teachers' preferences for sources of software evaluation information. *Journal of Special Education Technology, 9,* 144–155.

Mank, D. M., & Horner, R. H. (1988). Instructional programming in vocational education. In R. Gaylord-Ross (Ed.), *Vocational education for persons with handicaps* (pp. 142–173). Mountain View, CA: Mayfield Publishers.

Mann, L., & Sabatino, D. A. (1985). *Foundations of cognitive process in remedial and special education*. Rockville, MD: Aspen.

Mann, V. A., Cowin, E., & Schoenheimer, J. (1989). Phonological processing, language comprehension, and reading ability. *Journal of Learning Disabilities, 22,* 76–89.

Marholin, II, D., O'Toole, K. M., Touchette, P. E., Berger, P. L, & Doyle, D. A. (1979). "I'll have a Big Mac, large fries, large Coke, and apple pie," . . . or teaching adaptive community skills. *Behavior Therapy, 10,* 236–248.

Marland, S. P. (1971, May). *Career education now.* Speech presented at the convention of the National Association of Secondary School Principals, Houston, TX.

Marland, S. P. (1974). *Career education: A proposal for reform.* New York: McGraw-Hill.

Marozas, D. S., & May, D. C. (1988). *Issues and practices in special education.* New York: Longman.

Marpet, L., & Prentky, J. (1974). Tips on teaching arithmetic concepts. *Journal for Special Educators of the Mentally Retarded, 10*(3), 197–199.

Marsh, G. E., & Price, B. J. (1980). *Methods for teaching the mildly handicapped adolescent.* St. Louis: C. V. Mosby.

Marsh, G. E., Price, B. J., & Smith, T. E. (1983). *Teaching mildly handicapped children.* St. Louis: C. V. Mosby.

Marston, D., & Magnusson, D. (1985). Implementing curriculum-based measurement in special and regular education settings. *Exceptional Children, 52,* 266–276.

Martin, G., & Pear, J. (1978). *Behavior modification: What it is and how to do it.* Englewood Cliffs, NJ: Prentice Hall.

Martin, M., Pallotta-Cornick, A., Johnstone, G., & Goyos, A. (1980). A supervisory strategy to improve work performance for lower functioning retarded clients in a sheltered workshop. *Journal of Applied Behavior Analysis, 13*(1), 183–190.

Marvin, C. A. (1989). Language and learning. In D. D. Smith (Ed.), *Teaching students with learning and behavior problems* (pp. 147–181). Englewood Cliffs, NJ: Prentice Hall.

Maslow, A. (1970). *Motivation and personality.* New York: Harper & Row.

Mastropieri, M. A., Emerick, K., & Scruggs, T. E. (1988). Mnemonic instruction of science concepts. *Behavioral Disorders, 14,* 48–56.

Mather, N. (1988). Computer-assisted instruction. In C. S. Bos & S. Vaughn, *Strategies for teaching students with learning and behavior problems* (pp. 282–301). Boston: Allyn and Bacon.

Mathes, P. G., & Proctor, T. J. (1988). Direct instruction for teaching "hard to teach" students. *Reading Improvement, 25,* 92–97.

Matson, J. L. (1980). Preventing home accidents: A training program for the retarded. *Behavior Modification, 4,* 397–410.

Matson, J. L. (1981). Use of independence training to teach shopping skills to mildly mentally retarded adults. *American Journal of Mental Deficiency, 86,* 178–183.

Maynard, M. (1976). The value of creative arts for the developmentally disabled child: Implications for recreation therapists in community day service programs. *Therapeutic Recreation Journal, 10,* 10–13.

McClellan, E. (1985). Introduction to microcomputers. In E. McClellan (Ed.), *Microcomputer applications in special education: A training manual for special education teacher educators* (pp. I-1–I-14). Reston, VA: The Council for Exceptional Children.

McConnell, S. R., & Odom, S. L. (1986). Sociometrics: Peer-referenced measures and the assessment of social competence. In P. S. Strain, M. J. Guralnick, & H. M. Walker (Eds.), *Children's social behavior: Development, assessment, and modification* (pp. 215–286). New York: Academic Press.

McCord, W. T. (1983). From theory to reality: Obstacles to the implementation of the normalization principle in human services. *Mental Retardation, 20,* 247–253.

McDaniel, C. O. (1971). Extra-curricular activities as a factor in social acceptance among EMR students. *Mental Retardation, 9,* 26–28.

McDaniel, T. (1980). Corporal punishment and teacher liability: Questions teachers ask. *The Clearing House, 54,* 10–13.

McDonough, K. M. (1989). Analysis of the expressive language characteristics of emotionally handicapped students in social interactions. *Behavioral Disorders, 14,* 127–139.

McKinney, J. D. (1984). The search for subtypes of specific learning disability. *Annual Review of Learning Disabilities, 2,* 19–26.

McLoughlin, C. S., Garner, J. B., & Callahan, M. (1987). *Getting employed, staying employed.* Baltimore: Paul H. Brooks.

McLoughlin, J. A., & Netick, A. (1983). Defining learning disabilities: A new and cooperative direction. *Journal of Learning Disabilities, 16,* 21–23.

McNutt, G., & Mandlebaum, L. H. (1980). General assessment competencies for special education teachers. *Exceptional Education Quarterly, 16,* 1–5.

McReynolds, L. V. (1969). Application of timeout from positive reinforcement for increasing the efficiency of speech training. *Journal of Applied Behavior Analysis, 2,* 199–205.

Meichenbaum, D., & Asarnow, J. (1979). Cognitive-behavioral modification and metacognitive development: Implications for the classroom. In P. C. Kendall & S. D. Hollon (Eds.), *Cognitive behavioral interventions: Theory, research, and procedures.* New York: Academic Press.

Meichenbaum, D., & Goodman, S. (1979). Clinical use of private speech and critical questions about its study in natural settings. In G. Zivin (Ed.), *The development of self-regulation through private speech.* New York: Wiley & Sons.

Mercer, C. D. (1987). *Students with learning disabilities* (3rd ed.). Columbus, OH: Charles E. Merrill.

Mercer, C. D., & Mercer, A. R. (1985). *Teaching students with learning problems* (2nd ed.). Columbus, OH: Charles E. Merrill.

Mercer, C. D., & Mercer, A. R. (1989). *Teaching students with learning problems* (3rd ed.). Columbus, OH: Charles E. Merrill.

Meyen, E. (1988). A commentary on special education. In E. Meyen & T. Skrtic (Eds.), *Exceptional children and youth* (3rd ed., pp. 3–48). Denver: Love Publishing.

Meyen, E., & Skrtic, T. (Eds.). (1988). *Exceptional children and youth* (3rd ed.). Denver: Love Publishing.

Meyer, A. (1983). Origins and prevention of emotional disturbances among learning disabled children. *Topics in Learning and Learning Disabilities, 3,* 59–70.

Meyers, J., & Lytle, S. (1986). Assessment of the learning process. *Exceptional Children, 53,* 138–144.

Milgram, N. A. (1967). Retention of mediation set in paired-associated learning of normal and retarded children. *Journal of Experimental Child Psychology, 5,* 341–349.

Miller, J. F. (1978). Assessing children's language behavior: A developmental process approach. In R. L. Schiefelbusch (Ed.), *The bases of language intervention* (pp. 269–318). Baltimore: University Park Press.

Miller, L. K. (1980). *Principles of everyday behavior analysis* (2nd ed.). Monterey, CA: Brooks/Cole.

Miller, P. W. (1978). Reinforcing metric concepts for EMR's. *School Shop, 38* (4), 33–34.

Miller, S. C., & Cooke, N. L. (1989). Mainstreaming students with learning disabilities for videodisc math instruction. *TEACHING Exceptional Children, 21,* 57–60.

Mitchell, J. (1983). *Tests in Print III.* Buros Institute of Mental Measurements, Lincoln, NE: University of Nebraska Press.

Mithaug, D. E., Martin, J. E., & Agran, M. (1987). Adaptability instruction: The goal of transitional programming. *Exceptional Children, 53,* 500–505.

Mittler, P. (1976). Assessment for language training. In P. Berry (Ed.), *Language and communication in the mentally handicapped* (pp. 5–35). London: Edward Arnold.

Mobily, K. E. (1989). Meanings of recreation and leisure among adolescents. *Leisure Studies, 8,* 11–23.

Mokros, J. R., & Russell, S. J. (1986). Learner centered software: A survey of microcomputer use with special needs students. *Journal of Learning Disabilities, 19,* 185–190.

Moldolfsky, P. (1983). Teaching students to determine the central story problem: A practical application of scheme theory. *Reading Teacher, 36,* 740–745.

Moon, S., & Renzaglia, A. (1982). Physical fitness and the mentally retarded: A critical review of the literature. *Journal of Special Education, 16,* 269–287.

Moran, M. R. (1979). Nine steps to the diagnostic prescriptive process in the classroom. In E. Meyen, G. A. Vergason, & R. J. Whelan (Eds.), *Instructional planning for exceptional children* (pp. 177–197). Denver: Love Publishing.

Moran, M. R. (1983). Analytical evaluation of formal written language skills as a diagnostic procedure. *Diagnostique, 8,* 17–31.

Morgan, D. (1981). Characteristics of a quality IEP. *Education Unlimited, 3,* 12–17.

Morgan, D. P., & Jenson, W. R. (1988). *Teaching behaviorally disordered students: Preferred practices,* Columbus, OH: Charles E. Merrill.

Mori, A. (1979). Vocational education and special education: A new partnership in career education. *Journal of Career Education, 6,* 55–69.

Morse, W. C. (1959). The life space interview. *American Journal of Orthopsychiatry, 29,* 27–44.

Morsink, C. (1984). *Teaching special needs students in regular classrooms.* Boston: Little, Brown.

Mulhern, T. J., & Koller, E. Z. (1977). Use of a pocket calculator to train arithmetic skills with trainable adolescents. *Education and Training of the Mentally Retarded, 12,* 322–325.

Nadler, B., & Shore, K. (1980). Individualized education programs: A look at realities. *Education Unlimited, 2* (3), 30–33.

National Commission on Secondary Vocational Education (1984). *The unfinished agenda: The role of vocational education in the high school.* Columbus: The Ohio State University, National Center for Research in Vocational Education.

National Institute of Child Health and Human Development. (1987). Report of the Federal Interagency Committee on Learning Disabilities. Bethesda, MD: National Institute on Health (NIH).

Neef, N., Walters, J., & Egel, A. (1984). Establishing generative yes/no responses in developmentally disabled children. *Journal of Applied Behavior Analysis, 17,* 453–460.

Neef, N. A., Iwata, B. A., & Page, T. J. (1978). Public transportation training: In vivo versus classroom instruction. *Journal of Applied Behavior Analysis, 11,* 331–344.

Neef, N. A., Iwata, B. A., & Page, T. J. (1980). The effects of interpersonal training versus high-density reinforcement on spelling acquisition and retention. *Journal of Applied Behavior Analysis, 13,* 153–158.

Neitupski, J., & Svoboda, R. (1982). Teaching a cooperative leisure skill to severely handicapped adults. *Education and Training of the Mentally Retarded, 17,* 38–43.

Nelson, C., & Rutherford, R. (1983). Time-out revisited: Guidelines for its use in special education. *Exceptional Education Quarterly, 3*(4), 56–67.

Neubert, D. A., Tilson, G. P. Jr., & Ianacone, R. N. (1989). Postsecondary transition needs and employment patterns of individuals with mild disabilities. *Exceptional Children, 55,* 494–500.

Newcomer, P. L., Barenbaum, E. M., & Noding, B. F. (1988). Comparison of the strong production of learning disabled, normal-achieving, and low-achieving children under two modes of production. *Learning Disability Quarterly, 11,* 82–96.

Nietupski, J., Certo, N., Pumpian, I., & Belmore, K. (1976). Supermarket shopping: Teaching severely handicapped students to generate a shopping list and make purchases functionally linked to meal preparation. In L. Brown, N. Certo, K. Belmore, & T. Crowner (Eds.), *Madison's alternative for zero exclusion: Papers and programs related to public schools services for secondary age severely handicapped students* (Vol. 7, p. 1). Madison, WI: Madison Public Schools.

Nietupski, J., Hamre-Nietupski, S., Houselog, M., Donder, D. J., & Anderson, R. J. (1988). Proactive administration strategies for implementing community based programs for students with moderate/severe handicaps. *Education and Training in Mental Retardation, 23,* 138–146.

Nihira, K., Foster, R., Shellhaas, M., & Leland, H. (1974). *Adaptive Behavior Scale: Manual* (rev. ed.). Washington, DC: American Association on Mental Deficiency.

Nutter, D., & Reid, D. H. (1978). Teaching retarded women a clothing selection skill using community norms. *Journal of Applied Behavior Analysis, 11,* 475–487.

Oakland, T. (1980). Nonbiased assessment of minority group children. *Exceptional Education Quarterly, 1*(3), 31–46.

Oberlin, L. (1982). How to teach children to hate mathematics. *School Science & Mathematics, 82,* 261.

O'Brien, F., Bugle, C., & Azrin, N. H. (1972). Training and maintaining a retarded child's proper eating. *Journal of Applied Behavior Analysis, 5,* 67–72.

O'Connor, W., & Hermelin, B. (1963). Recall in normals and subnormals of like mental age. *Journal of Abnormal and Social Psychology, 66,* 81–84.

Oetting, G., & Miller, C. D. (1977). Work and the disadvantaged: The work adjustment hierarchy. *Personnel and Guidance Journal, 55,* 29–35.

Ogletree, E. J. (1977). Teaching the four arithmetic processes to the EMR child. *Journal for Special Educators of the Mentally Retarded, 13*(3), 146–153.

Ogletree, E. J., & Ujlaki, V. (1976). A motoric approach to teaching multiplication to the mentally retarded child. *Education and Training of the Mentally Retarded, 11,* 129–134.

Okolo, C. M. (1988). Instructional environments in secondary vocational education programs: Implications for LD adolescents. *Learning Disability Quarterly, 11,* 136–148.

Okolo, C. M., & Sitlington, P. (1988). The role of special education in LD adolescents' transition from school to work. *Learning Disabilities Quarterly, 11,* 292–306.

Olson, J., Algozzine, B., & Schmid, R. E. (1980). Mild, moderate, and severe EH: An empty distinction? *Behavioral Disorders, 5,* 96–101.

Orelove, F. P. (1982). Developing daily schedules for classrooms of severely handicapped students. *Education and Treatment of Children, 5,* 59–64.

Orr, G. J. (1977). Money management in life situations. *Education and Training of the Mentally Retarded, 12,* 65–67.

Page, T. J., Iwata, B. A., & Neff, N. A. (1976). Teaching pedestrian skills to retarded persons: Generalization from the classroom to the natural environment. *Journal of Applied Behavior Analysis, 9,* 433–444.

Pany, D., & McCoy, K. M. (1988). Effects of corrective feedback on word accuracy and reading comprehension of readers with learning disabilities. *Journal of Learning Disabilities, 21,* 546–550.

Panyan, M. V., Hummel, J., & Jackson, L. B. (1988). The integration of technology in the curriculum. *Journal of Special Education Technology, 9,* 109–119.

Paris, S. G., & Oka, E. R. (1989). Strategies for comprehending text and coping with reading difficulties. *Learning Disabilities Quarterly, 12,* 32–42.

Payne, J. S., & Patton, J. R. (1981). *Mental retardation.* Columbus, OH: Charles E. Merrill.

Payne, J. S., Polloway, E. A., Smith, J. E., & Payne, R. A. (1981). *Strategies for teaching the mentally retarded* (2nd ed.). Columbus, OH: Charles E. Merrill.

Peter, L. J. (1975). *Competencies for teaching: Classroom instruction.* Belmont, CA: Wadsworth.

Peterson, J., Heistad, D., Peterson, D., & Reynolds, M. (1985). Montevideo individualized prescriptive instructional management system. *Exceptional Children, 52,* 239–243.

Phelps, L. A., & Lutz, R. J. (1977). *Career exploration and preparation for the special needs learner.* Boston: Allyn and Bacon.

Phillips, E. L., Phillips, E. A., Fixsen, D., & Wolfe, M. M. (1971). Achievement place: Modification of the behaviors of pre-delinquent boys within a token economy. *Journal of Applied Behavior Analysis, 4,* 45–49.

Polloway, E. A., Patton, J. R., Payne, J. S., & Payne, R. A. (1989). *Strategies for teaching learners with special needs* (4th ed.). Columbus, OH: Charles E. Merrill.

Polloway, E. A., Payne, J. S., Patton, J. R., & Payne, R. A. (1985). *Strategies for teaching retarded and special needs learners* (3rd ed.). Columbus, OH: Charles E. Merrill.

Polloway, E. A., & Polloway, C. H. (1980). Remediating reversals through stimulus fading. *Academic Therapy, 15,* 539–543.

Polloway, E. A., & Polloway, C. H. (1981). Survival words for disabled readers. *Academic Therapy, 16,* 443–448.

Polloway, E. A., & Smith, J. D. (1983). Changes in mild mental retardation: Population, programs, and perspectives. *Exceptional Children, 50,* 149.

Polloway, E. A., & Smith, J. E. (1982). *Teaching language skills to exceptional learners.* Denver: Love Publishing.

Pomerantz, D., & Marholin, D. (1977). Vocational habilitation: A time for change. In E. Sontag (Ed.), *Educational programming for the severely and profoundly handicapped* (pp. 129–141). Reston, VA: The Council for Exceptional Children.

Poorman, C. (1980). Mainstreaming in reverse. *TEACHING Exceptional Children, 12,* 136–142.

Poplin, M. S. (1981). The severely learning disabled: Neglected or forgotten? *Learning Disability Quarterly, 4,* 330–335.

Porterfield, J., Herbert-Jackson, E., & Risley, T. (1976). Contingent observation: An effective and acceptable procedure for reducing disruptive behavior of young children in a group setting. *Journal of Applied Behavior Analysis, 9,* 55–64.

Poteet, J. A. (1980). Informal assessment of written expression. *Learning Disabilities Quarterly, 3*(4), 88–98.

Premack, D. (1959). Toward empirical behavior laws: Positive reinforcement. *Psychological Review, 66,* 219–233.

Pressley, M., Johnson, C. J., & Symons, S. (1987). Elaborating to learn and learning to elaborate. *Journal of Learning Disabilities, 20,* 76–91.

Price, M., & Goodman, L. (1980). Individualized education programs: A cost study. *Exceptional Children, 46,* 446–458.

Prillaman, D., & Abbott, J. C. (1983). *Educational diagnosis and prescriptive teaching.* Belmont, CA: Pitman Learning.

Public Law 94-142. Education for All Handicapped Children Act of 1975. 94th Congress, First Session, 1975.

Public Law 98-524. The Carl D. Perkins Vocational Educational Act of 1984. 98th Congress, 2nd Session, 1984.

Public Law 98-199. The Education of the Handicapped Act Amendments of 1983, reference of Public Statutes at large, Volume 97 (1983).

Public Law 98-524. The Carl D. Perkins Vocational Education Act, reference of Public Statues at large, Volume 98 (1984).

Pyecha, J. (1979). *A national survey of individualized education programs for handicapped children.* Research Triangle Park, NC: Research Triangle Institute.

Quay, H. C. (1975). Classification in the treatment of delinquency and antisocial behavior. In N. Hobbs (Ed.), *Issues in the classification of children* (Vol. 1). San Francisco: Jossey-Bass.

Quay, H. C. (1979). Classification. In H. C. Quay & J. S. Werry (Eds.), *Psychopathological disorders of children* (2nd ed., pp. 5–30). New York: Wiley.

Radabaugh, M. T., & Yukish, J. F. (1982). *Curriculum and methods for the mildly handicapped.* Boston: Allyn and Bacon.

Rakes, T. A., & Choate, J. S. (1989). *Language arts: Detecting and correcting special needs.* Boston: Allyn and Bacon.

Rau, D., Spooner, F., & Fimian, M. (1989). Career education needs of students with exceptionalities: One states case. *Exceptional Children, 55,* 501–507.

Rauth, M. (1981). What can be expected of the regular education teacher? Ideas and realities. *Exceptional Education Quarterly, 2,* 27–36.

Reichle, J. E., & Yoder, D. R. (1979). Assessment and early stimulation of communication in the severely and profoundly mentally retarded. In R. L. York & E. Edgar (Eds.), *Teaching the severely handicapped* (Vol. 4, pp. 79–98). Columbus, OH: Special Press.

Reid, D. K. (1988). *Teaching the learning disabled: A cognitive development approach.* Boston: Allyn and Bacon.

Reisman, F. K. (1982). *A guide to the diagnostic teaching of arithmetic* (3rd ed.). Columbus, OH: Charles E. Merrill.

Reiss, S., Levitan, G. W., & McNally, R. J. (1982). Emotionally disturbed mentally retarded people. *American Psychologist, 37,* 361–367.

Repp, A. (1983). *Teaching the mentally retarded.* Englewood Cliffs, NJ: Prentice Hall.

Repp, A., & Deitz, D. (1979). Reinforcement-based reductive procedures: Training and monitoring performances of institutional staff. *Mental Retardation, 17,* 221–226.

Repp, A. C., Klett, S. Z., Sosebee, L. H., & Speir, N. C. (1975). Differential effects of four token conditions on rate and choice of responding in a matching-to-sample task. *American Journal of Mental Deficiency, 80,* 51–56.

Repp, A. C., Nieminen, G. S., Olinger, E., & Brusca, R. (1988). Direct observation: Factors affecting the accuracy of observers. *Exceptional Children, 55,* 29–36.

Retish, P. (1989). Education and transition: Is there a relationship? *Career Development for Exceptional Individuals, 12,* 36–39.

Reynolds, M. C. (1988). A reaction to the JLD special series on the regular education initiative. *Journal of Learning Disabilities, 21,* 352–356.

Reynolds, M. C., & Birch, J. W. (1977). *Teaching exceptional children in all America's schools.* Reston, VA: The Council for Exceptional Children.

Reynolds, M. C., & Birch, J. W., (1988). *Adaptive mainstreaming: A primer for teachers and principals* (3rd ed.). New York: Longman.

Reynolds, M. C., Wang, M. C., & Walberg, H. J. (1987). The necessary restructuring of special and regular education. *Exceptional Children, 53,* 391–398.

Rhode, G., Morgan, D. P., & Young, K. R. (1983). Generalization and maintenance of treatment gains of behaviorally handicapped students from resource rooms to regular classrooms using self-evaluation procedures. *Journal of Applied Behavior Analysis, 16,* 171–188.

Rich, H. L. (1980). Managing interfering behavior. In J. W. Schifani, R. M. Anderson, & S. J. Odle (Eds.), *Implementing learning in the least restrictive environment.* Baltimore: University Park Press.

Richman, G., Reiss, M., Bauman, K., & Bailey, J. (1984). Teaching menstrual care to mentally retarded women: Acquisition, generalization, & maintenance. *Journal of Applied Behavior Analysis, 17,* 441–451.

Riordan, M., Iwata, B., Finney, J., Wohl, M., & Stanley, A. (1984). Behavioral assessment and treatment of chronic food refusal in handicapped children. *Journal of Applied Behavior Analysis, 17,* 327–342.

Risley, R., & Cuvo, A. J. (1980). Training mentally retarded adults to make emergency telephone calls. *Behavior Modification, 4,* 513–525.

Rizzo, J. V., & Zabel, R. H. (1988). *Educating children and adolescents with behavioral disorders: An integrative approach.* Boston: Allyn and Bacon.

Roberts, G. H. (1968). The failure strategies of third grade arithmetic pupils. *The Arithmetic Teacher, 15,* 442–446.

Robinson, N. M., & Robinson, H. B. (1976). *The mentally retarded child: A psychological approach* (2nd ed.). New York: McGraw-Hill.

Robinson, S. M., & Deshler, D. D. (1988). Learning disabled. In E. Meyen & T. M. Skrtic (Eds.), *Exceptional children and youth: An introduction* (3rd ed., pp. 109–138). Denver: Love Publishing.

Robinson-Wilson, M. A. (1976). Picture recipe cards as an approach to teaching severely retarded adults to cook. In G. T. Bellamy (Ed.), *Habilitation of the severely and profoundly retarded: Reports from the specialized training program* (pp. 99–108). Eugene: University of Oregon.

Robinson-Wilson, M. A. (1977). Picture recipe cards: An approach to teaching severely and profoundly retarded adults to cook. *Education and Training of the Mentally Retarded, 12,* 69–73.

Roe, B. D., Stoodt, B. D., & Burns, P. C. (1983). *Secondary school reading instruction: The content areas* (2nd ed.). Boston: Houghton Mifflin.

Rose, T. (1979). Reducing self-injurious behavior by DRO. *AAEPSH Review, 4,* 179–186.

Rose, T. (1983). A survey of corporal punishment of mildly handicapped students. *Exceptional Education Quarterly, 3*(4), 9–19.

Rupley, W. H., & Blair, T. R. (1983). *Reading diagnosis and remediation: Classroom and clinic* (2nd ed.). Boston: Houghton Mifflin.

Rusch, F. R., & Mithaug, D. E. (1980). *Vocational training for mentally retarded adults: A behavior analytic approach.* Champaign, IL: Research Press.

Rusch, F. R., & Phelps, L. A. (1987). Secondary special education and transition from school to work: A national priority. *Exceptional Children, 53,* 487–492.

Russell, B. E. (1982). Calculators in the special education classroom. *The Directive Teacher, 4*(1), 6 & 11.

Ryan, R. D. (1988). School-to-work transition for special needs students. *The Journal for Vocational Special Needs Education, 11,* 9–12.

Sabornie, E. J., & Kauffman, J. M. (1986). Social acceptance of learning disabled adolescents. *Learning Disability Quarterly, 9,* 55–60.

Sailor, W., & Guess, D. (1983). *Severely handicapped students: An instructional design.* Boston: Houghton Mifflin.

Sailor, W., Guess, D., Goetz, L., Schuler, A., Utley, B., & Baldwin, M. (1980). Language and severely handicapped persons. In W. Sailor, B. Wilcox, & L. Brown (Eds.), *Methods of instruction for severely handicapped students* (pp. 71–105). Baltimore: Paul H. Brooks.

Salend, S. J., & Kovalich, B. (1981). A group response-cost system mediated by free tokens: An alternative to token reinforcement. *American Journal of Mental Deficiency, 86*(2), 184–187.

Salvia, J., & Ysseldyke, J. E. (1985). *Assessment in special and remedial education* (3rd ed.). Boston: Houghton Mifflin.

Sander, M. (1981). Getting ready for arithmetic: Prerequisites for learning to add. *TEACHING Exceptional Children, 13,* 54–57.

Sarber, R., & Halasz, M. (1983). Teaching menu planning and grocery shopping skills to a mentally retarded mother. *Mental Retardation, 21*(3), 107–110.

Schalock, R. L., Harper, R. S., & Genung, T. (1981). Community integration of mentally retarded adults: Community placement and program success. *American Journal of Mental Deficiency, 85,* 478–488.

Schiefelbusch, R. L., & McCormick, L. (1981). Language and speech disorders. In J. M. Kauffman & D. P. Hallahan (Eds.), *Handbook of special education* (pp. 108–140). Englewood Cliffs, NJ: Prentice Hall.

Schilling, D., & Cuvo, A. J. (1983). The effects of a contingency-based lottery on the behavior of a special education class. *Education and Training of the Mentally Retarded, 18,* 52–58.

Schleien, S. (1982). Leisure education for the learning disabled student. *Learning Disabilities: An Interdisciplinary Journal, 1*(9), 105–122.

Schleien, S., Certo, N., & Muccino, A. (1984). Acquisition of leisure skills by a severely handicapped adolescent: A data based instructional program. *Education and Training of the Mentally Retarded, 19,* 297–305.

Schmid, R., Moneypenny, J., & Johnston, R. (1977). *Contemporary issues in special education.* New York: McGraw-Hill.

Schuler, A. L., & Perez, L. (1988). The role of social interaction in the development of thinking skills. In E. Meyen, G. A. Vergason, & R. J. Whelan (Eds.), *Effective instructional strategies for exceptional children* (pp. 259–275). Denver: Love Publishing.

Schulz, J. B., & Turnbull, A. (1983). *Mainstreaming handicapped students* (2nd ed.). Boston: Allyn and Bacon.

Schulman, E. D. (1980). *Focus on the retarded adult.* St. Louis: C. V. Mosby.

Schutz, R., Jostes, K., Rusch, F., & Lamson, D. (1980). Acquisition, transfer, and social validation of two vocational skills in a competitive employment setting. *Education and Training of the Mentally Retarded, 15,* 306–311.

Schwartz, L., & Oseroff, A. (1975). *Clinical teacher in special education.* Tallahassee: Florida State University.

Schwartz, S. E. (1977). *Real life math.* Chicago: Hubbard.

Schwartz, S. E., & Budd, D. (1983). Mathematics for handicapped learners: A functional approach for adolescents. In E. Meyen, G. A. Vergason, & B. R. Whelan (Eds.), *Promising practices for exceptional children* (pp. 321–340). Denver: Love Publishing.

Scott, L., & Goetz, E. (1980). Issues in the collection of in-class data by teachers. *Education and Treatment of Children, 3,* 65–71.

Seaman, J. A. (1973). Right up their alley. *TEACHING Exceptional Children, 5,* 196–198.

Sedlak, R. A., & Fitzmaurice, A. M. (1981). Teaching arithmetic. In J. M. Kauffman & D. P. Hallahan (Eds.), *Handbook of special education* (pp. 475–490). Englewood Cliffs, NJ: Prentice Hall.

Semel, E., & Wiig, E. (1982). *Clinical language intervention program.* Columbus, OH: Charles E. Merrill.

Sengstock, W. L., & Wyatt, K. E. (1976). Meters, liters, and grams: The metric system and its implications for curriculum for exceptional children. *TEACHING Exceptional Children, 8,* 58–65.

Shafer, M., Egel, A., & Neef, N. (1984). Training mildly handicapped peers to facilitate changes in the social interaction skills of autistic children. *Journal of Applied Behavior Analysis, 17,* 461–476.

Sherburne, S., Utley, B., McConnell, S., & Gannon, J. (1988). Decreasing violent or aggressive theme play among preschool children with behavior disorders. *Exceptional Children, 55,* 166–172.

Siders, J. A., & Whorton, J. (1982). The relationship of individual ability and IEP goal statements. *Elementary School Guidance and Counseling, 16,* 187–193.

Sidman, M., & Cresson, O. (1973). Reading and cross model transfer of stimulus equivalence in severe retardation. *American Journal of Mental Deficiency, 77,* 515–523.

Siegel, S. (1988). The career ladder program: Implementing Re-Ed principals in vocational settings. *Behavior Disorders, 14,* 16–26.

Siegel, S., Greener, K., Prieur, J., Robert, M., & Gaylord-Ross, R. (1989). The community vocational training program: A transition program for youths with mild handicaps. *Career Development for Exceptional Individuals, 12,* 48–64.

Silbert, J., Carnine, D., & Stein, M. (1981). *Direct instruction mathematics.* Columbus, OH: Charles E. Merrill.

Sileo, T. W., Rude, H. A., & Luckner, J. L. (1988). Collaborative consultation: A model for transition planning for handicapped youth. *Education and Training in Mental Retardation, 23,* 333–339.

Simon, C. (Ed.), (1985). *Communication skills and classroom success: Assessment of language-learning disabled students.* San Diego: College-Hill Press.

Sinclair, E., Forness, S. R., & Axleson, J. (1985). Psychiatric diagnosis: A study of its relationship to school needs. *Journal of Special Education, 19,* 333–344.

Sinclair, N. (1975). Cross country skiing for the mentally retarded. *Challenge, 5,* 33–35.

Singh, N., & Singh, J. (1984). Antecedent control of oral reading errors and self-corrections by mentally retarded children. *Journal of Applied Behavior Analysis, 17,* 111–120.

Skinner, B. F. (1953). *Science and human behavior.* New York: Macmillan.

Smeenge, M., Page, T., Iwata, B., & Ivancic, M. (1980). Teaching measurement skills to mentally retarded students: Training, generalization, and follow up. *Education and Training of the Mentally Retarded, 15,* 224–229.

Smeets, P. M., & Kleinloog, D. (1980). Teaching retarded women to use an experimental pocket calculator for making financial transactions. *Behavior Research of Severe Developmental Disabilities, 1,* 1–20.

Smith, A. L., Piersel, W., Filbeck, K., & Gross, E. (1983). The elimination of mealtime food stealing and scavenging behavior in an institutionalized severely mentally retarded adult. *Mental Retardation, 21* (6), 255–259.

Smith, D. D. (1989). *Teaching students learning and behavior problems* (2nd ed.). Englewood Cliffs, NJ: Prentice Hall.

Smith, G., & Smith, D. (1989). Schoolwide study skills program: The key to mainstreaming. *TEACHING Exceptional Children, 21,* 20–23.

Smith, G. J., & Edelen, P. J. (in press). A commencement model of secondary education and training in mild mental retardation. *Education and Training on Mental Retardation.*

Smith, J. O. (1988). Social and vocational problems of adults with learning disabilities. *Learning Disabilities Focus, 4,* 46–58.

Smith, M., & Meyers, A. (1979). Telephone skills training for retarded adults: Group and individual demonstrations with and without verbal instruction. *American Journal of Mental Deficiency, 83,* 581–587.

Smith, R. M. (Ed.) (1969). *Teacher diagnosis of educational difficulties.* Columbus, OH: Charles E. Merrill.

Smith, R. M. (1974). *Clinical teaching: Methods of instruction for the retarded* (2nd ed.). New York: McGraw-Hill.

Smith, R. M., & Neisworth, J. T. (1969). Fundamentals of informal educational assessment. In R. M. Smith (Ed.), *Teacher diagnosis of educational difficulties.* Columbus, OH: Charles E. Merrill.

Smith, R. M., Neisworth, J. T., & Greer, J. G. (1978). *Evaluating educational environments.* Columbus, OH: Charles E. Merrill.

Snell, M. E. (1981). Daily living skills. In J. M. Kauffman & D. P. Hallahan (Eds.), *Handbook of special education* (pp. 142–165). Englewood Cliffs, NJ: Prentice Hall.

Snell, M. E. (1983). Functional reading. In M. E. Snell (Ed.), *Systematic instruction of the moderately and severely handicapped* (2nd ed., pp. 324–385). Columbus, OH: Charles E. Merrill.

Snell, M. E. (1983). Implementation and monitoring of the IEP: Intervention strategies. In M. E. Snell (Ed.), *Systematic instruction of the moderately and severely handicapped* (2nd ed., pp. 113–145). Columbus, OH: Charles E. Merrill.

Snell, M. E., & Browder, D. M. (1986). Community-referenced instruction: Research and issues. *Journal of the Association for Persons with Severe Handicaps, 11,* 1–11.

Snell, M. E., & Smith, D. D. (1978). Intervention strategies. In M. E. Snell (Ed.), *Systematic instruction of the moderately and severely handicapped* (pp. 74–99). Columbus, OH: Charles E. Merrill.

Soffer, R. (1982). IEP decisions in which parents desire greater participation. *Education and Training of the Mentally Retarded, 17,* 67–70.

Sowers, J., Rusch, F., Connis, R., & Cummings, L. (1980). Teaching mentally retarded adults to time-manage in a vocational setting. *Journal of Applied Behavior Analysis, 13,* 119–128.

Sowers, J., Rusch, F. R., & Hudson, C. (1979). Training a severely retarded young adult to ride the city bus to and from work. *AAESPH Review, 4,* 15–23.

Sparrow, S. S., Balla, D. A., & Cicchetti, D. V. (1984). *Vineland Adaptive Behavior Scales-R.* Circle Pines, MN: American Guidance Service.

Sparzo, F. J., & Poteet, J. A. (1989). *Classroom behavior: Detecting and correcting special problems.* Boston: Allyn and Bacon.

Spears, D. L., Rusch, F. R., York, R., & Lilly, M. S. (1981). Training independent arrival behaviors to a severely mentally retarded child. *Journal of the Association for the Severely Handicapped, 6,* 40–45.

Spellman, C., DeBriere, T., Jarboe, D., Campbell, S., & Harris, C. (1978). Pictorial instruction: Training daily living skills. In M. E. Snell (Ed.), *Systematic instruction of the moderately and severely handicapped* (pp. 391–413). Columbus, OH: Charles E. Merrill.

Spikman, N., & Roth, F. (1984). Intervention strategies for learning disabled children with oral communication disorders. *Learning Disability Quarterly, 7*, 7–18.

Spitz, H. H. (1966). The role of input organization in the learning and memory of mental retardates. In N. Ellis (Ed.), *International review of mental retardation* (Vol. 2). New York: Academic Press.

Sprague, J., & Horner, R. (1984). The effects of single instance, multiple instance, and general case training on generalized vending machine use by moderately and severely handicapped students. *Journal of Applied Behavior Analysis, 17*, 273–278.

Stainback, W., & Stainback, S. (1984). A rationale for the merger of special and regular education. *Exceptional Children, 51*, 102–111.

Staples, K. S. (1975). *Coding from pictures.* Fargo, ND: North Dakota State University.

Stauffer, R. (1969). *Directing reading maturity as a cognitive process.* New York: Harper & Row.

Stephens, T. M., Blackhurst, A. E., & Magliocca, L. A. (1988). *Teaching mainstreamed students* (2nd ed.). New York: Pergamon Press.

Stephens, T. M., Hartman, A. C., & Lucas, V. H. (1982). *Teaching children basic skills: A curriculum handbook* (2nd ed.). Columbus, OH: Charles E. Merrill.

Sternberg, L., & Fair, G. W. (1982). Mathematics programs and materials. In T. Miller & E. Davis (Eds.), *The mildly handicapped student* (pp. 345–366). New York: Grune & Stratton.

Sternberg, L., Sedlak, R., Cherkes, M., & Minick, B. (1978). *Essential math and language skills program.* Northbrook, IL: Hubbard.

Sternberg, L., & Taylor, R. (1982). The insignificance of pyscholinguistic training: A reply to Kavale. *Exceptional Children, 49*, 254–256.

Sternberg, R. J., & Wagner, R. K. (1982). Automatization failure in learning disabilities. In H. L. Swanson (Ed.), Controversy: Strategy of capacity deficit. *Topics in Learning and Learning Disabilities, 2*(2), 1–11.

Stokes, T. F., & Baer, D. M. (1977). An implicit technology of generalization. *Journal of Applied Behavior Analysis, 10*, 349–367.

Stokes, T. F., & Baer, D. M. (1978). Am implicit technology of generalization. *Journal of Applied Behavior Technology, 10*, 349–367.

Stuckey, P. E., & Newbrough, J. R. (1981). Mental health of mentally retarded persons: Social-ecological consideration. In H. C. Haywood & J. R. Newbrough (Eds.), *Living environments for developmentally retarded persons.* Baltimore: University Park Press.

Sulzer-Azaroff, B., & Mayer, G. R. (1977). *Applying behavior-analysis procedures with children and youth.* New York: Holt, Rinehart, & Winston.

Super, D. E. (1976). Career education and the meanings of work. *Monographs on Career Education.* Washington, DC: Office of Education, U.S. Department of Health, Education and Welfare.

Swanson, H. L. (1988). Memory subtypes in learning disabled readers. *Learning Disability Quarterly, 11*, 342–357.

Swanson, H. L. (1982). Controversy: Strategy or capacity deficit. *Topics in Learning and Learning Disabilities, 2*(2), x–xiv.

Szmanski, E. M., & King, J. (1989). Rehabilitation counseling in transition planning and preparation. *Career Development for Exceptional Individuals, 12*, 3–10.

Tanner, D., & Tanner, L. N. (1980). *Curriculum development* (2nd ed.). New York: Macmillan.

Tarpley, H., & Schroeder, S. (1979). Comparison of DRO and DRI on rate of suppression of self injurious behavior. *American Journal of Mental Deficiency, 84,* 188–194.

Tarver, S., & Dawson, M. (1978). Modality preference and the teaching of reading: A review. *Journal of Learning Disabilities, 11,* 5–17.

Taylor, A., Thurlow, M., & Turnure, J. (1977). Vocabulary development of educable retarded children. *Exceptional Children, 43,* 444–450.

Taylor, R. L. (1989). *Assessment of Exceptional Students* (2nd ed.). Englewood Cliffs, NJ: Prentice Hall.

Test, D. W. (1985). Evaluating educational software for the microcomputer. *Journal of Special Education Technology, 7,* 37–46.

Test, D. W., Keul, P. K., & Grossi, T. (1988). Transitional services for mildly handicapped youth. *The Journal for Vocational Special Needs Education, 10,* 7–11.

Thomas, C. M., Sulzer-Azaroff, B., Lukeris, S., & Palmer, M. (1977). Teaching daily self-help skills for "long term" maintenance. In B. Etzel, J. LeBlanc, & D. Baer (Eds.), *New developments in behavioral research: Theory, method and application* (pp. 543–557). Hillsdale, NJ: Lawrence Erlbaum.

Thorkildsen, R. J., & Reid, R. (1989). An investigation of the reinforcing effects of feedback on computer-assisted instruction. *Journal of Special Education Technology, 9,* 125–135.

Thornton, C. A. (1979). Basic fact mastery: Guides to success for the LD child. *Focus on Learning Problems in Mathematics, 1*(1), 146–153.

Thurber, D. N. (1986). *D'Nealian handwriting.* Glenview, IL: Scott, Foresman.

Thurlow, M. L., & Turnure, James, E. (1977). Children's knowledge of time and money: Effective instruction for the mentally retarded. *Education and Training of the Mentally Retarded, 12,* 203–212.

Tiegs, E. W., & Clarke, W. W. (1970). California Achievement Test. Monterey, CA: CTB/McGraw-Hill.

Tobin, D. (1988). Computer assisted instruction in special education. In M. M. Behrmann (Ed.), *Integrating computers into the curriculum: A handbook for special educators* (pp. 145–178). Boston: College Hill Press.

Torgesen, J. K. (1984). Instructional uses of microcomputers with elementary-aged mildly handicapped children. *Specialized Services in the Schools, 1,* 37–48.

Torgesen, J. K., Waters, M. D., Cohen, A. L., Torgeson, J. L. (1988). Improving sight-word recognition skills in learning disabled children: An evaluation of three computer-program variations. *Learning Disability Quarterly, 11,* 125–132.

Trace, M. W., Cuvo, A. J., & Criswell, S. L. (1977). Teaching coin equivalence to the mentally retarded. *Journal of Applied Behavior Analysis, 10,* 85–92.

Trupin, E. W., Gilchrist, L., Maiuro. R. D., & Fay, G. (1979). Social skills training for learning disabled children. In L. A. Hamerlynck (Ed.), *Behavioral systems for the developmentally disabled: Vol. 2. Institutional, clinical, and community environments.* New York: Brunner/Mazel.

Tucker, J. A. (1985). Curriculum-based assessment: An introduction. *Exceptional Children, 52,* 199–204.

Turla, P. A., & Hawkins, K. L. (1983). *Time management made easy.* New York: E. P. Dutton.

Turnbull, A. P., Strickland, B. B., & Brantley, J. C. (1982). *Developing and implementing individualized education programs* (2nd ed.). Columbus, OH: Charles E. Merrill.

Tymitz-Wolf, B. (1982). Guidelines for assessing IEP goals and objectives. *TEACHING Exceptional Children, 14*, 198–201.

Usnick, V., & McCoy, K. (1987). Mathematics instruction. In K. McCoy, & H. J. Prehm (Eds.), *Teaching mainstreamed students: Methods and techniques* (pp. 359–402). Denver: Love Publishing.

Utley, B. L., Zigmond, N., & Strain, P. S. (1987). How various forms of data affect teacher analysis of student performance. *Exceptional Children, 53*, 411–422.

van den Pol, R. A., Iwata, B., Ivancic, M., Page, T. J., Neef, N., & Whitley, F. (1981). Teaching handicapped to eat in public places: Acquisition, generalization, and maintenance of restaurant skills. *Journal of Applied Behavior Analysis, 41*, 61–69.

Vandever, T. R. (1983). Comparisons of suspensions of EMR and nonretarded students. *American Journal of Mental Deficiency, 87* (4), 430–434.

Vaughn, S., Lancelotta, G. X., & Minnis, S. (1988). Social strategy training and peer involvement: Increasing peer acceptance of a female LD student. *Learning Disability Focus, 4*, 32–37.

Vitello, S. J. (1976). Quantitative abilities of mentally retarded children. *Education and Training of the Mentally Retarded, 11*, 125–129.

Vocational Evaluation and Work Adjustment Association. (1975, July). Vocational evaluation project final report. *Vocational Evaluation and Work Adjustment Bulletin* (special ed.), 8.

Voeltz, L. M., & Apffel, J. A. (1981). A leisure activities curricular component for severely handicapped youth: Why and how. *Viewpoints in Teaching and Learning, 57*, (1), 82–93.

Voeltz, L. M., Wuerch, B. B., & Bockhout, C. H. (1982). Social validation of leisure activities training with severely handicapped youth. *Journal of the Association for the Severely Handicapped, 7* (4), 3–13.

Voeltz, L. M., Wuerch, B. B., & Wilcox, B. (1982). Leisure/recreation: Preparation for independence, integration and self-fulfillment. In B. Wilcox & G. T. Bellamy (Eds.), *Design of high school programs for severely handicapped students* (pp. 175–209). Baltimore: Paul H. Brooks.

Vogel, S. A. (1983). A qualitative analysis of morphological ability in learning disabled and achieving children. *Journal of Learning Disabilities, 16*, 416–420.

Vogelsberg, R. T., & Rusch, F. R. (1979). Training severely handicapped students to cross partially controlled intersections. *AAESPH Review, 4*, 264–273.

Wacker, D., & Berg, W. (1983). Effects of picture prompts on the acquisition of complex vocational tasks by mentally retarded adolescents. *Journal of Applied Behavior Analysis, 16*, 417–434.

Wahler, R. G., & Fox, J. J. (1980). Solitary toy play and time out: A family treatment package for children with aggressive and oppositional behavior. *Journal of Applied Behavior Analysis, 13*, 23–29.

Walker, H. M. (1983). Applications of response cost in school settings: Outcomes, issues, and recommendations. *Exceptional Education Quarterly, 3* (4), 47–55.

Walker, H., McConnell, S., Holmes, D., Todis, B., Walker, J., & Golden, N. (1983). *The Walker social skills curriculum.* Austin, TX: ProEd.

Walker, J., & Shea, T. (1984). *Behavior management: A practical approach for educators.* St. Louis: Times Mirror/Mosby.

Walker, J. E., & Shea, T. M. (1988). *Behavior management: A practical approach for educators* (4th ed.). Columbus, OH: Charles E. Merrill.

Wallace, G., & Kauffman, J. M. (1978). *Teaching children with learning problems* (2nd ed.). Columbus, OH: Charles E. Merrill.

Wallace, G., & Larsen, S. C. (1978). *Educational assessment of learning problems: Testing for teaching.* Boston: Allyn and Bacon.

Wang, M. C. (1980). Adaptive instruction: Building on diversity. *Theory into Practice, 19,* 122–128.

Wang, M. C., & Walberg, H. J. (1988). Four fallacies of segregationism. *Exceptional Children, 55,* 128–137.

Warren, S., Rogers-Warren, A., Baer, D., & Guess, D. (1980). Assessment and facilitation of language generalization. In W. Sailor, B. Wilcox, & L. Brown (Eds.), *Methods of instruction for severely handicapped students* (pp. 227–258). Baltimore: Paul H. Brooks.

Watkins, M. W. (1989). Computerized drill-and-practice and academic attitudes of learning disabled students. *Journal of Special Education Technology, 9,* 167–172.

Watson, J. (1981). A communication training program for mildly retarded school children. *Educational Studies, 7*(3), 185–196.

Webber, J., & Coleman, M. (1988). Using rational-emotive therapy to prevent classroom problems. *TEACHING Exceptional Children, 21,* 32–35.

Wehman, P. (1977a). *Helping the mentally retarded acquire play skills.* Springfield, IL: Charles C. Thomas.

Wehman, P. (1977b). Research on leisure time and the severely developmentally disabled. *Rehabilitation Literature, 38,* 98–105.

Wehman, P. (1978). Effects of different environmental conditions on leisure time activity of the severely and profoundly handicapped. *Journal of Special Education, 12,* 183–193.

Wehman, P. (1979a). Toy play. In P. Wehman (Ed.), *Recreation programming for developmentally disabled persons.* Baltimore: University Park Press.

Wehman, P. (1979b). *Curriculum design for the severely and profoundly handicapped.* New York: Human Science Press.

Wehman, P. (1980). *Competitive employment: New horizons for severely disabled individuals.* Baltimore: Paul H. Brooks.

Wehman, P. (1988). Jobs for the 21st Century Symposium overview: Vocational programming looking ahead into the 21st century. *Mental Retardation, 26,* 335–336.

Wehman, P., Abramson, M., & Norman, C. (1977). Transfer of training in behavior modification programs: An evaluative review. *The Journal of Special Education, 11,* 127–131.

Wehman, P., Hill, M., Goodall, P., Cleveland, P., Brooke, U., & Pentecost, J. (1982). Job placement and followup of moderately and severely handicapped individuals after three years. *Journal of the Association for the Severely Handicapped, 7,* 5–16.

Wehman, P., Moon, M. S., Everson, J. M., Wood, W., & Barcus, J. M. (1988). *Transition from school to work.* Baltimore: Paul H. Brooks.

Wehman, P., & Schleien, S. (1980). Assessment and selection of leisure skills for severely handicapped individuals. *Education and Training of the Mentally Retarded, 15,* 50–57.

Wehman, P., & Schleien, S. (1981). *Leisure programs for handicapped persons.* Baltimore: University Park Press.

Weir, S., & Watt, D. (1981). LOGO: A computer environment for learning disabled students. *Computing Teacher, 8,* 11–17.

Weisberg, R. (1988). 1980's: A change in focus at Reading Comprehension Research: A view of reading/learning disabilities research based on an interactive model of reading. *Learning Disabilities Quarterly, 11,* 149–159.

Weisgerber, R. A., Dahl, P. R., & Appleby, J. A. (1981). *Training the handicapped for productive employment.* Rockville, MD: Aspen Systems.

Welch, S. J., & Holborn, S. W. (1988). Contingency contracting with delinquents: Effects of a brief training manual on staff contract negotiation and writing skills. *Journal of Applied Behavior Analysis, 21,* 357–368.

Weller, C., & Buchanan, M. (1988). *Educator's desk reference for special learning problems.* Boston: Allyn and Bacon.

Wesson, C. L., & Keefe, M. (1989). Teaching library skills to students with mild and moderate handicaps. *TEACHING Exceptional Children, 21,* 28–31.

Wesson, C. L., King, R. P., & Deno, S. L. (1984). Direct and frequent measurement of student performance: If it's good for us, why don't we do it? *Learning Disability Quarterly, 7,* 45–48.

Westling, D. L., & Koorland, M. A. (1979). Some considerations and tactics for improving discrimination learning. *TEACHING Exceptional Children, 11,* 97–100.

Westling, D. L., & Koorland, M. A. (1988). *The special educator's handbook.* Boston: Allyn and Bacon.

Wheeler, J., Ford, A., Nietupski, J., Loomis, R., & Brown, L. (1980). Teaching moderately and severely handicapped to shop in supermarkets using pocket calculators. *Education and Training of the Mentally Retarded, 15,* 105–112.

Whelan, R. J. (1988). Emotionally disturbed. In E. L. Meyen & T. M. Skrtic (Eds.), *Exceptional children and youth: An introduction* (3rd ed., pp. 183–232). Denver: Love Publishing.

White, G. D., Neilsen, G., & Johnson, S. M. (1972). Timeout duration and the suppression of deviant behavior in children. *Journal of Applied Behavior Analysis, 5,* 111–120.

White, O. R., & Haring, N. G. (1980). *Exceptional teaching* (2nd ed.). Columbus, OH: Charles E. Merrill.

Whitman, T. L., & Scibak, J. W. (1979). Behavior modification with the severely and profoundly retarded. In N. Ellis (Ed.), *Handbook of mental deficiency, psychological theory and research* (2nd ed., pp. 289–340). Hillsdale, NJ: Lawrence Erlbaum.

Wiederholt, J. L., Hammill, D. D., & Brown, V. L. (1983). *The resource teacher: A guide to effective practices* (2nd ed.). Boston: Allyn and Bacon.

Wiggins, S. B., & Behrmann, M. M. (1988). Increasing independence through community learning. *TEACHING Exceptional Children, 21,* 20–24.

Wiig, E., & Secord, W. (1985). Test of Language Competence. San Antonio, TX: The Psychological Corporation.

Wiig, E. H., & Semel, E. M. (1984). *Language assessment and intervention for the learning disabled* (2nd ed.). Columbus, OH: Charles E. Merrill.

Will, M. (1984). OSERS programming for the transition of youth with disabilities: Bridges from school to working life. Washington, DC: Office of Special Education and Rehabilitative Services, U.S. Department of Health and Human Services.

Will, M. (1986). Educating children with learning problems: A shared responsibility. *Exceptional Children, 52,* 411–415.

Williams, R. D., & Ewing, S. (1981). Consumer roulette: The shopping patterns of mentally retarded persons. *Mental Retardation, 19,* 145–149.

Wilson, C. R. (1983). Teaching reading comprehension by connecting the known to the new. *The Reading Teacher, 36,* 382–390.

Wilson, P., Reid, D., Phillips, J., & Burgio, L. (1984). Normalization of institutional mealtimes for profoundly retarded persons: Effects and non-effects of teaching family-style dining. *Journal of Applied Behavior Analysis, 17,* 189–202.

Wilson, P., Casella, V. R., & Wilson, W. C. (1989). Microcomputers and new technologies. In R. Gaylord-Ross (Ed.), *Integration strategies for students with handicaps* (pp. 96–132). Baltimore: Paul H. Brooks.

Wilson, R., Majsterer, D., & Southern, W. (1989). Content area programming for secondary learning disabled students. *Reading Improvement, 24,* 193–197.

Witt, J. C., Elliott, S. N., Gresham, F. M., & Kramer, J. J. (1988). *Assessment of special children: Tests and the problem solving process.* Glenview, IL: Scott, Foresman.

Witt, S. J. (1980). Increase in adaptive behavior level for mentally retarded persons. *Mental Retardation, 19,* 75–79.

Wolery, M., Bailey, D. B., & Sugai, G. M. (1988). *Effective teaching: Principles and procedures of applied behavior analysis with exceptional students.* Boston: Allyn and Bacon.

Wolf, M. M. (1978). Social validity: The case for subjective measurement, or How applied behavior analysis is finding it's heart. *Journal of Applied Behavior Analysis, 11,* 203–214.

Wong, B. Y. (1987). How do the results of metacognitive research impact on the learning disabled individual? *Learning Disability Quarterly, 10,* 189–195.

Wood, F. H. (1985). Issues in the identification and placement of behaviorally disordered students. *Behavioral Disorders, 10,* 219–228.

Wood, K. D., & Mateja, J. (1983). Adopting secondary level strategies for use in elementary school. *The Reading Teacher, 36,* 492–496.

Wood, R., & Flynn, J. (1978). A self evaluation token system vs. an external evaluation token system alone in a residential setting with predelinquent youth. *Journal of Applied Behavior Analysis, 11,* 503–512.

Woodcock, R. W. (1987). Woodcock Reading Mastery Test—Revised. Circle Pines, MN: American Guidance Service.

Woodcock, R. W., Clark, C. R., & Davis, C. O. (1979). *Peabody rebus reading program.* Circle Pines, MN: American Guidance Service.

Woods, M. L., & Moe, A. J. (1985). *Analytical reading inventory* (3rd ed.). Columbus, OH: Charles E. Merrill.

Worden, P. E., Malgren, I., & Gabourie, P. (1982). Memory for stories in learning disabled adults. *Journal of Learning Disabilities, 15,* 145–152.

Worrall, N., & Singh, Y. (1983). Teaching TMR children to read using integrated picture cueing. *American Journal of Mental Deficiency, 87,* 422–429.

Wuerch, B. B., & Voeltz, L. M. (1982). *Longitudinal leisure skills for severely handicapped learners: The Ho'onanea curriculum component.* Baltimore: Paul H. Brooks.

Yeaton, W. H., & Bailey, J. S. (1978). Teaching pedestrian safety skills to young children: An analysis and one-year follow-up. *Journal of Applied Behavior Analysis, 11,* 315–329.

Your Life Your Feelings: Growing Up and Understanding (1976). Salt Lake City: Utah Association for Retarded Citizens.

Zeaman, D., & House, B. J. (1963). The role of attention in retardate discrimination learning. In N. Ellis (Ed.), *International review of research in mental retardation,* (Vol. 1). New York: Academic Press.

Zentall, S. (1983). Learning environments: A review of physical and temporal factors. *Exceptional Education Quarterly, 4* (2), 90–109.

Zigler, E. (1961). Social deprivation and rigidity in the performance of feebleminded children. *Journal of Abnormal and Social Psychology, 62,* 413–421.

Zigler, E., & Balla, D. (1972). Developmental course of responsiveness to social reinforcement in normal children and institutionalized children. *Developmental Psychology, 6,* 66–73.

AUTHOR INDEX

SUBJECT INDEX